The Keys to Banking Law

A Handbook for Lawyers

THIRD EDITION

Karol K. Sparks

AMERICAN BAR ASSOCIATION
Business Law Section

Cover design by Catherine Zaccarine.

Page layout by Quadrum Solutions.

Printed in the United States of America.

24 5 4 3 2

ISBN: 978-1-64105-810-0

Discounts are available for books ordered in bulk. Special consideration is given to state bars, CLE programs, and other bar-related organizations. Inquire at Book Publishing, ABA Publishing, American Bar Association, 321 N. Clark Street, Chicago, Illinois 60654-7598.

www.shopABA.org

Contents

Acknowledgements

Dedication: Saying "*thank you" is never enough for those who help shape your perception, hone your self-confidence, build your knowledge and your wisdom; who challenge you to be the best professional you can be; who always offer support when you need it. Jim Scott and Marty Lybecker, I miss you – we all miss you. Rest in peace, my friends.*

From my beginning quest to share what I learned as a bank regulatory lawyer and teacher, I have aspired to open the doors to all the "rooms" in my brain and spill out the banking law and the tricks that make it work for me before the doors to those figurative rooms get too rusty. *The Keys to Banking Law* is the product of the brain dump. Thankfully, I had Harding Williams' original text *Federal Banking Law and Regulation* as my base. So, thanks first to Harding for paving the way and making this complex area of law manageable. When I tackled the Second Edition, I found I had more to dump, much more, and, with the Third Edition, my OCD took over and I moved from the initial concept of a 30,000 foot flyover to a much deeper dive. I have now pretty well exhausted my knowledge base from forty years in this business. Shame on me if I left something unsaid that is important to my readers.

I find myself extremely sentimental as I finish this Third Edition of *Keys* because there will not be a fourth (not by me anyway) and because of how grateful I am to those who blessed my professional life. I am indebted to so many people for their contributions, from my study group in law school, to those who hired me, to those who trusted me with their legal conundrums, to those who inspired and supported me. I fall woefully short of naming everyone who shared my passage.

So first, how did it all start? How does a junior high school English teacher, new mother, and night school law graduate (with no legal experience) become a bank regulatory lawyer? Not easily. It was John Alexander and Randy Wilson at Krieg DeVault Alexander & Capehart back in 1979 who saw something in me that said "banking lawyer." It was a tough road from there to now, and part of my passion for teaching and writing is to make the learning curve less steep for those who follow.

I could not have done it without the Banking Law Committee of the Business Law Section of the American Bar Association. That committee has been my backbone, my security blanket, my safety net, and my launching pad (you get the picture) and has housed countless brilliant lawyers with great generosity of spirit and mind. One of the first people I met on the committee back in 1985 was a former naval commander who frankly scared me to death on first impression. Yet, no one has taught me more than Ted McAniff. Thank you, Ted, for being the best mentor, fellow educator, and friend. I am honored. We have taught Banking Law Basics and then Fundamentals of Banking Law together twice a year since 1998, and, over forty times, I have listened to him mesmerize a classroom as he spun fascinating tales of banking law … and I learn every time. There is a lot of Ted in this book. But, thanks also to my other fellow legacy Banking Law Basics/Fundamentals faculty members for the many pieces of lore they have contributed: Jim Scott (for so many years of limericks, songs, eccentric hats, and, yes, we will never forget the gorilla suit, but also for his fine legal mind that he could not hide behind his outlandishness), Bill Kroener and Sara Kelsey, and our co-founders, who passed from this life long ago but remain in our hearts as we teach this class, John Baerst and Ed Lane-Reticker from Boston University. I have endeavored to write this book as we teach the course, with the hope that it will help guide lawyers to love this area of the law.

There are many more who have contributed along the way, but one is especially deserving of accolades: Marty Lybecker, who, regardless of how busy he was, never failed to respond to a "sanity check" from me and impart his wisdom with overwhelming patience. Thank you as well to so many others who sat at lunch or dinner or in a meeting with me and shared your expertise over the years. I was a sponge.

Acknowledgments also go to my firm Barack Ferrazzano Kirschbaum and Nagelberg in Chicago (2001–present), who unselfishly supported my growth as a lawyer and let me find balance in my life by teaching and writing and living away from them and never (almost never) asking more of me than I was interested in giving. I am so fortunate in my managing partners over these many years, Paul DeVault, Paul Lindemann, and Mike Williams at Krieg DeVault and now Howard Kirschbaum, and in my boss, John Freechack. And, I cannot forget the myriad clients who have been my ultimate cheerleaders. Each time a client made me learn a new area of the law (insurance? broker-dealer? adviser? prepaid cards? Treasury management?), he or she contributed to my career in countless ways. My other published treatise, Insurance Activities of Banks, in its Second Edition and now grown gargantuan from annual updates, is a direct result of a client who, when I told him I did not know the area, said, "Learn it." I did.

My thanks to the lawyers at Barack Ferrazzano who contributed to this book and especially to:

> Judy Muncy, who edited every word of the original book and several chapters of the Second Edition and originally authored the description of the control rules that introduces Chapter 10;
>
> John Geiringer, who was an original author of Chapter 11 on examination and enforcement, and added segments in Chapters 7 and 8 on cybersecurity, AML/BSA, and the impact of the coronavirus pandemic, and edited several chapters;
>
> Stan Orszula, who updated Chapter 11;
>
> Andrea Sill and Brent McCauley, who chimed in on Chapters 6 and 10, respectively; and
>
> Fritzi Getz for her help on Chapter 3.

Plus, my heartfelt thanks to Sara Kelsey—who is an amazing teacher, cheerleader, and banking law expert, and who immediately volunteered to author Chapter 12 on bank failure and brought it in before the deadline.

On a personal note, being a grandmother is the best gig ever. Steve and I are blessed with our lovely children, Ashley and Austin, and their spouses, Brendan and Kara, and the five boys who light up our lives, Jack, William, and Colin Sparks and Emmett and Ryan Creedon. And my beloved mother, Elisabeth Kroetz, who always had my back, deserves a special prayer of thanks. Never lose sight of the really important things! That is the best "key" of them all.

Karol Sparks
Salem, South Carolina

1

Understanding Banking Law

Where Do We Start?

How does one approach a body of law as vast and multifaceted as banking law in the United States? It is daunting to learn it, and in some respects, even more daunting to teach it. In the words of John D. Hawke, Jr., Comptroller of the Currency from 1998–2004, "Students of probability theory tell us that if enough monkeys pounded away for a sufficiently long time, they will eventually reproduce the entire works of Shakespeare. It seems unlikely, however, that even those intrepid monkeys could recreate our present system of financial regulation."[1]

While a gross exaggeration (monkeys crafting Shakespeare??), Mr. Hawke makes an excellent point that our system of financial regulation is not rational, and it is unlike anything else in the world. Why do we have a dual banking system, with federal and state charters competing across every kind of "bank"? For that matter, why do we have drastically different types of financial institution charters? Why does the predominant corporate structure in the financial services sector in America start at the top with a parent company? Why are many activities conducted in subsidiaries and affiliates? And, on that point, why do the charters, subsidiaries, and affiliates have diverse powers? Why are there myriad federal and state regulators divided into distinct silos for banking, for insurance, and for securities regulation?

1. Legal Times, June 13, 1983, at 34.

To understand it, we must first dig into our history and assess the factors that motivated legislative action in this sector. Congress does not enact banking legislation except when highly motivated, typically by crisis, innovation, or societal/economic pressure. Thus, its actions are reactive, and the result is foreseeably improvisational.

To understand it, we must grasp that banks[2] are "special."[3] They are financial intermediaries that have the distinct advantage of funding through cheap deposits—demand deposit accounts (*aka* transaction accounts *aka* your checking account). They literally create money by taking in deposits payable on demand at par and lending the money longer term to customers or investing in high-grade debt. Because they are susceptible to runs, they are protected by a federal "subsidy" of FDIC insurance. Does that subsidy alone rationalize so much regulation? Does it justify the extent of supervision and enforcement we find in this country?

To understand it, we must understand our client's structure. What kind of "bank" or "banks" are in the family? What kind of parent company? Who are the regulators? And we must find the law applicable to each entity. Do we look to federal law or state law or both? In any event, we start with a statute and then turn to the regulation promulgated by the applicable agency. Finally, we proceed deeper into interpretive guidance in the form of letters and releases, interagency statements, handbooks, and approval letters.

To understand it in today's world, we must understand the particular importance of capital.

To understand it, we must learn a new language replete with acronyms and inside-the-Beltway "*Bank-Speak.*" *See* Appendix A for the jargon, which is now keyed to chapters in this book.

And so, this book is dedicated to the "explaining":

Chapter 2 addresses the complicated **history** of our laws and how we achieved the complexity of today's regime;

Chapter 3 details **structure options** in the bank family, with special emphasis on our unique dual banking system;

Chapter 4 takes on the significance of **capital**;

2. Note: this book differentiates in many discussions between banks (both national and state) and savings and loan associations (both federal and state); however, for any generic discussion, unless the context is otherwise clear, this book will frequently use "bank" or "financial institution" or "FDIC-insured institution" to cover all depository financial institutions.
3. E. Gerald Corrigan, *Are Banks Special?*, 1982 Annual Report of the Federal Reserve Bank of Minneapolis.

Chapter 5 examines the **safety net** and discusses bank deposits and short-term liabilities and the myriad applicable laws;

Chapters 6, 7, 8, and 9 drill down into the myriad restrictions on banking in the United States justified by "specialness": **prudential regulation**, laws motivated by **societal objectives**, limitations on **expansion**, and finally the umbrella for it all, **safety and soundness**;

Chapter 10 focuses in greater detail on the regulation, rights, and restrictions associated with concepts of control and **holding companies**;

Chapter 11 addresses bank **examination and enforcement**; and

Chapter 12 concludes with an explanation of the consequences of **bank failure** and the **resolution** process.

We begin, however, with the summary below of our system of regulation, supervision, and enforcement as described in a prototype (pre–coronavirus disease [COVID-19])[4] Form 10-K Annual Report of a simple bank holding company (referred to below as the "Company" or "we") with between $3 billion and $10 billion in assets and owning a national bank subsidiary (referred to below as the "Bank"). It sets the stage for what you will find in the rest of this book.

Summary of the U.S. System of Bank Supervision, Regulation, and Enforcement

General

FDIC-insured institutions, their holding companies, and their affiliates are extensively regulated under federal and state law. As a result, our growth and earnings performance may be affected not only by management decisions and general economic conditions, but also by the requirements of federal statutes and by the regulations and policies of various bank regulatory agencies, including the Office of the Comptroller of the Currency (the "OCC"), the Federal Deposit Insurance Corporation (the "FDIC"), the Board of Governors of the Federal Reserve System (the "Federal Reserve"), and the Consumer Financial Protection Bureau (the "CFPB"). Furthermore, taxation laws administered by the Internal Revenue Service and state taxing authorities, accounting rules developed by the Financial Accounting Standards Board, securities laws administered by the Securities and Exchange Commission (the "SEC") and state securities authorities, and anti-money laundering laws enforced by the

4. Congress and the bank regulatory agencies developed special programs in response to the 2020 COVID-19 pandemic, some of which impacted aspects of this disclosure on a temporary basis.

U.S. Department of the Treasury ("Treasury") have an impact on our business. The effect of these statutes, regulations, regulatory policies, and accounting rules are significant to our operations and results.

Federal and state banking laws impose a comprehensive system of supervision, regulation, and enforcement on the operations of FDIC-insured institutions, their holding companies, and affiliates that is intended primarily for the protection of the FDIC-insured deposits and depositors of banks, rather than shareholders. These laws, and the regulations of the bank regulatory agencies issued under them, affect, among other things, the scope of our business; the kinds and amounts of investments we may make; reserve requirements; required capital levels relative to assets; the nature and amount of collateral for loans; the Bank's establishment of branches; our ability to merge, consolidate, and acquire; dealings with our insiders and affiliates; and our payment of dividends. In reaction to the global financial crisis and particularly following passage of the Dodd-Frank Wall Street Reform and Consumer Protection Act of 2010 ("Dodd-Frank Act"), we experienced heightened regulatory requirements and scrutiny. Although the reforms primarily targeted systemically important financial service providers, their influence filtered down in varying degrees to community banks over time and caused our compliance and risk management processes, and the costs thereof, to increase. However, in May 2018, the Economic Growth, Regulatory Relief and Consumer Protection Act ("Regulatory Relief Act") was enacted by Congress in part to provide regulatory relief for community banks and their holding companies. To that end, the law eliminated questions about the applicability of certain Dodd-Frank Act reforms to community bank systems, including relieving us of any requirement to engage in mandatory stress tests, maintain a risk committee, or comply with the Volker Rule's complicated prohibitions on proprietary trading and ownership of private funds. We believe these reforms are favorable to our operations.

This supervisory and regulatory framework subjects banks and bank holding companies to regular examination by their respective regulatory agencies, which results in examination reports and ratings that are not publicly available and that can impact the conduct and growth of their business. These examinations consider not only compliance with applicable laws and regulations, but also capital levels, asset quality and risk, management ability and performance, earnings, liquidity, and various other factors. The regulatory agencies generally have broad discretion to impose restrictions and limitations on the operations of a regulated entity where the agencies determine, among other things, that such operations are unsafe or unsound, fail to comply with applicable law or are otherwise inconsistent with laws and regulations or with the supervisory policies of these agencies.

The following is a summary of the material elements of the supervisory and regulatory framework applicable to us, beginning with a discussion of the continuing regulatory emphasis on our capital levels. It does not describe all of the statutes, regulations, and regulatory policies that apply, nor does it restate all of the requirements of those that are described. The descriptions are qualified in their entirety by reference to the particular statutory and regulatory provision.

Regulatory Emphasis on Capital

Regulatory capital represents the net assets of a banking organization available to absorb losses. Because of the risks attendant to their business, FDIC-insured institutions are generally required to hold more capital than other businesses, which directly affects our earnings capabilities. While capital has historically been one of the key measures of the financial health of both bank holding companies and banks, its role became fundamentally more important in the wake of the global financial crisis, as the banking regulators recognized that the amount and quality of capital held by banks prior to the crisis was insufficient to absorb losses during periods of severe stress. Certain provisions of the Dodd-Frank Act and Basel III, discussed below, establish strengthened capital standards for banks and bank holding companies that are meaningfully more stringent than those in place previously.

Minimum Required Capital Levels. Banks have been required to hold minimum levels of capital based on guidelines established by the bank regulatory agencies since 1983. The minimums have been expressed in terms of ratios of "capital" divided by "total assets." As discussed below, bank capital measures have become more sophisticated over the years and have focused more on the quality of capital and the risk of assets. Bank holding companies have historically had to comply with less stringent capital standards than their bank subsidiaries and have been able to raise capital with hybrid instruments such as trust preferred securities. The Dodd-Frank Act mandated the Federal Reserve to establish minimum capital levels for holding companies on a consolidated basis as stringent as those required for FDIC-insured institutions. A result of this change is that the proceeds of hybrid instruments, such as trust preferred securities, are being excluded from capital over a phase-out period. However, if such securities were issued prior to May 19, 2010, by bank holding companies with less than $15 billion of assets, they may be retained, subject to certain restrictions. Because we have assets of less than $15 billion, we are able to maintain our trust preferred proceeds as capital but we have to comply with new capital mandates in other respects and will not be able to raise capital in the future through the issuance of trust preferred securities.

The Basel International Capital Accords. The risk-based capital guidelines for U.S. banks since 1989 were based upon the 1988 capital accord known as "Basel I" adopted by the international Basel Committee on Banking Supervision, a committee of central banks and bank supervisors that acts as the primary global standard-setter for prudential regulation, as implemented by the U.S. bank regulatory agencies on an interagency basis. The accord recognized that bank assets for the purpose of the capital ratio calculations needed to be risk weighted (the theory being that riskier assets should require more capital) and that off-balance sheet exposures needed to be factored in the calculations. Basel I had a very simple formula for assigning risk weights to bank assets from 0% to 100% based on four categories. In 2008, the banking agencies collaboratively began to phase-in capital standards based on a second capital accord, referred to as "Basel II," for large or "core" international banks (generally defined for U.S. purposes as having total assets of $250 billion or more, or consolidated foreign exposures of $10 billion or more) known as "advanced approaches" banks. The primary focus of Basel II was on the calculation of risk weights based on complex models developed by each advanced approaches bank. Because most banks were not subject to Basel II, the U.S. bank regulators worked to improve the risk sensitivity of Basel I standards without imposing the complexities of Basel II. This "standardized approach" increased the number of risk-weight categories and recognized risks well above the original 100% risk weighting. The standardized approach is institutionalized by the Dodd-Frank Act for all banking organizations as a floor.

On September 12, 2010, the Group of Governors and Heads of Supervision, the oversight body of the Basel Committee on Banking Supervision, announced agreement on a strengthened set of capital requirements for banking organizations around the world, known as Basel III, to address deficiencies recognized in connection with the global financial crisis.

The Basel III Rule. In July of 2013, the U.S. federal banking agencies approved the implementation of the Basel III regulatory capital reforms in pertinent part, and, at the same time, promulgated rules effecting certain changes required by the Dodd-Frank Act (the "Basel III Rule"). In contrast to capital requirements historically, which were in the form of guidelines, Basel III was released in the form of enforceable regulations by each of the regulatory agencies. The Basel III Rule is applicable to all banking organizations that are subject to minimum capital requirements, including federal and state banks and savings and loan associations, as well as to bank and savings and loan holding companies, other than "small bank holding companies" (generally holding companies with consolidated assets of less than $3 billion) and certain qualifying community banking organizations that may elect a simplified framework.

The Basel III Rule impacts both the definitions of the various forms of capital used to calculate the ratios and how assets will be weighted for the purpose of calculating such ratios. It increased the required quantity and quality of capital and required more detailed categories of risk weights of riskier, more opaque assets. For nearly every class of assets, the Basel III Rule requires a more complex, detailed, and calibrated assessment of risk in the calculation of risk-weight amounts.

Not only did the Basel III Rule increase most of the required minimum capital ratios in effect prior to January 1, 2015, but it introduced the concept of Common Equity Tier 1 Capital, which consists primarily of common stock, related surplus (net of Treasury stock), retained earnings, and Common Equity Tier 1 minority interests subject to certain regulatory adjustments. The Basel III Rule also changed the definition of capital by establishing more stringent criteria that instruments must meet to be considered Additional Tier 1 Capital (primarily noncumulative perpetual preferred stock that meets certain requirements) and Tier 2 Capital (primarily other types of preferred stock and subordinated debt, subject to limitations). A number of instruments that qualified as Tier 1 Capital under Basel I do not qualify, or their qualifications changed. For example, noncumulative perpetual preferred stock, which qualified as simple Tier 1 Capital under Basel I, does not qualify as Common Equity Tier 1 Capital, but qualifies as Additional Tier 1 Capital. The Basel III Rule also constrained the inclusion of minority interests, mortgage-servicing assets, and deferred tax assets in capital and requires deductions from Common Equity Tier 1 Capital in the event that such assets exceed a certain percentage of a banking institution's Common Equity Tier 1 Capital.

The Basel III Rule required **minimum** capital ratios as of January 1, 2015, as follows:

- A ratio of minimum Common Equity Tier 1 Capital equal to 4.5% of risk-weighted assets;
- An increase in the minimum required amount of Tier 1 Capital from 4% to 6% of risk-weighted assets;
- A continuation of the minimum required amount of Total Capital (Tier 1 plus Tier 2) at 8% of risk-weighted assets; and
- A minimum leverage ratio of Tier 1 Capital to total quarterly average assets equal to 4% in all circumstances.

In addition, institutions that seek the freedom to make capital distributions (including for dividends and repurchases of stock) and pay discretionary bonuses to executive officers without restriction must also maintain 2.5% in Common Equity Tier 1 Capital attributable to a capital conservation buffer. The purpose of the conservation buffer is to ensure that banking institutions maintain a buffer of capital that can be used to absorb losses during periods of financial and economic stress. Factoring in the fully phased-in conservation buffer increases the minimum ratios depicted above to 7% for Common Equity Tier 1 Capital, 8.5% for Tier 1 Capital, and 10.5% for Total Capital.

Well-Capitalized Requirements. The ratios described above are minimum standards in order for banking organizations to be considered "adequately capitalized." Bank regulatory agencies uniformly encourage banks to hold more capital and be "well-capitalized" and, to that end, federal law and regulations provide various incentives for banking organizations to maintain regulatory capital at levels in excess of minimum regulatory requirements. For example, a banking organization that is well-capitalized may: (i) qualify for exemptions from prior notice or application requirements otherwise applicable to certain types of activities; (ii) qualify for expedited processing of other required notices or applications; and (iii) accept, roll-over or renew brokered deposits. Higher capital levels could also be required if warranted by the particular circumstances or risk profiles of individual banking organizations. For example, the Federal Reserve's capital guidelines contemplate that additional capital may be required to take adequate account of, among other things, interest rate risk, or the risks posed by concentrations of credit, nontraditional activities, or securities trading activities. Further, any banking organization experiencing or anticipating significant growth would be expected to maintain capital ratios, including tangible capital positions (i.e., Tier 1 Capital less all intangible assets), well above the minimum levels.

Under the capital regulations of the OCC, in order to be well-capitalized, a banking organization must maintain:

- A Common Equity Tier 1 Capital ratio to risk-weighted assets of 6.5% or more;
- A ratio of Tier 1 Capital to total risk-weighted assets of 8% or more (6% under Basel I);
- A ratio of Total Capital to total risk-weighted assets of 10% or more (the same as Basel I); and
- A leverage ratio of Tier 1 Capital to total adjusted average quarterly assets of 5% or greater.

It is possible under the Basel III Rule to be well-capitalized while remaining out of compliance with the capital conservation buffer discussed above.

As of December 31, 2019: (i) the Bank was not subject to a directive from the OCC to increase its capital, and (ii) the Bank was well-capitalized, as defined by OCC regulations. As of December 31, 2019, we had regulatory capital in excess of the Federal Reserve's requirements and met the Basel III Rule requirements to be well-capitalized. We are also in compliance with the Capital Conservation Buffer.

Prompt Corrective Action. An FDIC-insured institution's capital plays an important role in connection with regulatory enforcement as well. Federal law provides the federal banking regulators with broad power to take prompt corrective action to resolve the problems of undercapitalized institutions. The extent of the regulators' powers depends on whether the institution in question is "adequately capitalized," "undercapitalized," "significantly undercapitalized," or "critically undercapitalized," in each case as defined by regulation. Depending upon the capital category to which an institution is assigned, the regulators' corrective powers include: (i) requiring the institution to submit a capital restoration plan; (ii) limiting the institution's asset growth and restricting its activities; (iii) requiring the institution to issue additional capital stock (including additional voting stock) or to sell itself; (iv) restricting transactions between the institution and its affiliates; (v) restricting the interest rate that the institution may pay on deposits; (vi) ordering a new election of directors of the institution; (vii) requiring that senior executive officers or directors be dismissed; (viii) prohibiting the institution from accepting deposits from correspondent banks; (ix) requiring the institution to divest certain subsidiaries; (x) prohibiting the payment of principal or interest on subordinated debt; and (xi) ultimately, appointing a receiver for the institution.

Community Bank Capital Simplification. Community banks have long raised concerns with bank regulators about the regulatory burden, complexity, and costs associated with certain provisions of the Basil III Rule. In response, Congress provided an "off-ramp" for institutions, like us, with total consolidated assets of less than $10 billion. Section 201 of the Regulatory Relief Act instructed the federal banking regulators to establish a single "Community Bank Leverage Ratio" ("CBLR") of between 8% and 10%. Under the final rule, a community banking organization is eligible to elect the new framework if it has: less than $10 billion in total consolidated assets, limited amounts of certain assets and off-balance sheet exposures, and a CBLR greater than 9%. We may elect the CBLR framework at any time but have not currently determined to do so.

Regulation and Supervision of the Company

General. The Company, as the sole shareholder of the Bank, is a bank holding company. As a bank holding company, we are registered with, and subject to regulation, supervision and enforcement by, the Federal Reserve under the Bank Holding Company Act of 1956, as amended (the "BHCA"). We are legally obligated to act as a source of financial and managerial strength to the Bank and to commit resources to support the Bank in circumstances where we might not otherwise do so. Under the BHCA, we are subject to periodic examination by the Federal Reserve and are required to file with the Federal Reserve periodic reports of our operations and such additional information as the Federal Reserve may require.

Acquisitions and Activities/Financial Holding Company Election. The primary purpose of a bank holding company is to control and manage banks. The BHCA generally requires the prior approval of the Federal Reserve for any merger involving a bank holding company or any acquisition by a bank holding company of another bank or bank holding company. Subject to certain conditions (including deposit concentration limits established by the BHCA), the Federal Reserve may allow a bank holding company to acquire banks located in any state of the United States. In approving interstate acquisitions, the Federal Reserve is required to give effect to applicable state law limitations on the aggregate amount of deposits that may be held by the acquiring bank holding company and its FDIC-insured institution affiliates in the state in which the target bank is located (provided that those limits do not discriminate against out-of-state institutions or their holding companies) and state laws that require that the target bank have been in existence for a minimum period of time (not to exceed five years) before being acquired by an out-of-state bank holding company. Furthermore, in accordance with the Dodd-Frank Act, bank holding companies must be well-capitalized and examiners must rate them well-managed in order to effect interstate mergers or acquisitions. For a discussion of the capital requirements, see "Regulatory Emphasis on Capital" above.

The BHCA generally prohibits us from acquiring direct or indirect ownership or control of more than 5% of the voting shares of any company that is not a bank and from engaging in any business other than that of banking, managing and controlling banks or furnishing services to banks and their subsidiaries. This general prohibition is subject to a number of exceptions. The principal exception allows bank holding companies to engage in, and to own shares of companies engaged in, certain businesses found by the Federal Reserve prior to November 11, 1999, to be "so closely related to banking ... as to be a proper incident thereto." This authority would permit us to engage in a variety of banking-related businesses, including the ownership and operation of a savings association, or any entity engaged in consumer finance, equipment leasing, the operation of a computer service bureau (including software development) and mortgage banking and brokerage services. The BHCA does not place territorial restrictions on the domestic activities of nonbank subsidiaries of bank holding companies.

Additionally, bank holding companies that meet certain eligibility requirements prescribed by the BHCA and elect to operate as financial holding companies may engage in, or own shares in companies engaged in, a wider range of nonbanking activities, including securities and insurance underwriting and sales, merchant banking and any other activity that the Federal Reserve, in consultation with the Secretary of the Treasury, determines by regulation or order is financial in nature or incidental to any such financial activity or that the Federal Reserve determines by order to be complementary to any such financial activity and does not pose a substantial risk to the safety or soundness of FDIC-insured institutions or the financial system generally. We have elected to operate as a financial holding company. In order to maintain our status as a financial holding company, both the Company and the Bank must be well-capitalized, well-managed, and have a least a satisfactory Community Reinvestment Act ("CRA") rating. If the Federal Reserve determines that we are not well-capitalized or well-managed, we will have a period of time in which to achieve compliance, but during the period of noncompliance, the Federal Reserve may place any limitations on us it believes to be appropriate. Furthermore, if the Federal Reserve determines that the Bank has not received a satisfactory CRA rating, we will not be able to commence any new financial activities or acquire a company that engages in such activities.

Change in Control. Federal law also prohibits any person or company from acquiring "control" of an FDIC-insured depository institution or its holding company without prior notice to the appropriate federal bank regulator. "Control" is conclusively presumed to exist upon the acquisition of 25% or more of the outstanding voting securities of a bank or bank holding company, but may arise under certain circumstances between 10% and 24.99% ownership.

Capital Requirements. Bank holding companies are required to maintain capital in accordance with Federal Reserve capital adequacy requirements. For a discussion of capital requirements, see "Regulatory Emphasis on Capital" above.

Dividend Payments. The Company's ability to pay dividends to its shareholders may be affected by both general corporate law considerations and policies of the Federal Reserve applicable to bank holding companies. As a Delaware corporation, we are subject to the limitations of the Delaware General Corporation Law (the "DGCL"). The DGCL allows us to pay dividends only out of its surplus (as defined and computed in accordance with the provisions of the DGCL) or, if we have no such surplus, out of its net profits for the fiscal year in which the dividend is declared and/or the preceding fiscal year. Consistent with the "source of strength" policy for subsidiary banks, the Federal Reserve has indicated that the board of directors of a bank holding company should eliminate, defer, or significantly reduce dividends to shareholders if: (i) the company's net income available to shareholders for the past four quarters, net of dividends previously paid during that period, is not sufficient to fully fund the dividends; (ii) the prospective rate of earnings retention is inconsistent with the company's capital needs and overall current and prospective financial condition; or (iii) the company will not meet, or is in danger of not meeting, its minimum regulatory capital adequacy ratios. The Federal Reserve also possesses enforcement powers over bank holding companies and their nonbank subsidiaries to prevent or remedy actions that represent unsafe or unsound practices or violations of applicable statutes and regulations. Among these powers is the ability to proscribe the payment of dividends by banks and bank holding companies. In addition, under the Basel III Rule, institutions that seek the freedom to pay dividends have to maintain 2.5% in Common Equity Tier 1 Capital attributable to the capital conservation buffer. See "Regulatory Emphasis on Capital" above.

Monetary Policy. The monetary policy of the Federal Reserve has a significant effect on the operating results of financial or bank holding companies and their subsidiaries. Among the tools available to the Federal Reserve to affect the money supply are open market transactions in U.S. government securities, changes in the discount rate on bank borrowings and changes in reserve requirements against bank deposits. These means are used in varying combinations to influence overall growth and distribution of bank loans, investments and deposits, and their use may affect interest rates charged on loans or paid on deposits.

Federal Securities Regulation. Our common stock is registered with the SEC under the Securities Exchange Act of 1934, as amended (the "Exchange Act"). Consequently, we are subject to the information, proxy solicitation, insider trading and other restrictions and requirements of the SEC under the Exchange Act.

Corporate Governance. The Dodd-Frank Act addressed many investor protection, corporate governance and executive compensation matters that will affect most U.S. publicly traded companies. It increased stockholder influence over boards of directors by requiring companies to give stockholders a nonbinding vote on executive compensation and so-called "golden parachute" payments, and authorizing the SEC to promulgate rules that would allow stockholders to nominate and solicit voters for their own candidates using a company's proxy materials. The legislation also directed the Federal Reserve to promulgate rules prohibiting excessive compensation paid to executives of bank holding companies, regardless of whether such companies are publicly traded.

Regulation and Supervision of the Bank

General. The Bank is a national bank, chartered by the OCC under the National Bank Act. The deposit accounts of the Bank are insured by the FDIC's Deposit Insurance Fund (the "DIF") to the maximum extent provided under federal law and FDIC regulations, currently $250,000 per insured depositor category, and the Bank is a member of the Federal Reserve System. As a national bank, the Bank is subject to the examination, supervision, reporting and enforcement requirements of the OCC, the chartering authority for national banks. The FDIC, as administrator of the DIF, also has regulatory authority over the Bank.

Deposit Insurance. As an FDIC-insured institution, the Bank is required to pay deposit insurance premium assessments to the FDIC. The FDIC has adopted a risk-based assessment system whereby FDIC-insured institutions pay insurance premiums at rates based on their risk classification. For institutions like the Bank that are not considered large and highly complex banking organizations, assessments are now based on examination ratings and financial ratios. The total base assessment rates currently range from 1.5 basis points to 30 basis points. At least semi-annually, the FDIC updates its loss and income projections for the DIF and, if needed, increases or decreases the assessment rates, following notice and comment on proposed rulemaking. The assessment base against which an FDIC-insured institution's deposit insurance premiums paid to the DIF are calculated is based on its average consolidated total assets less its average tangible equity. This method shifted the burden of deposit insurance premiums toward those large depository institutions that rely on funding sources other than U.S. deposits.

The reserve ratio is the FDIC insurance fund balance divided by estimated insured deposits. The Dodd-Frank Act altered the minimum reserve ratio of the DIF, increasing the minimum from 1.15% to 1.35% of the estimated amount of total insured deposits, and eliminating the requirement that the FDIC pay dividends to FDIC-insured institutions when the reserve ratio exceeds certain thresholds. The reserve ratio reached 1.36% as of September 30, 2018, exceeding the statutory required minimum reserve ratio of 1.35%. As a result, the FDIC is providing assessment credits to insured depository institutions, like the Bank, with total consolidated assets of less than $10 billion for the portion of their regular assessments that contributed to growth in the reserve ratio between 1.15% and 1.35%. The share of the aggregate small bank credits allocated to each insured institution is proportional to its credit base, defined as the average of its regular assessment base during the credit calculation period. The FDIC is currently applying the credits for quarterly assessment periods beginning July 1, 2019, and, as long as the reserve ratio is at least 1.35%, the FDIC will remit the full nominal value of any remaining credits in a lump-sum payment.

Supervisory Assessments. National banks are required to pay supervisory assessments to the OCC to fund the operations of the OCC. The amount of the assessment is calculated using a formula that takes into account the bank's size and its supervisory condition. During the year ended December 31, 2016, the Bank paid supervisory assessments to the OCC totaling $[____].

Capital Requirements. Banks are generally required to maintain capital levels in excess of other businesses. For a discussion of capital requirements, see "Regulatory Emphasis on Capital" above.

Liquidity Requirements. Liquidity is a measure of the ability and ease with which bank assets may be converted to cash. Liquid assets are those that can be converted to cash quickly if needed to meet financial obligations. To remain viable, FDIC-insured institutions must have enough liquid assets to meet their near-term obligations, such as withdrawals by depositors. Because the global financial crisis was in part a liquidity crisis, Basel III also includes a liquidity framework that requires FDIC-insured institutions to measure their liquidity against specific liquidity tests. One test, referred to as the Liquidity Coverage Ratio ("LCR"), is designed to ensure that the banking entity has an adequate stock of unencumbered high-quality liquid assets that can be converted easily and immediately in private markets into cash to meet liquidity needs for a 30-calendar day liquidity stress scenario. The other test, known as the Net Stable Funding Ratio ("NSFR"), is designed to promote more medium- and long-term funding of the assets and activities of FDIC-insured institutions over a one-year horizon. These tests provide an incentive for banks and holding companies to increase their holdings in Treasury securities and other sovereign debt as a component of assets, increase the use of long-term debt as a funding source and rely on stable funding like core deposits (in lieu of brokered deposits).

In addition to liquidity guidelines already in place, the federal bank regulatory agencies implemented the Basel III LCR in 2014 and have proposed the NSFR. While the LCR only applies to the largest banking organizations in the country, as will the NSFR, certain elements are expected to filter down to all FDIC-insured institutions. The Bank continues to review its liquidity risk management policies in light of the LCR and NSFR.

Stress Testing. A stress test is an analysis or simulation designed to determine the ability of a given FDIC-insured institution to deal with an economic crisis. In October 2012, U.S. bank regulators unveiled new rules mandated by the Dodd-Frank Act that require the largest U.S. banks to undergo stress tests twice per year, once internally and once conducted by the regulators. Stress tests are not required for banks with less than

$10 billion in assets; however, the FDIC now recommends stress testing as means to identify and quantify loan portfolio risk and the Bank is engaged in the process.

Dividend Payments. Our primary source of funds is dividends from the Bank. Under the National Bank Act, a national bank may pay dividends out of its undivided profits in such amounts and at such times as the bank's board of directors deems prudent. Without prior OCC approval, however, a national bank may not pay dividends in any calendar year that, in the aggregate, exceed the bank's year-to-date net income plus the bank's retained net income for the two preceding years.

The payment of dividends by any FDIC-insured institution is affected by the requirement to maintain adequate capital pursuant to applicable capital adequacy guidelines and regulations, and an FDIC-insured institution generally is prohibited from paying any dividends if, following payment thereof, the institution would be undercapitalized. As described above, the Bank exceeded its capital requirements under applicable guidelines as of December 31, 2019. Notwithstanding the availability of funds for dividends, however, the OCC may prohibit the payment of dividends by the Bank if it determines such payment would constitute an unsafe or unsound practice. In addition, under the Basel III Rule, institutions that seek the freedom to pay dividends have to maintain 2.5% in Common Equity Tier 1 Capital attributable to the capital conservation buffer. See "Regulatory Emphasis on Capital" above.

Insider Transactions. The Bank is subject to certain restrictions imposed by federal law on "covered transactions" between the Bank and its "affiliates." The Company is an affiliate of the Bank for purposes of these restrictions, and covered transactions subject to the restrictions include extensions of credit to us, investments in our stock or other securities and the acceptance of our stock or other securities as collateral for loans made by the Bank. The Dodd-Frank Act enhanced the requirements for certain transactions with affiliates, including an expansion of the definition of "covered transactions" and an increase in the amount of time for which collateral requirements regarding covered transactions must be maintained.

Certain limitations and reporting requirements are also placed on extensions of credit by the Bank to its directors and officers, to our directors and officers and our subsidiaries, to our principal shareholders and to "related interests" of such directors, officers and principal shareholders. In addition, federal law and regulations may affect the terms upon which any person who is a director or officer of the Company or the Bank, or our principal shareholder, may obtain credit from banks with which the Bank maintains a correspondent relationship.

Safety and Soundness Standards/Risk Management. FDIC-insured institutions are expected to operate in a safe and sound manner. The federal banking agencies have adopted operational and managerial standards to promote the safety and soundness of such institutions that address internal controls, information systems, internal audit systems, loan documentation, credit underwriting, interest rate exposure, asset growth, compensation, fees and benefits, asset quality, and earnings.

In general, the safety and soundness standards prescribe the goals to be achieved in each area, and each institution is responsible for establishing its own procedures to achieve those goals. If an institution fails to operate in a safe and sound manner, the FDIC-insured institution's primary federal regulator may require the institution to submit a plan for achieving and maintaining compliance. If an FDIC-insured institution fails to submit an acceptable compliance plan, or fails in any material respect to implement a compliance plan that has been accepted by its primary federal regulator, the regulator is required to issue an order directing the institution to cure the deficiency. Until the deficiency cited in the regulator's order is cured, the regulator may restrict the FDIC-insured institution's rate of growth, require the FDIC-insured institution to increase its capital, restrict the rates the institution pays on deposits, or require the institution to take any action the regulator deems appropriate under the circumstances. Operating in an unsafe or unsound manner will also constitute grounds for other enforcement action by the federal bank regulatory agencies, including cease and desist orders and civil money penalty assessments.

During the past decade, the bank regulatory agencies have increasingly emphasized the importance of sound risk management processes and strong internal controls when evaluating the activities of the FDIC-insured institutions they supervise. Properly managing risks has been identified as critical to the conduct of safe and sound banking activities and has become even more important as new technologies, product innovation, and the size and speed of financial transactions have changed the nature of banking markets. The agencies have identified a spectrum of risks facing a banking institution including, but not limited to, credit, market, liquidity, operational, legal, and reputational risk. Key risk themes for 2020 have been identified as: (i) elevated operational risk as banks adapt to an evolving technology environment and persistent cybersecurity risks; (ii) the need for banks to prepare for a cyclical change in credit risk while credit performance is strong; (iii) elevated interest rate risk due to lower rates continuing to compress net interest margins; and (iv) strategic risks from nondepository financial institutions, use of innovative and evolving technology, and progressive data analysis capabilities. The Bank is expected to have active board and senior management oversight; adequate policies, procedures, and limits; adequate risk measurement, monitoring, and management information systems; and comprehensive internal controls.

Privacy and Cybersecurity. The Bank is subject to many U.S. federal and state laws and regulations governing requirements for maintaining policies and procedures to protect nonpublic confidential information of their customers. These laws require the Bank to periodically disclose their privacy policies and practices relating to sharing such information and permit consumers to opt out of their ability to share information with unaffiliated third parties under certain circumstances. They also impact the Bank's ability to share certain information with affiliates and nonaffiliates for marketing and/or nonmarketing purposes, or to contact customers with marketing offers. In addition, as a part of its operational risk mitigation, the Bank is required to implement a comprehensive information security program that includes administrative, technical, and physical safeguards to ensure the security and confidentiality of customer records and information and to require the same of its service providers. These security and privacy policies and procedures, for the protection of personal and confidential information, are in effect across all business lines and geographic locations.

Branching Authority. National banks headquartered in __________, such as the Bank, have the same branching rights in ______________________ as banks chartered under ______________ law, subject to OCC approval. _______________ law grants _______________________-chartered banks the authority to establish branches anywhere in the State of _____________, subject to receipt of all required regulatory approvals. The Dodd-Frank Act permits well-capitalized and well-managed banks to establish new interstate branches or acquire individual branches of a bank in another state (rather than the acquisition of an out-of-state bank in its entirety) without impediments.

Transaction Account Reserves. Federal law requires FDIC-insured institutions to maintain reserves against their transaction accounts (primarily NOW and regular checking accounts). These reserve requirements are subject to annual adjustment by the Federal Reserve. For 2020, the Federal Reserve originally announced that the first $16.9 million of otherwise reservable balances were exempt from reserves and have a zero percent reserve requirement; for transaction accounts aggregating between $16.9 million and $127.5 million, the reserve requirement was 3% of those transaction account balances; and for net transaction accounts in excess of $127.5 million, the reserve requirement was 10% of the aggregate amount of total transaction account balances in excess of $127.5 million. However, in March of 2020, during the COVID-19 pandemic shutdown, the Federal Reserve announced that the system had ample reserves and reduced all reserve tranches to zero. That action permits us to loan those funds if necessary.

Community Reinvestment Act Requirements. The Community Reinvestment Act requires the Bank to have a continuing and affirmative obligation in a safe and sound manner to help meet the credit needs of its entire community, including low- and moderate-income neighborhoods. Federal regulators regularly assess the Bank's record of meeting the credit needs of its communities. Applications for additional acquisitions would be affected by the evaluation of the Bank's effectiveness in meeting its Community Reinvestment Act requirements.

Anti-Money Laundering. The Uniting and Strengthening America by Providing Appropriate Tools Required to Intercept and Obstruct Terrorism Act of 2001 (the "Patriot Act") is designed to deny terrorists and criminals the ability to obtain access to the U.S. financial system and has significant implications for FDIC-insured institutions, brokers, dealers and other businesses involved in the transfer of money. The Patriot Act mandates financial services companies to have policies and procedures with respect to measures designed to address any or all of the following matters: (i) customer identification programs; (ii) money laundering; (iii) terrorist financing; (iv) identifying and reporting suspicious activities and currency transactions; (v) currency crimes; and (vi) cooperation between FDIC-insured institutions and law enforcement authorities.

Concentrations in Commercial Real Estate. Concentration risk exists when FDIC-insured institutions deploy too many assets to any one industry or segment. A concentration in commercial real estate is one example of regulatory concern. The interagency Concentrations in Commercial Real Estate Lending, Sound Risk Management Practices guidance ("CRE Guidance") provides supervisory criteria, including the following numerical indicators, to assist bank examiners in identifying banks with potentially significant commercial real estate loan concentrations that may warrant greater supervisory scrutiny: (i) commercial real estate loans exceeding 300% of capital and increasing 50% or more in the preceding three years; or (ii) construction and land development loans exceeding 100% of capital. The CRE Guidance does not limit banks' levels of commercial real estate lending activities, but rather guides institutions in developing risk management practices and levels of capital that are commensurate with the level and nature of their commercial real estate concentrations. On December 18, 2015, the federal banking agencies issued a statement to reinforce prudent risk-management practices related to CRE lending, having observed substantial growth in many CRE asset and lending markets, increased competitive pressures, rising CRE concentrations in banks, and an easing of CRE underwriting standards. The federal bank agencies reminded FDIC-insured institutions to maintain underwriting discipline and exercise prudent risk-management practices to identify, measure, monitor, and manage the risks arising from CRE lending. In addition, FDIC-insured institutions must maintain capital commensurate with the level and nature of their CRE concentration risk. Based on the Bank's loan portfolio as of December 31, 2019, it did not exceed the 300% guideline for commercial real estate loans.

Consumer Financial Services. The historical structure of federal consumer protection regulation applicable to all providers of consumer financial products and services changed significantly on July 21, 2011, when the CFPB commenced operations to supervise and enforce consumer protection laws. The CFPB has broad rulemaking authority for a wide range of consumer protection laws that apply to all providers of consumer products and services, including the Bank, as well as the authority to prohibit "unfair, deceptive or abusive" acts and practices. The CFPB has examination and enforcement authority over providers with more than $10 billion in assets. FDIC-insured institutions with $10 billion or less in assets, like the Bank, continue to be examined by their applicable bank regulators.

Because abuses in connection with residential mortgages were a significant factor contributing to the financial crisis, many new rules issued by the CFPB and required by the Dodd-Frank Act addressed mortgage and mortgage-related products, their underwriting, origination, servicing, and sales. The Dodd-Frank

Act significantly expanded underwriting requirements applicable to loans secured by 1-4 family residential real property and augmented federal law combating predatory lending practices. In addition to numerous disclosure requirements, the Dodd-Frank Act imposed new standards for mortgage loan originations on all lenders, including banks and savings associations, in an effort to strongly encourage lenders to verify a borrower's ability to repay, while also establishing a presumption of compliance for certain "qualified mortgages." The Regulatory Relief Act provided relief in connection with mortgages for banks with assets of less than $10 billion, and, as a result, mortgages the Bank makes are now considered to be qualified mortgages if they are held in portfolio for the life of the loan.

The CFPB's rules have not had a significant impact on the Bank's operations, except for higher compliance costs.

2

The Development of Banking Law

How and Why Did We Get Here?

When you read the Form 10-K disclosure at the end of Chapter 1, you must be struck by the complexities of our system of bank regulation, supervision, examination, and enforcement. And that discussion is about one national bank wholly owned by a parent bank holding company (BHC), a fairly vanilla corporate structure reminiscent of many community banks in this country. It can be much more complicated. In the United States, we have a dual banking system composed of national banks, state-chartered banks, state-chartered industrial loan companies, federal savings and loan associations, and state-chartered savings and loan associations; we have a corporate structure that involves BHCs that may become financial holding companies, and thrift holding companies that may be exempt or nonexempt, some of which may now be designated "systemically important." Moreover, our financial institutions have a variety of subsidiary organizations, including traditional operating subsidiaries, financial subsidiaries, service corporations, and service organizations.

We have as many as four federal regulatory agencies vested with supervisory authority over these entities under countless different federal laws: the Office of the Comptroller of the Currency, the Board of Governors of the Federal Reserve System, the Federal Deposit Insurance Corporation, and the Bureau of Consumer Financial Protection (not to mention all the state chartering authorities under applicable state laws). And then there are all of the other federal agencies with specialized authority over financial institutions and/or their affiliates. One need only take a quick peek at the list of acronyms and "*Bank-Speak*" in Appendix A of this book to understand that our system of banking regulation and supervision is ridiculously complex.

How did we get here; why did we get here? John D. Hawke, Jr., Comptroller of the Currency from 1998–2004, summed it up as follows:

> The answer to this is obvious: the current bank regulatory structure offends all of our aesthetic and logical instincts. It's complicated; it's irrational; it probably has inefficiencies; and it takes a great deal of explaining.
>
> It's the product of historical accident, improvisation, and expediency, rather than a methodically crafted plan.
>
> It reflects the accretion of legislative enactments, each passed at a very different time—and under different circumstances—in our history.[1]

This chapter is designed to give readers unfamiliar with federal banking law a sense of the "accretion of legislative enactments" that shaped the history of, and current regulatory structure for, our system of banking regulation.

Catalysts for Change

Before we proceed step-by-step through history, it is enlightening to view legislative developments through the lens of Congress and the factors that caused it to put aside political differences and enact comprehensive banking legislation through the decades. The underlying catalysts include the following: crisis, innovation, and economic/societal pressures.

Crisis

What of crisis as a catalyst? Crisis is indeed the primary engine for change in the financial services sector in the United States. So much may be laid at the door of recessions, depressions, and financial disarray. We reflect back and find crisis at the root of legislation enacted after the Civil War that created our uniform currency and, as a by-product, our national banking system; we find it after the panic of 1907 that brought us the Federal Reserve System as our central bank; we find it after the Great Depression with the creation of federal deposit insurance and the erection of the purportedly impenetratable barrier between Wall Street and commercial banking; and we find it after the thrift crisis with fundamental changes in accountability of bankers and institution-affiliated parties. The financial

1. Remarks of John D. Hawke, Jr., Comptroller of the Currency, before the Exchequer Club (Apr. 16, 2003).

crisis we witnessed in 2008–2009 proves the point yet again, with Congress delivering the Dodd-Frank Wall Street Reform and Consumer Protection Act of 2010, right on cue.

Innovation

What of innovation as a catalyst? Time and again Congress is called upon to assess an activity it never authorized, either to step in to halt the activity or to ratify it. Further to that point, many years ago, an enterprising banker with a national charter (no doubt acting under the advice of counsel) decided to branch where a state bank could not branch, and we have the McFadden Act, restricting national bank branching rights to those of state banks in the state. Another figured out how to avoid the interstate banking restrictions through regional reciprocal compacts, and we have the Riegle-Neal Interstate Branching and Efficiency Act of 1994, opening up nationwide expansion opportunities for all. Another avoided the limitations on bank activities through a parent company, and we have the Bank Holding Company Act of 1956 and the Savings and Loan Holding Company Act of 1959. Someone elected to merge Citicorp and Travelers Insurance, and we have the Gramm-Leach-Bliley Act of 1999, permitting the conglomeration of banking, securities, and insurance activities in a bank family.

Economic Trends and Societal Objectives

What of economic trends as a catalyst? A foreign bank defrauds U.S. customers, and we have the International Banking Act of 1978, subjecting foreign banks that come onshore to U.S. supervision and consolidated home country supervision. Terrorism raises its ugly head, and we have the International Money Laundering Abatement and Financial Anti-Terrorism Act of 2001, codifying "know your customer" requirements. Enron and its brethren display a shocking failure of ethics, and we have the Sarbanes-Oxley Act of 2002, bringing a whole new depth to corporate governance. Our financial system is on the brink of catastrophe, and we have the Emergency Economic Stabilization Act of 2008, permitting the U.S. Department of Treasury to make unprecedented equity investments directly in our banks under the Troubled Asset Relief Program: Capital Purchase Program. Most recently, we witnessed enactment of the Coronavirus Aid, Relief, and Economic Security ("CARES") Act to bolster the economy in part through special bank lending programs and regulatory relief.

Watch as we proceed through history how these catalysts developed and provoked change.

In the Beginning...

Acknowledging the catalysts helps us appreciate what provokes Congress to act, but swirling behind those are the themes that play out on virtually every banking issue: centralization versus decentralization; agrarian versus mercantile; small business and the small farm versus big business; societal objective versus profit motive; and ultimately community banks versus systemically important banks. Think about the Electoral College versus the popular vote for our president and you see the perfect example of this tension, a tension that began as early as the birth of our country with the competing visions of Thomas Jefferson, Secretary of State for President George Washington, and Alexander Hamilton, Secretary of the Treasury. Jefferson embraced an agrarian view of our future, small and decentralized, with minimal federal intervention. Hamilton, however, embraced centralization with a strong federal government.

This tension has played out in connection with development of our unique banking system as well. Hamilton championed creation of a national bank to act as a central bank for the country, to issue currency, and to perform certain central functions, designed along the lines of the formidable Bank of England. Jefferson staunchly opposed this approach. In this, Hamilton won the first round and the Bank of the United States was authorized by Congress. But this was an experiment, and the bank was permitted a charter of only 20 years (1791–1811); round two went to the Jeffersonians when the charter was not renewed. Five years passed and the Second Bank of the United States arose from the ashes (1816–1836), but it plummeted in the face of insider abuse and fraud and the vigorous opposition of President Andrew Jackson who vetoed an attempt to renew the charter.

Developments in Banking before the Civil War

While the federal government battled over the issue of a central bank, banking found other ways to proliferate, and the states stepped into the void. State-chartered banking institutions created by special acts of state legislatures began to appear. Bank of New York (1784/1791) and Manhattan Company (1799) led the way.

Proliferation of State Banks

By 1811, when the Bank of the United States was cashing in its charter, there were 88 state banks in existence that took deposits and made short-term commercial loans. After the demise of the Second Bank of the United States, commercial banking was conducted exclusively by more than 1,500 state-chartered banks. Banking systems varied from state to state. Some states required a special act of the legislature before prospective bankers could obtain an operating charter. Other states adopted "free banking," under which charters were granted to all applicants that met established conditions. In such states as Indiana and Tennessee, banks were state operated and owned; elsewhere, ownership was vested in public-private partnerships.

And in states like Ohio, several of these institutional arrangements were in use at the same time.[2]

The currency these banks created was in the form of their respective notes (essentially promissory notes) issued in exchange for, and backed by, their customers' gold and silver. The money supply, thus, consisted of various types of gold and silver coins along with these paper notes issued in multiple denominations by each of the thousands of individual banks. In theory, holders of notes could return them to the issuer and receive their face value in precious metal. However, especially where state supervision and oversight were weak, banks tended to issue notes beyond their redemption capabilities, which led to bank runs and failures. Worse yet, banks (referred to as "wild cat banks," because that was all that lived close to the bank office) were formed far away in the territories. At each destination, long-distance travelers had to convert their bank notes into local money, usually sustaining a loss with each exchange.[3] As a result of this profusion of notes and widespread counterfeiting, merchants and other note holders often had no idea whether the currency they held was genuine and, if so, what it would be worth when presented at their local bank.

There were several efforts to solve these problems, including a state insurance system in New York in 1829, which worked well for about 10 years, and a system initiated by the Suffolk Bank in Boston, which began in the early 1820s and lasted until 1858. By 1825, most New England banks were members. After early difficulties with the volatile notes of some rural banks, the Suffolk Bank became an ad hoc miniature central bank for New England, redeeming at par the notes of an increasing number of rural banks that maintained reserves at Suffolk. As a result of this system, the money supply was more stable in New England during most of this period than it was in most other parts of the country. Private clearinghouses also evolved after 1836 as lenders of last resort to perform some of the liquidity functions of the Second United States Bank and were able to increase the money supply by 2% to 4% during the financial panics of 1883 and 1907.[4]

Commercial banks at this time dealt primarily with business loans and other commercial activities, and no one was serving the banking needs of ordinary citizens. Enter the first of an assortment of savings associations, which today we frequently collectively call "thrifts."

2. The Office of the Comptroller of the Currency: *A Short History*, p. 1.
3. *Id.*
4. Edward Flaherty, *A Brief History of Central Banking in the United States*, University of Groningen, The Netherlands, 2001, ch. 9. *See also*, George Trivoli, *The Suffolk Bank—A Study of a Free-Enterprise Clearing System*, The Adam Smith Institute, 1979.

MSBs and State Savings Associations

Savings associations were organized in the early 1800s to provide banking services for ordinary citizens whose needs were not met by commercial banks. These institutions included mutual savings banks ("MSBs") and savings and loan associations, frequently called "building and loan associations" originally in the states.

MSBs were organized on a philanthropic basis by public-spirited citizens to provide wage earners with a safe place to deposit funds and earn interest. Unlike other kinds of depository institutions, they were organized as trusts and were run for the benefit of savers by a board of trustees supervised by state banking regulators. The first savings bank charter was issued to the Provident Institution for Savings in Boston in 1816, and the Philadelphia Savings Fund Society began operations on a voluntary basis the same year. Between 1820 and 1910, the number of MSBs increased from 10 to 637, and their aggregate assets increased from $1 million to more than $3 billion.[5] Among the investments permitted for these institutions were first mortgages on real estate and high-grade industrial bonds as well as blue-chip common and preferred stock.

More than 95% of MSBs were concentrated in nine states—Connecticut, Maine, Massachusetts, New Hampshire, New Jersey, New York, Pennsylvania, Rhode Island, and Washington. The initial concentration of MSBs in the northeast, and particularly in the large port cities, resulted primarily from the large influx of immigrants and their need for basic banking services. The names of the original New York savings banks reflect this market, for example, The Bowery, Dime, Emigrant, and Seamen's Savings Banks.

The first savings and loan association was the Oxford Provident Building Association of Philadelphia County founded in 1831. Patterned on British building societies, these early associations were organized to provide a way for members to pool their funds to provide loans to buy or build a home. Unlike MSBs, however, savings associations were owned by their members, who subscribed to "shares" in the institution at the time of its organization. In Massachusetts these early building societies were called "cooperative banks"—a name they retain today.

During and After the Civil War

It was not until the country required a means to finance the Civil War that the concept of a "national" bank was seriously considered once again. One of the purposes of the federal banking legislation introduced in

5. This discussion is based on FDIC, *History of the Eighties, Lessons for the Future*, ch. 6.

December 1862 was to stimulate bond sales and generate a rush of cash for the hard-pressed U.S. Treasury. That was a popular concept:

> Some members of Congress supported the national banking legislation as a simple act of patriotism. But the legislation's leading proponents—President Abraham Lincoln, Treasury Secretary Salmon P. Chase, and Ohio Senator John Sherman—saw the legislation not only as a way to tap the North's wealth and win the war but also as a means to assure the future greatness and permanence of the United States. At the heart of their vision was a safe, sound, and reliable banking and monetary system.[6]

Enter National Banks and the OCC

The Currency Act

The national bank contemplated by the Civil War legislation was a "charter," or type of bank, as opposed to one central bank. The first contemporary federal banking agency, the Office of the Comptroller of the Currency ("OCC" or the "Comptroller"), was created by legislation signed on February 23, 1863, generally referred to as the Currency Act of 1863. The OCC was structured as an office in the Treasury Department to charter and supervise national banks and to regulate the distribution of currency these banks were authorized to issue (hence the name "Comptroller *of the Currency*"). The OCC was to write uniform rules that would apply to all national banks and send examiners into the banks to make sure those rules were being followed.

The National Bank Act

The Currency Act was replaced by the National Bank Act of 1864 ("NBA"), which was signed on June 3, 1864.[7] The law required national banks to buy U.S. bonds in an amount equal to one third of their paid-in capital.[8] Banks would then issue uniform National Bank Notes, printed under the supervision of the OCC, equal to 90% of the market value of these bonds to create a uniform national currency. To counter the problem of discounting

---

6. OCC, *supra* note 2, at 3.
7. In 1874, Congress designated this Act "The National Bank Act" as a matter of law (12 U.S.C. § 38).
8. Under the 1864 Act, the minimum capital requirement for national banks ranged from $50,000 for banks in places with a population of 6,000 or less, $100,000 for banks in cities with a population of 6,000 to 50,000, and $200,000 for banks in cities with populations exceeding 50,000.

state bank notes and "wildcat banking," the NBA required that notes issued by national banks be redeemable on demand and at par at any national bank in the country.[9] The tying of currency issuance to U.S. bond holdings in this manner had a role in helping to finance the Civil War:

> If [a] bank wished to extend additional loans to generate more profits, then the bank had to increase its holdings of Treasury bonds. This provision . . . was designed to create a more active secondary market for Treasury bonds and thus lower the cost of borrowing for the federal government.[10]

The authorization of the national bank charter created a parallel scheme of state and federally chartered banks, which still is a cornerstone of our current dual banking system discussed in depth in Chapter 3. However, at the time, many advocates of the NBA hoped that the advantages of the new currency and other features of the act would drive the currency issued by state banks out of existence and induce state banks to convert to national banks, thereby ensuring a single national currency and a single banking system. This approach seemed to be working at first. Of the 1,600 state banks that existed in 1860, only 300 remained by 1866.[11] The number of national banks increased from 66 to 1,294 during this period, of which about 800 were converted state banks and the remainder *de novo*, or newly established, banks.[12] But, between 1870 and 1890, the number of state banks increased from 325 to 4,016, compared to an increase in the number of national banks from 1,612 to 3,715. Assets of state banks as a percentage of national bank assets increased from 12.8% to 56.3% during this period.[13] The beat goes on even today, with state-chartered banks outnumbering national banks, but holding decidedly less market share.

Panic and the Birth of the Federal Reserve System

The NBA was successful in producing a unified national currency and creating a network of banks subject to uniform regulations and examinations. It did not, however, put an end to financial panics, which occurred once in each of the four decades following its enactment, with a particularly severe crisis in 1907. These panics were caused in part by two restrictions imposed on national banks by the NBA. The first restricted the elasticity

9. National Banking Act of 1864, Sections 22 & 23.
10. Flaherty, *supra* note 4, ch. 10.
11. OCC, *supra* note 2, at 9.
12. Flaherty, *supra* note 4, ch. 10.
13. Richard Grossman, *US Banking History*, Civil War to World War II, EH.Net Encyclopedia, edited by Robert Whaples (Mar. 17, 2003).

of the currency each bank could have in circulation to a percentage of the market price of its government bonds, as follows:

> If prices in the Treasury bond market declined substantially, then the national banks had to reduce the amount of currency they had in circulation. This could be done by refusing new loans or, in a more draconian *way, by calling-in loans already outstanding. . . .* Consequently, the size of the money supply was tied more closely to the performance of the bond market *rather than* needs *of the economy.* (Emphasis added.)[14]

If loans were called and a critical number of borrowers declared bankruptcy because they could not repay their loans, the bank failed, and many depositors lost their funds.

The second restriction provided that a bank whose reserves fell below statutory requirements could be placed in receivership if it did not make up the shortfall within thirty days of being notified of the deficiency by the Comptroller. These shortfalls could occur when rural banks, in response to seasonal demand for farm credit, withdrew funds they had deposited with national banks in urban areas. If too many urban banks tried to restore their reserves at the same time by selling securities or calling in outstanding loans, the securities market would collapse, runs on certain banks would begin (sparked by rumors of impending failure), and a crisis would result. "Anyone unable to withdraw their deposits before the bank's till ran dry lost their savings all together. Private deposit insurance was scant and unreliable. Federal deposit insurance was nonexistent."[15]

Also contributing to these panics was the rise of demand deposits, which were supported only fractionally by cash reserves. There was no outside source of liquidity for the banking system so that "any excess cash reserves in the banking system were quickly exhausted whenever much of the public sought to convert deposits into currency."[16]

The Federal Reserve Act

These challenges led to the enactment of the Federal Reserve Act of 1913 ("FRA").[17] The FRA created the Federal Reserve System ("Federal Reserve"), headed by a board of seven members (later named the Board of Governors of the Federal Reserve System—the "Board"). To counter the fears by many bankers, businessmen, and others about the centralized control of the

14. Flaherty, *supra* note 4, ch. 11.
15. *Id.*
16. Kenneth Spong, *Banking Regulation, Its Purpose, Implementation and Effect*, Fed. Res. Bank of Kansas City, 2000, p. 20.
17. Act of Dec. 23, 1913, ch. 6 (38 Stat. 260).

banking system (the Hamilton-Jefferson debate still being alive and well), Federal Reserve operations were placed in 12 Federal Reserve Banks to be governed by nine directors, six of whom were elected by Federal Reserve member banks.

The FRA addressed the problem of the inelasticity of currency by granting the Federal Reserve the power to "rediscount"—or make loans secured by—eligible paper of member banks. By borrowing against eligible assets, member banks could obtain funds to meet sizable cash withdrawals or rapid increases in the demand for credit. The Federal Reserve was also authorized to hold reserves of member banks and to conduct monetary policy through open-market operations. In addition, as authorized by the FRA, Federal Reserve Banks issued Federal Reserve Bank Notes as legal currency in 1914 to begin to replace the Treasury notes, which had been the mainstay of U.S. currency until then.

National banks were required to join the system, and state-chartered banks were permitted to join voluntarily. State banks that join the Federal Reserve are referred to as "state member banks." The FRA granted the Federal Reserve the power to examine and supervise state member banks, requiring that these banks comply with the Board's capital and reserve requirements. This authority made the Federal Reserve the first contemporary federal agency to examine and supervise state-chartered banks.

Amendments to the FRA in 1917 also provided that a state bank that joined the system could "retain its full charter and statutory rights as a state bank or trust company, and may continue to exercise all the corporate powers granted it by the State in which it was created."[18] The FRA does, however, subject state member banks to investment restrictions imposed on national banks by the NBA.

The Great Depression

And then there was the Great Depression. Congressional response to the financial crisis of the Depression included an intense period of legislative activity during 1932–1934, which was designed to restore confidence in the banking system.[19] This period saw the enactment of laws providing federal deposit insurance for accounts in banks and savings associations, federal charters and a federal liquidity facility for savings associations, and extensive amendments to the NBA and FRA.

---

18. 12 U.S.C. § 330.
19. This period also saw the enactment of the acts that imposed federal regulation on the securities industry, the Securities Act of 1933 and the Securities Exchange Act of 1934.

The Banking Act of 1933[20] created the Federal Deposit Insurance Corporation ("FDIC"), prohibited member banks from paying interest on demand deposits, authorized the Federal Reserve to set interest rate ceilings on time deposits, and added Section 23A, relating to transactions with affiliates, to the FRA. The act also adopted the four statutory provisions known as the Glass-Steagall Act ("Glass-Steagall"), which prohibited banks from engaging in certain securities activities.[21]

Enter the FDIC, Federal Savings and Loan Associations, and the FHLBB

Federal Deposit Insurance Act

Perhaps the most far-reaching legislation relating to the banking system was the authorization in 1933 of federal insurance for deposits of banks.[22] This program, which was originally enacted as Section 12B of the FRA, became law on June 16, 1933.[23] The legislation initially offered deposit insurance of accounts in commercial and savings banks for up to $2,500. This insurance program was to be administered by the FDIC, an independent agency headed by a three-person board of directors, which was required to begin a temporary insurance program on January 1, 1934.

The establishment of the FDIC was funded by a capital contribution of $150 million by the Treasury and subscriptions to Class B stock by each Federal Reserve Bank in an amount equal to one-half of its surplus as of January 1, 1933. The initial annual insurance premium assessment was one-half of 1% of insurable deposits. One-half of this amount was payable immediately and the remainder payable on call by the FDIC.

National banks and state member banks were required to obtain deposit insurance. Originally, state nonmember banks could join the fund upon certification of solvency by their state regulator and after examination and approval by the FDIC. Because of the short time between the signing of the 1933 Banking Act and the starting date of January 1, 1934, the FDIC had to examine almost 8,000 state nonmember banks in three months. These banks had been examined and supervised by state banking agencies, but the quality varied greatly. In addition to restoring public confidence in the banking system by insuring individual accounts, deposit insurance was

20. June 16, 1933, ch. 89, 48 Stat. 163.
21. This act, which was partially repealed in 1999, is discussed further in Chapter 9, *infra*.
22. Proposals for some form of federal deposit insurance had been introduced in Congress since 1886, and insurance programs had been adopted by several states during 1829–1866 and 1908–1930.
23. June 16, 1933, ch. 89, 48 Stat. 163.

viewed as a way to bring state banks under uniform federal supervision as the "price" for these benefits.

The FDIC, with its powers of examination and supervision, thus became the primary federal regulator of state nonmember banks and the secondary federal regulator of national banks and state member banks. After its initial examinations to determine minimal acceptability for deposit insurance, and later examinations to determine capital adequacy, the FDIC shifted its attention to developing standards for safety and soundness examinations, which would be the foundation of the examinations the agency performs today. These examinations were designed to:

- appraise assets to determine net worth;
- assess asset quality;
- identify practices that could lead to financial difficulties;
- evaluate bank management; and
- assess compliance with law and regulations.

The FDIC was also granted supervisory powers at that time, including the authority to approve branch applications and capital reductions by insured nonmember banks and to approve mergers of all insured banks with uninsured institutions. The insurance of an insured bank could be terminated for failure to correct unsafe and unsound practices.

The Banking Act of 1935[24] provided that all institutions that were insured under the temporary program, which ended on September 1, 1935, would be admitted to the permanent program unless they decided to withdraw. At that time, 34 banks withdrew and 14,219 banks became federally insured.[25]

Federal supervision of MSBs began, as it did with state nonmember banks, with the authorization of federal deposit insurance in 1933. Deposit insurance was voluntary for MSBs, and many savings banks were opposed to the program. Only 56 savings banks, less than 12% of all MSBs, were admitted to the permanent program on September 1, 1935.[26] One of the reasons for this lower participation was that MSBs had not been subject to the kinds of "runs" that had affected commercial banks. MSBs had no demand deposits and could restrict early withdrawal of their savings accounts. As a result, many savings banks believed they did not need deposit insurance. Others regarded themselves as "preferred risks" and objected to being assessed for deposit insurance at the rates applied to commercial banks. A third factor was political: some were simply opposed

24. August 23, 1935, ch. 619 (49 Stat. 209).
25. In 1950, the federal deposit insurance program, which had been enacted in 1933 as Section 12B of the Federal Reserve Act, was removed from that Act by the Federal Deposit Insurance Act of 1950; Sept. 21, 1950, 64 Stat. 873 and codified separately in the U.S. Code at 12 U.S.C. § 1811 *et seq*.
26. FDIC, History, *supra* note 24, at 37.

to deposit insurance because it was a Roosevelt "New Deal" program.[27] By 1975, however, 70% of all MSBs were federally insured and the remainder, primarily cooperative banks in Massachusetts, were privately insured. These banks applied for federal deposit insurance in 1985 as a result of private insurance crises in Ohio and Maryland.

Federal Home Loan Bank Act and Home Owners Loan Act

Federal involvement in the savings association industry began with the enactment of the Federal Home Loan Bank Act of 1932 ("FHL Bank Act"),[28] also a piece of post-Depression legislation, which established the Federal Home Loan Bank System ("FHL Bank System") under the administration of a new agency, the Federal Home Loan Bank Board ("FHLBB"). The FHL Bank System was designed to reduce foreclosures and to encourage home ownership by providing an alternative source of funds for savings associations in the form of low-cost advances. The FHL Bank System consists of 12 regional Federal Home Loan Banks, which are government sponsored but owned by their members who are required to purchase stock as a condition of membership. Commercial banks and credit unions became eligible for membership in the FHL Bank System in 1989.

The Home Owners' Loan Act of 1933 ("HOLA")[29] ushered in the dual system for savings associations by authorizing the FHLBB to approve federal mutual charters for *de novo* savings associations and for those converting from a state charter. Federal supervisory authority over state-chartered savings associations began in 1934 with the creation of the Federal Savings and Loan Insurance Corporation ("FSLIC")[30] to insure deposits of federal and state savings associations. The FHLBB was designated as the board of directors of the FSLIC, thereby combining the deposit insurance and chartering function (for federal associations) in a single agency.

Between Crises

As a result of the accretion of legislative developments from the founding of our country until after the Great Depression, we developed the dual banking system across commercial banks and savings associations, and we added four federal bank regulatory agencies: the OCC, administrator of national banks; the Federal Reserve, central bank and primary federal regulator for

27. *Id.* at 29.
28. July 22, 1932, ch. 522, 47 Stat. 725, 12 U.S.C. §§ 1422, *et seq.*
29. June 13, 1933, ch. 64, 48 Stat. 128, 12 U.S.C. §§ 1461, *et seq.*
30. Title IV of the National Housing Act of 1934, June 27, 1934, 48 Stat. 1246 (12 U.S.C. § 1724 *et seq.*). Title IV was repealed by Section 407 of Public Law 101-73 (Aug. 9, 1989, 103 Stat. 183) in connection with the creation of the Savings Association Insurance Fund administered by the FDIC.

state member banks; the FDIC, the deposit insurer and primary federal regulator for state nonmember banks; and the FHLBB, primary regulator of savings associations.

From the Great Depression until the 1950s, the country was busy at war and healing from World War II, and no financial crises sparked new banking laws. That does not necessarily eliminate the possibility of banking legislation; although there is nothing like a financial crisis to create regulatory change. In fact, good times led to "loophole lawyering" or "innovative lawyering"—determining how to avoid the restrictions of banking laws.

Regulation of Holding Companies

At this time, many state laws impinged on the ability of banks to grow geographically, and both federal and state banking laws limited the activities in which banks and savings associations could engage. Enterprising bankers found ways around the restrictive laws by using corporations to own banks in more than one state and offer new products, like insurance. Congress reacted to close the loopholes and, between 1956 and 1970, enacted legislation to deal with the expansion of bank and savings and loan holding companies. As a result, the U.S. banking system distinguished itself from banking systems anywhere else in the world both then and now by developing banking families that were vertical and horizontal in structure (north to south, east to west) with a company, not a bank, at the pinnacle.

The Bank Holding Company Act

The Bank Holding Company Act of 1956[31] was enacted to curb the expansion of multiple-bank holding companies, holding companies that controlled more than one commercial bank, both geographically and with respect to powers. The BHCA included the "Douglas Amendment,"[32] which prohibited BHCs from acquiring banks in other states unless the law of that state specifically permitted such acquisitions. It also included Section 4, which restricted nonbanking activities of multibank holding companies.

But, Congress came back again and scooped up all companies that controlled a bank into the BHC regime. The Bank Holding Company Act Amendments of 1970[33] gave the Federal Reserve the authority to regulate the formation and operation of holding companies that only owned one bank—so called one-bank holding companies. The amended Bank Holding Company Act (the "BHCA") limited the nonbanking activities of all BHCs (subject to narrow exemptive authority) to "those that are so closely related

---

31. May 9, 1956, ch. 240, 70 Stat. 133.
32. Formerly codified in Section 3(d) (12 U.S.C. § 1842(d)) and repealed by the 1994 interstate branching legislation discussed in Chapter 9.
33. Pub. Law 91-607, Dec. 31, 1970, 84 Stat. 1760, codified at 12 U.S.C. §§ 1841 *et seq.*

to banking as to be a proper incident thereto."[34] Accordingly, the Federal Reserve added a new authority to its supervisory responsibilities—it became the supervisor of all BHCs and the ultimate arbitrator on the activities in which BHCs and their nonbank affiliates could engage.

The BHCA, and Regulation Y promulgated by the Federal Reserve thereunder, are intrinsically driven by the definitions that are found in Section 2 of the BHCA.[35] The concept of "control" in particular is critical in the determination of which entities come under the authority of the Federal Reserve and are subject to the restrictions of the BHCA. Section 3 of the BHCA[36] is dedicated to the formation of BHCs and their acquisitions of other BHCAs and banks. Section 4[37] contains the infamous limitations on nonbanking powers.

The Savings and Loan Holding Company Act

At the time of the enactment of the Savings and Loan Holding Company Act ("S&LHCA") of 1959 (the "Spence Act"),[38] the only savings associations organized in stock (rather than mutual) form were state chartered. Congressional concerns included the possibility of the holding company diverting the financial resources of the savings and loan subsidiary to the parent. The activities of associations at that time were limited primarily to residential mortgage lending in limited geographic areas, but there was some concern about multiple S&LHCs (i.e., those S&LHCs that owned more than one savings association).

To allow time for study of S&L holding companies, the Spence Act imposed a moratorium on the acquisition of additional associations by existing S&LHCs and limited new holding companies to the acquisition of a single association. The S&L Holding Company Act Amendments of 1967 imposed activity restrictions on multiple S&LHCs but permitted any company engaged in a lawful business to acquire a single association. From that emerged the "unitary thrift holding company"—a company that controlled one depository institution that was permitted to engage in commerce. Interestingly, while Congress closed that loophole for BHCs in 1970, the activities of unitary thrift holding companies were not curbed until 1999.

34. 12 U.S.C. § 1843(c)(8). The Federal Reserve was permitted to exempt certain BHCs in existence before July 1, 1968, from these restrictions.
35. 12 U.S.C. § 1841.
36. 12 U.S.C. § 1842. The concept of control is developed in Chapter 10, *infra*.
37. 12 U.S.C. § 1843. Discussed in depth in Chapter 10, *infra*.
38. Pub. Law 86-374, Sept. 23, 1959, 78 Stat. 691.

The Thrift Crisis

The sharp increase in interest rates to double-digit levels in late 1979 and early 1980 as a result of high rates of inflation, coupled with the limitation on the rates paid on deposits in effect since the Great Depression, made saving less attractive and at the same time reduced banks' traditionally important role in financial markets. Deregulation of interest rates then placed savings and loan associations—which loaned long term on one- to four-family homes and were trapped with 30-year loans priced at low interest rates—in a perilous financial position that eventually spiraled out of control.

Fix the Deposit Rates and Reserves

Depository Institutions Deregulation and Monetary Control Act

Congress, faced with monetary controls in need of buttressing and the steady flow of deposits away from traditional FDIC-insured depository institutions (a process called, "disintermediation") into higher paying funds, enacted the Depository Institutions Deregulation and Monetary Control Act ("DIDMCA")[39] in 1980 to facilitate the implementation of monetary policy, to provide for the gradual elimination of all limitations on the rates of interest payable on deposits, and to authorize interest-bearing transaction accounts.

Title I of the act was the Monetary Control Act of 1980. It required all institutions that accepted deposits to meet reserve requirements. (Reserve requirements are an important tool the Federal Reserve uses to achieve desired changes in the money supply.) Thrifts had not been required to hold reserves previously. In addition, the act provided for the gradual elimination of all limitations on the rates of interest payable on deposits and to authorize interest-bearing transaction accounts.

> Up until this time, the maximum interest rate that banks and other institutions could pay on deposits was regulated by the federal government under what was known as Regulation Q. In fact, banks were not allowed to pay any interest on checking accounts (or "demand deposit" accounts), and at the time the act was signed, the rate on savings accounts at banks was set at 5.25 percent. But market interest rates were in double digits, with short-term Treasury securities of over 12 percent.[40]

39. Pub. L. No. 96-221, 94 Stat. 132 (1980).
40. *See*, Federal Reserve History, *Depository Institutions Deregulation and Monetary Control Act of 1980*, Mar. 1980.

Fix the Thrifts and Enter the OTS

Garn-St Germain Depository Institutions Act

Congress' reaction to the threat to the thrift industry was then to enact the Garn-St Germain Depository Institutions Act of 1982 ("Garn-St Germain").[41] Garn-St Germain expanded the powers of thrift institutions in an effort to return them to profitability and keep them from failing. "The immediate effect of Garn-St. Germain was to turn the thrifts from a problem into a catastrophe. The fact is that deregulation in effect gave the industry—whose deposits were federally insured—a license to gamble with taxpayers' money, at best, or simply to loot it, at worst."[42] In any event, between 1980 and 1988, nearly 1,200 savings associations failed. Taxpayers lost an estimated $130–$150 billion.[43]

Garn-St Germain also expanded FDIC powers to assist troubled banks and, in response to intense lobbying efforts from the insurance industry, limited the insurance powers of BHCs.

Financial Institutions Reform, Recovery, and Enforcement Act

In order to restore the public's confidence in the savings and loan industry, Congress then enacted the Financial Institutions Reform, Recovery and Enforcement Act of 1989 ("FIRREA")[44] that made extensive changes in the way savings associations were regulated and insured. FIRREA rewrote HOLA to abolish the FHLBB, repeal title IV of the National Housing Act ("NHA"), and to make the following additional changes in the way savings associations were regulated:

- The authority to charter and supervise federal savings associations and federal savings banks was transferred from the FHLBB to the Office of Thrift Supervision ("OTS"), a new office in the Treasury;
- The insurance fund FSLIC was abolished, and its deposit insurance functions were transferred to a new Savings Association Insurance Fund ("SAIF") to be administered by the FDIC;
- The former FDIC insurance fund was redesignated the Bank Insurance Fund ("BIF"); BIF and SAIF were to be funded and administered separately by the FDIC;[45]

41. P.L. 97-320, 96 Stat. 1469.
42. Paul Krugman, *Reagan Did It*, NY Times, May 31, 2009.
43. Discussed in depth in Chapter 5, *infra*.
44. Pub. Law 101-73, Aug. 9, 1989, 103 Stat. 183.
45. BIF and SAIF were merged on March 31, 2006, in accordance with the terms of the FDIC Reform Act of 2005, Pub. Law 109-171, Title II, Subtitle B, Feb. 8, 2006, 120 Stat. 9.

- Supervision of the FHL Bank System was transferred to a new independent agency—the Federal Housing Finance Board;
- Several provisions of former title IV of the National Housing Act, including the S&L Holding Company Act and certain other powers of the former FSLIC with respect to state-chartered savings associations, were added into HOLA; and
- The Federal Home Loan Mortgage Corporation was made a separate government-sponsored enterprise under the supervision of the Department of Housing and Urban Development.

With the FHLBB folded and the FSLIC insurance fund insolvent, the industry needed a mechanism to resolve and liquidate assets (primarily mortgage loans and the underlying real property collateral) of all the failed federal savings associations. To that end, FIRREA created the Resolution Trust Corporation ("RTC"), which essentially became an enormous property management company. Between 1989 and mid-1995, the RTC closed or otherwise resolved 747 thrifts with total assets of $394 billion.[46] Its funding was provided by the Resolution Funding Corporation ("REFCORP").

Federal Deposit Insurance Corporation Improvement Act

But Congress was not finished because what had been a crisis in the thrift industry not only spread to the commercial banking industry but also peeled back the veil on untold examples of bank fraud and gross misbehavior by bankers and institution-related parties, like lawyers, accountants, and appraisers. And so, there was then the Federal Deposit Insurance Corporation Improvement Act of 1991 ("FDICIA").[47]

FDICIA scattered shot across many areas of banking in an effort to curb problems. It greatly increased the powers and authority of the FDIC in connection with resolutions of failed depository institutions. Major provisions recapitalized the BIF and allowed the FDIC to strengthen the fund by borrowing from the Treasury. FDICIA mandated a least-cost resolution method and prompt resolution approach to problem and failing banks and ordered the creation of a risk-based deposit insurance assessment scheme. Brokered deposits and the solicitation of deposits were restricted. FDICIA created new supervisory and regulatory examination standards and put forth new capital requirements for banks. It also expanded prohibitions against insider activities and created new truth-in-savings provisions.

Moreover, FDICIA limited the authority of state banks and their subsidiaries to act as principal in activities prohibited to national banks without approval of the FDIC and prohibited insurance underwriting through state banks, except to the extent permitted to national banks.

46. FDIC Analytics.
47. P.L. 102-242, 105 Stat. 2236.

Between Crises Redux

The amazing fact is that the country not only survived the thrift crisis, but prospered. We went from depository institution failures of 464 in 1988 and 533 in 1989 to one in 1997.[48] With the crisis in the rearview mirror, the industry turned once again to expansion, both geographically and in diversification of products. And the industry started winning.

Geographic and Powers Expansion

Riegle-Neal Interstate Banking and Branching Efficiency Act

Innovation, as pointed out at the beginning of this chapter, is an engine for change in the financial institution's sector in this country, and innovation typically has expansion as its objective. Thus, not surprisingly, the 1990s saw recovery from the thrift crisis and a significant quest by banks to get bigger and break out of the chains of the Douglas Amendment[49] to the BHCA and the McFadden Act[50] that restrained them in-state and sometimes in-county. The gist of the Douglas Amendment was to ban BHCs from bank acquisitions interstate unless state law in the state a BHC sought to enter specifically permitted it.

Was there a way to go state by state and free the restraints? Turned out the answer was "yes." On its face, the act permitted states to lift the ban and open their state up for bank expansion. Better yet, was there a way to do it that kept the big New York banks out of the game? Turned out the answer was also "yes" through regional reciprocal compacts—a state would limit the BHCs that could enter based on named states only and a requirement of reciprocity with the home state of those BHCs. The states in the Southeast created the Southeastern Regional Bank Compact,[51] and Massachusetts and Connecticut formed a New England Compact (intentionally excluding New York). The Supreme Court[52] upheld the New England compact and the rest of the country began carving itself up into similar reciprocal regions.

Congress, faced with interstate banking a-go-go without its blessing, eventually reacted and ratified the innovation with the Riegle-Neal Interstate

48. FDIC Division of Research and Statistics.
49. Section 3(d) of the BHCA (previously codified at 12 U.S.C. § 1842(d)).
50. P.L. 69-639, 44 STAT. 1224 (1927). The act prohibited interstate banking of national banks, unless permitted for state banks and is discussed in Chapter 9, *infra*.
51. *See,* Thomas D. Hills, *The Rise of Southern Banking and The Disparities among The States Following The Southeastern Regional Banking Compact,* XI North Carolina Banking Institute L.J. 57 (Feb. 27, 2007); *see also,* Arthur E. Wilmarth Jr., *The Case for the Validity of State Regional Banking Laws,* 18 Loy. L.A. L. Rev. 1017 (1985)
52. Northeast Bancorp, Inc. v. Board of Governors of Federal Reserve System, 472 U.S. 159 (1985).

Banking and Branching Efficiency Act of 1994,[53] which repealed the Douglas Amendment and the McFadden Act, permitted bank holding companies to acquire banks in any state, and allowed interstate mergers between banks, subject to conditions and concentration limits, state laws, and evaluations. So, gone were most of the impediments to national expansion. But that then required the law to construct an elaborate scheme for applicability of state laws to out-of-state bank branches.

Gramm-Leach-Bliley Act

With geography no longer a hindrance, the industry focused on powers. BHC powers were still limited under Section 4 of the BHCA, and bank powers were limited by the respective law of charter. Banks and BHCs desperately wanted to liberalize those laws, especially to permit them to enter the sacred realms of securities and insurance sales and underwriting. Over the ensuing years in the late 1990s, there were countless inroads by banks and BHCs into these realms. Step by step, the OCC permitted national banks to engage in broader activities, and the Federal Reserve did its share in expanding BHC securities powers. Each step engendered a lawsuit, many of which went all the way to the Supreme Court.

So, years went by as powers developed incrementally . . . and then came Citicorp and Travelers Group, a bank holding company and an insurance conglomerate, respectively. Together, they proposed to form Citigroup, the prototype for a domestic diversified financial services company, the likes of which had not been permitted in the United States since the Great Depression. The Federal Reserve approved the merger, predicated on the clear wording of the BHCA to the effect that otherwise illegal activities could be held by a new bank holding company for two years (with extensions).[54] The parties needed a little help from Congress to supply permanent legality. Congress complied.

Enactment of the Gramm-Leach-Bliley Act of 1999 ("Gramm-Leach-Bliley" or "GLBA")[55] concluded years of emotion-laden negotiations between the banking, securities, and insurance industries and among the administration, federal agencies, and state regulators. All existing statutory schemes for bank powers were affected by Gramm-Leach-Bliley, at least in terms of establishing or ratifying opportunities for financial institutions to engage in insurance and securities activities:

---

53. P.L. 103-328, 108 Stat. 2338 (1994).
54. Section 4(a)(2) of the BHCA (codified at 12 U.S.C. § 1843(a)(2)) permits any new BHC, for a period of two years, to engage in impermissible activities. By regulation, the Board may grant requests for three additional one-year extensions. 12 C.F.R. § 225.22(f).
55. Pub. L. No. 106-102, 133 Stat. 1338 (1999).

- Section 103 of Gramm-Leach-Bliley amended the BHCA to create *financial holding companies*, companies that engage in activities financial in nature, or incidental or complementary thereto, including insurance underwriting and agency, securities underwriting and brokerage, and merchant banking;
- Section 121 of Gramm-Leach-Bliley amended the NBA, Federal Deposit Insurance Act ("FDIA"), and the FRA to permit qualifying banks to own *financial subsidiaries* that may engage in many activities financial in nature or incidental thereto, including securities underwriting and brokerage and insurance agency activities, but generally excluding broad forms of insurance underwriting; and
- Section 401 of Gramm-Leach-Bliley amended HOLA to permit thrift holding companies to engage in activities financial in nature, without the necessity of otherwise meeting the requirements for financial holding companies.

But the currency for the new powers was a complex web of regulatory schemes, compliance burdens, and preemption rules that were codified primarily in Titles II, III, and V of the act. Title II required banks to push out most broker and dealer activities to registered broker-dealers (leading to years of nasty negotiations between the Securities and Exchange Commission ("SEC") and the Federal Reserve on joint rulemaking). Title III subjected bank insurance activities to state insurance law but established an elaborate preemption scheme for certain types of state law, and required cumbersome bank insurance sales disclosures. Title V gave us privacy disclosure requirements and sharing restrictions.

One of the hallmarks of Gramm-Leach-Bliley was the concept of "functional regulation," the goal being that banking would be supervised and regulated by the banking agencies; insurance activities by the state departments of insurance; and securities transactions by the SEC and state securities divisions. The financial crisis of 2008–2009 unveiled fundamental gaps in the regulatory scheme.

The Global Financial Crisis

Even when the Second Edition of *Keys* originally went to press in 2017, we remained haunted by the images of 2008 and the near collapse of our financial markets. There was no question but that reform was required. The system was broken and fault lay at the doorstep of many of the conglomerates created post-Gramm-Leach-Bliley. Yet Congress was tasked with creating solutions before the causes of the crisis were fully understood and wading into the weeds of our complex system of banking that was, after all, created improvisationally over the history of the United States.

Enter SIGTARP, FSOC, CFPB ... and Farewell OTS

Emergency Economic Stabilization Act

The first step in healing the broken system was the unprecedented authority for Treasury to invest in BHCs and S&LHCs. On October 3, 2008, Congress passed, and President Bush signed into law, the Emergency Economic Stabilization Act of 2008 ("EESA"). EESA authorized the Secretary of the Treasury to implement various temporary emergency programs designed to strengthen the capital positions of financial institutions and stimulate the availability of credit within the U.S. financial system. Ultimately, Treasury invested approximately $245 billion across five distinct bank programs.[56] Each of these programs was established to accomplish different goals as part of the overall effort to stabilize America's banking system.

The most noteworthy of the EESA programs and the largest bank program under TARP, known as the TARP Capital Purchase Program (the "CPP"), was Treasury's plan to provide Tier 1 capital (in the form of perpetual preferred stock) to eligible financial institutions. This program was allocated $250 billion from the $700 billion authorized by the EESA to Treasury for the purchase of senior preferred shares from qualifying financial institutions (the "CPP Preferred Stock"). Under the program, eligible institutions were able to sell equity interests to the Treasury in amounts equal to between 1% and 3% of the institution's risk-weighted assets. The CPP Preferred Stock was nonvoting and paid dividends at the rate of 5% per annum for the first five years and thereafter at a rate of 9% per annum. In conjunction with the purchase of the CPP Preferred Stock, the Treasury received warrants to purchase common stock from the participating public institutions with an aggregate market price equal to 15% of the preferred stock investment. Participating financial institutions were required to adopt Treasury's standards for executive compensation and corporate governance for the period during which Treasury holds equity securities issued under the CPP.

Treasury has reported that it provided capital to 707 financial institutions in 48 states. The final investment under the CPP was made in December 2009. TARP dispersed a total of $433.7 billion and Treasury has since focused on recovering the investments. Most banks repaid TARP funds using capital raised from the issuance of equity securities and debt not guaranteed by the federal government. As of August 31, 2016, cumulative collections under TARP, together with Treasury's additional proceeds from

56. Information on TARP as reported by Treasury is at treasury.gov under TARP-Programs.

the sale of non-TARP shares of AIG, totaled $442.1 billion, exceeding disbursements by $8.4 billion.[57]

Sadly, when money is provided, fraud often follows, and Congress, in anticipating that consequence with TARP, included in EESA the creation of the Office of the Special Inspector General for the Troubled Asset Relief Program ("SIGTARP"), with a Special Inspector General appointed by the President and confirmed by the U.S. Senate. The Special Inspector General's purpose is to monitor, audit, and investigate TARP-related activities, including those of the Treasury in the administration of the program, and report findings to Congress every quarter. Since 2009 more than $10 billion has been recovered as a result of SIGTARP investigations. In fiscal year 2019, SIGTARP investigations resulted in approximately $900 million recovered, criminal charges against 13 defendants, 4 arrests, criminal convictions of 18 defendants, courts sentencing 28 defendants to prison, and federal criminal or civil enforcement activity against 3 corporations/organizations.[58]

Dodd-Frank Wall Street Reform and Consumer Protection Act

More was needed than a bailout. Most agreed that substantial reformation of our banking system was required and Congress responded, delivering the Dodd-Frank Wall Street Reform and Consumer Protection Act of 2010 ("Dodd-Frank"),[59] signed into law by President Obama on July 21, 2010. Dodd-Frank boasts over 2,300 pages (848 pages of substance in the Conference Report) covering 16 separate titles. To put that in perspective, the Gramm-Leach-Bliley Conference Report had 185 substantive pages covering six titles, and that has taken us a decade to sort out. Moreover, those Dodd-Frank titles house many "Acts," such as the "Financial Stability Act of 2010," the "Enhancing Financial Institution Safety and Soundness Act of 2010," and the "Federal Insurance Office Act of 2010," each of which is sure to blur the already difficult world of "bank-speak."

And then there are the "inside the beltway" references to amendments and rules: the "Collins Amendment" (capital requirements for BHCs); the "Volcker Rule" (limitations on proprietary trading) and "Hotel California" ("you can check out but never leave" . . . a reference to Morgan Stanley and its ilk, which elected to become BHCs during the 2008 financial crisis and took CPP and are now banned from debanking to escape Federal Reserve regulation).

New Federal Offices. Let us not forget that Dodd-Frank creates 13 new federal offices, the acronyms for which are guaranteed to create havoc:

57. *Id.*
58. SIGTARP Semi-Annual Report to Congress Apr. 1, 2019, to Sept. 30, 2019.
59. Pub. L. No. 111-203 (2010). There are a number of terrific summaries of Dodd-Frank available on the Internet. Especially helpful is the American Bankers Association website, where the summaries have links to the actual law.

- Bureau of Consumer Financial Protection ("independent" within the Federal Reserve) (the "Bureau" or "CFPB"),
- Financial Stability Oversight Council (stand-alone) ("FSOC"),
- Federal Insurance Office (Treasury) ("FIO"),
- New Offices of Minority and Women Inclusion (banking and securities regulators) ("OMWI"),
- Investor Advisory Committee (stand-alone; to advise SEC) ("IAC"),
- Office of Investor Advocate (SEC) ("OIA"),
- Office of Credit Ratings (SEC) ("OCR"),
- Credit Rating Agency Board (SEC) ("CRAB"—did they think that one through?),
- Office of Financial Literacy ("OFL"),
- Office of Financial Research (Treasury) ("OFR"),
- Office of Housing Counseling (HUD) ("OHC"),
- Office of Fair Lending and Equal Opportunity (Federal Reserve) ("OFLEO"), and
- Office of Financial Protection for Older Americans (Federal Reserve) ("OFPOA").

Systemic Risk. Title I of Dodd-Frank tackled systemic risk—the risk of a chain reaction of failures of major, interconnected, highly leveraged institutions that would bring our economy to its knees—through increasing oversight and imposing more stringent prudential standards. Title I established a new supervisory structure for the risk-based oversight of the U.S. financial system that will focus on:

- Identifying and addressing systemic risks to the stability of the U.S. financial system;
- Bringing nonbank financial companies (companies that are predominantly engaged in financial activities but are not bank holding companies) that are determined to be significant to U.S. financial stability under comprehensive financial regulation and supervision; and
- Imposing new and heightened prudential standards for the operation of financial institutions and financial markets in the United States.

To this end, Title I created a new Financial Services Oversight Council ("FSOC"), chaired by the Secretary of the Treasury and composed of representatives from the principal federal financial regulatory agencies and a representative of the insurance industry, with its principal mission to prevent systemic risk from threatening the financial system. In so doing, FSOC is to fill gaps in supervision, monitor financial market developments, identify emerging risks in firms and market activities, and facilitate coordination of interagency policy and resolution of disputes.

For the purpose of meeting these obligations, FSOC is charged with collecting information necessary to recognize systemic risk early and monitor the financial system through the newly created Office of Financial Research ("OFR"). FSOC has no direct regulatory authority over financial firms. That is left to the Federal Reserve. To that end, the Federal Reserve was tasked with being a single point of accountability over financial firms, the failure of any of which could pose a threat to financial stability, regardless of whether they own banks. This includes nonbank firms designated by FSOC as systemically important financial institutions ("SIFIs") (no nonbank SIFIs remained in 2019), as well as all bank holding companies with total consolidated assets equal to or greater than $50 billion.

Title I mandated that the Federal Reserve establish, for the institutions under its purview: capital, leverage, and liquidity requirements; overall risk management requirements; and concentration limits. Covered institutions were also required to submit credible resolution plans (the so-called "living wills"). There are limits on acquisitions, requirements for applications, and other fundamental changes in how these institutions may operate and grow. The Federal Reserve's authority extends to an FHC's parent company and all of its subsidiaries, irrespective of whether any one of them is unregulated, is regulated by another federal agency, or is a domestic or foreign concern. These issues are addressed in more detail in Chapter 10, dealing with bank holding company regulation.

Orderly Liquidation. Title II is designed to handle "too big to fail" through the authorization of a new "orderly liquidation authority" ("OLA") by the FDIC in the case of the failure of a systemically important financial institution. OLA is intended to proceed like a bankruptcy, with the FDIC as receiver.

OTS Elimination. In a move contemplated by reform proposals for over two decades, Title III of Dodd-Frank eliminated the OTS on July 21, 2011 (the "transfer date") by merging it into the OCC. This is the only change in Dodd-Frank that affects the fundamental "who's who" of the existing bank regulatory agencies, although, as indicated above, there is some reshuffling as to supervisory responsibility. The thrift charter, however, survived; it just operates under a different supervisor—the OCC for federal thrifts and the FDIC for state charters. The thrift holding company also survived but under the supervision of the Federal Reserve. Ironically, Dodd-Frank's impact in this regard has been on insurance companies that entered banking through the federal thrift charter to avoid regulation by the Federal Reserve as bank holding companies. That privilege ended abruptly. Otherwise, the legal separation between banking and commercial activities was retained, reaffirmed, and strengthened.

Funds and Insurance. Title IV required registration of advisors to private funds. Title V established the Federal Insurance Office ("FIO") within Treasury and gave it authority with respect to all lines of insurance except health insurance, crop insurance, and certain types of long-term care insurance. Its mandate is not to be a regulator or supervisor—that role stayed with the states—but to monitor all aspects of insurance, assist Treasury and coordinate efforts in certain respects, recommend insurers who may be nonbank companies that should be subject to supervision by the Federal Reserve, make preemption determinations, and consult with state insurance regulators. Title V also included state-based insurance reform of the surplus lines and reinsurance markets.

Bank Regulatory Changes. Title VI meanwhile drove a stake into functional regulation as articulated by Gramm-Leach-Bliley, removing Section 10A from the BHCA, which limited the Federal Reserve's rulemaking and enforcement authority over functionally regulated affiliates. No longer would the Federal Reserve be asked to stay on the sidelines until the affiliate's actions "pose a threat to the safety and soundness of the depository institution affiliate." Moreover, Title VI delved into much of the minutiae of prudential bank regulation discussed in this book, making intricate changes designed to close loopholes that were exploited.

Swaps Regulation. Title VII addressed the regulation of swaps markets, and Section 716, also known as the "Swaps Push-Out Rule," or the "Lincoln Amendment," would have required FDIC-insured banks that are registered swap dealers to spin off certain commodity, equity swaps and uncleared credit default swaps into separate non-FDIC insured units (not including the two most actively-traded asset classes, interest rate and foreign exchange swaps). In December 2014, an omnibus spending bill was enacted by Congress and signed into law by President Obama. A provision in that bill repealed most of Section 716, so as to ease the limitations on the types of swap activities. Under the amended version of the Swaps Push-Out Rule, a push out is solely required with certain "structured finance swaps."[60]

Investor Protection. Title IX dealt with investor protections and improvements to the regulation of securities and rather provocatively required the SEC to study and report on the current broker-dealer standard of care and then, in its discretion, to begin rulemaking on the standard of care conundrum. While the report was ultimately released, the SEC did not immediately press the issue until June 5, 2019, when it issued Regulation Best Interest,[61] which requires associated persons of a broker-dealer (frequently referred to as "registered representatives") to act in the best interest of the retail customer when making a recommendation of any securities transaction or investment strategy, without placing the reps' financial or other interest.

---

60. Practical Law Finance, *Dodd-Frank Swaps Pushout Rule Substantially Repealed*, Dec. 17, 2014.
61. Regulation BI, 17 C.F.R. Part 240.

CFPB. In order to protect consumers, Title X of Dodd-Frank created the CFPB, housed independently within the Federal Reserve, with supervisory, examination, and enforcement authority over consumer-related financial services offered by financial entities. These services include mortgages and other credit or payment products, but do not generally include insurance products. As of July 21, 2011, the CFPB absorbed and consolidated the powers previously held by the federal regulators of depository institutions with respect to financial consumer protection laws, such as enforcement of the Truth in Lending Act and the alphabet soup of current Federal Reserve consumer regulations, but left jurisdiction over already-regulated investment products and services with the SEC or the Commodities Futures Trading Commission.

Title X is also infamous for bringing us the "Durbin Amendment," popular with retail merchants, but not so much with banks, that required the Federal Reserve to limit the amount of interchange fees large issuing banks could charge on debit card transactions, as well as restricting network exclusivity.

Mortgage Reform. Title XIII winds down TARP. And finally, Title XIV provided the much-needed reformation of our consumer mortgage market and hopefully spells the end of predatory lending practices at long last.

Lots of law and an unprecedented required promulgation of 390 rulemakings by as many as 11 different federal agencies. The law delivered many ways for bank lawyers to stay engaged.

Between Crises Redux (yet again)

As the Global Financial Crisis faded into a decidedly uncomfortable memory and the regulators were able to objectively view the results of Dodd-Frank, it was universally recognized that certain Dodd-Frank reforms needed rightsizing. It turned out that risk, especially systemic risk, is not based on an arbitrary asset size. Rather, risk is based on risk—reliance on short-term funding sources, excessive off-balance sheet exposures, interdependence in bank families, and the like. Thus, a look-back in better times revealed that asset thresholds for systemically important financial institutions of $50 billion and for certain prudential requirements to kick in at $10 billion were overly conservative; thus, the time had come to better align supervision with the risks posed by the largest banking institutions.

Economic Growth, Regulatory Relief and Consumer Protection Act

Along came Congress, enacting the Economic Growth, Regulatory Relief and Consumer Protection Act of 2018 ("Regulatory Relief Act" also known as "Crapo" or, the worst acronym ever, "EGRRCPA")[62] in May 2018 to modify or remove certain financial reform rules and regulations. The law rolls back a number of Dodd-Frank provisions, especially dealing with community and regional banks: the SIFI test was increased to $250 billion (from $50 billion); less than $10 billion are generally exempt from Volcker Rule and risk committee requirement; between $50 billion and $100 billion are exempt from enhanced prudential standards (resolution planning, stress tests, single party credit limits) immediately and no longer subject to stress testing; between $100 billion and $250 billion the bank regulatory agencies may exercise discretion to determine the appropriate standards to apply (so-called "tailoring"); less than $10 billion may adopt a simplified capital framework, the Community Bank Leverage Ratio of 9% ("CBLR") (an off-ramp for the complex consolidated capital rules known as Basel III); and small holding companies of $3 billion and less may qualify for an exception from complex consolidated capital reporting.

In addition, Crapo provided mortgage relief for community bank residential real estate mortgages held in portfolio; reciprocal deposit relief from brokered deposit restrictions; and simplified reporting requirements for less complex banks with under $5 billion in assets, in addition to addressing a variety of other Dodd-Frank remedial issues.

Global Pandemic

The coronavirus pandemic, unlike the previous crises, did not emanate from financial misdeeds, and its primary impact was not felt directly by financial institutions, but it still affected the industry in myriad ways. People demanding cash and loan modifications impacted liquidity, capital adequacy, and safety and soundness. As bank lawyers, we were faced with all kinds of unique challenges: e-signature and remote notarization issues, CALL report delays, disclosure conundrums, partial bank branch closings, and physical bank examinations on hold. So, Congress turned to tools it sharpened in the Global Financial Crisis and developed new tools to relieve the economy, hopefully developing an arsenal for future emergencies.

Coronavirus Aid, Relief, and Economic Security Act

The CARES Act of 2020[63] and its progeny represent the largest ever economic stimulus package in the history of the United States. Unprecedented in scope but still temporary. Most of this will roll-off at the end of 2020.

62. Economic Growth, Regulatory Relief and Consumer Protection Act of 2018 (Pub. Law 115–174, S. 2155) was signed into law by President Donald Trump on May 24, 2018.
63. Pub.L. 116–136 (2020) signed into law on Mar. 27, 2020.

For the banking industry (from a regulatory perspective, not an employer, taxpayer perspective), it is Title IV—Economic Stabilization and Assistance to Severely Distressed Sectors of the United States Economy—and, more particularly, Subtitle A—Coronavirus Economic Stabilization Act of 2020—that is impactful. For the purposes of this book, the CARES Act brought back the Transaction Account Guarantee Program first utilized by the FDIC during the Global Financial Crisis as an FDIC option; it temporarily waived lending limits and decreased community bank capital requirements; and it permitted an optional two-year delay in implementing a change in loan loss accounting that was expected to impact bank capital. Note: no material bank regulatory changes played out with this crisis.

Paycheck Protection. The act addressed a variety of lending modification and troubled debt issues outside the scope of this book. But, one lending program is noteworthy: the Paycheck Protection Program ("PPP"), added by Section 1102 of the CARES Act.[64] It was designed as a Small Business Administration ("SBA") loan to provide direct incentives for small businesses (including independent contractors and nonprofits) to keep their workers on the payroll. The SBA will forgive the loans if all employees were kept on the payroll for a designated number of weeks and the money was used for payroll, rent, mortgage interest, or utilities. Applications for the $350 billion in allocated funds were processed through existing SBA 7(a) lenders and through any insured depository institutions ("IDIs"). Lenders began processing loan applications on April 3, 2020. The funds in the original PPP were quickly exhausted with a reported burn rate of around $50 billion per day, and many small businesses were left waiting in line. Congress went back to work, allocating an additional $310 billion in PPP on April 24, 2020. With a nod to community banks, $60 billion at a minimum was set aside for smaller banks and credit unions, including $30 billion for institutions under $10 billion in assets, and $30 billion for those with between $10 billion and $50 billion in assets.

Where to Find the Law?

Given that our clients may have a variety of charters and may have any number of affiliates, we must know where to find the applicable law. Banking law moves from the statutes like those summarized above, to the regulations promulgated by the agency with rulemaking authority, to the abundant sources of less formal guidance in the form of interpretive letters, application approvals, financial institution letters and notices, and various types of handbooks. All of this creates our "law."

64. Codified as Subsection (36) of Section 7(a) of the Small Business Act.

Statutes

Rule number one: most of our statutes are codified in Title 12 of the U.S. Code ("U.S.C.") They are codified in the order of enactment. Thus, the NBA commands pole position, followed by the FRA and FDIA. It sounds easy but what complicates the process is that many of the laws described above, and many not mentioned, are "amending" statutes, meaning you cannot simply open 12 U.S.C. and find them. You find bits and pieces strewn throughout. To read the actual act, you must locate the conference report and work your way through it. As can be seen below, only the laws in bold have a formal place in the code.

National Bank Act 1864 (NBA) .... 12 U.S.C. § 1

Federal Reserve Act of 1913 (FRA) .... 12 U.S.C. § 241

McFadden Act 1927, 1933

Home Owners' Loan Act (HOLA) .... 12 U.S.C. § 1462

Federal Credit Union Act .... 12 U.S.C. § 1752

Glass-Steagall Act 1933

Federal Deposit Insurance Act 1935, 1950 (FDIA) .... 12 U.S.C. § 1811

Bank Holding Company Act of 1956, 1970 (BHCA) .... 12 U.S.C. § 1841

International Banking Act of 1978 .... 12 U.S.C. § 1878

Depository Institutions Deregulation and Monetary Control Act of 1980

Garn-St Germain Act 1982

Money Laundering Control Act of 1986

Competitive Equality Banking Act of 1987

Financial Institutions Reform, Recovery and Enforcement Act of 1989

Federal Deposit Insurance Corporation Improvement Act of 1991

Riegle-Neal Interstate Banking and Branching Efficiency Act of 1994

Gramm-Leach-Bliley Act of 1999

Emergency Economic Stabilization Act of 2008

Dodd-Frank Wall Street Reform and Consumer Protection Act of 2010

Economic Growth, Regulatory Relief and Consumer Protection Act of 2018

Regulations

Regulations are formal rulemakings promulgated under federal statutes and subject to the rigors of public comment under the Administrative Procedures Act. Notices of Proposed Rulemaking ("NPR") and Final Rules are published in the *Federal Register.*

Rule number two: the regulations are then codified in Title 12 of the Code of Federal Regulations ("C.F.R."). They are also in order from the first agency created to the last. Thus, the OCC holds pole position, followed by the Federal Reserve, the FDIC, and the newest kid on the block, the CFPB.

12 C.F.R. 1–199	Comptroller of the Currency
12 C.F.R. 200's	Federal Reserve System (conveniently identified by letter of the alphabet, the order of which coincides with the part of the C.F.R. Thus, Regulation D—the fourth letter of the alphabet—is 12 C.F.R. 204)
12 C.F.R. 300's	Federal Deposit Insurance Corporation
12 C.F.R. 500's	Office of Thrift Supervision (moved as shown below)
12 C.F.R. 1000's	Bureau of Consumer Financial Protection (Using the same letter system as the Federal Reserve. Thus, Regulation E—the fifth letter of the alphabet—is 12 C.F.R. 1005)

The former OTS Regulations have been moved as follows:

12 C.F.R. 100's	OCC—Federal Thrifts (many of these have been removed and regulations applicable previously to national banks are now allocable to both)
12 C.F.R. 390/391	FDIC—State thrifts
12 C.F.R. 238/239	Federal Reserve—Thrift holding companies (Reg LL) and mutual holding companies (Reg MM)

Interpretations, Guidelines, Bulletins, and Other Resources

Thankfully, the Internet creates a convenient location for our less formal law:

www.occ.treas.gov
www.federalreserve.gov[65]
www.fdic.gov
www.consumerfinance.gov

A Note on Guidance and Other Sources of "Law"

Each one of the websites listed above is a treasure trove of supervisory guidance, interagency statements, bulletins, policy statements, examination manuals and checklists, speeches of import, decisions on cases and applications, and "FAQs" (frequently asked questions). The amount of information is overwhelming, and it has been historically difficult to parse the line between what is enforceable and what is really merely guidance.

More problematic, examiners have been increasingly prone to treat supervisory guidance as law, noncompliance with which is subject to "MRAs" (matters requiring attention) and "MRIAs" (matters requiring immediate attention) and sometimes to regulatory enforcement actions.[66] **But guidance is not law.** Finally, all of the bank regulatory agencies (yes, even the CFPB) realized the necessity of transparency in this regard and, in 2018, collectively issued what they like to call "guidance on guidance"—officially titled, "The Interagency Statement Clarifying the Role of Supervisory Guidance."[67] Therein, the agencies clarified that "unlike a law or regulation, supervisory guidance does not have the force and effect of law, and the agencies do not take enforcement actions based on supervisory guidance. Rather, supervisory guidance outlines the agencies' supervisory expectations or priorities and articulates the agencies' general views regarding appropriate practices for a given subject area."

Among the points clarified in the guidance are answers to two critical questions:

- What if the guidance includes bright-line tests or numerical expectations? Answer: *Where numerical thresholds are used, the agencies intend to clarify that the thresholds are exemplary only and not suggestive of requirements.*

---

65. The Federal Reserve makes available all of its regulations plus related statutes, interpretations, policy statements, rulings, and staff opinions in the Federal Reserve Regulatory Services (FRRS), which may be ordered at www.federalreserve.gov.
66. The examination process and enforcement framework for banking is discussed in Chapter 11, *infra*.
67. The Federal Reserve issued the interagency Statement as SR 18-5/CA 18-7 (Sept. 12, 2018).

- May examiners criticize a bank for a violation of supervisory guidance? Answer: *Examiners will not criticize a supervised financial institution for a "violation" of supervisory guidance. . . . In some situations, examiners may reference (including in writing) supervisory guidance to provide examples of safe and sound conduct, appropriate consumer protection and risk management practices, and other actions for addressing compliance with laws or regulations.*

Ultimately, however, there is always the issue of safety and soundness, and you should not doubt that egregious violations of supervisory guidance that present risk may yet lead to a finding of unsafe and unsound banking practices, opening up the panoply of enforcement options.[68]

And, a Note on Administrative Law and Deference

When banking issues come before the courts, whether it be on the appropriateness of an approval of an application, or an enforcement against a bank or affiliated party, or in connection with rulemaking or whatever final agency action is ripe for review, the scope of review by the courts is generally under the Administrative Procedures Act,[69] and the standard to set aside agency action is often, "arbitrary, capricious, an abuse of discretion or otherwise not in accordance with law."

When final federal agency action is under the judicial microscope, the courts are bound to give the banking agency "deference," if deserving. Our banking law is rife with examples of significant cases where deference has been the deciding factor, especially in the arena of new powers.

In this regard, the seminal *Chevron*[70] doctrine of administrative deference has a two-part test established by the Supreme Court for reviewing the construction of a statute by a regulatory agency charged with the duty to administer the statute. To this end, the court must first determine whether "Congress has directly spoken to the precise question at issue. If the intent of Congress is clear, this is the end of the matter; for the court, as well as the agency, must give effect to the unambiguously expressed intent of Congress."[71] If, however, the court determines that Congress has not directly addressed the precise question, the court may not simply impose its own construction on the statute: "Rather, if the statute is silent or ambiguous, with respect to the specific issue, the question for the court is whether the agency's answer is based on a permissible construction of the statute.

68. Chapter 8, *infra.* is dedicated to the principles of safety and soundness.
69. 5 U.S.C. § 706.
70. Chevron USA v. Natural Resources Defense Council, 467 U.S. 837 (1984) ("*Chevron*").
71. 467 U.S. 837, 842–845.

A court may not substitute its own construction of a statutory provision for a reasonable interpretation made by the administrator of an agency."[72]

That last sentence is powerful stuff, precluding a court's *de novo* construction of the law. There are so many examples of this application, but no more than when the OCC was pushing the envelope of national bank insurance powers. For example, in an early case applying the *Chevron* doctrine to a decision of the OCC regarding the insurance powers of national banks, the D.C. Circuit Court reasoned:

> To overturn the Comptroller's construction, we would have to conclude that it is "so inconsistent" with a "sufficiently clear" statutory policy as to demonstrate that "Congress's clear intent has been violated."[73]

The OCC was undefeated with a string of successful deference cases throughout the 1980s and 1990s. But it lost its streak in 2000, when the D.C. Circuit affirmed the district court decision that national banks could not sell crop insurance outside of small towns. The court blasted the OCC for transgressing "both common sense and two traditional rules of statutory interpretation: the presumption against surplusage and *expressio unius est exclusio alterius*."[74] In short order, the D.C. Circuit, in applying *Chevron*, found applicable law (12 U.S.C. Section 24(Seventh)) to be unambiguous and to the extent of any ambiguity, found the OCC's interpretation to be not reasonable. Ouch.

The courts continue to refine deference. After *Chevron*, there was "*Auer* deference,"[75] arising from a case in which the Supreme Court held the Department of Labor's interpretation of its own regulation was "controlling unless plainly erroneous or inconsistent with the regulation." Note, *Chevron* is about *statutes*: *Auer* dealt with an "interpretation" of a *regulation*, giving agencies two levels to make law, the second without notice and comment.

There has been a constriction of *Auer* recently, and the Supreme Court, in an opinion authored by Justice Kagan, "cabined Auer's scope in varied and critical ways":

> First and foremost, a court should not afford Auer deference unless, after exhausting all the "traditional tools" of construction, [citing *Chevron*] the regulation is

72. *Id.*
73. Independent Ins. Agents of Am. v. Ludwig, 997 F.2d at 961 (citing Investment Co. Inst. v. Conover, 790 F.2d 925, 935 (D.C. Cir. 1986)). *See also,* NationsBank of North Carolina, N.A. v. Variable Annuity Life Ins. Co., 513 U.S. 251 (1995) regarding annuity sales.
74. Independent. Ins. Agents of Am. v. Hawke, 211 F.3d 638 (D.C. Cir. 2000).
75. Auer v. Robbins, 519 U.S. 452 (1997) ("*Auer*").

> genuinely ambiguous. A court must carefully consider the text, structure, history, and purpose of a regulation before resorting to deference. If genuine ambiguity remains, the agency's reading must still fall "within the bounds of reasonable interpretation." [Citation omitted] And even then, not every reasonable agency reading of a genuinely ambiguous rule should receive Auer deference. Rather, a court must also make an independent inquiry into whether the character and context of the agency interpretation entitles it to controlling weight.[76]

This rings eerily like the discussion above about the enforceability of agency guidance.

76. Kisor v. Wilkie, 139 S. Ct. 2400 (June 26, 2019).

3

Structure Choices in the Bank Family

Do You Know Your Client?

As can be seen from the discussions in Chapters 1 and 2, you cannot find the applicable law to respond to an issue raised by a banking client unless you identify the charter and regulators of that client. Seldom will you discover that your client is only one entity. So, it is not only the bank charter that should concern you, but the other members of the family: the parent (holding company), children (subsidiaries), and sisters and brothers (commonly controlled financial institutions and nonbank companies). There is thus a fundamentally important "know your client" exercise at the outset of any engagement, and it is an exercise to be repeated when your client decides to engage in a new activity, offer an additional product or service, or acquire an operating company. You will need to render advice as to where that activity should be conducted.

In a nutshell, a bank family has the following basic structure options:

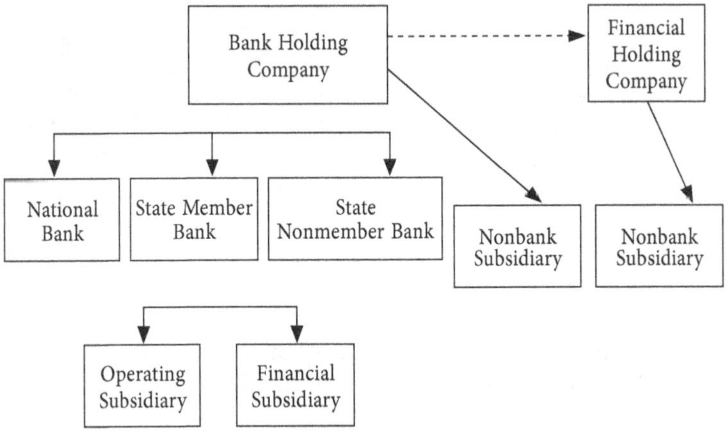

While there is no "rule" in this regard, the common practice of bankers and their lawyers is to create a bank family chart like the above example and depict the banking entities owned by the parent company on the left side (as we look at the chart) and the nonbank entities on the right, with arrows to show ownership. Ultimately, it helps to visually identify which entities are protected by the safety net (banks and operating subsidiaries) and which are not (the other affiliates).

Do all bank families look like this? Of course not. Some may be just a bank and a subsidiary or just a holding company owning one bank. Large banks may have dozens of subs with their own subsidiaries so the chart goes down vertically through many levels. The modern thrift holding company family composed of an insurance company may have the most complicated structure, with lots of affiliates that may not be involved in banking, and with lots of different regulators, as follows:

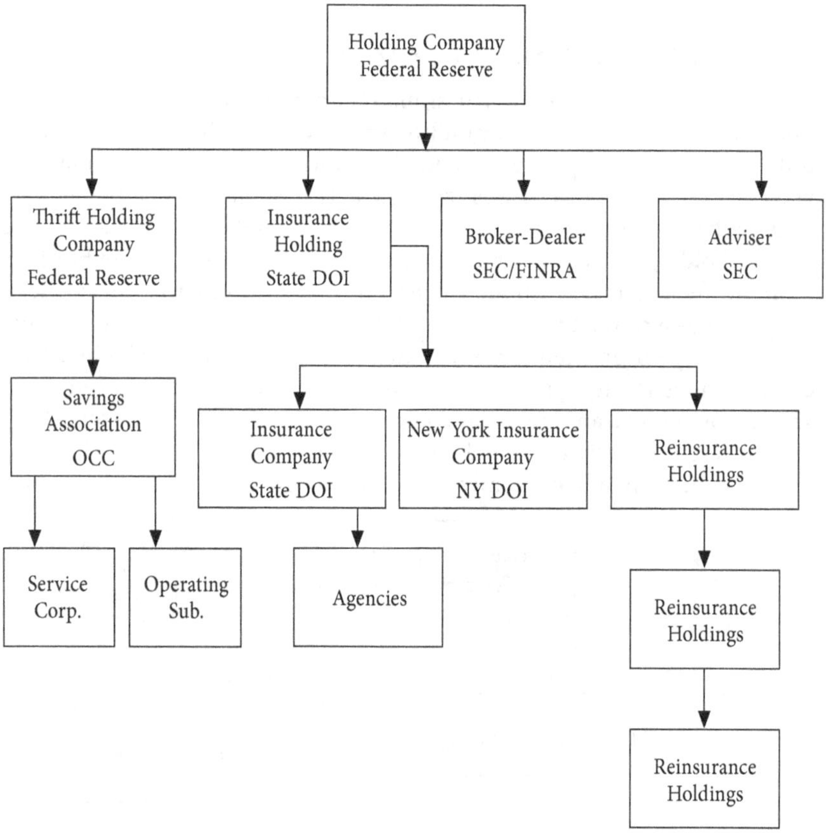

We were introduced to the banking entities you see in the above charts and how they were created legislatively in Chapter 2. This chapter will drill down a little further into who they are and how they are regulated, beginning with the dual banking system and the financial institution charters that comprise it, and then will address subsidiary and parent organizations. Subsequent chapters will dig deeper into the details of what these entities can and cannot do, as well as their advantages and disadvantages, including prudential regulation, activities restrictions, and geographic expansion opportunities.

The Dual Banking System

We have national banks and state banks; we have federal savings associations and state associations. That is our dual banking system. The survival and vitality of the dual banking system is remarkable considering the fact that state governments and the federal government each tried at different times to tax the other's banking system out of existence. These efforts were a result of "the dynamic tension between centralization and decentralization in U.S. banking [that] is as old as the debate between Thomas Jefferson and Alexander Hamilton over the First Bank of the United States."[1] In the end, the conflicts have been worked out "in typically American fashion," which is "to have it both ways."[2]

Even today, in the wake of the Global Financial Crisis, the dual banking system lies at the heart of American banking. In some respects it reflects the best of Hamilton and Jefferson: large national banking institutions imbued with the right to preempt state laws that significantly interfere with their operations (*a la* Hamilton's vision) versus state-chartered, community-focused banks and savings and loans (*a la* Jefferson's vision—sort of; Jefferson reportedly abhorred corporations of all types so even this may have been too organized for him). That does not mean all big banks and thrifts are nationally chartered and all small banks and thrifts are state chartered, but, as time goes by, it is getting closer to being true.

Attempts to Eliminate the Other's Charter

Attempts to eliminate the competing system's charter date back to the Second Bank of the United States. At issue then was whether the Constitution permitted the federal government to create banks. One of the bulwarks of the dual banking system became, and remains, the U.S. Supreme Court's 1819 ruling in *McCulloch v. Maryland*,[3] in which the court considered both

1. Former Federal Reserve Governor Mark W. Olson, *Dual Banking System and the Current Condition of the Banking Industry*, remarks at the annual meeting of the Conference of State Bank Supervisors, Salt Lake City, Utah, May 31, 2002.
2. *Id.*
3. McCulloch v. Maryland, 17 U.S. (4 Wheat.) 316 (1819).

the constitutionality of the national bank charter and a tax imposed on the operations of the Second Bank of the United States.

By way of background, Maryland had enacted a measure in February 1818 that imposed a tax on banks not chartered in the state. The tax, which was assessed against the Baltimore branch of the Second Bank, consisted of either a tax on the notes issued by the bank (ranging from 10 cents for a $5 note to $20 for a $1,000 note) or a flat tax of $1,500 per year. The Second Bank refused to pay the tax, the state sued, and judgment was rendered against the branch's cashier, J.W. McCulloch. On appeal by the bank, a unanimous Supreme Court declared that the chartering of a national bank by the U.S. government was constitutional and that the Maryland tax was unconstitutional. The opinion, penned by then Chief Justice Marshall cited the Constitution's Supremacy Clause, which asserts that the Constitution and the laws made under it "are the supreme law of the land, and the judges in every state shall be bound thereby, [any provisions] of the constitution or laws of any state to the contrary notwithstanding."[4]

"The states," Marshall wrote, in a frequently quoted passage, "have no power, by taxation or otherwise, to retard, impede, burden, or in any manner control, the operations of the constitutional laws enacted by congress to carry into execution the powers vested in the general government . . . this [case involves] a tax on the operations of the bank, and is, consequently, a tax on the operation of an instrument employed by the government of the Union to carry its powers into execution. Such a tax must be unconstitutional."[5]

Over forty years later, Congress created the national bank charter that we have today under this authority. An objective of the National Bank Act (the "NBA") was to create a nationwide system of banks subject to uniform rules. The expectation of Congress was that all banks would flock to the uniform charter. At first this appeared to be the case. Between 1863 and 1865, the number of state banks declined from 1,466 to 349—a decrease of 76%—and their assets declined by 86%. The number of national banks increased from 66 to 1,294 during this period, of which about 800 were converted state banks and the remainder were *de novo* (newly chartered) banks.[6] But there were still all those state banks. Accordingly, to further the objective of putting state banks out of business, Congress adopted an amendment to the NBA in 1866, championed by President Lincoln's Treasury Secretary, Salmon P. Chase, that required every national and state bank to pay a tax of 10% "on the amount of notes of any person, State bank, or

4. U.S. Const. Article VI, paragraph 2.
5. McCulloch, 17 U.S. at 436.
6. Edward Flaherty, *A Brief History of Central Banking in the United States*, University of Groningen, The Netherlands, 2001, Ch. 9.

State banking association, used for circulation and paid out by them after [August 1, 1866]."[7]

This tax made state banking unprofitable. During 1866 through the end of 1868, the first three years in which the tax was in effect, the number of state banks declined another 29% to 247—the lowest number they would reach after the creation of the national bank system. Conveniently, former Treasury Secretary, Salmon P. Chase became Chief Justice of the Supreme Court in the nick of time to author the majority opinion upholding the constitutionality of the tax in 1869.[8]

Nonetheless, state banks, evoking the innovative spirit that has marked the charter for decades, climbed back into popularity by inventing the checking account as a loophole around the tax. These checking accounts became so popular that by 1890 the Comptroller of the Currency estimated that only 10% of the nation's money supply was in the form of currency. Combined with lower capital and reserve requirements, as well as the ease with which states issued banking charters, state banks again became the dominant banking structure by the late 1880s.[9] They continue to flourish, as has the "doomed" dual banking system.

Charter Choices

Our unique dual banking system is composed of the following federal and state charters, each with its own regulators and characteristics.

National Banks

A national bank is merely a commercial bank, the organizers of which elect regulation under federal law. The laws that apply to national banks are crafted by the Congress of the United States and are codified primarily in Title 12 of the U.S. Code. The Office of the Comptroller of the Currency ("OCC" or "Comptroller"), a bureau of the Department of Treasury, regulates national banks. The Comptroller of the Currency is actually a person appointed by Congress, and when the OCC is sued, the Comptroller gets sued in his own name. The regulations of the OCC as to national bank operations are found in Title 12 of the Code of Federal Regulations ("C.F.R."), Chapter I, Parts 1 to 99. Much of the "law" with respect to national bank activities is found in OCC interpretive letters, approvals of applications, supervisory letters, and regulatory guidance. This treasure trove of informal law is now available on the Comptroller's website: www.occ.treas.gov.

7. Act of June 13, 1866 (14 Stat. 98, 146).
8. Veazie Bank v. Fenno, 75 U.S. 533 (1869).
9. Flaherty, *supra* note 6.

National banks must comply with a complex web of laws and regulations. This includes not only supervision and regulation by the Comptroller, but also by the Federal Reserve System ("Federal Reserve"), because national banks are required to be members of the Federal Reserve, and the Federal Deposit Insurance Corporation ("FDIC"), because the deposits of national banks are FDIC-insured. The activities of national banks are highly regulated under 12 U.S.C. Section 24,[10] which limits bank powers to the "business of banking" and activities "incident thereto," and, in some respects, the powers are different from those of state banks; so too are the locations at which they do business. In this regard, certain core banking activities—lending money, taking deposits, and cashing checks—may be conducted solely at legally established branches.[11]

What particularly distinguishes national banks from their state bank brethren is that they enjoy enormous benefit from preemption, as discussed later in this chapter. As a consequence, most of the largest banks in the nation flocked to national bank charters in the 1980s and 1990s as the OCC pushed the preemption envelope further and further.

State Banks

A state bank is a commercial bank organized under the laws of a particular state. Each of the 50 commonwealths and states, the District of Columbia, and the U.S. territories charter banks under the authority of state law. Notwithstanding state chartering authority, state banks are subject to federal supervision and regulation by either the FDIC or the Federal Reserve. The function of the FDIC and Federal Reserve in this regard is oversight. Their role as federal regulatory agencies is to assure the safety and soundness of the conduct of the state-authorized activities.

Nonmember Banks. Unless they voluntarily become members of the Federal Reserve, state banks are "nonmember banks" and are supervised and regulated by the FDIC.[12] Regulations of the FDIC are codified in 12 C.F.R. Chapter III, Parts 300 to 399. The informal law of the FDIC, in the form of interpretive letters, FILs (financial institution letters), application approvals, and regulatory guidelines, is available on the FDIC's website at: www.fdic.gov.

Member Banks. If a state bank chooses to join the Federal Reserve, it is characterized as a "member bank" with supervision and regulation by the Federal Reserve.[13] Regulations of the Federal Reserve are codified in 12 C.F.R. Chapter II, Parts 200–299 and carry names associated with letters

10. Discussed in Chapter 9, *infra*.
11. *Id.*
12. 12 U.S.C. §§ 1811 *et seq.*
13. 12 U.S.C. §§ 321 *et seq.*

of the alphabet, e.g., Regulation H, Regulation O, etc. General counsel's letters, staff interpretations, application orders, and regulatory guidelines are available on the Board's website: www.federalreserve.gov.

Powers. The federal regulators do not determine bank powers. Each state legislature generally determines the powers of the banks organized domestically. While the statutory schemes are somewhat disparate from state to state, the powers of banks are generally confined to those that are closely related to banking. The authority for state banks to engage in activities derives from three types of statutory sources: express statutory authorization; incidental powers determined by the state regulator; and so-called "wild card" or parity provisions, which permit state banks to exercise any power permitted to national banks or other financial institutions. That said, states may not go too far in authorizing state banks to engage in risky activities—under federal law, they may not engage as principal in any activity not permissible for a national bank, unless the FDIC determines that the activity would not pose a significant risk to the federal deposit insurance funds and the state bank is in compliance with federal capital requirements.[14]

Federal Savings Associations

Federal savings associations, including federal savings banks, are financial institutions organized under the Home Owners' Loan Act ("HOLA").[15] They are frequently referred to as "thrifts." They were originally organized in mutual form, meaning they were owned by their depositors (many converted to stock form in later years). The charter was conceived in order to stimulate savings by consumers and to provide funds for retail mortgages. Although the law still provides that such associations are organized, in part, to provide "for the extension of credit for homes and other goods and services,"[16] in recent decades, their banking powers have veered more closely to those of national banks.

Federal associations had been supervised and regulated by the Office of Thrift Supervision ("OTS"), formerly an office of the U.S. Treasury Department,[17] since its predecessor, the Federal Home Loan Bank Board ("FHLBB") was abolished by Congress in the Financial Institutions Reform, Recovery and Enforcement Act of 1989.[18] The deposits of federal associations are insured by the FDIC, by virtue of which the FDIC obtains certain supervisory authority over federal thrifts.

14. 12 U.S.C. § 1831a(a).
15. 12 U.S.C. §§ 1461 *et seq.*
16. 12 U.S.C. § 1464(a).
17. 12 U.S.C. § 1462a.
18. Pub. L. No. 101-73, 103 Stat. 183, Title III.

The thrift charter itself, as well as its regulator, have been the subject of elimination proposals for over two decades. So, it was not a surprise that the Dodd-Frank Wall Street Reform and Consumer Financial Protection Act of 2010 ("Dodd-Frank")[19] addressed the issue. What is perhaps surprising is that it left the charter intact, both in stock and mutual form, abolishing only the regulator. The OTS was eliminated on July 21, 2011, through a merger with the OCC. The OTS's supervisory responsibilities with respect to federal savings associations were allocated to the OCC.

Dodd-Frank continued the powers and authorities of federal savings associations under HOLA without change, except, as discussed below, with respect to federal law preemption of state consumer protection law. All orders, resolutions, determinations, agreements, interpretations, guidelines, procedures, and advisory materials issued by the OTS relating to federal savings associations remain in effect and are enforceable by or against the OCC until modified, terminated, or superseded by the regulatory agency, a court, or operation of law. While the OCC originally deposited the former OTS regulations in 12 C.F.R. Chapter 1, Parts 100–199, over time since 2011, the OCC has systematically brought federal associations under the same regulations as national banks, where possible. As a result, the regulatory differences between the charters are diminishing.

That said, one unique aspect of the federal thrift charter continues—it is required under HOLA to be and remain a "qualified thrift lender"[20] in order to preserve its original focus on mortgage lending. A QTL is a savings association that qualifies as a domestic building and loan association under Section 7701(a)(19) of the Internal Revenue Code or that has at least 65% of its portfolio assets in "qualified thrift investments." Investments that are considered "qualified thrift investments" include, among other things, loans and investments relating to domestic residential real estate or manufactured housing and mortgage-backed securities relating to the same, home equity loans, small business loans, educational loans, loans made through credit cards or credit card accounts, and shares of stock issued by any Federal Home Loan Bank, without limitation; and shares of stock issued by the Federal Home Loan Mortgage Corporation or the Federal National Mortgage Association, and 50% of the dollar amount of residential mortgage loans originated by the association and sold within 90 days, the aggregate of which is subject to a 20% of portfolio assets limitation.[21]

---

19. Pub. L. No. 111-203.
20. 12 U.S.C. § 1467a(c)(3).
21. 12 U.S.C. § 1467a(m)(4)(c); 12 U.S.C. § 1464(c)(1).

State Savings Associations

Savings associations may also be chartered by the several states in mutual or stock form. The states use a variety of names for this charter, including building and loan associations, cooperative banks, and the like. These institutions, like federal associations, were created to facilitate the availability of credit for housing. Several states also charter savings banks under statutory schemes separate from those governing state savings associations.

The OTS had operated as the primary federal regulator of state associations, until, as discussed above, Dodd-Frank eliminated the agency. Under Section 312 of Dodd-Frank, all of the powers, authorities, and duties of the OTS related to state savings associations were transferred to the FDIC on July 21, 2011. Now the FDIC operates with respect to state thrifts much as it does with state nonmember banks. The transfer included all functions of the OTS related to state savings associations in the same manner with respect to the FDIC as described above in regard to the OCC with federal associations. The FDIC's remaining regulations unique to state savings associations are deposited in 12 C.F.R. Chapter III, Parts 390–391.

The activities of state-chartered savings associations are determined in the first instance by the state chartering authority. In a parallel scheme to what was effected by Congress regarding state bank powers, a state savings association may not engage as principal in any activity not permissible for a federal savings association, unless the FDIC determines that the activity would not pose a significant risk to the federal deposit insurance funds and the savings association is in compliance with federal capital requirements.[22]

Industrial Loan Companies

Industrial loan companies ("ILCs") are slightly different from traditional bank charters. They are state-chartered institutions that originated in the early 1900s as finance companies for lower-income borrowers. These early ILCs offered relatively high interest unsecured loans to factory workers who could not otherwise obtain credit. They were not originally FDIC-insured and, instead of receiving deposits, these companies typically raised funds by issuing "certificates of investment" or "certificates of indebtedness." However, Colorado and Rhode Island began to authorize ILCs to receive deposits, sometimes denoted as "thrift certificates," and the FDIC began to issue federal deposit insurance in these states as early as 1958. At least six became federally insured from 1958 through 1979. Several states required ILCs to obtain federal deposit insurance as a condition of keeping their charters. Notwithstanding, most ILCs were not qualified to become federally

22. 12 U.S.C. § 1831e(a).

insured until the Garn-St Germain Act of 1982[23] authorized FDIC insurance for ILCs meeting regulatory standards.[24]

Nonbank Holding Companies. ILCs are currently only chartered by California, Hawaii, Minnesota, Nevada, and Utah. But, it is really all about Utah, which became a favorite "nonbank bank" charterer for commercial companies that were not eligible to become BHCs because of the powers' restrictions of the Bank Holding Company Act ("BHCA"). Most of the modern law regarding ILCs derives from these commercial companies that sought to enter banking through the ILC loophole. However, combining commerce and banking is always controversial, and the charter was back-burnered for years through Congressional and FDIC-inspired successive moratoria. And then came 2020, not a moratorium in sight, and the FDIC started approving deposit insurance applications. That story is told in Chapter 10 in the context of the BHCA and the way in which companies like BMW and Target, to name a few, are able to own FDIC-insured ILCs without being BHCs.

FDIA Definitions

The definitions of depository institutions in Section 3 of the Federal Deposit Insurance Act ("FDIA")[25] can be summarized as follows:

Banks

National banks	Banks chartered by the OCC.
State banks	State-chartered banks, which include trust companies, savings banks, industrial banks (or similar institutions that the FDIC finds to be operating in the same manner as an industrial bank), or other banking institutions that are "engaged in the business of receiving deposits, other than trust funds" and any cooperative bank or other unincorporated bank the deposits of which were insured by the FDIC on August 8, 1989 (the day before the Financial Institutions Reform, Recovery and Enforcement Act of 1989 was enacted).

23. Pub. L. 97–320, H.R. 6267, enacted Oct. 15, 1982, and codified as amended in scattered sections of 12 U.S.C.
24. Raymond Natter, The Industrial Loan Company Controversy," eNewsletter, Aug. 2005, ABA Banking Law Committee, Section on Business Law.
25. Codified at 12 U.S.C. § 1813.

Savings Associations

Federal associations	Insured institutions with a federal savings association or federal savings bank charter that is chartered under 12 U.S.C. Section 1464 (granted by the OCC or the former OTS/Federal Home Loan Bank Board).
State associations	Any building and loan association, savings and loan association, or homestead association; or any cooperative bank (other than a cooperative bank that is a state bank) that is organized and operating according to the laws of the state in which it is chartered or organized.

Special Purpose Charters

There are a variety of charters issued by the bank regulatory agencies that are banks, except for one reason or another they are not "banks." Some of these charters were historically denominated as "nonbank banks" and their purpose was primarily to avoid BHC status for the parent company. Industrial loan companies and credit card banks are examples of this phenomenon, and they are discussed further in Chapter 10 in connection with their ramifications under the BHCA.

The chartering authority of the OCC and the states includes the authority to charter special purpose banks.[26] These banks may offer only a small number of products, target a limited customer base, incorporate nontraditional elements, or have narrowly targeted business plans. They are primarily trust banks, credit card banks, community development banks, and bankers' banks. The organizers seek bank charters so they may exercise powers or extend consumer credit with the benefit of interest rate exportation (discussed below), but they do not intend to accept deposits (except that state trust companies have historically been required to hold one deposit account and be FDIC-insured). Some prudential regulation applies to them. Some does not. Antimoney laundering laws and the Community Reinvestment Act typically do. You have to parse the statutes to figure it out on an entity-by-entity basis and review the approval documents for the specific charter because the regulator may customize the charter and make approval conditional on compliance with certain laws.

Credit Card Banks. Credit card banks are institutions with a state or national bank charter that limits their activities exclusively to credit card operations. In order to assure that owners of these banks are not considered

26. The OCC devotes a portion of its Charters Booklet of the Comptroller's Licensing Manual (Sept. 2016) to Special Purpose Proposals starting at page 50. *See*, https://www.occ.gov/publications/publications-by-type/licensing-manuals/charters.pdf.

BHCs, organizers generally secure a regular national or state bank charter and voluntarily limit activities to conform to the BHCA exclusion.[27]

Delaware, however, does have a special charter for credit card institutions that conforms to the BHCA requirements.[28] As insured institutions, credit card banks are subject to virtually all of the rules and regulations of the FDIC and their chartering agency, including those pertaining to transactions with affiliates and tying arrangements.

Fintech Special Purpose Charters. As an example of what appeared to be the agility of the bank charter to respond to technology, on December 2, 2016, Thomas Curry, then Comptroller of the Currency, announced the OCC's intention to offer limited-purpose national charters to financial technology ("fintech") companies that are engaged in certain banking-related activities.[29] Despite several years of planning on the part of the OCC, the issuance of a licensing manual supplement and an announcement that the OCC was accepting applications, the agency lost on substance in the first round in the courts (despite earlier wins on issues of ripeness and standing). The opponents on behalf of the banking industry are the Conference of State Bank Supervisors and the New York State Department of Financial Services, both of which filed lawsuits claiming the agency lacked the power to create a federal charter for nonbanks. On October 19, 2019, the U.S. District Court for the Southern District of New York ruled in favor of the state regulator. Judge Victor Marrero held that the National Bank Act's "business of banking" clause unambiguously requires that, absent a statutory provision to the contrary, only depository institutions (in other words those that receive deposits) are eligible to receive national bank charters from the OCC.[30]

The OCC filed an appeal in December 2019. Its rationale for the charter is noteworthy:

> First, applying a bank regulatory framework to fintech companies will help ensure that these companies operate in a safe and sound manner so that they can effectively serve the needs of customers, businesses, and communities, just as banks do that operate under full-service charters. Second, applying the OCC's uniform supervision over national banks, including fintech companies, will help promote consistency in the application of law and regulation across the

27. Discussed in Chapter 10 *infra*.
28. Del. Code, Title 5, Ch. 15.
29. OCC NR 2016-152 (Dec. 2016), https://www.occ.gov/news-issuances/news-releases/2016/nr-occ-2016-152.html.
30. Lacewell v. Office of the Comptroller of the Currency (No. 18-cv-8377).

> country and ensure that consumers are treated fairly. Third, providing a path for fintech companies to become national banks can make the federal banking system stronger.[31]

By way of background, under the OCC's program, chartered fintech entities must first engage in one of the core banking activities (take deposits, make loans, cash checks) and offer services such as mobile payment platforms or online lending. They would then benefit from the same preemption of state laws as national banks, allowing them greater flexibility to operate nationally without tripping localized regulatory schemes and without having to partner with brick-and-mortar banks. Such entities would be required to meet rigorous chartering standards and would still not be able to accept federally insured deposits without the approval of the FDIC.

The Bank Regulators

Federal and state banking laws impose a comprehensive system of regulation, supervision, and enforcement on the operations of these financial institutions that is intended primarily for the protection of the FDIC-insured deposits and depositors of banks. In this regard:

- *Regulation* means that the federal or state agency has rulemaking authority under the applicable statute and the authority to interpret the law, typically with some degree of judicial deference.
- *Supervision* means examination authority and licensing authority—the ability to require applications, notices, and registrations.
- *Enforcement* means the ability of the agency to force compliance with laws.

If we drill down a little deeper, regulation is the basic topic of this book—our search for the law and how to apply it. But we also need to be keenly aware of the other pieces. On the examination front, financial institutions are subject to regular examination by their respective regulatory authorities, which results in examination reports and ratings (that are not publicly available) that can impact the conduct and growth of business. These examinations consider not only compliance with applicable laws and regulations, but also capital levels, asset quality and risk, management ability and performance, earnings, liquidity, and various other factors. On the enforcement front, the regulatory agencies generally have broad discretion

31. *Exploring Special Purpose National Bank Charters for Fintech Companies* (Dec. 2016), https://www.occ.gov/topics/bank-operations/innovation/special-purpose-national-bank-charters-for-fintech.pdf.

to impose restrictions and limitations on the operations of a regulated entity where the agencies determine, among other things, that such operations are unsafe or unsound, fail to comply with applicable law, or are otherwise inconsistent with laws and regulations or with the supervisory policies of these agencies.[32]

The regulatory agencies fall into categories as to whether they are the "chartering authority" or the "primary federal regulator" or have a secondary or targeted role in the supervision of financial institutions.

Chartering Authorities

In order to form a financial institution, the organizers will approach the chartering authority. The OCC is the chartering authority for national banks and, in the wake of Dodd-Frank, of federal thrifts. The state departments of financial institutions are chartering authorities for state banks and state associations.

Primary Federal Regulators

The Financial Institutions Reform, Recovery and Enforcement Act of 1989 ("FIRREA")[33] adopted Section 3(q) of the FDIA to revise the definition of the federal agencies that have the primary authority to examine and supervise insured banks and savings associations. Section 3(q) defines these agencies as the "appropriate federal banking agency." These agencies are referred to in many publications, and in this book, as "primary federal regulators." Responsibilities of the primary federal regulators include:

- conducting examinations;
- initiating supervisory and enforcement actions;
- assigning composite examination ratings;
- approving branch and other applications;
- reviewing change of control applications; and
- approving mergers (if it is the primary federal regulator of the resulting institution).

Accordingly, the FDIC is the primary federal regulatory agency for state nonmember banks and state savings associations; the Federal Reserve is the same for state member banks; and the OCC is for national banks and federal thrifts, making the OCC both a chartering authority and a primary federal regulatory agency.

32. Examination and enforcement are topics of discussion in Chapter 11, *infra*.
33. Pub. Law 101-73, Aug. 9, 1989, 103 Stat. 183.

Secondary Federal Regulators

This term is not defined in the FDIA. It has been used in several charts published by regulatory agencies in order to distinguish the authority the agencies exercise as primary federal regulators and the authority the FDIC and Federal Reserve exercise in their respective capacities as insurers of deposits and supervisors of institutions in the Federal Reserve System.

Other Regulators

As noted throughout this book, there are not only other lines of authority within these agencies (the FDIC, for example, has authority to approve certain activities of state banks and their subsidiaries), but there are also nonbanking agencies that have rulemaking authority affecting depository institutions. For instance, offices in the Treasury Department, such as the Financial Crimes Enforcement Network ("FinCEN"), enforce money laundering and currency transactions regulations.[34]

Consumer Financial Protection

Among the "other regulators," Title X of Dodd-Frank introduced us to what is being referred to as a "superagency"—the Bureau of Consumer Financial Protection (yes, "Bureau" is the first word in the name in the statute, but the acronym adopted by the agency is "CFPB"). It is "super" in its power over all consumer financial products and services. It is also "super" in its funding—off the federal budget, right out of the Federal Reserve's pockets (unless Congress changes that in light of the structural issues discussed below). The CFPB began operations formally on July 21, 2011, at which time it succeeded to all regulatory authority to prescribe rules or issue orders or guidelines (the so-called "consumer financial protection functions") transferred from the Federal Reserve, OCC, FDIC, FTC (with some limits), and HUD.

CFPB Mandate. The rulemaking authority of the CFPB includes a mandate to define unfair, deceptive, and "abusive" trade practices[35] and

34. Chapter 8, *infra*, focuses on the role of FinCEN.
35. The CFPB used the term in lawsuits against CashCall Inc. in December 2013 and NDG Financial Corp. in July 2015. That definition goes beyond contract terms that are potentially abusive and crosses into questions of information asymmetry between lenders and borrowers. *See*, http://www.law360.com/articles/692083/cfpb-suits-bring-some-clarity-to-its-definition-of-abusive.

to consider restricting mandatory predispute arbitration requirements.[36] The enumerated laws that are under its jurisdiction are:

Alternative Mortgage Transactions Parity Act

Consumer Leasing Act

Electronic Funds Transfer Act

Equal Credit Opportunity Act

Fair Credit Billing Act

Fair Debt Collection Practices Act

Home Mortgage Disclosure Act

Home Owners Protection Act

Home Ownership and Equity Protection Act

Real Estate Settlement Procedures Act

Privacy under the Gramm-Leach-Bliley Act

SAFE Mortgage Licensing Act

Truth in Lending Act

Truth in Savings Act

The primary federal regulatory agencies maintain jurisdiction over the Community Reinvestment Act, the Bank Secrecy Act and anti-money laundering laws, insider transactions under Regulation O, affiliate transactions under Federal Reserve Act Sections 23A and B, and flood insurance.

The CFPB also examines banks that have total assets over $10 billion and it has a unit that collects, tracks, and routes consumer complaints. It did not take long for the last to take root—many banks of all shapes and sizes experience the routing of consumer complaints their way. The CFPB's regulations (many of which were formerly those of the Federal Reserve) are found in 12 C.F.R. Chapter X, Part 1001 *et seq*.

Constitutionality of CFPB Structure. The CFPB is structured with one person, the director, charged with effectuating its mandate and who may be removed only for cause by the President. Since 2016 there have been a number of challenges to the constitutionality of the structure of the Bureau based on the for-cause removal restriction and the separation of powers doctrine. At issue is whether Congress, in creating the CFPB,

36. The CFPB proposed a rule in this regard on May 24, 2016. *See*, Arbitration Agreements, Bureau of Consumer Financial Protection, Proposed Rule, 81 Fed. Reg. 32,830. Pursuant to section 1028(b) of Dodd-Frank, the CFPB proposed to establish 12 CFR Part 1040, which would contain regulations governing consumer finance dispute resolution. President Trump, however, killed the rule by executive resolution.

infringed on the authority of the President by concentrating so much power in the single head of an agency.

The answer going into 2020 depended on what circuit you were in, beginning with the D.C. Circuit. The first challenge in this regard was in early 2016 and was brought by PHH Corporation, a mortgage service company that was ordered by Director Cordray of the CFPB to pay $109 million in restitution for illegal kickbacks it gave to mortgage insurers. *PHH Corporation v. CFPB* focused on the ability of the CFPB Director to order such restitution.

D.C. Circuit. On October 11, 2016, the U.S. Court of Appeals for the D.C. Circuit issued a controversial 2-1 ruling against the CFPB and its constitutional independent authority to protect consumers by regulating the financial industry.[37] In the 110-page landmark decision by Judge Kavanaugh, the court found that the single-Director structure violated constitutional separation-of-powers principles. The court's holding is strongly worded:

> In this case, the single-Director structure of the CFPB represents a gross departure from settled historical practice. [Citation omitted.] Never before has an independent agency exercising substantial executive authority been headed by just one person. The CFPB's concentration of enormous executive power in a single, unaccountable, unchecked Director not only departs from settled historical practice, but also poses a far greater risk of arbitrary decisionmaking and abuse of power, and a far greater threat to individual liberty, than does a multi-member independent agency.

If upheld, the decision would have permitted the President to replace the Bureau's Director at will. However, the CFPB filed a motion for the court to reconsider *en banc* in late 2016, and, notwithstanding the eloquent arguments of Judge Kavanaugh, the D.C. Circuit granted reconsideration and then issued its decision, holding that the Bureau's structure was constitutional, overruling the earlier decision,[38] and asserting that the for-cause removal restriction protecting the Director does not impede the President's ability to perform his constitutional duty to ensure laws are faithfully executed. Not surprisingly, Judge Kavanaugh authored the dissent.

New York, District Court, the Fifth and Ninth Circuits Ring In. Meanwhile, other circuits were split as to three cases making their way through the appeals process and predicated on similar facts (the CFPB having brought charges or assessed fines against the plaintiff): *CFPB v. Seila Law LLC* was brought

37. PHH Corporation v. CFPB, 839 F.3d 1 (D.C. Cir. 2016).
38. PHH Corporation v. CFPB, 881 F3d 75 (D.C. Cir. 2018) (*en banc*).

in the Ninth Circuit, which held that the structure is constitutional;[39] *All-American Check Cashing v. CFPB*[40] is still pending before the U.S. Court of Appeals for the Fifth Circuit; and in *CFPB v. RD Legal Funding*, a New York federal district court held the for-cause removal structure unconstitutional and not severable[41] and adopted the views expressed by Judge Kavanaugh in the original PHH opinion and in his dissent from the *en banc* opinion. That case is on appeal before the Second Circuit.[42]

The Supreme Court Speaks. Ah, but we were not finished. The Supreme Court granted cert on *Seila Law LLC v. CFPB*[43] and, after COVID-19 delays, issued its opinion on June 29, 2020.[44] Remember, Judge Kavanaugh is now Justice Kavanaugh. More interesting, the CFPB Director agreed with the Department of Justice and argued her position is unconstitutional.[45] Ultimately, it is not a surprise that the Court held with Justice Kavanaugh. In an opinion authored by Chief Justice Roberts, the Court determined that the for cause removal standard was unconstitutional because the CFPB's single-director structure "contravenes [the] carefully crafted system" of separation of powers created by our founders by "vesting significant governmental power in the hands of a singe individual who is neither elected by the people not meaningfully controlled (through threat of removal) by someone who is."[46] However, the Court also held that the director removal protection is severable from the provisions of Dodd-Frank that established the bureau.

That should keep law students challenged for a while. (So who thought *McCulloch v. Maryland*,[47] was our only fun Constitutional case in banking?) But, for banking lawyers, we still deal with the CFPB, so our everyday lives go on notwithstanding the sound and fury. But, henceforth, the President may remove the CFPB director without cause.

39. CFPB v. Seila Law LLC, 923 F.3d 680 (9th Cir. 2019).
40. All-American Check Cashing v. CFPB, No. 18-60302 (5th Cir. Sept. 17, 2018).
41. Consumer Financial Protection Bureau et al. v. RD Legal Funding, LLC et al. 332 F.Supp.3d 729 (S.D. N.Y. 2018).
42. CFPB v. RD Legal Funding, LLC, No. 18-2743 (2nd Cir. Mar. 22, 2019).
43. Supreme Court Case Number 19-7, Cert Petition Granted Oct. 18, 2019.
44. Seila Law LLC v. CFPB, *id.*
45. https://www.cnbc.com/2019/09/17/cfpb-head-tells-supreme-court-agency-is-unconstitutional.html.
46. *Supra* note 43, at 4.
47. *Supra* note 3.

The Regulators' Universe

All of this boils down to the following:

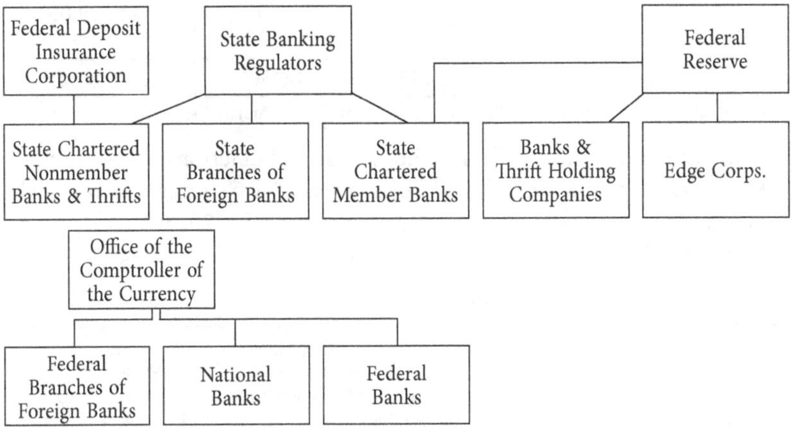

How many banks and thrifts does each regulator oversee? The chart below illustrates the distribution of deposits and offices by charter class as of June 30, 2019.

National Totals—by Charter Class as of June 30, 2019[48]

Charter Class	Number of Institutions	Number of Offices	Deposits ($000) for June 30, 2019
Commercial Banks	4,630	80,368	11,847,205,785
National Charter	798	39,297	7,688,135,007
State Charter	3,832	41,071	4,159,070,778
Federal Reserve Member	746	15,177	2,038,002,340
Federal Reserve Nonmember	3,086	25,894	2,121,068,438
Savings Institutions	673	5,989	924,329,603
Federal Charter Savings Associations	305	2,313	619,574,595
State Charter Savings Institutions	368	3,676	304,755,008
FDIC-Supervised Savings Banks	332	3,342	280,446,502
Federal Reserve-Supervised	36	334	24,308,506

48. The FDIC provides bank data and statistics on insured institutions at https://www5.fdic.gov/sod/sodSummary.asp?barItem=3.

Charter Class	Number of Institutions	Number of Offices	Deposits ($000) for June 30, 2019
U.S. Branches of Foreign Banks	10	10	41,189,034
Total	5,313	86,367	12,812,724,422

* Includes deposits in domestic offices (50 states and DC), Puerto Rico, and U.S. Territories.

The following chart drills into additions and deletions of charters from 2000 to 2015. The impact of the Global Financial Crisis is stunning when you look at the new charters versus failures for 2010–2015. Moreover, note that we had almost 3,000 fewer potential clients since 2000.

Additions and Deletions[49]

Year	Additions		Deletions				Total Institutions at Year End
				Failures			
	New Charters	Conversions	Unassisted Mergers	Mergers	Paid Off	Other	
2015	1	14	264	8	0	4	5,349
2014	0	23	238	14	0	12	5,610
2013	1	13	203	22	1	25	5,851
2012	0	22	172	39	1	2	6,088
2011	0	19	166	84	0	22	6,280
2010	5	8	183	130	3	-6	6,533
2009	24	10	157	114	6	14	6,830
2008	90	12	260	19	0	25	7,087
2007	175	19	293	1	0	14	7,289
2006	178	11	309	0	0	1	7,403
2005	167	11	271	0	0	17	7,524
2004	120	25	263	3	0	20	7,634
2003	110	16	225	2	0	13	7,775
2002	90	12	276	6	4	25	7,889
2001	125	16	359	3	0	-2	8,098
2000	188	22	456	6	0	17	8,317

49. *Id.*

Preemption

There were significant differences between the various charter options for many decades—substantive differences in powers, in geographic expansion rights, and in access to the Federal Reserve discount window and check clearing services. Those distinctions are mostly gone, and the choice of charter game now typically involves soft issues—how much you like one regulator over the other, the proximity of the legislature, the complexity of applications, and the cost of examinations. That is except for one gaping difference—preemption. Federal charters have it; state charters don't have it. Imagine the difference—federal charters may offer products across the country and largely ignore state laws; state banks that venture outside of their home state are subjected to a vast assortment of licensing requirements and substantive laws. The one area where preemption does not lie for the most part is in the realm of bank insurance activities. Section 104 of the Gramm-Leach-Bliley Act ("Gramm-Leach-Bliley")[50] recognized that state insurance laws reign supreme, and they are, thus, equally applicable to all bank charters.[51]

Preemption derives directly from the Supremacy Clause of the U.S. Constitution. Federal courts have historically upheld the assertions of the OCC and OTS that Congress, in creating the national bank system and authorizing the creation of federally chartered savings associations, intended that these institutions be able to exercise the powers granted to them by federal law on a nationwide basis without interference from the laws of the state or states in which they operate. These assertions are grounded in the history of the U.S. banking system beginning with *McCulloch v. Maryland*,[52] with its application of the Supremacy Clause and the legislative history of the NBA, both of which are discussed above.

National Banks

National banks are federal instrumentalities. Their powers derive from federal law: "An attempt by a State to define [a national bank's] duties or control the conduct of [a national bank's] affairs is absolutely void wherever such attempted exercise of authority expressly conflicts with the laws of the United States and either frustrates the purposes of the national legislation or impairs the efficiency of these agencies of the federal government to discharge the duties for the performance of which they were created."[53] The OCC asserts that it is the principles of preemption that "make the

50. Public Law 106-102, Nov. 12, 1999, 113 Stat. 1338.
51. Section 104, 113 Stat. 1352 (1999) (codified at 15 U.S.C. § 6701).
52. *Supra* note 3.
53. Davis v. Elmira Savings Bank, 161 U.S. 275, 283 (1896).

system dual."[54] The grounds for preemption as characterized by the OCC are as follows:

> First, Congress can adopt *express* language setting forth the existence and scope of preemption. Second, Congress can adopt a framework for regulation that "*occupies the field*" and leaves no room for states to adopt supplemental laws. Third, preemption may be found when state law actually conflicts with Federal law. *Conflict* will be found when either: (i) compliance with both laws is a "physical impossibility;" or (ii) when the state law stands "as an obstacle to the accomplishment and execution of the full purposes and objectives of Congress."[55] (Citations omitted.) (Emphasis added.)

The Supreme Court Speaks in *Barnett*. Over a few decades the OCC adopted principles of conflict preemption in many national bank cases and even flirted with field preemption in connection with lending. Ultimately the U.S. Supreme Court was called upon to determine the grounds for declaring a national bank law preemptive of a state law in *Barnett Bank of Marion County, N.A. v. Nelson*.[56] *Barnett* provided an instance of a state law that was an obstacle to an authorized activity of a national bank (selling insurance). The Court summed up the "many formulations" of conflicts standards defined by the courts in analyzing preemption cases and stated:

> In defining the pre-emptive scope of statutes and regulations granting a power to national banks, these cases take the view that normally Congress would not want States to forbid, or impair significantly, the exercise of a power that Congress explicitly granted. To say this is not to deprive States of the power to regulate national banks, where (unlike here) doing so does not *prevent or significantly interfere* with the national bank's exercise of its powers.[57] (Emphasis added.)

The unanimous Court then held that the Florida law that prohibited banks from selling insurance was preempted, thereby adding to the OCC's preemption arsenal. That started a presumptive game of "dodgeball" as

54. OCC, *National Banks and the Dual System*, Sept. 2003, p. 2.
55. Preamble to OCC, Bank Activities and Operations; Real Estate Lending and Appraisals, Final Rule, 69 Fed. Reg. 1,904 (Jan. 13, 2004) at 1910.
56. Barnett Bank of Marion County, N.A. v. Nelson, 517 U.S. 25 (1996).
57. *Id.* at 33.

Congress and the OCC kept spiking the preemption ball at each other over the extent of the OCC's reach.

Gramm-Leach-Bliley Impact. Prior to *Barnett*, the OCC had opined that national banks were not subject to state insurance licensing schemes or other insurance laws because the laws were preempted. Congress was quick to dispel that notion in 1999 in Section 104 of Gramm-Leach-Bliley,[58] when it tackled the issue of preemption with respect to the powers of banks and their affiliates conferred by the act. Section 104 begins with the recognition that state law is the law of the land in connection with insurance sales, and it makes it clear that insurance licensing laws apply. But it put limits on the states by first adopting a prohibition against any state action the effect of which would *prevent or restrict* a depository institution or an affiliate from engaging in any activity authorized by the act and by then expressly adopting the *prevent or significantly interfere* language from *Barnett* quoted above in connection with the sales, solicitation, and cross-marketing of insurance.[59] The law also prohibits discrimination by the states in connection with an activity authorized by it.

The OCC took its turn in January 2004, when it adopted final regulations[60] on preemption in connection with deposit-taking and lending and on state visitorial rights. In so doing, the OCC incorporated *Barnett* but also other principles the courts have developed in preemption cases over the years involving national banks and included additional verbs used by other courts, like "obstruct, impair or condition."

Dodd-Frank Impact. Congress then resumed control in Dodd-Frank[61] when it rolled back OCC preemption as of July 21, 2011, and once again stressed that *Barnett* ruled in connection with preemption of state consumer financial protection laws. Dodd-Frank also established procedural requirements for future preemption determinations, most remarkably, eliminating judicial deference to the OCC in this space and requiring case-by-case determinations supported by substantial evidence in the record. Significantly, it overturned the Supreme Court's decision

58. Section 104, 113 Stat. 1352 (1999) (codified at 15 U.S.C. § 6701).
59. Gramm-Leach-Bliley had a narrow focus on powers and covered more than national banks.
60. Bank Activities and Operations; Real Estate Lending and Appraisals, 69 Fed. Reg. 1,904 (Jan. 2004), codified at 12 C.F.R. § 7.4000, Visitorial Powers; § 7.4007, Deposit-taking; § 7.4008, Lending.
61. Sections 1044–1046, 124 Stat. at 2014–2017 (codified at 12 U.S.C. 25b, 1465). Section 1044, which amends chapter one of title LXII of the Revised Statutes by inserting a new Section 5136C (codified at 12 U.S.C. § 25b), contains the principal national bank preemption provisions.

in *Watters v. Wachovia*,[62] which had extended preemption to operating subsidiaries of national banks.

All would agree that Congress won, right? Except the OCC may not see it that way. In a May 12, 2011, letter to Senator Tom Carper (D-Del.), the OCC provided its interpretation of Section 1044 and also provided long-awaited insight into the changes it planned to propose to the preemption regulations it adopted in 2004. Interestingly, the OCC opined that the preemption standard it applied when issuing the regulations was consistent with the preemption standard under Dodd-Frank and thus it preserved the regulations, except for changes that were required as to removing references to operating subsidiaries. The OCC did not back off an iota from its view that the conflict preemption standard under *Barnett* was not limited to a state law that "prevents or significantly interferes with exercise by the national bank of its powers."[63] Instead, the OCC interpreted Dodd-Frank as requiring consideration of the whole conflict preemption analysis in the *Barnett* decision, including any verbs used by the court. The OCC, however, capitulated on one point—that its effort to distill the preemption principles from the *Barnett* case (and the cases cited in *Barnett*) into an abbreviated regulatory preemption standard may have caused uncertainty. As a result, the OCC amended its regulations effective July 21, 2011,[64] to remove the "obstruct, impair or condition" formulation from its preemption regulations and make it clear that Barnett is the standard. The respective preemption regulations actually list the state laws that are not applicable to national banks (licensing, loan-to-value ratios, terms of credit, etc.) and those few that are (contracts, criminal law, taxation, zoning, etc.) and on that note conclude with the catch-all:

> Any other law that the OCC determines to be applicable to national banks in accordance with the decision of the Supreme Court in *Barnett Bank of Marion County, N.A. v. Nelson, Florida Insurance Commissioner* [citation omitted] or that is made applicable by Federal law.

Where are we? Both Congress and the OCC cite *Barnett* as providing the appropriate standard for national bank preemption, but there may still be significant disagreement about what the *Barnett* case means. There may be more to come on this point if the OCC's appetite for pushing the envelope on preemption rises from the ashes of the Global Financial Crisis.

---

62. Watters v. Wachovia Bank, N.A., 550 U.S. 1 (May 22, 2007).
63. 12 U.S.C. § 25b.
64. 76 Fed. Reg. 43,565 (July 21, 2011), *amending* 12 C.F.R. §§ 7.4000, 7.4007 and 7.4008 and adding § 7.4010 as to federal savings associations being subject to the same standards as national banks (as required by Section 1046 of Dodd-Frank).

Visitorial Powers. The above discussion considers the OCC's visitorial powers position as part of preemption, and it is, sort of; while there is some controversy hanging over the OCC's preemption regulations and precedent, there is little surrounding its pronouncement that only the OCC or an authorized representative of the OCC may exercise visitorial powers with respect to national banks.[65] Thus, state officials may not conduct examinations, inspect or require the production of books or records of national banks, or prosecute enforcement actions, except in limited circumstances authorized by federal law.

What happens if state officials do not mind? The OCC says: "If a bank receives a request from a state or local official seeking information that constitutes an attempt to exercise visitation over the bank, the bank is not required to provide this information and should contact its examiner-in-charge as soon as possible."[66]

There is one hitch. Dodd-Frank[67] adopted the Supreme Court's visitorial powers decision in *Cuomo v. Clearing House Association, L.L.C.*,[68] recognizing the ability of state attorneys general to bring enforcement actions in court to enforce applicable laws against national banks as authorized by such laws.

Federal Savings Associations

Federal savings associations, like national banks, have a long history of favorable court cases involving state laws that interfere with their operations. In fact, until Dodd-Frank, federal thrifts enjoyed "field preemption"—a complete occupation of the field in connection with consumer and mortgage lending. The source of the authority is the 1982 decision in *Fidelity Federal Savings and Loan Assn. v. de la Cuesta*,[69] in which the U.S. Supreme Court upheld a rule by the FHLBB that preempted a California law prohibiting the enforcement of "due on sale" clauses in mortgage loans made by federal associations. These clauses declare a mortgage loan due and payable at the time the underlying property is sold or otherwise conveyed. The Court held that the FHLBB acted within its statutory authority in issuing the regulation.

> The [FHLB], an independent federal regulatory agency, was formed in 1932 and thereafter was vested with plenary authority to administer the Home Owners' Loan Act of 1933. . . . Section 5(a) of the HOLA, 12 U.S.C. 1464(a) (1976 ed., Supp. IV), empowers

65. 12 U.S.C. § 484; 12 C.F.R. § 7.400.
66. OCC Bulletin 2020-43 (Apr. 24, 2020).
67. Section 1047, adding Section 5136C to the NBA (codified at 12 U.S.C. § 25b).
68. Cuomo v. Clearing House Assoc. L.L.C., 557 U.S. 519 (June 29, 2009).
69. Fidelity Fed. Sav. and Loan Assn. v. de la Cuesta, 458 U.S. 141 (1982).

> the [FHLB] "under such rules and regulations as it may prescribe, to provide for the organization, incorporation, examination, operation, and regulation of associations to be known as 'Federal Savings and Loan Associations.'" Pursuant to this authorization, the Board has promulgated regulations governing "the powers and operations of every Federal savings and loan association *from its cradle to its corporate grave*."[70] (Citations omitted.) (Emphasis added.)

The Court went on to conclude:

> When the administrator promulgates regulations intended to pre-empt state law, the court's inquiry [is the following]:
>
> "If [h]is choice represents a reasonable accommodation of conflicting policies that were committed to the agency's care by the statute, we should not disturb it unless it appears from the statute or its legislative history that the accommodation is not one that Congress would have sanctioned."[71]

The Court found that the preemption of the California due-on-sale prohibition was beneficial to the residential mortgage market and housing finance in several ways, including the maintenance of a healthy secondary market for these loans, and upheld the FHLBB's preemption.

The *de la Cuesta* case was one of many in this vein that substantiated the preemptive position that federal thrifts held. None of these cases is particularly relevant post-Dodd-Frank, because as of July 21, 2011, federal thrifts have the same preemption rights as national banks as determined by the OCC,[72] and the OCC has the same visitorial rights.

State Charters

State banks and savings associations do not enjoy the benefit of preemption, except in the realm of interest rate exportation discussed immediately below.

---

70. *Id.* at p. 144, *quoting* People v. Coast Federal Savings & Loan Assn., 98 F. Supp. 311, 316 (SD Cal. 1951).
71. *Id.* at 154, *quoting* United States v. Shimer, 367 U.S. 374, 381, 383 (1961).
72. *See*, 76 Fed. Reg. 43,565 (July 21, 2011), adding 12 C.F.R. § 7.4010 to the OCC's preemption regulations, as required by Section 1046 of Dodd-Frank, making federal savings associations subject to the same standards of preemption and visitation as national banks.

Exportation of Interest Rates—Most Favored Lender Laws

Now and again Congress levels the playing field and recognizes that all banks should enjoy parallel rights. However, the level playing field is frequently achieved by reducing one charter's rights to those of another. We see that in federal restrictions on branching and state bank activities as principal, for instance. But the result is different in connection with interest rate exportation, which involves the use by a bank of the favorable interest laws of its home state in certain transactions with out-of-state borrowers. This practice, which arises from national most favored lending ("MFL") laws applicable to banks and savings associations, is essential to today's credit card and mortgage industries. Under these MFL laws, institutions can take advantage of favorable home state usury rates in transactions with customers in other states. They can also export home state rules on charges, such as late fees, that qualify as interest under state law.

The original MFL provision for national banks was enacted as Section 30 of the National Banking Act of 1864,[73] and it is now found in Section 85 of the NBA.[74] In 1978, the U.S. Supreme Court in its seminal *Marquette*[75] decision held that exportation of favorable home state usury rates by a national bank in Nebraska to customers in Minnesota was permissible under Section 85 and did not violate the usury laws of Minnesota. The *Marquette* opinion is based on an extensive discussion of the legislative history of the 1864 act as it related to exportation. In a statement that might be the theme for the developments discussed in this section, the Court said:

> Petitioners' final argument is that the "exportation" of interest rates, such as occurred in this case, will significantly impair the ability of States to enact effective usury laws. This impairment, however, *has always been implicit in the structure of the National Bank Act,* since citizens of one State were free to visit a neighboring State to receive credit at foreign interest rates. . . . This impairment may in fact be accentuated by the ease with which interstate credit is available by mail through the *use of* modern credit cards.[76] (Emphasis added.)

73. June 3, 1984, ch. 106, 13 Stat. 100, Section 30.
74. 12 U.S.C. § 85.
75. Marquette Nat. Bank v. First of Omaha Corp., 439 U.S. 299 (1978).
76. *Id.* at 318.

Within two years after *Marquette,* Congress amended the federal banking laws to extend the benefits of Section 85 to state banks and savings associations.

National Banks

Section 30 was enacted in part to prevent states from discriminating against national banks by subjecting them to lower rates ceilings than those that applied to state banks. This section provided in part that national banks may "take, receive, reserve, and charge on any loan or discount made, or upon any notes, bills of exchange, or other evidences of debt, interest at the rate allowed by the laws of the State, Territory or District where the bank is located, whichever may be greater and no more; *except that where, by the laws of any State, a different rate is limited for banks, organized or existing under State laws, the rate so limited shall be allowed for associations organized in any such State [under the act.]*"[77] (Emphasis added.)

Section 30 was given its current interpretation as an MFL statute in *Tiffany v. National Bank of Missouri*[78] in which a national bank in Missouri had charged 9% on a loan when the rate allowed by "the laws of the state" was 10% and state banks were limited to 8%. The plaintiff claimed that Section 30 limited the national bank to the state bank rate of 8%. The court rejected these interpretations saying that:

> [National banks] were established for the purpose, in part, of providing a currency for the whole country, and in part to create a market for the loans of the General government. It could not have been intended, therefore, to expose them to the hazard of unfriendly legislation by the States, or to ruinous competition with State banks. The only mode of guarding against such contingencies was that which, we think, Congress adopted [in Section 30]. It was to allow to National [banks] the rate allowed by the State to natural persons generally, and a higher rate, if State banks . . . were authorized to charge a higher rate.[79]

Section 85 of the NBA, which, as noted, is the current version of Section 30, is similar to the original version and permits a national bank to charge interest on any loan at the rate that is the greater of the rate allowed by the state in which the bank is located. If a state has a different rate for banks chartered in that state, national banks "organized or existing in that

77. June 3, 1984, ch. 106 13 Stat. 100, Section 30.
78. Tiffany v. National Bank of Missouri, 85 U.S. 409 (1873).
79. *Id.* at 413.

state" may charge that rate. It is this section of the NBA that the Supreme Court interpreted in its 1978 *Marquette* decision as permitting national banks to export interest rates. At that time, there were no federal statutes applicable to other insured institutions relating to MFL and interest rate exportation. As noted below, these companion statutes were enacted two years later.

The OCC's policy on interest rates on intrastate transactions (which are exportable under *Marquette),* states in part:

> A national bank located in a state may charge interest at the maximum rate permitted to any state-chartered or licensed lending institution by the law of that state. *If state law permits different interest charges on specified classes of loans, a national bank making such loans is subject only to the provisions of state law relating to that class of loans that are material to the determination of the permitted interest.* For example, a national bank may lawfully charge the highest rate permitted to be charged by a state-licensed small loan company, without being so licensed, but subject to state law limitations on the size of loans made by small loan companies.[80] (Emphasis added.)

On another note, Section 85 appears to create a default federal usury rate when it provides that if "no rate is fixed by the laws of the State, Territory or District [where the bank is located]," the bank may charge the greater of 7% or 1% above the discount rate on 90-day commercial paper in effect in the bank's Federal Reserve District.[81] However, that provision has been read out of the statute and interpreted to mean when no rate is "allowed by the laws"—or, in other words, when the state does not permit interest to be charged at all.[82] Thus, if the home state of the bank does not have a usury limit, then there is no limit on the interest the bank may export.

Most banks charge fees in addition to interest on loans, and many state laws include limits on those types of fees and the amounts that may be charged, especially in connection with consumer lending. In February 1996, the OCC published final interpretive rulings on several subjects, including MFL issues.[83] The OCC's definition of interest as used in 12 U.S.C. § 85 is set out at 12 C.F.R. § 7.4001 and includes the following:

---

80. 12 C.F.R. § 7.4001.
81. 12 U.S.C. § 85.
82. Daggs v. Phoenix National Bank, 117 U.S. 549 (1900 at 735). *See also,* Hiatt v. San Francisco Nat'l Bank, 361 F.2d 504 (9th Cir. 1966).
83. Interpretive Rulings, Final Rule. 61 Fed. Reg. 4,849 (Feb. 9, 1996).

> . . . late fees, [fees for returned checks], over limit fees, annual fees, cash advance fees, and membership fees. It does not ordinarily include appraisal fees, fees for document preparation or notarization, or fees incurred to obtain credit reports.

In 1996, the Court, in *Smiley v. Citibank (South Dakota)*,[84] held that Section 85 permitted national banks to export late fees on credit card balances.[85]

The OTS published its MFL interpretations in September 1996, which were substantially the same as those of the OCC and have been continued by the OCC:

> Given the similarities between Section 4(g) of the HOLA and the national bank most favored lender provision, OTS believes that the term "interest" as it appears in Section 4(g) and OTS's implementing regulation should be interpreted in a manner consistent with the OCC regulation and the Supreme Court's decision . . . Therefore, rather than perpetuate nonsubstantive differences in syntax that could create confusion, OTS has decided *to* conform new Sec. 560.110 to the OCC regulation.[86]

The OTS noted that this position was consistent with Congressional policy calling for greater uniformity in banking agency regulations.

State Banks and Savings Associations

In a 1998 legal opinion, the FDIC observed that as interest rates rose in the late 1970s, "Congress recognized that Section 85 of the National Bank Act [as evidenced by *Marquette*] provided national banks with a distinct competitive advantage over state-chartered lending institutions whose

84. Smiley v. Citibank (South Dakota), N.A., 517 U.S. 735 (1996).
85. Exportation of late fees by state banks had been upheld in 1992 in the First Circuit in Greenwood Trust Co. v. Massachusetts, 971 F. 2d 818, 829–831 (1st Cir. 1992), *cert. denied*, 506 U.S. 1052 (1993).
86. Lending and Investment, Federal Regulatory Reform, Final Rule, 61 Fed. Reg. 50,951, 50,968 (Sept. 30, 1996). The reference to Sec. 560.110 is now renumbered as an OCC regulation at 12 C.F.R. § 160.110. Additional regulations that are now OCC regulations are at 12 C.F.R. Part 190 (preemption of usury laws) and Part 191 (preemption of state due on sale clauses).

interest rates were constrained by state laws."[87] As a result, in 1980 Congress added Section 27 to the FDIA and Section 4(g) to the HOLA.

Section 27 of the FDIA. Section 27 was intended to give state-chartered banks the benefit of Section 85 and purposely engrafted, at several points, language from the NBA.[88] This section applies to state commercial and savings banks, ILCs, and other institutions whose primary federal regulator is the FDIC.[89] Section 27(a) provides in relevant part:

> In order to prevent discrimination against State-chartered depository institutions, including insured savings banks . . . with respect to interest rates, if the applicable rate prescribed in this subsection exceeds the rate such State bank . . . would be permitted to charge in the absence of this subsection, such State bank . . . may, notwithstanding any State constitution or statute which is hereby preempted for the purpose of this section . . . charge on any loan . . . interest at a rate of not more than [the Federal Reserve discount rate] or at the rate allowed by the laws of the State . . . where the bank is located, whichever may be greater.

Competitive equality goes to the components of interest as well. The FDIC addressed several MFL issues in General Counsel's Opinion No. 10, *Interest Charges Under Section 27 of the Federal Deposit Insurance Act,* which concluded that "the term 'interest,' for purposes of Section 27 [of the FDIA], includes those charges that a national bank is authorized to charge as interest under Section 85 of the NBA . . ."[90]

Savings Associations. Section 4(g)(1) of HOLA,[91] which applies to state and federal savings associations and federal savings banks, provides as follows:

> Notwithstanding any State law, a savings association may charge interest on any extension of credit at a rate of [the Federal Reserve discount rate], or at the rate

87. FDIC, General Counsel's Opinion No. 10, *Interest Rate Charges Under Section 27 of the Federal Deposit Insurance Act*, 63 Fed. Reg. 19,258 (Apr. 17, 1998), p. 19,258.
88. Greenwood Trust (*see* footnote 83 *supra*), among other cases.
89. 12 U.S.C. § 1831d(a) added by Section 512 of the Depository Institutions Deregulation and Monetary Control Act (DIDMCA), Pub. Law 96-221, Mar. 31, 1980, 94 Stat. 164. The state of Iowa continues to have opted out of this scheme.
90. 63 Fed. Reg. 19,258 (Apr. 17, 1998).
91. 12 U.S.C. § 1463(g)(1), added by Section 513 of DIDMCA, new Section 533 of the National Housing Act (12 U.S.C. § 1730g(a)) and reenacted as 4(g) of HOLA by Section 301 of FIRREA, Pub. Law 101-73, Aug. 9, 1989, 103 Stat. 183.

> allowed by the laws of the state in which such savings association is located, whichever is greater.

Exportation of Interest Rates by Interstate Banks

The above discussions dealt primarily with exportation of interest rates to states by banks that do not have branches outside their home state. Thus, the state where a state bank was chartered had been established as the state in which a bank was "located" for purposes of exporting interest rates. As banks began to branch across state lines after the enactment of the Riegle-Neal Interstate Banking and Branching Efficiency Act of 1994 ("Riegle-Neal I")[92] and the Riegle-Neal Amendments Act of 1997 ("Riegle-Neal II"),[93] questions were raised as to, in the words of the FDIC in a 1998 General Counsel's Opinion:

> [What is the] appropriate state law for purposes of [exportation of interest rates] that should govern the interest charges on loans made to customers of a State bank that is chartered in one state (the bank's home state) but has a branch or branches in another state (the host state).[94]

The FDIC was asking: is it possible for an interstate state bank to make loans to customers either from the state in which it is chartered or from an out-of-state branch and export interest rates from one or the other? Although the courts had not addressed this issue, the OCC issued several interpretive letters in 1988 indicating that an interstate national bank may be "located" for purposes of Section 85 in the state where its main office is located, as well, under certain circumstances, as in the state or states where it maintains branches.[95] The FDIC agreed,[96] as did the OTS.[97] The following discussion is based on these interpretations.

Example:
Bank B, located in state A, has branches in states C and D and credit card customers throughout the country. Under the Bank's MFL authority in Section 85 of the NBA and Section 27 of the FDIA (collectively the "MFL

92. Pub. L. 103-328, Sept. 29, 1994, 108 Stat. 2338.
93. Pub. L. 105-24, 111 Stat. 238 (1997).
94. General Counsel's Opinion No. 11, *Interest Charges by Interstate State Banks*, 63 Fed. Reg. 27,282 (May 18, 1998), at p. 27,282.
95. *See*, OCC Interpretive Letter # 822 (Feb. 17, 1988).
96. General Counsel's Opinion No. 11, *supra* note 75.
97. *Powers of Federal Savings Associations*, Office of Thrift Supervision, Mar. 1, 2002.

statutes"), it is able to export interest at the rate allowed by the laws of the state where it is "located."

For purposes of the MFL statutes, B is "located" in its home state and in every state in which it has a branch.

A branch in state C may export the interest rates of state C on loans to customers in any other state, including customers in state D and in the bank's home state, if the loan is "made" at that branch. This conclusion is based on the legislative history of Riegle-Neal I.[98]

This legislative history also provided guidance on the activities relating to a loan that determines where a loan is made. These activities are classified as "ministerial," or routine activities relating to making a loan, and "nonministerial" activities, which are activities essential to making a loan.[99] These activities are illustrated as follows:

- *Ministerial activities* (Routine): include providing loan applications, assembling documents, providing a location for returning documents necessary for making a loan, providing loan account information, and receiving payments.
- *Nonministerial activities* (Essential): the decision to extend credit, the extension of credit itself, and the disbursal of the proceeds of the loan.

Thus, ministerial duties may be conducted anywhere, but the essential nonministerial ones must be at the location selected for the purpose of interest rate exportation.[100] As explained by the FDIC in applying OCC precedent[101]:

> The Interstate Banking Statutes do not affect the ability of an Interstate State Bank to export interest rates on loans made to out-of-state borrowers from that bank's home state, even if the bank maintains a branch in the state where the borrower resides. If an out-of-state branch or branches of an Interstate Bank in a single host state performs all the non-ministerial functions (approval of an extension of credit, extension of the

98. *Id.*, citing a statement by Sen. William Roth (R-Del.) during Senate debate on Riegle-Neal I referring to "the widespread congressional understanding that, in the context of nationwide interstate branching, it is the office of the bank or branch making the loan that determines which state law applies" (25140 Cong. Rec. S12789 (daily ed., Sept. 13, 1994)).
99. *Id.* at 8, citing 140 Cong. Rec. S12789 (daily ed., Sept. 13, 1994).
100. The OCC has issued several interpretive letters on this point: see Interpretive Letter Nos. 686, 707, 782, and 822.
101. FDIC Opinion 5500 (May 20, 2015), https://www.fdic.gov/regulations/laws/rules/5500-800.html.

> credit, and disbursal of loan proceeds to a customer) related to a loan, it "makes" the loan to the customer for purposes of the Interstate Banking Statutes and the loan should be governed by the usury provisions of the host state.

That said, most of the time banks share credit functions across their footprint, and nonministerial functions may not all be effected at one office. What happens then? The FDIC addressed this issue as well:

> If the three non-ministerial functions occur in different states or if some of the non-ministerial functions occur in an office that is not considered to be the home office or branch of the bank, then home state rates may be used. Alternatively, in those situations the interest rates permitted by the host state where a non-ministerial function occurs may be applied, if based on an assessment of all of the facts and circumstances, the loan has a clear nexus to the host state. To avoid uncertainty regarding which state's interest rates apply to a loan Interstate State Banks should make an appropriate disclosure to the customer that the interest to be charged on the loan is governed by applicable federal law and the law of the relevant state which will govern the transaction.[102]

Judicial and Regulatory Developments—Applicability to Assignees[103]

Loans are sold; loans are securitized. Such loans are made in reliance on interest rate exportation. What happens when they are in the hands of a nonbank assignee? Are they "valid when made" or does the assignment blow MFL? This depends on whom you ask and, maybe, in what circuit.

Madden Case. In this regard, the Second Circuit Court of Appeals handed the banking industry a bombshell in 2015 with its decision in *Madden v. Midland Funding, LLC*[104] that a nonbank assignee of credit card accounts originated by a national bank and transferred to the assignee for collection is not entitled to the preemption of state usury laws applicable

102. *Id.*
103. Thanks to Fritzi Getz of Barack Ferrazzano, LLP, for this discussion.
104. Madden v. Midland Funding, LLC, 786 F.3d 246 (2d Cir. 2015), *cert. denied.*

to the originating bank.[105] In so holding, the Second Circuit departed from longstanding "valid-when-made"[106] principles that have been historically applied in the usury context and cast uncertainty on the ability of nonbank assignees to rely on the preemption of state usury laws available to bank loan originators under Section 85 and Section 27. The defendants in the case petitioned the Supreme Court for a writ of certiorari on the question of "whether the [NBA] . . . continues to have preemptive effect after [a] national bank has sold or otherwise assigned [a] loan to another entity."[107] Upon the Court's invitation, the Solicitor General submitted a brief joined by the OCC criticizing the Second Circuit's reasoning for, among other deficiencies, failing to recognize that "a national bank's Section 85 power to charge certain interest rates carries with it the power to assign to others the right to charge the same rates."[108]

Notwithstanding its rejection of the Second Circuit's holding, the Solicitor General recommended against a hearing, and the Supreme Court subsequently denied the petitioners' request, leaving participants in the lending marketplace to grapple with *Madden*'s uncertainties and risks. Despite initial hopes that Congress would step in to legislate a path forward, congressional discussions on the topic become mired in debates regarding Federalism, predatory lending, and the well-being of the U.S. credit markets.[109]

Unsurprisingly, a variety of cases have emerged from the confusion to test the teeth of the *Madden* decision. In New York, two putative class actions have been brought against nonbank depositor, securitization trust, and trustee-purchasers of credit card account receivables.[110] The complaints allege that, following from *Madden*, state usury laws are not federally

105. The plaintiff in *Madden*, a New York resident, opened a credit card account from a national bank that was subsequently charged-off and sold to Midland Funding, LLC, a non-bank purchaser of charged-off debts ("Midland"). When an affiliate of Midland attempted to collect on the plaintiff's debt, the plaintiff filed suit on the claim that, because New York state usury law caps annual interest at 25%, Midland's attempt to collect 27% interest (the contracted rate permissible under Delaware law) violated the Fair Debt Collection Practices Act, 15 U.S.C. §§ 1692e, 1692f. Ruling against the defendants, the Second Circuit held that because the defendant was neither a national bank nor an agent of a national bank, application of state usury laws against the defendant would not "significantly interfere" with any national bank's ability to exercise its powers under the NBA. *Madden* at 250.

106. Historically courts have held that "the non-usurious character of a note should not change when the note changes hands." FDIC v. Lattimore Land Corp., 656 F.2d 139, 148-9 & n.17, 18 (5th Cir. 1981).

107. Petition for a Writ of Certiorari, at I (Nov. 10, 2015), *In re Madden*.

108. Brief for the United States as Amicus Curiae, at 12 (May 24, 2016), *In re Madden*.

109. *See e.g.*, H.R. 3299 ("Protecting Consumers' Access to Credit Act of 2017").

110. Petersen v. Chase Card Funding, LLC, No. 1:19-cv-00741 (W.D.N.Y.); Cohen v. Capital One Funding LLC, No. 19-cv-03479 (E.D.N.Y).

preempted with respect to receivables transferred to nonbank third parties. In a different vein, two actions brought by the Administrator of Colorado's Uniform Consumer Credit Code against FinTech lending platforms level *Madden*-styled challenges to the ability of state-chartered banks to assign their interest rate exportation rights.[111] None of these cases had reached an ultimate resolution as of the time this edition of *Keys* went to print.

The Regulators Respond with Valid When Made. However, all is not chaos. Each of the OCC and the FDIC stepped forward to help fill the void created by the Supreme Court's reticence and the inaction of Congress by engaging in a joint rulemaking to explicitly redress the uncertainties of *Madden*. The OCC's rule, which was adopted as proposed in June 2020, codifies the "valid-when-made" doctrine, affirming that when a national bank or savings association sells or assigns a loan, the interest permissible before the transfer continues to be permissible following the transfer.[112] Similarly, the FDIC's proposed rule clarifies that a bank's statutory right to make loans carries with it the authority to assign loans.[113] Though neither rule can definitively unwind *Madden*, each is likely to reduce the likelihood that courts outside of the Second Circuit will follow *Madden* and, in the absence of a legislative solution, support stability in the marketplace for loans and fintech partnerships with banks.

Bank Subsidiary Structures

Virtually every activity engaged in by financial institutions, except deposit-taking, which requires a bank charter, may be conducted in a subsidiary of the institution. For a variety of business reasons, banks and thrifts may select a subsidiary structure for:

- Marketing purposes—because a subsidiary will use a nonbank name which may be more readily identifiable with the product;
- Operational purposes—because a subsidiary operates as a separate corporation with its own, often specialized, board of directors and officers; and
- Liability-containment purposes—because a subsidiary, which appropriately conducts its activities separate and apart from those of the parent bank, will contain its liabilities and not expose the parent bank's assets and capital.

111. Meade v. Avant of Colorado, LLC, 307 F. Supp. 3d 1134 (D. Col. 2018); Meade v. Marlette Funding LLC, 2018 U.S. Dist. LEXIS 46814 (D. Col 2018).
112. Permissible Interest on Loans that are Sold, Assigned or Otherwise Transferred, OCC Final Rules, 84 Fed. Reg. 64299 (Nov. 21, 2019), codified at 12 C.F.R. § 7.4001 (national banks) and § 160.110 (federal savings associations).
113. Federal Interest Rate Authority, 12 CFR Part 331 (Dec. 6, 2019).

Moreover, there are legal reasons that may force the use of a subsidiary. For instance, there are structures that require subsidiary usage for bank regulatory reasons, such as certain partnerships and joint ventures.

What Is a Subsidiary?

Subsidiaries are entities that are wholly owned or *controlled* by a depository institution. There are a number of different types of financial institution subsidiaries, some of which provide institutions with the opportunity to engage in activities that they cannot engage in directly, such as real estate development for savings associations. Others provide operational flexibility by providing institutions a choice of conducting activities in a subsidiary or in the bank itself. This section discusses the principal types of subsidiaries permitted to be owned by financial institutions. Subsidiaries of holding companies are discussed separately in Chapter 10.

As separate corporate entities, subsidiaries may protect the parent bank from legal liability and may enhance the safety and soundness of conducting new activities by distinguishing the subsidiary's activities from those of the parent bank (as a legal matter) and allowing more focused management and monitoring of its operations.[114] In this regard, the FDIC says:

> [S]uch separation insulates banks and the deposit insurance fund from undue risk and potential liability stemming from litigation. To protect against 'piercing the corporate veil' between the subsidiary and parent, thus mitigating litigation risks, the FDIC [for example] usually has required that the bank conduct real estate investment activities in a majority-owned subsidiary which is adequately capitalized; is physically separate and distinct in its operations from the operations of the bank; maintains separate accounting and other corporate records; observes corporate formalities such as holding separate board of directors' meetings.[115]

Principal Kinds of Subsidiaries

The regulatory agencies recognize the following subsidiary structures:

114. Policies and Procedures for Corporate Activities, OCC Final Rules, 61 Fed. Reg. 60,341, 60,354 (Nov. 11, 1996).
115. Activities and Investments of Insured State Banks, FDIC Proposed Rules, 61 Fed. Reg. 43,486, 43,491 (Aug. 23, 1996).

Operating subsidiaries are corporations or similar entities that may engage in activities in which the bank or savings association may engage in directly.

Bank service companies are sometimes called bank service corporations. These companies can be organized and controlled by one or more depository institutions to perform services for banks and other depository institutions including credit unions.

Statutory subsidiaries are companies in which banks are authorized to invest by law, such as bank service companies, small business development corporations, safe deposit companies, companies that hold the premises of the bank, and, for national banks and state member banks, Edge Act and agreement corporations for foreign investment.

"Section 24" subsidiaries are subsidiaries of state banks that may engage in activities that are prohibited for subsidiaries of national banks, if approved by the FDIC under Section 24 of the FDIA.[116]

Service corporations are subsidiaries of savings associations, not banks, which have broader powers than the parent savings association.

Financial subsidiaries are subsidiaries authorized by Gramm-Leach-Bliley, in which banks may provide most of the financial services not permissible for the bank itself, such as general securities underwriting, that are authorized for financial holding companies ("FHCs").

Bank Traditional Operating Subsidiaries

Traditional operating subsidiaries are subsidiaries that may only engage in activities that are permissible for the parent bank. Operating subsidiaries do not include:

- financial subsidiaries or bank service companies;
- certain "statutory subsidiaries," which are summarized above; and
- subsidiaries acquired through foreclosure or to avoid a loss in connection with a debt previously contracted.

The OCC has long recognized that national banks have the organizational flexibility to conduct activities indirectly through forming subsidiaries.[117] The OCC's regulations in 12 C.F.R. Part 5 deal with the rules, policies, and procedures for corporate activities of national banks, and include Section 5.34 with respect to traditional operating subsidiaries. State banks, likewise, have the authority under state laws to operate through subsidiaries under virtually the same rules, and subject to the same restrictions as national banks.

116. 12 U.S.C. 1831a.
117. *See*, 12 C.F.R. § 5.34.

Corporate Form. An operating subsidiary may be a corporation, limited liability company ("LLC"), limited partnership, or similar entity controlled at least 50% by the bank. Operating subsidiaries do not include general partnerships. National banks lack the authority to assume liability for the actions of partners, as do most state banks, and thus may not enter into a general partnership directly.[118] They may, however, invest in limited partnerships where the bank's partnership liability is limited and the partnership's activities are restricted to those permissible for national banks.[119] Moreover, the Comptroller permits operating subsidiaries of national banks to participate as partners with other banks and nonbanking companies in general partnerships engaged in activities otherwise permissible for the bank.[120] In allowing national bank subsidiaries to participate in general partnerships, the Comptroller typically imposes a number of requirements in order to address legal, policy, and prudential concerns. State bank regulators generally follow suit.

Permitted Activities. Operating subsidiaries may only engage in activities permitted to the parent bank. As a result, they tend to act as incorporated departments of the parent bank. Generally, an application or notice to the OCC or the state bank regulator is required; however, the FDIC and Federal Reserve generally do not require an application or a notice for a state bank to form or acquire a subsidiary.

In the 1980s and early 1990s the extent of subsidiary powers was unclear for state banks owned by bank holding companies. These "grandchildren" of bank holding companies were permitted to exercise state powers granted to state banks under federal law.[121] However, on December 5, 1988, the Federal Reserve issued for public comment a proposal to rescind this regulation, thereby subjecting subsidiaries of state banks to the limitations of Section 4(c)(8) of the BHCA.[122] No further action was taken on that proposal, but the Federal Reserve was subsequently challenged when it attempted to assert jurisdiction over an insurance subsidiary of a Citicorp bank subsidiary in the State of Delaware. The Second Circuit ruled that the BHCA limitations do not apply to subsidiaries of state banks.[123] From time to time, staff members

118. *See*, Merchants' Nat'l Bank v. Wehrmann, 202 U.S. 295 (1906).
119. *See, e.g.*, Letter dated Nov. 13, 1986, from William B. Glidden, Assistant Director, Legal Advisory Services; OCC Interpretive Letter No. 435 (June 30, 1988).
120. *See, e.g.*, OCC Interpretive Letter No. 622 (Apr. 9, 1993); OCC Interpretive Letter No. 516 (July 12, 1990); OCC Interpretive Letter No. 411 (Jan. 20, 1988); OCC Interpretive Letter No. 419 (Feb. 16, 1988); OCC Interpretive Letter No. 289 (May 15, 1984).
121. *See*, 12 C.F.R. § 225.22(d)(2)(ii).
122. 53 Fed. Reg. 48,915 (1988).
123. Citicorp v. Board of Governors of the Federal Reserve System, 936 F.2d 66 (2d Cir. 1991), *cert. denied*, 112 S. Ct. 869 (1992).

of the Federal Reserve hint that they may raise this issue again and they apply it to less-than wholly owned operating subsidiaries, as noted below.

Control Requirement. Historically, operating subsidiaries were permitted as long as the bank owned at least 80% of the subsidiary. As indicated above, banks may now own merely 50% or more of the voting control of an operating subsidiary or otherwise control the subsidiary as long as no other person has voting control of the subsidiary.[124] Nonetheless, the Federal Reserve continues to take the position that the ownership of less than 100% of an operating subsidiary by a state bank that is a subsidiary of a BHC is subject to the activities limitations applicable to BHCs under Section 4(c)(8) of the BHCA[125] and requires Board approval. Because, for instance, insurance activities permissible under Section 4(c)(8) are so limited, the Board's position generally precludes state bank investments of less than 100% in insurance agencies and underwriters unless the product is credit insurance.

Regulatory Treatment. As a regulatory matter, traditional operating subsidiaries are treated for the most part as separately incorporated divisions of the parent bank and, as such, are treated like banks, not as affiliates for the purposes of many prudential regulations, like Sections 23A and B of the Federal Reserve Act[126] and the antitying provisions of the BHCA.[127]

Bank Service Companies

These are corporations or LLCs authorized by the Bank Service Corporation Act ("BSCA")[128] that may be organized and controlled by one or more banks to perform services for banks and other depository institutions including credit unions. The BSCA generally requires the banks that control the corporation to be located in the same state, limits the performance of services to locations within the state at which the bank could perform the services, and limits the services to be performed to those permissible for the bank or banks involved, except taking deposits. These subsidiaries may also provide services that are permissible for bank holding companies under Section 4(c)(8) of the BHCA.[129] The OCC regulations are found at 12 C.F.R. § 5.35.

Banks must apply to their primary federal regulator to acquire the company and to perform these services, and state banks would also apply

124. 12 C.F.R. § 5.34(d)(2). Noncontrolling investments in "operating subsidiaries" are permitted and are discussed at the end of Chapter 9 in the context of bank investments.
125. Discussed in Chapter 10, *supra*.
126. Discussed in Chapter 6, *infra*.
127. Discussed in Chapter 9, *infra*.
128. 12 U.S.C. §§ 1861 *et seq.*
129. 12 U.S.C. § 1843(c)(4), discussed in Chapter 10, *infra*.

to the state bank regulator. No application is required, however, for one or more controlling banks to acquire a service company to perform, for depository institutions only, certain clerical and accounting services, including the following:

- check and deposit sorting and posting;
- posting of interest and other credits and charges; and
- preparing and mailing checks, statements, and notices.

Statutory Subsidiaries

National banks are permitted to invest in certain corporations by statute, including bank service companies, which are discussed above.[130] The corporations and their statutory authority also include:

- *Agricultural credit corporations* (12 U.S.C. § 24 (7th))—corporations organized to make loans to farmers and ranchers.
- *Bankers banks* (12 U.S.C. § 24 (7th))—a national or state bank engaged exclusively in providing services for other depository institutions and their officers, directors, and employees.
- *Safe deposit corporations* (12 U.S.C. § 24 (7th))—corporations organized under state law to conduct a safe deposit business.
- *State housing corporations* (12 U.S.C. § 24 (7th))—investments in any state housing corporation that is incorporated in the state in which the bank is located.
- *Small business investment companies* (12 U.S.C. § 682(b))—venture capital firms licensed by the Small Business Administration to provide debt and equity financing for small businesses.
- *Edge Act and agreement corporations* (12 U.S.C. §§ 601-604(a), 611–631)—Edge Act and agreement corporations are chartered by the Board and state banking agencies, respectively, generally as subsidiaries of member banks, as a means of financing international business transactions, particularly exports. They may conduct deposit and loan businesses in other states other than their parent bank's home state, so long as the business is related to international transactions. They may also make certain foreign investments that member banks may not make.

Bank Financial Subsidiaries

Section 121 of Gramm-Leach-Bliley permits qualifying national banks to engage in a broader range of activities through what was a new type of

130. OCC, Comptrollers Handbook, Related Organizations, Aug. 2004.

subsidiary called a *financial subsidiary*. State banks are also permitted to own financial subsidiaries, as long as state law permits. A financial subsidiary is a company controlled by one or more banks that engages in activities that are financial in nature or incidental to such activities. A bank is deemed to control a financial subsidiary if it owns or controls more than 25% of the shares of the subsidiary. The OCC final rule as to financial subsidiaries is in 12 C.F.R. § 5.39.

Financial subsidiaries have a broad range of securities powers—essentially the same as FHCs, as discussed below. Because national banks have more limited insurance powers than most state banks,[131] national banks may equal the playing field and sell all lines of insurance from any location through the mechanism of a financial subsidiary. However, Gramm-Leach-Bliley prohibits financial subsidiaries from underwriting insurance, except for the underwriting authority in place as of January 1, 1999 (essentially credit insurance and captive risks). Even those permitted underwriting activities are further limited to generally exclude title insurance (except for title insurance underwriting conducted as of January 1, 1999) and annuities.

Authority for financial subsidiaries is as follows:

- National banks—Section 5136A of the Revised Statutes,[132] added by Section 121(a) of GLBA.
- State banks—Section 46 of the FDIA[133] added by Section 121(d) of GLBA.
- Savings associations—not authorized. They have authority for service corporations, which are similar.

Prudential Qualifications. Banks seeking to own financial subsidiaries must qualify to engage in the new activities. In essence, they must be the "best and brightest." To qualify to operate a financial subsidiary, a bank must, among other things:

- be well-capitalized and well-managed, along with each of its depository institution affiliates, if any;
- have a Community Reinvestment Act ("CRA") rating of at least "Satisfactory";
- comply with the GLBA amendments that apply the restrictions of Sections 23A and 23B of the Federal Reserve Act to transactions with financial subsidiaries.

A financial subsidiary may lose its status if it becomes less than "well-capitalized" or if it is rated as less than "well-managed." There is generally

131. Discussed in Chapter 9, *infra*.
132. Codified at 12 U.S.C. § 24a.
133. Codified at 12 U.S.C. § 1831w.

a 180-day cure period after notice from the federal regulator, or a longer period as prescribed by the agency. If the violation is not cured, the financial subsidiary must stop engaging in activities other than activities otherwise permissible for a subsidiary.

Additional Safeguards for the Bank. Moreover, because financial subsidiaries were permitted a broader range of riskier activities than the bank parent, GLBA imposed the following additional restrictions on the operation of a financial subsidiary[134]:

- *Rating requirements.* A national bank that is one of the 100 largest insured banks must have at least one issue of outstanding debt that meets standards of creditworthiness determined by the Board and Treasury (credit ratings may no longer be used as the test). These requirements do not apply if the financial subsidiary is providing financial services only as agent.
- *Asset limits.* The total consolidated assets of all financial subs may not exceed the lesser of 45% of the consolidated assets of the parent bank or $50 billion.
- *Capital deduction and financial statement requirements.* A national bank must deduct the aggregate amount of its outstanding equity investment, including retained earnings, in all financial subsidiaries from its total assets and tangible equity; may not consolidate the assets of the subsidiary with those of the bank; and must separately present financial information relating to these investments in published financial statements.
- *Safeguards for the bank.* A national bank that establishes a financial subsidiary must ensure that it has procedures:
    - for identifying and managing financial and operational risks within the bank and the subsidiary that protect the bank from these risks; and
    - to preserve the separate corporate identity and limited liability of the bank and its financial subsidiaries.

State Bank Section 24 Subsidiaries

The laws of several states, including South Dakota and Delaware, historically permitted state banks to underwrite insurance. In response to those laws and other perceived state bank risks, Congress enacted Section 24 of FDICIA and eliminated the ability of state banks to operate as principal (as opposed to agent) except to the extent of national banks, unless they applied to the FDIC for a finding that the activity was not a risk to the deposit insurance

134. 12 C.F.R. § 5.39(g).

fund and that the bank was well capitalized. In addition, FDICIA prohibited state banks from underwriting insurance products except to the extent permitted for national banks and except for grandfathered activities.

Section 121(d) of Gramm-Leach-Bliley expressly preserves the authority of the FDIC under Section 24 to permit any activity that it determines is not a risk to the deposit insurance fund as long as the bank is well capitalized, so this structure option remains viable for state banks. The FDIC has preapproved, subject to various conditions, the following activities for majority-owned Section 24 subsidiaries, which are subjected to an expedited approval process as long as they meet the requirements of Part 362[135]:

- ownership of preferred stock and shares of investment companies;
- real estate investment, development, and leasing; and
- general securities underwriting and distribution that had been approved for the subsidiary before Nov. 12, 1999, the date of enactment of GLBA (by which this activity became a financial subsidiary activity under Section 46, which is discussed below).[136]

Most applications from state banks under this authority are to engage in real estate investment and securities underwriting. The FDIC lists its approvals on its website.[137] These lists are very instructive because they provide a snapshot of the kinds of activities permitted, the limitations the FDIC imposes based on a percentage of capital, and the associated conditions.

As noted above, state banks are permitted to organize financial subsidiaries to engage in many of the financial-in-nature activities authorized by GLBA in 1999 for FHCs. However, the FDIC has construed this authority as arising only for activities that may not be engaged in through financial subsidiaries.[138] That means state nonmember banks may not apply generally under Section 24 for activities that may be engaged in through financial subsidiaries.

---

135. FDIC, Activities of Insured State Banks and Insured Savings Associations, Final Rule, 63 Fed. Reg. 66,275 (Dec. 1, 1998), pp. 66,294–66,295. The application procedures are codified at 12 C.F.R. § 303.122 and relate to certain activities defined in 12 C.F.R. §§ 362.3 and 362.4.
136. The U.S. Court of Appeals, in Investment Company Institute v. FDIC, 815 F.2d 1540 (D.C. Cir. 1987), upheld an FDIC opinion stating that Section 21 of the Glass-Steagall Act, which bars banks from underwriting securities, did not apply to subsidiaries of state nonmember banks.
137. FDIC, Activities of State Banks, p. 66,276. http://www.fdic.gov/regulations/laws/bankdecisions/InvestActivity/index.html.
138. 12 C.F.R. § 362.18(d)(2).

Thrift Subsidiary Organizations

Savings associations may operate indirectly through two types of subordinate organizations in which they invest: *service corporations*, which are entities either formed as subsidiaries or as joint ventures, are permitted to engage in activities reasonably related to the activities of federal associations as the OCC may determine and approve.[139] This authority is contrasted to *operating subsidiaries* of federal associations, which are more akin to departments of associations, albeit separately incorporated.

Operating Subsidiaries. Operating subsidiaries of federal associations may be organized in any state and may conduct any activity that the parent federal association may conduct after notifying the OCC of the creation of the subsidiary. The association must control 50% or more of the voting shares of the subsidiary, and no other entity may exercise operating control.[140] OCC regulations on operating subsidiaries of savings associations are found at 12 C.F.R. § 5.38.

Service Corporations. A federal association may invest up to 3% of its assets in one or more service corporations as long as the excess investment over 2% serves primarily community, inner-city, or community development needs.[141] OCC regulations on service corporations of savings associations are found at 12 C.F.R. § 5.59.

Other characteristics and requirements of service corporations include the following:

- Service corporations are corporations chartered under state law, but the OCC will consider applications to organize a first-tier service corporation as an LLC or a limited partnership on a case-by-case basis.
- First-tier service corporation ownership is limited to associations that have their home office in the state in which the corporation is chartered and are organized under the laws of the home state.
- There is no minimum percentage of ownership that the association is required to hold, and there is no requirement that the association control the service corporation.
- The investments of service corporations are not aggregated with those of the parent.
- Service corporations may invest in lower-tier entities that engage solely in activities permissible for the parent service corporation, which need not be located in the same state as the parent.

139. 12 U.S.C. § 1464(c)(4)(B); 12 C.F.R. § 5.59.
140. *See*, 12 C.F.R. § 5.38(e)(2).
141. 12 U.S.C. § 1464(c)(4)(B) as implemented by the OCC in 12 C.F.R. § 5.59(v).

- Generally, an association that controls, or has a minority interest in, certain subsidiaries that are engaged as principal in activities not permissible for a national bank, must deduct its entire debt and equity investment in such subsidiaries in calculating its core capital.[142]
- Lending limits do not apply to loans between the parent and the corporation, but loans by a service corporation to entities other than the association or entities it controls are aggregated with the loans of the association for loan to one borrower purposes.
- Service corporations are generally not affiliates for purposes of transactions with affiliate limits, with certain exceptions noted for operating subsidiaries.

Permissible Activities. In addition to any activity that all federal savings associations may conduct directly, except taking deposits, these permissible activities include[143]:

- *Finance-related activities.* Accounting or internal audit; advertising and marketing research; data processing and data storage facilities operation; personnel benefit program development and administration; software development and systems integration; and operation, leasing, ownership, and establishment of remote service units.
- *Credit-related activities.* Acquiring and leasing personal property; appraising; operating a collection agency, check or credit card guaranty and verification; and acting as escrow agent or trustee.
- *Consumer services.* Financial advice or consulting; income tax return preparation; postal services; stored value instrument sales; welfare benefit distribution; and check printing and related services.
- *Real estate related services.* Acquiring real estate for development, construction, resale or leasing to others for construction; acquiring improved real estate or manufactured homes to be held for rental or resale; acquiring improved real estate for remodeling, renovating, or demolishing and redevelopment; real estate management; and real estate brokerage for property owned by a savings association that controls or has an ownership interest in the service corporation.
- *Securities brokerage, insurance, and related services.* Retail brokerage services; investment advice, insurance brokerage or

---

142. 12 C.F.R. § 167.5(a)(2)(iv). Subsidiaries for which this deduction is not required include those engaged solely in mortgage banking, subsidiaries that are themselves insured depository institutions, and subsidiaries of certain federal associations that converted from a state savings bank charter before Oct. 15, 1982.
143. 12 C.F.R. § 5.59(f).

agency for liability, casualty, automobile, life, health, accident, or title insurance; and issuing notes, bonds, debentures, or other obligations or securities.

- *Investments.* Tax-exempt bonds used to finance residential real estate; tax-exempt obligations of public housing agencies used to finance housing projects with rental assistance subsidies; and investment in small business investment companies licensed by the U.S. Small Business Administration to invest in small businesses engaged exclusively in activities permissible for service corporations of federal associations.
- *Community development and charitable activities.* Investments in community development projects that benefit low- and moderate-income borrowers; low-income housing tax credit projects and entities authorized by statute to promote community, inner-city, and community development.

Noncontrolling Investments in Subsidiaries

Originally all subsidiaries had to be "controlled" in order for the investment to be permissible. Otherwise, the bank was making an impermissible equity investment in an entity. However, the historical resistance has given way, and banks may make noncontrolling investments in "subsidiaries" under strict rules.

National Banks. Subject to certain conditions, the Comptroller permits national banks to make noncontrolling investments in companies that engage in activities permitted to national banks upon 10 days' after-the-fact notice to the OCC.[144] National banks must be well capitalized and well managed in order to take advantage of the after-the-fact notice.[145] Generally, a national bank may make the noncontrolling investment either directly or through an operating subsidiary.

There are quirky requirements to this notice, including requiring a description of (i) how the bank has the ability to prevent the enterprise from engaging in activities that are not permitted or not contained in published OCC precedent approving a noncontrolling investment by a national bank or its operating subsidiary, and (ii) how the bank otherwise has the ability to withdraw its investment if the enterprise commences an impermissible activity; and further requiring a certification that the bank's loss exposure will be limited, as a legal and accounting matter, and that the bank does

144. 12 C.F.R. § 5.36(e).
145. The definition of *well capitalized* is found in 12 C.F.R. § 6.4(b)(1) and the definition of *well managed* is found in 12 C.F.R. § 5.34(d)(3); both are the same in this context as for formation of a financial subsidiary.

not have open-ended liability for the obligations of the enterprise. What happens if the investment is structured such that the requirements of the notice cannot be met? For instance, if the bank cannot make changes in the shareholder documents to include some of the provisions required above? Or what happens if the bank fails to meet the well-capitalized or well-managed tests? In either event, the investor must seek the prior approval of the Comptroller.

State Banks. The investments of state banks are determined by state law with federal law overlaid. As discussed above, state banks may not make any equity investment directly or indirectly of a type not permitted for national banks.[146] Thus, noncontrolling investments by state banks would fall within the FDICIA rule and be tied to national bank authority and would be subject to the Federal Reserve policy on powers discussed above. Further, states may impose more restrictive conditions, and state banks would have to follow the application or notice requirements of their respective state regulator.

Savings Associations. As indicated above, federal savings associations have the authority to invest in service corporations in any amount, so noncontrolling investments are contemplated for federal associations and are, thus, permitted for state associations unless otherwise provided by applicable state law.

Holding Companies

A large number of banks and thrifts in this country have bank holding companies. The back story is told in Chapter 2, but suffice it to say for the purposes of this chapter that they were utilized almost exclusively to avoid legal restrictions on banks, including both geographic and activity-related restrictions. As such, they came under fire by regulators and eventually came under scrutiny by Congress, which led to various degrees of regulatory supervision. The following is a summary of key points regarding holding companies as structure choices. The detail is in Chapter 10.

Bank Holding Companies

Bank holding companies ("BHCs") are state-chartered corporations or limited liability companies that are federally regulated by the Federal Reserve pursuant to the BHCA[147] and Regulation Y.[148] The primary business of BHCs has historically been the management and control of banks.

146. 12 C.F.R. § 362.3(a).
147. 12 U.S.C. §§ 1841 *et seq.*
148. 12 C.F.R. Part 225.

Today, any company (broadly defined in Section 2 of the BHCA) that controls (defined with great complexity in Section 2 of the BHCA and numerous Federal Reserve pronouncements) a bank and/or savings association (as defined in Section 2 of the BHCA to include any FDIC-insured depository institution) is regulated, supervised, and examined by the Federal Reserve. Holding companies conduct most nonbanking activities through subsidiary organizations that may be wholly owned or partially owned by the parent. The holding company and the nonbank subsidiaries are the quintessential "affiliates" of banks for the purposes of prudential regulation, in contrast to operating subsidiaries discussed above.

A hallmark of the BHC Act is not only the fact that every entity that controls a bank gains Federal Reserve jurisdiction, but the fact that Section 4(c)(8) of the BHCA limits BHCs to activities "closely related to banking and a proper incident thereto."[149] However, under Section 102 of Gramm-Leach-Bliley, these activities were "frozen" as of November 11, 1999 (the day prior to enactment of the GLB Act). Thus, there will be no further expansion of Section 4(c)(8) activities absent Congressional intervention, and BHCs that do not qualify as FHCs must continue to operate under these restrictions.

Financial Holding Companies

FHCs are not separate entities. They are BHCs that certify with the Federal Reserve and are permitted a broader range of activities financial in nature or incidental or complementary thereto under Section 4(k) of the BHCA,[150] inducing the sale and underwriting of all lines of insurance and securities, as well as merchant banking. However, the subsidiary banks (and, under Dodd-Frank, the BHC itself) must be well capitalized, well managed, and CRA compliant (as discussed under the discussion of financial subsidiaries above).

Thrift Holding Companies

A thrift holding company is any company that directly or indirectly controls a federal or state savings association.[151] These holding companies in stock form are general business corporations incorporated under state law; they may be in mutual form, in which event they were created by the OTS and the OCC now has the chartering power. These entities were regulated primarily at the federal level by the OTS. Under Dodd-Frank, thrift holding companies are now regulated and examined by the Federal Reserve. Existing

149. 12 U.S.C. § 1843(c)(8).
150. 12 U.S.C. § 1843(k).
151. 12 U.S.C. § 1467a(a)(1)(D).

OTS regulations, as amended in some respects, were moved to the Federal Reserve's Regulation LL and MM on July 21, 2011.

The scope of permissible activities of thrift holding companies and their nonbank affiliates depended historically on whether the holding company was "unitary"—owning one thrift—or "multiple"—owning more than one thrift.[152] A unitary holding company was permitted to engage in any commercial activity; a multiple was limited to bank holding company activities with a few extras tossed in. The expanded authority of unitaries was eliminated by Section 401 of Gramm-Leach-Bliley as of May 4, 1999.[153] Under this provision, all thrift holding companies approved after May 4, 1999, could engage in activities that were financial in nature or incidental or complementary thereto, like FHCs. The others may continue to exercise commercial powers. The OTS differentiated the two types by referring to former unitaries with broad powers as "exempt" holding companies and the others as "nonexempt" holding companies.

Today, under Section 606(b) of Dodd-Frank, all thrift holding companies may exercise FHC powers, subject to the conditions and limits imposed by the Federal Reserve. Any pre-Gramm-Leach-Bliley unitary thrift holding company that met the test as a unitary continues to be essentially restriction-free as to activities. It may be a manufacturer or a department store or an insurance underwriter, and it may add activities willy-nilly.

152. Multiple savings association holding companies were treated as unitary thrift holding companies for purposes of the activity restrictions if all but one of their subsidiary savings associations were acquired as failing institutions and all of their subsidiary savings associations met the QTL test. 12 U.S.C. § 1467a(c)(3)(B).

153. Section 401 amended 10(c) of HOLA, adding (9)(C) (12 U.S.C. § 1467a(c)(9)(C)).

4

Regulatory Emphasis on Capital

Is Capital "King"?

The oft-repeated mantra "Capital is King" remains true despite more than a decade having passed since the Global Financial Crisis exposed weaknesses in our capital architecture. In fact, bank and bank families were found to have held too little capital, both quantitatively and qualitatively. As a consequence, not only did capital requirements increase after 2008, but the type of instruments that constitute capital changed, and, as a result of the so-called Collins Amendment to the Dodd-Frank Act,[1] most bank and saving association holding companies must hold capital on a consolidated basis under rules as stringent as those for insured depository institutions. Moreover, the actions of the international Basel Committee on Banking Supervision, a committee of central banks and bank supervisors headquartered in Basel, Switzerland, to reassess the nature and uses of capital in connection with "Basel III," the latest Basel capital accord (discussed below), have a significant impact on the capital requirements applicable to U.S. depository institutions and their holding companies.

Why Is Capital Important in Banking?

"The primary function of capital is to support the bank's operations, act as a cushion to absorb unanticipated losses and declines in asset values that could otherwise cause the bank to fail, and provide protection to uninsured depositors and debt holders in the case of liquidation."[2] That is certainly

1. The Dodd-Frank Wall Street Reform and Consumer Protection Act of 2010 ("Dodd-Frank"), Pub. L. No. 111-203 (2010), is discussed *supra* in Chapter 2. Section 171, the "Collins Amendment," is discussed later in this chapter.
2. *Commercial Bank Examination Manual*, Federal Reserve Board, Section 3020.1, p. 1.

a start in demystifying this subject, but the need for, and importance of, capital is far more complex today. When we view capital as lawyers (not from a macroeconomic perspective—we leave that to the Federal Reserve), we unveil not only its capacity for loss absorption, but its role as a constraint (sometimes a binding constraint) on, and prerequisite for, activities and investments, and as a tool of prudential regulation.

Loss Absorption. Capital is a snapshot of a bank's balance sheet at any given time. For us lawyers, we look at the balance sheet and subtract liabilities from assets and the difference is the basic amount of capital (like our net worth when we subtract our personal liabilities from our assets). In that regard, capital is built first by investors purchasing securities and then built up by retained earnings year after year. When a banking institution loses money on bad loans or investments, the loss reduces earnings and reduces assets such that both capital and the ability to rebuild capital decrease. It is more complicated because there are reserves (such as the allowance for loan and lease losses) that are hit for losses first, but reserves must be replenished from earnings. All the bank crises through the years taught us that capital depletes quickly when things go bad and that there are better forms of capital to absorb loss than others. The Global Financial Crisis taught us that forward-looking capital planning is essential to assure the success of the loss absorption properties of capital in times of financial stress. The coronavirus pandemic then added the exclamation point.

Constraint. When we look at capital as a constraint, we flip the script and view it not while looking at the balance sheet as a whole but while looking at each dollar of capital and what it supports. How does this work? Capital is literally held on a per asset basis. So, a bank that seeks to engage in a risky investment or loan needs to assure that it has enough capital to support that asset. This can be a binding constraint in that the bank may not make the investment or loan if it cannot allocate the required amount of capital to it. To this end, the Basel capital accords introduced the concept of "risk weighting" assets on the bank balance sheet such that more capital must be held against higher-risk assets and on off-balance sheet assets. As an example, with very easy math, a bank wants to buy a $1 million bond, which the capital rules assign a risk weight of 50% (so the asset is valued at $500,000—50% of $1 million). The capital rules say the bank needs to have a ratio of 10% capital to risk-weighted assets, or $50,000 in capital, for that investment. Lawyers who represent banks in swaps, structured finance, and other complex financial instruments have to be savvy with the capital treatment to assure capital is not indeed a binding constraint.

Regulatory Prerequisite. Capital is also used by the regulators as a prerequisite for many activities and expedited approvals. They liberally use being "well capitalized" as that threshold. For instance, if a banking institution seeks to help fund its activities with "brokered deposits" (deposits sourced by third parties), it must hold capital at levels considered well capitalized or seek a waiver.

Tool of Prudential Regulation. Much of this book addresses the need to keep banks "safe," and from that concept we have lots and lots of law that is prudential in nature—the root being "prudence." Capital serves as a valuable tool in that regard, as banking law frequently uses a percentage of capital as the maximum limit a bank may engage in an activity or make an investment. For instance, a bank may loan an affiliate no more than 10% of its capital.

Why Does a Lawyer Need to Understand Capital?

As lawyers, we certainly will not be asked to do the calculations (thank goodness). To make the point, the following is a simple Basel III calculation in HTML (the PDF version is replete with the Greek letters):

```
max {0, [([Sigma]E - [Sigma]C) + [Sigma](Es
x Hs) + [Sigma](Efx x Hfx)]{time}
```

So, unless we understand Greek symbols and algorithms, we will not even be able to follow many of the modern calculations. Yet, almost every aspect of our clients' businesses will be dependent on how much capital they hold. When we factor in the constraints and prerequisites discussed above, capital levels will determine whether they can pay dividends to shareholders; whether they can repurchase stock; whether they can accept brokered deposits; whether they can branch and merge across state lines; whether they can engage in new activities; the extent to which they can make certain investments; what kind of applications they will need to file; and their ability to make capital distributions and pay discretionary bonuses to executive officers. We also need to factor in capital calculations of lending limits, loans to insiders, affiliate transactions, and investments in certain types of instruments and subsidiaries. If our client is capital-deficient, enforcement actions will ensue. If capital dissipates completely, our client will fail.

We render legal advice in connection with each of these matters. That means, in a nutshell: capital colors our world.

Capital Basics

Immediately below we strip capital down to its most simple concepts. The history, details, and the drill-down into many of the specifics follow this primer.

Who Is Subject to Capital Requirements?

Historically, concepts of capital adequacy applied only to insured depository institutions. Thus, all commercial banks and all savings associations were under relatively uniform guidelines, but the parent companies, not so much. Recognizing once again that what worked before the Global Financial Crisis would not work going forward, Congress required that holding company capital requirements be the same as those applied to insured depository institutions. As a result, capital is now measured on the individual depository institution and on the bank family as a consolidated group (except for most holding companies with $3 billion or less in assets). For the purposes of the following discussions, assume any reference to "institutions" or "banking organizations" means all depository institutions and the covered parent companies.

What Is Capital and How Is It Measured?

As indicated above, at its heart and soul, capital is money paid in by persons buying the stock of the holding company or bank from the issuer that the issuer does not owe back, including its retained earnings. Yes, that is too simplistic, and the capital rules permit a number of other instruments, some of which must be repaid, to qualify for capital treatment, but that is a start. Its sufficiency in the world of banking is measured as a *ratio to assets*. To determine a ratio, of course, we must have a numerator and a denominator.

In the past, this was pretty basic. One looked at the bank balance sheet: the numerator was the sum of the paid-in capital, surplus, and retained earnings of each category of equity issued by the institution; the denominator was the total assets. If banks held about 8% capital to assets, that was a good number. This "balance sheet" calculation came to be known as the "leverage ratio."

Flash-forward to today, and the modern capital framework known as Basel III, as promulgated by the U.S. bank regulators, is the law of the land on measuring capital, and it favors several risk-weighted calculations. Thus, under Basel III, the numerator and denominator are sliced and diced several ways.

Basel III Numerators. Because different kinds of equity have different levels of quality, what constitutes "capital" for regulatory purposes has three different levels based on its ability to absorb loss:

Tier 1 capital (the best kind), which gets subdivided into *Common Equity Tier 1* ("CET 1") and *Additional Tier 1* (basically noncumulative perpetual preferred stock);

Tier 2 capital, basically other preferred stock, some forms of subordinated debt, and part of the allowance for loan and lease losses ("ALLL")[3]; and

Total capital (Tier 1 plus Tier 2).

Basel III Denominators. There are also two different denominators that factor into the required ratios:

Risk-weighted assets

- Assets that are weighted according to risk and include off-balance sheet exposures brought back on the balance sheet based on risk. There are two approaches that determine the risk weighting: the "Advanced Approach" for the largest banking entities (basically $250 billion or more in consolidated assets) (the "Advanced Approaches" institutions) and the "Standardized Approach" for all banking entities.

Adjusted book assets

- Total balance sheet assets, minus some intangibles.

Basel III Ratios. From these come a number of different ratios:

CET 1 capital to risk-weighted assets,

Tier 1 capital to risk-weighted assets,

Total capital to risk-weighted assets, and

Tier 1 capital to adjusted book assets (the current version of the leverage ratio).

Capital Adequacy

There are then several layers of capital adequacy.

Minimum Requirements. The adequacy of capital is first determined based on the **minimum** required. Under Basel III, the minimum capital ratios for all covered institutions as of January 1, 2015, are as follows:

CET 1 capital equal to 4.5% of risk-weighted assets,

Tier 1 capital equal to 6% of risk-weighted assets,

Total capital equal to 8% of risk-weighted assets, and

3. The ALLL is a contra account on the bank's balance sheet that constitutes the reserve for bad debts.

> A leverage ratio of Tier 1 capital to total quarterly average assets equal to 4%.

Capital Conservation Buffer. *But there is more.* Institutions that seek the freedom to make capital distributions (including for dividends and repurchases of stock) and pay discretionary bonuses to executive officers without restriction must also maintain 2.5% of risk-weighted assets in CET 1 attributable to a Capital Conservation Buffer. The purpose of the conservation buffer is to ensure that banking institutions maintain a buffer of capital that can be used to absorb losses during periods of financial and economic stress. The buffers got their first test during the coronavirus pandemic when regulators encouraged banks to use them—after all that is what they are there for.

Factoring in the fully phased-in conservation buffer increases the minimum ratios depicted above to 7% for CET 1 capital, 8.5% for Tier 1 capital, and 10.5% for Total capital.

Well Capitalized. *And there is more.* To be "well capitalized," which is the regulatory objective, a banking organization must maintain no less than:

> CET 1 capital to risk-weighted assets of 6.5%,
> Tier 1 capital to total risk-weighted assets of 8%,
> Total capital to total risk-weighted assets of 10%, and
> A leverage ratio of Tier 1 capital to total adjusted average quarterly assets of 5%.

It is possible under the Basel III Rule to be well capitalized while remaining out of compliance with the Capital Conservation Buffer mentioned above.

And there is still more for the largest banking institutions, countercyclical buffers and all kinds of surcharges and enhancements, discussed later in this chapter.

Capital Measures for Purposes of Prudential Regulation

When capital is also used as a limitation on certain riskier activities, it finds its way into the prudential regulation that applies to all insured depository institutions, including loans to one borrower, affiliate lending, insider lending, and certain investments.[4] Despite the statutory wording in this regard, the federal banking agencies apply a uniform definition of "capital" to these rules:

> Tier 1 capital plus Tier 2 capital plus the remainder of the ALLL not already included in Tier 2.

4. Discussed in Chapter 6, *infra.*

Drill-Down

Practically every word set forth above requires pages of explanation and some require complex calculations and computer modeling. From "what is capital?" to the required ratios, there is so much more nuance. And there is so much history that helps build the premises.

GAAP versus Regulatory Capital

From an accounting perspective, capital may be defined as "the residual interest in assets of an entity after deducting its liabilities."[5] Or as "assets that have no offsetting liability on the bank's balance sheet." If an entity is liquidated, capital is "what's left after all of its assets have been sold and its creditors paid." For going concerns, capital, much like a personal savings account, allows the business to absorb losses without becoming insolvent.

GAAP Capital Standards for Public Companies. Companies that register securities under the federal securities laws, including bank and savings and loan holding companies, are required to file financial reports with the Securities and Exchange Commission ("SEC") that are presented in accordance with generally accepted accounting principles ("GAAP").[6] GAAP are designed to provide a workable, transparent, and accurate representation of the economic condition of public companies. They are also designed to provide comparable statements of financial results across the entire spectrum of domestic capital markets so that investors, creditors, and other parties can make meaningful comparisons of earnings, assets, stockholders' equity, and other financial data of individual companies. The most authoritative accounting principles are those developed by the Financial Accounting Standards Board ("FASB"), a private organization established in 1974.

Regulatory Capital versus GAAP Capital. Insured depository institutions and their holding companies are required to file quarterly reports of financial results with their primary federal regulator. Financial data in these reports is prepared in accordance with GAAP, and the balance sheets in these reports reflect the institution's GAAP capital, or stockholders' equity. Regulatory capital standards for banks, savings associations, and their holding companies are based on GAAP, as it is modified to meet supervisory requirements.

The Federal Reserve describes the different purposes of GAAP capital and regulatory capital as follows:

5. *GAAP 2002*, John Wiley & Sons, p. 733.
6. Section 19(b)(1) of the Securities Act of 1933 (12 U.S.C. § 77a, *et seq.*), Section 77s(b)(1); Section 13(b)(2) of the Securities Exchange Act of 1934 (12 U.S.C. § 78a, *et seq.*), Section 78m(b)(2).

> Although GAAP informs the definition of regulatory capital, the Board is not bound to use GAAP accounting concepts in its definition of [regulatory capital components] because regulatory capital requirements *are regulatory constructs designed to ensure the safety and soundness of banking organizations not accounting designations established to ensure the transparency of financial statements.* In this regard, the definition of [certain regulatory capital components] since the Board adopted its risk-based capital rule in 1989 has differed from GAAP equity in a number of ways. The Board has determined that these differences are consistent with its responsibility for ensuring the soundness of the capital bases of banking organizations under its supervision. These differences are not differences between regulatory reporting and GAAP accounting requirements, but rather are differences only between the definition of equity for purposes of GAAP and the definition of [regulatory capital] for purposes of the Board's regulatory capital requirements for banking organizations.[7] (Emphasis added.)

If GAAP capital were the end-all and be-all in this world, one would merely look at the GAAP balance sheet of a financial institution, use the "Total Assets" amount as the denominator and the "Total Stockholders' Equity" amount as the numerator, divide, and determine the percentage. Alas, nothing is that simple.

The only way to really grasp the capital process is to walk through it from the historical regime through the Dodd-Frank and Basel III rules, understanding that from 2015 forward, everything got tougher.

Source of Current Regulatory Capital Standards

Current regulatory capital standards have evolved from principles developed by the Bank for International Settlements ("BIS"). Its committee, the Basel Committee on Bank Supervision ("Basel Committee" or "BCBS"), bills itself as the "global standard setter for the prudential regulation of banks," and it is the source of the Basel capital accords. One might ask about the role of BIS and BCBS. Former Federal Reserve Board Vice Chairman Roger W. Ferguson, Jr. notes that the Committee "has no formal authority":

7. Risk-Based Capital Standards: Trust Preferred Securities and the Definition of Capital, Final Rule, 70 Fed. Reg. 11,827, 11,828 (Mar. 10, 2005).

> Rather, it works to develop broad supervisory standards and promote best practices in the expectation that each country will implement the standards in ways most appropriate to its circumstances. Agreements are developed by consensus, but decisions about which parts of the agreements to implement and how to implement them are left to each nation's regulatory authorities.[8]

Basel I. The oil crisis of the 1970s and later developments prompted the Basel Committee to focus its attention on the issue of regulatory supervision of internationally active banks. International risk-based capital standards were endorsed in 1988 by the governors of the central banks of the G-10 countries in the "International Convergence of Capital Measurement and Capital Standards," referred to as the Basel Capital Accord, or "Basel I."

One of the purposes of the first Basel Accord was the development of uniform capital measures for large internationally active banks in order to enhance the soundness of the international banking system, among other things, and to reduce competitive inequalities among these banks that result from differences in international capital standards. In practice, Basel I, which has been adopted in various versions in over 100 countries, has been applied beyond the largest institutions to cover most banking organizations in the United States and worldwide.[9] The U.S. agencies adopted it as part of the 1989 risk-based capital framework for banks and bank holding companies ("BHCs").[10]

Basel II. As the size and complexity of large banking organizations increased after 1988, bank regulators realized that more sophisticated capital standards were needed, especially in connection with risk weighting assets. As a result, the Basel Committee began work on a second round of international capital standards, known as "Basel II." Basel II only applies to the largest banking organizations in the United States and other organizations that volunteer to be governed by its standards.

Basel III. The Global Financial Crisis spawned a new initiative, the Basel III accord, rolled out incrementally in the United States from 2015 to 2019. Basel III focuses more on the quality of capital instruments because a number of instruments permitted under Basel I turned out to be weak sources of capital when faced with crisis.

---

8. *Capital Standards for Banks: The Evolving Basel Accord*, Federal Reserve Bulletin, Sept. 2003, p. 396. This article is based on testimony by Vice Chairman Ferguson on June 18 and 19, 2003, before the Senate Committee on Banking, Housing and Urban Affairs and the House Committee on Financial Services, respectively.
9. *Id.* at 401.
10. Released at 54 Fed. Reg. 4186 (Jan. 27, 1989) (Federal Reserve); 54 Fed. Reg. 4168 (Jan. 27, 1989) (OCC); and 54 Fed. Reg. 1150 (Mar. 21, 1989) (FDIC).

Basel I Structure

Basel I introduced the concept of risk weighting assets and bringing off-balance sheet exposures back on the balance sheet. It then added market risk as an element of capital.

Risk-Based Ratios

Risk-based capital ratios were designed to reflect the credit risks posed to an institution by various categories of assets in its portfolio and are expressed in terms of capital required against a percentage of "risk-weighted assets," that is, total assets after their face amounts have been adjusted to reflect their credit risk. Under the Basel I system, lesser amounts of capital were required to be held against lower-risk assets. Bank assets were divided into four basic risk-weighted categories of zero, 20%, 50%, and 100%. Consumer and residential mortgage loans, for example, pose more credit risk to an institution than U.S. government bonds, and more capital is required to back these loans than is required with respect to government bonds. The minimum amount of capital required for assets in each category was determined by multiplying the amount of the assets in each category by their risk weight and then by the percentage of capital required.

The Basel I risk-weight categories and typical assets within each category are instructive to understand the *concept of risk weighting*; however, they turned out to be way too simplistic and have been replaced with more complex and nuanced calibrations under Basel II and III:

Zero percent category: Cash; gold bullion; obligations of the U.S. Treasury; obligations of central governments of countries that are members of the Organization for Economic Cooperation and Development ("OECD countries"); deposit reserves and other balances at Federal Reserve Banks; and securities issued by, and other direct claims on, the U.S. government or its agencies, or the central government of an OECD country.[11]

11. OECD member countries in 2020 are Australia, Austria, Belgium, Canada, Chile, Czech Republic, Denmark, Estonia, Finland, France, Germany, Greece, Hungary, Iceland, Ireland, Israel, Italy, Japan, Latvia, Lithuania, Luxembourg, Mexico, Netherlands, New Zealand, Norway, Poland, Portugal, Slovenia, South Korea, Spain, Sweden, Switzerland, Turkey, the United Kingdom, and the United States.

20 percent category:

- Included securities of Government-Sponsored Enterprises ("GSEs")[12] and general obligation claims on, or portions of claims guaranteed by, the full faith and credit of states or other political subdivisions of the United States or other OECD countries.
- This category also included certain privately issued mortgage-backed securities, e.g., collateralized mortgage obligations ("CMOs") and real estate mortgage investment conduits ("REMICs"), if the underlying pool is composed solely of mortgage-related securities issued by Ginnie Mae, Fannie Mae, and Freddie Mac, and claims on, or guaranteed by, official multilateral lending institutions or regional development institutions in which the U.S. government is a shareholder or contributing member.

50 percent category:

- First mortgages on one- to four-family residential properties, either owner occupied or rented, and on multifamily residential properties that meet certain criteria; and loans to builders with substantial project equity for construction of one- to four-family homes that have been presold to buyers who have firm mortgage commitments.
- Privately issued mortgage-backed securities, i.e., those that do not carry the guarantee of a government or government-sponsored agency, if they meet other underwriting criteria.
- Revenue bonds of states or other political subdivisions of the United States and other OECD countries; and the credit equivalent amount of certain derivative contracts that do not qualify for inclusion in a lower risk category.

100 percent category:

- Most assets not included in the above categories were assigned to this category, which included commercial, consumer, and residential property loans that do not qualify for a lower risk weight. Federal Reserve documents say the bulk of the assets typically found in a loan portfolio would have been assigned to the 100% category.[13]

---

12. These agencies were originally established or chartered by the federal government to serve public purposes specified by the U.S. Congress, whose obligations are not explicitly guaranteed by the full faith and credit of the U.S. government. They include the Federal Home Loan Mortgage Corporation ("Freddie Mac"), the Federal National Mortgage Association ("Fannie Mae"), the Government National Mortgage Association ("Ginnie Mae"), the Farm Credit System, and the Federal Home Loan Bank ("FHLB") System. GSE claims include capital stock in an FHL Bank that is held by banks and savings associations as a condition of membership in the FHLB System.
13. Regulation H (12 C.F.R. Part 208), Appendix A.

- Certain claims on non-OECD banks and central governments; investments in fixed assets, premises, and other real estate owned; common and preferred stock of corporations, including stock acquired in settlement of debts previously contracted; all stripped mortgage-backed securities and similar instruments.
- Industrial-development bonds and similar obligations issued under the auspices of states or political subdivisions of the United States and other OECD countries.

Thus, when risk weighting the assets of a banking institution: the first asset on the balance sheet is "Cash and Due from Banks" with a risk weight of zero, so even if the balance sheet shows millions of dollars in this category, it would be adjusted to "0" for the purposes of calculating the risk-weighted denominator. On the other hand, the balance sheet entry for commercial loans would remain at 100%. Note that the amount of total assets under Basel I would always be *reduced* from book assets by risk weighting because no risk weights were greater than 100%.

Off-Balance-Sheet Assets

Another predicate of Basel I was a recognition of risk associated with large amounts of bank obligations that are contingent and are therefore held "off balance sheet." These exposures include loan commitments, letters of credit, sales with recourse and repurchase agreements, and other obligations that are contingent on future events or actions of another party. They are not booked until they are drawn on and then become a booked asset. Historically, no capital was held to hedge these off-balance sheet obligations, but that changed under Basel I. In most cases, the capital requirements of off-balance-sheet items were calculated in two steps: (i) the face amount of the item was multiplied by one of four credit-conversion factors, or percentages, which were designed to reflect the risk characteristics of the activity in terms of an on-balance-sheet equivalent; and (ii) this credit equivalent was then assigned to its proper on-balance-sheet risk-weight category for a determination of the amount of capital it required. The credit conversion factors used the same simplistic 0%, 20%, 50%, and 100% as the risk-weight categories. So, if an off-balance sheet obligation had a credit conversion factor of 50%, it would be put on the balance sheet at 50%. Then if the risk-weight category was also 50%, it would be reduced by another half.

Tier 3 Capital—Market Risk

In 1995, the Basel Committee amended Basel I to add a market risk measure to the regulatory capital of banks engaged in substantial trading activities. The U.S. banking agencies amended their risk-based capital standards in 1996 to incorporate a "Tier 3" capital measure for market risk for banks and

BHCs whose trading activity equals 10% or more of its total assets or equals $1 billion or more.[14] An institution subject to the rule must hold capital to support its exposure to general market risk arising from fluctuations in interest rates, equity prices, foreign exchange rates, and commodity prices.

Capital also must be held against specific risks associated with certain debt and equity positions, which refers to changes in the market value of specific positions resulting, for example, from insolvency or other adverse changes in the financial condition of counterparties or issuers of a particular instrument. These risks include potential losses caused by mismatches in maturities of assets and liabilities, the timing of their repricing, and shifts in indexes used in interest rate swaps and other transactions.

Banks subject to these rules must measure their market risk "using their internal value-at-risk ('VaR') measurement model and, subject to parameters in the market risk rule, hold sufficient levels of capital to cover the exposure."[15] Tier 3 capital generally "consists of short-term subordinated debt subject to certain criteria, including a lock-in provision that prevents the issuer from repaying the debt even at maturity if the issuer's risk-based capital ratio [would be] less than 8.0% following the payment."[16] The regulations include a formula for integrating Tier 3 capital into the bank's Tier 1 and Tier 2 holdings.

The Basel III Final Rule, discussed below, includes a change to the market risk calculations primarily related to securitizations.[17]

The Basel II Project

On June 26, 2004, the central bank governors and bank supervisors of the Group of Ten (G-10) countries endorsed the publication of a proposed amendment[18] to the 1998 Basel I capital standards that was drafted by the BCBS. This new document, known as the Revised Framework, or simply as Basel II, was designed to strengthen capital standards for large internationally active banks. Interestingly, the hallmark of Basel II is, in calculating capital,

---

14. Risk-Based Capital Standards: Market Risk, Joint Final Rule, 61 Fed. Reg. 47,357 (Sept. 6, 1996).
15. Federal Reserve Board, Commercial Bank Examination Manual, Section 3020.1, p. 7. Further information on VaR and related issues is available at Risk Glossary, http://www.riskglossary.com, which provides links to additional information, and Michael Gordy, *A Risk Factor Model Foundation for Risk-Based Bank Capital Rules, Journal of Financial Intermediation*, July, 2003, p. 119.
16. Joint Final Rule, *supra* note 14, at 47,359.
17. The market risk rule is in each of the primary federal regulator's Basel III regulations at Subpart F. *See, e.g.*, 12 C.F.R. § 217.201 *et seq.*
18. This document, *International Convergence of Capital Measurement and Capital Standards: A Revised Framework*, was approved by the Basel Committee on Bank Supervision on June 25, 2004.

banks were given greater latitude to use their own internal rating systems or metrics to assess risk. As it turned out, those metrics often resulted in capital requirements that were less than required under Basel I.

Reasons for Amendments to Basel I

Basel I "is widely viewed as having achieved its purpose of promoting financial stability and providing an equitable basis for competition among larger banks."[19] As larger banks grew in size, risk, and complexity, however, the Basel I standards became less useful as a measure of the capital adequacy of these banks.

Many of these banks were developing new internal methodologies to measure the "real" economic risk underlying their increasingly complex activities, but these economic capital requirements bore little relationship to regulatory capital measured under the four risk categories of Basel I. One of the results of the disparity between economic and regulatory capital standards was that banks could be regarded as well capitalized under regulatory capital rules while being undercapitalized on an economic basis. One of the dangers of this capital "arbitrage" was recognized as follows:

> [N]ominally high regulatory capital ratios can be used to mask the true level of insolvency probability. For example, consider the case where the bank's own risk analysis calls for a 15 percent internal economic capital assessment against its portfolio. If the bank actually holds 12 percent [regulatory] capital, it would, in all likelihood, be deemed to be "well-capitalized" in a regulatory sense, even though it might be undercapitalized in the economic sense.[20]

Another problem with Basel I as a capital measure for large banks was that, until 1996, Basel I covered only credit risk and ignored other banking risks, such as market, operational, and interest rate risk. As noted above, market risk was added in 1996,[21] but there was a consensus among international bank regulators that if there were to be a convergence of capital standards for large, complex banking organizations ("LCBOs")

---

19. Ferguson, *supra* note 8, at 396.
20. Alan Greenspan, Former Chairman, Federal Reserve Board, *The Role of Capital in Optimal Banking Supervision and Regulation*, Conference on Capital Regulation in the 21st Century, Federal Reserve Bank of New York, Apr. 26, 1998.
21. Market risk was added as a component of Basel I in 1996 by the three U.S. banking agencies: Risk-Based Capital Standards: Market Risk, Joint Final Rule, 61 Fed. Reg. 47,357 (Sept. 6, 1996).

across national boundaries (one of the goals of Basel I), international capital standards had to cover other risks.

In addition, the measure of credit risk itself in Basel I was inadequate, as noted by Federal Reserve Chairman Alan Greenspan in 1998, because, among other things:

> The formal capital ratio requirements, because they do not flow from any particular insolvency probability standard, are, for the most part, arbitrary. All corporate loans, for example, are placed into a single 8 percent "bucket."[22]

In remarks a year later, the Chairman commented:

> In recent years it has become clear that the largely arbitrary treatment of risks within [Basel I] has distorted risk-management practices and encouraged massive regulatory capital arbitrage. That is, our rules have induced bank transactions that have the effect of reducing regulatory capital requirements more than they reduce a bank's risk position. Consequently, the fundamental credibility of regulatory capital standards as a tool for prudential oversight and prompt corrective action at the largest banking organizations has been seriously undermined.[23]

Moreover, regulators were concerned about the systemic risk to the international financial system posed by the concentration of assets held by large banks and the increasing risk embedded in these assets. The Basel II amendment revised the methodology for calculating credit risk and extended risk-based coverage to operational risk. Interest rate risk in the bank's loan portfolio was determined by bank supervisors on a case-by-case basis.

Implementation

The Basel Committee suggested that provisions relating to credit and operating risks would be available for implementation by G-10 members at year end 2006, with the most technical approaches to risk measurement available for implementation January 1, 2008. A one-year "parallel run" trial period to test Basel II standards was to begin January 1, 2006, and

22. Before the Conference on Capital Regulation in the 21st Century, Federal Reserve Bank of New York, Feb. 26, 1998.
23. *The Evolution of Bank Supervision*, remarks of Chairman Greenspan before the American Bankers Association, Phoenix, Arizona, Oct. 11, 1999.

was to continue for two additional years for institutions using the advanced implementation approaches, and one year for banks in other countries using the less advanced approaches system.

Implementation by U.S. Banking Agencies. The U.S. adopted that portion of Basel II that applied to the most complex institutions, known as the "Advanced Approaches" institutions—these were institutions with $250 billion in consolidated assets or $10 billion in foreign exposures and others who could opt in. The U.S. institutions began "parallel runs" (using both Basel I and II capital standards) in 2009. The preliminary results of this exercise, called the Fourth Quantitative Impact Study (QIS-4), showed that implementation of the Basel II framework by participants would have resulted in an average *decrease* in minimum required capital ("MRC") of 15.5% from Basel I requirements and a median decrease in MRC of 26.3%. The study also showed a "significant dispersion of results across institutions and portfolio types," with regulatory capital changes ranging from an MRC increase of 55% for one institution to a decrease of 47% for another. Changes in capital requirements for specific portfolios varied from an average increase of 66% for credit card portfolios to an average decrease of 61.4% for residential mortgages.[24]

Ultimately, no U.S. institutions were permitted to exit parallel runs until Basel III was implemented (which does not permit Basel II to apply alone, as discussed below). Advanced Approaches institutions were then permitted to exit parallel runs from 2014 to 2015.

Application of a New Basel to Smaller U.S. Banks. As most U.S. banks were not subject to Basel II, U.S. bank regulators worked to improve the risk sensitivity of Basel I standards without imposing the complexities of Basel II and to narrow the anticipated differences in capital rates that some believe would have placed non–Basel II banks at a competitive disadvantage to those that adopted Basel II standards. On October 20, 2005,[25] the agencies requested comment on a new version of Basel for smaller banks (sometimes referred to as "Basel I.5"). The subjects included the following:

- increasing the number of risk-weight categories;
- expanding the use of external credit ratings as an indicator of credit risk for externally rated exposures;
- using loan-to-value ratios, credit assessments, and other broad measures of credit risk for assigning risk weights to residential mortgages;

24. *Basel II and the Potential Effect on Insured Institutions in the United States*: Results of the Fourth Quantitative Impact Study, Capital and Accounting News, Supervisory Insights, FDIC, Winter, 2005.
25. Joint advance notice of proposed rulemaking, Risk-Based Capital Guidelines; Capital Adequacy Guidelines, 70 Fed. Reg. 61,068 (Oct. 20, 2005).

- requiring that certain loans 90 days or more past due or in a nonaccrual status be assigned to a higher risk-weight category; and
- modifying the risk-based capital requirements for certain commercial and real estate loans.

All of this found purchase in Basel III.

Basel III

The Global Financial Crisis exposed the need for more and better capital. Thus, on September 12, 2010, the Group of Governors and Heads of Supervision, the oversight body of the Basel Committee, announced agreement to a strengthened set of capital requirements for banking organizations in the United States and around the world, known as Basel III. The agreement was supported by the U.S. federal banking agencies, which released three joint proposals in June 2012 to roll out the Basel III reforms for all financial institutions and parent companies (except bank and savings association holding companies with consolidated assets of less than $3 billion (formerly $1 billion) that are subject to the Small BHC Policy Statement, as discussed below) and released final rules in 2013[26]: the Basel III final rule ("Basel III Rule"), the Standardized Approach Rule; and the Advanced Approach and Market Risk Rule (for large institutions) (collectively "Basel III"). Basel III was intended to be fully phased in on January 1, 2019.

To avoid confusion, the agencies designed the framework so that references to one set of regulations (for instance the OCC's) would be the correct reference to another set of regulations (for instance the FDIC's), even though they are placed in different parts of 12 C.F.R.[27] Under the revised structure:

- Definitions are found in Subpart A.
- The minimum risk-based and leverage capital requirements and buffers are contained in Subpart B.
- The definition of regulatory capital is included in Subpart C.

26. Regulatory Capital Rules: Regulatory Capital, Implementation of Basel III, Final Rule (OCC and Federal Reserve) 78 Fed. Reg. 62,157 (Oct. 11, 2013); Interim Final Rule (FDIC) 78 Fed. Reg. 55,471(Sept. 10, 2013).
27. Basel III is codified in the respective regulations as: (OCC) 12 C.F.R. Part 3 for national banks and Part 167 for savings and loan associations; (Federal Reserve) 12 C.F.R. Part 217 (Regulation Q) for bank holding companies, savings association holding companies and state member banks, and (FDIC) 12 C.F.R. Part 324 for nonmember banks. For ease of reference, the remainder of this chapter will reference citations in Regulation Q.

- Subpart D includes the risk-weighted asset calculations required of all banking organizations; these risk-weighted asset calculations are described in the Standardized Approach Basel III Rule.
- Subpart E contains the advanced approaches rules for the largest banks, including changes made pursuant to the Advanced Approach Basel III Rule.
- The market risk rule is in Subpart F.
- Transition provisions are in Subpart G.

Minimum Capital Ratios and Capital Conservation Buffer

Minimums are indeed minimums, and most depository institutions and parent companies are not going to want to just meet the minimums. Nevertheless, the minimum ratios are important as a beginning point to understand the changes made by Basel III. Basel III requires, among other things: (i) a new required ratio of minimum **common equity Tier 1** ("CET 1") equal to 4.5% of total risk-weighted assets; (ii) an increase in the minimum required amount of Tier 1 capital from the current level of 4% of risk-weighted assets to 6%; and (iii) a continuation of the minimum required amount of total capital at 8% of risk-weighted assets. The rule also requires a minimum leverage ratio (Tier 1 capital divided by adjusted book assets) of 4%.[28]

In addition, institutions that seek the freedom to make capital distributions (including for dividends and repurchases of stock) and pay discretionary bonuses to executive officers without restriction must also maintain 2.5% in CET 1 attributable to a Capital Conservation Buffer (fully phased in on January 1, 2019). The addition of the Capital Conservation Buffer raises the above minimums by 2.5% to 7%, 8.5% and 10.5%, respectively. Institutions that fail to maintain a Capital Conservation Buffer of 2.5% or greater will be unable to make capital distributions or pay discretionary bonuses to executive officers in an aggregate amount exceeding a "maximum payout ratio," calculated as follows[29]:

28. 12 C.F.R. § 217.10.
29. 12 C.F.R. § 217.11(a)(4) Table 1. This section also covers the countercyclical buffer for Advanced Approaches institutions and the G-SIB surcharge for global systemically important BHCs.

Common Equity Capital Conservation Buffer (as a percentage of risk-weighted assets)	Maximum payout ratio (as a percentage of eligible retained income)
Greater than 2.5%	No payout limitation applies
Greater than 1.875% and less than or equal to 2.5%	60%
Greater than 1.25% and less than or equal to 1.875%	40%
Greater than 0.625% and less than or equal to 1.25%	20%
Less than or equal to 0.625%	0%

Changes to the Numerator

Basel III tightened all the capital categories so that capital has more intrinsic quality than under Basel I, adding the new CET 1 numerator to the mix.[30]

CET 1. The new numerator of "Common Equity" means exactly what it says—common stock and its related surplus, and retained earnings, with a few other refinements. It is the most loss-absorbing form of capital. As a consequence, to ensure that a banking organization's CET 1 is available to absorb losses as they occur, the agencies require that common equity capital instruments issued by a banking organization satisfy the following criteria:

- The instrument is paid in, issued directly by the banking organization, and represents the most subordinated claim in a receivership, insolvency, liquidation, or similar proceeding of the banking organization.
- The holder of the instrument is entitled to a claim on the residual assets of the banking organization that is proportional with the holder's share of the banking organization's issued capital after all senior claims have been satisfied in a receivership, insolvency, liquidation, or similar proceeding. That is, the holder has an unlimited and variable claim, not a fixed or capped claim.

30. 12 C.F.R. § 217.120(b).

- The instrument has no maturity date, can only be redeemed via discretionary repurchases with the prior approval of the issuer's primary federal regulator, and does not contain any term or feature that creates an incentive to redeem.
- The banking organization did not create at issuance of the instrument through any action or communication an expectation that it will buy back, cancel, or redeem the instrument, and the instrument does not include any term or feature that might give rise to such an expectation.
- Any cash dividend payments on the instrument are paid out of the banking organization's net income and retained earnings and are not subject to a limit imposed by the contractual terms governing the instrument.
- The banking organization has full discretion at all times to refrain from paying any dividends and making any other capital distributions on the instrument without triggering an event of default, a requirement to make a payment-in-kind, or an imposition of any other restrictions on the banking organization.
- Dividend payments and any other capital distributions on the instrument may be paid only after all legal and contractual obligations of the banking organization have been satisfied, including payments due on more senior claims.
- The holders of the instrument bear losses as they occur equally, proportionately, and simultaneously with the holders of all other common stock instruments before any losses are borne by holders of claims on the banking organization with greater priority in a receivership, insolvency, liquidation, or similar proceeding.
- The paid-in amount is classified as equity under GAAP.
- The banking organization, or an entity that the banking organization controls, did not purchase or directly or indirectly fund the purchase of the instrument.
- The instrument is not secured, not covered by a guarantee of the banking organization or of an affiliate of the banking organization, and is not subject to any other arrangement that legally or economically enhances the seniority of the instrument.
- The instrument has been issued in accordance with applicable laws and regulations. In most cases, the agencies understand that the issuance of these instruments would require the approval of the board of directors of the banking organization or, where applicable, of the banking organization's shareholders or of other persons duly authorized by the banking organization's shareholders.
- The instrument is reported on the banking organization's regulatory financial statements separately from other capital instruments.

Pursuant to Basel III, certain deductions and prudential filters, including minority interests in financial institutions, mortgage servicing rights, and deferred tax assets from timing differences, are fully deducted from CET 1. Certain instruments that no longer qualify as Tier 1 capital, such as trust preferred securities, were also phased out (except for BHCs with assets of less than $15 billion).

Additional Tier 1 Capital. The definition of Additional Tier I capital[31] includes similar concepts to assure that instruments included in that category are indeed permanent, such as perpetual noncumulative preferred stock. In addition, the agencies allow banking organizations to include in additional Tier 1 capital instruments that were (i) issued under the Small Business Jobs Act of 2010 or, prior to October 4, 2010, under the Emergency Economic Stabilization Act of 2008, and (ii) included in Tier 1 capital under the agencies' former general risk-based capital rules. These instruments would be included in Tier 1 capital whether or not they meet the qualifying criteria for CET 1 or additional Tier 1 capital instruments.

Tier 2 Capital. Under the rule, the Tier 2 capital elements[32] include:

- Subordinated debt and preferred stock that satisfy specified criteria in the rule, as long as they are reduced in the last five years prior to maturity. This will include most of the subordinated debt currently included in Tier 2 capital according to the agencies' existing risk-based capital rules;
- Total capital minority interest (as defined in the rule), subject to the limitations, and not included in the banking organization's Tier 1 capital;
- Allowance for ALLL not exceeding 1.25% of the banking organization's total risk-weighted assets; and
- Instruments that qualified as Tier 2 capital under the agencies' general risk-based capital rules and that were issued under the Small Business Jobs Act of 2010, or, prior to October 4, 2010, under the Emergency Economic Stabilization Act of 2008.

AOCI. In another complicating wrinkle, Basel III required unrealized gains and losses on available-for-sale securities to flow through to regulatory capital as opposed to the previous treatment, which neutralized such effects. Recognizing the problem for smaller banks, the U.S. bank regulatory agencies adopted a one-time election for all institutions other than Advanced Approaches to opt out of including most elements of accumulated other comprehensive income ("AOCI") in regulatory capital.[33] This opt-out had

31. 12 C.F.R. § 217.20(c).
32. 12 C.F.R. § 217.20(d).
33. 12 C.F.R. § 217.22(b). The opt-out is addressed at (b)(2).

to be made in the first quarter of 2015 and permitted exclusion from regulatory capital of both unrealized gains and losses on available-for-sale debt securities and accumulated net gains and losses on cash-flow hedges and amounts attributable to defined benefit postretirement plans.

Changes to the Denominator

Basel III installs a much more complex and nuanced protocol to risk weight assets for the purposes of the capital calculations, which generally increase the risk weighting of riskier assets, requiring more capital to be held against them.

Standardized Approach. The Standardized Approach[34] is a nonmodels approach to risk weighting that applies to all institutions subject to minimum capital requirements, including Advanced Approaches institutions (because the approach is the floor required by the Collins Amendment to Dodd-Frank).[35] It uses the same technique introduced by Basel I in listing assets to assigned risk-weight categories, but it significantly increases the categories and adds conditions. For instance, residential mortgage exposures remain at 50% for prudently underwritten first lien mortgage loans that are not past due, reported as nonaccrual or restructured, but there is a 100% risk weight for all other residential mortgages. Highly volatile commercial loans can be 150% and exposures to other banks run from 20% to 100%—in other words, everything is more risk based. Risk-weight categories go as high as 250% for certain commercial real estate exposures and into the stratosphere for certain derivatives. Moreover, the regulations assign each OECD country a "country risk classification" from 1 to 7 (1 being highly rated and 7 being really bad) to calibrate the risk weight of their respective bank obligations. For instance, a senior unsecured bond issued by an Argentine bank has a risk weight of 150% because Argentina has a country risk classification of 7. Compare that to a country with a country risk classification of 2, with a risk weight of 50%.

Like with Basel I, off-balance sheet exposures are brought onto the balance sheet but using many more credit conversion factors. As a result, a banking institution with a risky business model could actually find that the sum of its balance sheet assets, with off-balance sheet exposures added and all assets risk weighted, increases from book assets—a result that was not possible under Basel I.

The cool thing about the Standardized Approach is that you just look up the asset type in the regulation and apply the required risk weight and conversion factor. Nonetheless, this is an evolving science as new types of

34. 12 C.F.R. §§ 217.30 *et seq.*, Subpart D.
35. *Supra* note 1.

assets go on the balance sheet. For instance, in response to issues arising out of the coronavirus pandemic, loans made under the Paycheck Protection Program ("PPP") receive a zero percent risk weight regardless of whether they are pledged as collateral to the Federal Reserve.[36]

Advanced Approach. This applies to the Advanced Approaches institutions and incorporates sophisticated models, approved by the applicable regulator, to determine the risk of assets.[37]

The Leverage Ratio

The leverage ratio, as described above, is not a risk-based calculation, rather it is essentially book assets (with adjustments) divided by Tier 1 capital. Why is it needed in light of all the risk-based measures? Again we look back at the Global Financial Crisis, when one of the causes was the buildup of excessive on- and off-balance sheet leverage (borrowed money) in the banking system.[38] While it seems counterintuitive, banks could have seemingly strong risk-based capital ratios yet build up excessive leverage. As the U.S. bank regulatory agencies articulated frequently, they believed that risk-based and leverage capital requirements work best as effective complements when leverage capital requirements serve as a backstop to risk-based capital requirements. Yet there was a fear that a leverage ratio could serve as too much of a binding constraint, and it needed to be calculated carefully, keeping in mind:

> If a leverage ratio is calibrated at a level that makes it generally a binding constraint, it can create negative incentives. For example, firms may reduce participation in or increase costs for low-risk, low return businesses. At the same time, a leverage requirement that is calibrated at too low of a level will not serve as an effective complement to a risk-based capital requirement.[39]

Similarly, the Basel Committee introduced a leverage ratio in Basel III as a simple, non-risk-based "backstop" to reduce the risk of periods of deleveraging.[40]

---

36. The PPP is discussed under the CARES Act in Chapter 2, *supra*, and the Federal Reserve's role is discussed in Chapter 5, *infra*.
37. 12 C.F.R. §§ 217.30 *et seq.*, Subpart E.
38. BCSB, Basel III Leverage Ratio Framework—Executive Summary (Oct. 25, 2017).
39. *See*, https://www.federalreserve.gov/newsevents/pressreleases/files/bcreg20180411a1.pdf, at 3.
40. The Basel Committee on Banking Supervision introduced a leverage ratio in the 2010 Basel III package of reforms, followed in January 2014 with detailed specification of the leverage ratio framework. However, the calculation of the denominator includes off-balance sheet exposures. *See*, https://www.bis.org/fsi/fsisummaries/b3_lrf.htm.

Simplification for Community Banks—CBLR

Over time, community banks raised continuing concerns with bank regulators about the regulatory burden, complexity, and costs associated with certain provisions of the Basel III Rule. In response, Congress provided a Basel III "off-ramp" for depository institutions and their holding companies with total consolidated assets of less than $10 billion. Section 201 of the Regulatory Relief Act[41] instructed the federal banking regulators to establish a single Community Bank Leverage Ratio ("CBLR") of between 8% and 10%.

On November 3, 2019, the agencies issued a final rule setting the CBLR at 9% of tangible equity to total assets for a qualifying bank to be well capitalized.[42] A community banking organization is eligible to elect the new framework if it has less than $10 billion in total consolidated assets, limited amounts of certain assets and off-balance sheet exposures, and a CBLR greater than 9%. The electing institution is not required to calculate the risk-based and leverage capital requirements of the Basel III Rule and does not need to risk weight its assets for purposes of capital calculations.

A qualifying community banking organization may opt into and out of the CBLR framework by completing the associated reporting requirements on its Call Report. Interestingly, many qualifying banking institutions have not elected the simplified framework, believing their investors need to see information that is comparable to what other banks would report.

What happens if an electing institution slips below the 9% leverage ratio? The regulatory agencies provided a two-quarter grace period (which begins at of the end of the calendar quarter in which the electing banking organization ceases to satisfy any of the qualifying criteria) to either meet the qualifying criteria again or to comply with the generally applicable capital rule. The grace period applies when a banking organization's leverage ratio is 9% or less but greater than 8%. A banking organization that fails to maintain a leverage ratio greater than 8% would not be permitted to use the grace period and must comply with the generally applicable capital rule, and file the appropriate regulatory reports.

CARES Act Modifications. In an effort to alleviate the adverse impact of the coronavirus pandemic on community banks, the federal bank regulatory agencies issued two interim final rules to provide temporary relief to community banking organizations to implement Section 4012 of the Coronavirus Aid, Relief, and Economic Security ("CARES") Act, which

41. Economic Growth, Regulatory Relief and Consumer Protection Act of 2018 (Pub. Law 115–174, S. 2155) was signed into law by President Donald Trump on May 24, 2018.
42. Final Rule, 84 Fed. Reg 61,804 (Nov. 13, 2019) (codified in their respective capital regulations [listed *supra* note 28]). They also issued a Fact Sheet on Sept. 17, 2019. *See, e.g.*, https://www.fdic.gov/regulations/resources/cbi/cblr-facts.pdf.

requires the agencies to temporarily lower the CBLR to 8%.[43] The two rules modified the framework so that:

- beginning in the second quarter 2020 and until the end of the year, an institution that has a leverage ratio of 8% or greater and meets certain other criteria may elect to use the community bank leverage ratio framework; and
- such institutions will have until January 1, 2022, before the community bank leverage ratio requirement is re-established at greater than 9%.

Under the interim final rules, the community bank leverage ratio was 8% beginning in the second quarter and for the remainder of calendar year 2020, 8.5% for calendar year 2021, and 9% thereafter. The interim final rules also maintain a two-quarter grace period for a qualifying community banking organization whose leverage ratio falls no more than 1% below the applicable CBLR.

The Impact of CECL

An issue to watch with respect to capital and its role in loss absorption is the potential impact of the Current Expected Credit Loss ("CECL") standard, which will force an institution to forecast and reserve for lifetime credit and certain investment losses as soon as a loan is made and investment made. It requires procyclical planning through data and modeling. Ultimately, it will reduce capital more upfront than over time. There have been several delays in the roll-out of CECL for all but the largest banks, and another in connection with the coronavirus pandemic.

By way of background (accounting not being a priority on most banking lawyers' learning curve), in 2016, FASB issued Accounting Standards Update No. 2016-13, Financial Instruments—Credit Losses, Topic 326, Measurement of Credit Losses 8 on Financial Instruments. The update resulted in significant changes to credit loss accounting under U.S. GAAP by rolling out CECL to replace the incurred loss methodology. CECL requires banking organizations to recognize lifetime expected credit losses and to incorporate reasonable and supportable forecasts in developing an estimate of lifetime expected credit losses, while also maintaining the current requirement that banking organizations consider past events and current conditions.

43. Regulatory Capital Rule: Temporary Changes to the Community Bank Leverage Ratio Framework, Interim Final Rule, 85 Fed. Reg. 22,924; Regulatory Capital Rule: Transition for the Community Bank Leverage Ratio Framework, Interim Final Rule, 85 Fed. Reg. 22,930 (Apr. 23, 2020).

The banking agencies issued a final rule in 2019 to address the impact of CECL.[44] CECL was to have taken effect in the first quarter of 2020 for insured depository institutions with holding companies that are registered with the SEC, and was delayed to 2023 for smaller reporting and nonreporting BHCs and institutions. The coronavirus pandemic then resulted in additional optional delays for smaller institutions.[45]

Regulatory Capital for Holding Companies

The Collins Amendment to the Dodd-Frank Act[46] mandated that the Federal Reserve establish minimum capital levels for BHCs on a consolidated basis that are as stringent as those required for insured depository institutions. This was made a part of Basel III, such that all BHCs with assets of $3 billion or more are required to meet the Basel III Rule. That change left many BHCs with capital instruments they could not maintain, or, even if they could maintain them, the instruments could no longer be used to raise capital.

Bank Holding Companies

Following are some of the principal differences between Basel III regulatory capital standards for BHCs and those that existed before the Collins Amendment.

Cumulative Preferred Stock and Trust Preferred Securities. Before the Global Financial Crisis, the quality of capital was less of an emphasis than today. In fact, up to 25% of BHC Tier 1 capital could be composed of qualifying *cumulative* perpetual preferred stock and related surplus that was issued directly by the BHC or which consisted of minority interests in consolidated subsidiaries. In 1996, the Federal Reserve expanded the definition of cumulative preferred stock to include trust preferred securities (so-called "TRuPS"), which could count as capital within this 25% Tier 1 sublimit. These instruments, which are issued by a special purpose entity ("SPE") created by the BHC, qualified under GAAP at that time as minority interests in a consolidated subsidiary and therefore as regulatory capital. Many U.S. BHCs used TruPS as a significant capital generation tool.

---

44. Final Rule, 84 Fed. Reg. 4222 (Feb. 14, 2019). (OCC) 12 CFR Part 3 (OCC); (Federal Reserve) 12 CFR Part 217; (FDIC) 12 CFR Part 324.
45. The agencies issued an interim final rule dated March 27, 2020, giving banks implementing CECL in 2020 the option to delay for two years the phase-in of the standard's regulatory capital effects. This is in addition to a three-year phase-in period that was previously established. *See, Joint Statement on the Interaction of the CECL Revised Transition Interim Final Rule with Section 4014 of the Coronavirus Aid, Relief, and Economic Security Act,* FDIC FIL 32-2020 (Mar. 31, 2020).
46. *Supra* note 1.

Characteristics of TRuPS. The Federal Reserve described TRuPS and a typical TRuPS offering as follows[47]:

- TRuPS are undated cumulative preferred securities issued by an SPE, usually a trust created by the BHC. The proceeds of the TRuPS are transferred to the BHC.
- The BHC owns all of the common stock of the SPE.
- The only asset of the SPE is a deeply subordinated note issued by the BHC that is senior only to the BHC's common and preferred stock.
- The note has terms that are generally the same as the TRuPS, except the note has a fixed maturity of thirty years.
- Dividends on the TRuPS can be deferred for twenty quarters.
- The failure of the BHC to pay the cumulative dividend owed to investors after the twenty-quarter deferral causes an event of default and acceleration. This gives the investors the right to take over the subordinated note issued by the BHC and causes the note to become immediately due and payable.

The Federal Reserve pointed out that "a key advantage of trust preferred securities to BHCs is that for tax purposes the dividends paid on trust preferred securities, unlike those paid on directly issued preferred stock, are a tax-deductible interest expense. The Internal Revenue Service ignores the trust and focuses on the interest payments on the underlying subordinated note."[48]

TRuPS as Capital. The Federal Reserve gave several reasons why it considered TRuPS capital for regulatory purposes, including "two key features . . . their long lives, approaching economic perpetuity, and their dividend deferral rights (deferral for 20 consecutive quarters) approaching economically indefinite deferral—were features that provide substantial capital support." Additional reasons included the following:

- While TRuPS are not equity capital and cannot forestall a BHC insolvency, they are able to absorb losses more widely than most other minority interests available to the BHC because the cash flow available from a deferred dividend payment can be deployed anywhere in the BHC's consolidated organization.
- TRuPS are widely traded, transparent, and well understood by the markets.

---

47. Risk-Based Capital Standards: Trust Preferred Securities and the Definition of Capital Final Rule, Board of Governors of the Federal Reserve System, 70 Fed. Reg. 11,827 (Mar. 4, 2005) (amending 12 CFR Parts 208 and 225).
48. *Id.* at 11,828.

- The favorable tax treatment of dividends lowers BHCs' cost of capital, and the inability to use this kind of funding would place an international BHC at a competitive disadvantage.
- Eliminating the ability to include trust preferred securities in Tier 1 capital would put BHCs at a disadvantage to domestic and foreign competitors. The agency noted that foreign competitors had issued as much as $125 billion of similar tax-efficient Tier 1 capital instruments.[49]

Nonetheless, TRuPS did not survive the Global Financial Crisis as a viable option for qualifying capital generation.

TRuPS under Dodd-Frank. As indicated previously, the components of Tier 1 capital for holding companies are now restricted to capital instruments that are considered to be Tier 1 capital for insured depository institutions. As a result:

- The proceeds of TRuPS are excluded from Tier 1 capital unless such securities were issued prior to May 19, 2010, by bank holding companies with less than $15 billion of assets.
- Holding companies having assets of less than $15 billion were able to maintain TRuPS proceeds as capital but have to comply with new capital mandates in other respects, and may not raise Tier 1 capital in the future through the issuance of TRuPS.
- Those holding companies with over $15 billion in assets were required to phase them out over three years beginning January 1, 2013.[50]

While the initial Basel III proposal would have required TRuPS and cumulative perpetual preferred stock to be phased out of Tier 1 capital even for those BHCs grandfathered under Dodd-Frank, the final rule paralleled Dodd-Frank and exempted depository institution holding companies with less than $15 billion in total consolidated assets as of December 31, 2009, or organized in mutual form as of May 19, 2010, from this requirement. Grandfathered capital instruments were limited to 25% of adjusted Tier 1 capital elements. Banking organizations with assets of $15 billion or greater that are not Advanced Approaches banks were required to begin to phase out TRuPS from Tier 1 capital by January 1, 2015; however, TRuPS may remain in Tier 2 capital until the instruments are redeemed or mature. Advanced Approaches banks began the phaseout of TRuPS from regulatory capital in January 2014.

---

49. *Id.* at 11,830.
50. *See, The Ticking Time Bomb of Trust Preferreds,* The Community Bank Monitor, Vol. XXXI, June 2012.

Small Holding Companies

The Small BHC Policy Statement of the Federal Reserve Board[51] was first released in 1980 in order to facilitate transfers of ownership of small banking organizations. Back then BHCs were formed to assume individuals' bank stock acquisition debt, and thus, the Policy Statement generally limited debt to 30% of equity. Flash forward and the small BHC treatment continues under Dodd-Frank and Basel III such that qualifying BHCs are able to apply the risk-based capital and leverage capital guidelines on a bank-only basis and meet the debt-to-equity ratio at the parent BHC level. In other words, they are not subject to the capital requirements of the Basel III Rule and are deemed to be "well-capitalized" as long as each subsidiary bank is well capitalized. The Policy Statement was extended to small thrift holding companies in the Basel III Rule.[52]

What is a "small" holding company for this purpose? Qualification for the special capital treatment is based primarily on asset size, and Congress' definition of "small" has changed over time: the threshold moved from BHCs with less than $500 million in assets to less than $1 billion in 2015 and, as a result of the Regulatory Relief Act, to less than $3 billion in 2018. The Federal Reserve issued an interim final rule, effective August 30, 2018, to raise the threshold as required by the new law.[53]

However, the exemption from capital reporting under the Policy Statement is more nuanced than asset size alone. To be precise, the Policy Statement exempts those holding companies with pro forma consolidated assets of under $3 billion, *as long as they do not*: engage in significant nonbanking activities, conduct significant off-balance sheet activities, or have a material amount of debt or equity securities registered with the SEC. Sound simple? Not so fast. Note that one of the qualifications for this treatment is that the holding company *not have a material amount of securities registered with the SEC*. Isn't that the case with any small BHC that is a publicly reporting company and has shares registered with the SEC (and there are a lot of them)? Read literally, those BHCs flunk the Policy Statement—right? The Federal Reserve has indicated informally that a strict reading of this condition may be "conservative," and in fact, we find many small SEC-reporting BHCs do not report Basel III consolidated capital.[54] Why? "Because our examiners told us not to."

---

51. 12 C.F.R. Part 225, Appendix C. *See,* Small Bank Holding Company Policy Statement and Related Regulations, 83 Fed. Reg. 44,195 (Aug. 30, 2018).
52. 12 C.F.R. § 217.1(c)(iii).
53. Interim Final Rule with request for comment; changes to reporting requirements, 83 FR 44,195 (Aug. 30, 2018).
54. The Federal Reserve requires holding companies to file the FR Y-9C form to report their consolidated capital calculations.

On what grounds are they excused by examiners? The releasing materials for the Policy Statement when it was updated in 2015[55] explained that qualitative requirements are at work and that determinations of materiality are made on a case-by-case basis in order to assess the complexity of a firm. Thus, in considering whether a holding company had a "material" amount of SEC-registered debt or equity securities outstanding that contributed to its complexity (other than trust preferred securities), the Federal Reserve said it may consider, among other factors:

- the number and type of classes and series of stock issued; the holding company's market capitalization;
- the number of outstanding shares;
- the average trading volume;
- the holding company's history of issuing equity and debt securities, including whether the entity has issued any other securities that are not registered with the SEC (e.g., privately placed securities);
- the nature and distribution of ownership;
- whether the securities are listed on a national exchange;
- whether the holding company qualifies as a "smaller reporting company" pursuant to the SEC's regulations and related interpretations; and
- the amount, type, and terms of any debt instruments issued by the entity.[56]

It is a little disconcerting to rely on 2015 language in releasing materials. Plus, does that language establish a rebuttable presumption that a holding company is in or out? Not clear. A little more certainty would be welcome.

S&L Holding Companies

Savings and loan holding companies are treated just like BHCs under Dodd-Frank, with a couple of exceptions. First, is the small BHC exception noted above that the Federal Reserve has extended to thrift holding companies. Second, the holding companies are excluded if they derive 50% of their consolidated assets or 50% of the total revenues from activities not considered financial in nature under the BHCA.[57] Third, Congress amended Dodd-Frank in 2014 to clarify that the Federal Reserve had authority to consider different capital requirements for holding companies that are insurance companies.[58] On that last note, while the Federal Reserve did

55. Small Bank Holding Company Policy Statement, Final Rule, 80 Fed. Reg. 20,153 (Apr. 15, 2015).
56. *Id.*
57. *See*, 12 C.F.R. § 217.2, definition of *Covered Savings and Loan Holding Company*.
58. The Insurance Capital Standards Clarification Act of 2014, ACLI Capital Hill Update.

not exactly act with alacrity in response to the mandate of Congress, it finally released an Advanced Notice of Proposed Rulemaking on June 14, 2016, and another on October 24, 2019, seeking comment on approaches to consolidated capital requirements for insurance depository institution holding companies and SIFI insurance companies.[59]

Additional Requirements for the Largest Holding Companies

We all understand there are "too big to fail banks" because they are systemically important institutions domestically and globally. The resiliency of these financial institutions is critical to the stability of our economy. This is where even more capital comes into play. As the Federal Reserve expressed in the background to its capital integration proposal for the largest banks[60]:

> As shown in the 2007–2008 financial crisis, problems at large financial institutions can lead to significant market disruption, spread rapidly throughout the financial system, and cause a credit crunch, worsening economic downturns. To be resilient, a financial institution must maintain sufficient levels of capital to support the risks associated with its exposures and activities. In the years leading up to the financial crisis, neither the regulatory capital regime nor financial institutions' own models sufficiently captured the actual risk exposures of financial institutions, resulting in a level of capital that was inadequate to cover losses as conditions deteriorated, putting the economic activity at risk.
>
> The risks to the ability of the financial system to support economic growth were exacerbated by actions taken by firms during the crisis. Rather than conserve loss-absorbing resources, many firms continued to distribute capital to shareholders in an attempt to reassure the market of their health and resiliency. Further, the lack of transparency into firms' actual risk profiles during the crisis increased uncertainty, left counterparties unable

59. Capital Requirements for Supervised Institutions Significantly Engaged in Insurance Activities, Proposed Rule, 81 Fed. Reg. 38,631 (June 14, 2016); 84 Fed. Reg. 57,240 (Oct. 24, 2019).
60. Notice of Proposed Rulemaking, 83 Fed. Reg. 18,160 (June 25, 2018) (to integrate the Board's regulatory capital rule [capital rule] and the Board's Comprehensive Capital Analysis and Review [CCAR] and stress test rules in order to simplify the capital regime applicable to firms subject to the capital plan rule).

> to distinguish between healthy and unhealthy banks, and prompted a large and sudden reaction from the markets as the full scale of risks was revealed.

As a consequence, the largest institutions became subject to further capital surcharges, enhancements, and other requirements to bolster financial stability. After rightsizing as per the Regulatory Relief Act, there are special additional capital requirements for:

- Advanced Approaches institutions—those with over $250 billion in assets or over $10 billion in foreign exposures; and
- G-SIBs—those globally systemically important financial institutions. The United States has eight G-SIBs identified by the Federal Reserve (Bank of America, Bank of New York, Citi, Goldman Sachs, J.P. Morgan Chase, Morgan Stanley, State Street, and Wells Fargo).

Countercyclical Buffer ("CCyB"). This buffer, intended to operate as an additional amount of the Capital Conservation Buffer (with the same consequences) for Advanced Approaches institutions, is established by the appropriate regulator at between 0% and 2.5% according to its perception of the systemic risk that has built up in the banking system. It has been set at 0% by the U.S. bank regulators to start.[61]

Supplemental Leverage Ratio ("SLR"). Advanced Approaches institutions are required to meet a 3% SLR, which differs from the leverage ratio that applies to all institutions by including off-balance sheet exposures.[62]

Enhanced Supplemental Leverage Ratio ("eSLR"). The eSLR standards[63] require even more capital to be held by G-SIBs and by the insured depository institution subsidiaries of those firms as well.[64] The eSLR assessment is 5%, which is the sum of the minimum 3% SLR requirement plus a buffer of 2%, for the institution to avoid limitations on capital distributions and certain discretionary bonus payments. The insured depository institution subsidiaries of the G-SIBs must maintain an eSLR of 6% to be considered well capitalized.

In connection with rightsizing of certain Dodd-Frank requirements after the Regulatory Relief Act was enacted, the Federal Reserve and OCC

61. 12 C.F.R. § 217.11(b)(2).
62. 12 C.F.R. § 217.10(a)(4).
63. 79 Fed. Reg. 24,528 (May 1, 2014), and as amended by the G-SIB surcharge rule. 80 Fed. Reg. 49,082 (Aug. 14, 2015).
64. Regulatory Capital Rules: Enhanced Supplementary Leverage Ratio Standards, Final Rule, 79 Fed. Reg 24,528 (May 1, 2014).

proposed changes to the eSLR in April 2018,[65] which would modify the fixed 2% buffer to be one-half of each institution's G-SIB Surcharge. The proposal would also tailor the current 6% requirement for the insured depository institution subsidiaries of G-SIBs based on risk.

G-SIB Surcharge. G-SIBs must also hold additional CET 1 capital of 1% to 4.5%, added to the Capital Conservation Buffer.[66] The scoring to determine the amount of surcharge is based on Basel Committee criteria of systemic risk indicators within five categories:

- *Size*—total exposures (20%)
- *Interconnectedness*—intrafinancial system assets (6.67%), intrafinancial system liabilities (6.67%), and securities outstanding (6.67%)
- *Substitutability*—payments activity (6.67%), assets under custody (6.67%), and underwritten transactions in debt and equity markets (6.67%)
- *Complexity*—notional amount of OTC derivatives (6.67%), trading and available-for-sale securities (6.67%), and level 3 assets (6.67%)
- *Cross-Border Activity*—cross-border claims (10%) and cross-border liabilities (10%)

The U.S. rules are tougher; G-SIBs have to apply these criteria (known as Method 1) and a second substitutability factor replaced with a score reflecting the institution's dependence on short-term wholesale funding (Method 2). They then have to apply the higher of the two to determine their surcharge.

The Basel Committee releases an annual list that places each G-SIB in a bucket corresponding to its surcharge. For instance, JP Morgan Chase was in bucket 4 (with 5 the highest), and its surcharge as of November 2019 was 2.5%; Wells Fargo was in bucket 2 with a surcharge of 1.5%.[67]

Total Loss Absorbing Capacity ("TLAC"). The Board released its final rule on TLAC on December 15, 2016,[68] applying it to domestic G-SIBs, as well as to the U.S. operations of foreign G-SIBs. These institutions are required to meet a new long-term debt requirement and a new TLAC requirement.

---

65. Regulatory Capital Rules: Regulatory Capital, Enhanced Supplementary Leverage Ratio Standards for U.S. Global Systemically Important Bank Holding Companies; Total Loss-Absorbing Capacity Requirements for U.S. Global Systemically Important Bank Holding Companies, Joint Notice of Proposed Rulemaking, 83 Fed. Reg. 17,317 (Apr. 19, 2018).
66. G-SIB Surcharge, Final Rule, 80 Fed. Reg. 49,082 (Aug. 14, 2015) (codified at 12 C.F.R. § 217.11(c) and Subpart H).
67. https://www.fsb.org/wp-content/uploads/P221119-1.pdf.
68. Total Loss-Absorbing Capacity, Long-Term Debt, and Clean Holding Company Requirements, 12 C.F.R. Part 252.

The requirements are intended to reduce the systemic impact of the failure of a G-SIB by permitting it to fail and cause its investors to suffer losses, while the critical operations of the firm continue to function. For domestic G-SIBs, the proposed long-term debt requirement will set a minimum level of long-term debt that could be used to recapitalize these firms' critical operations upon failure. The complementary TLAC requirement would set a new minimum level of total loss-absorbing capacity, which can be met with both regulatory capital and long-term debt. Under the rule, domestic G-SIBs would be required to hold at a minimum:

- a long-term debt amount of the greater of 6% plus its G-SIB surcharge of risk-weighted assets and 4.5% of total leverage exposure; and
- a TLAC amount of the greater of 18% of risk-weighted assets and 9.5% of total leverage exposure.

Stress Capital Buffer ("SCB"). Yes, there is more. In April 2018, the Federal Reserve proposed replacing the Capital Conservation Buffer for those firms that go through the Comprehensive Capital Analysis and Review ("CCAR") stress test process with a new "stress capital buffer" consisting of maximum projected decline (peak-to-trough) in a firm's CET1 ratio during the nine-quarter stress horizon under the "severely adverse" scenario, plus four quarters of the firm's planned common stock dividends.[69]

Prompt Corrective Action

What happens when capital starts to dissipate in a financial institution? What actions can the regulators take? Can they catch the problem before the bank fails? Historically, there was no road map, and sometimes regulators were powerless. At its worst in modern times, we witnessed "zombie" thrifts operating recklessly with negative capital in the thrift crisis of the 1980s. The insurance fund at the time could not handle the exceptional number of receiverships. There needed to be an early detection regime.

In the midst of a lot of finger pointing, Congress responded and granted the federal banking agencies the power to impose increasingly severe sanctions on institutions whose capital levels fall.[70] This regime, called Prompt Corrective Action ("PCA"),[71] creates levels of capital adequacy ranging from "well-capitalized" through "undercapitalized" to "critically undercapitalized."

---

69. Notice of Proposed Rulemaking, 83 Fed. Reg. 18,160 (Apr. 25, 2018).
70. FDIC Improvement Act of 1991, Pub. L. 102–242, title I, § 131(a) (codified at 12 U.S.C. § 1831o).
71. PCA only applies to insured depository institutions. The agency implementing regulations are: (OCC) 12 C.F.R. Part 6; (Federal Reserve) 12 C.F.R. § 208.40 (Regulation H applicable to member banks); (FDIC) 12 C.F.R. Part 324, Subpart H.

Capital Categories

Capital Category	Total Risk-Based Capital Ratio	Tier 1 Risk-Based Capital Ratio	Common Equity Tier 1 Risk-Based Capital Ratio	Tier 1 Leverage Ratio	Other
Well-capitalized	10%	8%	6.5%	5%	[Not subject to formal action to maintain a specific capital level]
Adequately Capitalized	8%	6%	4.5%	4%	[Leverage ratio of 3% or more if bank is 1 rated and not growing]
Undercapitalized	< 8%	< 6%	< 4.5%	< 4%	[Leverage ratio of 3% or more if bank is 1 rated and not growing]
Significantly Undercapitalized	< 6%	< 4%	< 3%	< 3%	[N/A]
Critically Undercapitalized	Tangible equity to total assets ratio is <= 2% regardless of other capital ratios				

Restrictions

The rubber hits the road under PCA in connection with the restrictions it imposes on a depository institution as its capital deteriorates.

Well and adequately capitalized institutions: May not pay dividends, with certain exceptions, or management fees if such payments would cause the institution to become undercapitalized.

Deposit insurance premiums: Institutions that are less than well capitalized are subject to higher deposit insurance premiums than those that are well capitalized.

Undercapitalized institutions: The banking agencies must take the following actions against institutions that become undercapitalized:

- restrict payment of capital distributions and management fees;
- require the institution to develop a capital restoration plan;

- monitor the condition of the institution and the implementation of its capital plan;
- restrict asset growth; and
- require prior approval of new activities, including acquisitions, branching, and new lines of business.

Significantly undercapitalized institutions: Institutions that reach this level of capitalization are subject to the above restrictions applicable to undercapitalized institutions. In addition, the institution may not pay bonuses to, or grant raises to, senior executive officers, until a capital restoration plan has been submitted by the institution and unless the bonus or raise is approved by the appropriate agency.

PCA provides that the agencies "shall take" the following actions unless they determine that such actions would not be effective:

- require the institution to be acquired by a depository institution holding company, or to combine with another insured depository institution, if one or more grounds exist for appointing a conservator or receiver for the institution;
- restrict transactions with affiliates; and
- restrict future interest rates paid on deposits to those prevailing in the institution's market area.

The agencies may also impose the following restrictions on institutions that become significantly undercapitalized:

- restrict asset growth;
- require the institution or any of its subsidiaries to alter, reduce, or terminate any activity that the agency determines poses excessive risk to the institution;
- improve management by requiring one or more of the following:
    - ordering the election of new directors;
    - ordering the dismissal of directors or senior executive officers; or
    - requiring the institution to employ qualified senior executive officers (who, if the agency so specifies, shall be subject to approval by the agency);
- prohibit the acceptance of deposits from correspondent banks, including renewals and rollovers of prior deposits;
- prohibit a bank holding company from making any capital distribution without the prior approval of the Federal Reserve Board;
- require the institution to divest subsidiaries that are deemed to pose a significant risk to the institution;

- require the parent of the institution to:
  - divest a nondepository affiliate if the "appropriate Federal banking agency for that company"[72] determines that the affiliate poses a significant risk to the institution,
  - divest the institution itself if the appropriate federal banking agency for that company determines that divestiture would improve the institution's financial condition and future prospects,
  - require the institution to take any other action that the agency deems advisable.

Critically Undercapitalized Institutions. The appropriate federal banking agency is required to appoint a receiver for an institution within 90 days after it becomes critically undercapitalized. There are several exceptions to this requirement, including a case in which the agency and the FDIC find that the institution has positive net worth, is viable, and is not expected to fail. The institution is also prohibited from making payments of principal and interest on its subordinated debt, except as permitted by the FDIC.

The FDIC is required "at a minimum" to prohibit the institution from doing any of the following without its prior written approval:

- entering into any material transaction other than in the usual course of business, including any investment, expansion, acquisition, sale of assets, or other similar action with respect to which the depository institution is required to provide notice to the appropriate banking agency;
- extending credit for any highly leveraged transaction;
- amending the institution's charter or bylaws, except to the extent necessary to carry out any other requirement of any law, regulation, or order;
- making any material change in accounting methods;
- engaging in any transaction that is a "covered transaction" under the transactions with affiliates rules of Section 23A of the Federal Reserve Act[73];
- paying excessive compensation or bonuses;
- paying interest on new or renewed liabilities at a rate that would increase the institution's weighted average cost of funds to a level

72. At the time of enactment of the PCA rules, the appropriate federal banking agency was the Board for bank holding companies and the OTS for S&L holding companies. As a result of the enactment of Dodd-Frank, the Board is the appropriate federal banking agency for both BHCs and S&LHCs.
73. 12 U.S.C. 371c.

significantly exceeding the prevailing rates of interest on insured deposits in the institution's normal market areas; and

- making any principal or interest payment on subordinated debt beginning 60 days after becoming critically undercapitalized.

Capital Restoration Plan

Institutions whose capital levels decline to undercapitalized or lower are required to submit a capital restoration plan to their regulator that must, among other things, specify the steps the institution will take to become adequately capitalized. The plan must include a guarantee executed by each company that controls the institution.[74] These companies must guarantee that the institution will comply with its capital plan until it is adequately capitalized for four consecutive calendar quarters. The PCA statute provides, however, that the aggregate amount of liability for all companies that control a specific bank is limited to the lesser of 5% of the institution's total assets or the institution's capital shortfall.

Relation to Other Authority

The provisions of PCA do not limit any authority of an appropriate banking agency or any state regulator "to take action in addition to (but not in derogation of) that required under this section." The FDIC regulations further state that nothing in PCA or its regulations "in any way limits the authority of the FDIC under any other provision of law to take supervisory actions to address unsafe or unsound practices, deficient capital levels, violations of law, unsafe or unsound conditions, or other practices."[75]

Capital Planning and Supervision

The capital rules scripted by BCBS in Basel III are only part of an overall plan. To that end, what is discussed in depth above in connection with "Capital Adequacy" is Pillar 1 of Basel III. Pillar 2 is "Supervisory Review," under which banking institutions are obligated to assess their internal capital adequacy for covering all risks they can potentially face in the course of their operations. In turn, the bank regulator is responsible for ascertaining whether the institution uses appropriate assessment approaches and covers

---

74. The Federal Reserve says it will "consider on a case-by-case basis the appropriate type of guarantee for multi-tier holding companies, or . . . shell [holding] companies that have limited resources." (Federal Reserve Board, Commercial Bank Examination Manual, Section 4133.1).
75. 12 C.F.R. § 325.101(d).

all associated risks.[76] As a result, there are critical parts to play by institutions and their regulators to assure that capital adequacy is not just a balance sheet exercise but supports real resiliency.

A Matter of Safety and Soundness

Chapter 8 of this book discusses the concept of "safety and soundness" as the backstop of prudential regulation. It is not a stretch to equate an institution's lack of adequate capital planning with an unsafe and unsound banking practice. In this regard, on June 7, 2012, the OCC, released a bulletin entitled "Guidance for Evaluating Capital Planning and Adequacy,"[77] in which it provided national banks and federal savings associations with its expectations in this area, linking capital planning with safety and soundness. The OCC expects every bank, regardless of size or charter type, to have an effective internal process to (i) assess its capital adequacy in relation to its overall risks *and* (ii) plan for maintaining appropriate capital levels. What is particularly striking about the guidance is that it emphasizes that the capital calculations are just one piece of the overall capital picture:

> The appropriate level of capital for an individual bank cannot be determined solely through the application of a mathematical formula or wholly quantitative criteria. In this regard, the regulatory minimum capital ratios are standards that address only a subset of risks faced by banks. Therefore, a bank should maintain capital well *above* regulatory minimum capital ratios, especially during expansionary periods when the economy may be growing robustly and bank earnings are strong but the inherent risks in a bank's operations and balance sheet may be increasing. Equally emphasized in this bulletin, a bank at the "*well-capitalized*" level under the Prompt Corrective Action rule should not automatically assume that it has sufficient capital to cover all of its risks.[78]

The planning process contemplated in the bulletin is much more comprehensive than banks conducted precrisis. It becomes part of the risk management processes generally, with both quantitative and qualitative measures, taking into consideration both short- and longer-term capital needs. In fact, the OCC expects bank boards and management to be actively involved in the process and coordinate capital planning with the bank's

76. https://www.bis.org/bcbs/basel3/b3summarytable.pdf.
77. *See*, OCC Bulletin 2012-16 (June 7, 2012).
78. *Id.*

overall strategy and planning cycles, usually with a forecast horizon of at least two years. The OCC identifies the following steps:

- identify risks, improve their understanding of the bank's overall risks, set risk tolerance levels, and assess strategic choices in longer-term planning;
- identify vulnerabilities such as concentrations and assess their impact on capital;
- integrate business strategy, risk management, capital, and liquidity planning decisions, including due diligence for a merger or acquisition; and
- have a forward-looking assessment of the bank's capital needs, including capital needs that may arise from rapid changes in the economic and financial environment.

The FDIC promulgated a capital maintenance regulation at 12 C.F.R. Part 325 that provides state nonmember banks and savings associations the FDIC's expectations in this regard.

Capital Planning for the Largest BHCs

In November 2011, the Federal Reserve began requiring BHCs with consolidated assets of $50 billion or more to turn capital planning strategies and processes into formal capital plans and to submit annual capital plans to the Federal Reserve for review.[79] The $50 billion threshold was rightsized by Section 401 of the Regulatory Relief Act by generally raising the minimum asset threshold for application of prudential standards under Section 165 for Dodd-Frank from $50 billion in total consolidated assets to $250 billion in total consolidated assets. However, for capital plans and periodic supervisory stress tests, the threshold was raised partway—to $100 billion.

The required annual capital plans must be filed with the Federal Reserve by April 5 of each year and must address four mandatory elements:

- assessment of expected uses and sources of capital over the nine-quarter planning horizon, reflecting the company's size, complexity, risk profile, and scope of operations under both expected and stressed conditions;
- description of company's processes for assessing capital adequacy;
- capital policies; and
- discussion of baseline changes to the company's business plan that would likely have a material impact on the capital adequacy and liquidity.[80]

79. 12 C.F.R. § 225.8(e).
80. 12 C.F.R. § 225.8(e)(2).

The Federal Reserve evaluates BHCs' capital plans[81] as part of the CCAR exercise discussed below. Until 2020, the evaluation involved two assessments:

- *Qualitative assessment*—focuses on the key areas of the capital planning process and the internal practices used to determine the amount and composition of capital needed in a period of stress (different expectations for institutions of different size and complexity). The Federal Reserve has most frequently objected to capital plans on qualitative grounds, but the qualitative assessment is to be phased out and only certain foreign banks will be covered for 2020.[82]
- *Quantitative assessment*—focuses on BHC's ability to take the capital actions described and maintain its capital ratios above the minimum in stressed conditions.

The Federal Reserve then must publish summary results of "object" or "no objection" in June of each year. There are numerous consequences to an objection, including that the BHC may not make any capital distributions without the prior written approval of the Federal Reserve, and it must submit a revised capital plan.[83]

CCAR and DFAST Stress Testing

In the wake of the financial crisis, Congress enacted Section 165(i) of Dodd-Frank Act,[84] which, among other "enhanced prudential standards," required the responsible federal banking agency to conduct an annual stress test of institutions with total consolidated assets of $50 billion or more as well as nonbank financial companies designated for supervision by the Board.[85] The threshold for this regime was rightsized by the Regulatory Relief Act to $100 billion in assets.

The Federal Reserve Board conducts these supervisory stress tests to help ensure that large bank holding companies operating in the United States will be able to continue operations by maintaining ready access to creditors and other counterparties and continuing to serve as credit intermediaries even in a severe recession.[86] The tests have two components: the Dodd-Frank Act stress test ("DFAST") and the Comprehensive Capital Analysis and

81. 12 C.F.R. § 225.8(f).
82. Final Rule, 84 Fed. Reg. 8953 (Mar. 13, 2019).
83. 12 C.F.R. § 225.8(f) and (g).
84. Codified in 12 U.S.C. § 252 (Regulation YY).
85. 12 C.F.R. § 225.8(f).
86. 12 C.F.R. §252.46.

Review ("CCAR").[87] DFAST is a forward-looking assessment of the capital adequacy of holding companies that uses standard assumptions across all covered firms. CCAR evaluates the capital planning practices and capital adequacy of holding companies using capital actions, such as dividend payments and share repurchases, planned by those firms.

Stress tests in 2020 evaluated 34 large banks with more than $100 billion in total assets.[88]

CCAR. CCAR is a process that evaluates a covered BHC's capital adequacy, capital planning process, and planned capital distributions, such as any dividend payments and common stock repurchases. As part of CCAR, the Federal Reserve evaluates whether institutions have sufficient capital to continue operations throughout times of economic and financial market stress and whether they have robust, forward-looking capital-planning processes that account for their unique risks. In conducting the CCAR, the Federal Reserve must project balance sheets, RWAs, net income, and resulting poststress capital levels and regulatory capital ratios over a nine-quarter "planning horizon," generally using a set of capital action assumptions prescribed in the Dodd-Frank stress test rules. The stress tests include two hypothetical scenarios: baseline and severely adverse developed annually by the Federal Reserve in concert with the OCC and FDIC.

Stress Tests. CCAR covered institutions must also run annual internal stress tests as part of their capital planning.[89] In 2012, the three federal banking agencies each published its final annual stress test rule,[90] which set out definitions and rules for scope of application, scenarios, reporting, and disclosure. For the annual company-run stress test, the institutions use the same planning horizon, capital action assumptions, and scenarios as those used in the CCAR in order to enhance the comparability of the supervisory and company-run results.

The objective of the annual company-run stress test is to ensure that institutions have robust, forward-looking capital planning processes that account for their unique risks, and to help ensure that institutions have

87. U.S. bank holding companies and U.S. intermediate holding companies of foreign banking organizations with $100 billion or more in assets are subject to the Federal Reserve Board's supervisory stress test rule (12 CFR 252, subpart E) and the capital plan rule (12 CFR 225.8). In addition, certain U.S. BHCs, U.S. IHCs, savings and loan holding companies, and state member banks must comply with the Board's company-run stress test rules. (12 CFR 238, subpart P; 12 CFR 252, subpart B; and 12 CFR 252, subpart F).
88. A list of the 34 companies subject to Federal Reserve stress tests in 2020 is found on the Federal Reserve website.
89. Section 165(i)(2) of Dodd-Frank.
90. (OCC) 12 C.F.R. Part 46; (Federal Reserve) 12 C.F.R. Part 252; (FDIC) 12 C.F.R. Part 325 Subpart C. *See also*, http://www.occ.treas.gov/tools-forms/forms/bank-operations/stress-test-reporting.html.

sufficient capital to continue operations throughout times of economic and financial stress.

Scenarios. The regulators provide the required scenarios to the covered institutions by February 15 of each year. For example, in the United States in 2012, an adverse scenario used in stress testing was all of the following:

- Unemployment at 13%;
- 50% drop in equity prices;
- 21% decline in housing prices.

On February 6, 2020,[91] the Federal Reserve released the stress test scenarios for the 2020 exercises. In pertinent part, the severely adverse scenario assumes:

- The U.S. unemployment rate will climb to a peak of 10% in the third quarter of 2021.
- In line with the increase in the unemployment rate, real GDP will fall about 8.5% from its prerecession peak, reaching a trough in the third quarter of 2021.
- The decline in activity will be accompanied by a lower headline CPI inflation rate, which will fall to an annual rate of about 1.25% after the first quarter of 2020, before gradually rising to average 1.75% in 2022.
- In line with the severe decline in real activity, the interest rate for three-month Treasury bills will immediately fall near zero and remain at that level through the end of the scenario. The ten-year Treasury yield will immediately fall to 0.78% during the first quarter of 2020 and rises gradually thereafter to 2.25% by the end of the stress-test period.

It seemed to be scary stuff. Coronavirus redefined scary stuff with unprecedented unemployment and the closing of the economy. As a result the Board went back to work.[92] While finding that all large banks were sufficiently capitalized in the first two quarters of 2020, the Board took additional action to preserve capital and to assess banks' capital plans more frequently during the time of COVID-19 uncertainty. In particular, the Board:

- suspended share repurchases,
- capped the growth of dividends and imposed a limit that does not exceed recent income,
- required banks to re-assess their capital needs and resubmit their capital plans later in the year, and

91. https://www.federalreserve.gov/newsevents/pressreleases/files/bcreg20200206a1.pdf.
92. *Assessment of Bank Capital during the Recent Coronavirus Event,* June 2020, https://www.federalreserve.gov/publications/files/2020-sensitivity-analysis-20200625.pdf.

- planned to conduct additional stress analyses later in 2020 as data from banks became available and economic conditions evolved.

The restrictions applied for the third quarter of 2020, with the possibility of extensions, as the economic situation continued to evolve.

The Federal Reserve also undertook a "sensitivity analysis"[93] to explore the vulnerabilities of banks to the downside risks to the economy posed by the COVID event. Finding the stress brought on by the COVID event was larger than anticipated and could result in an unusual relationship between the economic and financial factors and credit losses, in part because of extraordinary government actions, the Board constructed three alternative downside scenarios for the institutions participating in the 2020 DFAST stress tests:

- a rapid V-shaped recovery that regains much of the output and employment lost by the end of 2020;
- a slower, more U-shaped recovery in which only a small share of lost output and employment is regained in 2020; and
- a W-shaped double dip recession with a short-lived recovery followed by a severe drop in activity later in 2020 due to a second COVID event.

93. *Id* at 1.

5

Bank Deposits and Short-Term Borrowing

Subsidy? What Subsidy?

It is difficult to imagine in retrospect, but a contentious debate raged for much of the 1990s and early 2000s as to whether American banks were subsidized by the federal government—it raged right up until it fizzled out on the doorstep of 2008, when we witnessed the full force and effect of subsidies, with the U.S. government literally hauling countless large banks and other "financial institutions" back from the brink of insolvency.

Why was there a debate in the first place? The largest banks in the land believed that the cost of federal government backing in terms of regulation was excessive and that they did not benefit from it. Pretty ironic in retrospect.

The express government backing of all American depository institutions is embodied in what we call the "federal safety net"—federal deposit insurance and discount window borrowing—but there is more to it for the largest banks. There is also what is frequently characterized as an "implicit" subsidy. The theory in this regard postulates that the largest banks in the land, which are potentially the most dangerous because of their sheer size and complexity, can borrow at lower rates, because creditors perceive them as too big to fail. That means banks have a powerful incentive to get big and unwieldy. The larger they are, the more disastrous their failure would be and the more certain creditors can be of a government bailout in an emergency. Multiplied by the total liabilities of the ten largest United States banks by assets, it is argued that the implicit subsidy amounts to $83 billion a year.[1] In estimating the funding advantage that the subsidy provides to too-big-to-fail banks, economists at the Federal Deposit Insurance Corporation

1. *Why Should Taxpayers Give Big Banks $83 Billion a Year,* https://www.bloomberg.com/view/articles/2013-02-20.

("FDIC") compared interest rates offered by small and large banks on money-market deposit accounts with balances exceeding FDIC insurance from 2005 through 2010. For banks with assets greater than $100 billion, they found the deposit funding advantage to be worth a 0.45 percentage point. For banks with assets greater than $200 billion, the advantage came to approximately 1.2 percentage points.[2] That amounts to significant earnings when multiplied by the amount of their respective deposits.

So, we have the safety net and then we have the funding advantage for banks that are too big to fail. Sounds like subsidies. Debate over?

The Safety Net

What is the "safety net"? The safety net is a term given by the financial industry to federal programs that underlie the stability and efficiency of the banking system. The focus in this regard is on the liability side of the bank balance sheet, and the primary liability of a bank, of course, is its deposit accounts. Deposits are borrowed money, much of which must be repaid on demand. Banking systems rely on the confidence of depositors that they will be able to access their funds whenever they need them. If that confidence is shaken—perhaps by the failure of an important bank or large commercial firm or sometimes just because of a rumor—people will instinctively rush to withdraw their deposits to avoid losing funds if their bank fails. Because banks hold only a fraction of the value of their customers' deposits in the form of cash and high quality liquid assets, a sudden, unexpected attempt to convert deposits into cash can leave banks short of funds. The result can be a liquidity crisis, and banks can quickly fail because of liquidity even if they remain technically solvent.

The challenge for the system is, thus, to avert a liquidity crisis in the first instance, and maintain depositor security so as to avert runs. The safety net responds to these challenges and features federal deposit insurance as its mainstay, so that depositors know exactly how much of their money is safe—literally backed by the federal government. But, it also includes the Federal Reserve Board's emergency and other "discount window" loans and critical elements of the federal payments system (the clearance and settlement of checks and other items).[3] The "protection of the safety net" is a key priority of federal banking laws, regulations, and supervision, and the safety net itself has been characterized as having "[provided] depository

2. *Remember That $83 Billion Bank Subsidy? We Weren't Kidding*, https://www.bloomberg.com/view/articles/2013-02-24.
3. The federal payments system, which is not covered in this book, is implemented in part by the Federal Reserve Board's Regulation J (12 C.F.R. Part 210).

institutions and financial market participants with safety, liquidity, and solvency unheard of in previous years."[4]

We experienced a rather astounding metamorphosis of the safety net extending to not only banks but the general economy in connection with the 2020 coronavirus pandemic, hopefully providing tools that will be equally effective to provide liquidity and stem future national economic emergencies.

We once again turn to our history for the backstory.

Why a Discount Window?

The Federal Reserve's role as "lender of last resort" or "central bank" is often referred to in terms of its discount window operations. As depicted in Chapter 2, from the birth of our country, Alexander Hamilton extoled the virtues of a central bank to serve as a banker's bank. With the demise of his brainchild (Bank of the United States) and its successor (Second Bank of the United States), each after a charter of 20 years, commercial banks in the country were left with no short-term liquidity providers to buttress them in a bank panic.

And we had bank panics, most notably the Panic of 1907, which in its most simple form, was a six-week run on banks from October to November 1907.[5] With no central bank, J.P. Morgan & Co., owned by New York financier J.P. Morgan, was the only institution with the experience and authority to act.[6] Morgan helped to save several trust companies and a leading brokerage house from insolvency, bailed out New York City and rescued the New York Stock Exchange. He also persuaded his fellow financiers to supply liquidity to the markets, including underwriting $30 million worth of New York City bonds to keep the city from defaulting.[7] His actions are not without controversy, but perhaps the highest testament to what he accomplished was that in the year of Morgan's death, President Woodrow Wilson passed into law the Federal Reserve Act ("FRA"), which established the Board of Governors of the Federal Reserve System as the central bank that might have prevented or minimized the Panics of 1893 and 1907 and was ultimately instrumental in mitigating the impact of future crisis.[8]

4. Remarks by Alan Greenspan, Chairman of the Federal Reserve Board, *The Financial Safety Net*, at the 37th Annual Conference on Bank Structure and Competition of the Federal Reserve Bank of Chicago, Chicago, Illinois (May 10, 2001).
5. Many of the causes and challenges of the 1907 Panic are discussed in Chapter 2 in connection with the birth of the Federal Reserve System.
6. *See, The Panic of 1907*, http://economicsofjpmorgan.yolasite.com/panic-of-1907.php.
7. *Easing the Panic*, https://www.jpmorgan.com/country/US/en/jpmorgan/about/history/month/oct.
8. *The Panic of 1907*, http://economicsofjpmorgan.yolasite.com/panic-of-1907.php.

Why FDIC Insurance?

The federal deposit insurance program is one of the cornerstones of our banking system and one of the principal components of the federal safety net. It was necessitated because bank insolvency means depositor losses. The Great Depression proved the point.

Starting in 1930, a series of banking panics rocked the U.S. financial system, quickly eclipsing the impact of the preceding panics. As depositors pulled funds out of banks, banks lost reserves and had to contract their loans and deposits, which reduced the nation's money supply. The monetary contraction, as well as the financial chaos associated with the failure of large numbers of banks, caused the economy to collapse. In the four years of 1930–1933 alone, nearly 10,000 banks failed or their business was suspended. These banks held deposits of over $6.8 billion ($1.00 in 1933 has the same buying power as $18.06 in 2016[9] so that is equivalent to perhaps $122 billion in modern dollars, but it represented a much larger share of each depositor's wealth back then). The depositors in these banks lost nearly 20% of their deposits when the banks failed. Because there was no federal deposit insurance yet, and most state attempts at deposit insurance schemes had shut down, this meant that everyday citizens lost their savings.[10] Thus, for these people a deposit in a bank turned out to be as speculative as an investment in stocks and bonds.

Bank Failures in the Great Depression[11]

Year	Number of Suspensions	Deposits ($)	Losses Borne by Depositors ($)	Losses to Depositors as percent of Deposits in All Suspended Banks	Losses to Depositors as percent of Deposits in All Comm. Banks
1929	659	230,643	76,659	33.24	0.18
1930	1,350	837,096	237,359	28.36	0.57
1931	2,293	1,690,232	390,476	23.10	1.01
1932	1,453	706,187	168,302	23.83	0.57
1933	4,000*	3,596,708	540,396	15.02	2.15

*Estimate

9. http://www.dollartimes.com/inflation/inflation.php?amount=1&year=1933.
10. *Banks Failures: The 1920's and The Great Depression*, https://econproph.com/2009/10/26.
11. *Id.*

During the Great Depression, many banks could not (or would not) borrow from the Federal Reserve because they either lacked acceptable collateral or did not belong to the Federal Reserve System.[12] Another solution was needed, and Congress acted. As discussed in Chapter 2, the Banking Act of 1933[13] added a section to the FRA to create the federal deposit insurance system, which is one of the Depression-era programs that revitalized the U.S. banking system. Although it was enacted temporarily in 1933, it was made permanent by Congress in 1935. The federal insurance system is now administered by the FDIC as a permanent agency under the Federal Deposit Insurance Act ("FDIA"), which was enacted as a free-standing statute in 1950.[14] The federal deposit insurance system underwent changes in 2006, when the Federal Deposit Insurance Reform Act of 2005[15] was enacted. Not surprisingly, in light of the Global Financial Crisis, the Dodd-Frank Act ("Dodd-Frank") made even more changes.

In the meantime, FSLIC—the Federal Savings and Loan Insurance Corporation—came (actually became insolvent in the late 1980s) and went as the deposit insurance fund for savings and loan associations.[16] Credit unions are insured by the NCUSIF—National Credit Union Share Insurance Fund—which was created by Congress in 1970 to insure members' deposits in federally insured credit unions.[17] The Share Insurance Fund is backed by the full faith and credit of the United States to the same extent as FDIC coverage for bank deposits.

Sources of Federal Law and Rulemaking Authority

Since passage of the FRA and then the FDIA, the statutory construct of the safety net has been under the auspices of the Federal Reserve's and the FDIC's respective rulemaking authority. The Federal Reserve was vested with authority for the discount window, the payments system and several laws deposited in the FRA dealing with deposit reserves, funds availability, rates and disclosures. The FDIC was gifted everything else with respect to deposits, deposit insurance and receivership of failed banks. However, that balance changed somewhat with the passage of Dodd-Frank and the grant

12. For many years following enactment of the FRA, banks had to be member banks—members of the Federal Reserve System—in order to participate.
13. Banking Act of 1933, June 16, 1933, ch. 89, 48 Stat. 163.
14. Federal Deposit Insurance Act of 1950, Sept. 21, 1950, ch. 967, 64 Stat. 873 (codified at 12 U.S.C. §§ 1811 *et seq.*).
15. The Federal Deposit Insurance Reform Act of 2005, Pub. Law 109-171, Title II, Subtitle B, 120 Stat. 9.
16. Discussed in Chapter 2, *supra*.
17. Federal Credit Union Act, Public Law 91-468, 1970, enacted Title II—Share Insurance (codified at 12 U.S.C. §§ 1751–1775).

of consumer regulatory authority to the Bureau of Consumer Financial Protection ("CFPB"). As a consequence, the CFPB inherited consumer protection statutes associated with deposit-taking.

The regulatory authority assignments now are as follows:

> **Federal Reserve**—Regulations are in 12 C.F.R. Part 200; Federal Reserve uses letters of the alphabet based on the order in the alphabet.
> Types of Deposits/Reserves—Regulation D
> Availability of Funds and Collection of Checks—Regulation CC
> Unlawful Internet Gambling—Regulation GG
>
> **FDIC**—Regulations are in 12 C.F.R. Part 300; deposit insurance rules are codified in 12 C.F.R. § 330.
> Deposit Insurance
> Receiverships
> Brokered/Core Deposit Classifications
>
> **CFPB**—Regulations are in 12 C.F.R. Part 1000; the CFPB has codified former Federal Reserve regulations by the same letters, except in the 1000's—for example, Regulation E is now 12 C.F.R. § 1005 (5th letter of the alphabet).
> Electronic Funds Transfer Act—Regulation E
> Truth in Savings—Regulation DD
> Unfair, Deceptive or Abusive Acts or Practices

In addition to these regulatory assignments, the Financial Crimes Enforcement Network ("FinCEN") of the Treasury Department enforces anti-money laundering and anti-terrorist financing requirements as to deposit accounts under the Bank Secrecy Act and the USA Patriot Act.[18]

The Role of the Federal Reserve

The Federal Reserve wears many hats. It is, like the FDIC, a primary federal banking regulatory agency for state banks—those insured depository institutions that are members of the Federal Reserve System. It regulates bank and thrift holding companies and systemically important financial institutions. It has rulemaking authority under the affiliate transaction rules and insider lending rules discussed in Chapter 6. Before Dodd-Frank, it had rulemaking authority under all the federal laws applicable to

18. Discussed in Chapter 7, *supra*.

consumer financial products and services. It is a principal player in our payments system.

As noted above, and most importantly for the purposes of this chapter, it is also our central bank and lender of last resort through its discount window operations, both of which have become part of its implementation of the monetary policy of the United States. The Federal Reserve's three instruments of monetary policy are:[19]

- Open market operations, which involve the buying and selling of government securities.
- The discount rate, which is the interest rate charged by Federal Reserve Banks to depository institutions on short-term loans.
- (Historically) Reserve requirements, which are the fractional portions of deposits that banks maintain either in their vaults or on deposit at one of the twelve Federal Reserve Banks.

Lender of Last Resort

The Federal Reserve is bestowed lending authority in two sections of the FRA, Section 10B dealing with its discount window operations and 13(3), a little used section that came into play in the rescue of several notable nonbanks in the Global Financial Crisis, not without residual controversy, and re-emerged in the 2020 coronavirus pandemic.

FRA Section 10B. The discount window functions as a safety valve in relieving pressures in reserve markets; its extensions of credit can help relieve liquidity strains in a depository institution and in the banking system as a whole.[20] The window also helps ensure the basic stability of the payment system more generally by supplying liquidity during times of systemic stress. Much of the statutory framework that governs lending to depository institutions is contained in Section 10B of the FRA.[21] The general policies that govern discount window lending are set forth in the Federal Reserve's Regulation A.[22]

The actual lending function is accomplished by the Federal Reserve Bank in the district where the borrowing institution is located (or where its parent BHC is assigned). All discount window loans must be collateralized to the satisfaction of the lending Federal Reserve Bank. The primary credit program is the principal facility for ensuring adequate liquidity in the banking system and a backup source of short-term funds for generally

19. https://www.frbdiscountwindow.org/en/Pages/General-Information/The-Discount-Window.aspx.
20. *Id.*
21. Codified as amended at 12 U.S.C. § 347b.
22. 12 C.F.R. Part 201.

sound depository institutions. Most depository institutions qualify for primary credit. Secondary credit is available to meet backup funding needs of depository institutions that do not qualify for primary credit. Seasonal credit is available to depository institutions that can demonstrate a clear pattern of recurring intra-yearly swings in funding needs.[23] The Federal Reserve describes these programs as follows:[24]

> *Primary credit* is a lending program available to depository institutions that are in generally sound financial condition. Primary credit is priced relative to the Federal Open Market Committee's ("FOMC") target range for the federal funds rate. On March 15, 2020, the Federal Reserve announced changes to primary credit by: (i) narrowing the spread of the primary credit rate relative to the general level of overnight interest rates to help encourage more active use of the window by depository institutions to meet unexpected funding needs; and (ii) providing discount window credit for periods as long as 90 days, prepayable and renewable by the borrower on a daily basis. These changes were effective March 16, 2020, and will remain in effect until the Board announces otherwise.
>
> *Secondary credit* is available to depository institutions that are not eligible for primary credit. It is extended on a very short-term basis, typically overnight, at a higher rate than primary credit rate. In contrast to primary credit, there are restrictions on the uses of secondary credit extensions. Secondary credit is available to meet backup liquidity needs when its use is consistent with a timely return by the borrower to a reliance on market sources of funding or the orderly resolution of a troubled institution. Secondary credit may not be used to fund an expansion of the borrower's assets. Moreover, the secondary credit program entails a higher level of Reserve Bank administration and oversight than the primary credit program. Reserve Banks typically apply higher haircuts on collateral pledged to secure secondary credit.

23. This information is available at https://www.federalreserve.gov/newsevents/reform_discount_window.htm.
24. *Id.*

> *The seasonal credit* is a lending program that is available to assist small depository institutions with demonstrated liquidity pressures of a seasonal nature and will not normally be available to institutions with deposits of $500 million or more. Institutions that experience and can demonstrate a clear pattern of recurring intra-yearly fluctuations in deposits and loans—caused by construction, college, farming, resort, municipal financing and other seasonal types of business—frequently qualify for the seasonal credit program. Eligible depository institutions may qualify for term funding for up to nine months of seasonal need during the calendar year, enabling them to carry fewer liquid assets during the rest of the year and, thus, allowing them to make more funds available for local lending. The interest rate applied to seasonal credit is a floating rate based on market rates.

FRA Section 13(3). Prior to Dodd-Frank, Section 13 paragraph 3 of the FRA[25] read: "In unusual and exigent circumstances, the Board of Governors of the Federal Reserve System, by the affirmative vote of not less than five members, may …," lend money to "any individual, partnership, or corporation," as long as certain requirements are met. The emphasis here is on the word "*any*"—not just depository institutions. During the early days of the mortgage crisis in 2008 (which then turned into the Global Financial Crisis), the Federal Reserve revived this obscure provision to extend credit to nonbank financial firms for the first time since the 1930s. Using this authority, the Federal Reserve created six broadly based facilities to provide liquidity to "primary dealers" (certain large investment firms) and to revive demand for short term funding (commercial paper) and asset-backed securities. More controversially, the Federal Reserve provided special, tailored assistance to four firms considered "too big to fail"—AIG, Bear Stearns, Citigroup, and Bank of America.[26]

The amount of credit extended (in the form of cash or securities) authorized by Section 13(3) during the Global Financial Crisis peaked at $710 billion in November of 2008. And it was all repaid with interest. "Contrary to popular belief, the Fed earned profits of more than $30 billion and did not suffer any losses on transactions authorized by Section 13(3)."[27]

---

25. 12 U.S.C. § 343 (2008).
26. Federal Reserve: *Emergency Lending* (Updated March 27, 2020), Congressional Research Report, R44185, Summary, https://fas.org/sgp/crs/misc/R44185.pdf.
27. *Id.*

Notwithstanding the fact that many in the industry lauded the efforts of the Federal Reserve under Section 13(3) in helping stem the consequences of the crisis, the action sparked an ongoing dialogue regarding the role of the Federal Reserve. Ultimately, Congress reacted and in Title XI of Dodd-Frank[28] amended Section 13(3) such that the Federal Reserve may only conduct emergency lending in the future for liquidity purposes through widely available programs approved by the Secretary of the Treasury—it may not save individual banks—and it is prohibited from lending to insolvent institutions. So, the old 13(3) tool has been rendered a creature of history.

Pandemic Facilities. But, the new 13(3) turned out to be exactly what we needed when the Federal Reserve invoked it again in early 2020 to unveil new lending facilities to stem the economic impact of the coronavirus pandemic and assist households and employers of all sizes and bolster the ability of state and local governments to deliver critical services during the national emergency. CNBC characterized these actions with a reference to Star Trek: "To boldly go where no man has gone before."

Technically, the Federal Reserve announced eleven credit facilities in March and April of 2020, reopening four of the broadly-based programs used in the Global Financial Crisis. Applicable requirements of Section 13(3) applied to these facilities.[29]

PPPL Facility. First, in connection with the Paycheck Protection Program ("PPP") created by Section 1102 of the Coronavirus Aid, Relief, and Economic Security Act ("CARES Act"),[30] and, recognizing the strain on the banking system in connection with holding the PPP loans in portfolio, the federal banking agencies announced the Federal Reserve's Paycheck Protection Program Lending Facility ("PPPL Facility") in an interim final rule on April 7, 2020.[31] The PPPL allows banking organizations to neutralize the regulatory capital effects of participating in the PPP. Under the PPPL Facility, each of the Federal Reserve Banks was to extend non-recourse loans to eligible lenders, including depository institutions, to fund loans under the PPP, taking the loans as collateral at face value.

Additional Facilities. But, thank goodness, the Federal Reserve was only beginning. The descriptions below are eerily similar to the Fall of 2008 when the effects of Global Financial Crisis needed to be stemmed, as

28. Section 1101 of Dodd-Frank amends Section 13(3) of the FRA (codified at 12 U.S.C. § 343).
29. Federal Reserve, *supra* note 26.
30. Pub.L. 116–136 (2020).
31. *See, e.g.*, the FDIC's announcement in FIL-37-2020 (April 9, 2020).

the Federal Reserve announced the following additional pandemic-related programs:[32]

- To backstop the market for commercial paper (unsecured, short-term notes issued by businesses and municipalities), the Federal Reserve revived this 2008 facility, the Commercial Paper Funding Facility, on March 27;
- To support money market funds (the primary purchasers of commercial paper), the Federal Reserve revived the Money Market Fund Liquidity Facility on March 19;
- To address liquidity and other needs of primary dealers (banks that purchase government securities for the Federal Reserve or Treasury), the Federal Reserve opened the Primary Dealer Credit Facility for a six-month period beginning March 20;
- To ensure credit flows to small and mid-sized businesses with the purchase of up to $600 billion in loans through the Main Street Lending Programs. The Department of the Treasury, using funding from the CARES Act, provided $75 billion in equity to the facility;
- To increase the flow of credit to households and businesses through capital markets, by expanding the size and scope of the Primary and Secondary Market Corporate Credit Facilities as well as the Term Asset-Backed Securities Loan Facility (now referred to as "TALF 2.0"). These three programs were to support up to $850 billion in credit backed by $85 billion in credit protection provided by the Treasury; and
- To help state and local governments manage cash flow stresses caused by the coronavirus pandemic by establishing a Municipal Liquidity Facility that offered up to $500 billion in lending to states and municipalities. The Treasury provided $35 billion of credit protection to the Federal Reserve for the Municipal Liquidity Facility using funds appropriated by the CARES Act.

Now that we have gone deep into that place where no man had gone before, these facilities may now be at the ready as we go forward to the next inevitable crisis.

Reserves

A basic fact of banking is that no bank actually holds all the funds it takes in deposits. Consider that checking accounts are "demand" deposit accounts,

32. Press Release, *Federal Reserve Takes Additional Actions to Provide up to $2.3 Trillion in Loans to Support The Economy,* (April 9, 2020). *See also*, Hannah Lang, *Cheat Sheet: 8 Ways the Federal Reserve Is Using Emergency Powers to Counter Pandemic,* Am. Banker, May 5, 2020.

meaning the funds must be paid to the depositor upon demand – when a check is written, when a debit card is used, when cash is withdrawn at the teller window or at an ATM, when an online or mobile or other electronic transfer is made. So there must be some fractional amount of cash and liquid assets on "reserve" to meet the demand.

The amount of the reserves that depository institutions must maintain are based on ratios established by statute.[33] In connection with its instrumental role in maintaining liquidity in the banking system, the Federal Reserve has rulemaking authority in connection with reserves, and has promulgated Regulation D[34] to that end. Regulation D sets uniform requirements for all depository institutions to maintain reserve balances either with their Federal Reserve Bank, a correspondent bank[35] or as vault cash. The Federal Reserve adjusts the amount of required reserves annually based on the amount of transaction account dollars in three tranches: a zero percent tranche, a 3% tranche and a 10% tranche.

Zero Required Reserves *circa* 2020. On March 15, 2020, however, the Board announced it had reduced the reserve requirement ratio to *zero* in all tranches on all deposits effective March 26, 2020. Translated: no required reserves. Although it did so to encourage banks to lend out all of their funds during the coronavirus pandemic, it emphasized that the change was not temporary, explaining that the industry had a surplus of reserves:

> [R]eserve balances are currently far in excess of banks' reserve requirements and the FOMC has indicated that it will in the longer-run conduct policy with ample reserves. With such a large quantity of reserves in the banking system, the Federal Reserve can no longer effectively influence the FFR [Federal Funds Rate] by small changes in the supply of reserves. For example, a relatively small increase in reserves will not lower interest rates, nor will a relatively small reduction in reserves raise short-term interest rates.[36]

There are so many ramifications to this startling change for banking lawyers. In many respects, it wiped out basic tenants of deposit law. For one, there is an established system of banks buying and selling excess reserves ("fed funds") and lots of banks run fed funds credit lines with other banks.

---

33. 12 U.S.C. § 461.
34. 12 C.F.R. Part 204.
35. The banking system is organized with contractual banking relationships known as correspondent banks, with "upstream correspondents" being the larger banks with access to more products and services and with greater capacity to aid smaller banks.
36. Scott A. Wolla, *A New Fortier: Monetary Policy with Ample Reserves*, Economic Research, Federal Reserve Bank of St. Louis (May 2019).

Moreover, there are products that have been patented based on algorithms to reduce bank reserve requirements. And there are reams of disclosures about kinds of accounts that may be irrelevant.

Types of Deposit Accounts. Reserves are held on demand deposit obligations, called net "transaction accounts" under the FRA and Regulation D. These have the following characteristics:

- are demand and NOW accounts (described below);
- permit a depositor or account holder to make unlimited transfers or payments to third parties; and
- permit a depositor to make unlimited transfers between accounts of the same depositor at the same institution.[37]

But the rubber hits the road in determining what accounts *do not* constitute transaction accounts and do not require reserves: broadly defined as savings accounts and time deposits. Regulation D provides key definitions in this regard:

> **Savings deposit** means a deposit or account with respect to which the depositor is not required by the deposit contract but may at any time be required by the depository institution to *give written notice of an intended withdrawal not less than seven days before withdrawal is made*, and that is not payable on a specified date or at the expiration of a specified time after the date of deposit.
>
> The term "savings deposit" also means: … a passbook savings account, a statement savings account, or a money market deposit account (MMDA), that otherwise meets the requirements of § 204.2(d)(1) and from which, under the terms of the deposit contract or by practice of the depository institution, the depositor is permitted or authorized to make *no more than six transfers and withdrawals*, or a combination of such transfers and withdrawals, per calendar month or statement cycle (or similar period) of at least four weeks, to another account (including a transaction account) of the depositor at the same institution or to a third party by means of a preauthorized or automatic transfer, or telephonic (including data transmission) agreement, order or instruction, or by check, draft, debit card, or

37. https://www.federalreserve.gov/boarddocs/supmanual/cch/int_depos.pdf.

> similar order made by the depositor and payable to third parties.[38] (Emphasis added.)

With the zero percent reserves in 2020, the distinction between these types of deposits may not be important until reserve requirements resurface. (Banking law students don't need to worry about this on the final exam.) Furthermore, that long definition of a savings account set forth above? The six transfer restriction was gone as of April 23, 2020, and until reinstated.[39] That means, MMDA owners could make any number of convenience transfers during the pendency of the rule change. But, the change was optional—banks could continue to enforce the rule.

Simplistically under the historical Regulation D regime, banks traditionally maintain the following basic types of accounts:

> *Demand Deposits.* Demand deposits or "DDAs" are regular checking accounts, both corporate and individual transaction accounts. They permit immediate withdrawal and are used for payments. They are quintessential transaction accounts.
>
> *Now (Negotiable Order of Withdrawal) Accounts.* A NOW account is a special type of transaction account. Like a savings account it pays interest, and like a checking account it can be used for payments. It is not available to businesses. They are also transaction accounts.
>
> *Savings and Time Deposits.* These include deposits that permit withdrawal but not checking, and deposits that have fixed maturities (certificates of deposit—CDs). As a result of the Regulation D rules, any deposit account agreement must disclose the right of the bank to require seven days' notice for withdrawal if the account is a savings account.
>
> *Money Market Accounts.* An MMDA is a special type of savings account permitting a limited number of transactions and originally intended, when interest rates were controlled, to permit the payment of a rate that is competitive with the return on money market mutual funds. MMDA accounts have been subject to a six transfer/withdrawal per month rule, which became

38. 12 C.F.R. § 204.2(d)(1).
39. The Federal Reserve issued an Interim Final Rule, including FAQs, to delete the six-per-month limit on convenience transfers, 85 Fed. Reg. 23,445 (Apr. 28, 2020).

optional for a period in 2020, and history is strewn with all kinds of arrangements that manage to avoid the restriction.[40]

Reserve Ratios. Basic reserve calculations are in the FRA, as amended:

- First, by the Garn-St Germain Act of 1982,[41] which exempted the first $2 million of reservable liabilities from reserve requirements; and
- Then by the Monetary Control Act of 1980,[42] which set the amount of net transaction accounts subject to a reserve requirement ratio of 3% at $25 million.

There is then a third 10% requirement for remaining balances. The tranches are adjusted annually by the Federal Reserve using statutory formulas specified in the FRA. Before they were set at zero, for 2020:

- The exemption amount was the first $16.9 million (up from $16.3 million in 2019) of otherwise reservable balances;
- The 3% tranche applied to transaction accounts aggregating more than $16.9 million up to $127.5 million (up from $124.2 million in 2019); and
- The reserve requirement was then 10% for net transaction accounts in excess of $127.5 million.[43]

Historically, reserves did not earn interest and were frequently (and one might say critically) referred to as "sterile reserves." Since 2008, Federal Reserve Banks must pay interest on reserves they hold[44] and they also pay interest on excess reserves, which is the interest paid on those balances that are above the level of reserves that the depository institution is required to hold.[45]

Fed Funds Lending of Excess Reserves. At any given time, banks may have a surplus of reserves and they may lend them to correspondent

---

40. For instance, withdrawals or transfers in person are not counted toward the six limit and many complex sweep programs rely on a carrier to make the transfers daily to avoid the restriction.
41. Garn-St Germain Depository Institutions Act of 1982, P.L. 97-320, 96 Stat. 1469.
42. Monetary Control Act of 1980, Pub. L. 96–22.
43. *See* https://www.federalreserve.gov/monetarypolicy/reservereq.htm.
44. 12 C.F.R. § 204.10. The Financial Services Regulatory Relief Act of 2006 authorized the Federal Reserve Banks to pay interest on balances held by or on behalf of depository institutions at Reserve Banks, subject to regulations of the Board of Governors, effective Oct. 1, 2011. The effective date of this authority was advanced to Oct. 1, 2008, by the Emergency Economic Stabilization Act of 2008.
45. https://www.newyorkfed.org/aboutthefed/fedpoint/fed15.html.

banks that have a deficit position, typically in overnight lending transactions based on lines of credit. These are commonly referred to as "fed funds" transactions. The average rate at which these transactions occur is called the fed funds rate. The daily federal funds effective rate, calculated by the Federal Reserve Bank of New York, is one measure of the overnight fed funds rate. The rate is based on data voluntarily provided to the New York Federal Reserve Bank by major fed funds brokers, and is a weighted-average rate of all overnight fed funds transactions arranged through these brokers each business day.[46]

Internal Sweeps to Minimize Reserves. Even with interest paid on excess reserves and fed funds transactions, there have been economic benefits to banks to minimize the amount of transaction accounts they hold and reduce their reserve requirements. As a consequence, there are a variety of sweep account mechanisms available that run complex algorithms to determine the amount of funds in the bank that are actually frequently used. The excess amounts are then swept internally into MMDA accounts every night at close of business. The funds are swept back the next morning. Depositors are in no way affected by the sweeps, but banks must disclose the existence of the sweep in their deposit terms and conditions.

Additional Federal Reserve Deposit Regulations

Interest Paid on Deposit Accounts. For years the interest rates that could be paid on savings accounts were fixed by law under Regulation Q.[47] A competitive advantage was even given to savings and loans, which could pay more by law than banks. That ended with the thrift crisis and the free market has reigned since then. Nonetheless, the law still did not permit interest to be paid on business checking accounts until that prohibition was repealed by Section 627 of Dodd-Frank.[48] The Federal Reserve then repealed Regulation Q in its entirety and it has been reissued as the Board's capital regulation.

That said there are interest rate restrictions that kick into place for all less than well-capitalized institutions under FDIC regulations.[49] The cap is based on the "national rate," which the FDIC defines as a simple average of rates paid by U.S. depository institutions as calculated by the FDIC.[50]

46. *Id.*
47. 12 C.F.R. Part 217.
48. Section 627 of Dodd-Frank repealed Section 371a(i) of the FRA (codified at 12 U.S.C. § 371a).
49. 12 C.F.R. § 337.6.
50. FDIC, Financial Institution Letter FIL-69-2009.

Rates for each week are posted online.[51] Not surprisingly, in 2020, they were very, very low: 1.67% for a 60 month Certificate of Deposit was the highest.

Availability of Funds. Consistent with its critical role in the payments system, the Federal Reserve was granted rulemaking authority by Congress with respect to funds availability, check collection and substitute checks under the Expedited Funds Availability Act[52] and what is known as "Check 21,"[53] respectively. The law with respect to funds availability addresses an historical hindrance that occurred when banks would impose long holds on checks without the knowledge or understanding of the depositor. As a consequence, the law is prescriptive and requires transparency. It applies to both consumer and business accounts.

The Board's Regulation CC requires a bank to make deposited funds available for withdrawal within a certain period after the banking day on which they are received. Cash deposits in person, wire transfers, and certain check deposits that pose little risk to the bank (such as Treasury checks and cashier's checks) generally are to be made available for withdrawal on or before the business day after the day of deposit.[54] The time when the bank must make other check deposits available for withdrawal depends on whether the check is local or nonlocal to the depositary bank. Proceeds of local and nonlocal checks must be available for withdrawal by the second and fifth business day following deposit, respectively.[55] However, Regulation CC allows a bank to set, within certain limits, cutoff hours, after which the bank will deem funds to be received on the next banking day for purposes of calculating the availability date. Different cutoff-hours apply to different types of deposits. There are a number of exceptions that permit longer hold periods for new accounts, large deposits, redeposited checks and repeated overdrafts, but banks must give provide notice of the delay.

Banks must provide the funds availability schedule in writing before a deposit account is opened, on deposit slips and ATMs and at branches where consumer checks are deposited.[56] The initial disclosure is typically included in the customer account agreement, along with a prescribed Check 21 notice on consumer rights when substitute checks are used in the collection process.[57]

---

51. See, https://www.fdic.gov/regulations/resources/rates/.
52. Codified at 12 U.S.C. §§ 4001–4010.
53. Check Clearing for the 21st Century Act (codified at 12 U.S.C. §§ 5001–5018).
54. 12 C.F.R. § 229.10.
55. 12 C.F.R. § 229.12.
56. 12 C.F.R. § 229.17–18.
57. 12 C.F.R. § 229.57. Substitute checks are accurate representations of the original check that are created for expedited collection purposes.

Unlawful Internet Gambling. The Unlawful Internet Gambling Enforcement Act of 2006 ("UIGEA")[58] prohibits "any person engaged in the business of betting or wagering from knowingly accepting payments in connection with the participation of another person in unlawful Internet gambling." The Federal Reserve's implementing regulations require a strengthened screening process at the time of account opening to deny commercial entities that may be acting as Internet casinos access to the payments system. It also requires that policies and procedures be implemented to prevent all debit and credit card payments to Internet casinos. It does not require that checks, ACH payments, or wire transactions related to Internet gambling be monitored or blocked. Banks include a certification by commercial customers at account-opening that accounts will not be used for this purpose. It is noteworthy that legal gambling proceeds may be deposited, and banks have procedures for those businesses to provide evidence of legality. To this end, the UIGEA specifically excludes fantasy sports that meet certain requirements, skill-games and legal intrastate and intertribal gaming.

The Role of the FDIC

The FDIC is a primary federal bank regulatory agency for state-chartered banks and thrifts that are not members of the Federal Reserve System as described in Chapters 2 and 3, but the focus here is on its role as insurer of bank and thrift deposits. It administers the deposit insurance fund ("DIF") for the benefit of depositors with the objective that insured depositors are protected from loss without recourse to taxpayer funding. Deposit insurance is a fundamental component of the safety net in maintaining stability and public confidence in the U.S. financial system. To that end, the FDIC is tasked with maintaining the DIF so that adequate funds are available to protect insured depositors in the event of an institution's failure.

FDIC Insurance Today

What Does the FDIC Insure? The FDIA defines "deposit," in pertinent part, as: "The unpaid balance of money or its equivalent received or held by a bank or savings association in the usual course of business and for which it has given or is obligated to give credit, either conditionally or unconditionally, to a commercial, checking, savings, time, or thrift account, or which is evidenced by its certificate of deposit, thrift certificate, investment

58. Regulation GG, 12 C.F.R. Part 233, was promulgated under the UIGEA, Pub. Law 109-347, 120 Stat. 1884 (codified at 31 U.S.C. §§ 5361–5367).

certificate, certificate of indebtedness, or other similar name, or a check or draft drawn against a deposit account and certified by the bank or savings association, or a letter of credit or a traveler's check on which the bank or savings association is primarily liable...."[59] Deposits that are guaranteed to be insured are those within the SMDIA: the "standard maximum deposit insurance amount" is now $250,000 per account ownership held in a given bank or thrift.[60]

The genesis of FDIC insurance is discussed in detail in Chapter 2 as an outgrowth of the Great Depression. Not surprisingly, each subsequent crisis exposed weaknesses in the system, and changes were made accordingly as lessons were learned. Thus, like most every topic in our regulatory universe, history is important to an understanding of the workings of FDIC insurance. But, we can start with today to work-through how this subsidy operates and how it is financed (hint, not by the federal government, although, the FDIC claims it is backed by the full faith and credit).

Key Concepts. There are three important concepts when studying the FDIC and FDIC insurance:

> *Reserve Ratio:* The reserve ratio is the DIF balance divided by estimated insured deposits. It is currently around 1.38%, as discussed below.
>
> *DRR:* The designated reserve ratio ("DRR") is then an estimation of the minimum level of funds needed to withstand future crises. It has been set by law somewhere between 1.15% and 1.50% of estimated deposits for the past decades. However, an analysis by the FDIC using historical fund losses and simulated income data from 1950 to 2010 showed that the reserve ratio would have had to exceed 2% before the onset of the two crises that occurred during the past 30 years to have maintained both a positive balance and stable assessment rates throughout both crises.[61] As a consequence, the DRR was raised to 2% effective January 1, 2011.[62]
>
> *Receivership.* The third concept is a recognition that deposit insurance has no intrinsic value that can be monetized. It comes into play only when an insured depository institution fails, and the FDIC takes over as

59. 12 U.S.C. § 1813(l)(1).
60. The SMDIA is set under 12 U.S.C. § 1821(a)(B), as implemented by 12 C.F.R. Part 330.
61. https://www.fdic.gov/deposit/insurance/.
62. Designated Reserve Ratio, Final Rule. 75 Fed. Reg. 79,286 (Dec. 20, 2010).

> receiver.[63] At that time, the FDIC has several statutory options as to the manner in which it will resolve the institution, any of which will guarantee all insured depositors their funds up to the SMDIA.

Assessment Base. Despite some interesting periods in our history, as detailed below, FDIC insurance is not free. It is paid for by all insured depository institutions. To that end, the FDIC maintains a sufficient DIF balance by collecting risk-based insurance premiums from insured depository institutions through quarterly assessments and through prudent fund investment strategies. The FDIC continually evaluates the adequacy of the DIF. It identifies risks to the insurance fund by analyzing regional, national, and global economic, financial, and financial institution developments, and by collecting and evaluating information through the supervisory process.

Assessments. Over the years, the calculation of FDIC insurance assessments has changed, but, after the Global Financial Crisis and after some Dodd-Frank tinkering, the FDIC fixes insurance premiums at rates based on bank risk classifications. For "smaller" institutions with assets of less than $10 billion, the FDIC simplified the process effective July 1, 2016, so that supervisory ratings are used to establish minimum and maximum assessment rates (i.e., CAMELS ratings).[64] The assessment base against which an FDIC-insured institution's deposit insurance premiums paid to the DIF are calculated is based on its average consolidated total assets less its average tangible equity (not based on domestic deposits). This method (employed under Dodd-Frank) shifts the burden of deposit insurance premiums toward those large depository institutions that rely on funding sources other than U.S. deposits.

The base assessment rates range from 3 basis points to 30 basis points. Total base assessment rates range from 1.5 basis points to 40 basis points. At least semi-annually, the FDIC updates its loss and income projections for the DIF and, if needed, increases or decreases the assessment rates, following notice and comment on proposed rulemaking.

To provide some perspective, the DIF balance was $104.9 billion in the first quarter of 2019.[65]

63. Discussed in Chapter 12, *infra*.
64. *See*, https://www.fdic.gov/deposit/insurance/assessments/.
65. https://www.fdic.gov/bank/analytical/qbp/2019mar/qbpdep.html is a wonderful source of data on DIF.

After the Thrift Crisis

Switching back in time to see how we journeyed to the current framework from the system put in place after the Great Depression, we begin with the thrift crisis, during which flaws in the system were exposed and Congress was called upon to make significant structural changes.

BIF and SAIF. The first flaw in the system was an unimaginable one: FSLIC, the savings and loan association insurer, failed. It did not hold anywhere near enough funds to cover losses sustained as thrifts large and small failed. As a result of the collapse of FSLIC and bankruptcy of the insurance fund for thrifts, Congress created two insurance funds, the Bank Insurance Fund ("BIF") and the Savings Association Insurance Fund ("SAIF") (each a "Fund"). To this end, the Financial Institutions Reform, Recovery and Enforcement Act of 1989 ("FIRREA")[66] amended FDIA to:

- rename FDIC's Federal Deposit Insurance Fund as the BIF; and
- require the FDIC to assume responsibility for the new SAIF, created to replace the former FSLIC.

Commingling of the assets of BIF and SAIF was prohibited by FIRREA so they were administered and funded separately. Moreover, On August 9, 1989, the date of enactment of FIRREA, institutions that were members of the FDIC, predominantly commercial and FDIC-supervised savings banks, became members of BIF, and institutions whose accounts were insured by the FSLIC, primarily state and federal savings associations, became SAIF members.

DRR and Premium Assessments. FIRREA set a DRR for each Fund of 1.25% (125 basis points) of estimated insured deposits, which could be increased to 150 basis points for either Fund if the FDIC determined that the higher percentage was justified by higher risks of default by the Fund's members. A new premium methodology was then imposed by the FDIC Improvement Act of 1991 ("FDICIA"),[67] which required the FDIC to develop a risk-based assessment system in which better-capitalized and financially healthy institutions would pay lower deposit insurance premiums than those that posed greater risk to their respective insurance Fund. In setting these rates, the FDIC was required to consider several factors, including each Fund's reserve ratio and earnings, the financial condition of the industry and potential future losses to the Funds from institution

66. Pub. Law 101-73, 103 Stat. 183 (1989) (codified as amended in scattered sections of 12 U.S.C.).
67. Federal Deposit Insurance Corporation Improvement Act of 1991, Pub. Law 102-242, 105 Stat. 2236, Section 302 amends Section 7(b) of the FDIA (codified at 12 U.S.C. § 1817(b)).

insolvencies. To meet these requirements, the FDIC developed the matrix format shown below, in which premiums were plotted by supervisory status and capital adequacy and set an initial premium range of 0-27 basis points for BIF and SAIF as follows.

BIF and SAIF Assessment Schedules

First Half of 1996:

Supervisory Subgroups (Assessments are in basis points)

Capitalization	A	B	C
Well capitalized	0	3	17
Adequately capitalized	3	10	24
Less than adequately capitalized	10	24	27

/1/ Premiums are a percentage of insured deposits expressed in basis points (each basis point equals one one-hundredth of one percent).

Capitalization standards (at the time):

- Well capitalized: Minimum total risk-based capital: 10%; Tier 1 capital: 6%; and Tier 1 leverage ratio: 5%.
- Adequately capitalized: Minimum total risk-based capital: 8%; Tier 1 capital: 4%; and Tier 1 leverage ratio: 4%.
- Less than adequately capitalized: Institutions that do not qualify as adequately capitalized.

Supervisory subgroups:

- *Subgroup A:* Financially sound institutions with only a few minor weaknesses.
- *Subgroup B:* Institutions with weaknesses that, if not corrected, could lead to significant deterioration of the institution and increased risk of loss to BIF or SAIF.
- *Subgroup C:* Institutions that pose a substantial probability of loss to BIF or SAIF unless effective corrective action is taken.

Fund Disparity. BIF reached its DRR in May 1996, and qualified effective January 1, 1999, for the zero-27 basis-point schedule depicted above. It had become clear much earlier, however, that SAIF, for several reasons,[68] would not reach its DRR for a few more years, if at all, thereby prolonging a premium disparity that would place SAIF members at a long-term competitive disadvantage. This disparity could have also led to diversion of insured deposits from SAIF to BIF, which happened briefly in 1995, thereby making it more difficult, if not impossible, for SAIF to reach its DRR.

These developments led to the eventual recapitalization of SAIF by means of a special assessment on SAIF members and on certain BIF member banks that held SAIF-insured deposits, approved in the Deposit Insurance Funds Act of 1996.[69] The assessment brought in $4.5 billion[70] and resulted in SAIF reaching its DRR on October 1, 1996, which also became the effective date of the zero-27 basis point deposit insurance assessment schedule for SAIF members. The BIF-SAIF premium disparity that ended with the recapitalization of SAIF in 1996 was replaced by another kind of disparity, free rides, which was one of the major contributors to deposit insurance reform in 2006.

Free Rides. Under the law, the FDIC was unable to impose premiums on any well-capitalized institutions. The agency could set higher assessments only for institutions that had financial, operational, or compliance problems or that were undercapitalized as shown below. Thus, not only well-capitalized existing banks qualified for the zero percent premium assessment but brand new banks which became members of BIF or SAIF after 1996 enjoyed the full benefits of deposit insurance coverage without paying insurance premiums because they were well-capitalized and had qualified for the zero percent premium rate from the time they were organized. As a result of the prosperity of the banking industry in the 2000s, increasing numbers of pre-1996 institutions qualified for the zero basis point premium rate, and the post-1996 institutions remained well-capitalized. By the end of 2004, over 93% of insured institutions holding over 98% of the deposit insurance assessment base were in the zero percent premium category.

---

68. These reasons included the fact that SAIF at its inception had a lower reserve ratio than BIF and the fact that a substantial portion of SAIF premiums were diverted to pay the interest on 30-year "FICO bonds" issued to pay the costs of the resolution of savings association failures that had occurred before 1987. FICO was the Financing Corporation, a mixed-ownership government corporation created by Competitive Equality Banking Act of 1987. The 30-year FICO bonds were issued between 1987 and 1989 to recapitalize FSLIC. The FDIC, as agent for FICO, then collected FICO Assessments from FDIC-insured institutions to pay interest on FICO bonds. The final collection was on the March 29, 2019 FDIC Quarterly Certified Statement Invoice.
69. The Funds Act is set out in Division A, Title II, Subtitle G, of the Omnibus Consolidated Appropriations Act, 1997, Public Law 104-863, 110 Stat. 3009 *et seq.* (The Funds Act can be found at 110 Stat. 3009-479, and p. 480 of the pdf version of Pub. Law 104-863.).
70. FDIC, A *Brief History of Deposit Insurance in the United States,* Sept. 1998, p. 58.

Translated—that means the vast majority of U.S. insured depository institutions did not pay premiums for the subsidy of deposit insurance for years.

The 2006 Federal Deposit Insurance Reform Act

Re-Creation of DIF. The FDI Reform Act of 2006[71] addressed the disparities in premium payments and the zero basis point conundrum in a number of regards. First, it merged the two deposit insurance Funds, BIF and SAIF, into a new DIF as of March 31, 2006. Importantly, it also ended the "free ride" by requiring all institutions to be assessed a premium based on a revised risk-based system. The FDIC was granted greater flexibility in setting premium schedules, and was no longer required to set premiums and reevaluate the premium schedule every six months. The FDIC was permitted to set the DRR of DIF to insured deposits at levels between 1.15% and 1.50% of insured deposits. If the ratio fell below 1.15%, the FDIC was required to develop a plan to restore the DIF to that level within five years. The restoration plan could include limits on use of the transitional assessment credit, which is discussed below, until the reserve ratio was restored to 1.15%.

DRR after the FDI Reform Act. Balancing techniques in the form of dividends, rebates and special assessments were employed by the FDIC over the years to maintain the DRR. For example, the FDI Reform Act required the FDIC to provide a dividend or rebate to insured institutions of 100% of their respective premium income in excess of that required to maintain the DIF's DRR at 1.50% of insured deposits. When the DIF's DRR reached 1.35%, the FDIC was required to pay a premium dividend equal to 50% of premium income in excess of that required to maintain the reserve ratio at 1.35%. The amount of the dividend that each eligible institution received was determined by FDIC regulations based on each eligible institution's relative contribution to the DIF and the former BIF and SAIF.

Further, a transitional deposit insurance premium credit of $4.7 billion, approximately the size of the 1996 special assessment that recapitalized SAIF, was made available to eligible institutions based on their respective percentage of total industry assessable deposits on December 31, 1996, and other factors to be considered by the FDIC. To be eligible for the credit, the institution must have been in existence on December 31, 1996, or be a successor to an institution in existence on that date, and must have paid at least one insurance assessment before that date. These credits were used to offset future insurance assessments. For institutions that exhibited financial, operational, or compliance weaknesses at the beginning of an assessment

71. Federal Deposit Insurance Reform Act (Title II, subtitle B of Pub. L. 109–171, 110 Stat. 9 (Feb. 8, 2006). *See,* Conference Report on the Reform Act, H. Rept. 109-171, and "Reg/Ops," March 2006, America's Community Bankers.

period, the credit was reduced to an amount equal to the average assessment rate on all institutions for that period.

Dodd-Frank Changes

Subtitle C of Title III of Dodd-Frank attempted to address a few remaining issues associated with FDIC insurance. Part of the impetus for change was that the large, risky banks had been paying lower premiums for being in the lower risk categories and were assessed premiums based on deposits, which tended to be much less than their total asset size. Dodd-Frank revised the FDIC's fund management authority by setting requirements for the DRR and redefining the assessment base. In response to these statutory revisions, the FDIC developed a comprehensive, long-term management plan for the DIF designed to reduce pro-cyclicality and achieve moderate, steady assessment rates throughout economic and credit cycles, while also maintaining a positive fund balance even during a banking crisis.

DRR and Assessments after Dodd-Frank. Section 331 of Dodd-Frank permitted the FDIC to change the assessment base to total assets, not deposits, thereby shifting more burden to maintain funding to the large banks.[72] Among other provisions to strengthen the DIF, Dodd-Frank: (i) raised the minimum reserve ratio for the DIF to 1.35% (from the former minimum of 1.15%);[73] (ii) required that the reserve ratio reach 1.35% by September 30, 2020;[74] and (iii) required that, in setting assessments, the FDIC "offset the effect of [the increase in the minimum reserve ratio] on insured depository institutions with total consolidated assets of less than $10 billion."[75] Both Dodd-Frank and the FDIA grant the FDIC broad authority to implement the requirement to achieve the 1.35% minimum reserve ratio.[76] The reserve ratio reached 1.15% effective as of June 30, 2016, and the FDIC began collecting large institution assessment surcharges. Surcharges were collected on invoices dated December 30, 2016, through December 30, 2018.[77] The reserve ratio reached 1.36% as of September 30, 2018, exceeding the statutory required minimum reserve ratio of 1.35%.

At this point, as required by Dodd-Frank, the FDIC provided assessment credits to insured depository institutions with total consolidated assets

72. Section 331(b) of Dodd-Frank required the FDIC to amend its regulations promulgated under Section 7(b)(2) of the FDIA to change the assessment base. The FDIC regulations on assessments are in 12 C.F.R. Part 327.
73. Section 334(a) of Dodd-Frank (codified at 12 U.S.C. § 1817(b)(3)(B)).
74. Section 334(d) of Dodd-Frank (codified at 12 U.S.C. § 1817).
75. Section 334(e) of Dodd-Frank, amends Section 7(b)(3)(B) of the FDIA (12 U.S.C. § 1817).
76. *See*, https://www.fdic.gov/news/board/2016/2016-03-15_notice_dis_b_fr.pdf 12 C.F.R. Part 327.11.
77. https://www.fdic.gov/deposit/insurance/assessments/changesassessments.html.

of less than $10 billion for the portion of their regular assessments that contributed to growth in the reserve ratio between 1.15% and 1.35%. The share of the aggregate small bank credits allocated to each insured institution was proportional to its credit base, defined as the average of its regular assessment base during the credit calculation period. The FDIC applied the credits for quarterly assessment periods beginning July 1, 2019, and remitted the full nominal value of any remaining credits in a lump-sum payment.

SMDIA. The SMDIA was also formally and permanently increased to $250,000, with a retroactive effective date of January 1, 2008.[78] Thus, simplistically, FDIC insurance covers:

- Single accounts (owned by one person with no beneficiaries): $250,000 per owner
- Joint Accounts (two or more persons with no beneficiaries): $250,000 per co-owner
- IRAs and other certain retirement accounts: $250,000 per owner
- Revocable trust accounts: Each owner is insured up to $250,000 for each unique eligible beneficiary named or identified in the revocable trust, subject to specific limitations and requirements.

The FDIC website has an insurance calculator for depositors to determine the amount of FDIC insurance they have in their accounts. It is called EDIE—Electronic Deposit Insurance Estimator.[79] Other accounts that are eligible for deposit insurance include the following:

- Accounts held by an agent, nominee, guardian, custodian, or conservator;
- Annuity contract accounts;
- Accounts of a corporation, partnership, or unincorporated association;
- Accounts held by a depository institution as the trustee of an irrevocable trust;
- Irrevocable trust accounts;
- Funds of the U.S. deposited by official custodians of such funds;
- Accounts of a state, county, municipality, or political subdivision; and
- Funds underlying stored value, payroll, and other kinds of access cards.

Transaction Account Guarantees. In the midst of the Global Financial Crisis, banks became susceptible to online runs when business customers

78. Section 335 of Dodd-Frank Amended Section 11(a)(1)(E) of the FDIA (codified at 12 U.S.C. § 1821(a)(1)(E)).
79. https://www.fdic.gov/edie/index.html.

transferred large accounts, like payroll and operating accounts, from banks that could be under financial duress into the "too big to fail" banks. One of the causes of the failure of Wachovia Bank was just such a run. The SMDIA did not provide nearly enough FDIC insurance coverage for these accounts.

A fairly brilliant solution was effected first by the FDIC and then ratified by Congress. First, as part of a coordinated response by the U.S. government to the disruption in the financial system and the collapse of credit market, the FDIC implemented a Transaction Account Guarantee Program ("TAGP") that guaranteed in full all domestic noninterest-bearing transaction deposits, low-interest NOW accounts, and Interest on Lawyers Trust Accounts (IOLTAs) held at participating banks and thrifts through December 31, 2009. The deadline was extended twice and expired on December 31, 2010.[80] The TAGP was replaced by Dodd-Frank when Section 1105[81] granted the FDIC and the Federal Reserve authority to create widely available programs for the FDIC to guarantee obligations of solvent financial institutions and holding companies. The deposit program created thereunder provided that non-interest bearing transaction accounts would have unlimited deposit insurance coverage through December 31, 2012. It covered all depository institution noninterest-bearing transaction accounts, but not low interest-bearing accounts. The coverage expired on schedule at the end of 2012.

Only to rise again when in Section 4008 of the CARES Act Congress granted the FDIC the power to once more establish a TAGP program and guarantee qualifying business deposit account until not later than December 31, 2020. The NCUA was granted the same power as to credit union accounts. However, because the coronavirus pandemic was not a bank crisis, it was not necessary to trigger the new TAGP.

Other Deposit Insurance Issues

FDIC Insurance Logo. Insured depositary institutions must display the FDIC logo at each place of business where deposits are taken.[82] Sounds simple, except technology has moved banks from brick and mortar branches and onto the internet and wireless networks. Watch for developments in this area as the FDIC reassesses the rule in light of modern banking methods.

Deposits in Foreign Branches. What happens if a depositor of a U.S.-based bank with offshore branches places deposits in a foreign branch? It is a U.S. bank, so the deposited funds are insured? The answer is no. As a matter of fact, historically, these were not even "deposits" for deposit preference purposes in bank receivership so depositors were general creditors

80. https://www.fdic.gov/regulations/resources/tlgp/index.html.
81. 12 U.S.C. § 5612.
82. 12 U.S.C. § 1828(a).

of the estate and were paid after all expenses and all deposits. In the post-Dodd-Frank environment, the United Kingdom bank regulators pushed the issue and in 2013, the FDIC revised its regulations so that deposits in foreign branches of U.S. banks are still not FDIC-insured, but they can be deposits for purposes of the national depositor preference statute as long as they are "dually payable" in the United States.[83] Consequently, banks must revise their deposit account agreement accordingly to give deposits in foreign branches a nudge up the receivership preference priority list. However, if banks make that change, they really have to make payment available at branches in the United States and most apparently do not want to do that.

Pass-Through Coverage (agent or custodial accounts). Frequently bank accounts are held for the benefit of other persons. These accounts may be brokered, as discussed below, or they may be custodial or agency accounts. When this occurs, technically there will be one SMDIA for the entire account. So, if there are 200 beneficial owners with millions of dollars in the account, there would only be $250,000 in FDIC insurance coverage for all beneficial owners. To avoid that potentially dastardly result, the FDIC recognizes "pass-through" insurance coverage when the underlying funds are owned by the beneficial owners not the named account holder.[84] With pass-through coverage, each beneficial owner has FDIC insurance up to the SMDIA—in other words, 200 SMDIAs with 200 beneficial owners. However, the FDIC rules must be carefully followed. First, the bank's account records must have a signpost indicating the agency nature of the account (XYZ Company as Custodian or Agent). Second, the bank's records or accountholder's records must indicate both the identities of the beneficial owners, as well as the ownership interest in the deposit. As a consequence, it is critical that the bank records either show that information, or indicate who holds that information (the named account holder or its agent). Lastly, the deposit terms (i.e., the interest rate and maturity date) for accounts opened at the bank must match the terms that the third party agent promised the customer and must be disclosed to the beneficial owner, along with disclosure of the identity of the bank.

Sweeps. A deposit sweep occurs when the depositor authorizes the bank to transfer money out of one bank account (typically a checking account) and deposit it into another account in or out of the bank. Thus, the funds are "swept" out. This sweep is effected at close of business on a banking day, and usually the funds are swept back into the original account

83. 12 C.F.R. § 330.3(e), revised 9-10-13.
84. 12 C.F.R. § 330.5 and § 330.14. *See also*, Financial Institution Letter: Guidance on Deposit Placement and Collection Activities, FIL-29-2010 (June 7, 2010) and letter to William Burdette, CEO, Institutional Deposits Corp., from Christopher L. Hencke, Counsel, FDIC (Sept. 23, 2010).

(sometimes called the "master" account") at the opening of business the next morning. Sweeps can be for (i) bank internal reserve purposes;[85] (ii) rate chasing by the customer—for instance to an MMDA that pays interest or into an internal or external investment account (typically a no-load mutual fund); (iii) into a repurchase agreement or "repo" (the purchase of a fractional interest in a government security); or (iv) into another bank for FDIC insurance coverage.

All of these sweep arrangements are blessed by the regulators as long as appropriate disclosures are made. However, the lingering issue for decades revolved around the FDIC's treatment of sweeps in connection with bank failures. Why was this an issue? The FDIC closes failing depository institutions at the close of business usually on a Friday. Sweeps are effected at the close of business. Which comes first? If the closure comes first, the funds stay in the bank and many times that means the funds are above the SMDIA. As a result, the FDIC issued a rule[86] and follow-up FAQ's in 2009[87] to address the treatment of sweeps upon bank failure. In a nutshell, if the parties comply with the FDIC's rules as to proper execution of the sweep and provide appropriate disclosures, the FDIC will honor the sweep.[88]

Brokered Deposits

A significant deposit issue that impacts not only the amount of a bank's FDIC-insurance assessment, but also liquidity and safety and soundness, is whether the bank's deposits consist significantly of "brokered" deposits. Historically, deposit accounts were sourced from each institution's local community and were considered "core" or stable funding because the deposits would stay in the bank. However, with brokered deposits, a whole host of third parties place funds of other parties, who have no relationship to the bank, in bank accounts for FDIC insurance and/or for returns. There are advantages to these deposits because they can constitute easy funding sources. But they can be expensive funding to the extent the bank has to attract them by paying more than the competition; they are not typically stable; and the funds are transferred out of the bank when there is a hint of trouble. Thus, these deposits are sometimes referred to as "hot money" and, because of their volatility, they can represent a liquidity strain and exacerbate precarious bank stability.

Background. Brokered deposit restrictions rose from the ashes of the thrift crisis (like so much of modern deposit law) because many failed

85. *See* discussion of reserve sweeps, *supra*.
86. 12 C.F.R. § 360.8.
87. Sweep Account Disclosure Requirements, FDIC FIL-39-2009 (July 6, 2009).
88. Chapter 12 on Bank Failure and Receiverships includes a further discussion of the FDIC's sweep rules.

institutions funded through large influxes of third-party-placed money, attracted by excessive interest rates. In a high-profile example, the Office of Thrift Supervision ("OTS") appointed a conservator to resolve Franklin Savings Association in part because 70% of the thrift's deposits were high-cost brokered deposits. The OTS found the thrift to be in an unsafe and unsound condition. Franklin and its parent company challenged the decision. The Tenth Circuit reversed the judgment of the District Court for the District of Kansas and upheld the action by the Director of the OTS,[89] holding:

> When Director made the decision that reliance upon brokered funds for seventy per cent of total deposits was an unsafe or unsound condition, Director was making first, a policy decision, i.e., seventy per cent of total deposits being brokered is an unacceptable level, and second, a predictive judgment, i.e., Franklin had created an unacceptable level of risk for the depositors' funds. Substantial evidence existed to support this decision.

While an extreme situation, Franklin Savings put a face to regulatory concerns related to funding through brokers. Congress reacted by enacting a new Section 29 of the FDIA[90] in FIRREA and the FDIC gave the issue special emphasis by promulgating its enabling rules as part of its Unsafe and Unsound Banking Practices regulations.[91] The law originally restricted troubled institutions (i.e., those that did not meet the minimum capital requirements) from (i) accepting deposits from a deposit broker without a waiver and (ii) soliciting deposits by offering rates of interest on deposits that were significantly higher than the prevailing rates of interest on deposits offered by other insured depository institutions having the same type of charter in such depository institution's normal market area.

FIRREA's thrift crisis twin, FDICIA, refined the picture two years later, adding the Prompt Corrective Action ("PCA") capital regime to the FDI Act.[92] FDICIA amended the threshold for the brokered deposit and interest rate restrictions from a troubled institution to a bank falling below the "well-capitalized" PCA level and authorized the FDIC to waive the restriction for "adequately capitalized" institutions.

---

89. Franklin Sav. Ass'n v. Director, Office of Thrift Supervision, 934 F.2d 1127, 1145 (1991).
90. Section 29 of the FDIA (12 U.S.C. § 1831f)
91. 12 C.F.R. § 337.6. Chapter 8 the import of unsafe and unsound banking practices are discussed in Chapter 8, infra.
92. PCA is discussed in depth in Chapter 4, *supra*.

As a consequence, banking law exacts its own penalties for holding these deposits. Brokered deposits must be shown separately on Call Reports[93] and are assessed higher FDIC insurance premiums. Furthermore, without a waiver, a bank MAY NOT ACCEPT, ROLL-OVER OR RENEW BROKERED DEPOSITS UNLESS IT IS WELL-CAPITALIZED.[94] As to the interest rate restrictions—to keep banks that are not well-capitalized from circumventing the prohibitions on brokered deposits by offering rates significantly above market rates, the FDIC will not permit those banks to offer deposit rates more than 75 basis points above average national rates for deposits of similar size and maturity.[95]

FDIC Guidance.[96] Despite FIRREA and FDICIA and the impediments noted above, brokered deposit programs grew in popularity over time and, as novel structures were developed by banks and prospective placement agents, the FDIC was faced with numerous requests to review a myriad of factual situations with the hope (of the party requesting the interpretation) that the FDIC would bless the plan and opine that the deposit arrangement did not meet the statutory tests.

A slew of FDIC staff letters interpreting the statutory definitions and exemptions followed for years until finally supplanted by the FDIC's July 14, 2016, Guidance on Identifying, Accepting and Reporting Brokered Deposits,[97] which compiled prior interpretations and was released in the form of Frequently Asked Questions ("2016 FAQs"). The guidance basically created a presumption that any deposit placed (i.e., funds delivered) by a third person is brokered unless an exemption applies. This list included: affiliate bank deposits, most prepaid card deposits, advertised deposits (where volume based fees are paid), insurance agent, lawyer and accountant referred deposits, bank network placed deposits, and some listing services. In other words, the statute was very narrowly construed and most, if not all, third party-placed deposits were considered brokered. But, at least we in the banking bar had more certainty.

Post-2016 Developments. It goes without saying that technology has changed the face of deposit generation, such that the industry is operating in a new gen environment but under stale rules. Internet-sourced deposits, prepaid card deposits, and health savings accounts, to name a few, have been deemed to be brokered and yet most in the industry assert that they

---

93. Call Reports are the quarterly financial statements filed by banking institutions with their respective federal regulatory agency. They are discussed in Chapter 11.

94. 12 C.F.R. § 337.6.

95. *See*, section G of 2016 FAQs.

96. For further reading on this topic, see, the FDIC's *Study on Core Deposits and Brokered Deposits*, issued in July 2011 and available on its website.

97. FDIC Financial Institution Letter 42-2016 (superseding FIL-2-2015 and FIL-51-2015 and replacing FAQ's issued on 12/24/2014).

can be a stable source of funding. As a result, there have been two major developments in this space following the release of the 2016 FAQs. First, the Economic Growth, Regulatory Relief, and Consumer Protection Act ("Regulatory Relief Act") eliminated brokered status on certain reciprocal deposits. Second, the FDIC rang in in early 2020 with a notice of proposed rulemaking to modernize the brokered deposit regulations after having previously solicitated industry thoughts on the matter.

Reciprocal Deposit Arrangements. Section 202 of the Regulatory Relief Act[98] amended the brokered deposit provisions of Section 29 of the FDIA,[99] effective on May 24, 2018, to permit certain insured depository institutions to accept a capped amount of reciprocal deposits without treatment as brokered deposits. According to the FDIC in its final rule,[100] a reciprocal deposit arrangement is based upon a network of banks that place funds at other participating banks in order for depositors to receive insurance coverage for the entire amount of their deposits.[101] In these arrangements, institutions within the network are both sending and receiving *identical amounts* of deposits simultaneously.

Under the final rule, reciprocal deposits of an institution are not considered to be funds obtained through a deposit broker to the extent that the total amount of such reciprocal deposits does not exceed the lesser of: (i) $5 billion; or (ii) an amount equal to 20% of the total liabilities of the institution. Such institutions must have a composite condition of outstanding or good; and either be well-capitalized or, if adequately capitalized, have obtained a waiver from the FDIC.

The challenge in designing deposits to meet this exception is matching the outflow and inflow to make them the same dollar amount (the bank's balance sheet actually does not change an iota). It is usually a matter of money movement to and from numerous banks based on complex algorithms and, not surprisingly, there are a number of professional deposit placement agents operating in this marketplace.

FDIC 2020 Proposal. The FDIC promised that it would address modernizing its approach to brokered deposits for over a year beginning in 2019, solicited industry comments and then released its notice of proposed rulemaking on February 10, 2020 ("2020 Proposal"),[102] which is intended to create a new framework for analyzing certain provisions of

98. Public Law 115–174, 132 Stat. 1296–1368 (2018).
99. *Supra* note 90.
100. Limited Exception for a Capped Amount of Reciprocal Deposits From Treatment as Brokered Deposits, FDIC, Final Rule, 84 Fed. Reg. 1346 (Feb. 4, 2019), codified at 12 C.F.R. § 337.6(e).
101. *See*, FDIC Advisory Opinion No. 03–03 (July 29, 2003).
102. Unsafe and Unsound Banking Practices: Brokered Deposit Restrictions, FDIC, Notice of Proposed Rulemaking, 85 Fed. Reg. 7453 (Feb.10, 2020).

the definition of "deposit broker" and to establish an application process for certain relationships.

The following discussion breaks down the major issues associated with brokered deposits as of the 2016 FAQs with commentary as to changes that would be made under the 2020 Proposal.

Brokered Deposit Definitions and Issues.

What is a Deposit Broker? A brokered deposit is essentially a deposit placed not by the owner of the funds, but by a placement agent or broker. The FDIC deals with this issue by defining a "deposit broker" primarily as:[103]

- any person engaged in the business of *placing deposits*, or *facilitating the placement of deposits*, of third parties with insured depository institutions or the business of placing deposits with insured depository institutions for the purpose of selling interests in those deposits to third parties; and
- an agent or trustee who establishes a deposit account to facilitate a business arrangement with an insured depository institution to use the proceeds of the account to fund a prearranged loan.

There is a lot packed into that first bullet and its language leads to many conundrums. There are three prongs: (i) placing deposits, (ii) facilitating the placement of deposits and (iii) selling interests in deposits. The last is the easiest—interests in deposits are securities and when they are sold by placement agents, the deposits are brokered. No nuance. The other prongs have more nuance and are developed further below in the context of the 2020 Proposal and the FDIC's guidance on specific relationships.

The 2020 Proposal leaves these definitions essentially intact with helpful commentary. In clarifying the first prong, the proposal indicates: "The FDIC would view a person to be engaged in the business of placing deposits if that person has a business relationship with its customers, and as part of that relationship, places deposits on behalf of the customer (e.g., acting as custodian or agent for the underlying depositor)."[104]

Most of the confusion, however, has derived from the second prong and, in that regard, the FDIC addresses more comprehensively what it means to be "engaged in the business of *facilitating* the placement of deposits." First on this point, the FDIC identified the following activities, engaging in any one of which makes the person a deposit broker:[105]

- The person directly or indirectly shares any third party information with the insured depository institution;

103. 12 C.F.R. § 337.6(a)(5)(i)(A).
104. 2020 Proposal, *supra* note 102, 7457.
105. *Id.* (proposed 12 C.F.R. § 337.6(a)(5)(ii)).

- The person has legal authority, contractual or otherwise, to close the account or move the third party's funds to another insured depository institution;
- The person provides assistance or is involved in setting rates, fees, terms, or conditions for the deposit account; or
- The person is acting, directly or indirectly, with respect to the placement of deposits, as an intermediary between a third party that is placing deposits on behalf of a depositor and an insured depository institution, other than in a purely administrative capacity.

According to the FDIC:[106]

> The proposed "facilitation" definition is intended to capture activities that indicate that the person takes an active role in the opening of an account or maintains a level of influence or control over the deposit account even after the account is open. It is the FDIC's view that a level of control or influence indicates that the deposit relationship is between the depositor and the person rather than the depositor and the insured depository institution. Having a level of control or influence over the depositor allows the person to influence the movement of funds between institutions and makes the deposits less stable than deposits brought to the insured depository institution through a single point of contact where that contact does not have influence over the movement of deposits between insured depository institutions.

The idea is that, if the person is not engaged in any of the activities above, then that person is not facilitating the placement of deposits. In other words, if you do not want a deposit to be characterized as brokered, you craft a contract that prohibits the listed activities.

What is not a Brokered Deposit? Obviously, anything that is not sourced or facilitated by a deposit broker. That is probably not as helpful as the list of ten exceptions in the law dealing with relationships like employers, trust departments and pension trustees.[107] However, the most important exception is: "An agent or nominee whose primary purpose is not the placement of funds with depository institutions." More on that below.

What is a Primary Purpose?

106. *Id.*
107. 12 C.F.R. § 337.6(a)(5)(ii).

And then there is the "primary purpose exception"[108] mentioned above, which has been applied in instances where the deposits at issue were made to:

- satisfy an SEC reserve requirement;
- allow for the creation of a perfected security interest; and
- facilitate brokerage customers' purchases and sales of securities, subject to certain conditions.

For this exception, the "primary purpose" means "primary intent"; that is, what is the primary intent behind the placement of the deposits? In a seminal interpretive letter on this point,[109] the FDIC considered: (i) the materiality of the activity in the context of the agent; (ii) the type and purpose of the deposit account; (iii) and the compensation arrangement. First, the FDIC determined that the primary purpose exception could be appropriately applied to investment manager funds swept into bank deposit accounts if the funds were limited to 10% of the total assets under the investment advisor's management, as applied and reported to the FDIC on a monthly basis. Second, the FDIC deemed significant the fact that the deposit accounts were not time deposits, because "the placement of funds into time deposit accounts would be inconsistent with the argument that the 'primary purpose' . . . is to facilitate the purchase and sale of securities, and not to provide a deposit placement service." Furthermore, in evaluating the compensation, the FDIC looked with favor on a "flat" per account or per customer fee associated with the accounts at issue (presumably as distinguished from fees based on the balance of funds maintained in the account) and paid to the investment advisor by the affiliated banks. Those flat fees "represent[ed] payment for [the investment advisor's] recordkeeping and administrative services and not for the placement of deposits," and accordingly, the FDIC stated that such fees do not change its conclusion that the investment advisor's role and activities in that regard satisfied the primary purpose exception.

Suffice it to say that over time we did not get a whole lot more detail and eventually the FDIC was no longer responding to interpretive requests regarding this issue. Nevertheless, every lawyer working in this space has heard the third party who seeks to source deposits exclaim: "But, this is not my primary purpose." The 2020 Proposal permits them to put their money where their mouths are as the FDIC proposes to create an application process and reporting process for anyone claiming to rely on the primary purpose

108. Section 29(g)(2)(I) of the FDIA (12 U.S.C. § 1831f(g)(2)(I)), implemented by 12 C.F.R. § 337.6(a)(5)(ii)(I).
109. FDIC Advisory Opinion No. 05-02 (Feb. 3, 2005).

exception.[110] The application may be filed by the bank or the third party and the FDIC promises to process each application in 120 days.

Most helpfully on this point, the FDIC proposed that the primary purpose of an agent's or nominee's business relationship with its customers will not be considered to be the placement of funds, subject to an application process, if less than 25% of the total assets that the agent or nominee has under management for its customers, in a particular business line, is placed at depository institutions.[111]

Referred Deposits. Perhaps most problematic under the 2016 FAQs was the assertion that certain referrers of persons to banks for deposit services may be considered deposit brokers. Thankfully, there appears to be a presumption that that is not the case, unless there is a formal, programmatic arrangement (by agreement between the referrer and the bank) for the referral of deposits and the referrer receives fees from the bank.[112] Once again, these are useful tips in designing arrangements.

Listing Services. A listing service is a company that compiles and publishes information about deposit accounts at many different banks. The information published by a listing service will include the interest rates offered by the various banks. Some listing services operate Internet sites open to the public, while others provide information solely to banks and institutional investors who are willing to pay subscription fees. The FDIC has long recognized factual situations in which a listing service qualifies as a deposit broker and some when it does not. If the listing service places deposits or facilitates the placement of deposits (in addition to compiling and publishing information on interest rates and other features of deposit accounts), the listing service is a deposit broker, and the deposits would be brokered. The FDIC does not treat the listing service as a deposit broker if the company satisfies each of the following requirements:[113] (i) The person or entity providing the listing service is compensated solely by means of subscription fees (i.e., the fees paid by subscribers as payment for their opportunity to see the rates gathered by the listing service) and/or listing fees (i.e., the fees paid by depository institutions as payment for their opportunity to list or "post" their rates). The listing service does not require a depository institution to pay for other services offered by the listing service or its affiliates as a condition precedent to being listed; (ii) The fees paid by depository institutions are flat fees, not calculated on the basis of the number or dollar amount of deposits accepted by the depository

110. 2020 Proposal, *supra* note 102, 7470 (proposed 12 C.F.R. § 303.243(b)).
111. *Id*, at 7459.
112. 2016 FAQs. Section B.6.
113. FDIC Advisory Opinion No. 04-04 (July 28, 2004).

institution as a result of the listing or posting of the depository institution's rates; (iii) In exchange for these fees, the listing service performs no services except: (1) the gathering and transmission of information concerning the availability of deposits; and/or (2) the transmission of messages between depositors and depository institutions including purchase orders and trade confirmations. In publishing or displaying information about depository institutions, the listing service must not attempt to steer funds toward particular institutions, except that the listing service may rank institutions according to interest rates and also may exclude institutions that do not pay the listing fee. Similarly, in any communications with depositors or potential depositors, the listing service must not attempt to steer funds toward particular institutions; (iv) The listing service is not involved in the physical placement of deposits. Any funds to be invested in deposit accounts are remitted directly by the depositor to the insured depository institution and not, directly or indirectly, by or through the listing service.

Risk Management. It is noteworthy that the brokered deposit rules are promulgated under the caption "Unsafe and Unsound Banking Practices." In 2001, the federal banking agencies issued a Joint Agency Advisory on Brokered and Rate-Sensitive Deposits.[114] The advisory sets forth guidelines for brokered deposits that require bank management to implement risk-management systems that are commensurate in complexity with the liquidity and funding risks that the bank undertakes.

The Role of the CFPB

As discussed in Chapter 3, Title X of Dodd-Frank created the CFPB and tasked it with regulating consumer financial products and services. As part of the transfer of power, the CFPB took over the Federal Reserve's former rulemaking role in connection with the Electronic Fund Transfer Act[115] and Regulation E[116] and the Truth in Savings Act[117] and Regulation DD.[118] In addition, the CFPB was conferred authority over enforcement of UDAAP—Prohibiting Unfair, Deceptive, or Abusive Acts or Practices.[119] Prepaid cards, overdrafts, account-opening disclosures, privacy, and account

114. The FDIC version is FDIC-PR-37-2001 (May 11, 2001), https://www.fdic.gov/news/news/press/2001/pr3701.html.
115. 15 U.S.C. § 1693 *et seq.*
116. 12 C.F.R. Part 1005.
117. 12 U.S.C. § 4301 *et seq.*
118. 12 C.F.R. Part 1030.
119. 12 U.S.C. §§ 5531–5536. *See also*, Prohibition of Unfair, Deceptive, or Abusive Acts or Practices in the Collection of Consumer Debts, CFPB Bulletin 2013-07 (July 10, 2013).

access devices, all affecting retail deposit accounts, are under its purview. The CFPB, however, only examines banking institutions of $10 billion in assets or greater. Each bank's prudential regulator otherwise exams consumer law compliance.

This book is not focused on consumer banking law—that is another book in and of itself—but it is critical for bank regulatory lawyers to be aware of the jurisdiction of the CFPB and its reach in rulemaking and enforcement.

The Role of FinCEN and OFAC

Deposit accounts can be used for all sorts of nefarious purposes, particularly to defraud, to launder proceeds of illegal activity, and to finance terrorism. Very scary stuff. As a consequence, Congress has created new departments, councils and offices with regulatory authority in this space and has enacted a host of laws, many of which focus on deposit-takers and put them on the frontline to detect suspicious activity. The role of banks in anti-money laundering and in combating terrorist finance is discussed in depth in Chapter 7.

Liquidity

If capital is indeed king, then liquidity is queen. As mentioned in the introduction to this chapter, depository institutions require liquid assets that may be turned to cash promptly so that they can pay depositors their funds on demand (if a transactional account) or pursuant to the contract of deposit (if savings or time deposits). Think about the fact that, as a financial intermediary, a bank takes deposit dollars, places them on its balance sheet as a liability (owed back to the depositor) and then invests those funds as principal out into the economy in the form primarily of investments and loans. Fractional amounts are held as cash and in reserves and the Federal Reserve discount window is open for borrowing, but those would never withstand a depositor run, which in our modern marketplace could be effected online—no standing in long lines like in the depression.

Liquidity Risk Management

In response to liquidity risk, financial institutions must establish and maintain liquidity management systems to assess their prospective funding needs and ensure that funds are available at appropriate times.[120] In this respect, they need to plan for any unexpected funding needs, regardless of whether they arise from firm-specific factors, such as a drop in the firm's collateral value, or from systemic (economy-wide) factors. They must be able to measure and forecast the prospective cash flows for assets, liabilities, off-balance-sheet commitments, and derivative positions over several time horizons, under both normal conditions and a range of stress scenarios and over multiple time horizons. [121]

LCR and NSFR

Because the Global Financial Crisis was in part a liquidity crisis, Basel III[122] also created a liquidity framework that requires certain large FDIC-insured institutions to measure their liquidity against specific liquidity tests. The objective was to provide an incentive for banks and holding companies to increase their holdings in unencumbered high-quality liquid assets ("HQLA") like Treasury securities and other sovereign debt as a component of assets, increase the use of long-term debt as a funding source and rely on stable funding like core deposits (in lieu of brokered deposits). Basel III introduced two tests for this purpose.

The first test, referred to as the Liquidity Coverage Ratio ("LCR"),[123] is designed to ensure that the banking entity has an adequate stock of HQLA that can be converted easily and immediately in private markets into cash to meet liquidity needs for a 30-calendar day liquidity stress scenario. The LCR requires covered institutions to measure inflows and outflows on a daily basis, such that the HQLA amount when divided by outflows on the same date is to be over 100%. In other words, the LCR tells institutions on a daily basis how much HQLA they must hold. The key questions are:

---

120. There is a plethora of guidance on this point. First is the Interagency Policy Statement on Funding and Liquidity Risk Management (Mar. 17, 2010). For national banks, *see* the Comptroller's Handbook on Liquidity. For state member banks and bank holding companies, *see* the Federal Reserve's Commercial Bank Examination Manual (section 4020), Bank Holding Company Supervision Manual (section 4010), and Trading and Capital Markets Activities Manual (section 2030). For state non-member banks, *see* the FDIC's Revised Examination Guidance for Liquidity and Funds Management, (section 6-1), as well as Financial Institution Letter 84-2008, Liquidity Risk Management (Aug. 2008).
121. What is Liquidity Risk? FRBSF Economic Letter, 2008-33 (Oct. 24, 2008).
122. *See* generally, Basel Committee on Banking Supervision. 2008a, Liquidity Risk: Management and Supervisory Challenges; Basel Committee on Banking Supervision. 2008b, Principles for Sound Liquidity Risk Management and Supervision, available at bis.org.
123. The Federal Reserve, OCC and FDIC issued the final LCR rule on October 10, 2014, 79 Fed. Reg. 61,440 (Oct 10, 2014), codified at (Federal Reserve) Regulation WW, 12 C.F.R. Part 249, (OCC) 12 C.F.R. Part 50, (FDIC) 12 C.F.R. Part 239.

- Does the transaction cause a liquidity drain under outflow assumptions?
- Does the transaction serve as a liquidity source or inflow?
- Can the instrument serve as a liquidity store, or "HQLA"?

The LCR was effective at January 1, 2015 for all Advanced Approaches institutions and their bank subsidiaries.[124]

The other test, the Net Stable Funding Ratio ("NSFR"), is designed to promote more medium- and long-term funding of the assets and activities of FDIC-insured institutions over a one-year horizon. The U.S. banking agencies proposed the NSFR in 2015 for the same group of bank holding companies[125] without finalizing the rule. They were expected to proceed with rulemaking in 2020.

Other Deposit Products and Sources of "Law"

Political subdivisions and commercial/business customers place funds in bank accounts for many purposes, most of it in DDAs. The accounts may be operating accounts, payroll accounts or investment accounts, but in almost all events the dollars will far exceed the SMDIA. Consequently, these depositors have special deposit needs and, as such needs became more faceted and complex and as technological advances leapt forward, banks and their service providers created scores of new products and services generally referred to as "treasury management" or "cash management" services.

Treasury Management Services

The suite of products and services considered to meet commercial deposit customer treasury needs tend to be executed through a business online banking platform, but they may have their own portals or they may even still be paper-based. The services, and the rules that apply, are primarily creatures of contract, so banks that offer them require robust contracts with appropriate provisions and limits of liability.

Examples. These services include:

- ACH (automated clearing house) origination – initiating and settling batch files of entries to credit or debit a receiver's account through ACH operators;

124. Advanced Approaches institutions are those bank holding companies with assets over $250 billion or over $10 billion in on-balance sheet foreign exposures). A modified requirement applies to those over $50 billion in assets.
125. Notice of Proposed Rulemaking, 81 Fed. Reg. 35,123 (June 1, 2016).

- Wire transfers - payment orders from a customer's account to a beneficiary's account, typically routed through the Federal Reserve;
- Remote deposit capture and mobile RDC- scanning or taking digital pictures of checks for electronic deposit and collection;
- Lockbox - payment remittance collection and posting;
- Sweeps - funds in a deposit account being transferred out to a destination within or outside the bank, usually at the close of business;
- Repurchase or Reverse Repurchase agreements - essentially a loan to or from the bank secured by government securities but formalized as a purchase and resale of a fractional interest in a government security;
- Coin and currency - making cash and currency available and collecting it for deposit;
- Cash vault - immediate credit of cash deposits placed in a secure safe;
- Check and ACH Positive Pay - processes to validate payments from customer accounts and block certain debits.

Applicable Law. There is for almost all purposes, no body of federal law that applies to these treasury management services, as long as they are used primarily for business purposes (not personal, household or family purposes). Importantly, Regulation E does not apply and, therefore, banks should not provide business customers the Regulation E error resolution disclosures or they will have given commercial customers, by contract, rights that do not otherwise apply.

However, that does not mean that there is no law or no standards. Network rules, clearinghouse rules and state law like the Uniform Commercial Code abide in this space. In addition, the bank regulators have examination authority and issue guidance from time to time on the way they expect these services to be executed. Lawyers need to be aware of the following laws and rules if they prepare contracts for these services or give legal advice:

- ACH origination - the ACH system is governed by complex operating rules issued by Nacha—the Electronic Payments Association, which cover every aspect of these transactions, including contract requirements.
- Wire transfers - UCC Article 4A governs wire transfers, but those that route through the Federal Reserve are under Regulation J (Fedwire), which is in the process of supplanting the UCC in this space.

- Remote deposit capture – there are networks that have rules on electronic check presentment (like ECCHO) and regulatory guidelines on risk management, but it is Check 21 that permits electronic check presentment and substitute checks, as implemented by Regulation CC. There are warranties in Check 21 that need to be included in contracts and special endorsement requirements.
- Lockbox – if the lockbox will accept remittances with protected health information, such as explanations of benefits (EOBs), then HIPAA/HiTech applies and the parties will need a business associate agreement that complies with the statutes.
- Repurchase agreements – the purchase and sale of the government security must be perfected under UCC Article 9 (as it defaults in part to Article 8) for proper execution under the FDIC rules.[126]

Thus, there is lots of "law" that pours into these contracts. And that means the contracts should be updated regularly as the rules are updated.

Security Procedures and Risk-Shifting

A number of the treasury management services listed above involve transfers out of business accounts, most of which are executed online or over a wireless network. Business bill pay, ACH entries and wire transfer orders are examples. As indicated above, consumer protections against fraud and unauthorized transfers do not abide in this space. So, we are back to the contract—for the protection of the institution and its customers, contracts must include clear allocations of risk and liability, and both parties must warrant that each has established secure networks, virus and malware protection and data breach reaction procedures. That said, as between the parties, the key component to mitigating against fraud is security procedures.

Verifying Payment Orders. The concept of security procedures is not new. It was established in Article 4A of the Uniform Commercial Code in order to authorize and validate wire transfer requests. UCC §§ 4A-201-202 are the operative provisions, with 4A-201 defining a security procedure as: "[A] procedure established by agreement of a customer and a receiving bank for the purpose of (i) verifying that a payment order … is that of the customer, or (ii) detecting error in the transmission or the content of the payment order or communication." Two important initial take-aways: There must be a contract and it must specify the security procedures. Too many contracts reference security procedures but never describe what they are. Strike one.

126. The Government Securities Act (15 U.S.C. § 78o-5) applies to certain aspects of repurchase transactions and, among other things, compels certain disclosures.

The beauty of the UCC in this regard is that it then creates a defense for the bank receiving and acting on the payment order: If a bank and its customer have agreed that the authenticity of payment orders will be verified pursuant to a security procedure, a payment order received by the receiving bank is effective as the order of the customer, whether or not authorized, if (i) the security procedure is a *commercially reasonable* method of providing security against unauthorized payment orders, and (ii) the bank proves that it accepted the payment order in good faith and in compliance with the security procedure. [127] Thus, in order to operate as a defense to bank liability, the security procedure must be commercially reasonable (ultimately, a question of law). The take-away here is the parties must agree in the contract that the security procedure is reasonable and appropriate for the customer's needs. The contract does not confirm commercial reasonableness? Strike two.

Security Procedure Examples. There are many security procedures and security devices in use today. For example:

> *Security Devices* include access ID's, personal identification numbers ("PINs") (including telephone PINs) and passwords, security questions, logon identifications, personal or location identification numbers, USB plug-ins and tokens (which electronically generate one-time passwords).
>
> *Security Procedures* include the use of algorithms, Security Devices and additional procedures, including call-backs, out-of-band authentication, dual control, biometrics, encryption and other systems and software that may be used in connection with an online service.

Multi-factor Authentication. Gone is the time when passwords or PINs get the job done. The banking agencies have rung in on this issue through the Federal Financial Institutions Examination Council ("FFIEC"). The FFIEC first issued guidance entitled *Authentication in an Internet Banking Environment* in 2001 and replaced it in 2016.[128] The Guidance describes authentication methodologies as involving the following factors: (i) something the user *knows* (e.g., password, PIN), (ii) something the user *has* (e.g., ATM card), and (iii) something the user *is* (e.g., fingerprint). Use of more than one of these methodologies is called "multi-factor authentication," which presents a more reliable and stronger fraud deterrent than single-factor methods. Accordingly, the Guidance states:

127. U.C.C. Article 4A-202(b). The UCC commentary is very insightful and recommended reading on this point.

128. *See*, https://www.ffiec.gov/pdf/authentication_guidance.pdf.

> The agencies consider single-factor authentication, as the only control mechanism, to be inadequate for high-risk transactions involving access to customer information or the movement of funds to other parties. Financial institutions offering Internet-based products and services to their customers should use effective methods to authenticate the identity of customers using those products and services. The authentication techniques employed by the financial institution should be appropriate to the risks associated with those products and services. Account fraud and identity theft are frequently the result of single-factor (e.g., ID/password) authentication exploitation. Where risk assessments indicate that the use of single-factor authentication is inadequate, financial institutions should implement multifactor authentication, layered security, or other controls reasonably calculated to mitigate those risks.

Accordingly, in this day and age, the security procedures should be multi-factor—one device may not work alone. You login into online banking with a user ID and password and then input a one-time passcode texted to your mobile device. It is that kind of combination of security devices that is effective. No multi-factor? Strike three.

Multi-level Authentication and Authorization Hierarchy. In addition, any external transfer is far riskier and may require two different authentications, such as:

> *Dual Control* – when a service requires a transfer order to be made by one user and confirmed by another, each using the security procedure described for the service.
>
> *Call-backs* – when the receiving bank places a confirming telephone call to an authorized user who has been authorized to confirm the specific transaction. Many times, especially in wire transfer, call-backs require use of a Telephone PIN assigned to the confirming user.

Treasury management services then work on a hierarchy of authorizations. What officers and employees have authority to access accounts for external transfers and what are their individual limits? Who can initiate and who can confirm?

Risk-Shifting. The UCC construct is intended to incentivize banks to provide reasonable security procedures by limiting their liability for unauthorized or fraudulent transfers. What happens if the customer finds the security procedures to be cumbersome and seeks to waive multi-factor, dual control or call-backs? You should add express language in the contract to shift the risk and, if the customer insists on a waiver, make them sign a release and indemnification form that has the customer accepting the risk of the decision. An example of contract language is:

> Client acknowledges that there is a growing risk of losses resulting from unauthorized transactions in accounts. Bank offers services that provide effective means for controlling such risk, including: (i) ACH Debit Block and ACH Positive Pay, (ii) Account Reconciliation and (iii) Positive Pay. In addition, Bank may recommend that Client use certain fraud prevention practices to reduce Client's exposure to online fraud. Each of these practices is an industry "best practice." An example of a best practice is Dual Control, which requires a payment or user modification initiated by one User to be approved by a second User on a different computer or Mobile Device before it takes effect. Client will be treated as having assumed the risk of any loss that could have been prevented by its use of any fraud prevention service or best practice Bank has recommended to Client, if Client: (A) declines to enroll in the fraud prevention Service(s); (B) enrolls in the fraud prevention service but fails to use it in accordance with the Service Terms applicable to it; or (C) fails to adopt and follow a best practice. In that event, Client will be precluded from asserting any claims against Bank for paying unauthorized, altered, counterfeit or other fraudulent items that such tool was designed to detect or deter, and Bank will not be required to re-credit Client's account or otherwise have any liability for paying such items.

There are numerous cases that support the risk allocation. In *Choice Escrow & Land Title v. BancorpSouth Bank,*[129] for example, the Eighth Circuit Court of Appeals issued a decision regarding cybersecurity and who should bear the loss for unauthorized funds transfers. The court of appeals affirmed the U.S. District Court for the District of Missouri's grant of summary judgment in favor of a receiving bank, BancorpSouth Bank, concluding that under Article 4A, the bank complied with its commercially reasonable security measures and was not responsible for its customer, Choice Escrow & Land Title's, loss resulting from a fraudulent payment. The customer was

129. 2014 U.S. App. LEXIS 10817. *See also, What Banks Should Know About the Eighth Circuit's Decision in Choice Escrow & Land Title, LLC v. BancorpSouth Bank*, https://www.americanbar.org/groups/business_law/publications/blt/2014/10/02_desjardins/.

victimized by a phishing scam involving a $440,000 fraudulent wire transfer from the customer's account at the bank.

As to the security procedures in question, the bank recommended four measures designed to ensure that access to its customers' accounts was available only to each customer's authorized users:

- A unique user ID and password
- Device authentication
- Daily dollar limits on the volume of wire transfer activity from a customer's account
- Dual control requiring a second authorized user to separately approve a pending payment order.

The customer declined two of the four security measures by not placing daily transfer limits on its account and by declining dual control. The customer signed a waiver of the security feature and declined dual control on two occasions.

The court held that the security procedures were commercially reasonable and the bank accepted the payment order in good faith, thus meeting the requirements of the UCC. The court characterized this as a case where "an informed customer refuses a security procedure that is commercially reasonable and suitable for that customer and insists on using a higher-risk procedure because it is more convenient or cheaper," and Choice "voluntarily assumed the risk of failure of the procedure and cannot shift the loss to" BancorpSouth.

Although there are no guarantees, cases like this demonstrate that the right system functions and contractual terms mitigate risk of bank loss.

6

Three Prudential Policies Applicable to All FDIC-Insured Institutions

How Great the Cost of "Specialness"?

Banks are special. They have cheap deposit funding. Time has taught us that this "specialness" must be protected: from deposit runs, from risky activities and investments, from bad decisions, from insider and affiliate abuse.... Thus, we have, for example, deposit insurance and access to the Federal Reserve's discount window as subsidies of enormous consequence.[1] Many argue that their very existence validates supervision, regulation, and enforcement on the scale described in this book.

This chapter discusses three regulatory policies applicable to all depository institutions that are intended to protect them from abuse. We tend to think of these as the foundation of "prudential regulation" because they require banks to exercise "prudence." Chapter 9 then presents another aspect of protectionism in terms of the restrictions on bank expansion into new and/or riskier activities. These chapters encompass the heart and soul of what a bank regulatory lawyer deals with on an everyday basis as we give advice on whether and how our clients may conduct business.

The policies discussed below apply to all banks and savings associations and frame the fundamentals of "prudential" regulation. Three impose significant restrictions on banks and one is expressed as a commandment instead of a negative and remains the backstop of it all. In a nutshell, all insured depository institutions SHALL:

- Limit transactions with affiliates;
- Limit insider loans;

1. The federal subsidies and the "safety net" are the subject of Chapter 5, *supra*.

- Limit loans to one borrower; and
- Not engage in unsafe and unsound banking practices.

The last commandment has become so great in import that it now commands Chapter 8 on its own.

Transactions with Affiliates

Sections 23A and 23B of the Federal Reserve Act (collectively, "Sections 23A and B")[2] impose quantitative and qualitative restrictions on transactions between banks and their affiliates. The Federal Reserve Board ("Board" or "Federal Reserve") has described these sections as follows:

> Sections 23A and 23B of the Federal Reserve Act are important statutory provisions designed to protect against a depository institution suffering losses in transactions with affiliates. They also limit the ability of a depository institution to transfer to its affiliates the subsidy arising from the institution's access to the Federal safety net.[3]

Section 23A, which was enacted in 1933, originally applied to banks that were members of the Federal Reserve System (member banks). In fact, the statute still refers solely to "member banks," causing no end of confusion for young lawyers who may still decide they do not have to read it if the client is a nonmember bank or savings association. Notwithstanding the express words of the statute, it now applies, along with Section 23B, which was enacted in 1987, to federally insured nonmember banks[4] and to all savings associations[5] (referred to collectively with member banks as "banks" in this discussion).

The Board has rulemaking authority under Sections 23A and B but declined to exercise it for decades, relying instead on staff interpretations and informal guidance, much of which was unofficial and some of which stretched beyond the statutory construction. These sections then assumed increasing importance with the enactment of the Gramm-Leach-Bliley Act of 1999 ("Gramm-Leach-Bliley").[6] Gramm-Leach-Bliley not only expanded the scope of activities in which banks and their subsidiaries could

---

2. Codified at 12 U.S.C. §§ 371c and 371c-1, respectively.
3. Federal Reserve Board, Transactions between Member Banks and Their Affiliates, Final Rule, 67 Fed. Reg. 76,604 (Dec. 12, 2002), as amended at 76 Fed. Reg. 56,531, Sept. 13, 2011 (codified at 12 C.F.R. Part 223).
4. Section 8(j) of the Federal Deposit Insurance Act (codified in 12 U.S.C. § 1828(j)).
5. Section 11(a) of the Home Owners' Loan Act (codified in 12 U.S.C. § 1468(a)). The former regulation at 12 C.F.R. § 163.41 now merely has a direction to Regulation W.
6. Pub. Law 106-102 Nov. 12, 1999, 113 Stat. 1338.

engage with affiliates, but also required the Board to adopt regulations under Section 23A relating to derivative transactions and intraday credit extensions. In response to these developments, the Board adopted final rules implementing these sections, captioned as Regulation W (conveniently the 23rd letter of the alphabet so it is codified at 12 C.F.R. Part 223) ("Regulation W"), and final rules repealing its interpretive rulings,[7] most of which found a home in Regulation W, along with a slew of others.

The principal restrictions under Sections 23A and B may be summarized as follows:

1. Extensions of credit to, asset purchases from, and certain other "covered transactions" by a bank with an affiliate are subject to the following quantitative limits (§§ 223.11–12):
   - 10% of the bank's capital and surplus to any single affiliate; and
   - 20% of the bank's capital and surplus to all affiliates;
2. Extensions of credit to and guarantees on behalf of an affiliate must be collateralized (§ 223.14);
3. A bank may not purchase low-quality assets from an affiliate (§ 223.15);
4. All covered transactions by a bank with affiliates must be consistent with safe and sound banking practices (§ 223.13);
5. Section 23B: all transactions by a bank with affiliates must be on market terms (§§ 223.51–52);
6. Attribution rule: transactions by a bank with a third party, the proceeds of which are transferred to an affiliate or that benefit an affiliate, are considered made to the affiliate (§ 223.16).

If a bank has one or more affiliates and contemplates any intrafamily transactions, it is incumbent upon the board of directors to adopt a policy statement with respect to its expectations in this area, including naming the responsible parties for approvals and compliance. The policy statement, and any procedures promulgated thereunder, should not merely recite the law. They should provide direction.

Section 23A

It is important to note in this regard that Section 23A is all about protecting the bank. For this reason, traditional operating subsidiaries (those that can only engage in the activities of the parent bank and a few others

7. The formal interpretations of Sections 23A and B were published in 12 C.F.R. Part 225. They were rescinded in 67 Fed. Reg. 76,620 (Dec. 12, 2002).

described below) are treated as part of the protected bank—as if they were an incorporated division. It is useful to imagine a net around the bank and the protected subsidiaries keeping the money from flowing out to affiliates without an express exit permitted under the rules.

Definitional Challenges

Section 23A is a very short statute. In its brevity, it depends on numerous definitions. As a consequence, it can only be approached by drilling down into the definitions (some of which are italicized in the following sentence). It limits the amount of a *member bank* and its *operating subsidiary's covered transactions* with a single *affiliate* to 10% of the bank's *capital stock and surplus*, and limits such transactions with all affiliates to 20% of this amount.

What is a Member Bank?[8] As indicated above, "member bank" when used in the statute means any bank or savings association that has Federal Deposit Insurance Corporation ("FDIC") insurance, or is an "insured depository institution." For example, any trust company that has FDIC insurance is a bank, but those that do not have insurance, are not.

What is an Operating Subsidiary?[9] A company that is a subsidiary of a bank is generally considered a part of the bank within the protection of Section 23A. A subsidiary is not an "affiliate" unless it is:

- a depository institution;
- directly controlled by one or more affiliates of the bank (other than a depository institution affiliate) or by a shareholder or group of shareholders that control the member bank;
- an employee stock option plan organized for the benefit of employees, shareholders, and others related to the bank; or
- a financial subsidiary,[10] other than one operating solely as an insurance agency.[11]

Treating subsidiaries as part of the bank for the purposes of the transactions with affiliates restrictions makes subsidiaries an ideal structure choice for a number of activities in which the existence of the corporate veil for liability containment purposes may be appropriate.

8. 12 C.F.R. § 223.
9. 12 C.F.R. § 223.
10. These subsidiaries are introduced in Chapter 2, *supra*, and discussed in Chapter 3, *supra*.
11. *See*, 12 C.F.R. § 223.3(p)(2)(i). This was a refinement added in Regulation W in deference to the fact that insurance activities did not represent principal risk as would other activities of financial subsidiaries.

What is an Affiliate?[12] Affiliates are the entities that the bank is protected from—they are outside the "net." They are not individuals, although individuals may control the bank and also control another entity that is an affiliate because of the common control. Section 23A defines "affiliates" of banks to include the following:

- a company that controls the bank (bank holding company or savings and loan holding company);
- companies that are under common control by the bank's parent company or certain other entities, including the common control of the same individual;
- a company a majority of whose directors or general partners comprise a majority of the persons holding similar positions at the bank or the bank's parent company;
- any investment fund advised by the bank or an affiliate of the bank;
- a company in which the bank and its affiliates control more than 5% of the voting securities or equity capital of the fund;
- a depository institution that is a subsidiary of the bank;
- a partnership or LLC in which the bank or affiliate, or any officer, director, or employee thereof, serves as a general partner or managing member, respectively;
- any subsidiary of the companies described above; and
- any company including a subsidiary of a bank that the Federal Reserve or the primary federal regulator determines to be an affiliate by regulation or order.

Entities excluded from the definition of "affiliate" include certain companies acquired from the exercise of rights arising out of a bona fide debt previously contracted (so-called "DPC" property) and companies engaged solely in: holding the premises of the member bank; a safe deposit box business; and holding U.S. and certain U.S.-guaranteed securities.

What is Control?[13] The concept of control is a significant feature of Section 23A in order to determine which entities constitute affiliates. If an entity is not under common control or controlled by the bank, it is not an affiliate. A company or shareholder controls another company if that company or shareholder, directly or indirectly, or acting through one or more other persons:

- owns, controls, or has power to vote 25% or more of any class of voting securities of the other company (including shares held by a subsidiary);

12. 12 C.F.R. § 223.2.
13. 12 C.F.R. § 223.3(g). This concept is discussed in depth in Chapter 10, *infra*.

- controls in any manner the election of a majority of the directors of the other company; or
- is found by the Federal Reserve, after notice and opportunity for hearing, to exercise a controlling influence over the management or policies of the other company.

What is a Covered Transaction?[14] Section 23A only applies to "covered transactions" between a bank and its operating subsidiary and an affiliate. These mostly involve funds leaving the bank. Transactions subject to the 10% and 20% quantitative limits under Section 23A include:

- extensions of credit to, or purchases of assets from, an affiliate, including loans to a third party that benefit an affiliate (see discussion of attribution rules below) and including:
    - any transaction that creates a repayment obligation, including accidental actions that result in accounts payable to an affiliate, including paying the taxes of an affiliate or paying for services rendered on behalf of the affiliate;
    - purchase of a note or obligation of an affiliate;
    - intraday credit (broadly defined);
    - a purchase of assets subject to a repurchase agreement;
- purchase of, or investment in, a security of an affiliate;
- the acceptance of a security issued by an affiliate as collateral for an extension of credit to any person or company, and the acceptance of other debt obligations of an affiliate as collateral;
- the issuance of a guarantee, acceptance, or letter of credit on behalf of an affiliate, and the confirmation of a letter of credit issued by the affiliate; and
- cross-affiliate netting arrangements.[15]

Section 608 of the Dodd-Frank Wall Street Reform and Consumer Protection Act of 2010 ("Dodd-Frank")[16] also adds, as of July 21, 2012:

- a transaction with an affiliate involving the borrowing or lending of securities to the extent the transaction causes the bank to have a credit exposure to the affiliate; and

---

14. 12 C.F.R. § 223.3(h).
15. A cross-affiliate netting arrangement is an arrangement between a member bank, one or more affiliates, and one or more nonaffiliates of the bank, in which a nonaffiliate can deduct any obligation of the affiliate to the bank when settling the nonaffiliate's own obligation to the bank, and when a bank is permitted or required to add any amount owed by the affiliate to the nonaffiliate when settling the bank's obligations to the nonaffiliate.
16. Pub. L. No. 111-203 (2010).

- a derivative transaction with an affiliate to the extent that it causes the bank to have a credit exposure to the affiliate. (There is no definition yet of the term "credit exposure.")

In addition, internal reorganizations and other transactions that are not specifically listed above typically involve covered transactions and, therefore, must be carefully scrutinized under the rules. For instance, the donation of a subsidiary by a parent company to a bank involves a covered transaction because the bank is deemed to have purchased the assets with an assumption of liabilities as the purchase price.[17]

Restrictions on Covered Transactions

When a bank seeks to engage in covered transactions with one or more affiliates, it must comply with all the rules discussed below and, as part of its policies and procedures to assure compliance with the law and Regulation W, it must establish internal controls to carefully monitor lines of credit to keep them under the quantitative limitations and must monitor collateral positions to assure they remain at the required levels.

Quantitative Limits.[18] Section 23A prohibits a bank or subsidiary from entering into a new covered transaction that would exceed for that affiliate 10% of the bank's capital stock and surplus, and for all affiliates 20% of this amount. The banking agencies have promulgated identical regulations as to how capital is calculated for the purpose of prudential regulations: it is a bank's Tier 1 and Tier 2 regulatory capital plus the allowance for loan and lease losses (ALLL) not used in the bank's Tier 2 capital as of the prior CALL report.[19]

Asset Quality.[20] A bank may not purchase a "low quality asset" from an affiliate unless, pursuant to an independent credit evaluation, the bank contracted to buy the asset before it was acquired by the affiliate. Low-quality assets include those that have been classified as "sub-standard" or lower in the affiliate's most recent examination or the bank's own internal loan rating system, assets on which principal and interest payments are more than 30 days past due, those that are on a nonaccrual basis, and those that have been renegotiated or compromised.

Collateral Requirements.[21] A bank's extension of credit to, or guarantees issued on behalf of, an affiliate must be secured by a statutorily mandated amount of collateral. Collateral requirements range from 100% of the loan

17. 12 C.F.R. § 223.31.
18. 12 C.F.R. §§ 223.11-12.
19. *See, e.g.*, 12 C.F.R. § 1.2(a). Capital is discussed in Chapter 4, *supra*.
20. 12 C.F.R. § 223.3(v).
21. 12 C.F.R. § 223.14.

if the collateral consists of U.S. government obligations or securities of equivalent safety to 130% of the loan if the collateral is stock, leases, or other real or personal property. Debt obligations of an affiliate (as well as securities issued by an affiliate) are not permitted to be used as collateral for an extension of credit to, guarantee on behalf of, or credit exposure on a derivative or securities lending or borrowing transaction with an affiliate. Under Section 608 of Dodd-Frank, beginning on July 21, 2012, a credit extension or guarantee is required to remain secured in accordance with the collateral requirements of Section 23A *so long as it is outstanding*. Under prior law, the collateral only needed to meet the requirements when the covered transaction was funded. In addition, the collateral requirements of Section 23A apply to the bank's credit exposure on derivative transactions with an affiliate and with respect to the credit exposure on borrowing or lending transactions with an affiliate.

Safety and Soundness.[22] The bank must conduct all covered transactions, including transactions that are exempt from other requirements of Section 23A, on a safe and sound basis.

Attribution Rule.[23] Under Section 23A, a loan made to a third party for the benefit of an affiliate is regarded as a loan to the affiliate for purposes of the restrictions. A loan by the bank to a third party used to purchase an item from an affiliate of the bank, or from a company, such as an automobile dealership, that is controlled by persons who also control the bank is deemed to be a loan to the affiliate. There are several notable exceptions to the attribution rule, including a provision that general purpose credit cards, such as Visa and MasterCard, issued by a member bank will be exempt from these attribution rules if less than 25% of the purchases with the card are from an affiliate of the bank. The preamble to the final rules points out that most banks issuing special purpose cards comply with Section 23A by selling receivables to an affiliate at the end of each day.[24]

Exemptions from the Provisions of Section 23A

The first list of exemptions and the lists following it closely track statutory exemptions in Section 23A(d)(6) from the quantitative limits and certain other restrictions of Section 23A.[25] All of the transactions listed, however, are subject to the requirements that any transactions with affiliates be conducted on a safe and sound basis. The transactions listed first below

22. 12 C.F.R. § 223.13.
23. 12 C.F.R. § 223.16.
24. Transactions between Member Banks, *supra* note 3, discussion of general purpose credit cards.
25. 12 C.F.R. § 223.4.

are also subject to the prohibition on transactions involving low-quality assets, discussed above. These exempt transactions are:

- transactions with another depository institution if the bank controls 80% or more of the voting securities of the institution or with an institution that controls 80% or more of the bank;
- transactions between a bank and a depository institution if the same company has 80% or more control of both institutions (the "sister bank" exemption);
- purchases of a loan by a bank from an affiliate on a nonrecourse basis; and
- purchase of assets from an affiliate and other transactions in connection with certain internal corporate reorganizations.

Sister Bank Transactions. Banks that are owned 80% or more by a company—often referred to as "sister banks"—are affiliates for the purposes of Section 23A, but benefit from an exemption from the qualitative and collateral value requirements shown above.[26] As indicated, that leaves them, however, subject to the prohibition on the purchase of low-quality assets and to the commandment as to safety and soundness. Interestingly, because operating subsidiaries are treated as being part of the banks, they are also under the sister bank exemption and may engage in covered transactions with each other. It is noteworthy that banks that are commonly controlled but with ownership at less than 80% are just plain affiliates, subject to all the rules.

Purchase of Securities. While purchases of securities from an affiliate are covered transactions, Regulation W recognizes that certain transactions can be objectively priced on an arm's length basis. These transactions are exempt from the quantitative limits, the collateral requirements, and the low-quality assets prohibition.[27] First in this regard, purchases from an affiliate of securities or other assets at or below their market value are exempt if the securities are listed on an exchange or whose market value is otherwise "readily identifiable and publicly available." In addition, securities purchased from an affiliate that is a registered broker-dealer are exempt if the securities conform to the Securities and Exchange Commission ("SEC") criteria for having a "ready market"[28] and the securities:

26. 12 C.F.R. § 223.41.
27. 12 C.F.R. § 223.42.
28. SEC Rule 240.153c3-1(c)(11)(i) defines a "ready market" as a "recognized securities market in which there exits independent bona fide offers to buy and sell so that a price reasonably related to the last sales price or current bona fide competitive bid and offer quotations can be determined for a particular security almost instantaneously and where payment will be received in settlement of a sale at such price."

- are not issued by an affiliate;
- are not purchased within thirty days of an underwriting by an affiliate (except for certain U.S. and U.S.-guaranteed obligations);
- are eligible for purchase by state member banks;
- are not low quality; and
- meet other requirements including having their prices quoted on an unaffiliated electronic service that provides data from real-time financial networks.

Other Exemptions.[29] Other activities that are exempt from the above provisions of Section 23A include:

- making deposits in correspondent banks;
- making a loan to, or issuing a guarantee on behalf of, an affiliate that is fully secured by U.S. obligations or a segregated, earmarked deposit account at the member bank (this one is particularly useful, permitting an affiliate to convey control of a securities account or deposit account to the bank with sufficient collateral to cover any covered transaction);
- purchasing an extension of credit from an affiliate on a nonrecourse basis subject to certain limits including the following: (i) the bank must make an independent evaluation of the borrower's creditworthiness before the loan is made, and (ii) the bank may not purchase each year more than 50% of the loans originated by the affiliate (historically called the "250-250 exception" because of its previous citation);
- purchasing a security from a securities affiliate of the member bank if the member bank or the securities affiliate is acting exclusively as a riskless principal, and the security purchased is not issued, underwritten, or sold as principal (other than as riskless principal) by any affiliate of the member bank;
- purchasing from an affiliate a loan originated by the bank and sold to the affiliate subject to a repurchase agreement or with recourse; and
- extensions of intraday credit to an affiliate if the bank maintains policies and procedures reasonably designed to manage the credit exposure of these transactions, the transactions comply with the "arm's length" requirements of Section 23B, and the bank ceases to treat the transaction as an extension of intraday credit at the end of the bank's business day in the United States.

29. 12 C.F.R. §§ 223.41–43.

"Super 23A"

A 23A wrinkle was introduced as part of the Volcker Rule's prohibition on investments in covered funds.[30] In the so-called "Super 23A" provision, outright prohibitions are imposed on certain transactions between banking entities and covered funds that they sponsor or advise—extensions of credit, guarantees issued on behalf of the fund, and purchases of assets or securities from the fund. There has been a lingering question as to whether typical Section 23 A exemptions, described above, would apply. In the banking agencies' 2019 final rule on Volcker,[31] they clarified that the historical Section 23A exemptions apply, and they provided an additional exemption for an extension of credit to, or purchase of asset from, a covered fund, as long as:

- the transaction is in the ordinary course of business in connection with payment transactions, settlement services, or futures, derivatives, and securities clearing;
- each extension of credit is repaid, sold, or terminated by the end of five business days; and
- the banking entity making each extension of credit has established and maintains policies and procedures reasonably designed to manage the credit exposure arising from the extension of credit in a safe and sound manner and ensure that it is on market terms, and has no reason to believe that the covered fund will have difficulty repaying the extension of credit in accordance with its terms.

Basic Provisions of Section 23B

Section 23B was added in order to assure that affiliates did not have sweetheart deals with banks and their subsidiaries. As a result, it sweeps more broadly in terms of the transactions that it covers. For purposes of Section 23B, the terms "subsidiary" and "affiliate" have the same meaning as in Section 23A except the term "affiliate" does not include an insured depository institution.

Market Terms Requirement.[32] Section 23B requires that certain transactions between a bank and its affiliates be on "market terms," that is, on terms including credit standards that are prevailing at the time for comparable transactions, or in the absence of comparable transactions, on terms that in good faith would be offered to nonaffiliated companies. This means that banks must either find comparables for the transaction

30. Discussed in Chapter 9, *infra*, in the context of bank investments.
31. Prohibitions and Restrictions on Proprietary Trading and Certain Interests in, and Relationships With, Hedge Funds and Private Equity Funds, 84 Fed. Reg. 61,974 (Nov. 14, 2019).
32. 12 C.F.R. § 223.51.

or validate that the terms would be offered to unaffiliated parties. It also means that banks and their affiliates need to have arms-length, negotiated contracts in place for the transactions to which Section 23B applies.

The market terms requirement applies to all transactions that are "covered transactions" under Section 23A, with certain exceptions[33]:

- making deposits in correspondent banks;
- making a loan to, or issuing a guarantee on behalf of, an affiliate that is fully secured by U.S. obligations or a segregated, earmarked deposit account at the bank;
- purchasing "marketable securities" from an affiliate and purchasing loans from an affiliate subject to a repurchase agreement;
- transactions between banks in which one has 80% control of the other;
- transactions between sister banks; and
- purchasing loans on a nonrecourse basis from an affiliated depository institution.

Furthermore, the requirement applies to the following transactions that are *not* "covered transactions" under Section 23A:

- payments of money or furnishing services to an affiliate;
- transactions in which an affiliate acts as an agent or broker or receives a fee for its services to the bank or to any other person; and
- transactions with a third party if an affiliate has a financial interest in the third party or is a participant in the transaction.

Prohibited Asset Purchases.[34] A bank or its subsidiary may not purchase as fiduciary any securities (as defined in Section 3(a)(10) of the Securities Exchange Act of 1934[35]) from an affiliate unless the purchase is permitted: (i) under the instrument creating the fiduciary relationship, (ii) by court order, or (iii) by the law of the jurisdiction governing the fiduciary relationship.

Banks either acting as principal or fiduciary are also prohibited from purchasing or otherwise acquiring any security during the existence of any underwriting or selling syndicate, if a principal underwriter of that security is an affiliate of such bank, unless: (i) the purchase was approved, before the securities were initially offered for sale to the public, by a majority of the directors of the bank; and (ii) the approval was based on a determination that the purchase is a sound investment for the bank irrespective of the fact that an affiliate of the bank is the principal underwriter.

33. 12 C.F.R. § 223.52.
34. 12 C.F.R. § 223.53.
35. 15 U.S.C. Section 78c(a)(10).

Advertising Rules.[36] A bank or any subsidiary or affiliate of a bank may not publish any advertisement or enter into any agreement stating or suggesting that the bank shall in any way be responsible for the obligations of its affiliates. This provision, however, does not prohibit a bank from issuing a guarantee, acceptance, or letter of credit on behalf of an affiliate, confirming a letter of credit, or entering into a cross-affiliate netting arrangement, to the extent the transaction satisfies the quantitative limits and collateral requirements of Section 23A.

Examples

Several simple transactions between a bank and the other members of the bank holding company family will be subject to the quantitative limitations and collateral requirements of Section 23A and the additional requirements of Section 23B.

Loan to Holding Company: If a subsidiary bank makes a loan to a holding company subsidiary, this transaction will fall within the category of "covered transactions." As a covered transaction, the bank would be subject to the quantitative limitations of Section 23A and the applicable restrictions of Section 23B. Further, since the loan is an extension of credit to an affiliate requiring collateral security, the transaction will be subject to the collateral requirements of Section 23A.

Holding Company Stock as Collateral for Bank Loan: If a customer of a subsidiary bank offers stock of a holding company to secure a loan from the subsidiary bank, this transaction will also fall within the category of "covered transactions." Since this transaction does not create a repayment obligation of an affiliate, the bank will not be subject to the collateral requirements of Section 23A, but will be subject to the quantitative limitations of Section 23A and the applicable restrictions of Section 23B. The affiliate for these purposes is the issuer of the stock—the holding company.

Bank Lease of Property from Holding Company: If a subsidiary bank leases property from a holding company, this transaction will not fall within the definition of "covered transactions," and the bank will not be subject to the limitations or requirements of Section 23A. However, as this transaction is one of the specified transactions under Section 23B, the lease must be on comparable terms as leases offered to nonaffiliates and it must comply with the other applicable restrictions of Section 23B.

Bank Loan of Operating Funds to Its Insurance Agency Subsidiary: A nonbank subsidiary of a bank engaged in insurance sales is excluded from the definition of "affiliate" by Regulation Y, even if it is a financial subsidiary otherwise. Therefore, neither the quantitative nor qualitative restrictions

36. 12 C.F.R. § 223.54.

of Section 23A nor the additional restrictions of Section 23B would apply to a bank loan to its nonbank subsidiary.

Insider Loans

Sections 22(g) and 22(h) of the Federal Reserve Act ("FRA")[37] impose restrictions on extensions of credit a bank may make to the bank's directors, executive officers, and principal stockholders. These restrictions also apply, with certain exceptions, to persons who hold these insider positions in the bank's affiliates.[38] Subsidiaries of banks are considered part of the bank itself under this law, as with Sections 23A and B. As a result, extensions of credit by bank subsidiaries to the bank's insiders are counted as loans made by the bank for purposes of the insider lending restrictions.

The Federal Reserve's insider loan rules are implemented by Regulation O.[39] As it did with the FRA's provisions on transactions with affiliates, Congress extended the FRA sections on insider loans to state nonmember banks and savings associations.[40] Regulation O also applies to credit card banks, industrial loan companies ("ILCs"), and certain other institutions that are excluded from the definition of "bank" under the Bank Holding Company Act ("BHCA")[41] and to the companies that control these institutions.

Principal Provisions of Regulation O

Regulation O applies to insiders, which are defined with the following permutations:

---

37. 12 U.S.C. Section 375a and 375b, respectively.
38. Affiliates include any parent company of the bank and any subsidiary of the parent company that represents 10% or more of the consolidated assets of the parent company.
39. 12 C.F.R. Part 215.
40. These rules are applied to state nonmember banks by Section 18(j) of the Federal Deposit Insurance Act (FDIA) (12 U.S.C. § 1828(j)). Section 22(h) of the FRA, which deals with loans to all insiders and executive officers, was applied to state nonmember banks in 1978 by Section 108 of Pub. Law 95-630 (Nov. 10, 1978), 92 Stat. 3664. Section 22(g), relating to loans to executive officers, was added to Section 18(j) by Section 306(k) of FDICIA, Pub. Law 102-242, Dec. 19, 1991, 105 Stat. 2236. Insider loan rules are applied to savings associations by Section 11(b) of the Home Owners' Loan Act (HOLA) (12 U.S.C. § 1468(b)). Section 22(h) of the FRA was applied to savings associations by Section 301 of FIRREA. Regulation O now applies to savings associations. *See*, 12 C.F.R. § 163.43.
41. 12 U.S.C. § 1811, *et seq*. Credit card banks and ILCs are excluded from this definition by Sec. 2(c)(2)(F) and (H), respectively, of the BHCA and are discussed in Chapter 10, *infra*.

- *Insiders* are defined as directors, executive officers, and principal shareholders. Regulation O imposes limits not only on extensions of credit the bank may make to its own insiders but also, with some exceptions, on extensions of credit to persons who are insiders of the bank's subsidiaries, parent company, if any, and certain subsidiaries of the parent company.[42]
- *Directors*. This term is given its normal meaning; Regulation O provides that a person's status as a director is not dependent on the person receiving compensation for his or her service. Advisory directors who are unelected, who do not vote and are not authorized to vote on matters before the board of directors, and who provide solely general policy advice are not "directors" for purposes of Regulation O.
- *Executive officers*. Executive officers of a company or bank are persons who participate or have authority to participate (other than in the capacity of a director) in major policymaking functions of the company or bank regardless of their title. It should be noted, however, that there are certain officer positions that are presumed under Regulation O to be executive officer positions, including:
    - chairman of the board;
    - president;
    - vice president;
    - secretary;
    - treasurer; or
    - cashier.

The above-mentioned officers will be considered "executive officers" for purposes of Regulation O, *unless* (i) the officer is excluded by resolution of the board of directors or by the bylaws of the entity, from participating (other than as a director) in major policymaking functions of the entity; and (ii) the person does not in fact participate in them.

Board resolutions excluding an individual from the designation of "executive officer" will only pass regulatory muster if the person may not participate in major policymaking functions, and in fact, does not participate in major policymaking functions. The terms "authority to participate" and "major policymaking functions" are not defined by Regulation O. However, when considering whether an individual is an "executive officer" for purposes of Regulation O, banking regulators may determine on a case-by-case basis whether an individual is responsible for the formulation and implementation of major policy. Regulators have a fair amount of discretion in determining

42. Subsidiaries of a parent company that represent 10% or less of the consolidated assets of the parent company are generally excluded from coverage under Regulation O.

the types of duties that constitute major policymaking functions, but have often focused on involvement in areas of key importance for a banking institution, such as lending, audit, investments, and trust activities. There tends to be a heavy regulatory presumption against excluding certain officers from the designation of executive officer, including: (i) any officer whose title contains the word "Chief;" and (ii) the chairman of the board.

Principal Shareholders. These are persons other than banks (and any company that controls the bank) that, directly or indirectly, or "acting through or in concert with others," own or control the power to vote more than 10% of any class of voting shares of a bank or company. For purposes of determining whether an individual is a principal shareholder for purposes of Regulation O, shares owned or controlled by a member of a person's "immediate family" are considered to be held by that person. "Immediate family" is defined in Regulation O to include the spouse of an individual, the individual's minor children, and any of the individual's children (including adults) residing in the individual's home. Although there is no definition of "acting in concert" in Regulation O, for purposes of determining whether an individual or an entity is **"acting in concert"** with other shareholders, Federal Reserve Regulation Y is instructive. Federal Reserve Regulation Y establishes various presumptions of concerted action that are applicable to a determination of acting in concert under Regulation O.[43] Because Regulation Y contains a much broader definition of "immediate family" than the one in Regulation O, it significantly broadens the scope of persons whose ownership may be aggregated together and treated as "principal shareholders" under Regulation O.

---

43. Federal Reserve Regulation Y presumes that the following individuals and entities are acting in concert:
    - a company and any controlling shareholder, partner, trustee, or management official of the company, if both the company and the person own voting securities of the related interest;
    - an individual and the individual's **"immediate family"**;
    - companies under common control;
    - persons who are parties to any agreement, contract, understanding, relationship, or other arrangement, whether written or otherwise, regarding the acquisition, voting, or transfer of control of voting securities of the related interest, other than through a revocable proxy;
    - persons that have made, or propose to make, a joint filing under laws and regulations of the Securities and Exchange Commission; and
    - a person and any trust for which the person serves as trustee.

    Regulation Y defines **"immediate family"** for purposes of the "acting in concert" standard to include an individual's father, mother, stepfather, stepmother, brother, sister, stepbrother, stepsister, son, daughter, stepson, stepdaughter, grandparent, grandson, granddaughter, father-in-law, mother-in-law, brother-in-law, sister-in-law, son-in-law, daughter-in-law, spouse of any of the aforementioned individuals, and spouse.

Related Interests. Regulation O covers extensions of credit to insiders and to their "related interests." These are businesses and other companies controlled by the insider and political or campaign committees that are controlled by an insider or that provide funds or services that benefit the insider. Regulation O establishes a conclusive presumption of control triggered when a person, directly or indirectly, or acting through or in concert with others: (i) owns, controls, or has the power to vote 25% or more of a class of the voting securities of an entity; (ii) controls in any manner over the election of a majority of the directors of the company; or (iii) has the ability to exercise a controlling influence over the management or policies of the company (regardless of the individual's percentage ownership interest in the company). Regulation O establishes rebuttable presumptions of control triggered when a person, directly or indirectly, or *acting in concert* with others,[44] owns, controls, or has the power to vote more than 10% and less than 25% of any class of the company's voting securities if the individual either: (i) is an executive officer or director of the company[45]; or (ii) is the company's single largest holder of the company's voting securities.

Loan Limits

An "extension of credit" is defined broadly under Regulation O to include virtually any transaction as a result of which a person becomes obligated to pay money or its equivalent to a bank. This includes not only loans and lines of credit, but also certain advances of unearned salary, overdraft advances,[46] certain standby letters of credit, and more. Moreover, the Dodd-Frank Act expanded the definition of "extension of credit" to include credit exposure to a person from a derivative transaction, repurchase agreement, reverse repurchase agreement, securities lending transaction, or securities borrowing transaction.

There are four sets of overlapping loan limits in Regulation O:

- loans to all insiders that require prior board approval;
- separate rules on loans to executive officers of the bank;

---

44. *Id.* for definition of "acting in concert."
45. A person is considered to be a "director" of a company for purposes of the above if the person is:
    - a member of a member-managed limited liability company;
    - a manager of a manager-managed limited liability company;
    - a trustee of a trust;
    - a partner of a general partnership; or
    - a general partner of a limited partnership.
46. Overdraft advances by executive officers and directors of a bank are subject to separate and distinct restrictions set forth in 12 C.F.R. § 215.4(e).

- a ceiling on the aggregate amount of loans a bank may have outstanding to all insiders at any one time; and
- a limit on the maximum amount of loans that may be outstanding to a single borrower.

Loans to insiders of the bank, its subsidiaries, and certain affiliates (except loans to executive officers of the bank) and loans to the related interests of those insiders, require prior approval of a majority of the entire bank's board of directors (with any interested director recusing themselves from discussion and abstaining from the vote) if, when combined with all other outstanding loans from the bank to that person and the person's related interests, they would exceed either: the greater of $25,000 or 5% of the bank's unimpaired capital and unimpaired surplus[47]; or $500,000. Prior board approval is not required if the loan is made pursuant to a line of credit approved by the board within 14 months of the loan.

Bank Executive Officer "Carve Out." Separate rules apply to extensions of credit to executive officers of the bank. These rules permit the following extensions of credit, subject to the bank's normal underwriting standards:

- Loans "in any amount" to executive officers for financing, subject to certain restrictions, the purchase, construction, or rehabilitation of their principal residence, for education of their children, and loans secured by certain interests in securities or by a segregated account.[48] The phrase "in any amount" in Regulation O means that the loans can be for any amount up to the loans to one borrower limit summarized below, so long as the loan is made on a non-preferential basis and the executive officer meets the bank's underwriting standards for the loan.
- Loans for "other purposes," which may not exceed at any one time the higher of 2.5% of the bank's unimpaired capital and unimpaired surplus or $25,000, but in no event more than $100,000.

Maximum Loan to One Borrower. Regulation O provides that the maximum extension of credit that may be outstanding by a member bank to any one insider and his or her related interests is the loans to one borrower ("LTOB") limit that is applied to national banks by Section 5200 of the Revised Statutes.[49] This limit is:

---

47. A bank's unimpaired capital and unimpaired surplus equals the bank's Tier 1 and Tier 2 capital plus the balance of the bank's allowance for loan and lease losses not included in its Tier 2 capital for regulatory reporting purposes.
48. Restrictions and parameters for these types of loans are set forth in 12 C.F.R. § 215.5(c)(2) and (c)(3).
49. 12 U.S.C. § 84. *See* discussion below.

- 15% of the bank's unimpaired capital and surplus for extensions of credit not fully secured; plus
- an additional 10% of the bank's unimpaired capital and unimpaired surplus in the case of extensions of credit that are fully secured by readily marketable collateral.

For state member banks chartered in a state that has a LTOB limit lower than that provided in Section 5200, the lower rate will prevail. Additional requirements and restrictions apply to overdrafts of directors and executive officers of member banks.[50]

Aggregate Loan Limit

Section 22(h) provides that, subject to certain exceptions, the aggregate amount of extensions of credit outstanding to all insiders may not exceed the bank's unimpaired capital and unimpaired surplus.[51] Banks with deposits of less than $100 million that are well managed and well capitalized may have up to twice that amount if authorized by an annual resolution of the bank's board of directors, which must determine, among other things, that the higher limit is consistent with safe and sound banking practices.[52]

In addition to the quantitative restrictions on extensions of credit to insiders described above, Regulation O also imposes qualitative requirements on insider loans. Regulation O requires that an extension of credit:

- be made on substantially the same terms as, and following underwriting standards that are no less stringent than, those prevailing at the time for comparable transactions with noninsiders; and
- does not involve more than the normal risk of repayment or present other unfavorable features.[53]

Temporary Relief from Regulation O Restrictions for Certain Insider Loans

In response to the coronavirus pandemic, Congress authorized the Paycheck Protection Program ("PPP") as part of the Coronavirus Aid, Relief, and Economic Security Act (the "CARES" Act),[54] designed to assist small businesses impacted by the pandemic. The Small Business Administration ("SBA") is responsible for the administration of the program. Since the initial

50. 12 C.F.R. § 215.4(e).
51. *Id. See also,* 12 C.F.R. § 215.4(d).
52. 12 C.F.R. § 215.4(d)(2).
53. 12 C.F.R § 215.4.
54. Pub.L. 116–136 (2020) signed into law on Mar. 27, 2020.

implementation of the PPP, the SBA has released a series of guidance and FAQs to clarify the scope and parameters of the program.

On April 14, 2020, the SBA issued written guidance clarifying that eligible businesses owned by outside bank directors and shareholders who own less than a 30% equity interest in their financial institution may obtain PPP loans from their banks. Such loans would normally be covered and limited by Regulation O. However, in response to the SBA's guidance, the Federal Reserve issued an Interim Final Rule, effective April 22, 2020, exempting certain PPP loans from the requirements of Regulation O. Under the Federal Reserve's Interim Final Rule, for purposes of Regulation O, "extensions of credit" to insiders (other than executive officers) do not include PPP loans made between February 15, 2020, and June 30, 2020, that are permissible under the SBA guidelines. PPP loans to insiders that do not meet applicable SBA lending requirements do not qualify for the exception contained in the Federal Reserve's Interim Final Rule.

Recordkeeping Requirements

Recordkeeping for Insiders of the Bank. Regulation O requires banks to adopt recordkeeping methods that:

- identify, through an annual survey, all insiders of the bank; and
- maintain records of all extensions of credit to insiders of the bank itself, including the amount and terms of each such extension of credit.[55]

Recordkeeping for Insiders of Affiliates. Regulation O has also required banks to identify all directors, officers, and principal shareholders of the bank and its affiliates and their related interests and to specify the amounts and terms of all credit extended to these insiders. By the time the Federal Reserve Board considered adoption of amendments to Regulation O in 1994, it was obvious that financial institution holding companies had become so large and widely dispersed that literal compliance with these requirements was not practical. The Federal Reserve realized that large banking organizations with "hundreds of affiliates with thousands of officers and directors would have no practical way to know who they are or whether they have a loan with the bank"[56] and adopted an amendment to Regulation O permitting banks to use one of the three following methods to make these reports:

55. 12 C.F.R. § 215.8(b).
56. Staff memo presented Jan. 24, 1994, during meeting at which the Board adopted final regulations amending Regulation O at 56 Fed. Reg. 8,837 (Feb. 24, 1994).

- *Survey method.* Identifying each insider of the bank's affiliates through an annual survey and keeping records of extensions of credit made to these insiders;
- *Borrower inquiry method.* Requiring as part of each extension of credit that the borrower indicate whether the borrower is an insider of an affiliate of the bank, and maintaining records that identify the amount and terms of each extension of credit by the bank to borrowers so identifying themselves; or
- *Alternative recordkeeping method.* As approved by the banks' principal federal regulator.[57]

Other Reports

Upon receipt of a written request from a member of the public, a bank must disclose the names of its executive officers and principal shareholders who, along with their related interests, received extensions of credit from the bank as of the latest previous quarter of the year, that in the aggregate equaled or exceeded 5% of the bank's capital and unimpaired surplus or $500,000, whichever amount is less.[58] Additionally, each executive officer or director of a bank that is not publicly traded must report annually to the board of directors the outstanding amount of any extension of credit that is secured by the stock of the bank.[59]

Purchases of Assets from Insiders

Section 615 of the Dodd-Frank Act extends the protections afforded by Regulation O by adding a section prohibiting an insured depository institution from purchasing an asset from an "insider" unless: the transaction is on market terms; and, if it represents more than 10% of the capital of the bank, it is approved in advance by a majority of the disinterested members of the board of directors.[60]

Loans to One Borrower

The oldest form of prudential regulation governs how much a bank may lend to one borrower. The "lending limit" or "loans to one borrower" (LTOB) limit is intended to assure that no concentration of credit exists such that one borrower could cause the failure of the bank. It also promotes diversification of the loan portfolio. The lending limit for national banks is

57. 12 C.F.R. § 215.8(c).
58. 12 C.F.R. § 215.9(b).
59. 12 C.F.R. § 215.10.
60. *Amending* Section 18 of the FDIA (12 U.S.C. § 2828) by adding a subsection (z).

codified at 12 U.S.C. § 84 (Section 5200 of the Revised Statutes), with the OCC regulations at 12 C.F.R. Part 32. The OCC published an Interim Final Rule on June 21, 2012,[61] in order to amend its regulation to consolidate the lending limit rules applicable to national banks and savings associations and remove its separate regulation governing lending limits for savings associations. Thus, the OCC rules apply to federal savings associations from July 21, 2012, forward. Note: the banking agencies also supervise concentrations at banks, and that is different from LTOB. A concentration could be numerous loans to one industry or in one segment (e.g., commercial loans) and the agencies have issued various guidelines, usually under the rubric of safety and soundness, with respect to concentrations of credit.

National banks and Federal Thrifts. The lending limit for national banks and federal savings associations is 15% of the institution's capital and surplus (defined in the same manner as for Regulation W and Regulation O), plus an additional 10% of the institution's capital and surplus if the loan is fully secured by readily marketable collateral (the "general lending limit").[62] Readily marketable collateral is narrowly defined to include financial instruments (securities traded on a national exchange, commercial paper, negotiated certificates of deposit, and shares of mutual funds) and bullion that are salable under ordinary market conditions with reasonable promptness at a fair value determined by quotations based on actual transactions at an auction or similarly available daily bid and ask price markets.[63]

In addition, loans made by a national bank to a corporate group may not, in the aggregate, exceed 50% of the lending bank's capital and surplus.[64] This 50% limitation applies even if loans to some or all of the members of the corporate group are not required to be combined for purposes of the general lending limit. OCC regulations define a corporate group as consisting of a person or entity and all other entities in which such person or entity owns 50% or more of the voting securities or voting interests.

State Banks. State banks and state savings associations are subject to similar provisions under state law, although they tend to be less stringent.

Disparity Relief. The regulations of the OCC include provisions that address, in part, this lending limit disparity between national banks and state-chartered banks in states that have higher lending limits than national banks. Under the OCC lending limit regulations,[65] an eligible national bank is able (subject to receipt of prior OCC approval) to increase its lending limit with respect to one- to four-family residential real estate loans, loans

---

61. 77 Fed. Reg. 37,265 (June 21, 2012).
62. 12 U.S.C. § 84(a).
63. 12 C.F.R. § 32.2(n).
64. 12 C.F.R. § 32.5(d).
65. 12 C.F.R. § 32.7.

to small businesses, and certain agricultural loans by an amount equal to the lesser of (i) 10% of its capital and surplus or (ii) the percent of its capital and surplus, in excess of 15%, that a state-chartered bank is permitted to lend under the applicable laws of the state in which the national bank's main office is located (the "increased lending limits"). A national bank's outstanding loans to any one borrower made under the increased lending limits, when aggregated with loans made to the same borrower under the OCC's general lending limit, may not exceed 25% of the lending bank's capital and surplus. Further, a national bank's total outstanding loans to all borrowers made under the increased lending limits may not exceed 100% of the bank's capital and surplus.

Extensions of Credit

Lending limits apply to a vast assortment of transactions defined generally as "loans or extensions of credit":

- a contractual commitment to advance funds
- purchase of securities subject to repurchase; exception for government securities where a bank has assured control over the collateral
- purchase of third-party paper subject to repurchase
- overdrafts, whether prearranged or not, but not intraday
- charged off loans, unless unenforceable
- Fed funds sold with a maturity of more than one day
- guarantee fund and initial margin to a clearing house.[66]

The OCC also implemented Section 610 of the Dodd-Frank Act, to amend the statutory definition of "loans and extensions of credit" to include credit exposures arising from derivative transactions, repurchase agreements, reverse repurchase agreements, securities lending transactions, and securities borrowing transactions, effective on January 1, 2013.[67]

The following are NOT loans or extensions of credit:

- additional advances for taxes, insurance, utilities to preserve the value of the collateral of the bank
- financed sale of a bank's own assets
- accrued interest
- renewal or restructured loans if no new money or new borrower
- nonrecourse participation where credit risk is shared
- commercial letters of credit, not standby or commitments.[68]

---

66. 12 C.F.R. § 32.2(k)(1).
67. 77 Fed. Reg. 37,265 (June 21, 2012).
68. 12 C.F.R. § 32.2(k)(2).

In addition, there are numerous exceptions, including:

- loans secured by U.S. obligations or those guaranteed by a federal agency
- loans to or guaranteed by the general obligations of a state or political subdivision loans secured by segregated deposit accounts
- loans secured by discount of commercial paper
- 35% limit for loans secured by bills of lading or warehouse receipts covering readily marketable staples
- loans participated without recourse to the originating bank—do not count the amount of participations.

Attribution Rules

What makes lending limit law more difficult is that "one borrower" is much broader in practice than one individual or one company. Section 84(d)(2) provides authority to the OCC to determine when a loan putatively made to one person shall be attributable to another person. The regulations of the OCC[69] require a loan to a named borrower to be attributed to other borrower(s) under a direct benefit test and a common enterprise test:

- If the named borrower is a partnership, joint venture, or association, the loan will be attributed to the partners or members of the entity unless: (i) the agreement establishing the partnership, joint venture, or association provides that the members of the entity are not personally liable for the obligations of the entity; and (ii) those provisions of the agreement are valid under applicable law.
- A loan to a named borrower will be attributed to the other borrower(s) if: (i) the proceeds of the loan, or assets purchased with loan proceeds, are transferred to the other borrower(s), other than in a bona fide arm's-length transaction where the proceeds are used to acquire goods, property, or services; or (ii) a common enterprise exists between the named borrower and the other borrower(s).
- A common enterprise will be found to exist if:
    - the expected source of repayment for loans made to both the named borrower and the other borrower(s) are the same and no borrower has another source of income from which the loan and the borrower's other obligations can be repaid;

---

69. 12 C.F.R. § 32.5.

- the named borrower and the other borrower(s) are related through common control[70] and there is substantial financial interdependence between the borrowers;[71]
- the named borrower and the other borrower(s) use the loan proceeds to acquire more than 50% of a business enterprise, without regard to whether each borrower is otherwise creditworthy independently of either the business enterprise or the other borrower(s); or
- the OCC determines that a common enterprise exists based on the facts and circumstances of a particular transaction.[72]

National banks would generally be required to combine loans to separate borrowers when the source of repayment for the loans is the same, the creditworthiness of the named borrower would not justify the loan without reliance on the creditworthiness of the other borrower(s), or the primary beneficiary of the loan was the other borrower(s) rather than the named borrower.

Noncompliant and Nonconforming Loans

When a bank makes a loan that is "overline," i.e., over the lending limit when it is made, the board of directors is deemed to be personally responsible for the loan until the last penny is paid.[73] That is pretty sobering news to any client and is a very effective prophylactic to assure compliance.

Loans are deemed nonconforming if they later exceed the lending limit. No remedy is required during the term of the loan if the loan complied with

70. For purposes of the OCC's lending limit rules, control is presumed to exist when a person or entity, directly or indirectly, or acting through or together with one or more persons or entities: (i) owns, controls, or has the power to vote 25% or more of the voting securities of an entity; (ii) controls in any manner the election of a majority of an entity's directors, trustees, or persons exercising similar functions; or (iii) has the power to exercise a controlling influence over the management and policies of an entity.
71. "Substantial financial interdependence" is deemed to exist if 50% or more of the annual gross receipts or gross expenditures of one borrower are derived from transactions with another person or entity.
72. Factors that have been considered by the OCC in making such a determination include whether the borrowers: (i) engage in supporting lines of business; (ii) interchange goods and services; (iii) share common ownership of assets, common management, or use of common facilities; (iv) commingle assets and liabilities; (v) engage in closely related business activities; (vi) have similar structures, financing, and holdings; (vii) may receive financial aid from each other; (viii) are members of the same family; and (ix) pledge assets to support another's loans.
73. del Junco v. Conover, *aff'd*, 682 F2d 1338 (9th Cir. 1982). This policy has now been codified in the FDIA, permitting the banking agencies to seek restitution form directors for violations of law. *See*, 12 U.S.C. § 1818(b)(6).

limits when made. However, if the collateral value declines, the borrower must post more collateral within 30 days. Additionally, before a bank can renew a nonconforming loan, it must make a good faith effort to bring the loan back into compliance with the lending limit.

Interplay among Prudential Regulations

There are numerous situations in which a given loan may be subject to the lending limit, as well as Regulation W and/or Regulation O. In addition, a bank may buy debt of a customer that is subject to different rules under investment limitations in 12 U.S.C. Section 24 (Seventh) and 12 C.F.R. Part 1. How are these reconciled? According to the OCC, the lending limit does not apply to covered transactions with affiliates; it does apply to Regulation O loans; and the investment limits provide additional leeway such that a bank may invest in debt up to the limit in Section 24 (Seventh) and 12 C.F.R. Part 1 (10%) and loan that borrower up to the lending limit.[74]

74. 12 C.F.R. § 32.1(c)(1)-(3).

7

Societal Objectives/ Purpose

Are Banks Charged with Societal Purpose?

With the safety net comes responsibility. "If finance succeeds for all of us, it helps to build a good society."[1] We have certainly witnessed times when finance failed us, and for that, we get lots of law forcing good behavior. The topics selected for this chapter are exemplary of banks serving on the frontline and leveraging their position for the betterment of, and protection of, us and our society.

Depository Institutions Meeting the Convenience and Needs of Their Communities

Depository institutions accept deposits willy-nilly. We rarely see discrimination in deposit-taking. It is cheap funding, and they get to redeploy those funds in the economy. Societal purpose demands fair lending and investing, meeting the convenience and needs of their communities.

Against a backdrop of redlining and discriminatory credit practices, Congress enacted numerous federal laws in the 1970s and 1980s intended to force banks to this end. Redlining refers to the presumed practice of lenders, especially mortgage lenders, of drawing red lines around portions of their service area map to indicate areas or neighborhoods in which they would not make loans.[2] Needless to say, these redlined areas were not golf course communities; they were low- and moderate-income ("LMI") neighborhoods.

1. Robert Shiller, FINANCE AND THE GOOD SOCIETY (Princeton University Press, 2012).
2. Federal Reserve, Consumer Compliance Handbook, Fair Housing Act, p. 1.

In other words, there was a practice of denying creditworthy applicants loans because they lived in an excluded neighborhood even though the applicants were otherwise eligible for the loan. The vast majority of laws enacted in this space are prescriptive and punitive in nature and are now under the jurisdiction of the Bureau of Consumer Financial Protection ("CFPB"), outside the scope of this book. But, one remains banking law, enforced by the prudential bank regulators, namely the Community Reinvestment Act ("CRA").[3]

Community Reinvestment

CRA, enacted by Congress in 1977, is different in most respects from its brethren. It is intended to incent depository institutions to help meet the credit needs of the entirety of the communities in which they operate through a system of "carrots and sticks." Each institution's record in this regard is evaluated periodically by the federal agencies that are responsible for supervising the depository institution: the Board of Governors of the Federal Reserve System ("Federal Reserve"), the Federal Deposit Insurance Corporation ("FDIC"), and the Office of the Comptroller of the Currency ("OCC"). Today, much of the guidance on CRA is deposited on the website of the Federal Financial Institutions Examination Council ("FFIEC") at www.ffiec.gov/cra/.

How did this begin? With Congressional findings that: (i) regulated financial institutions are required by law to demonstrate that their deposit facilities serve the convenience and needs of the communities in which they are chartered to do business; (ii) the convenience and needs of communities include the need for credit services as well as deposit services; and (iii) regulated financial institutions have continuing and affirmative obligation to help meet the credit needs of the local communities in which they are chartered.[4] Note, however, there remains an emphasis on safe and sound lending. Nothing about CRA says banks should make bad loans or bad investments.

CRA as Leverage

The tools to enforce CRA are unique. The law is not about consumer compliance (although a bad CRA record no doubt means other antidiscrimination laws are probably in play). The law relies on a system

---

3. 12 U.S.C. § 2901, implemented by Regulations 12 CFR Parts 25 (OCC), 228 (Federal Reserve), and 345 (FDIC). The agencies have released helpful FAQs: Community Reinvestment Act; Interagency Questions and Answers Regarding Community Reinvestment, 81 Fed. Reg 48,506 (July 25, 2016).
4. 12 U.S.C. § 2901.

of leverage (those carrots and sticks), because it rewards good behavior and punishes bad behavior differently from the enforcement regime for violations of other laws.

Application Considerations. The first element of this regime rewards (and punishes) through the application approval process, such that, in connection with every application for:[5]

- a charter for a national bank or federal thrift;
- deposit insurance for a newly chartered bank;
- establishment of a branch;
- relocation of a main office or branch;
- a merger, consolidation, or deposit assumption under the Bank Merger Act; and
- a BHC acquisition of shares of a regulated financial institution under Section 3 of the Bank Holding Company Act ("BHCA"),

the responsible agency must assess the applicant's, or each party's, history of meeting the convenience and needs of the community, and to that end, it must review the CRA record of the applicant and, if relevant, the target. But there is more. Notice of all these covered transactions must be published in one or more newspapers of general circulation, comments are solicited, and hearings may be held.[6]

Our history is rife with CRA protests arising from this process that were so emotional at times that rocks have been thrown and bank executive offices have been stormed. Moreover, tens of thousands of protest letters have been sent, raising issues on numerous applications—in connection with the Citicorp and Travelers Insurance merger alone, hundreds of CRA comment letters had to be addressed.[7] To avoid the possibility of a denied or delayed application, lending institutions have an incentive to negotiate with, and make formal agreements with, community organizations. By intervening in the CRA review process, nonprofit groups have been able to gain control over pools of dedicated bank capital, which they in turn parcel out to individual low-income mortgage seekers. According to former Comptroller of the Currency, Joseph Otting, literally trillions of dollars have flown into the communities banks serve.[8] ACORN Housing received

---

5. 12 U.S.C. § 2902.
6. As discussed in Chapter 9, *infra*, in connection with applications.
7. The Board's approval of the Travelers Group Inc. application to become a BHC by acquiring Citicorp date Sept. 23, 1998, is recommended reading on how CRA comes into play in applications, https://www.federalreserve.gov/boarddocs/press/BHC/1998/19980923/19980923.pdf.
8. Joseph Otting, BankThink, *The Final CRA Rule Is In. Here's Why It's Better*, https://www.americanbanker.com/opinion/the-final-cra-rule-is-in-heres-why-its-better, May 20, 2020.

a $760 million commitment from the Bank of New York, the Boston-based Neighborhood Assistance Corporation of America negotiated a $3 billion agreement with Bank of America; and a coalition of groups headed by New Jersey Citizen Action negotiated a five-year, $13-billion agreement with First Union Corporation. Similar deals operate in almost every major U.S. city.[9] And so, deals get done.

Examination. As discussed in Chapter 11, bank regulatory agencies conduct specialized CRA examinations,[10] where banks are assigned an overall CRA Rating using a four-tiered rating system: Outstanding, Satisfactory, Needs to Improve, and Substantial Noncompliance. Unlike other examination ratings, these ratings are available to the public.

FHC Status. Further, a bank holding company ("BHC") may not become a financial holding company ("FHC") unless each subsidiary depository institution has at least a satisfactory rating. In this regard, the BHCA directs the Federal Reserve to prohibit FHCs from establishing or acquiring financial companies if any bank or thrifts controlled by the FHC have received a less than satisfactory CRA rating in their most recent CRA exam. It also renders ineffective any FHC declaration made when the CRA test is not met.[11]

Standards for Assessing CRA Performance

The agencies use three tests in assessing CRA performance: a lending test, an investment test, and a service test based on the assessment area. Banks may also use strategic plans if approved by the appropriate regulator. There are special rules for wholesale banks, limited purpose banks, and community banks.

Assessment Areas.[12] Remember the map with the redlines? CRA requires that map to accurately reflect a bank's various service areas with no exclusions and no detours—no red lines. Thus, at the core of CRA are the geographic zones tied to the physical components of financial institutions: offices, branches, and ATMs. Banks must delineate one or more of these areas based generally on metropolitan statistical areas ("MSAs"). They must be whole geographies.

Lending Test.[13] The lending test evaluates a bank's record of helping to meet the credit needs of its assessment area(s) through its lending

9. https://www.city-journal.org/html/trillion-dollar-bank-shakedown-bodes-ill-cities-12096.html.
10. 12 U.S.C. § 2903(a).
11. Section 103(b) of the Gramm-Leach-Bliley Act amends Section 804 of the CRA to this end (codified at 12 U.S.C. § 2903).
12. *See, e.g.*, 12 C.F.R. § 228.41 (Federal Reserve).
13. *See, e.g.*, 12 C.F.R. § 228.22 (Federal Reserve).

activities by considering a bank's home mortgage, small business, small farm, and community development lending. If consumer lending constitutes a substantial majority of a bank's business, the agency will evaluate the bank's consumer lending in one or more of the following categories: motor vehicle, credit card, other secured, and other unsecured loans. In addition, at a bank's option, the agency will evaluate one or more categories of consumer lending, if the bank has collected and maintained data for each category that the bank elects to have the agency evaluate. The agency considers originations and purchases of loans. The agency will also consider any other loan data the bank may choose to provide, including data on loans outstanding, commitments, and letters of credit.

Investment Test.[14] The investment test evaluates a bank's record of helping to meet the credit needs of its assessment area(s) through qualified investments that benefit its assessment area(s) or a broader statewide or regional area that includes the bank's assessment area(s). Activities considered under the lending or service tests may not be considered under the investment test.

Service Test.[15] The service test evaluates a bank's record of helping to meet the credit needs of its assessment area(s) by analyzing both the availability and effectiveness of a bank's systems for delivering retail banking services and the extent and innovativeness of its community development services.

Coronavirus Implications

The coronavirus pandemic raised interesting questions about CRA and unveiled unique needs for revitalization and stabilization activities that differ from those typically undertaken in response to natural disasters or other emergencies. As such, the federal banking agencies released a March 19, 2020, Joint Statement[16] effective through the six-month period after the national emergency declaration lifted, unless extended by the agencies, and followed with Frequently Asked Questions ("FAQs") related to COVID-19. Examples of qualified activities include loans, investments, or community development services that support, on a temporary basis:

- emergency medical care, including medical facility services and supplies, temporary medical facilities, and enhanced medical/hospital capacity;

14. *See, e.g.*, 12 C.F.R. § 228.23 (Federal Reserve).
15. *See, e.g.*, 12 C.F.R. § 228.24 (Federal Reserve).
16. https://www.federalreserve.gov/supervisionreg/caletters/CA%2020-4%20Attachment.pdf; https://www.fdic.gov/news/news/financial/2020/fil20019a.pdf; https://www.occ.gov/news-issuances/bulletins/2020/bulletin-2020-19.html.

- purchase and distribution of personal protective equipment;
- provision of emergency food supplies; or
- assistance to state, tribal, territorial, or local governments for emergency management and to support communications of general health and safety information to the public.

Certain qualifying Paycheck Protection Plan ("PPP") loans were also included for small business CRA credit.

2020 CRA Proposal

Over the years, there have been CRA studies and requests for comment made for or by the federal banking agencies, and a massive amount of criticism has targeted them, with many a promise made to improve. Finally, the OCC and FDIC proposed to modernize CRA[17] to better achieve the law's underlying statutory purpose, in their words, "by making the regulatory framework more objective, transparent, consistent, and easy to understand."[18] To accomplish these goals, the proposed rule would strengthen the CRA regulations by (i) clarifying which activities qualify for CRA credit, (ii) updating where activities count for CRA credit, (iii) creating a more transparent and objective method for measuring CRA performance, and (iv) providing for more transparent, consistent, and timely CRA-related data collection, recordkeeping, and reporting. Yes, that marks a sea change on the horizon.

OCC Goes It Alone. Ultimately, the OCC decided not to wait out its fellow regulators but to go it alone on CRA reform. To that end, on May 20, 2020, the agency issued its final rule substantially rewriting 12 C.F.R. Part 25 and Part 195, its CRA regulations for national banks and federal savings associations, respectively.[19] The objective was transparency: clarity on what counts; where it counts; how to count it; and to make recordkeeping more transparent and timelier.[20] Specifically, the final rule: (i) clarifies and expands the bank lending, investment, and services (collectively, qualifying activities or CRA activities) that qualify for positive CRA consideration; (ii) updates how banks delineate the assessment areas in which they are evaluated; (iii) provides additional methods for evaluating CRA performance in a consistent and objective manner; and (iv) requires reporting that is timely and transparent. It is fair to say that the OCC came out swinging,

17. Joint Notice of Proposed Rulemaking, 85 Fed. Reg. 1204 (Jan. 9, 2020).
18. *Id.* at 1204.
19. Community Reinvestment Act Regulations, Final Rule, 85 Fed. Reg. 34, 734 (June 5, 2020).
20. Otting, *supra* note 8.

criticizing the subjectivity of CRA application in numerous ways and vowing objectivity:

> By moving from a system that is primarily subjective to one that is primarily objective and that increases clarity for all banks, CRA ratings will be more reliable, reproducible, and comparable overtime. Under the agency's final rule, the same facts and circumstances will be evaluated in a similar manner regardless of the particular region or particular examiner. CRA activities will be treated in a consistent manner from bank to bank.[21]

On the point of objectivity and clarity, a very handy tool came with: The OCC's "CRA Illustrative List," which is a nonexhaustive list of examples of activities that would qualify under 12 C.F.R. 25.04. It is keyed to subsections and paragraphs of the rule, so it is twenty-two pages that take a lot of the guesswork out of this area.

Financial Institutions Protecting Our Personal Financial Information

Financial institutions create, use, and store a myriad of our personal financial information. They obtain our social security numbers; they see our credit reports; they create our deposit account numbers and credit card numbers; they have our routing numbers; they know our passwords for online and mobile banking; they know how much we owe and the terms of the loans; and they know our payment and purchasing habits. And that intimate knowledge is shared.

Prior to the Gramm-Leach-Bliley Act of 1999 ("Gramm-Leach-Bliley"), privacy laws were inconsistent at best, and the concept of electronic data security resided somewhere in the ether of the future. There were several states that had adopted limitations on the sharing of financial and health information in the context of banking and/or insurance, and there were a handful of states that recognized a common law right to financial privacy. But the only major legislation on both the federal and state fronts was in the form of right to financial privacy laws that imposed rules on providing customer financial information to the government.[22]

21. Final Rule, *supra* note 19, 34,734-34,735.
22. The Right to Financial Privacy Act of 1978 (codified at 12 U.S.C. ch. 35, § 3401 et seq).

Gramm-Leach-Bliley

For the first time under federal law, Title V of Gramm-Leach-Bliley[23] imposed obligations on all financial institutions as to the privacy and confidentiality of nonpublic personal information ("NPPI"). To that end, the federal law[24] begins: "It is the policy of the Congress that each financial institution has an affirmative and continuing obligation to respect the privacy of its customers and to protect the security and confidentiality of those customers' nonpublic personal information." The first objective is known as the "Privacy Rule"; the second piece is known as the "Safeguards Rule." The Privacy Rule is policed by the CFPB.[25] The Safeguards Rule is policed for depository institutions by their respective primary federal banking agency.[26] This section of Keys addresses the Privacy Rule as a societal objective/compliance and disclosure matter. Chapter 8 addresses the Safeguards Rule as a matter of safety and soundness.

When the CFPB was transferred jurisdiction over the Privacy Rule under Title X of the Dodd-Frank Act Wall Street Reform and Consumer Protection Act ("Dodd-Frank"), it re-codified the prior regulations of the banking agencies in its Regulation P.[27] A valuable tool in this space is the CFPB GLBA Privacy Examination Manual posted on its website at consumerfinance.gov.

NPPI. According to Gramm-Leach-Bliley and the implementing regulation: information is NPPI subject to this law if it is personally identifiable financial information regarding consumer customers, including lists that are generated from this information. Personally identifiable financial information is any information collected about a consumer in conjunction with providing a financial product or service. This includes:

- information provided by the consumer during the application process (e.g., name, phone number, address, income);
- information resulting from the financial product or service transaction (e.g., payment history, loan or deposit balances, credit card purchases);
- information from other sources about the consumer obtained in connection with providing the financial product or service

23. Title V, Subtitle A (codified at 15 U.S.C. § 6801-6809).
24. 15 U.S.C. § 6801(a).
25. Dodd-Frank Sections 1002(12)(J), 1024(b)-(c), and 1025(b)-(c); 12 U.S.C. §§ 5481(12)(J), 5514(b)-(c), and 5515(b)-(c).
26. Section 1002(12)(J) of Dodd-Frank excluded financial institutions' information security safeguards under Gramm-Leach-Bliley Section 501(b) from the CFPB's rulemaking, examination, and enforcement authority.
27. 12 C.F.R. Part 1016.

(e.g., information from a consumer credit report or from court records); and

- any information that is disclosed in a manner that indicates that the individual is or has been a customer. Thus, the very fact that an individual is a customer is personally identifiable financial information.

State Law Issues. Keep in mind that Gramm-Leach-Bliley was enacted at a time before our lives unfolded digitally. As a result, the definition of NPPI is almost sophomoric in comparison to the information that is now created, maintained, and stored by banking institutions and their vendors. More recent state laws can be far more expansive. For instance, the California Consumer Privacy Act of 2018 ("CCPA")[28] defines "Personal information"[29] as information that identifies, relates to, describes, is reasonably capable of being associated with, or could reasonably be linked, directly or indirectly, with a particular consumer or household, including (i) identifiers such as a real name, alias, postal address, unique personal identifier, online identifier, internet protocol address, email address, account name, social security number, driver's license number, passport number, or other similar identifiers; (ii) biometric information; (iii) internet or other electronic network activity information, including, but not limited to, browsing history, search history, and information regarding a consumer's interaction with an internet website, application, or advertisement; (iv) geolocation data; (v) audio, electronic, visual, thermal, olfactory, or similar information; (vi) professional or employment-related information; (vii) education information (not otherwise publicly available); and (viii) inferences drawn from any of the information identified in this subdivision to create a profile about a consumer reflecting the consumer's preferences, characteristics, psychological trends, predispositions, behavior, attitudes, intelligence, abilities, and aptitudes.

Moreover, some state laws also cover commercial customer information. So, state law must always be factored in.

Privacy Notice. Under the Privacy Rule, banks must disclose to consumer customers how they acquire NPPI, how they use it, and how they share it and with whom. They must provide opt-outs for certain types of sharing. Banking organizations were required to release their initial written privacy notices under Gramm-Leach-Bliley on or before July 1, 2001, and annually thereafter and in connection with account opening. The agencies released model forms for the disclosure on November 17, 2009, which are

28. CAL. CIV. Code, Title 1.81.5, [1798.100 - 1798.199], added by 2018 Cal. Stat. Ch. 55, Sec. 3.
29. CAL. CIV. Code 1798.140(o)(1).

now the CFPB's model forms, so most privacy notices have the same or similar appearance.[30]

For years, privacy notices were printed and mailed annually and provided in all new account packets and loan packets. Suffice it to say, that process cost a lot of dollars and tons of paper for consumers to receive a disclosure they had seen many times before. Finally, on October 28, 2014, the CFPB imposed some common sense on the process and published a final rule, effective immediately, creating an alternative delivery method that financial institutions may use under certain circumstances.[31] The alternative delivery method allows a financial institution to provide an annual privacy notice by posting the notice on its website, if it only shares NPPI under certain exceptions.[32] If material changes are made (an opt-out is added or changes are made as to whom NPPI is shared), a written notice is once more required for that cycle.

Opt-out Exceptions. The basic rule of Gramm-Leach-Bliley is that financial institutions may not share NPPI without disclosure of their practices and without providing an opt-out. To this end, an opt-out is a clear and conspicuous notice that the financial institution reserves the right to share NPPI, the consumer has the right to withhold approval by opting out, and there must be a reasonable means for the consumer to exercise that right.[33]

The law recognizes an array of exceptions when banks may share information without an opt-out. The exceptions are in Subpart C of Regulation P, and they include sharing to process transactions, with service providers and joint marketers, in connection with mergers, and a myriad of other routine transactions. Noteworthy are:

- Service providers and joint marketers[34] – this exemption hinges on agreement terms with the provider/joint marketer and that must include use and sharing restrictions (the provider will not use the NPPI except for the purposes of the agreement and will not share the information except as needed, provided the other party is subject to the same use and sharing restrictions).
  - For the joint marketer, there must be a "joint marketing agreement," and there must be disclosure in the privacy notice

30. The model forms are in the Appendix to Regulation P. They are available online at https://www.consumerfinance.gov/policy-compliance/guidance/gramm-leach-bliley-act/model-privacy-form/.
31. 79 Fed. Reg. 64,057.
32. Delivery requirements are set forth in 12 C.F.R. § 1016.5. The exceptions are in §§ 1016.13, 1016.14, and 1016.15.
33. 12 C.F.R. § 1016.7(a).
34. 12 C.F.R. § 1016.13.

of the practice and the categories of joint marketing partners (broker-dealers, insurance agencies, credit card companies, fintechs). Joint marketing is limited under some state laws without an opt-out or opt-in.

- Affiliate sharing, as discussed further below.
- With the consent of the consumer[35] – perhaps the easiest of all options if there is any question about sharing, is to get the written consent of the customer.

Privacy Policy Considerations. There are a whole host of policy decisions each financial institution must make before it rolls out its privacy notice. Whether an institution is subject only to Gramm-Leach-Bliley or has state law applicable as well, it must know what it collects, how it is to be used, and to whom it will be disclosed. This information is then made part of an institution-wide privacy policy, and perhaps a separate website privacy policy, which describe the bank's policies and procedures with respect to NPPI. From the self-analysis and the decisions in the privacy policy, the institution may then prepare the required disclosures and develop any required functionality.

Under Gramm-Leach-Bliley, decisions must be made on sharing:

- Will the bank share NPPI among affiliates? If so, what will be shared?
    - Transaction and experience NPPI (known as "eligibility information") may be shared without limits.
    - Information from credit applications and credit reports ("creditworthiness information") may only be shared in compliance with the Fair Credit Reporting Act ("FCRA")[36] requirements. FCRA permits sharing of such information solely among affiliates, but only if an *opt-out* is provided and not exercised.

35. 12 C.F.R. § 1016.15(a)(1).
36. 15 U.S.C. § 1681 *et seq.*

    - NPPI for affiliates to market to consumer customers may only be shared if an *opt-out* is provided and not exercised.[37]
- Will the bank share with joint marketing partners to market products and services to consumer customers? The financial institution must determine what categories of parties with whom it will share. (Watch state law on this point—there are opt-out and even opt-in states.)
- Will the bank share NPPI with nonaffiliates to market products? An *opt-out* must be provided and not exercised.

When these decisions are made and the bank intends to share in a situation where an opt-out is required, it must build the functionality in its systems to block the information from being shared. In addition, let's say the bank decides to authorize sharing of lists of maturing CD holders with a broker-dealer under joint marketing, then it needs a procedure for who has authority to release the list and under what circumstances.

Obviously, the Privacy Rule is just the tip of the iceberg. It is the posting, storing, and transmittal of all that information that puts the safety and soundness of financial institutions at risk of data security breaches. That is where the Safeguards Rule and lots of state law come into play.[38]

Depository Institutions as the Frontline on Money Laundering and Terrorism Finance[39]

Deposit accounts can be used for all sorts of nefarious purposes, particularly to defraud, to launder proceeds of illegal activity, and to finance terrorism. Very scary stuff. As a consequence, Congress has created new departments, councils, and offices with regulatory authority in this space and has enacted

---

37. Affiliate sharing rules changed significantly as a result of Section 214 of the FACT Act (Pub. L. No. 108-159 (Dec. 2, 2003). The FACT Act amended FCRA as to the use of bank transaction and experience information by affiliates to market their products. Under this law, any person who receives information from an affiliate regarding the transactions of a consumer, or the institution's experience with a consumer, may not use the information to make a solicitation for marketing purposes unless the party collecting the information discloses that the information may be shared among affiliates for purposes of making such solicitations, and the consumer is provided an opportunity to opt out from receiving such solicitations. A consumer may elect to opt out of solicitations for at least five years. Financial institutions, however, are able to have shared databases with their affiliates without an opt-out. It is noteworthy that the FACT Act provisions preempt all state laws on affiliate sharing.
38. Discussed in Chapter 8, *infra*.
39. The section of this book on BSA/AML was authored by John M. Geiringer, partner, Barack Ferrazzano LLP, and Joseph E. Silvia, Counselor Howard & Howard, who are in the process of drafting a comprehensive chapter for a book on the subject.

a host of laws, many of which focus on deposit-takers and put depository institutions on the frontline to detect suspicious activity.

Statutory Authority

The federal statutory scheme is intended to combat money laundering and the financing of terrorism and other financial crimes, as well as to establish a comprehensive economic sanctions regime against terrorists and other threats to the United States, including the following:

- The Currency and Foreign Transactions Reporting Act of 1970, commonly known as the Bank Secrecy Act (the "BSA"), which has been revised by the following legislation[40]:
  - Money Laundering Control Act of 1986
  - Anti-Drug Abuse Act of 1988
  - Annunzio-Wylie Anti-Money Laundering Act of 1992
  - Money Laundering Suppression Act of 1994
  - Money Laundering and Financial Crimes Strategy Act of 1998
  - Uniting and Strengthening America by Providing Appropriate Tools to Restrict, Intercept and Obstruct Terrorism (the "USA PATRIOT") Act of 2001
  - Intelligence Reform and Terrorism Prevention Act of 2004
  - USA PATRIOT Improvement and Reauthorization Act of 2005
- Anti-Terrorism Act of 1990.[41]

Together these laws are referred to as "BSA/AML."

Government Agencies

Special federal departments, offices, and councils undertake specific roles in connection with combating money-laundering and terrorist financing ("CFT").

Office of Terrorism and Financial Intelligence. The Treasury Department maintains an Office of Terrorism and Financial Intelligence (the "OTFI"), which was established in 2004. The OTFI is responsible for providing policy, strategic, and operational direction to the Treasury Department on issues relating to the BSA, economic sanctions programs, CFT, financial crimes, and related enforcement, intelligence, and security functions.[42]

40. 12 U.S.C. §§ 1829b, 1951-1959 and 31 U.S.C. §§ 5311-5314, 5316-5332.
41. 18 U.S.C. § 2333.
42. 31 U.S.C. § 312(a)(4).

FinCEN. FinCEN, the government's financial intelligence unit, safeguards the U.S. financial system from illicit use, combats money laundering, and promotes U.S. national security through the collection, analysis, and dissemination of financial intelligence and the strategic use of financial authorities.[43] The BSA authorizes the Treasury Department, which has in turn designated FinCEN, to require banks and other financial institutions to prepare and maintain "certain reports or records where they have a high degree of usefulness in criminal, tax, or regulatory investigations or proceedings, or in the conduct of intelligence or counterintelligence activities, including analysis, to protect against international terrorism."[44] Based on that authority, FinCEN promulgates regulations that govern BSA/AML requirements for U.S. financial institutions.[45]

OFAC. OFAC currently administers and enforces almost forty economic and trade sanctions programs against certain targeted countries, entities, and individuals, based on U.S. foreign policy, national security goals, and applicable domestic and international authority, as described above. OFAC maintains and publishes an evolving list of over 6,000 individuals, groups, companies, and governmental entities ("blocked persons"), called the Specially Designated Nationals and Blocked Persons ("SDN") list.[46] The SDN list is based on various U.S. embargoes and economic sanctions programs, and includes numerous entities and individuals involved in terrorism-related activities that have been designated by the government as Foreign Terrorist Organizations, Specially Designated Terrorists, or Specially Designated Global Terrorists. Since 9/11, OFAC has designated over 800 individuals and entities under the government's various counterterrorism sanctions programs.[47]

Federal Financial Institutions Examination Council. The Federal Financial Institutions Examination Council (the "FFIEC") was established in 1979 to provide uniform principles, standards, and reporting forms for the federal examination of banks.[48] The FFIEC's member agencies include, among others, the federal banking agencies, the National Credit Union Administration, and the Consumer Financial Protection Bureau. In 2006, the State Liaison Committee ("SLC") was added to the FFIEC as a voting member. The SLC includes the Conference of State Bank Supervisors, an association that represents the interests of state banking agencies, as well

43. http://www.fincen.gov/.
44. 31 U.S.C. § 5311.
45. 31 U.S.C. § 310.
46. http://www.treasury.gov/ofac/downloads/t11sdn.pdf.
47. Written Testimony of Department of the Treasury under Secretary David S. Cohen before the U.S. Senate Subcommittee on Financial Services and General Government, Apr. 2, 2014.
48. http://www.ffiec.gov/about.htm.

as the American Council of State Savings Supervisors and the National Association of State Credit Union Supervisors.[49] The FFIEC maintains a BSA Working Group to coordinate BSA examination issues, and publishes the "Bank Secrecy Act/Anti-Money Laundering Examination Manual," which summarizes the various BSA/AML requirements with which banks must comply (the "BSA Manual").[50]

Compliance Program

At the heart of BSA/AML is the requirement that banking institutions must establish and implement an effective BSA/AML program.[51] This program must be individually tailored to take into account the bank's size, complexity, geographic footprint, customer base, and products and services. At a minimum, the compliance program must contain the following elements, commonly known as the "four pillars."[52]

Internal Controls. Banks must maintain a system of internal controls to ensure ongoing compliance with BSA/AML requirements. One aspect of such internal controls involves policies, procedures, and processes designed to limit and control risks and achieve compliance. These must be clearly written, comprehensive and current, organized and tailored to the bank, useful to train employees, and able to document evidence of adherence to applicable standards.

Another aspect of internal controls is the maintenance of a monitoring and reporting system, which should include the identification of unusual activity, SAR[53] decision-making, completion and filing, escalation criteria to close accounts and notify law enforcement, and an analysis of the customer relationship when repeat SARs are necessary.

Independent Testing. Banks also must provide for annual independent BSA/AML compliance testing to be conducted by internal personnel or by an outside party. This testing should be independent, have the proper level of scope, involve appropriate transaction testing, include an assessment and validation of the Bank's automated monitoring system, and be provided directly to the Bank's board of directors.

BSA Officer. A bank's board of directors must designate an individual responsible for coordinating and monitoring day-to-day BSA/AML

---

49. *Id.*
50. The most recent version of the BSA Manual is the 2020 version, which was released by the FFIEC on Apr. 15, 2020, and can be accessed at https://www.ffiec.gov/press/PDF/FFIEC%20BSA-AML%20Exam%20Manual.pdf.
51. 31 U.S.C. §§ 5318(a)(2) and 5318(h). *See*, FFIEC BSA/AML Examination Manual (2014 version), pp. 28–39.
52. 31 U.S.C. § 5318(h)(1); 12 U.S.C. § 1818(s); 12 C.F.R. §§ 21.21 (OCC); 208.63 (Federal Reserve); 326.8(c) (FDIC).
53. Suspicious activity reports are discussed *infra*.

compliance, implementing policies and directives, ensuring that employees adhere to policies, procedures, and processes. This individual, known as the BSA Officer, must have appropriate expertise, time, and resources, periodically meet with individuals throughout the Bank, and ensure the existence of a succession plan.

Training. Banks should provide comprehensive, ongoing, and documented training for appropriate personnel, including directors. Each person must receive appropriate training relevant to their responsibilities that includes the Bank's policies and procedures, changes to the Bank's compliance program, updated requirements, and compliance trends and hot topics.

Customer Identification Program

For centuries, banks were the place to hide money. Secret bank accounts were legendary. But, that practice stood in the way of law enforcement. As a consequence, in December 1998, the federal banking agencies issued for public comment a proposed "Know Your Customer" rule, which required banks to have policies and procedures to have sufficient knowledge of their customers to assist in the detection and prevention of illicit activity.[54] The proposed rule was not received well by the industry. In fact, thousands of comment letters poured in expressing concern about information privacy and regulatory burden, and the agencies eventually capitulated and withdrew the rule in March 1999.[55]

The events of 9/11 drastically changed attitudes both in the government and the financial industry about the necessity of a customer profiling regime that would be mandated for all financial institutions, regardless of size. This was highlighted by the fact that the 9/11 plotters utilized both large money center banks, as well as smaller regional banks, to facilitate their plan.[56] With the enactment of the USA PATRIOT Act shortly after 9/11, "Know Your Customer" was resurrected, and rebranded, as the "Customer Identification Program" ("CIP").

As a part of their BSA/AML compliance program, each bank must implement a board of directors–approved written CIP that includes risk-based procedures to verify, to the extent reasonable and practicable, the identity of each of its customers.[57] These procedures must be based on the bank's assessment of the relevant risks, including those presented by the types of accounts maintained by the bank, methods of opening accounts

54. *See*, OCC proposal at 63 Fed. Reg. 67,524 (Dec. 7, 1998).
55. Joint Statement, Proposed "Know Your Customer" Rule.
56. 9/11 Monograph, p. 53.
57. 31 C.F.R. § 1020.220(a)(1).

provided by the bank, types of identifying information available, and the bank's size, location, and customer base.

Customer Information Required. At a minimum, banks must obtain the following information from customers before opening an account: (i) name; (ii) date of birth (for individuals); (iii) address (residential or principal place of business), or if unavailable, comparable information such as military post office or next of kin's address; (iv) identification number, such as a taxpayer identification number for U.S. persons and a government-issued document bearing a photograph or similar safeguard (if an individual) or if an entity, alternative government-issued documentation certifying its existence.[58]

Customer Verification. The CIP must contain procedures for verifying the identity of the customer, using the information described above, within a reasonable time period after the account is opened.[59] The procedures must describe when the bank will use documents, nondocumentary methods, or a combination of both methods.

Lack of Verification. The CIP must include procedures for responding to circumstances in which the bank cannot form a reasonable belief that it knows the true identity of a customer. These procedures should describe when the bank should not open an account, the terms under which a customer may use an account while the bank attempts to verify the customer's identity, when the bank should close an account after attempts to verify a customer's identity have failed, and when the bank should file a SAR.[60]

Customer Notice. The CIP must include procedures for providing bank customers with adequate notice that the bank is requesting information to verify their identities. This typically appears in the deposit account-opening agreement and says:

> **IMPORTANT INFORMATION ABOUT PROCEDURES FOR OPENING A NEW ACCOUNT** – To help the government fight the funding of terrorism and money laundering activities, federal law requires all financial institutions to obtain, verify, and record information that identifies each person who opens an account.
>
> What this means for you: When you open an account, we will ask for your name, address, date of birth, and other information that will allow us to identify you.

58. 31 C.F.R. § 1020.220(a)(2)(i).
59. 31 C.F.R. § 1020.220(a)(2)(ii).
60. 31 C.F.R. § 1020.220(a)(2)(iii).

> We may also ask to see your driver's license or other identifying documents.

Due Diligence

Banks must also adopt and implement a customer due diligence ("CDD") program for all of its customers that allows the bank to understand the normal and expected transactions in which those customers are likely to engage throughout the course of the relationship. This allows a bank to distinguish between lower-risk and higher-risk customers, and to determine if its customers change their risk profile such that more robust surveillance is necessary to detect, monitor, and report suspicious activity.

Significantly, in 2016, FinCEN finalized its CDD rules for financial institutions.[61] These rules require financial institutions to collect beneficial owner information on the natural persons behind legal entity customers. The identification and verification requirements for such beneficial owners is a new, separate legal requirement for banks, subject to limited exemptions. The new rules also add explicit CDD requirements with respect to understanding the nature and purpose of customer relationship and conducting ongoing monitoring as components in each bank's core BSA/AML program requirements.

Banks must also establish risk-based enhanced due diligence ("EDD") for customers that pose a higher risk. These customers may include, for example, cash intensive businesses, nonbank financial institutions, nongovernment organizations and charities, nonresident aliens and foreign individuals, politically exposed persons (senior foreign political figures, their families, and their associates), privately owned automated teller machines, and professional service providers. Banks should ensure that these higher-risk customers are more closely reviewed when they open accounts and that their transactions are more closely scrutinized throughout the entire relationship.

Compliance Culture

To ensure that senior officers and directors understand the importance of a robust BSA/AML program, in August 2014, FinCEN issued its Advisory to U.S. Financial Institutions on Promoting a Culture of Compliance (the "Advisory").[62] The Advisory "highlight[s] general principles illustrating how financial institutions and their leadership may improve and strengthen organizational compliance with BSA obligations."[63] In particular, the Advisory

61. 81 Fed. Reg. 29397 (2016) (codified at 31 C.F.R. § 1010.230 and 31 C.F.R. § 1020.210).
62. FinCEN Advisory FIN-2014-A007 (Aug. 11, 2014).
63. *Id.*

notes that a financial institution may strengthen its BSA and compliance culture by ensuring that:

1. The financial institution's leadership actively supports and understands the compliance efforts of the institution;
2. Efforts to manage risks and mitigate any deficiencies in BSA/AML compliance are not compromised by the institution's search for revenue;
3. Relevant information from the institution's departments is shared with compliance staff for BSA/AML compliance purposes;
4. The financial institution devotes adequate resources to its compliance function;
5. The compliance program is effective and tested by an independent and competent party; and
6. The financial institution's leadership and staff understand the purpose of its BSA/AML efforts and how its reporting is used.

As with other aspects of the BSA/AML compliance program requirements, banks, and financial institutions generally, need to implement the concepts of this guidance in a manner that is consistent with the institutions' risk profile and business model.

Reporting Requirements

The reporting and the transparency that financial institutions provide under FinCEN's regulations result in some of the most important information available to law enforcement and others safeguarding the nation.[64] More specifically, the reports that financial institutions submit under the BSA/AML reporting regime are used to serve as tips to initiate investigations, expand existing investigations, promote international information exchange, and identify significant relationships, trends, and patterns.[65] These reports include, but are not limited to, Suspicious Activity Reports ("SARs"), Currency Transaction Reports ("CTRs"), monetary instruments logs, and funds transfer reports.

Suspicious Activity Reports. SARs[66] are the primary reporting requirement under the BSA. They must be filed when a bank believes that it was either an actual or potential victim of a criminal violation, or series of criminal violations, or that the bank was used to facilitate a criminal transaction.[67] Specifically, a bank must file a SAR when it detects a transaction that it knows, suspects, or has reason to suspect:

64. *See,* FinCEN Advisory FIN-2014-A007, p. 4 (Aug. 11, 2014).
65. *Id.* at 5.
66. FinCEN Form 111.
67. *See,* 31 C.F.R. § 1020.320.

- involves funds derived from illegal activities or is intended or conducted to hide or disguise funds or assets derived from illegal activities;
- is designed to evade any requirements of the BSA and its implementing regulations;
- has no business or apparent lawful purpose or is not the sort in which the particular customer would normally be expected to engage, and the bank knows of no reasonable explanation for the transaction after examining the available facts, including the background and possible purpose of the transaction; or
- is otherwise relevant to the possible violation of any law or regulation.[68]

Through SARs, banks must submit detailed information about themselves, the suspicious activity in question, and any potential suspects involved in the activity. To help the government analyze suspicious activities throughout the financial system, SAR instructions require filers to categorize the suspicious activity using an enumerated list of potential crimes, including money laundering, fraud, false statements, and as of 2003, terrorist financing. From 2003 until 2012, the amount of SARs filed annually by banks increased from 288,343 to 860,858.[69] Even more striking are the more recent filing numbers. For example, between March 1, 2012, and December 31, 2014, over three million unique SARs were filed.[70]

Filing. Banks must electronically file SARs with FinCEN no later than thirty calendar days after the date of the initial detection of facts constituting the basis for filing the SAR. If no suspect is immediately identified, the bank may delay filing a SAR for an additional thirty calendar days to identify a suspect.[71] Banks may also subsequently file amended or corrective SARs as necessary. Upon receipt, FinCEN disseminates SARs to other regulatory and law enforcement agencies.

If particular suspicious situations require immediate attention, such as violations that are ongoing or exigent, the bank must immediately notify, by telephone, an appropriate law enforcement authority and its regulator(s), in addition to filing a timely SAR. FinCEN encourages banks to immediately report suspicious activity relating to terrorist activity by either contacting their local FBI field office, or by calling FinCEN's Financial Institutions Hotline (1-866-556-3974), which is constantly operational and

---

68. 31 U.S.C. 5318(g); 31 C.F.R. § 1020.320(a). *See also,* 12 C.F.R. § 21.1(c) (OCC); 12 C.F.R. § 208.62(c) (Federal Reserve); 12 C.F.R. § 353.3(a) (FDIC).
69. *See,* SAR Activity Review, By the Numbers, Issue 18.
70. *See,* FinCEN's SAR Stats Technical Bulletin, Oct. 2015, p. 1.
71. 31 C.F.R. 1020.320(b)(3) (FinCEN); 12 C.F.R. § 21.1(d) (OCC); 12 C.F.R. § 208.62(d) (Federal Reserve); 12 C.F.R. § 353.3(b) (FDIC).

was established to facilitate the immediate transmittal of this information to appropriate law enforcement officials.[72]

Confidentiality. The government considers SARs to be extremely sensitive in nature. Except to their advisors, banks are generally prohibited from disclosing SARs, or any information that would reveal their existence, outside of their organization.[73] According to FinCEN, the unauthorized disclosure of SARs could "undermine ongoing and future investigations by tipping off suspects, deterring financial institutions from filing SARs, and threatening the safety and security of institutions and individuals who file such reports."[74]

Notification. Bank management must, however, promptly notify the bank's board of directors of any SARs to allow directors to fulfill their fiduciary duties.[75] Banks must maintain a copy of any SARs, along with supporting information, for five years so that the banking agencies or law enforcement may subsequently review such information.[76] In those situations, law enforcement does not require legal process to obtain such information. To encourage banks to file SARs when appropriate, they are provided a legal safe harbor from liability with respect to SAR filings.[77] This means that banks are "protected from civil liability for all reports of suspicious transactions made to appropriate authorities, including supporting documentation, regardless of whether such reports are filed pursuant to the SAR instructions."[78]

Currency Transaction Reports. Currency is defined as coin and paper money of the United States (or any country) that is circulated and accepted as money.[79] Banks are required to file CTRs[80] in connection with each deposit, withdrawal, exchange of currency, or other payment or transfer, by, or to such bank involving a transaction in currency of over $10,000, with some exceptions.[81] CTRs must be electronically filed with FinCEN

72. http://www.fincen.gov/fi_hotline.html.
73. 31 C.F.R. § 1020.320(e) (FinCEN); 12 C.F.R. § 21.1(k) (OCC); 12 C.F.R. § 208.62(j) (Federal Reserve); 12 C.F.R. § 353.3(g) (FDIC).
74. FinCEN, SAR Confidentiality Reminder for Internal and External Counsel of Financial Institutions, Mar. 2, 2012 (FIN-2012-A002).
75. 12 C.F.R. § 21.1(h) (OCC); 12 C.F.R. § 208.62(h) (Federal Reserve); 12 C.F.R. § 353.3(f) (FDIC), Manual, p. 79.
76. 31 C.F.R. § 1020.320(d) (FinCEN); 12 C.F.R. § 21.1(g) (OCC); 12 C.F.R. § 208.62(g) (Federal Reserve); 12 C.F.R. § 353.3(e) (FDIC).
77. 31 U.S.C. § 5318(g)(3); 31 C.F.R. § 1020.320(f) (FinCEN); 12 C.F.R. § 21.1(l) (OCC); 12 C.F.R. § 208.62(j) (Federal Reserve); 12 C.F.R. § 353.3(g) (FDIC).
78. FFIEC BSA/AML Examination Manual, p. 61 (2020).
79. 31 C.F.R. § 1010.100(m).
80. FinCEN's electronic CTR form is the "Bank Secrecy Act Currency Transaction Report (referred to as the "BCTR")."
81. 31 C.F.R. § 1010.311.

within fifteen days after the date of the transaction. Each CTR requires information about the individuals involved in the transaction, the amount and type of the transaction, and the financial institution where the transaction took place. In 2015 alone, banks and other financial institutions filed over 15 million CTRs.[82]

Aggregation. Multiple currency transactions in a single business day that total more than $10,000 are treated as a single transaction for CTR purposes, assuming that the bank had knowledge that the transactions are by, or for the benefit of, the same person.[83] To determine whether the CTR threshold has been met, each bank must establish a monitoring system to aggregate multiple transactions by one person across all of its offices on a single business day.[84]

Structuring. If an individual intentionally manipulates his or her transactions to avoid CTR filings being made for those transactions, such as by making deposits just under the CTR filing threshold, they are engaged in an activity known as "structuring."[85] Because structuring is a federal crime and therefore requires the filing of a SAR, banks must maintain tracking systems to identify potential structuring among their customers.

Exemptions. To avoid the necessity for banks to file, and for the government to analyze, CTRs that may have no significant investigative value, FinCEN allows banks to exempt certain types of entities from CTR filings, including government agencies, domestic banks, publicly traded companies, and certain cash-intensive "nonlisted businesses" or payroll customers.[86]

Monetary Instruments Log. Banks issuing or selling a bank check or draft, cashier's check, money order, or traveler's check for $3,000 to $10,000 inclusive to any purchaser must maintain a monetary instrument log that contains information, such as the name of the purchaser, the date of purchase, the type(s) of instrument(s) purchased, the serial number(s) of each of the instrument(s) purchased, and the amount in dollars of each of the instrument(s) purchased.[87]

Funds Transfers. Banks involved in funds transfers must collect and retain information in connection with funds transfers of $3,000 or more. The extent of this information depends on a bank's role in the funds transfer, whether the originator or beneficiary is a bank customer, and whether a payment order is made in person.[88]

82. 81 Fed. Reg. 5518, 5519 (Feb. 2, 2016).
83. FFIEC BSA/AML Examination Manual, p. 81 (2014).
84. 31 C.F.R. § 1010.313.
85. 31 C.F.R. § 1010.314.
86. 31 C.F.R. § 1020.315.
87. 31 C.F.R. § 1010.415.
88. 31 C.F.R. § 1020.410(a).

Enforcement Actions

Banks that fail to adhere to this complicated regime, and their employees, can find themselves subject to significant regulatory and law enforcement actions. In 2018, a California-based national bank named Rabobank pled guilty to conspiracy to obstruct an OCC examination and paid a forfeiture in the amount of $368,701,259, and a CMP to the OCC in the amount of $50 million. The following year, the OCC issued a consent order of prohibition and a $50,000 CMP against its former General Counsel for participating in the continuous concealment of a third-party report assessing Rabobank's BSA program from the OCC, and making false statements to the OCC.[89]

Pandemic Planning Guidance

Banks and their counsel who experienced the Great Recession could not imagine anything as impactful occurring to their industry again, but that was before the COVID-19 pandemic (the "2020 Pandemic") descended on our nation and our world. It was an event that profoundly altered how Americans lived and worked, and the banking sector was on the forefront of the nation's recovery. As summarized below, the federal banking regulators (the "Agencies"), along with their state counterparts, issued a steady stream of guidance, and took a number of unprecedented steps, to help banks fulfill that mission.

Pandemic Planning Guidance

As the 2020 Pandemic began, the FFIEC issued an Interagency Statement on Pandemic Planning (the "Pandemic Planning Guidance"), which updated guidance originally promulgated over a decade earlier in the wake of a prior pandemic.[90] The Pandemic Planning Guidance described both "business continuity" and "pandemic planning" as requiring a cyclical process of planning, preparing, responding, and recovering. It then distinguished pandemic planning as being more challenging because it involves a more expansive scope, duration, and geographic reach than the malicious activity, technical disruptions, and other typical natural and man-made disasters to which bankers were accustomed to responding.

To help banks address the unique challenges posed by pandemics, the Pandemic Planning Guidance makes a number of recommendations, including the following:

89. OCC Issues Consent Order of Prohibition and $50,000 Civil Money Penalty Against Former General Counsel of Rabobank N.A. (July 23, 2019).
90. FFIEC Interagency Statement on Pandemic Planning (Mar. 6, 2020).

Business Continuity Plan. Each bank should have a pandemic Business Continuity Plan that provides for: (i) a preventative program to reduce the likelihood that the bank's operations will be significantly affected; (ii) a documented strategy providing for scaling the bank's pandemic efforts to be aligned with the stage of the pandemic; (iii) a comprehensive framework of facilities, systems, or procedures to continue critical operations if staff is unavailable for prolonged periods; (iv) a testing program to ensure that the bank's practices and capabilities are effective, and will allow critical operations to continue; and (v) an oversight program to ensure ongoing review and updates to the pandemic plan.

Risk Assessment and Management. Risk assessment and management should include: (i) coordination with third parties, such as critical service providers; (ii) identification of pandemic triggering events; (iii) employee protection strategies, including enhanced hygiene programs and social distancing; (iv) mitigating controls, such as employee cross-training; and (v) remote access protocols.

Risk Monitoring and Testing. Testing surrounding the aforementioned should include: (i) stakeholder roles and responsibilities, (ii) planning assumptions, (iii) increased reliance on remote banking operation, and (iv) remote access and telecommuting capabilities for employees.

Customer Assistance Initiatives

Congressional Response. The Coronavirus Aid, Relief, and Economic Security Act (the "CARES Act"), which President Trump signed on March 27, 2020, was enacted to provide emergency assistance and health care response for individuals, families, and businesses affected by the 2020 Pandemic.[91] The CARES Act temporarily added a new product, the Paycheck Protection Program (the "PPP"), to the U.S. Small Business Administration's ("SBA's") 7(a) Loan Program, and provides for forgiveness of up to the full principal amount of qualifying loans guaranteed under the PPP.

Initial Customer Assistance Guidance. Even before Congress enacted the CARES Act, the Agencies began issuing guidance to encourage banks to work with customers affected by the 2020 Pandemic. For example, the FDIC issued its Statement on Financial Institutions Working with Customers Affected by the Coronavirus and Regulatory and Supervisory Assistance (the "Preliminary FDIC Statement"), which encouraged banks to work with depositors impacted by the 2020 Pandemic by such actions as:

- waiving certain fees,
- increasing ATM cash withdrawal limits, and
- easing restrictions on cashing out-of-state and noncustomer checks.

---

91. Pub. L. 116–136, 134 Stat. 281 (Mar. 27, 2020).

The FDIC also encouraged banks to address 2020 Pandemic-related borrower needs by prudently:

- increasing credit card limits for creditworthy borrowers,
- offering loan payment accommodations, and
- modifying and otherwise restructuring the debt obligations of its borrowers.[92]

To help assuage banks' fears, the Preliminary FDIC Statement said that the FDIC would not criticize banks that accommodate customers in a safe and sound manner (thereby preserving the agency's maneuverability), and that its examiners were directed "to exercise significant flexibility in determining whether to adversely classify credits that are impacted by COVID-19, including those designated as TDRs."

Loan Modifications. The Agencies issued guidance, confirmed with the Financial Accounting Standards Board ("FASB"), that short-term modifications (e.g., six months in duration) made on a good faith basis in response to the 2020 Pandemic, to previously current borrowers, would not be deemed as troubled debt restructurings ("TDRs") under ASC Subtopic 310-40.[93] The Agencies clarified that such guidance continues to apply with respect to loan modifications related to the 2020 Pandemic that are not addressed by Section 4013 of the CARES Act, which provides full relief from TDR classification for certain loan modifications.[94]

Mortgage Borrower Relief. Acknowledging the significant impact of the 2020 Pandemic on mortgage borrowers, the Agencies encouraged banks to consider prudent arrangements to ease cash flow pressures on those borrowers, improve their capacity to service debt, increase the potential for financially stressed residential borrowers to keep their homes, and facilitate the banks' ability to collect on its loans.[95]

Moreover, the Agencies announced a flexible supervisory and enforcement approach during the 2020 Pandemic regarding certain consumer communications required by the mortgage servicing rules.[96] Among other things, they clarified that if a mortgage servicer provides

92. FDIC, Federal Banking Agencies Provide Banks Additional Flexibility to Support Households and Businesses (Mar. 17, 2020).

93. FDIC-FIL-22-2020, Interagency Statement on Loan Modifications by Financial Institutions Working with Customers Affected by the Coronavirus (Mar. 22, 2020).

94. FDIC FIL-36-2020, Revised Interagency Statement on Loan Modifications by Financial Institutions Working with Customers Affected by the Coronavirus (Apr. 7, 2020).

95. Statement of Jelena McWilliams, Chairman, Federal Deposit Insurance Corporation on Oversight of Financial Regulators before the Committee on Banking, Housing, and Urban Affairs, U.S. Senate, May 12, 2020.

96. FDIC FIL-40-2020, *Supervisory and Enforcement Practices Regarding the Mortgage Servicing Rules in Response to COVID-19 and the CARES Act* (Apr. 10, 2020).

a borrower a short-term forbearance payment option, the Agencies would not take supervisory or enforcement action for failing to meet certain timing requirements for consumer communications related to incomplete application acknowledgement, loss mitigation and early intervention, and annual escrow statements, if the servicer makes good faith efforts to provide these notices within a reasonable time.

Small Dollar Loans. A joint statement encouraged banks to offer responsible small-dollar loans to both individuals and small businesses in a manner that is consistent with safe and sound practices, provides fair treatment of consumers, and complies with applicable laws and regulations, including consumer protection laws.[97]

Community Reinvestment Act. Another joint statement announced favorable Community Reinvestment Act ("CRA") consideration for banks providing retail banking services and lending activities in their assessment areas, consistent with safe and sound banking practices, that are responsive to the needs of low- and moderate-income individuals, small businesses, and small farms affected by the 2020 Pandemic.[98] Those activities include waiving certain fees, easing restrictions on out-of-state and noncustomer checks, expanding credit products, increasing credit limits for creditworthy borrowers, providing alternative service options, and offering prudent payment accommodations. That joint statement also provided favorable CRA consideration for certain 2020 Pandemic-related community development activities.

Regulatory Flexibility and Capacity Building Initiatives

Capital and Liquidity Buffers. A joint statement provided that capital and liquidity buffers were meant to give banks the means to support the economy in adverse situations, and that the Agencies would support banks that use the buffers for that purpose if undertaken in a safe and sound manner.[99] The Agencies later issued an interim final rule revising the definition of eligible retained income to make more gradual any automatic limitations on capital distributions under the Agencies' capital rules.[100]

Current Expected Credit Losses. An interim final rule provided banking organizations implementing the current expected credit losses

97. FDIC FIL-26-2020, Statement Encouraging Responsible Small-Dollar Lending to Consumers and Small Businesses in Response to COVID-19 (Mar. 26, 2020).

98. FDIC FIL-19-2020, *Joint Statement on CRA Consideration for Activities in Response to COVID-19* (Mar. 19, 2020).

99. FDIC, Federal Banking Agencies Provide Banks Additional Flexibility to Support Households and Businesses (Mar. 17, 2020).

100. Regulatory Capital Rule: Eligible Retained Income, 85 Fed. Reg. 15909 (Mar. 20, 2020).

("CECL") methodology before the end of 2020 the option to delay for two years an estimate of CECL's effect on regulatory capital, relative to the incurred loss methodology's effect on regulatory capital, followed by a three-year transition period.[101] A joint statement later clarified that no banking organization is required to comply with CECL during the relief period established by Section 4014 of the CARES Act, including institutions otherwise required to adopt CECL in 2020.[102]

Community Bank Leverage Ratio. The community bank leverage ratio ("CBLR") framework, which became effective January 1, 2020, provides a simplified measure of capital adequacy for banking organizations with less than $10 billion in total consolidated assets that meet certain risk-based qualifying criteria.[103] Qualifying organizations having a CBLR of greater than 9% can opt into the CBLR framework, by which they would not be subject to other risk-based and leverage capital requirements, and would be considered to have met the well-capitalized ratio requirements under the applicable regulatory capital requirements.

In responding to the 2020 Pandemic, the Agencies issued two interim final rules implementing Section 4012 of the CARES Act by temporarily modifying the CBLR to:

- establish a temporary 8% CBLR, starting the second quarter of 2020, with a gradual stepped transition back to 9% in the first quarter of 2022, and
- permit a two-quarter grace period, for organizations whose CBLR falls no more than one percentage point below the then-applicable CBLR during that transition process, to still be considered well capitalized under applicable capital regulations.[104]

Regulatory Reporting Extensions. In an unprecedented manner, the Agencies also increased the flexibility for banks to comply with certain regulatory reporting obligations. The Preliminary FDIC Statement said that the FDIC would "work with" banks experiencing challenges in their reporting responsibilities, taking into account each bank's circumstances. For example, the Agencies gave banks a thirty-day grace period to file their

101. Regulatory Capital Rule: Revised Transition of the Current Expected Credit Losses Methodology for Allowances, 85 Fed. Reg. 17723 (Mar. 31, 2020).
102. FDIC FIL-32-2-2020, *Joint Statement on the Interaction of the CECL Revised Transition Interim Final Rule with Section 4014 of the Coronavirus Aid, Relief, and Economic Security Act* (Mar. 31, 2020).
103. 84 FR 61776 (Nov. 13, 2019).
104. Regulatory Capital Rule: Temporary Changes to the Community Bank Leverage Ratio Framework, 85 Fed. Reg. 22924 (Apr. 23, 2020).

Call Reports for the first quarter of 2020.[105] Additionally, the FDIC gave banking institutions a forty-five-day grace period to submit the annual reports required under Part 363 of its regulations.[106]

Examinations. Because of the need for 2020 Pandemic-related social distancing measures by the Agencies and the banks that they examine, the Agencies revamped the manner in which they conducted their periodic examinations of their regulated institutions. For example, the FDIC Preliminary Statement announced that the FDIC would work with banks to reduce burden when scheduling examinations, including making greater use of off-site reviews, consistent with applicable legal and regulatory requirements.

Federal Reserve Liquidity Programs. The Federal Reserve issued guidance encouraging banking institutions to utilize its discount window and the intraday credit extended by its Reserve Banks to help households and businesses impacted by the 2020 Pandemic.[107] Additionally, the Federal Reserve established the following additional credit facilities:

Primary Market Corporate Credit Facility ("PMCCF"). Open to investment-grade companies and provides bridge financing of up to four years;

Secondary Market Corporate Credit Facility ("SMCCF"). Purchases in the secondary market corporate bonds issued by investment-grade U.S. companies and U.S.-listed exchange-traded funds whose investment objective is to provide broad exposure to the market for U.S. investment-grade corporate bonds;

Term Asset-Backed Securities Loan Facility ("TALF"). Lends on a nonrecourse basis to holders of certain AAA-rated asset-backed securities backed by newly and recently originated consumer and small business loans;

Money Market Mutual Fund Liquidity Facility ("MMLF"). Makes loans available to eligible financial institutions secured by high-quality assets purchased by the institutions from money market mutual funds ("MMFs") (including certain high-quality assets purchased from single state and other tax-exempt municipal MMFs, and municipal rate demand notes, and certificates of deposit);

Commercial Paper Funding Facility ("CPFF"). Purchases unsecured and asset-backed commercial paper rated A1/P1 (as of March 17, 2020) directly from eligible companies, as well as high-quality, tax-exempt commercial paper; and

105. FDIC FIL-28-2020, *The FDIC Announces a 30-Day Grace Period for the Call Report for the First Quarter of 2020* (Mar. 26, 2020).

106. FDIC FIL-30-2020, *Statement on Part 363 Annual Reports in Response to the Coronavirus* (Mar. 27, 2020).

107. https://www.federalreserve.gov/newsevents/pressreleases/monetary20200315b.htm. Discussed in more depth in Chapter 5, *supra*.

Primary Dealer Credit Facility ("PDCF"). Offers primary dealers overnight and term funding with maturities up to ninety days.[108]

Conclusion

Taken together, these legislative, regulatory, and supervisory initiatives created an environment in which the banking sector could help the nation, its businesses, and its citizens recover from the 2020 Pandemic. Those initiatives also left an updated playbook for future crises that we may face.

108. https://www.federalreserve.gov/covid-19-supervisory-regulatory-faqs.htm.

8

Safety and Soundness/Risk Management

What Is Risky about the Business of Banking?

If you were to describe the core business of banking, you would no doubt start with a phrase similar to "making loans to individuals and businesses funded with depositor dollars." After considering the ramifications of that description for a minute, you would probably restate the above inquiry to ask: "What is *not risky* about the business of banking?"

The antonym of "risk" is "safety" (check the Thesaurus) and keeping banks "safe and sound" is the primary purpose of our banking laws and our bank regulatory regime. At the end of the day, this concept is the backstop for all other rules discussed in this book. The objective is safety and soundness on a macro level, of the industry as a whole. But that starts bank-by-bank.

This chapter views safety and soundness with a focus on institutional objectives, and a key component of that in the wake of the Global Financial Crisis is the management of all that risk.

Safety and Soundness

While in many ways safety and soundness is conceptual in nature, the federal banking agencies have provided context by adopting interagency rules that establish operational and managerial standards to promote the safety and soundness of federally insured depository institutions.[1] The rules include the following noteworthy interagency appendices:

Appendix A covers standards for internal controls, information systems, internal audit systems, loan documentation, credit underwriting, interest rate exposure, asset growth, excessive compensation, fees and benefits, asset quality, and earnings.

Appendix B includes the *Interagency Guidelines Establishing Information Security Systems*, the rules banks must follow to assure that they and their vendors protect customer information under the requirements of the Gramm-Leach-Bliley Act.

Appendix C is entitled *Guidelines Establishing Standards for Residential Mortgage Practices.*

Appendix D is where the regulators deposited the heightened standards for risk management in large institutions.

But, there is more to safety and soundness. It comes into play in underwriting loans, asset growth and concentrations of credit, all aspects of consumer services, interest rate exposure, brokered deposits, new products, compensation practices, and anywhere else the agencies identify risk. It serves as the regulatory predicate to make behavior subject to penalty that is not otherwise a violation of law. In essence, the pursuit of safety and soundness propels regulatory guidance (which by its terms is recommended, not required) into enforceable law where risk is perceived.

The failure of an institution to manage to safety and soundness standards manifests in "unsafe and unsound" banking practices.

Unsafe and Unsound Banking Practices

Interestingly, given that the Federal Deposit Insurance Act and other federal banking laws sprinkle the concept of engaging in unsafe and unsound practices liberally, Congress has not defined the term, leaving it to the regulators and the courts. To that end, the Comptroller of the Currency ("OCC") suggests that unsafe and unsound banking practices "encompass ... conduct deemed contrary to accepted standards of banking operations which might result in abnormal risk or loss to a banking institution or shareholder."[2] Courts point out that this is a fact-based inquiry:

---

1. As contemplated by 12 U.S.C. § 1831(p)-1. *See,* (OCC) 12 C.F.R. § 30; (Federal Reserve) 12 C.F.R. § 208 (Regulation H), Appendix D-1 and D-2; (FDIC) 12 C.F.R. § 364. The FDIC also has promulgated regulations at Part 337 that address unsafe and unsound banking practices in connection with other areas, including letters of credit and brokered deposits.
2. Sinclair v. Hawke, 314 F.3d 934 n. 2 (2003), citing First Nat'l Bank of Eden v. Dept. of the Treasury, 568 F.2d 610, 611 n. 2 (8th Cir.1978). *See also,* Michael v. F.D.I.C., 687 F.3d 337 (2012) and Doolittle v. National Credit Union Ass'n, 992 F.2d 1531 (1993).

> What constitutes an unsafe and unsound condition is somewhat of an amorphous concept, as it varies depending on the circumstances involved. It is clear, however, that an unsafe or unsound condition exists where a financial institution is operated in such a manner as to cause unacceptable levels of risk to its depositors' funds. Since a particular condition may not necessarily be unsafe or unsound in every circumstance, it must be judged in relation to all relevant facts.[3]

How do we police safety and soundness? As discussed in Chapter 11, federal law provides an arsenal of enforcement weapons to bank regulatory agencies. Unsafe and unsound banking practices, along with violations of law and breaches of fiduciary duty, define bad bank behavior and serve as the predicate for enforcement.[4]

Enforcement. There is a waterfall of potential regulatory reaction to unsafe and unsound practices, depending on the severity of the misbehavior. If an agency identifies an unsafe and unsound banking practice, it may start more informally and require the bank to submit a plan for achieving and maintaining compliance. If a bank fails to submit an acceptable compliance plan, or fails in any material respect to implement a compliance plan that has been accepted by its primary federal regulator, the regulator is required to issue an order directing the bank to cure the deficiency. Until the deficiency cited in the regulator's order is cured, the regulator may restrict the bank's rate of growth, require the bank to increase its capital, restrict the rates the bank pays on deposits or require the bank to take any action the regulator deems appropriate under the circumstances. Noncompliance with safety and soundness may also constitute grounds for cease and desist orders and civil money penalty assessments, as discussed in Chapter 11, or even result in bank failure, as discussed in Chapter 12.

Risk Management

The definitions of unsafe and unsound banking practices set forth above each emphasize the existence of "abnormal risk" and "unacceptable levels of risk." From the perspective of the bank regulatory agencies, the failure of an insured depository institution to provide effective risk management constitutes an unsafe and unsound banking practice. While we cannot de-risk banking, we can manage it. Thus, from the foundation of safety and soundness springs the construct of risk management—perhaps the

3. Franklin Sav. Ass'n v. Director, Office of Thrift Supervision, 934 F.2d 1127 (1991).
4. *See*, 12 U.S.C Section 1818 where each of these three misbehaviors triggers various enforcement actions.

most important commandment in the regulatory lexicon of the early 21st century.

The regulators "heightened" focus on this area has altered the way banks function and the way in which lawyers advise our financial institution clients.

Catalyst

What engendered the heightened focus on risk management? It cannot be a surprise that the Global Financial Crisis unveiled a systemic failure of corporate governance and risk management. According to a study by the Group of Thirty, regulators, boards, and management all played a role[5]:

> [M]ost observers have agreed that a combination of "light touch" supervision, which relied too heavily on self-governance in financial firms, and weak corporate governance and risk management at many systemically important financial institutions contributed to the 2008 meltdown in the United States. Regulators also missed the potential systemic impact of entire classes of financial products, such as subprime mortgages, and in general failed to spot the large systemic risks that had been growing during the previous two decades.... In this context, boards of directors failed to grasp the risks their institutions had taken on. They did not understand their vulnerability to major shocks, or they failed to act with appropriate prudence. Management, whose decisions and actions determine the organization's risk status, clearly failed to understand and control risks. In many cases, spurred on by shareholders, both management and the board focused on performance to the detriment of prudence.

Clearly, there was a lot of work to be done.

Identifying Risk

The banking agencies posit that a risk is effectively managed when it is *identified, understood, measured, monitored, and controlled.* To start the

5. *Toward Effective Governance of Financial Institutions*, Group of Thirty, at 11 (2012). https://group30.org/images/uploads/publications/G30_TowardEffectiveGovernance.pdf. The Group of Thirty is an international body of leading financiers and academics which aims to deepen understanding of economic and financial issues and to examine consequences of decisions made in the public and private sectors related to these issues. *See*, www.group30.org.

process and identify risks, the agencies have defined eight categories of risk for bank supervisory purposes, generally including[6]:

> *Credit Risk* is the most basic and recognizable bank risk as it is a part of every bank's lending business and arises from an obligor's failure to meet the terms of any contract with the bank or otherwise perform as agreed. Credit risk is found in all activities in which settlement or repayment depends on counterparty, issuer, or borrower performance. This risk exists any time bank funds are extended, committed, invested, or otherwise exposed through actual or implied contractual agreements, whether reflected on or off the balance sheet. But it is more than lending. Credit risk also arises in conjunction with a broad range of bank activities, including selecting investment portfolio products, derivatives trading partners, or foreign exchange counterparties. Moreover, country or sovereign exposure, as well as indirectly through guarantor performance, give rise to credit risk exposure.
>
> *Interest Rate Risk* is also at the core of banking because the major source of bank earnings is net interest income—interest earned on loans and investments less interest expense on deposits and other borrowing. Interest rate risk results from differences between the timing of rate changes and the timing of cash flows (repricing risk); from changing rate relationships among different yield curves affecting bank activities (basis risk); from changing rate relationships across the spectrum of maturities (yield curve risk); and from interest-related options embedded in bank products (options risk).
>
> *Liquidity Risk* is a product of taking demand deposits and incurring other short-term indebtedness with only a fraction of cash on hand to meet demand. It arises from an inability to meet obligations when they come due. This risk includes the inability to access funding sources

6. *See, e.g.*, Comptroller of the Currency Bank Supervision Process Handbook discussion of categories of risk at Appendix H, https://www.occ.gov/publications/publications-by-type/comptrollers-handbook/pub-ch-ep-bsp.pdf. The Federal Reserve has issued a Framework for Risk-Focused Supervision at Large Complex Institutions, https://www.federalreserve.gov/boarddocs/srletters/1997/sr9724a1.pdf.

or manage fluctuations in funding levels. Liquidity risk also results from a bank's failure to recognize or address changes in market conditions that affect its ability to liquidate assets quickly and with minimal loss in value.

Price Risk is a newer risk identified by the OCC and arises from changes in the value of either trading portfolios or other obligations that are entered into as part of distributing risk. These portfolios typically are subject to daily price movements and are accounted for primarily on a mark-to-market basis. This risk occurs most significantly from market-making, dealing, and position-taking in interest rate, foreign exchange, equity, commodities, and credit markets. Price risk also arises from bank activities whose value changes are reflected in the income statement, such as in lending pipelines, other real estate owned, and mortgage servicing rights.

Operational Risk is often referenced as the scariest risk because it arises from inadequate or failed internal processes or systems, human errors or misconduct, or adverse external events. Operational losses result from internal fraud; external fraud; inadequate or inappropriate employment practices and workplace safety; failure to meet professional obligations involving clients, products, and business practices; damage to physical assets; business disruption and systems failures; and failures in execution, delivery, and process management. The quantity of operational risk and the quality of operational risk management are heavily influenced by the quality and effectiveness of a bank's system of internal controls.

Compliance Risk (sometimes referred to as "legal" or "regulatory" risk) arises from violations of laws or regulations, or from nonconformance with prescribed practices, internal policies and procedures, or ethical standards. This risk exposes a bank to fines, civil money penalties, payment of damages, and the voiding of contracts. Compliance risk can result in diminished reputation, limited business opportunities, and lessened expansion potential.

Strategic Risk arises from adverse business decisions, poor implementation of business decisions, or lack of responsiveness to changes in the banking industry

> and operating environment. This risk is a function of a bank's strategic goals, business strategies, resources, and quality of implementation. The resources needed to carry out business strategies are both tangible and intangible. They include communication channels, operating systems, delivery networks, and managerial capacities and capabilities.
>
> *Reputation Risk* is the one that is the most difficult to measure and is inherent in all bank activities. A bank that actively associates its name with products and services offered through outsourced arrangements or asset management affiliates is more likely to have higher reputation risk exposure. Significant threats to a bank's reputation also may result from negative publicity regarding matters such as unethical or deceptive business practices, violations of laws or regulations, high-profile litigation, or poor financial performance. The assessment of reputation risk needs to take into account the bank's culture, the effectiveness of its problem-escalation processes and rapid-response plans, and its deployment of media.

Financial institutions of all shapes and sizes are expected to analyze each product, each service, each activity, and in some cases, types of customers, and assess which risks exist. Note: most bank activities give rise to a number of these risks—rarely are we dealing with an isolated type of risk. Further note: risk management is enterprise wide, not entity by entity.

A simple example—a bank wants to accept deposits from a payment processor and initiate ACH debits as originating depository financial institution to consumer accounts (that means initiating debits of consumer bank accounts for club fees or other payments). How many risks? Operational (the processor website is hacked or fraud occurs); compliance (lots of laws will be implicated, including anti-money laundering laws and know your customer requirements and state licensing requirements); reputation (the processor absconds with funds); and credit risk (the bank is not protected on returned items).

Another example—a bank wants to start a nondeposit investment program with a third-party broker-dealer that will sell stocks and bonds and mutual funds to the bank's clients. What risks? Reputation, compliance and operational. Plus, the broker-dealer is a service provider—stay tuned for third-party risk issues discussed below.

Setting the Tone at the Top

This risk management process begins at the top, and the board of directors is expected to establish the bank's risk appetite. "Setting an appropriate tone at the top is critical to establishing an ethical culture."[7]

Boards of directors play the pivotal role in financial institution governance through their control of the three factors that ultimately determine the success of the institution: (i) the choice of strategy; (ii) the assessment of risk taking; (iii) and the assurance that the necessary talent is in place, starting with the chief executive officer ("CEO"), to implement the agreed strategy.[8]

Management in turn must play a continuous proactive role in the overall governance process, upward to the board and downward through the organization. Those accountable for key risk policies in financial institutions, on the board and within management, must be sufficiently empowered to put the brakes on the firm's risk taking, as well as play a critical role in enabling the firm to conduct well-measured, profitable risk-taking activities that support the firm's long-term sustainable success.[9]

Risk Governance Framework

Consider that different banks engage in the same activity in different ways, or engage in different activities in different ways, or offer different new products and services to different customers, and it is clear that there is no one-size-fits-all solution for banking organizations. Tailoring is the key to this process, such that "the sophistication of risk management systems should be proportionate to the risks present and the size and complexity of an institution."[10] Consequently, as an organization grows more diverse and complex, the sophistication of its risk management must keep pace. While publicly traded bank holding companies of $50 billion or more in average total consolidated assets are subject to heightened standards,[11] risk management systems in other banks will vary according to the type, complexity, and volume of risk the bank assumes.

The guidance set forth below for the big banks, although not applicable to smaller banks and holding companies, provides valuable insight into the structure and processes they should consider.

---

7. Comptroller of the Currency Bank Supervision Process Handbook, *supra* note 6, at 23.
8. Group of Thirty, *supra* note 5. In addition, Part III of the OCC's heightened standards for risk management rule includes a comprehensive description of the obligations of boards of directors. *See*, 12 C.F.R. Part 30, Appendix D.
9. Group of Thirty, *supra* note 5.
10. Comptroller of the Currency Bank Supervision Process Handbook, *supra* note 6 at 22.
11. *See, e.g.*, (OCC) 12 C.F.R. Part 30, Appendix D.

Enhanced Standards for Enterprise Risk Management

As part of the "enhanced prudential standards" expectations of the Dodd-Frank Act ("Dodd-Frank"),[12] Section 165(h) required certain publicly traded bank holding companies to establish a risk committee to be "responsible for the oversight of the enterprise-wide risk management practices." The Regulatory Relief Act[13] in turn raised the threshold for mandatory application of the risk-committee requirement from publicly traded bank holding companies with $10 billion or more in total consolidated assets to publicly traded bank holding companies with $50 billion or more in total consolidated assets.[14]

In 2014, the OCC finalized safety and soundness standards requiring covered national banks to establish and adhere to a formal written risk governance framework, approved by the board (or the board's risk committee), that would set the overall risk appetite for the bank and risk limits for all material activities.[15] The Federal Reserve adopted a similar approach for large bank holding companies.[16]

Organizational Framework. The framework is predicated on a three-function process, known as the "three lines of defense":

> *1st line of Defense*: Business/frontline units;
>
> *2nd line of Defense*: Risk, Control and Compliance functions independent of the business/frontline units;
>
> *3rd Line of Defense*: Internal Audit function that provides an independent and objective periodic evaluation of all key governance, risk management, and internal control processes.

The following descriptions are from the OCC's risk governance regulations.[17]

First Line of Defense: Role and Responsibilities of Frontline Units. Supervisors generally expect the frontline units to:

12. Pub. L. No. 111-203 (2010).
13. Economic Growth, Regulatory Relief and Consumer Protection Act of 2018 (Pub. L. 115–174, S. 2155).
14. However, the Board has discretion to apply risk-committee requirements to publicly traded bank holding companies with under $50 billion in total consolidated assets if the Board determines doing so would be necessary or appropriate to promote sound risk-management practices.
15. 12 CFR 30, Appendix D.
16. *See, e.g.*, Federal Reserve Supervisory Letter SR 12-17, Dec. 17, 2012; Federal Reserve Bank Holding Company Supervision Manual, Sections 2124.07 and 4070.1.
17. *Supra* note 15, at Part II.

- take responsibility and be held accountable by the CEO and the board of directors for appropriately assessing and effectively managing all of the risks associated with their activities;
- assess, on an ongoing basis, the material risks associated with their activities;
- establish and adhere to a set of written policies that include:
    - frontline unit risk limits as set forth in the risk governance framework,
    - processes for ensuring the frontline unit's activities are effectively identified, measured, monitored, and controlled, consistent with the bank's risk appetite statement, concentration risk limits, and risk governance framework;
- adhere to all policies, procedures, and processes established by independent risk management;
- develop, attract, and retain talent and maintain staffing levels required to carry out the unit's role and responsibilities effectively; and
- establish and adhere to effective compensation and performance management programs.

Second Line of Defense: Role and Responsibilities of Independent Risk Management. The Chief Risk Executive supervises the independent risk management function, which is responsible for overseeing the firm's risk-taking activities and assessing risks and issues independent of frontline units, including by:

- taking primary responsibility for designing a comprehensive written risk governance framework that is commensurate with the size, complexity, and risk profile of the bank;
- identifying and assessing, on an ongoing basis, the bank's material aggregate risks and determining if actions are needed to strengthen risk management or reduce risk given changes in the bank's risk profile or other conditions;
- establishing and ensuring compliance with enterprise policies that include concentration risk limits, policies for determining how aggregate risks within the bank will be identified, measured, monitored, and controlled, consistent with the bank's risk appetite statement and risk governance framework;
- identifying and communicating to the CEO and the board of directors material risks and significant instances where independent risk management's assessment of risk differs from that of a frontline unit and significant instances where a frontline unit is not adhering to the risk governance framework;

- identifying and communicating to the board material risks and significant instances where independent risk management's assessment of risk differs from that of the CEO, and significant instances where the CEO is not adhering to, or holding frontline units accountable for adhering to, the risk governance framework; and
- developing, attracting, and retaining talent and staffing levels needed to carry out its role effectively.

Third Line of Defense: Role and Responsibilities of Internal Audit. Internal audit is overseen by the Chief Audit Executive and should:

- ensure the firm's risk governance framework is appropriate for the size, complexity, and risk profile of the firm;
- carry out an audit plan that takes into account the firm's risk profile, emerging risks, and issues, and that includes evaluation of the adequacy of and compliance with policies, procedures, and processes established by frontline units and independent risk management under the risk governance framework;
- report to the board's audit committee its conclusions and material issues and recommendations, including identifying the root cause of any material issues and whether the root cause creates an issue for other units of the firm, and assessing the effectiveness of frontline units and independent risk management in identifying and resolving issues in a timely manner;
- independently assess the design and ongoing effectiveness of the risk governance framework on at least an annual basis;
- identify and communicate to the board's audit committee significant instances where frontline units or independent risk management are not adhering to the risk governance framework;
- establish a quality assurance program that ensures internal audit's policies, procedures, and processes comply with law and industry guidance, are appropriate for the size, complexity, and risk profile of the firm, are updated to reflect changes to internal, external, and emerging risks and improvements in industry internal audit practices, and are consistently followed; and
- develop, attract, and retain talent and maintain staffing levels required to effectively carry out its role.

Of course, there is much more detail on the risk framework, risk appetite, concentration limits, and the like in the OCC and Federal Reserve guidance.

Role of Lawyers

What does this regime mean for the bank lawyer? In the old days, we would opine on the legality of a proposed activity and provide insight into process and the rules, but leave the business judgement with bank management. Our day-to-day activities were primarily framed in black and white—the client could do it or could not. If we identified a loophole or the law was otherwise unclear, we might ask the appropriate agency for an interpretive letter on point. We rarely wrote policies and procedures. We rarely rang in on organizational structure. And may I repeat, we were warned off venturing into business decisions.

Today, nothing has changed up front. We have to take the same steps, but now we advise on structure, we draft board committee charters, we review minutes, we draft (or at least review) policies and procedures, and we must tackle risk. On any new product or activity, we ask: "What risks have you identified? What is your risk assessment? Does this need to go to the risk committee? Can the bank manage the risks? What policies and procedures are, or will be, in place? Do you have the right people in place? Do you have the right controls?" And sometimes we still have to be prepared to say, "Consider this carefully." (It sounds better than "No" [which feeds the protype] or "Are you crazy?" [which is probably best not uttered out loud.])

Selected Risk Management Topics

As you can see from the examples provided above, risk management requirements go across the spectrum of bank activities, products and services: from the asset side to the deposit side to operations, from commercial lending to banking payment processors to cybersecurity to nondeposit investment programs to bank-owned life insurance to hedging and derivatives trading. Banks have to constantly identify the risks, measure them, monitor them and put controls in place. This chapter could literally go on forever if every aspect of this lifecycle were addressed. It makes no sense to rephrase all of the excellent regulatory guidance you can find online and dump it here. Instead, this chapter will focus on areas of particular concern to lawyers as they counsel clients as we head forward from 2020 when the third edition of *Keys* went to press. In that regard, nothing has commanded more attention in the headlines than data security/cybersecurity, vendor management (third-party risk), and incentive compensation. And then, of course, the coronavirus pandemic created its own risks and processes, as discussed previously in Chapter 7.

Data Security/Cybersecurity

For the first time under federal law, Title V of the Gramm-Leach-Bliley Act of 1999 ("Gramm-Leach-Bliley")[18] imposed obligations on all financial

18. Title V, Subtitle A (codified at 15 U.S.C. § 6801-6809).

institutions as to the privacy and confidentiality of nonpublic personal information ("NPPI") (personally identifiable financial information regarding consumer customers, collected in conjunction with providing a financial product or service). To that end, the federal law begins[19]: "It is the policy of the Congress that each financial institution has an affirmative and continuing obligation to respect the privacy of its customers and to protect the security and confidentiality of those customers' nonpublic personal information."

The legal framework around privacy and the Gramm-Leach-Bliley requirements (the "Privacy Rule") is discussed in Chapter 7 as a societal regulatory/compliance matter. But, what it spawned in recognizing our rights as consumers, was that financial institutions had to keep that information safe. Data security and cybersecurity are now at the top of the risk pyramid, within a "heightened risk environment" warning around every corner.[20]

Data Security

In addition to the Privacy Rule, Gramm-Leach-Bliley requires that any party who creates or receives NPPI must have in place data security procedures to protect it (the "Safeguards Rule").[21] The statute and the Interagency Guidelines Establishing Information Security Standards[22] require these parties to have established and to maintain an information security program that is designed to (i) ensure the security and confidentiality of NPPI, (ii) protect against any anticipated threats or hazards to the security or integrity of NPPI, (iii) protect against unauthorized access to or use of NPPI, and (iv) properly dispose of NPPI. Covered institutions must have the safeguards in place themselves and must require all third parties who receive NPPI from them to have equally stringent safeguards in place.

Cybersecurity[23]

Even at the time of Gramm-Leach-Bliley, Congress and the agencies did not foresee the enormous influx of financial information that would be downloaded electronically and stored on servers or in a cloud somewhere. The risks associated with data breaches, ransomware, and identity theft are unprecedented, and "electronic crimes are dynamic as cyber criminals

19. 15 U.S.C. § 6801(a).
20. *See, e.g.*, FDIC, OCC, Joint Statement on Heightened Cybersecurity Risk, Jan. 16, 2020, https://www.fdic.gov/news/news/financial/2020/fil20003a.pdf.
21. 15. U.S.C. § 6801(b).
22. The guidelines are found at Appendix B to the banking agencies safety and soundness regulations. *See*, (OCC) 12 C.F.R. Part 170; (Federal Reserve) 12 C.F.R. Part 208 (Regulation H); (FDIC) 12 C.F.R. Part 364.
23. Thank you to John. M. Geiringer, partner, Barack Ferrazzano, LLP, for providing portions of this discussion of cybersecurity.

continually change their techniques."[24] Thus, the Safeguards Rule has morphed from data security and conflated with cybersecurity, with ever-evolving risk management processes required.

There is a vast supply of law and guidance in this area. Where do we look for that law and guidance? The banking agencies release guidance regularly and examine their financial institutions on information security, but the true force is the Federal Financial Institutions Examination Council ("FFIEC"), a formal U.S. government interagency body that includes all five banking regulators. It has taken the lead in information technology initiatives of the agencies for a number of years. However, we cannot ignore the states, some of which are more aggressive than federal law and claim extraterritorial reach if a bank has customers residing in the jurisdiction.

Admittedly, there is far too much law to summarize in any meaningful manner. But, lawyers are typically not down in the bowels of the bank with the technology wizards checking for resiliency, disaster recovery, and breaches. We need to know where to find the law and how to use the law to advise our clients, coach on risk management, and draft robust contracts to protect our client, to the extent possible, from its vendors' faults. Please excuse the mountain of footnotes—there are just so many places to look.

Bank Regulatory Guidance. The best place to start on an issue in constant evolution is recent pronouncements (not history on this point). For that, we look to the January 16, 2020, *Joint Statement on Heightened Cybersecurity Risk*[25] issued by the FDIC and OCC, not in response to the pandemic but to threats from Iran. Nonetheless, it appears equally applicable and reminds institutions: "Implementing and maintaining effective cybersecurity controls is critical to protecting financial institutions from malicious activity, especially in periods of heightened risk."[26]

The regulators identify the following as the cornerstones of sound risk management for cybersecurity:

- *Response and resilience capabilities*: Review, update, and test incident response and business continuity plans.
- *Authentication*: Protect against unauthorized access.
- *System configuration*: Securely configure systems and services.

Previously, the federal banking agencies issued an advance notice of proposed rulemaking regarding enhanced cyber risk management standards for large (consolidated assets of $250 billion or more) and interconnected

24. Texas Bankers Electronic Crimes Task Force, *Best Practices: Reducing the Risks of Corporate Account Takeovers*, Sept. 2011, at 1.
25. The FDIC issued the bulletin as FIL 2003a, https://www.fdic.gov/news/news/financial/2020/fil20003a.pdf.
26. *Id.*

banks (the "Enhanced Standards"),[27] and, because of the complexity of the issues, reopened the comment period on January 24, 2017.[28] The Enhanced Standards are meant to increase the operational resilience of those entities and reduce the impact on the financial system in case of a cyber event experienced by one of them. The Enhanced Standards include the following categories: (i) cyber risk governance; (ii) cyber risk management; (iii) internal dependency management; (iv) external dependency management; and (v) incident response, cyber resilience, and situational awareness. The agencies are considering implementing the Enhanced Standards in a tiered manner, imposing more stringent standards on the systems of banks that are critical to the functioning of the financial sector.

FFIEC Guidance. The FFIEC has released numerous examination manuals and supplements on IT infrastructure and risk management, all available through its Cybersecurity Awareness website.[29]

This process started officially in 2014, when the FFIEC evaluated over five hundred community banks to assess their inherent cybersecurity risks, current risk management practices, and potential best practices for determining organizational preparedness (the "Assessment").[30] On November 3, 2014, the FFIEC released a report detailing general observations regarding the Assessment,[31] and based on these findings developed the Cybersecurity Assessment Tool (the "Assessment Tool") to help banks measure and improve their cybersecurity preparedness (updated in May 2017).[32] It provides that a bank's procedures, information technology sophistication, and data protection infrastructure must be consistent with the extent of its risk-creating practices. Moreover, on October 17, 2016, the FFIEC issued a Frequently Asked Questions guide to the Assessment Tool.[33] While use of the tool by banks is discretionary, it is a really good idea because examiners are using it.

Process Flow. The Assessment Tool measures a bank's cybersecurity preparedness by comparing the level of inherent risk in the bank's operations and the maturity of the bank's cybersecurity infrastructure. Here is how the FFIEC recommends financial institutions approach the Assessment:

---

27. Enhanced Cyber Risk Management Standards, Proposed Rule, 81 Fed. Reg. 74,315 (2016).
28. Notice of Proposed Rulemaking, 82 Fed. Reg. 8172 (2017).
29. https://www.ffiec.gov/cybersecurity.htm.
30. *See,* FFIEC Cybersecurity Assessment General Observations 1 (2014), https://www.ffiec.gov/press/PDF/FFIEC_Cybersecurity_Assessment_Observations.pdf [hereinafter "FFIEC General Observations"].
31. *Id.*
32. FFIEC Cybersecurity Assessment Tool (2017), https://www.ffiec.gov/cyberassessmenttool.htm. [hereinafter in footnotes, FFIEC Assessment Tool].
33. FFIEC Cybersecurity Assessment Tool Frequently Asked Questions (Oct. 17, 2016).

Step 1: *Read Overview for Chief Executive Officers and Boards of Directors* to gain insights on the benefits to institutions of using the Assessment, the roles of the CEO and Board of Directors, a high-level explanation of the Assessment, and how to support implementation of the Assessment.
Step 2: *Read the User's Guide* (Update May 2017) to understand all of the different aspects of the Assessment, how the inherent risk profile and cybersecurity maturity relate, and the process for conducting the Assessment.
Step 3: *Complete Part 1: Inherent Risk Profile of the Cybersecurity Assessment Tool* (Update May 2017) to understand how each activity, service, and product contribute to the institution's inherent risk and determine the institution's overall inherent risk profile and whether a specific category poses additional risk.
Step 4: *Complete Part 2: Cybersecurity Maturity of the Cybersecurity Assessment Tool* (Update May 2017) to determine the institution's cybersecurity maturity levels across each of the five domains.
Step 5: *Interpret and Analyze Assessment Results* to understand whether the institution's inherent risk profile is appropriate in relation to its cybersecurity maturity and whether specific areas are not aligned. If management determines that the institution's maturity levels are not appropriate in relation to the inherent risk profile, management should consider reducing inherent risk or developing a strategy to improve the maturity levels.

FFIEC Assessment Tool. Under the Assessment Tool, a bank's inherent risk profile depends on the "type, volume, and complexity of the bank's operations," measured by its: (i) technologies and connection types; (ii) delivery channels; (iii) online or mobile products and services; (iv) organizational characteristics; and (v) number of external threats. For each of these factors, a bank should measure its risk level for several subcategories along a scale from least to most inherent risk. For example, one subcategory of "delivery channels" asks to what extent the bank uses ATM services, with "No ATM services" yielding the least risk and international, internally managed ATM services provided to other financial institutions yielding the most risk. After ranking each of these subcategories, a bank can assess how many entries it maintains at each risk level, as well as specific areas of particularly high risk in determining the overall risk profile. The FFIEC does not prescribe or recommend a strict system for tallying inherent risk based on these results, but provides in the attendant "overview" document several questions that managers might consider when reviewing the results.[34]

After determining its inherent risk profile, banks are expected to complete a similar questionnaire to assess the maturity of their cybersecurity procedures and infrastructure, ranking the level of sophistication from "baseline" to "innovative" within five domains: (i) cyber risk management and oversight; (ii) threat intelligence and collaboration; (iii) cybersecurity controls; (iv) external dependency management; and (v) cyber incident management and resilience. The FFIEC notes that the Assessment Tool is "not designed to identify an overall cybersecurity maturity level," but that comparing the results in each domain with the bank's inherent risk can inform whether it has adequate measures in place.[35] Banks with greater inherent risk should have greater cybersecurity maturity, and imbalanced results suggest that a bank should conduct a "gap analysis," and ultimately either reduce its inherent risk or improve its maturity levels.[36] Finally, the FFIEC recommends that all banks—regardless of the results of their Assessment—continue to reevaluate their cybersecurity preparedness regularly over time, and that independent evaluation through an audit or similar process can augment the Assessment Tool analysis.

It is also critical to remember that cybersecurity exposure is a significant risk in connection with acquisitions. An overall cyber risk assessment early in the process can provide a general idea of the cyber maturity of the target.[37] In addition, a diligence review of the target's cyber documentation (*e.g.*, security policy, incident response policy, access control policy, etc.) is essential.

State Action. Watch the states in this space.

New York. The New York Department of Financial Services has been especially proficient and led the pack in 2017 with its *Cybersecurity Requirements for Financial Services Companies* regulation[38] ("NYDFS Rule") in order to promote the protection of customer information as well as the information technology systems of regulated entities. Any person operating under or required to operate under a license, registration, charter, certificate,

---

34. One question asks banks to determine current areas of highest risk, and another asks how management and the board can support improvements to the Assessment process. *FFIEC Tool Overview* at 4–5. The 2014 *General Observations* document also lists additional questions to consider for each of the inherent risk factors. For example, when considering the "connection types" results, a bank should ask if it needs all of its connections, and how these connections collectively affect the overall inherent risk. *Id.* at 1.
35. FFIEC Assessment Tool at 8.
36. FFIEC Assessment Tool at 9.
37. *See*, Business Law Section of the American Bar Association publication, a *Cybersecurity M&A Due Diligence Checklist.*
38. *See*, 23 NYCRR 500 (eff. Mar. 1, 2017).

permit, accreditation, or similar authorization under the New York Banking Law, the Insurance Law, or the Financial Services Law is covered by the rule; except smaller entities are exempt from most provisions (*i.e.,* those with (i) fewer than ten employees, including any independent contractors, of the entity or its affiliates located in New York or responsible for business of the entity, or (ii) less than $5,000,000 in gross annual revenue in each of the last three fiscal years from New York business operations of the entity and its affiliates, or (iii) less than $10,000,000 in year-end total assets, calculated in accordance with generally accepted accounting principles, including assets of all affiliates).

The NYFDS Rule is a comprehensive tool for any financial institution to review in the context of its cybersecurity risk management. Essentially, each covered person must conduct a periodic risk assessment and then scale its cybersecurity program and cybersecurity policy accordingly. Each must name a chief information security officer, conduct penetration and vulnerability assessments, encrypt nonpublic information, limit personnel access to systems and nonpublic information, maintain an audit trail, and have an incident response plan, in addition to training and monitoring. Covered persons must also take steps to ensure that their affiliates and service providers safeguard the customer information in their care as well. Boards of directors must certify compliance with the NYFDS Rule and file the certification form with the department.

California. The California Consumer Privacy Act ("CCPA")[39] introduces new privacy rights for consumers and forces companies that conduct business in California to implement structural changes to their privacy programs. The CCPA took effect on January 1, 2020, with enforcement beginning in July 1, 2020. The CCPA applies to businesses, defined as any "for-profit entity that collects 'consumer' (in this case California residents') personal data and meets at least one of the following:

- The business annually buys, receives, sells or shares the personal information of 50,000 or more consumers, households, or devices.
- The business has an annual gross revenue of over $25 million.
- The business derives 50% or more of its annual revenue from selling consumer personal information."

The CCPA puts a premium on institutions knowing and disclosing what they collect and store and the consumer understanding his or her rights to the personal data. Under key provisions, consumers may request to access, delete, or port the personal information they have provided to a company, up to two times in a twelve-month period. To protect consumers' privacy

39. California Consumer Privacy Act of 2018, Cal. Civil Code, Title 1.81.5, added by 2018 Cal. Stat. Ch. 55, Sec. 3. 1798.100-1798.199.

and security, the law requires companies establish processes to verify consumers' identity and authorization.

Third-Party Risk

A significant focus of risk management involves third-party risk management. The bank regulatory agencies view outsourcing to service providers as the bank engaging in the activity itself and consider affiliates of a bank to be third parties with respect to the bank. They believe that a bank cannot contractually transfer its liability to a third party, and they believe that vendors expose financial institutions to risks that may result in financial loss, litigation, and loss of reputation. Think about that for a minute and you recognize that vendor management—the obligation of banks to manage the risks attendant to delegating functions to third parties—is a process, not something that is accomplished only before the contract is inked. The process starts with due diligence of third parties at the outset, but requires that it continue over the course of a relationship; it requires effective contractual provisions to mitigate risk; and it requires continuous monitoring. Once again, the agencies provide a wealth of information in this regard on their respective websites.[40]

But, it gets worse. In the wake of the Global Financial Crisis (and borrowing a term from Dodd-Frank that demanded "heightened" prudential standards for systemically important financial institutions), the bank regulatory agencies started using the phrase "heightened expectations" when they really, really wanted to get the immediate attention of their bankers. It means "pay attention now—you are going to have to work harder than ever." Thus, when all three federal bank regulatory agencies and the CFPB began using the phrase in connection with vendor management, it meant banks had to redesign vendor management programs from top to bottom and build layers of ongoing requirements into the process. What was behind the new emphasis? The agencies recognized an increase in the number and complexity of bank third-party relationships and expressed concern that risk management was not keeping pace.

In a nutshell, the general premises underlying the regulatory construct for vendor management are:

---

40. A helpful tool in this regard is the FDIC's Compliance Examiner Questionnaire for Reviewing Third-Party Risk Relationships, Appendix A to Part VII of its Compliance Manual ("FDIC Questionnaire"). *See also*, OCC Bulletin 2013-29, Third-Party Relationships (Oct. 30, 2013) ("OCC Bulletin") and FRB SR 13-19, Guidance on Managing Outsourcing Risk (Dec. 5, 2013). In addition, the CFPB released its expectations as to service providers in connection with consumer financial law compliance in Bulletin 2012-13.

- Each bank owns the responsibility and accountability to manage vendor risk as if it were conducting the service or function directly;
- The vendor management process must be commensurate with the level of risk/complexity of each third-party relationship and organizational structure;
- Banks must employ more comprehensive and rigorous oversight and management of third-party relationships involving critical functions and activities;
- The process follows a continuous life cycle from due diligence through termination.[41]

"Heightened expectations" has also come to mean that the agencies want the attention and involvement of the board of directors and senior management. Thus, more is expected from the top of the organization—yes, on each significant vendor relationship. The board of directors is expected to initially approve, oversee and review significant vendor relationships at least annually and review arrangements/written agreements whenever there is a material change. Management is expected to periodically review the vendor's operations to verify consistency with the agreement and ensure that risks are controlled.

Importantly, the Bank Service Company Act[42] applies to vendors, and financial institutions must notify their federal regulator of contracts with technology service providers that provide the following services: data processing, internet banking, mobile banking, as well as check and deposit sorting and posting, computation and posting of interest, preparation and mailing of checks or statements, and other clerical, bookkeeping, accounting, statistical, or similar functions. The regulatory agencies have authority to audit such vendors under the law.

Starting the Process. The bank will start by identifying the functions to be outsourced, will create a request for proposal ("RFP"), and will narrow its focus to the viable contenders. As part of that initial process, it needs to determine how complex the task and how critical the function to establish how heightened the process must be. Some of this is easy: core processing—the most complex, the most risk, the most critical; internet banking—not far behind. What other considerations factor into determining a critical function? Are the delegated functions significant bank functions or shared services (e.g., cybersecurity, privacy and data protection, payments, clearing, settlements and custody; shared information technology; and marketing of consumer products)? Is there customer impact? Is this a significant resource investment? Will there be a major impact if alternatives are needed? It is

41. OCC Bulletin, at 1. Appendix A of this document lists all the risks associated with vendors and Appendix B lists all the OCC guidance in this area.
42. 12 U.S.C. § 1867.

safe to say that access to a bank's electronic systems or networks, in the protection of sensitive data and in maintenance of anti-money-laundering and Bank Secrecy Act programs land pretty squarely in the arena of critical functions.

In summary, the risk assessment must:

- Be consistent with strategic planning and overall business strategy
- Identify all categories of potential risk
- Identify all applicable consumer laws and regulations and others that may impact compliance function
- Analyze benefits, costs, legal aspects and potential risks
- Ascertain the vendor's knowledge and skills to adequately perform risk analysis
- Identify performance criteria, internal controls, reporting needs and contractual requirements.[43]

And then there is due diligence, which must be conducted prior to selection and periodically during course of relationship and must be of a scope and depth commiserate with the importance and magnitude of the proposed relationship and the risks.[44]

Vendor Contract Highpoints. The responsibility for vendor contracts is owned by different parties in different banks. Most significant contracts will require review by counsel. The bank regulatory agency guidelines cited above include examiner checklists for vendor contracts that are extremely helpful tools in reviewing and revising vendor service agreements. It is good practice to use the checklists with every contract review and then create for the file a summary of the reasons that any key element is not included—for instance, it was not relevant to the particular service or, despite multiple attempts to negotiate, the vendor would not accept the change requested. If there are too many variances from the checklist or the variances are material, there is a point at which the decision-maker at the bank must be able to say, "We will not sign this contract."

Without attempting to reproduce or even summarize all those comprehensive tools, the following are basic considerations that the regulators find important, followed by bullet points on several key contract concepts.

- **Scope of outsourced services** – while this seems self-evident, may vendor agreements today fail to provide any specificity as to exactly what services the vendor will provide. Literally, there is no promise to enforce.

43. FDIC Questionnaire, at 1–2.
44. Due diligence considerations are provided in the FDIC Questionnaire beginning on page 5 and in the OCC Bulletin beginning on page 3.

- **Bank's service-level expectations** - typically a vendor should provide (for most services) an SLA—service level agreement—that drills down on a service-by-service basis how efficiently it will perform and typically includes a criticality escalation table detailing contact persons and response times for certain events.
- **The type of information reporting required of the vendor** - for the avoidance of doubt, list the reports and their coverage.
- **Dispute resolution mechanisms** - will there be a waiver of trial by jury and/or class actions or will there be mandatory mediation and/or arbitration? If arbitration, before whom and under what rules?
- **Default and termination provisions** - consider all the things that could go wrong and make sure the bank can get out for the worst without going through cumbersome breach and cure periods.
- **Insurance requirements** - don't forget a fidelity bond where applicable and cyber insurance coverage.

Selected Contract Concepts. The following is a summary of recurring key issues that frequently arise in connection with the negotiation of vendor agreements.

Will the services involve consumer compliance?

- Ensure that consumer protection laws are taken into account and specify critical applicable laws
- Require the vendor to warrant legal compliance
- Provide specific allocation of responsibility
- Monitor and analyze consumer complaints and satisfaction
    - Contract should include a process to report, escalate and resolve
- Review vendor's controls, processes, disclosures, call center scripts…
- Include immediate termination rights in the event of breach of consumer laws.

Will the bank share NPPI?

- Include robust Gramm-Leach-Bliley/State Law use and disclosure restrictions - the vendor needs to promise that it will only use the information for the purposes of effectuating the agreement and will not share the information except as permitted by law with persons who have a need to know and are subject to confidentiality agreements at least as strict as the vendor agreement.
- Include Interagency Guidelines Establishing Information Security Standards - this starts with the four requirements of the standards

addressed above, but more robust language that covers encryption and storing requirements is the norm.

- Develop breach notification requirements – to avoid confusion, consider adding a definition of security breach and specific protocols and time frames for criticality escalation and breach notice procedures.
- Require data destruction at termination.

Can the vendor recover in a business interruption?[45]

- Require maintenance and testing of a disaster recovery plan ("DRP") with recovery standards
- Include requirements for reporting disruption
- Define terms and contractual remedies.

What are the rights to audit the vendor?

- Bank and its agents should have audit rights (include forensics)
- Regulatory audit rights should be recognized
- Require sharing of audit reports, such as SSAE 16, AUP, Security, Disaster Recovery, PCI, GLBA, NACHA, PIN, or equivalent independent audit results.

Will the vendor subcontract services or assign the contract?

- Will the vendor assume responsibility for its subcontractors?
    - Otherwise, the bank must conduct due diligence either directly or indirectly as if the subcontractor were providing the services directly.
- Prohibit foreign subcontractors?
- Prohibit assignment without consent.

After the operative provisions and the vendors representations and warranties are negotiated, come the risk allocation parts of the contract, which is actually private law developed in the contract for the resolution of disputes and breaches.

Damage Limitations

- Balance vendor's need to mitigate against excessive damages and bank's need for redress
- Vendors typically disclaim all special damages

45. In 2019, the FDIC issued a special alert regarding deficiencies examiners found in disaster recover contractual provisions in contracts between banks and technology service providers. FIL-19-2019 (Apr. 2, 2019).

- Vendors may limit direct damages to fees for amount of months (1, 3, 6, or 12)
- Exclude from the limit of liability:
  - Gross negligence and willful disregard
  - Indemnification rights
  - Breach of confidentiality – this is becoming more difficult to carve out because of the possible cyber exposure, but in any event it should be limited to an amount that is more than the general limit of liability, and the vendor should have data security insurance to back it up.

Indemnification – this is a promise to defend and hold harmless the counterparty for third-party claims arising from contract when one party is at fault

- Rarely offered by vendors – usually the only indemnification is from the bank
- Get coverage for gross negligent and willful acts
- Indemnification should be free from damage limitations and any mandatory arbitration provision
- MUST HAVE – intellectual property infringement indemnification – if the vendor is providing intellectual property (software, a patented product or process or a trademark) of any sort, it should agree to defend, indemnify and hold harmless the bank in the event the bank is sued for using an infringing product.

Banking as a Service ("BaaS"). Fintech provides a number of challenges in this area. The first is defining the relationship between the financial institution and the fintech provider. Oftentimes, the fintech in these relationships is part commercial deposit customer, so that the bank is providing services to the fintech and its customers (hence, "Banking as a Service"), and part service provider to the bank, thus subject to the vendor management regime discussed above. A clear delineation of relationship is required in these contracts to know what checklist and guidance applies.

Cloud Computing. At the conversion of vendor management and data security, we find banking in the cloud (and in case you thought you knew what that meant, it is defined as "a model for enabling ubiquitous, convenient, on-demand network access to a shared pool of configurable computing resources (e.g., networks, servers, storage, applications, and services) that can be rapidly provisioned and released with minimal management effort or third-party service provider interaction)."[46] Yes, it is as fraught with risk as it sounds. The FFIEC has chimed in here as well and

46. *Infra* note 47, fn 2.

issued a joint statement on the use of cloud computing services on May 1, 2020.[47] The statement highlights risk management practices and controls for the safe and sound use of cloud computing services and includes a list of resources to assist financial institutions using cloud computing services. The primary concern is with resiliency and security controls and assuring that the parties have a contractual allocation of responsibilities.

Incentive Compensation

If anything defined banking in terms of the headlines in 2016 it was "incentive compensation gone bad," layered on the already recognized abuses in this area exposed during the Global Financial Crisis. It is evident that incentive compensation programs can go wrong from the top down or from the bottom up. Wells Fargo has emerged as the poster child for abuse in this space[48] and it became clear as the scandal unfolded that the culture went bad from the top when the actual incentive plan itself may have been facially neutral. Other plans may induce inappropriate employee behavior because of perverse incentives in favor of one product sale or referral over another and may impact from the bottom up. In any event, the effectiveness of any incentive program must be judged not only on results but must be aligned with the institution's risk management regime to assure that the program does not incentivize the wrong type of behavior.

And this is not just an issue with the big banks. Excessive compensation and incentive compensation plans may support allegations of unsafe and

47. Joint Statement released at FDIC FIL-52-2020, OCC Bulletin 2020-46.
48. *See, e.g.*, E. Scott Reckard, *Times Investigation of Wells Fargo Culture Provokes Strong Reaction* (Dec. 28, 2013) http://articles.latimes.com/2013/dec/28/business/la-fi-mo-wells-fargo-sales-pressure-20131228; Emily Glazer, *At Wells Fargo, How Far Did Bank's Sales Culture Go?*, The Wall Street Journal (Nov. 30, 2015), http://www.wsj,com/articles/at-wells-fargo-how-far-did-banks-sales-culture-go; Evan Weinberger, *Feds Dig into Wells Fargo Sales Tactics, Report Says* (Sept. 14, 2016), http://www.law360.com/articles/840153/feds-dig-into-wells-fargo-sales-tactics-report-says; James Rufus Koren, *California Attorney General Investigating Wells Fargo on Allegations of Criminal Identity Theft* (Oct. 19, 2010), http://www.latimes.com/business/la-fi-wells-fargo-harris-20161018-snap-story.html.

unsound banking practices, certainly when on the scale of Wells Fargo, but also at small banks.[49]

Interagency Guidance. In October 2009, the Federal Reserve demonstrated a bit of prescience and first requested comment on a *Proposed Guidance on Sound Incentive Compensation Policies,*[50] predicated on the fact that banks "can provide executives and employees with incentives to take imprudent risks that are not consistent with the long-term health of the organization." While the proposal was driven by events that occurred in advance of the Global Financial Crisis, it looked more broadly at the issues and swept incentive compensation plans of all types, from senior executive packages to employee programs, into the risk management matrix. To that end, the Federal Reserve recognized three core principles:

Effective incentive plans should:

- Provide employees incentives that appropriately balance risk and reward;
- Be compatible with effective controls and risk-management; and
- Be supported by strong corporate governance, including active and effective oversight by the organization's board of directors.

Recognizing that flawed incentive compensation practices in the financial industry were one of many factors contributing to the Global Financial Crisis, the other banking agencies joined with the Federal Reserve in 2010 to release an *Interagency Guidance on Sound Incentive Compensation Practices*[51] *in line with, and expanding upon, the Board's original core principles. Much of the guidance addresses large banking organizations and, because of the size and complexity of their operations, the regulators expect those organizations* to maintain systematic and formalized policies, procedures, and systems for ensuring that the incentive compensation arrangements for all executive and nonexecutive employees covered by this guidance are identified and reviewed, and appropriately balance risks and rewards. Smaller banking organizations that use incentive compensation arrangements are

---

49. *See, e.g.*, In the Matter of First National Bank of Eden, South Dakota v. Department of the Treasury, Office of the Comptroller of the Currency, 568 F.2d 610 (1st Cir. 1978), in which the court affirmed the actions of the OCC in determining that the bank's compensation to executives constituted an unsafe and unsound banking practice. The OCC had required the bank to develop a salary plan for executive officers specifically limiting the amount of salaries and bonuses so that the bank's total personnel expenses would not exceed 1.5% of its average assets. The order also included a requirement that the bank President and Vice-President reimburse the bank in the amount of $61,000 for bonuses paid to them in 1975.
50. Proposed Guidance on Sound Incentive Compensation Policies, 74 Fed. Reg. 55,227 (Oct. 27, 2009).
51. Guidance on Sound Incentive Compensation Policies, Final Guidance, 75 Fed. Reg. 36,395 (June 25, 2010).

expected to be less extensive, formalized, and detailed than those of the larger banks. According to the agencies' releasing materials,[52] supervisory reviews of incentive compensation arrangements at smaller, less complex banking organizations will be conducted by each regulator as part of the evaluation of those organizations' risk management, internal controls, and corporate governance during the regular, risk-focused examination process. These reviews will be tailored to reflect the scope and complexity of an organization's activities, as well as the prevalence and scope of its incentive compensation arrangements. Little, if any, additional examination work is expected for smaller banking organizations that do not use, to a significant extent, incentive compensation arrangements.

Among pages of guidance on risk mitigation, controls and oversight, the interagency guidance includes the following summary of essential steps for risk management in this area:[53]

- Identify employees who are eligible to receive incentive compensation and whose activities may expose the organization to material risks;
- Identify the types and time horizons of risks to the organization from the activities of these employees;
- Assess the potential for the performance measures included in the incentive compensation arrangements for these employees to encourage the employees to take imprudent risks;
- Include balancing elements, such as risk adjustments or deferral periods, within the incentive compensation arrangements for these employees that are reasonably designed to ensure that the arrangement will be balanced in light of the size, type, and time horizon of the inherent risks of the employees' activities;
- Communicate to the employees the ways in which their incentive compensation awards or payments will be adjusted to reflect the risks of their activities to the organization; and
- Monitor incentive compensation awards, payments, risks taken, and risk outcomes for these employees and modify the relevant arrangements if payments made are not appropriately sensitive to risk and risk outcomes.

Regardless of the size of the bank, or the scope of incentive plans, those steps represent the keystone for establishing process around this area.

This ultimately means incentive plans must be "balanced." The regulators assert that an unbalanced arrangement can be moved toward balance by

52. *See, e.g.*, OCC Bulletin 2010-24 (June 10, 2010).
53. 75 Fed. Reg. 36,395 at 36,413. While these steps are articulated for large banking organizations, they provide valuable insight into the process for all institutions.

adding or modifying features that cause the amounts ultimately received by employees to appropriately reflect risk and risk outcomes. This theme plays out in both the bank agencies' guidance, the actions and pronouncements of the CFPB and the requirement for Level 1 and 2 institutions under the proposed § 956 Rules discussed below in the concept of "deferral"—should the incentive plan for product sales include a deferral mechanism that eliminates credits or payments when a product is cancelled or replaced and perhaps increases credit or payments based on retention? In this event, the actual payout of an award to a recipient would be delayed significantly beyond the end of the performance period, and the amounts paid would be adjusted for actual losses or other aspects of performance that are realized or become better known only during the deferral period. To be most effective, the banking agencies suggest that deferral period should be sufficiently long to allow for the realization of a substantial portion of the risks from employee activities.

The interagency guidelines drill down on the concept of balance as follows[54]:

Risk Adjustment of Awards: The amount of an incentive compensation award for an employee is adjusted based on measures that take into account the risk that the employee's activities may pose to the organization. Such measures may be quantitative, or the size of a risk adjustment may be set judgmentally, subject to appropriate oversight.

Deferral of Payment: The actual payout of an award to an employee is delayed significantly beyond the end of the performance period, and the amounts paid are adjusted for actual losses or other aspects of performance that are realized or become better known only during the deferral period. The deferral-of-payment may also use a "clawback" under which an employee must return incentive compensation payments previously received by the employee (and not just deferred) if certain risk outcomes occur. To be most effective, the deferral period should be sufficiently long to allow for the realization of a substantial portion of the risks from employee activities, and the measures of loss should be clearly explained to employees and closely tied to their activities during the relevant performance period.

Longer Performance Periods: The time period covered by the performance measures used in determining an employee's award is extended (for example, from one year to two or more years). Longer performance periods and deferral of payment are related in that both methods allow awards or payments to be made after some or all risk outcomes are realized or better known.

54. 75 Fed. Reg. 36,395 at 36,408–409.

Reduced Sensitivity to Short-Term Performance: The banking organization reduces the rate at which awards increase as an employee achieves higher levels of the relevant performance measure(s). Rather than offsetting risk-taking incentives associated with the use of short-term performance measures, this method reduces the magnitude of such incentives. This method also can include improving the quality and reliability of performance measures in taking into account both short-term and long-term risks, for example improving the reliability and accuracy of estimates of revenues and long-term profits upon which performance measures depend.

The regulatory guidance reflects the expectation that large banks will have robust procedures for collecting information about the effects of their incentive compensation programs on employee risk-taking, as well as systems and processes for adjusting compensation arrangements to eliminate or reduce unintended incentives for risk-taking.

Dodd-Frank § 956 Rulemaking.[55] The gist of the compensation guidance was later turned into a joint proposed rulemaking to implement § 956 of Dodd-Frank in 2011. Almost five years later, on June 10, 2016, the agencies released an updated proposed rule for comment.[56] The regulatory focus in this regard is triggered by the risky practices associated with the mortgage crisis and on plans "with material amounts of risk." By 2020, these rules were on a far back burner, but the agencies were promising at various conferences that § 956 rulemaking was back on the to-do list.

Section 956 of Dodd-Frank required the banking agencies, the National Credit Union Administration, the Securities and Exchange Commission and the Federal Housing Finance Agency to jointly prescribe regulations that prohibit types of incentive-based compensation that encourage inappropriate types of behavior and to disclose certain information regarding such plans. The proposed rules implementing Dodd-Frank (the "§ 956 Rules") prohibit "incentive-based compensation arrangements" that encourage inappropriate risks "by providing excessive compensation" or that "could lead to material financial loss." As we delve into this area, the first step is to grasp what the regulators are targeting in the § 956 Rules. For this purpose, "incentive-based compensation" is defined broadly to mean any variable compensation that serves as an incentive for performance. The form of payment, whether it is cash, an equity award, or other property, does not affect whether compensation is "incentive-based compensation." Thus, the universe of payments and the associated incentive plans covered by the proposed rules is broad. The group of individuals covered by the

55. Thanks to Donald L. Norman, Jr. and Andrew K. Strimaitis of Barack Ferrazzano Kirschbaum & Nagelberg LLP for their Client Alerts that contributed to this section.

56. Incentive-Based Compensation Arrangements, Proposed Rule, 81 Fed. Reg. 37,669 (June 10, 2016).

requirements includes senior executives as well as "significant risk-takers"—a new category designed to target employees whose actions could serve to increase the risk undertaken by an institution.

The second issue is then to whom will the proposed rules apply? In this, as in many other regards, Dodd-Frank focused on larger banks, and in fact § 956 expressly excludes applicability to financial institution with assets of less than $1 billion—note, the $1 billion threshold includes many community banks, so not all that large. Covered institutions have escalating responsibilities and restrictions and are divided into three categories:

- Level 1 (consolidated assets greater than or equal to $250 billion);
- Level 2 (consolidated assets greater than or equal to $50 billion and less than $250 billion); and
- Level 3 (consolidated assets greater than or equal to $1 billion and less than $50 billion).

The proposed rules are comprehensive and have four key components:

- Prohibition of incentive-based compensation arrangements for covered persons that would encourage inappropriate risks by providing excessive compensation;
- Prohibition of incentive-based compensation arrangements for covered persons that would expose the institution to inappropriate risks by providing compensation that could lead to a material financial loss;
- Requirement of annual reports on incentive compensation structures to the institution's primary Federal regulator; and
- Requirement of policies and procedures for incentive-based compensation arrangements that is commensurate with the size and complexity of the institution.

While the rules are mostly principles and reporting-based for Level 3 institutions, they delve into detailed requirements for Levels 1 and 2 institutions (and certain Level 3s, if determined in the discretion of their regulators). For example:

- From 40% to 60% of incentive compensation for senior executives and significant risk-takers must be deferred for up to four years following the end of the incentive period.
- A seven-year "clawback" provision must be included as a term of incentive compensation arrangements.
- Other provisions include prohibitions on accelerated vesting of deferred awards, caps on incentive compensation payouts, and minimum performance vesting requirements.

It is anticipated that the proposed regulated, while providing beneficial guidance, will not survive the policies of the Trump administration.

The CFPB Rings in. The CFPB, with its focus on protecting consumers, has also been very active in this area and has pursued at least 12 financial firms in cases involving improper practices to market credit card add-on products alone.[57] Its agenda is not as expansive as that of the federal banking agencies and its primary concern is with consumer product sales and cross-marketing. In this regard, it issued a compliance bulletin at the end of 2016[58] outlining expectations for incentive compensation programs. The bulletin compiles guidance previously issued by in other contexts and highlights examples from the agency's supervisory and enforcement experience.

While most of the CFPB's expectations and recommended components for compliance are similar to the banking agency expectations (board of directors and management oversight; compliance program, which includes policies and procedures, training, and monitoring and corrective action; consumer complaint management program; and independent compliance audit), it provides specific examples of compensation problems that build substance into some of the principles:

- Sales goals may encourage employees, either directly or indirectly, to open accounts or enroll consumers in services without their knowledge or consent. Depending on the type of account, this may further result in, for example: (i) improperly incurred fees; (ii) improper collections activities; and/or (iii) negative effects on consumer credit scores.
- Sales benchmarks may encourage employees or service providers to market a product deceptively to consumers who may not benefit from or even qualify for it;
- Paying compensation based on the terms or conditions of transactions (such as interest rate) may encourage employees or service providers to overcharge consumers, to place them in less favorable products than they qualify for, or to sell them more credit or services than they had requested or needed;
- Paying more compensation for some types of transactions than for others that were or could have been offered to meet consumer needs, which could lead employees or service providers to steer consumers to transactions not in their interests; and

57. The Bureau's website includes a description of these cases at http://www.consumerfinance.gov/policy-compliance/enforcement/actions/.
58. *Detecting and Preventing Consumer Harm from Production Incentives*, CFPB Compliance Bulletin 2016-03 (Nov. 28, 2016).

- Unrealistic quotas to sign consumers up for financial services may incentivize employees to achieve this result without actual consent or by means of deception.[59]

At the end of the day, it is safe to say that incentive compensation arrangements are no longer under the exclusive purview of employment lawyers. They are now a regulatory matter for us bank regulatory lawyers too.

59. *Id.* at 2.

9

Bank Expansion

How Do Banks Branch, Merge, and Offer New Products?

Unregulated entities have few legal constraints in connection with growth. They do not worry about authority for the activities they are conducting; they are not concerned with the need for prior approval to conduct a new activity or to acquire someone to that end (at least absent antitrust issues); they have no geographic restraints, at least while within the borders of the United States; and they certainly do not have to balance growth based on externally imposed capital requirements.

Contrast that with banks. It is sobering to consider all of the barriers that must be discussed in this chapter—branching barriers, growth contingent on capital barriers, new product barriers. It adds up to rules, rules, and more rules . . . more rules in fact than can be done justice in less than forty pages, but the good news is that the regulatory agencies have terrific resources on their respective websites that help demystify the issues, many of which are noted below.

Banks "grow" first and foremost by deposit gathering, and, historically, to do so they needed additional offices, and so they grew, and continue to grow, by opening or acquiring new branches or by opening nonbranch satellite offices. They grow through mergers (when another financial institution becomes a part of them), consolidations (when two institutions become a part of a new institution), and deposit assumptions (when parts of the selling or failed bank are left behind). They grow through offering new products to capture fee income. The following discussions walk through the various barriers and requirements associated with bank growth.

One proviso: many of these transactions require approval of the applicable regulator(s), so a review of licensing/prior approval/notice requirements is almost always necessary.

Branching

The concept of "branching" is novel to depository institutions because it means more than just opening a satellite office in a new location. In fact, the National Bank Act ("NBA")[1] defines a "branch" of a national bank as an office of the bank "at which deposits are received, or checks paid, or money lent." The definition of "domestic branch" in the Federal Deposit Insurance Act ("FDIA")[2] for both state member and nonmember banks is identical in all material respects to the NBA definition. These three activities—receiving deposits, cashing checks, and lending money—are frequently referred to as the "core banking activities." As a consequence, when a depository institution seeks to open a new office (known as a "*de novo*" office) or acquire an office at which it will engage in a core banking activity (as defined by the agencies as discussed below), that office is a "branch" and the establishment or acquisition will generally require an application or notice to the applicable regulator(s) and will have regulatory consequence, for instance, with respect to its obligations to the community and how the branch may be closed.

It is important to note that because operating subsidiaries of banks may only engage in activities permissible to the parent bank, they are also restricted to making loans and cashing checks at the legally established main office or branch offices of the parent bank (only a bank may accept deposits, so that requirement is irrelevant to a subsidiary). This rule can get tricky when a bank has a finance company or mortgage company as a subsidiary because they have the same geographic restrictions.

Background

The current ability of state and national banks to branch across state lines is a relatively recent development. Historically, states not only prohibited branching across state lines but also imposed limits on the ability of state-chartered banks to branch within the state. National banks could not branch at all until Congress enacted the McFadden Act[3] in 1927, which permitted them to open branches in cities or towns in which they were located to the extent state banks could do so. In 1933, this restriction was eased to permit national banks to branch within their state in the same manner as

1. 12 U.S.C. § 36(j).
2. Section 3(o), FDIA, 12 U.S.C. § 1813(o).
3. Feb. 25, 1927, 44 Stat. 1228, 12 U.S.C. § 36.

state banks. Yet state law anomalies like home office protection (a bank could not open a branch in a city where another bank had its main office), restrictions on the number of branches, and limitations on branching outside of the home county persisted. Yes, Thomas Jefferson was smiling.

In 1965, seventeen states prohibited their banks from establishing any branches; seventeen permitted limited intrastate branching; and sixteen states permitted statewide branching. By the early 1990s, state restrictions on intrastate branching had eased. At the end of 1992, the number of states that permitted some form of statewide branching had risen to thirty-nine, while eleven states retained stricter limits on branching within the state. As state restrictions on intrastate branching were being reduced, pressures for interstate branching were building. Maine enacted a bill permitting nationwide interstate banking in 1978. By mid-1994, as Congress was considering interstate branching legislation, thirty-four states permitted nationwide interstate banking, fifteen were members of regional interstate reciprocal banking compacts (i.e., your state banks can *de novo* branch into my state as long as my state banks can branch into yours), and only one state, Montana, banned interstate banking.[4]

Riegle-Neal Advances. In 1994, Congress enacted the Riegle-Neal Interstate Branching and Banking Efficiency Act of 1994 ("Riegle-Neal"),[5] which provided a comprehensive framework for interstate branching by national and state banks. It essentially permitted interstate mergers, but *de novo* branching required an opt-in by each state. In the best tradition of the dual banking system, Congress, as it drafted the bill, was able to draw on the experience of the forty-nine states that had already approved some form of interstate branching directly or through reciprocal compacts.

Dodd-Frank Eliminates Impediments. Section 613 of the Dodd-Frank Wall Street Reform and Consumer Protection Act of 2010 ("Dodd-Frank")[6] put the issues to rest at long last and eliminated the requirements of Riegle-Neal, amending the federal branching laws applicable to national[7] and state[8] banks to provide that a bank may branch into a state if "the law of the State in which the branch is located, or is to be located, would permit establishment of the branch, if the bank were a State bank chartered by such State …."

Accordingly, Dodd-Frank opens the doors to unlimited geographic expansion through *de novo* branching, a power federal savings associations already had, so all depository institutions have the same ability. It is

4. The discussion of developments in branching law is from H. Rept. 103-448 on the 1994 interstate legislation, footnote 5, *infra*, 19–21.
5. (Interstate Branching Act), Pub. Law 103-328, Sept. 29, 1994, 108 Stat. 2315.
6. Pub. L. No. 111-203 (2010).
7. 12 U.S.C. § 36(g)(1)(a).
8. 12 U.S.C. § 1828(d)(4)(A)(i).

noteworthy, however, that Dodd-Frank continues to predicate entry by an out-of-state bank into each state on what an in-state bank can do in the state, and that means, if an in-state state bank must file an application or notice to open a branch, so must the out-of-state national[9] or state bank.[10]

Nonbranch Facilities and Activities

As a result of the historical impediments to branching, and even today as a result of applications and branch requirements, banks seek ways to enter new markets efficiently. The concept of a "nonbranch" office was, thus, born to accommodate these interests.

The core banking activities are not the only activities in which banks engage, and such noncore activities do not need to be conducted at a branch office—for instance, banks may sell insurance or provide investment advice at nonbranch locations. So, the nonbranch facility issue does not deal with noncore activities (those are easy); rather the question is: how close may a bank come to providing one or more core banking activities at a nonbranch location?

ATMs take deposits. Are they branches? In 1996, the definition of "branch" for national and state banks was amended to clarify that ATMs and other remote facilities were excluded.[11] The amendment to federal law on this point was designed to resolve persistent questions about the kinds of off-premises services that banks could offer in remote facilities for the convenience of customers without going to great lengths to avoid having the facility considered to be a branch. With this amendment, banks could operate their own ATMs and other remote facilities without definitional issues.

In 1999, the Office of the Comptroller of the Currency ("OCC"), the primary federal regulator for national banks, adopted regulations[12] relating to remote service units ("RSUs"), deposit production offices ("DPOs"), and facilities that combined these services with loan production offices ("LPOs"), asserting that as long as the services performed at these facilities met the regulatory standards, they were not branches. In essence, the OCC gutted the core banking activities and the NBA branching provisions in connection with this pursuit, providing gaping holes for any national bank with a little

9. 12 U.S.C. § 36(g)(2) provides that an application by a national bank to establish and operate a *de novo* branch in a host state shall be subject to the same requirements and conditions to which an application for an interstate merger transaction is subject under paragraphs (1), (3), and (4) of Section 1831u (b) (12 U.S.C. § 1831u(b)).
10. *See*, 12 U.S.C. § 1831u(b), discussed in the previous note.
11. The Economic Growth and Paperwork Reduction Act of 1996, Pub. Law 104-208 (Sept. 30, 1996), 110 Stat. 3009-394, Section 2205, amending Section 5155(j) of the Revised Statutes (12 U.S.C. § 36(j)) and Section 3(o) of the FDIA (12 U.S.C. § 1813(o)).
12. Investment Securities; Rules, Policies, and Procedures for Corporate Activities; Bank Activities and Operations, Final Rule, 64 Fed. Reg. 60,092 (Nov. 4, 1999).

bit of flexibility to exploit. Moreover, most state banks achieved the same ability either expressly or through interpretation by the state departments of financial institutions.[13]

Remote Service Unit (RSU)—§ 7.400s. This is an automated facility, as noted above, that performs core branching services but is not a branch. It is defined in the regulation as a facility operated by a customer of the bank that:

> [C]onducts banking functions, such as receiving deposits, paying withdrawals, or lending money. . . . An RSU includes an automated teller machine, automated loan machine, and automated device for receiving deposits. An RSU may be equipped with a telephone or televideo device that allows contact with bank personnel. An RSU is not a "branch" within the meaning of [the McFadden Act] and is not subject to state geographic or operational restrictions or licensing laws.

It is also noteworthy in this regard that branching issues arose in connection with remote deposit terminals—essentially scanners that are sold or leased to commercial customers so that they could capture a check image and deposit the check without walking into the bank. The bank regulators determined informally that the deposits were received technically at the office of the bank where the scanned images were processed and, thus, the scanners were not branches.

Deposit Production Office (DPO)—§ 7.4004. DPOs are offices that can be operated by the bank or an operating subsidiary at a site other than the main office or a branch of the bank for the origination of deposits. While deposits may be made by the customer at an ATM located on the premises of the DPO, bank employees at these offices may only solicit deposits, provide customers with forms necessary for opening an account, and assist them in completing these forms, but may not accept the customer's deposit. That would be a "receipt" of a deposit, which is prohibited in a facility that is not a branch. The rule provides:

> All deposit and withdrawal transactions of a bank customer using a DPO must be performed by the customer, either in person at the main office or a branch office of the bank, or by mail, electronic transfer, or a similar method of transfer.

---

13. State laws, however, may require out-of-state state banks to register to do business in the state and/or to file representative office or similar applications to enter the host state. These issues have to be addressed on a state-by-state basis. National banks generally have the benefit of preemption in this space.

Loan Production Offices (LPOs)—§§ 7.1003, 7.1004 and 7.1005. In contrast to its DPO policy, OCC interpretations permit LPOs to engage in virtually all aspects of making a "loan" without the facility being characterized as a branch. The OCC's policies with respect to permissible activities of LPOs evolved originally through Interpretive Letters rather than by regulation, but were then codified in §§ 7.1003, 7.1004 and 7.1005.

In this regard, an OCC 2001 Interpretive Letter held that an LPO could do the following without being a "branch" under federal law:

- accept loan applications;
- underwrite the loan using credit standards developed by the bank;
- have a loan officer at the LPO approve or deny the loan based on these criteria (with certain authority to make exceptions based upon personal judgment); and
- give the loan proceeds to the borrower.

These activities were performed by an LPO in State *A* operated by an out-of-state national bank that had no branches in State *A*. State *A* asserted that the LPO was a branch under the laws of State *A*. Since State *A* had not adopted laws permitting out-of-state institutions to organize *de novo* branches in the state, the state claimed that the LPO was an impermissible *de novo* branch of the national bank. In its response, the OCC said "while [State *A*] may define a 'branch' for purposes of state law, the definition of a national bank 'branch' is governed by federal law."[14] The OCC then provided its analysis of the "make loans" element of the core banking activities definition, citing cases and earlier Interpretive Letters, holding that the activities of the LPO in question did not fall within this definition. The OCC asserted, for example, that its regulation at 12 USC § 7.1004, providing that an LPO will not be regarded as a branch if its loans are approved at the bank's main office or at a branch, is not a legal requirement that approvals must be made at these locations, but was merely a "safe harbor." The agency asserted:

> [M]oreover, the core branching function that is required under the McFadden Act is "making" loans. It is apparent that neither loan origination nor the technical act of loan approval, taken separately, constitutes the making of a loan.[15]

14. First National Bank in Plant City v. Dickinson, 396 U.S. 122 (1969).
15. OCC Interpretive Letter # 902, Jan. 2001.

In summary, the OCC's regulations:

- define "money lent" as being where the borrower receives loan proceeds, but then acknowledges that proceeds may be disbursed by third parties, such as an attorney or escrow agent[16];
- requires the credit decision to be made by a bank employee at the main office or branch,[17] but then permits credit decisions elsewhere.[18] (Generally considered to apply to credit scoring models.)

That circular reasoning appears to mean that about anything in terms of lending may be done at an LPO, as long as the bank colors within those lines.

Combination of Loan Production Office, Deposit Production Office, and Remote Service Unit—§ 7.4005. This section provides that since a loan production office, a deposit production office, and a remote service unit are not branches, the combining of these facilities at a single site does not create a branch.

Federal Associations

As noted above, federal savings associations historically have been able to branch across state lines. This authority is found in Section 5(r) of the Home Owners' Loan Act ("HOLA"),[19] which conditions this authority on the association's meeting Community Reinvestment Act and capital standards, as well as one of two asset composition tests: the qualified thrift lender ("QTL") test at 12 U.S.C. 1467a(m) or the "tax test" in the tax code at 26 U.S.C. 7701(a)(19), both of which are discussed below. This exercise of OCC authority is preemptive of any state law purporting to address the subject of branching by a federal savings association.[20]

For federal savings associations, a branch does not include electronic facilities. A "branch" is defined as "any office *other than* its home office, agency office, administrative office, data processing office, or an electronic means or facility under part 555 of this chapter [relating to Electronic Operations]." (Emphasis added.) HOLA provides that a federal association may establish remote service units for the purpose of crediting savings or demand accounts, debiting such accounts, crediting payments on loans, and the disposition of related financial transactions, as provided in regulations developed by the OTS.[21]

---

16. 12 C.F.R. § 7.1003.
17. 12 C.F.R. § 7.1004(b).
18. 12 C.F.R. § 7.1005.
19. 12 U.S.C. § 1461 *et seq.*
20. 12 C.F.R. § 145.92(c).
21. 12 C.F.R. § 145.92(a) and Sec. 5(b)(1)(F) of HOLA (12 U.S.C. § 1464(b)(1)(F)).

State Savings Associations

The ability of state savings associations to branch across state lines depends on state law. A state association that is prevented from interstate branching by state law may convert to a federal association and branch in accordance with Section 5(r) of HOLA.

Affiliate Bank Agency Activities

Any bank subsidiary of a bank holding company may act as agent for a depository institution affiliate of the holding company and the agency will not be considered a branch.[22] Agency activities include closing, servicing, and receiving payments on loans, receiving deposits, and renewing certificates of deposits and other time deposits. As with any other activity, however, state institutions require state law authority for this initiative.

Branch Closings

Section 42 of the FDIA[23] requires all insured depositories to file a notice with their primary federal regulator 90 days before closing a branch. A "branch" for purposes of this policy excludes ATMs, RSUs, and LPOs. A closing does not include the relocation of a branch to another site in the same neighborhood or a closing of a branch of a failing institution.

The institution must also mail a notice of the planned closing to customers of the branch at least ninety days prior to the proposed closing date and post a notice in the branch at least thirty days before the closing.[24] If the bank maintains branches in multiple states and proposes to close a branch that is located in a low- or moderate-income area, the notice to customers must tell customers that they may send comments on the closing to the institution's primary regulator and provide that agency's address and the agency in its discretion may hold a meeting of interested parties to discuss, among other things, alternative ways to replace the branch. The agencies do not have the authority to approve or disapprove the closing. This procedure ensures that the bank receives public comment on the planned closing, but the final decision is left to the business judgment of the bank.

During the coronavirus pandemic national emergency, banks had to limit branch activity to a different degree in various states, but, to what extent that amounted to a temporary branch closure raised interesting regulatory issues, discussed in Chapter 7.

---

22. 12 U.S.C. § 1828r.
23. 12 U.S.C. § 1831r-1.
24. Branch Closings (Joint Policy Statement), 64 Fed. Reg. 34,844 (June 29, 1999).

Mergers, Consolidations, and Deposit Assumptions

Mergers, consolidations, and deposit assumptions between depository institutions are governed by the terms of the Bank Merger Act ("BMA").[25] Riegle-Neal eliminated any prohibition on interstate mergers, so those impediments are long gone, but keep in mind streamlined applications, and even some authority issues, depend on the bank being well capitalized.

Mergers Generally

The BMA provides, among other things, that covered transactions are subject to final approval by the primary federal regulator of the resulting institution (which the BMA defines as the "responsible agency"). This means that no insured depository institution may merge with another unless the transaction has been approved by the "responsible agency," which is

- The OCC if the resulting institution is a national bank or federal savings association;[26]
- The Federal Reserve Board ("Federal Reserve") if the resulting institution is a state member bank; or
- The Federal Deposit Insurance Corporation ("FDIC") if the resulting institution is a state nonmember bank or a savings bank or state savings association.[27]

State banks and thrifts will also need approval from the state regulatory authority for the resulting institution.

Application. The federal banking agencies use an Interagency Bank Merger Application for mergers and similar transactions. The form is available on each agency's website, along with instructions, some of which vary from agency to agency.

Evaluation Criteria. The responsible agency, among other things, must request a report from the U.S. Attorney General and other federal banking agencies on the competitive effects of the transaction and may not approve the transaction if the proposed merger would result in a monopoly, or restraint of trade, unless it finds that the anticompetitive effects of the transaction are outweighed by the benefits to the community. The agency must also evaluate the:

---

25. Sec. 8(c) of FDIA (12 U.S.C. § 1828(c)).
26. Applicable law is found in the National Bank Act at 12 U.S.C. §§ 215, 215a and 215a(1), dealing respectively with mergers and consolidations within the same state, acquisition transactions with state banks, and interstate transactions. The OCC codified its operative regulations in 12 C.F.R. § 5.33.
27. The FDIC codified its merger procedures in 12 C.F.R. Part 303, Subpart D.

- financial and managerial resources of the participants;
- future prospects of the existing and proposed institutions;
- convenience and needs of the community to be served; and
- effectiveness of the parties in combating money laundering.

Risk to the Financial System. In addition, Section 604(f) of Dodd-Frank amended the BMA to require the responsible agency to consider the "risk to the stability of the United States banking or financial system" in connection with all merger transactions (not only involving larger banks). The discussion of the financial stability factor by the OCC, for instance, in recent orders approving applications under the BMA,[28] indicates that the agencies will consider the following six criteria:

(i) whether the proposed transaction would result in a material increase in risks to financial system stability due to an increase in size of the combining firms;
(ii) whether the transaction would result in a reduction in the availability of substitute providers for the services offered by the combining firms;
(iii) whether the transaction would materially increase the extent of the interconnectedness of the financial system;
(iv) whether the transaction would materially increase the extent to which the combining firms contribute to the complexity of the financial system;
(v) whether the transaction would materially increase the extent of cross-border activities of the combining firms; and
(vi) the relative degree of difficulty of resolving the combined firm.

Community Reinvestment Act. The agencies must also take into consideration, in connection with reviewing the convenience and needs of the community, the record of each participating bank's performance under the Community Reinvestment Act ("CRA"). This is an area that historically engendered numerous comments to, and protests of, high-profile applications, as discussed in Chapter 7.

Public Notice. Each of the federal agencies requires public notice be made of mergers and the like in a newspaper of general circulation in the

28. *See, e.g.*, OCC CRA Decision No. 186, Conditional Approval of Application to Merge Capital Bank Corporation, Raleigh, North Carolina, with and into First Tennessee Bank National Association, Memphis, Tennessee (Oct. 16, 2017); OCC CRA Decision No. 177, Condition Approval of Merger of First Niagara Bank, National Association, Buffalo, New York, into KeyBank National Association, Cleveland, Ohio (Sept. 22, 2016).

participating banks' main locations. The public has the right to comment and protest during the comment period.[29]

Additional Merger Requisites. The respective chartering laws of the institution—NBA for national banks, HOLA for federal savings associations, and state law for state institutions—also impose requirements on the proposed transaction, such as required shareholders' or members' vote and rights of dissenting shareholders.

Exit Notice. Notice must be given to the OCC that a national bank or federal savings bank was merged into another institution when the application was not filed with the OCC.[30] States typically require a similar notice.

Post-Merger Branch Names. In some situations, institutions merge but seek to keep the name of the target bank (the one that is merged away) on its former branches and for marketing purposes. Sometimes it is a long-term plan when the target bank wishes to maintain its local goodwill. Or, it may be on a short-term basis while the parties complete conversion and roll out new signage. An example in 2020 was the merger of BB&T and SunTrust in which both banks intended to maintain their respective former name on branch signage and for marketing purposes for a period of about 18 months before converting to the new bank name, Truist. This practice typically requires assumed/fictitious name filings in states where the affected branches are located.

The federal banking agencies permit merged banks to engage in this practice and continue to use their previous name for certain purposes as an assumed business name of the resulting institution. However, they share a concern that depositors will be confused with respect to the extent of FDIC deposit insurance coverage if a branch or division carries an assumed name. In this regard, use of two names is inherently susceptible to confusion that may only be overcome by standards and procedures of identification that would cause a reasonable person to conclude that the assumed name appearing in signage, disclosures, and contracts is in reference to the official charter name.[31]

In order to address these issues, on May 1, 1998, the federal bank regulatory agencies issued an Interagency Policy Statement on Branch Names (the "branch Name Policy Statement").[32] Such Policy Statement requires an insured depository institution that intends to use different names for

---

29. *See, e.g.*, (FDIC) 12 C.F.R. § 303.7. Publication is also required for establishment or relocation of a branch, relocation of a main office, change in control or application for deposit insurance.
30. 12 C.F.R. § 5.33(k).
31. For a discussion of these issues as applied to a bank merger, *see*, State of Washington, Department of Financial Institutions, Division of Banks, ISGC-2005-013-DOB.
32. FIL-46-98 (May 1, 1998), available at https://www.fdic.gov/news/news/financial/1998/fil9846b.html.

various branches to take reasonable steps to ensure that its customers will not become confused and inadvertently exceed the FDIC insurance limit.

The Branch Name Policy Statement and interpretive letters issued under it provide the following examples of steps or measures to consider in order to mitigate or eliminate customer confusion with respect to insurance of deposits:

- disclosing, clearly and conspicuously, in signs, advertising, and similar materials that the facility is a branch, division, or other unit of the insured institution, and assuring that signs and advertising do not create a deceptive and/or misleading impression;
- using the legal name of the insured institution for legal documents, certificates of deposits, signature cards, loan agreements, account statements, checks, drafts, and other similar documents;
- educating the staff of the insured institution regarding the possibility of customer confusion with respect to deposit insurance, and requiring that staff inquire of customers, prior to opening any new accounts, whether the customers have deposits at the institution's other branches;
- providing a customer notification to all existing branch customers to include a FAQ brochure disclosing that branches are a part of the insured depository institution, and the division is not a separate institution for purposes of FDIC insurance coverage;
- requiring an acknowledgment by a customer opening a deposit account in a branch (in bold, above the customer's signature) that the customer understands that the branch is a division of the insured depository institution and that accounts at the branch and at the insured institution are not separately insured;
- requiring prior approval of the institution's legal or compliance departments for all documentation, including website screens, to ensure that the branch customers are given full and conspicuous disclosure that they are doing business with the insured institution, and to otherwise ensure compliance with the Policy Statement.

The banking agencies have the same customer concern with respect to an institution using a different assumed name over the internet. Examples of internet-related practices that may create, rather than mitigate, confusion for customers include: (i) statements on an institution's website that suggest that the branch or division (operating under a trade or assumed name) is a separate entity, or (ii) a listing on the branch or division website of certain employees as executive officers of the branch or division, without clarification that the branch or division is part of the insured financial institution. The FDIC has issued cease and desist letters to institutions that have been found to engage in these practices.

The internet branch's homepage and any pages that allow a customer to initiate deposit transactions should make clear that the customer is dealing with the insured institution. Such disclosures must be clear, prominent, and easy to understand.

Deposit Assumptions

Historically, deposit assumptions occurred when one depository institution either effected an acquisition of another depository institution as a "P&A"—purchase and assumption transaction—or merely bought a few branches. In either event, the purchasing institution buys part of the target bank. These transactions are subject to the BMA, just like mergers. The same application goes to the same agency(ies); the approval considerations are the same; they require public notice and CRA consideration. The remaining assets and liabilities remain in the target bank, either for it to continue operations a bit skinnier or to be liquidated.

An interesting example in 2020 involved State Farm Bank, FSB, selling all of its deposits to U.S. Bank. Why interesting? State Farm Bank had no branches and funded exclusively through its network of insurance agents and from the internet. It accumulated over $10 billion in deposits in that manner. The transaction was a major part of State Farm exiting the business of banking.

In recent years, there has been a new spin on deposit assumptions. Banks have begun restructuring their balance sheets in order to increase capital. In so doing, many have attempted to move deposits associated with a line of business to another institution. For instance, they would seek to transfer all of the prepaid card deposits, or all of the portable health account deposits or all the deposits of a deposit broker. The law in this regard is not well-settled and many of these transactions will require a full application under the BMA. If the account to be moved is a pure brokered deposit and the broker has the authority from the accountholders to move the account, it probably does not require an application.[33] Otherwise, it probably does. Lawyers need to check with the responsible agency for the assuming bank until such time as the regulatory policy on this issue is formally articulated.

Antitrust Implications

Every financial institution business combination, whether it be structured as a merger, acquisition, purchase of assets, or consolidation, is destined to be tested to assure that it does not "substantially lessen competition in any

33. Brokered deposits involve another area of the law, subject to rules of the FDIC generally requiring that the depository institution be "well-capitalized" to accept them. *See*, 12 U.S.C. § 1831f. Brokered deposits are discussed in depth in Chapter 5, *supra*.

section of the country"[34] first by the responsible agency for the acquiring or surviving entity and then again by the enforcement arm of the federal government, the Department of Justice ("DOJ").[35]

Antitrust becomes an issue when an acquisition involves the loss of a competitor in a market. These are called "horizontal mergers" and involve parties that compete in the same market or markets. The acquisition of a failing or failed depository institution, as well as a merger of controlled affiliates, each constitutes an exception to the antitrust rules.

The banking agencies provide delegated authority[36] to review most merger applications at the local office (local Federal Reserve Bank or regional office of the OCC or FDIC), but if the pro forma market share of the acquiror will exceed 35% of the market, the application will go to Washington, DC.

Defining the Market. In order to determine if the transaction is horizontal, there must be a defined geographic and product market.

Geographic Market. The agencies must first define a geographic market in order to have borders inside which they may measure competition. The general rule for determining the extent of a relevant geographic market in a bank acquisition comes from the Supreme Court's decision in *U.S. v. Philadelphia National Bank,*[37] *to wit*: That localized area where customers of the participating institutions can practicably turn for alternative financial services. Banking markets may be counties or in proximity to counties, statistical areas, or Rand McNally metro areas (a favorite of DOJ). But, in the first instance, we merely look to the Federal Reserve. Banking markets for this purpose have been predefined across the country by the Federal Reserve, and horizontal merger transactions are screened for the impact on competition by using the Federal Reserve definition of the market. If the parties do not agree on the definition, the applicant should provide an analysis of competition (in a so-called economic brief) as part of any application.

Product Market. There must also be a definition of the product overlap. Traditionally, the definition of the relevant product market for evaluating bank mergers evolved from the Supreme Court's analysis in *Philadelphia National Bank,* which defined commercial banking as a "cluster of products

---

34. The federal banking laws establish essentially the standard of Section 7 of the Clayton Act, 15 U.S.C. § 18.
35. 12 U.S.C. § 1828(c).
36. The federal banking agencies are headquartered in Washington, D.C., but they each have numerous branch offices in the case of the OCC and FDIC, and the Federal Reserve has the twelve Federal Reserve Banks, which have local offices. Delegated authority means that the branch offices/Federal Reserve Bank have authority under the applicable statute to act on applications and notices.
37. U.S. v. Philadelphia National Bank, 374 U.S. 321 (1963).

and services." This has been followed by bank regulatory agencies, who tend to view all products offered by financial institutions as being within a distinct line of commerce and, therefore, within one product market. They have not generally distinguished between consumer services and commercial services or between particular products such as mortgage lending, transaction accounts, cash management, and the like, accepting that the cluster is vested with economic significance beyond the individual products and services that constitute it.[38] In adopting the cluster analysis, each agency has recognized that competitors other than commercial banks provide equivalent products and services. They, however, have not consistently agreed on the competitive importance of alternative providers such as thrifts and credit unions in a given market. This resulted in counting thrifts as less than whole competitors by discounting their share in the market by 50% for screening purposes. Lesser treatment has been accorded to credit unions. Today, however, all will count these providers as 100% competitors with evidence that they offer commercial bank-like services in the market.

Role of DOJ. Most mergers and acquisitions do not require special scrutiny by DOJ because they either do not involve a horizontal merger or because they do not adversely impact competition in a significant manner. DOJ will issue a summary report to the banking agencies listing the transactions that do not cause problems. If the DOJ determines to scrutinize a transaction, it will initiate an independent investigation of the market. There is no secret in this regard. Staff members of the Antitrust Division will contact the applicant as early as the public announcement of the transaction to discuss preliminary concerns. They will typically take the lead in the investigation, with the banking agency looking on; although the Federal Reserve economists and lawyers may stay more involved than the other agencies.

The DOJ now applies a novel approach to the product market that involves disaggregating the market. To this end, DOJ analyzes distinct market segments of banking or "mini-clusters," such as small and medium-size business lending. DOJ typically admits that consumer services are provided by a myriad of in- and out-of-market providers and, unless factors in a given market indicate otherwise, focuses exclusively on the commercial segment.

Screening with the HHI. Any proposed transaction that involves competitors in the same market needs to be screened under the guidelines based on the market definitions maintained by the Federal Reserve Bank for the region. To guide participants through the process, the DOJ issued revised Horizontal Merger Guidelines on August 19, 2010,[39] but in so doing

38. U.S. v. Phillipsburg National Bank, 399 U.S. 350 (1969).
39. Horizontal Merger Guidelines (Aug. 19, 2010).

failed to liberalize the historical standards for financial institution mergers. Guidance DOJ released as to bank mergers in 1995 continues to abide.[40]

The DOJ's screening tool is called the Herfindahl-Hirschman Index (HHI) and it is calculated on each market in which there is a horizontal merger proposal as follows (work sheets for the calculations are provided by DOJ):[41]

1. List each competitor in the market (based on the Federal Reserve definition) and their respective deposits (large to small).
2. All savings association deposits need to be reduced by 50%. (No credit unions are counted at this stage.)
3. Determine the market share of each competitor in the market (expressed as a percent of total deposits).
4. Square each market share.
5. Sum the squares.

The pre-merger HHI is calculated before the transaction; the post-merger HHI is after the transaction. However, there is a shortcut to calculate the increase off of the pre-merger HHI analysis: take the market share of acquirer × the market share of target × 2.

The DOJ's test for concentration in the market for financial institution mergers is both a post-merger HHI of 1800 or more and an increase of 200 or more.

Mitigating Circumstances. Any proposed transaction that exceeds these limits will generally require greater scrutiny by the primary federal regulatory agency and the DOJ and the applicant will want to provide an ancillary analysis, including the following types of information[42]:

- evidence that the merging parties do not significantly compete with one another or that the target institution does not offer full suites of modern banking products;
- evidence that rapid economic change has resulted in an outdated geographic market definition, and that an alternate market is more appropriate;
- evidence that market shares are not an adequate indicator of the extent of competition in the market, such as:
    - evidence that institutions in the market would be likely to expand current levels of commercial lending. Such evidence might include current loan-to-deposit ratios, recent hiring of new commercial loan officers, pending branch applications or

40. Bank Merger Competitive Review—Introduction and Overview (1995).
41. *Id.* The HHI worksheets are provided at the end of the Guidelines.
42. *Id.* at Section 2.

significant out-of-market resources that would be shifted into the market in response to new loan opportunities;

- evidence that a particular institution's market share overstates or understates its competitive significance (such as evidence that an institution is rapidly gaining or losing market share or that the institution is not competitively viable or is operating under regulatory restrictions on its activities);
- in the market where the main office of one or more of the banks is located, evidence that the deposits booked at the main office significantly overstate the actual amount of local deposits because the bank books brokered deposits, online and national accounts, government deposits, and the like at its main office.[43]

- evidence concerning entry conditions, including evidence of entry by institutions within the last two years and the growth of those institutions that have entered; evidence of likely entry within the next two years, such as pending branch applications; and expectations about potential entry by institutions not now in the market area and the reasons for such expectations, including legal requirements for entry.

Additional information that may be relevant includes evidence of competition from sources not included in the scree, such as[44]:

- evidence that a thrift institution is actively engaged in providing services to commercial customers, particularly loans for business startup or working capital purposes and cash management services;
- evidence that a credit union has such membership restrictions, or lack of restrictions, and offers such services to commercial customers that it should be considered to be in the market;
- evidence of actual competition by out-of-market institutions for commercial customers, particularly competition for loans for business startup or working capital purposes;
- evidence of actual competition by nonbank institutions for commercial customers, particularly competition for loans for business startup or working capital purposes.

Divestiture as a Cure. Should the applicant's arguments not be sufficient to outweigh the anticompetitive effects of a transaction, all is not lost. The applicant has the opportunity to cure the problem through divestiture.

43. *See, e.g.*, Federal Reserve Board, Public Memorandum on Competitive Considerations and Statistical Annex regarding BB&T Corporation, Mar. 8, 2019.
44. *Supra* note 40 at Section 2.

Typically, DOJ will determine the branches to be divested and will provide a list of possible bidders. Some of this is negotiable, but only with solid data to support any proposed change.

Role of Hart-Scott-Rodino. There are instances involving thrift acquisitions that may trigger Hart-Scott-Rodino notices to the Federal Trade Commission; however, those issues typically only arise when there is no BMA application. This area is discussed in Chapter 10 in the context of financial holding company acquisitions where HSR comes into play most notably.

Relocation of a National Bank's Main Office

A national bank, upon approval of two-thirds of its shareholders (and a certificate of approval by the OCC), may move its main office to "any . . . location" that is not more than 30 miles from the limits of the "city, town or village" where the office was originally located. This authority, which was enacted in 1886,[45] was interpreted by the OCC prior to Riegle-Neal as permitting a national bank that relocates its main office to retain the former office as a branch even if the bank could not have opened a branch at the old location under the McFadden Act. The agency also permitted national banks to move their main office to another state so long as the 30-mile limit was observed and to retain the office in the former state as a branch—thereby permitting the bank to operate on an interstate basis. Not surprisingly, these policies gave rise to considerable litigation with the OCC prevailing in virtually all of these cases.[46] The OCC successfully argued, among other things, that there was nothing in Section 30 that imposed a geographic limit on the location of the new office, and nothing that conferred McFadden Act jurisdiction over the use of the former main office.

Limitations on Interstate Activity

As indicated above, prohibitions on interstate mergers and similar transactions were eliminated in Riegle-Neal. However, Dodd-Frank added several new twists. Section 623 of Dodd-Frank amends the BMA to prohibit the responsible agency from approving any merger that would result in the resulting institution controlling more than 10% of the total deposits of all insured depository institutions in the United States. Moreover, as of July 21, 2012, the BMA was amended by Section 607 of Dodd-Frank to require

45. May 1, 1886, ch. 73, 24 Stat. 18, 12 U.S.C. § 30.

46. *See, e.g.*, Ramapo Bank v. Camp, 425 F.2d 333, 344 (3d Cir. 1970), *cert. denied*, 400 U.S. 828 (1970), and Interpretations—Corporate Decision #96-58, Sept. 30, 1996, Published in Interpretations and Actions, Oct. 1996.

that an interstate transaction subject to the BMA may only be approved if each bank will continue to be "well-capitalized and well-managed."[47]

In considering an interstate application, the primary federal regulator of the resulting institution must take into account the federal CRA compliance record of the applicant and banks that would be an affiliate of the resulting bank, and the compliance of the applicant with state CRA laws. An unsatisfactory CRA compliance rating can be grounds for disapproval of the application.[48]

In addition, under Riegle-Neal, a state may adopt a law or regulation limiting interstate activity in some respects:

Age Requirements. A state is permitted to enact a requirement that a bank in that state must have been in existence for up to five years before it, or any of its branches, may be acquired by an out-of-state bank.[49] A host state may also apply this age limit to acquisitions of banks by bank holding companies. In cases in which an interstate acquisition presents technical problems, the acquirer may charter a "shell bank" in the host state for the sole purpose of acquiring control of, or acquiring the assets of, the target bank or any of its branches. Shell banks are deemed to have the age of the target bank for purposes of the host state's age laws.[50]

Concentration Limits. An interstate merger may not be approved if the resulting bank and its depository institution affiliates:

- control more than 10% of the total amount of deposits of insured depository institutions in the United States; or
- other than its first time entry into the state, control more than 30% of the deposits of all insured banks and savings associations in any state in which both banks participating in the merger had a branch prior to the merger.[51]

Example:

- Bank X, headquartered in state A, has branches in states B, C, and D
- Bank Y, headquartered in state B, has branches in states A, C, and D
- Bank X and Y propose to merge with Bank X as the resulting institution.

The merger would not be approved under this provision if, after the merger, Bank X would control more than 30% of the deposits of all insured

47. *Amending* 12 U.S.C. § 1828u(b)(4)(B). The concept of "well-managed" is discussed in Chapter 11, *infra*.
48. 12 U.S.C. § 1831u(b)(3).
49. 12 U.S.C. § 1831u(a)(5).
50. *See, e.g.*, OCC Corp. Dec. # 97-33, Application of Bank One Wisconsin Trust Co., N.A., et al. (June 1, 1997). Codified at 12 U.S.C. § 1831u(a)(6).
51. 12 U.S.C. § 1831u(b)(2).

banks and savings associations in *any one* of the following states: A, B, C, or D.

A state may, by law or policy, set a concentration limit higher than 30% of deposits so long as the law or policy does not discriminate against out-of-state banks, bank holding companies, or their subsidiaries. These concentration limits do not apply to mergers between affiliated banks or acquisitions of failed institutions.

Mergers Primarily for Deposit Production

In keeping with the principle that banks should serve the credit needs of their communities, Section 109 of Riegle-Neal requires the banking agencies to promulgate regulations to prohibit the use of interstate branching primarily for deposit production, that is, gathering deposits in a host state that are used primarily to make loans in the bank's home state or in a third state. To this end, the regulations relating to this practice[52] require each agency to determine whether the loan-to-deposit ratio of each branch established under Riegle-Neal in a host state is at least 50% of the statewide ratio for all banks in that state. If an interstate branch's ratio is below the 50% level, the responsible agency, after pursuing certain administrative proceedings and analyzing mitigating circumstances, may prohibit the bank from opening additional branches. It could also order the bank to close one or more branches, unless the bank provides an acceptable plan to meet the credit needs of the communities it serves in the host state.

State Law Issues in Connection with Interstate Expansion

When a bank headquartered in one state (the "home" state) enters another state (the "host" state) through a new branch or acquisition, it will have potentially inconsistent laws that may apply to its operations. Congress addressed these issues in Riegle-Neal and, in an attempt to level the playing field for various institutions, in a 1997 amendment to the law.

National Bank Branches in Host States

National banks have the benefit of preemption of many state laws. Yet certain laws need to apply in order to balance the interests of residents of host states. Section 102 of Riegle-Neal addressed this issue by listing the laws of a host state that apply to a branch of a national bank:

52. Agency regulations on this subject are found at: (OCC) 12 C.F.R. Part 25, Subpart E; (FDIC) 12 C.F.R. Part 369; (Federal Reserve) 12 C.F.R. § 208.28.

- community reinvestment,
- fair lending, consumer protection, and
- intrastate branching.[53]

Each is intended to apply to the same extent the law applies to a branch of a bank chartered in that state. So far so good, but then the law goes rogue and gives the OCC an out: those laws do not apply if application of the law to the branch is preempted by federal law; or the OCC finds that it is discriminatory in its application to the branch as compared to its application to the branch of a bank chartered in that state.

Moreover, some host state laws apply to a branch of an out-of-state national bank because the OCC has determined that state law is not preempted under its general preemptive powers derived from the Constitution's Supremacy Clause. These include state laws relating to:

- contracts,
- collection of debts,
- acquisition and transfer of property,
- taxation,
- zoning,
- crimes,
- torts, and
- homestead rights.[54]

Note, however, the power to enforce a state law applicable to a branch of a national bank is vested in the OCC and, to the extent permitted under Dodd-Frank, the state attorneys general. State laws, other than those listed above and certain tax laws, apply to a branch of a national bank in a host state in the same manner as they apply to a branch of a national bank headquartered in the host state.

"Out-of-State" State Bank Branches in Host State

The extent to which the laws of a host state apply to branches established in such state by an out-of-state bank is established by Section 24(j) of the FDIA,[55] as amended by the Riegle-Neal Amendments Act of 1997 ("Riegle-Neal II").[56]

The amendment was intended to remedy deficiencies in the original version and align the rights of state banks with national banks, and to that end, it provides that the laws of a host state, including laws relating

53. Codified at 12 U.S.C. § 36(f).
54. 12 C.F.R. §§ 7.4007–7.4009.
55. Codified at 12 U.S.C. § 1831a(j)(1).
56. Pub. Law 105-24 (July 3, 1997), 111 Stat. 238.

to community investment, consumer protection, fair lending, and the establishment of intrastate branches, apply to host state branches of out-of-state, state banks to the same extent that host state laws apply to a branch of an out-of-state *national* bank located in the host state.

In other words, host state laws can be applicable to a state bank branch if they are applicable to a national bank and inapplicable to the same extent (as the result of federal preemption of the state law, or otherwise). Circular reasoning to an extent because you have to figure out where a national bank stands to figure out the result for a similarly situated state bank. Once a determination is made that host state law is inapplicable to a branch in that state of an out-of-state, state bank, the law of the home state of the out-of-state bank will apply to its branch in the host state.

Activities of Branches of Out-of-State State Banks

Riegle-Neal treated activities treated in the same manner, with perhaps less clarity. Section 24(j)(2)[57] provides that an out-of-state, state bank can conduct any activities at its host state branch that are permissible under the bank's home state "to the extent" such activity is permissible for a bank chartered in the host state, or for a branch in the host state of an out-of-state national bank.

Many in the banking industry believed that even after the Riegle-Neal II amendment, Section 24 still did not achieve the stated congressional goal of providing parity between national banks and state banks with respect to interstate activities. As a result, the Financial Services Roundtable filed a petition with the FDIC requesting rulemaking to clarify certain laws relating to interstate activities of insured state banks and their subsidiaries, including Section 24.[58] In response to the petition, the FDIC published a notice of proposed rulemaking, which would have, among other things, created a new Subpart F, "Preemption," to its branching rules at 12 C.F.R. Part 362. The proposal would have defined "activity conducted at a branch" to mean an activity "of, by, through, in, from, or substantially involving, a branch."[59]

Since a national bank branch gets the benefit of preemption whether or not the entire activity is performed in its branch, and since Congress intended to grant state banks full parity with national banks in this area, the definition in the proposed rule was designed to clarify that a branch of an out-of-state state bank gets the benefit of preemption whether or not the

57. 12 U.S.C. § 1831a(j)(2).
58. *Petition for FDIC Rulemaking Providing Interstate Banking Parity for Insured State Banks*, filed Mar. 4, 2005, and published at 70 Fed. Reg. 13,413 (Mar. 21, 2005).
59. *Id.* at 60,030.

entire activity is performed in the branch.[60] The FDIC has not taken further action on the proposed rule and is not expected to do so, but it highlights some of the issues that remain outstanding in this space.

Activities Restrictions

Another hallmark of the "specialness" of banks is the extensive amount of law that restricts their activities and ultimately keeps them out of commerce. As pointed out in the introduction to this chapter, banks are essentially the opposite in this regard from unregulated entities: bank powers must be express or implied; whereas corporations and LLCs have all powers permitted under law, unless limited by their governing documents. History has designed a patchwork of powers for depository institutions—national banks have different powers in a number of respects than state banks and the same is true for savings associations. Thus, once again, legal advice may not be provided until the charter to conduct the activity is identified and applicable law is researched, it being understood that if no law, regulation, or interpretation permits the activity, it is impermissible.

Much of the law in this space derives from statutory tests that tie activities to the "business of banking" and the way in which the appropriate regulator has interpreted such tests. The OCC is the chief architect of powers in this respect, so we begin with national bank powers.

National Banks

The general powers of national banks are expressly delineated in portions of Title 12 of the U.S. Code, primarily in 12 U.S.C. § 24. It is in paragraph seventh of this law ("Section 24 (Seventh)") that the Comptroller is granted by Congress discretion to broaden the express powers of national banks. Specifically, that paragraph permits national banks.

> [T]o exercise...*all such incidental powers as shall be necessary to carry on the business of banking*; by discounting and negotiating promissory notes, drafts, bills of exchange, and other evidences of debt; by receiving deposits; by buying and selling exchange, coin, and bullion; by loaning money on personal security; and by obtaining, issuing, and circulating notes according to the provisions of this title.[61] [Emphasis added.]

60. *Id.* at 60,027.
61. 12 U.S.C. § 24 (Seventh) (emphasis added).

The first clause, the so-called incidental powers clause, grants banks the power to conduct activities incidental to the "business of banking." Since the late 1800s, the Comptroller has used this clause as a predicate to permit additional activities for national banks—activities ranging from certifying checks to leasing personal property to underwriting municipal bond insurance.[62] On occasion, courts have found that the Comptroller went too far in construing this clause.[63]

The cases have struggled with two essential issues: (i) defining the "business of banking" as that term is used in Section 24 (Seventh), and (ii) establishing a test for determining what is "incidental thereto." Neither term is defined in the statute. They are, thus, subject to interpretation by the Comptroller and the courts. The legal controversy in this regard has primarily involved whether the business of banking is limited to the express enumerated powers that follow its reference in the statute after the semicolon or whether it constitutes a separate grant of power. Although this issue was litigated and argued for decades, the U.S. Supreme Court only definitively resolved it in 1995 in connection with its unanimous *NationsBank/VALIC* decision, when it inserted in a footnote that the business of banking "is not limited to the enumerated powers in § 24 (Seventh) and that the Comptroller therefore has discretion to authorize activities beyond those specifically enumerated."[64]

This decision of the Supreme Court confirmed the Comptroller's latitude in authorizing activities for national banks under Section 24 (Seventh). Finally, it was clear that the "business of banking" went beyond the enumerated powers. Moreover, as the business of banking expanded conceptually, so too must activities "incidental thereto."

The "Business of Banking"

Shortly after the *NationsBank/VALIC* decision, and presumably in response to its grant of authority, Julie Williams, then Chief Counsel of the OCC, coauthored an article exploring the definition of the business of banking

62. Merchants' Nat'l Bank v. State Nat'l Bank, 77 U.S. 604 (1871) (certifying checks); M&M Leasing Corp. v. Seattle First Nat'l Bank, 563 F.2d 1377 (9th Cir. 1977), *cert. denied*, 436 U.S. 956 (1978) (leasing); American Ins. Ass'n v. Clarke, 656 F. Supp. 404 (D.D.C. 1987), *aff'd in part*, 865 F.2d 278 (D.C. Cir. 1988) (municipal bond insurance). *See also*, First Nat'l Bank of Eastern Ark. v. Taylor, 907 F.2d 775, 778 (8th Cir.), *cert. denied*, 498 U.S. 972 (1990), for a list of approved activities and relevant citations.
63. *See, e.g.*, Arnold Tours, Inc. v. Camp, 472 F.2d 427 (1st Cir. 1972), rejecting the authority of national banks to operate travel agencies. The court used a strict reading of the incidental powers clause: requiring incidental powers to be directly related to one of the express powers set forth in Section 24 (Seventh).
64. NationsBank of North Carolina, N.A. v. Variable Annuity Life Ins. Co., 513 U.S. 251, n.2 (1995).

in contemporary contexts.[65] She concluded that the business of banking is an evolving activity and that the national bank charter should be treated as an organic entity whose powers may respond, over time and within certain parameters, to developments in the financial marketplace and the needs of banks' customers. She then proposed three principles for determining whether an activity was within the business of banking:

- Is the activity functionally equivalent to or a logical outgrowth of a recognized banking activity?
- Will the activity respond to customers' needs or otherwise benefit the bank or its customers?
- Does the activity involve risks similar in nature to those already assumed by banks?[66]

These principles were then adopted as the interpretive position of the OCC in connection with the next authorization of a new banking power—reinsurance of private mortgage insurance—and appear in any interpretive letter in which the Comptroller considers whether a proposed activity is authorized.[67]

"Incidental Thereto"

Once the Comptroller established parameters for defining the business of banking, the agency faced reformulating the definition of incidental powers—the premise being that this language constituted a separate grant of authority to undertake activities inherently not part of the business of banking.[68] In a separate article,[69] the Chief Counsel again comprehensively clarified her views on incidental powers, asserting that such powers must evolve along with the business of banking.

The Chief Counsel first acknowledged that Section 24 (Seventh) requires that incidental powers be "necessary" to the business of banking. In that regard, she recognized the definition of "necessary" previously developed by the First Circuit Court of Appeals in the seminal *Arnold Tours* decision.[70] Under this authority, incidental powers must be "convenient" or "useful" to authorized activities.

65. Julie L. Williams & Mark P. Jacobson, *The Business of Banking: Looking to the Future,* 50 Bus. Law 783 (May 1995).
66. *Id.* at 785.
67. *See,* OCC Interpretive Letter No. 743 (Oct. 17, 1996).
68. Julie L. Williams & James F. E. Gillespie, Jr., *The Business of Banking: Looking to the Future—Part II,* 52 Bus. Law 1279 (Aug. 1997).
69. *Id.*
70. Arnold Tours v. Camp, 473 F.2d 427 (1st Cir. 1972).

After reconciling and distinguishing precedent, the Chief Counsel concluded that incidental powers authorize:

- Activities that facilitate aspects of operating a bank as a business enterprise;
- Activities functionally equivalent to the business of banking that enhance the quality and efficiency of its content and delivery; and
- Activities that optimize the use and value of a bank's facilities and competencies or enable a bank to avoid economic waste in its franchise.[71]

These principles were then followed in connection with the Comptroller's approval of national bank sales of crop insurance.[72] In this regard, the Comptroller found the activity to be incidental to banking because it enhanced a bank's ability to receive repayment for its loans, promoted a bank's lending business by making available a credit-related product sought by borrowers, and enabled the bank to avoid economic waste in connection with its lending activities. Despite the fact that the OCC's decision on crop insurance was subsequently reversed by the D.C. Circuit, its theory as to incidental powers continues to be espoused, and the three tests appear in OCC interpretive letters as to all activities that may be authorized as "incidental."

Authorized Activities

The OCC has used the above tests countless times to approve numerous activities through the vehicles of interpretive letters and application approvals. As a consequence, most powers will not be found in regulations, with the exception of those found in Part 7.[73] Most are in the informal law, never subjected to notice and comment (although a number were litigated as far as the Supreme Court).

The OCC has cut the corner on research in this regard and includes on its website an invaluable tool: *Activities Permissible for National Banks and Federal Savings Associations, Cumulative*. The powers are listed there, along with the developmental history with citations to OCC interpretive letters. These are worth their weight in gold to the bank regulatory lawyer. Note: in July of 2020, the OCC issued a notice of proposed rulemaking to revise and reorganize its regulations relating to the activities and operations of

71. Williams, *supra*, note 58 at 1280–1281.
72. OCC Interpretive Letter No. 812 (Dec. 29, 1997).
73. 12 C.F.R. Part 7. This part includes activities as finder, insurance agent, payroll issuer, messenger service, and the like.

national banks and federal savings associations.[74] This proposal would clarify and codify OCC interpretations, integrate certain regulations for national banks and federal savings associations, and update or eliminate outdated regulatory requirements. As a result, OCC regulations at 12 C.F.R. Parts 7, 145 and 160, where the activities rules reside, are undergoing an overhaul.

State Banks

State banks have those powers permissible under applicable state law. It may be an express power, an implied power, or a power derived from another source under a wild card or parity provision. However, state legislatures and regulators are curtailed in some respects by federal law to keep them from racing to the bottom when it involves activities conducted as principal (as opposed to activities conducted as agent or custodian).

Express Authorization

Express authorization is obviously found in the applicable state statute. Many states have lists of approved activities on their websites.

Beware there is a "gotcha"—a few state laws have banks begin life as general corporations, with general corporate powers, and then they are granted bank licenses.[75] Oftentimes, the banks in these states may have few express powers (everything being implied) and more laws and regulations that list what they may not do.

"Wild Card" Authority

The primary source of authority for state bank activities beyond those expressly authorized by statute historically was found in state "wild card" or parity provisions. These banking statutes essentially authorize state banks to exercise the same powers permitted to national banks and, sometimes, federal savings associations.

Virtually all states now have some variety of wild card. Wild card statutes are not all self-effecting. While many are unlimited in nature, a majority have limitations on the scope of the authority conferred. They may require some action on the part of the bank regulator to effectuate the authority, or they may require state bank regulators to promulgate rules before the

74. Activities and Operations of National Banks and Federal Savings Associations, OCC Notice of Proposed Rulemaking, 85 Fed. Reg. 40,794 (July 7, 2020).
75. California, North Carolina, and Ohio banks, for example, are corporations. Not only do these banks have general corporate powers, but they file documents directly with the respective secretaries of state. That is something most state banks may not do.

activity is authorized. This is especially true when a state bank is seeking to exercise a power granted uniquely to a federal savings association.

In the late 1990s, a new type of wild card, the so-called "Super Wild Card," was first enacted by the legislature of the State of Illinois. Illinois chartered banks had enjoyed parity with national banks for 30 years and even had parity with savings associations,[76] but the legislature went even further by permitting state banks parity with any other state bank in the United States.[77] Thus, an Illinois state bank could engage in any activity permitted in another state, subject to the same limitations and restrictions that would be applicable to a state-chartered institution in that state, except that real estate brokerage was prohibited and insurance activities must be conducted in compliance with Illinois law.[78] Additional states, such as Utah, have now enacted super wild cards and obtained powers without the limitations applicable to national banks.

Incidental Powers

A number of state banking statutes include incidental powers provisions similar in nature to Section 24 (Seventh). These provisions present the applicable state banking regulator with the ability to broaden state bank powers either proactively by designing specific approvals or reactively by following the lead of the Comptroller.

An example is the State of New York, where the banking department issued two interpretive letters in 1991 agreeing with the Comptroller's approval for national banks to sell fixed and variable annuities. The banking department opined that the Comptroller's analysis applied equally to New York state-chartered banks. The New York Supreme Court initially annulled the determination of the state banking department. However, the appellate division reversed, holding that the department properly interpreted the New York incidental powers clause.[79] The court of appeals affirmed. In a decision that predated the *NationsBank/VALIC* decision and foreshadowed it, the court held that the department's construction of the incidental powers clause was not unreasonable or irrational.[80] Thus, it deserved deference. The court rejected the argument that annuities were insurance for these purposes.

---

76. Sections 5(11) and 5(25), respectively, of the Illinois Banking Act, 205 ILCS 5/5(11) and (25).
77. House Bill 2204; Public Act 91-330, amending Section 5(25) of the Illinois Banking Act.
78. *See,* Illinois Office of Banks and Real Estate Interpretive Letter 2000-02 (Jan. 12, 2000).
79. New York State Ass'n of Life Underwriters v. New York State Banking Dep't, 598 N.Y.S.2d 824 (App. Div. 1993).
80. New York State Ass'n of Life Underwriters v. New York State Banking Dep't, 610 N.Y.S.2d 470, 632 N.E.2d 876 (1994).

The Effect of FDICIA

Until December 19, 1992, state law exclusively controlled the powers of state banks. Federal law did not interfere with the dominion of the states in this regard. However, Congress' passage of the Federal Deposit Insurance Corporation Improvement Act of 1992 ("FDICIA")[81] added a new Section 24 to the Federal Deposit Insurance Act limiting activities and equity investments of state banks. Specifically, the law restricts:

- Activities of state banks acting *as principal* (i.e., an activity that is conducted other than as agent for a customer or a brokerage, custodial, advisory, or administrative capacity or is conducted other than as a trustee);
- Insurance underwriting;
- Equity investments (excluding majority owned subsidiaries);
- Activities of bank subsidiaries acting *as principal*; and
- Common and preferred stock investments.

Essentially all such limitations tie the activity or investment authority of state banks to that authorized for national banks and require FDIC approval for any other activities. Such approval may be granted if the bank meets its capital requirements and the FDIC determines that conducting the activity would not pose a significant risk to the deposit insurance fund. The FDIC released its regulations under FDICIA in two parts: the first deals with equity investments and common and preferred stock investments and the second deals with activities.[82] The FDIC posts its Section 24 approvals on its website.[83]

Importantly, note that FDICIA does not apply to *agency* activities. So state banks are unencumbered in exercising state-granted powers to be an insurance agent/broker or travel agent or real estate agent, etc.

Bank Activities in a Nutshell

So, what about those "non-traditional" activities that banks always seem to want to conduct in the pursuit of fee income? Remember first: if a national bank can do it, a state bank probably can do it as well through at least a wild card and sometimes even more expansively. Suffice it to say, decades of turf battles (with national banks and the OCC fighting the industries which were trying to keep banks off their turf) have written a complicated script on most of these powers. The thirty-second rundown is as follows:

---

81. Pub. L. No. 102-242 (1991) (codified at 12 U.S.C. § 1831a).
82. *See*, 12 C.F.R. §§ 362.3 and 362.4.
83. Search for Section 24 approvals.

Real Estate. Except in the event of foreclosure (when banks may own "OREO"—other real estate owned—subject to complex rules on holding and disposal) and as necessary to conduct their business (i.e., own their office buildings) under 12 U.S.C. § 29[84] or to hold as trustee, banks are extremely limited in this space. Real estate brokerage and development is forbidden to national banks, but some state laws permit state banks to engage in one or both. Even with state law authorization, real estate development, as a principal activity, is subject to the FDICIA restrictions addressed above.

Insurance.[85] Because of case law, national banks may sell annuities and credit insurance directly[86] but all other sales must follow the "place of 5,000" rules developed by the OCC under 12 U.S.C. § 92.[87] As to state banks, a majority of states permit state banks to sell all lines of insurance.

Because of the Gramm-Leach-Bliley Act of 1999[88] ("Gramm-Leach-Bliley") (which gave new powers but also took a few away), title insurance is treated with a reverse wild card: it may be sold by national banks in states where state banks have the express authority. But, watch the states on this issue. The title industry's lobbyists were resourceful in the legislatures, and many state laws expressly forbid the sale of title insurance by banks.

Prior to Gramm-Leach-Bliley, national banks were permitted to reinsure credit insurance and private mortgage insurance, and those powers were grandfathered. Otherwise, insurance underwriting is limited to credit insurance for all charters.

Not only is the insurance powers' matrix complicated, but Section 301 of Gramm-Leach-Bliley made it clear all insurance activities are functionally regulated by the states. That means state licensing regimes apply, as do most insurance laws.

Securities. Sections 201 and 202 of Gramm-Leach-Bliley established a new playing field for bank securities activities and, by amending the definitions of "broker"[89] and "dealer"[90] under the Securities Exchange Act of

84. *See also*, 12 C.F.R. § 7.1000, which also applies to federal savings associations.
85. There are hundreds of pages on this issue in Chapter 3 of Karol K. Sparks, Insurance Activities of Banks (2nd ed. Wolters Kluwer Law and Business 2012).
86. The OCC adopted 12 C.F.R. Part 2 permitting credit insurance sales, *aff'd*, Independent Bankers Ass'n of Am. v. Heimann, 613 F.2d 1164 (D.C. Cir. 1979), cert. denied, 449 U.S. 823 (1980). The OCC then authorized debt cancellation contracts as an alternative to credit insurance in 12 C.F.R. § 7.013, *aff'd*, First Nat'l Bank of E. Ark. v. Taylor, 907 F.2d 775 (8th Cir.), cert. denied, 498 U.S. 972 (1990). As to annuities, *see*, OCC Interpretive Letter No. 331 (Apr. 4, 1985), (variable annuities); OCC Interpretive Letter No. 499 (Feb. 12, 1990), (fixed annuities), *aff'd*, NationsBank of N.C. N.A. v. Variable Annuity Life Ins. Co., 513 U.S. 251 (1995).
87. *See also*, 12 C.F.R. § 7.1001 and numerous related interpretations.
88. Section 303 of Gramm-Leach-Bliley, Pub. L. No. 106-102, 133 Stat. 1338 (1999).
89. Section 3(a)(4) of the Exchange Act (codified at 12 U.S.C. §§ 78c(a)(4)).
90. Section 3(a)(5) of the Exchange Act (codified at 12 U.S.C. §§ 78c(a)(5)).

1934, basically required almost all broker and dealer activities to be pushed out of the depository institution to affiliated or nonaffiliated registered broker-dealers. There are numerous exceptions to the push-out requirements based on traditional bank activities: for third-party brokerage arrangements, trust activities (based on the kind and amount of compensation), transactions in commercial paper, stock purchase plans, sweep accounts, affiliate transactions, private securities offerings, safekeeping and custody, certain identified banking products, and municipal securities, and there is a de minimus shelter provision. The devil is in all the details found in the statute and the enabling Regulation R,[91] which must be read together.

Banks may provide investment advice, but only if they have trust powers. If they provide advice to funds, they must be registered as investment advisers.

Travel Agency. No, national banks may not conduct this activity based once again on case law.[92] Many state laws permit this activity for state banks, but, if the state bank will pre-book rooms or airline tickets for resale, they are engaging in a principal activity subject to FDICIA.

And then there is **finder**, under which authority banks can do almost everything indirectly that they cannot do directly,[93] and, maybe even better, electronic finder authority.[94]

Note what banks may not do: lotteries,[95] loans on their own stock,[96] transfers in contemplation of insolvency,[97] and guarantees (except for letters of credit and those transactions in which the bank has an interest).[98]

Federal Savings Associations

The powers of federal savings associations are determined under HOLA.[99] Savings associations were created to make mortgage loans and stimulate savings by individuals. Thus, most of the statutory and regulatory language regarding activities deals with making loans and taking deposits.[100] As described below, the OTS expanded powers somewhat through

91. Technically this was a joint rulemaking by the Securities and Exchange Commission and Federal Reserve Board. It is Federal Reserve Regulation R (12 C.F.R. Part 18), and it defines many of the statutory terms.
92. Arnold Tours v. Camp, 400 U.S. 45 (Nov. 23, 1970).
93. 12 C.F.R. § 7.1002.
94. 12 C.F.R. Part 7, Subpart E.
95. 12 U.S.C. § 25a; 12 U.S.C. § 339.
96. 12 U.S.C. § 83; 12 U.S.C. § 324.
97. 12 U.S.C. § 91.
98. 12 C.F.R. §§ 7.1016 and 7.1017.
99. 12 U.S.C. §§ 1461 *et seq.*
100. *See, e.g.*, the Deposit Regulations at 12 C.F.R. Part 157 and the Lending and Investment Regulations at 12 C.F.R. Part 160.

interpretations, but, for the most part, other activities are authorized for service corporations.[101]

The OCC has prepared a *Comparison of the Powers of National Banks and Federal Savings Associations*, which is another handy tool to familiarize lawyers with the powers of their clients and the differences between them.[102]

Qualified Thrift Lender Test

Because of its unique purpose, a federal thrift is required under HOLA to be and remain a QTL[103] in order to preserve its original focus on mortgage lending. A QTL is a savings association that qualifies as a domestic building and loan association under Section 7701(a)(19) of the Internal Revenue Code or that has at least 65% of its portfolio assets in "qualified thrift investments." Investments that are considered "qualified thrift investments" include, among other things, loans and investments relating to domestic residential real estate or manufactured housing and mortgage-backed securities relating to the same, home equity loans, small business loans, educational loans, loans made through credit cards or credit card accounts, and shares of stock issued by any Federal Home Loan Bank, without limitation; and shares of stock issued by the Federal Home Loan Mortgage Corporation or the Federal National Mortgage Association, and 50% of the dollar amount of residential mortgage loans originated by the association and sold within ninety days, the aggregate of which is subject to a 20% of portfolio assets limitation.[104]

Section 624 of Dodd-Frank[105] makes this regime take on greater significance. If a savings association fails to remain a QTL, it is immediately subject to certain restrictions and possible enforcement action. This is in contrast to the HOLA provisions that required QTL failing savings associations to either become banks or become subject to certain restrictions. Dodd-Frank provides that if a savings association fails the QTL test, it will be limited to paying only those dividends that would be permissible for a national bank, that are necessary to meet the obligations of any company that controls the savings association, and that are specifically approved by the OCC.

101. Discussed in Chapter 3, *supra.*

102. As of July 1, 2019, and updated from time to time. *See also* the companion document entitled *Key Differences Among National Bank, Federal Savings Association, and Covered Savings Association Requirements* on the OCC website.

103. 12 U.S.C. § 1467a(c)(3).

104. 12 U.S.C. § 1467a(m)(4)(c); 12 U.S.C. § 1464(c)(1).

105. Section 624 amends Section 10(m)(3) of HOLA (codified in 12 U.S.C. § 1467a(m)(3)).

Incidental Powers

Federal thrifts have incidental powers under HOLA, just as national banks do under the NBA. In 1994, the OTS crafted a four-part test for assessing what activities fall within the incidental powers of federal savings associations:

- Is the activity consistent with the purpose and function Congress envisioned for federal savings associations, as evidenced in the relevant banking statutes and the legislative history?
- Does the activity facilitate the conduct of an activity expressly authorized by Congress for federal savings associations, or is the activity similar to an activity that Congress has expressly authorized for federal savings associations?
- Does the activity relate to the financial intermediary role that all federal savings associations were intended to play?
- Is the activity necessary to enable federal savings associations to remain competitive and relevant in a modern economy, thereby permitting federal savings associations to fulfill the purposes for which they were created?[106]

The OTS then used these tests to permit federal savings associations, among other things, to sell credit insurance and annuities, and the OCC has continued these authorities.

State Savings Associations

The powers of state savings associations are determined by state law, with some clarification by the FDIC.[107] Like state banks, their powers are impinged by FDICIA in connection with principal activities. They may not engage as principal in any activity not permissible for a federal savings association, unless the FDIC determines that the activity would not pose a significant risk to the federal deposit insurance fund and the savings association is in compliance with federal capital requirements.[108]

Savings banks chartered under the laws of Massachusetts, New York, and Connecticut have the unique power to issue and underwrite SBLI—savings bank life insurance, free from the restrictions imposed by FDICIA.[109]

---

106. Memorandum from Karen Solomon, Deputy Chief Counsel of OTS, *et al.*, re: Direct Sale of Credit Insurance and Fixed-Rate Annuities by Federal Savings Associations (Oct. 17, 1994).
107. The FDIC deposited the former OTS regulations in 12 C.F.R. § 390, including sections dedicated to powers.
108. 12 U.S.C. § 1831e(a).
109. SBLI is discussed in Sparks, *supra* note 85.

New Product Roll-outs

The decision to exercise these powers and introduce a new product or service raises a whole host of safety and soundness and risk management issues of the sort discussed in Chapter 8. At the outset, the institution needs a process, complete with policies and procedures, to follow from the first day the idea is floated through product roll-out. It needs to consider the needs of its customers, its ability to staff and train employees, the potential risks, compliance requirements and financial costs and benefits. If it will outsource any part of the service, the institution must follow its vendor management protocol as well. The Federal Reserve offers a helpful tool in this regard for community banks in its FedLinks article "Introducing a New Product or Service."[110]

The OCC in turn released a bulletin in 2004 outlining its expectations that bank management and the board will oversee all new, expanded, or modified products and services through an effective risk management process, including (i) performing adequate due diligence prior to introducing the product, (ii) developing and implementing controls and processes to ensure risks are properly measured, monitored, and controlled, and (iii) developing and implementing appropriate performance monitoring and review systems.[111]

Tying Arrangements

As financial institutions broadened their product lines in the 1960s and were permitted to have affiliates, Congress, under pressure from a number of constituencies, including insurance agent trade groups, became concerned that banks would coerce customers into buying new products or affiliate products by tying them to bank products. A typical tying arrangement is one in which a seller conditions the sale of a product or service on the buyer's purchase of another product or service from the seller. The product offered by the seller that is wanted by the customer is best thought of as the "desired product;" the product the buyer is required to buy is the "tied product." An example would be a bank conditioning the approval of an auto loan or the granting of a lower rate on the loan if the customer opened a checking account at the bank or bought homeowner's insurance from an affiliate.

These arrangements can result in federal antitrust law violations if the seller has a dominant market position in the tying product and can stifle competition even if falling short of antitrust violations. The anticompetitive

110. FedLinks, *Introducing a New Product or Service* (Sept. 2014).
111. OCC Bulletin 2004-20, May 10, 2004.

potential of tying arrangements led Congress to impose restrictions on tying arrangements by banks and their operating subsidiaries by adopting Section 106 of the Bank Holding Company Act Amendments of 1970 ("Section 106").[112] Tying restrictions were imposed on savings associations by Section 5(q) of HOLA in 1982[113] and are basically the same as those in Section 106. As such, when the OCC adopted the former OTS regulations, it eliminated the thrift antitying provisions and amended the rule to refer to the Board's regulations.[114]

Unless an exception applies, "tying" in the context of Section 106 means offering a bank loan or other bank product or service *or* varying the consideration on a bank loan or other bank product or service on any of the following conditions:

- the customer's obtaining another product or service from a bank or its affiliate, or
- the customer's providing some additional credit, property, or service to the bank or its affiliates, or
- the customer's agreeing not to obtain credit, property, or services from a competitor.

The entities subject to the antitying rules line up like they do under Sections 23A and B of the Federal Reserve Act:[115] banks and their operating subsidiaries may not impose a tie of their own products or the products of their affiliates. However, the affiliates are not subject to the restrictions on their own products and may impose a tie absent antitrust issues.

The "Traditional Bank Product" Exception

Section 106 has a number of exceptions, many of which are extremely useful. Furthermore, the Board has exemptive authority under Section 106, which it has used on several occasions. One major exemption is the traditional bank product exemption. This exemption permits tying of a bank product if the tie is to a "traditional" bank product. Traditional bank products include loans, discounts, deposits, trust services, and credit derivatives. In 1997, the Board adopted extensive amendments to the regulations implementing Section 106.[116] Among these changes were the following:

112. Pub. L. 91-607, title I, § 106(b), Dec. 31, 1970, 84 Stat. 1766, (12 U.S.C. § 1972). The Board's tying rules are published at 12 C.F.R. § 225.7.
113. 12 U.S.C. Sec. 1464(q), added by Section 331 of the Garn-St. Germain Depository Institutions Act of 1982, Publ. L. 97-320, Oct. 15, 1982.
114. 12 C.F.R. § 163.36.
115. Discussed in Chapter 4, *supra*.
116. *Id.*

- The traditional bank product exception was extended to transactions by a bank in which a bank tied one of its products or services to a tied product of an affiliate.
- Any exemptions afforded to banks generally would also be available to credit card banks, industrial loan companies ("ILCs"), and entities that are excluded from the definition of "bank" in the BHCA.

Combined Balance Discounts

In 1995, the Federal Reserve amended Regulation Y to permit banking organizations to offer customers a discount on the cost of certain products if they maintained a minimum balance in one or more "eligible products" specified by the bank, including nontraditional products such as securities brokerage and insurance products.[117] The agency said it adopted this "combined-balance discount" safe harbor because it would, among other things, "permit banks to market products more efficiently and compete more effectively with their nonbanking competitors who currently offer combined-balance discount arrangements [and] would permit banks to package these products and therefore attract and retain more customers."[118]

The combined-balance discount program must meet the following requirements:

- the bank involved in the program must offer deposits;
- all such deposits must be eligible products; and
- deposit balances must receive equal or greater weight than nondeposit product balances in calculating the required minimum balance.

The agency pointed out that "a bank could count toward the minimum balance 100% of demand deposits, 80% of certificates of deposit, 70% of mutual fund shares, and 60% of stock held in a brokerage account. So long as the percentages assigned to all deposits are higher than [or equal to] the percentages assigned to the nondeposits, the safe harbor would apply."[119] The purpose of these provisions is to prevent banks from using product weighting to require the purchase of certain higher-cost, nontraditional products in order to qualify for the discount.

The variety of eligible products that may be included in combined-balance discount programs is exemplified in a 2001 inquiry by Citibank (South Dakota), N.A. and its banking affiliates (collectively, "bank") describing a combined-balance discount program that the bank wished to

117. Revisions Regarding Tying Restrictions (Combined-balance Discounts), Final Rule 60 Fed. Reg. 20,186 (Apr. 25, 1995).
118. *Id.* at 20,187.
119. *Id.* at 20,188.

offer its customers.[120] The program would offer incentives to the bank's credit card, mortgage, or loan customers who maintained "a combined minimum balance in a package of products and services that included annuities, auto, homeowners, life, and/or long-term care insurance from insurance affiliates of Citibank.[121] The incentives would include lower interest rates and/or other items, such as airline frequent flyer miles or contributions to accounts maintained by a customer with other Citibank affiliates."

On the question of product weighting, the bank had "indicated that in [its] combined-balance discount program, deposits, credit card balances, and insurance premiums would count equally, dollar for dollar, towards the minimum balance." The bank requested confirmation that insurance products may be included among the eligible products in the program and if so, "asked for confirmation that the principal amount of annuity products may be counted towards the minimum balance, and that insurance premiums may be counted towards the minimum balance for non-annuity insurance products." The agency agreed that Citi's combined balances may include these items.

Relationship Banking

In the wake of the Gramm-Leach-Bliley, which permitted the affiliation of banks and investment banks, there were a number of high-profile allegations that large banks and their investment banking affiliates were tying loans to securities underwriting. The Board took the rather unprecedented course of issuing a "proposed interpretation" of the antitying restrictions of Section 106 with a request for public comment.[122] The proposed interpretation has never been adopted formally, but remains as an excellent resource for "seeing into the mind" of Board staff on these issues.

One of the developments in the "interpretation" was a liberalization of the combined-balance discount exemption into what the Board called "relationship banking." In this regard, the Board opined that it is permissible and consistent with industry practice to offer "mixed product arrangements," in which a bank:

- offers a customer a "menu" of products and services,
- measures each customer's total relationship over a period of time, including establishing a "hurdle rate," and

120. Board: Legal Interpretations—Clarification of Antitying Exemption in Regulation Y—May 16. All quotes in this discussion are from the Board document.
121. Tying of bank products and insurance products is the subject of numerous restrictions under state insurance laws.
122. Antitying Restrictions of Section 106 of the Bank Holding Company Amendments of 1970, Proposed interpretation and supervisory guidance with request for public comment, 68 Fed. Reg. 52,024 (Aug. 29, 2003).

- makes a determination about continuing such relationship based on such review;
- provided that: the practice must conform to: antitying rules and interpretations; Section 23B of the Federal Reserve Act (which requires that a bank's extensions of credit made in transactions where an affiliate has a financial interest must be on market terms); safe and sound credit underwriting standards; and other applicable laws and regulations.

In so doing, the Board established the combined-balance discount rule as a safe harbor, but permits bank to exceed the safe harbor as long as the bank offers the customer a meaningful option to satisfy the "hurdle rate" by selecting traditional bank products. The bank must have "policies, procedures and documentation that reflect a good faith belief that a customer offered a mixed-product arrangement would be able to satisfy the condition associated with the arrangement solely through the purchase of traditional bank products." This test is workable with commercial customers but it is a difficult test to meet for customers who are individuals.

Investments

Banking statutes frequently combine the concepts of authorized activities and authorized investments. Section 24 (Seventh) and FDICIA are prime examples. Notwithstanding, there is a fundamental distinction under banking law between a bank activity, as discussed above, and a bank investment. A bank activity is the exercise of a power granted by law. Thus, a bank engages in an activity by making a loan or selling insurance itself. On the other hand, an investment is the redeployment of deposit liabilities through the purchase of an instrument. Activities involve growth, the subject of this chapter; investments typically do not.

That said, investments pertain to growth when a bank decides to establish or acquire a subsidiary. The ownership interest in another entity as a subsidiary is an investment, typically an equity investment. These equity investments are permitted, both in the form of controlling and noncontrolling interests, as discussed in Chapter 3.

Glass-Steagall Background

After the Great Depression, Congress constructed a "wall" to separate commercial banking and investment banking. At the time, what was considered overzealous commercial bank involvement in stock market investment, was deemed a culprit of the financial crash. According to that reasoning, commercial banks took on too much risk with depositors' money. In response, the Glass-Steagall Act's[123] statutory framework included four provisions:

- Section 16, 12 U.S.C. § 24 (Seventh): National banks may purchase and sell securities "without recourse, solely upon the order . . . of customers," and purchase "investment securities." May only underwrite limited types of securities; may not purchase equities.
- Section 20, 12 U.S.C. § 377: Barred member banks from being affiliated with companies that are "engaged principally in the issue, flotation, underwriting, public sale or distribution at wholesale or retail or through syndicate participation of stocks, bonds, debentures, notes or other securities. . . ."
- Section 21, 12 U.S.C. § 378: No person or organization engaged in the business of "issuing, underwriting, selling or distributing" securities (except as permitted under Section 16) may engage "at the same time to any extent whatever" in deposit taking (same approach as Section 16, but from the investment banking side).
- Section 32, 12 U.S.C. § 78: Barred personnel interlocks between member banks and entities "primarily engaged" in the issuance, underwriting, public sale, or distribution of securities.

The "affiliation" provisions of Sections 20 and 32 were repealed by Section 101 of Gramm-Leach-Bliley. But, the "activities/powers" restrictions of Section 16 (prohibiting commercial banks from conducting securities activities in the bank) and Section 21 (prohibiting investment banks from taking deposits) were retained. For depository institutions, their authority post-Gramm-Leach-Bliley to act as principal with respect to securities is addressed below. Chapter 10 tackles holding companies and affiliates.

Authority and Limitations

As a general proposition, depository institutions are not permitted to make equity investments; instead, they may invest funds in "bank-eligible" instruments, mainly high-grade debt instruments as permitted under the law of the charter. So for national banks, the authority is in the NBA[124]; for federal associations, it is in HOLA[125]; and for state banks and savings associations, it is state law, except that, under the Federal Reserve Act, state member banks only have the investment powers of national banks.[126] Thus, Section 24 of the NBA and the regulations of the OCC at 12 C.F.R. Part 1 define the investment limitations of all member banks (flashback to

123. This was part of the banking Act of 1933. June 16, 1933, ch. 89, 48 Stat. 163.
124. 12 U.S.C. § 24 (Seventh).
125. 12 U.S.C. § 1464.
126. 12 U.S.C. § 335.

Chapter 2, all national banks are Federal Reserve member banks). OCC regulations at Part 160 define the limitations for federal savings associations.

One additional twist: FDICIA prohibits *equity* investments by all insured state banks, except for investments national banks may make and except for certain qualified housing projects.[127]

National Banks and State Member Banks. Section 24 (Seventh), as modified by the Glass-Steagall Act, limits member banks in connection with acting as a principal with respect to securities: purchasing for their own account, dealing in, and underwriting, except (subject to certain limits based on the capital of the bank), member banks may:

- purchase and sell securities "without recourse," solely upon the order and for the account of customers—i.e., act as broker, subject to the Gramm-Leach-Bliley push-out requirements (discussed above).
- underwrite, deal in, purchase and sell certain government, agency, and municipal securities.
- purchase and sell (but not underwrite or deal in) other investment grade and marketable corporate debt, small-business and mortgage-related securities, and securitizations of similar loan pools.

Generally, such securities must be:

Marketable – registered under the federal securities laws, issued and sold under SEC Rule 144A, municipal revenue bonds, or ones that "can be sold with reasonable promptness at a price that corresponds reasonably to its fair value."[128]

Investment grade – Section 939A of Dodd-Frank required the federal agencies to reduce reliance on external credit ratings. In the updated OCC definition, "investment grade" means[129]:

- the issuer of a security has adequate capacity to meet financial commitments under the security for the projected life of the asset or exposure, and
- "adequate capacity" can be found if "the risk of default by the obligor is low and the full and timely repayment of principal and interest is expected."

To this end, Part 1 divides securities into Types I–V, based on risk, what roles a bank may play, and percentage of capital that may be expended. On the unrestricted end, Type I covers federal government and agency obligations, and the bank may purchase, deal, and underwrite these obligations without

127. 12 U.S.C. § 1831a(c).
128. 12 C.F.R. § 1.2(f).
129. 12 C.F.R. § 1.2(d).

capital limitations. Whereas, by the time you get to Type V, a bank may only purchase them up to 25% of capital (defined, as for all prudential regulation, as Tier 1 plus Tier 2 capital plus the remainder the allowance for loan and lease losses not counted in Tier 2).

Held in Satisfaction of Debt Previously Contracted. So called, DPC securities (acquired through foreclosure, compromise of claim, or to avoid a loss under a debt previously contracted) may be held for five years, plus a possible five-year extension.[130]

Volcker Rule

There are a lot of loopholes in Part 1. All kinds of risk-shifting strategies were permitted by the agencies over the roaring 1990s such that suddenly banks actually traded equities for their own account and held all kinds of roles with respect to non-SEC registered funds. Section 619 of Dodd-Frank, known colloquially as the "Volcker Rule" (amends the Bank Holding Company Act, adding a new Section 13[131]) because of its patronage by former Federal Reserve Board chairman Paul Volcker, restricts banks, parent companies, and their affiliates (defined as "banking entities"[132]) from making certain of these "speculative" investments that do not benefit their customers. Investments in terms of proprietary trading and in covered hedge and private equity funds are subject to the Volcker Rule.[133] Specifically, it: prohibits insured depository institutions and their affiliates from: (i) engaging in proprietary trading[134]; (ii) acquiring or retaining any equity, partnership, or other ownership interest in a hedge fund or private equity fund; and (iii) sponsoring a hedge fund or a private equity fund.[135]

The statute expressly exempts from these prohibitions various activities, including among other things:

- underwriting and market making related activities;
- risk-mitigating hedging activities;
- activities on behalf of customers;
- activities for the general account of insurance companies; and
- trading and covered fund activities and investments by non-U.S. banking entities solely outside the United States.

130. 12 C.F.R. § 1.7.

131. Codified at 12 U.S.C. § 1851.

132. *See*, (OCC) 12 C.F.R. § 44.2(c).

133. The Final Rule was released at 79 Fed. Reg. 5536 (Jan. 31, 2014), and the banking agencies have codified it at: (OCC) 12 C.F.R. Part 44; (Board) 12 C.F.R. Part 248; and (FDIC) 12 C.F.R. Part 351. Accompanying statements, fact sheets, and related documents can be found on the websites of the agencies.

134. These provisions are found in Subpart B of the above cited regulations.

135. Provisions as to funds are found in Subpart C of the above cited regulations.

In addition, the law contains an exemption that permits banking entities to organize and offer, including sponsor, covered funds, subject to certain restrictions, including that banking entities do not rescue investors in those funds from loss, and are not themselves exposed to significant losses due to investments in or other relationships with these funds.

The amount of detail in the Volcker Rule and the enabling regulations is excruciating. And there has been an enormous amount of uncertainty in the years following Dodd-Frank. Hordes of lawyers in large firms have been dedicated to demystifying this rule for their clients for years. But, it is getting slightly better.

Notably, Section 203 of the Economic Growth, Regulatory Relief and Consumer Protection Act of 2018[136] exempted banks with assets of $10 billion or less and total trading assets and liabilities equal to 5% or less of total consolidated assets from the Volcker Rule. The agencies also revised the restrictions applicable to the naming of a hedge fund or private equity fund to permit an investment adviser that is a banking entity to share a name with the fund under certain circumstances.[137]

Fine-tuning continues. In 2019, the agencies issued a final rule[138] to provide greater clarity and certainty about what activities are prohibited under the rule, in particular, under the prohibition on proprietary trading, and to better tailor the compliance requirements based on the risk of a banking entity's activities. Those provisions became effective in January 2020. As to covered funds, the original rule allowed banks to take direct stakes in individual startup companies but not funds containing multiple investments. A comprehensive 2020 proposal[139] would ease that provision by allowing banks to invest in instruments such as credit funds, venture capital funds, customer facilitation funds, and family wealth management vehicles—even if those funds contained multiple investments.

The agencies also have addressed issues concerning the regulations implementing the rule through a series of staff Frequently Asked Questions (FAQs).[140]

136. Publ. L. 115–174, S. 2155. Revisions to Prohibitions and Restrictions on Proprietary Trading and Certain Interests In, and Relationships With, Hedge Funds and Private Equity Funds, Final Rule, 84 Fed. Reg. 35,008 (July 22, 2019). *See, e.g.*, (OCC) 12 C.F.R. § 44.2(r)(2).

137. *Id.* at 35,103.

138. Prohibitions and Restrictions on Proprietary Trading and Certain Interests in, and Relationships With, Hedge Funds and Private Equity Funds, 84 Fed. Reg. 61,974 (Nov. 14, 2019).

139. Joint Notice of Proposed Rulemaking, 85 Fed. Reg. 12, 120 (Feb. 28, 2020).

140. Search for Volcker Rule FAQs on the agency websites.

10

Concepts of Control/ Holding Companies

Who Can Own a Bank?

The uncomplicated answer? Any person can own a bank: an individual, a family, a group acting in concert, a corporation, LLC or partnership, a trust, an ESOP (employee stock ownership plan), an investment fund .... More to the point is the complicated reality that a bank owner faces in terms of supervision and regulation—the themes of this book. There are no real advantages to bank ownership (other than esteem in the community and higher dividends, maybe). Yes, the bank has the safety net but it cannot be exploited for other purposes—preferential terms for loans are prohibited, and as an "institution affiliated person," the whole arsenal of enforcement weapons may be unleashed on principal shareholders. Just the probing process of regulatory approval is sufficient to turn many potential investors away. Applications require completion of intrusive biographical and financial questionnaires.

The triggering device for all the delights of bank ownership is "control." But first, a rundown of the key laws and their coverage is in order.

Applicable Law and Key Terms

First, all three federal bank regulators have jurisdiction under certain laws to determine who may own a banking entity under their jurisdiction. By now this is old news: the Board of Governors of the Federal Reserve System ("Federal Reserve" or "Board"), as to state-chartered banks that are members of the Federal Reserve, bank holding companies, and savings and loan holding companies; the Office of the Comptroller of the Currency ("OCC"), as to national banks and federal savings associations; and the Federal Deposit

Insurance Corporation ("FDIC"), as to state-chartered banks that are not member banks and state-chartered savings associations.

There are three statutes that may apply to an acquisition of an ownership interest in a banking organization.

The Change in Bank Control Act ("CBCA")[1] applies to acquisitions of an ownership interest in a banking organization by one or more "persons."

- The term "person," for purposes of CBCA, includes both natural persons and entities.[2]
- The term "insured depository institution" is defined in CBCA to include FDIC-insured banks and savings associations as well as any holding company for an FDIC-insured bank or savings association.[3]
- Each of the three federal banking agencies has the authority to enforce the requirements of CBCA with respect to investments in those banking organizations for which it is the designated primary federal regulator, and each agency has promulgated regulations to implement the requirements of CBCA.[4]

Section 3 of the Bank Holding Company Act ("BHCA")[5] applies to the acquisition of an ownership interest in a bank or bank holding company by a company. Section 3 of the BHCA establishes the conditions under which a company will be deemed to be the holding company for a bank, and is enforced by the Federal Reserve in its capacity as the primary federal regulator of bank holding companies.[6] The BHCA is intrinsically driven

1. CBCA is codified at 12 U.S.C. § 1817(j).
2. 12 U.S.C. § 1817(j)(8)(A).
3. 12 U.S.C. § 1817(j)(18).
4. The regulations of the Federal Reserve implementing CBCA are set forth in Subpart E of Regulation Y (12 C.F.R. §§ 225.41–225.44) and Subpart D of Regulation LL (12 C.F.R. §§ 238.31–238.33). The provisions of Regulation Y apply to acquisitions of interests in state member banks and bank holding companies, while the provisions of Regulation LL apply to acquisitions of interests in savings and loan holding companies. The regulations of the OCC implementing CBCA are set forth at 12 C.F.R. § 5.50 (national banks) and 12 C.F.R. §§ 174.1–174.7 (federal savings associations). The regulations of the FDIC implementing CBCA are found at 12 C.F.R. §§ 303.80–303.86 (state nonmember banks) and §§ 391.40–391.49 (state savings associations).
5. Section 3 of the BHCA is codified at 12 U.S.C. § 1842.
6. The implementing regulations of the BHCA are found in Subpart B of Regulation Y (12 C.F.R. §§ 225.11–225.17). Because financial holding companies ("FHCs") are merely bank holding companies that meet certain eligibility requirements allowing them to elect to operate as FHCs, Section 3 of the BHCA and Subpart B of Regulation Y also apply to acquisitions of FHCs.*

by the definitions that are found in Section 2.[7] That is where you find the answers to:

- What is a "company?" – it can be a corporation, partnership, business trust, limited liability company, or similar organization and includes certain trusts.
- What is a "bank?" – any insured depository institution (with few exceptions discussed later in this chapter), except savings associations are treated as nonbanks under the BHCA.
- What is "control"? – this concept is critical in the determination of which entities come under the authority of the Federal Reserve and are subject to the restrictions of the BHCA, and the law on this point is developed below.

The Board's rulemaking under the BHCA is found in Regulation Y.[8]

Section 10(e) of the Home Owners' Loan Act ("HOLA")[9] applies to the acquisition of an ownership interest in a savings association or savings and loan holding company by an entity. Section 10 of HOLA establishes the conditions under which an entity will be deemed to be the holding company for a savings association (whether state or federally chartered), and is enforced by the Federal Reserve in its capacity as the primary federal regulator of savings and loan holding companies.[10] The Savings and Loan Holding Company Act ("S&LHCA")[11] applies to the companies that meet the definitions in HOLA. The Board's rulemaking under the S&LHCA is found in Regulations LL and MM.[12]

Issues of Control[13]

In general, the statutes listed above and the respective regulations establish notice and application requirements that apply to the acquisition of a controlling ownership interest in a FDIC-insured financial institution

7. A key to surviving the BHCA is knowing how to slice and dice it to find what you seek. A note when finding the law on BHCs: the sections in the BHCA (that we cite all the time and no one can find because they do not know this trick) move down one number when codified in the U.S.C. So, we say Section **2** of the BHCA and that is 12 U.S.C. § 1841; likewise, Section **3** is 12 U.S.C. § 184**2**.
8. 12 C.F.R. Part 225.
9. Section 10(e) of HOLA is codified at 12 U.S.C. § 1467a(e).
10. HOLA implementing regulations are found in Subpart B of Regulation LL (12 C.F.R. §§ 238.11–238.15).
11. The BHCA and S&LHCA are codified, respectively, at 12 U.S.C. § 1841 *et seq.*, and 12 U.S.C. § 1467a.
12. 12 C.F.R. Part 238 (S&LHCs) and Part 239 (mutual holding companies).
13. The control section of this chapter was originally authored by Judith K. Muncy, Counsel, and was updated for the Third Edition by Brent McCauley, Barack Ferrazzano, LLP.

or its holding company (for the purposes of this discussion, each is a "banking organization"). As discussed below, however, determining when an acquisition results in control is not always straightforward, and may require an analysis not only of a particular proposed investment, but also of the ownership interests of other existing and proposed investors, and the relationships of existing and proposed investors to each other and to the banking organization in which they have invested or propose to invest.

The following discussion addresses the requirements imposed by federal law and regulations on acquisitions of ownership interests in banking organizations. Additional requirements may be established by state banking laws with respect to investments in state-chartered financial institutions and their holding companies.

The Change in Bank Control Act

CBCA provides, in pertinent part:

> [N]o person, acting directly or indirectly or through or in concert with one or more other persons, shall acquire control of any insured depository institution through a purchase, assignment, transfer, pledge, or other disposition of voting stock of such insured depository institution unless the appropriate Federal banking agency has been given 60 days' prior written notice of such proposed acquisition and within that time period the agency has not issued a notice disapproving the proposed acquisition or, in the discretion of the agency, extending for an additional 30 days the period during which such a disapproval may issue.[14]

Applicability. Under CBCA, the acquisition of 25% or more of a class of voting securities of a financial institution or its holding company conclusively constitutes "control."[15] The regulations of the federal banking agencies, however, also create a rebuttable presumption of control triggered by the acquisition of 10% or more, but less than 25%, of a class of voting

14. 12 U.S.C. § 1817(j)(1).
15. 12 U.S.C. § 1817(j)(8)(B).

securities of a financial institution or its holding company.[16] An acquisition of between 10% and 25% of a class of voting securities of a state or national bank, BHC, or savings and loan holding company will trigger the rebuttable presumption of control if:

- The banking organization whose securities are being acquired has registered securities under Section 12 of the Securities Exchange Act of 1934; or
- Immediately following the proposed acquisition, no other person will own, control, or hold the power to vote a greater percentage of that class of voting securities.[17]

The acquisition of between 10% and 25% of a class of voting stock of a savings association—whether state or federally chartered—will likewise trigger a rebuttable presumption of control if the acquiring person is subject to one or more of the control factors set out in the applicable regulations, one of which is that the acquiring person will be one of the savings association's two largest shareholders.[18]

If a proposed acquisition triggers the rebuttable presumption of control, the acquiring person has the option of seeking to rebut the presumption of control, rather than filing the required notice under CBCA. If, however, the rebuttal is not successful, the acquiring person must then file the required notice under CBCA before the proposed stock acquisition may be completed. The procedures for filing rebuttals and notices under CBCA are specified in each federal banking agency's regulations.

The regulations of the federal banking agencies implementing CBCA also include various exemptions from the prior notice requirement established by the statute, which in some cases allow an acquisition to proceed

---

16. Note that both the conclusive presumption of control and the rebuttable presumption of control are triggered by the acquisition of a stated percentage of a *class* of voting securities, and not total outstanding voting securities. Thus, for example, if a banking organization has multiple classes of voting stock, each of which has separate class voting rights, the acquisition of a controlling interest in any class will trigger the applicability of CBCA even though the acquiring person may have a less than controlling ownership interest in the banking organization's total issued and outstanding voting stock. For the definition of the term "voting securities" *see,* 12 C.F.R. §§ 5.50(d)(7) (national banks), 174.1 (federal savings associations), 225.2(q) (state member banks and bank holding companies), 238.2(r) (savings and loan holding companies), and 391.41 (state savings associations). The FDIC's regulations implementing CBCA with respect to state nonmember banks do not include a definition of "voting securities."
17. 12 C.F.R. §§ 5.50(f)(2)(iii) (national banks); 225.41(c)(2) (state member banks and bank holding companies); 238.31(c)(2) (savings and loan holding companies).
18. 12 C.F.R. §§ 174.4(b) and (c) (federal savings associations) and 391.43(b) and (c) (state savings associations).

without any filing at all and in other cases permit a postacquisition filing (for instance, when the shareholder exceeds a control trigger inadvertently).

Acting in Concert Issues. Determining control under CBCA is often complicated by the concept of "acting in concert." The regulations of the federal banking agencies define "acting in concert" generally as including "knowing participation in a joint activity or parallel action towards a common goal of acquiring control" and, in some cases, specify relationships that are presumed (subject to rebuttal) to constitute concerted action.[19]

If a proposed investor in a banking organization is found to be acting in concert with one or more other proposed investors in, or existing stockholders of, that same banking organization, then it will be the aggregate ownership interest of the members of this group that will determine whether a filing must be made under CBCA. In other words, if Investor A is found to act in concert with Investor B and Existing Stockholder C, and the combined ownership interests of Investor A, Investor B, and Existing Stockholder C would constitute control (under either the conclusive or rebuttable presumptions of control described above), then all three would be subject to the filing requirements established under CBCA, even if none of the three, considered individually, has an ownership interest large enough to trigger a control presumption.

Grounds for Disapproval. An acquisition of control under CBCA may be disapproved if, among other things, the appropriate federal banking agency concludes that the proposed transaction would be anticompetitive, or the integrity or financial capacity of the acquiring person is such that the proposed acquisition would be detrimental to the interests of the target banking organization, its depositors, or the community served by the banking organization.[20]

---

19. The regulatory definition of acting in concert is set out in 12 C.F.R. §§ 5.50(d)(2) (national banks), 174.2(c) (federal savings associations), 225.41(b)(2) (state member banks and bank holding companies), 238.31(b) (savings and loan holding companies), 303.81(b) (state nonmember banks), and 391.41 (state savings associations). The regulations of the Federal Reserve applicable to state member banks, bank holding companies and savings and loan holding companies (specifically, 12 C.F.R. §§ 225.41(d) and 238.31(d)), as well as the regulations of the OCC applicable to federal savings associations (specifically, 12 C.F.R. § 174.4(d)) and the regulations of the FDIC applicable to state savings associations (specifically, 12 C.F.R. § 391.43(d)), specify relationships which are presumed, subject to rebuttal, to constitute concerted action. The regulations of the OCC applicable to national banks include a rebuttable presumption of concerted action among members of the same immediate family (12 C.F.R. § 5.50(f)(2)(ii)), but the regulations of the FDIC applicable to state-chartered nonmember banks are silent as to specific relationships that may constitute concerted action.
20. 12 U.S.C. § 1817(j)(7).

Sections 3 of the BHCA and 10(e) of HOLA

Before you venture further, understand the task at hand. Randy Quarles, vice chair for supervision of the Board since October 2017, has described the Federal Reserve's treatment of "control" under the BHCA on numerous, occasions, but never more colorfully than when he said that control was understood only by those with "a long apprenticeship in the subtle hermeneutics of Federal Reserve lore, receiving the wisdom of their elders through oral tradition like the tribes of Orinoco." "Subtle hermeneutics"? "Orinoco"?

Under the BHCA, a company that controls a bank is deemed to be a bank holding company ("BHC"); likewise, under HOLA, a company that controls a savings association is deemed to be a savings and loan holding company ("S&LHC"). In either case, a company that directly or indirectly acquires control of a bank or savings association must register with, and submit to regulation by, the Federal Reserve, in its capacity as the primary federal regulator of bank holding companies and savings and loan holding companies. The regulations of the Federal Reserve[21] provide that "control," in this context, means:

- Ownership or control of, or power to vote, 25% or more of the outstanding shares of any class of voting securities of a banking organization, directly or indirectly or acting through one or more other persons (the "ownership test");
- Control in any manner over the election of a majority of the directors, trustees or general partners (or individuals exercising similar functions) of a banking organization (the "board control test"); or
- The power to exercise, directly or indirectly, a controlling influence over the management or policies of a banking organization (the "controlling influence test").

If control is found to exist under either the ownership test or the board control test, the controlling influence test is irrelevant; that is, an entity that acquires control of a banking organization under the ownership test or the board control test is presumed to have the ability to exercise a controlling influence over that banking organization. If an investing entity's interest in a banking organization does not constitute control under the ownership test or the board control test, only then will the Federal Reserve analyze the investor's interest under the controlling influence test.

Controlling Influence. A finding of control under the controlling influence test will depend on the specific facts and circumstances of the

21. 12 C.F.R. §§ 225.2(e) and 238.2(e).

proposed investment and any other relationships between the proposed investor and the target banking organization. As such, the Federal Reserve has not established specific rules that will determine, in every case, whether a proposed investor has the ability to exercise a controlling influence over the management or policies of a banking organization; rather, the Federal Reserve has provided written guidance on the principles it will apply in analyzing investments under the controlling influence test. Those principles, as established in 2008,[22] and, as amended by the Federal Reserve's final rule for Control and Divestiture Proceedings, adopted on January 30, 2020 (the "Control Rule Changes"),[23] are as follows[24]:

- *Amount and Type of Total Investment.* As noted above, an entity that owns, controls, or has the power to vote 25% or more of a class of the *voting securities* of a banking organization is conclusively presumed to control the banking organization under the ownership test. But what of *nonvoting securities*? If a proposed investor's ownership in a banking organization consists of a combination of voting and nonvoting securities that, in the aggregate, represents more than 25% of the banking organization's total equity,[25] the proposed investor will often be deemed to have a controlling influence over the management and policies of the banking organization and, thus, will be deemed to control the banking organization. Absent other indicia of control, however, the Board may determine that an investment representing less than 25% of a class of a banking

22. Policy Statement on Equity Investments in Banks and Bank Holding Companies (Sept. 22, 2008).
23. On Jan. 30, 2020, the Federal Reserve adopted a final rule for Control and Divestiture Proceedings (the "Final Rule") to clarify considerations it will use to determine whether a company has the ability to exercise control or a controlling influence over another company under the BHCA and HOLA. 85 FR 12,398, Mar. 2, 2020. Regulations to implement the Final Rule will be added under the Federal Reserve's Regulation Y, 12 C.F.R. Part 225, for BHCs and Regulation LL, 12 C.F.R. Part 238, for SHLCs. The original effective date of the Final Rule was Apr. 1, 2020; however, the Federal Reserve delayed the effective date to Sept. 30, 2020. 85 FR 18,427, Apr. 2, 2020.
24. The following discussion assumes that a proposed investor is acting independently of other investors and/or other shareholders of the banking organization. If a proposed investor is deemed to be part of a group "acting in concert" with other investors or shareholders, the interests of all members of the group will be aggregated in applying the control factors discussed below.
25. In general, a banking organization's total equity includes any instrument that qualifies as a component of the banking organization's regulatory capital. Thus, for example, an investment that consists of a combination of voting or nonvoting equity securities and subordinated debt representing, in the aggregate, over 25% of the banking organization's regulatory capital may raise similar issues.

organization's voting securities, but more than 25% of the banking organization's total equity, does not constitute control if:

- the aggregate investment represents less than one-third of the banking organization's total equity for BHCs and less than one-quarter of the banking organization's total equity for SLHCs;
- the investment does not allow the proposed investor to own, hold, or vote 15% or more of any class of voting securities of the banking organization; and
- in the case of any nonvoting securities that are convertible into voting securities:
- the convertible nonvoting securities, when aggregated with any voting securities held by the proposed investor, represent less than one-third of any class of the banking organization's voting securities, assuming the conversion of all convertible securities; and
- the convertible nonvoting securities may not be converted into voting securities in the hands of the proposed investor and may be transferred by the proposed investor only: (i) to an affiliate of the investor or to the banking organization; (ii) in a widespread public distribution; (iii) in transfers in which no transferee, or group of related transferees, would acquire 2% or more of any class of the banking organization's voting securities; or (iv) to a transferee that would control more than 50% of the voting securities of the banking organization without any transfer from the proposed investor.

- *Board Representation.* As noted above, a company that controls a majority of the board seats of a banking organization is conclusively presumed to have control over the banking organization under the board control test. Prior to the Control Rule Changes, a proposed investor was generally permitted to have one representative on the banking organization's board of directors, and possibly two representatives if the proposed investor's aggregate director representation was proportionate to its total equity interest in the banking organization, but does not exceed 25% of the voting members of the board. The Control Rule Changes, however, are a bit more lenient and provide that a proposed investor may have representation on the banking organization's board of directors:
    - of less than half of the number of directors when investing less than 5%;
    - of less than a quarter of the number of directors (as long as such directors do not have the power to make or block major

operational or policy decisions) when investing between 5% and 24.9%.

- *Board Committees.* Additionally, proposed investors that will make an investment that represents more than 10% but less than 24.99% of the banking organization's voting securities may serve on committees of the banking organization's board of directors, provided that the proposed investor's representatives do not hold more than 25% of the committee memberships and do not have the authority or ability to make or block committee decisions that are binding on the banking organization's board of directors or management. Prior to the Control Rule Changes, a proposed investor's representative was not permitted to serve as chairman of the board of directors or chairman of a committee of the board. The Control Rule Changes have clarified that this presumption of control is triggered only by investors that make investments that amount to 15% or more but less than 24.99% of the banking organization's voting securities.
- *Officer/Employee Interlocks.* The Control Rule Changes permit only one interlock (never the chief executive officer) for investments between 5% and 14.99%. None are permitted for greater ownership.
- *Business Relationships.* Business relationships between a proposed investor and the target banking organization may be viewed as providing the proposed investor with a controlling influence over the banking organization, depending on the size of the business relationship and whether the business relationship is on market terms, nonexclusive, and terminable without penalty by the banking organization. The Control Rule Changes provide, in general, the more equity that a "first company" (to use the language introduced in the Federal Reserve's rulemaking) owns in the "second company," the fewer and less significant the first company's relationships with the second company must be in other areas to trigger a rebuttable presumption of control. This tiered approach adopted in the Control Rule Changes to trigger a rebuttable presumption of control is set forth below:

Between 5% and 9.99% voting securities	**Between 10% and 14.99% voting securities**	**Between 15% and 24.99% voting securities**
Less than 10% of revenues or expenses of the second company	Less than 5% of revenues or expenses of the second company	Less than 2% of revenues or expenses of the second company

- *Covenants.* If the terms and conditions of the investment or other contractual arrangements between a proposed investor and a banking organization place restrictions on, or otherwise inhibit, the ability of the banking organization's management to exercise discretion over major policies and decisions with respect to the operations of the banking organization (e.g., with respect to personnel, business activities, capital structure, or mergers or acquisitions), the proposed investor will likely be deemed to exercise a controlling influence over the banking organization.[26]

Application Requirement. An entity that will acquire control of a banking organization must file an application with, and obtain the approval of, the Federal Reserve prior to making its proposed investment in the banking organization. The Federal Reserve may deny approval of a particular investment if, among other things, the proposed acquisition would be anticompetitive or would be detrimental to the interests of the target banking organization, the community served by the banking organization, or the FDIC's deposit insurance fund.[27]

As noted above, CBCA is also applicable to investments in banking organizations by entities. CBCA provides an express exemption for transactions subject to approval under Section 3 of the BHCA or Section 10(e) of HOLA,[28] but a proposed investment that does not constitute control under Section 3 of the BHCA or Section 10(e) of HOLA may nonetheless constitute control as defined in CBCA and require the filing of a notice under that statute. In such a case, the investing entity, together with any entities or natural persons that control the investing entity and any other entities or natural persons with which the investing entity is acting in concert, as described above, will be required to satisfy the filing requirements of CBCA. If a notice under CBCA is required, the Board typically requires the proposed investor to enter into commitments with the Board, designed to ensure that the relationship between the proposed investor and the banking organization is not modified in a way that would provide the proposed investor with the ability to exercise a controlling influence over the management and policies of the banking organization. Any change in the relationship between the proposed investor and the banking organization that is inconsistent with the passivity commitments made by the proposed investor to the Board would constitute grounds for

---

26. Such terms and conditions, if included in the terms and conditions of securities issued by the banking organization to the investor, will likely also preclude the securities from being treated as part of the banking organization's regulatory capital under the Federal Reserve's capital rules.
27. 12 U.S.C. §§ 1842(c) and 1467a(e)(2).
28. 12 U.S.C. § 1817(j)(17).

administrative enforcement action by the Board against the proposed investor unless the proposed investor obtained Board approval of a modification to the passivity commitments to accommodate the change.

Bank Holding Companies

Today's BHCs may be large global conglomerates, or they may be parent companies of community banks. Regardless of size, they share the Federal Reserve as their federal regulator. They are unlimited in geographic scope but strictly restricted on the activities in which they may engage.

The Form 10-K disclosure at the end of Chapter 1 discusses the regulation and supervision of one BHC under the heading "The Company" and is worth reviewing as a snapshot of what this section will address.

History of BHC Regulation

The holding companies we think of today evolved over the last 100 years from early "chain banks," which generally involved control of two or more banks by an individual or group of individuals. Dating back to at least the 1890s,[29] these chains, which originated in the Northwest and the South, were organized primarily to overcome intrastate, and in some cases, interstate, branching restrictions. They grew rapidly between 1900 and 1920, and by 1931, 176 chain banking organizations were operating 908 banks with assets of $927 million. By the end of 1945, there were 115 chain organizations operating 522 banks with combined assets of $4.62 billion.

A variation of chain banks that arose prior to the 1920s were "group banks," which were essentially bank holding companies as we know them today. The group consisted of two or more banks controlled by a corporation, which held controlling stock in each of its subsidiary banks. The principal advantage of group banks was their ability, as corporations, to finance their growth by raising capital in the financial markets. The growth of chain banks, by contrast, was limited by the financial resources of the individual or individuals who formed the chain.[30] Group banks experienced rapid growth during the 1920s, fueled in part by the stock market boom. By 1931, there were 97 group banking organizations operating 978 banks with 1,219 additional branch offices. In 1930, the Board reported that ten of the thirty-four largest operated in more than one state, one of which controlled banks in eight states.

29. The discussion in this section is based on Robert T. Clair and Paula K. Tucker, *Interstate Banking and the Federal Reserve: A Historical Perspective, Federal Reserve Bank of Dallas*, Economic Review, Nov. 1989.

30. *Id.* at 5.

These chain bank and group bank organizations were devices structured to evade branching and affiliation limitations of state law. It is not surprising that Congress was paying attention and revisited the issues several times over a span of almost forty years, beginning in 1933, when Congress granted the Board limited authority to supervise BHCs that controlled at least one bank that was a member of the Federal Reserve System. The parent company, then called a "holding company affiliate," included a company that owned or controlled a majority of the outstanding shares of the capital stock of a member bank or more than 50% of the number of shares voted for the election of directors in the preceding election.

The Board was not originally given the extensive powers over BHCs that it has today. It was given the power to examine and supervise BHCs only when the parent company had to make a decision that required a formal vote of the shares of the subsidiary bank (most likely including cases in which state or federal law required approval of the decision by a majority of the bank's shareholders). In these cases, the BHC had to acquire a "voting permit" from the Board. The granting of this permit entitled the Board to examine and supervise the BHC, and to implement certain restrictions on the BHC's activities.

Multibank Holding Companies. Several bills relating to BHCs were introduced in Congress after 1933 to strengthen the agency's authority to regulate BHCs, but it was not until the enactment of the BHCA in 1956[31] that Congress subjected BHCs to broader federal regulation. The 1956 Act strengthened the Board's authority with respect to BHCs that controlled more than one bank ("multibank holding companies"). During its consideration of the proposed holding company legislation, the Senate Banking Committee observed that by December 31, 1954, eighteen BHCs had obtained voting permits from the Board in accordance with the 1933 Act. The agency estimated that at least forty-six holding companies would be covered by the terms of the pending bill, which applied to companies that controlled more than 25% of the stock of each of two or more banks. The Senate committee report on the 1956 bill cited testimony of then-Board Chairman William McChesney Martin, Jr., stating:

> [T]he two principal concerns posed by multibank holding companies were: the unrestricted activity of a holding company group to add to the number of its banking units, making possible the concentration of commercial bank facilities in a particular [geographic] area under a single control and management; and the combination under single control of both banking and

31. May 9, 1956, ch. 240, 70 Stat. 133.

> nonbanking enterprises, permitting departure from the principle that banking institutions should not engage in business wholly unrelated to banking. Such a combination involves the lending of depositors' money, whereas other types of [businesses], not connected with banking, do not involve this element of trusteeship.[32]

Other concerns included:

- The possibility that the parent company would either force the bank to make loans to finance speculative business projects, or force it to compensate the parent for losses incurred in business ventures; and
- The potential for the parent company to use the deposits of the bank as "capital" to fund businesses of the parent, for the parent to use its market power to discriminate against persons who were not depositors, and charging holding company competitors higher interest rates on commercial loans than it charged noncompetitors.

The 1956 BHCA required holding companies to register with the Board before acquiring control of a second bank, and gave the agency the power to regulate and supervise the operation of multibank holding companies. The Act restricted certain BHC activities but did not prohibit permitting the company from acquiring shares:

> [O]f any company all the activities of which are of a financial, fiduciary or insurance nature and which the Board by order has determined to be *so closely related to the business of banking or of managing or controlling banks as to be a proper incident thereto.*[33] (Emphasis added.)

One-Bank Holding Companies. At the time of the enactment of the BHCA, Congress did not believe that coverage of one-bank holding companies under the act was warranted. This issue was revisited in 1966, with the Senate Banking Committee concluding that after reviewing all of the testimony presented at hearings on the bill, "there was no substantial evidence of abuses occurring in one-bank holding companies."[34] The committee further concluded that repeal of the one-bank holding company exemption would make it more difficult for individuals to hold or form

32. S. Rept. No. 1095 July 25, 1958, p. 2483, U.S. CONG. AND ADMN. NEWS, 85th Cong., 2nd sess.
33. 1956 Act, Section 5(c)(6), 70 Stat. 173.
34. S. Rept. No. 1179, June 7, 1966, p. 2385, U.S. CODE CONG. AND ADMN. NEWS, 89th Cong., 2nd sess. on the bill that became "An Act to Amend the BHCA of 1956," Pub. Law 89-485, July 1, 1966, 80 Stat. 236.

small independent banks. In order to minimize potential conflicts, however, the committee voted to extend the provisions of Section 23A of the Federal Reserve Act, relating to transactions of Federal Reserve member banks with their affiliates,[35] to state nonmember banks supervised by the FDIC.

In 1967, however, the Senate Banking Committee found that 23 banks with more than $1 billion in assets were subsidiaries of one-bank holding companies. These included the six largest banks in the country, which held more than 20% of the deposits of the country's entire banking system. The committee also found that the percentage of deposits held by all banks in one-bank holding companies had increased from 10% in early 1967 to more than 40% in 1970.[36] Because of their exemption from the BHCA of 1956, one-bank holding companies were not prevented by the federal banking laws from engaging in any nonbanking business, subject only to the restrictions of the antitrust laws. At hearings held by the Senate Banking Committee in 1969, Chairman Martin reiterated his concerns about the potential for anticompetitive practices arising from the combination of banking and commerce:

> If a holding company combines a bank with a typical business firm, there is a strong possibility that the bank might deny credit to competing firms or grant credit to other borrowers only on the condition that they agree to do business with the affiliated firm. If we allow the line between banking and commerce to be eased, we run the risk of cartelizing our economy [and] we could later see the country's business firms clustering about banks in holding company systems in the belief that such an affiliation would be advantageous or even necessary to their survival.[37]

Thus, Congress amended the BHCA to include companies that controlled one bank in the BHCA Amendments of 1970[38] and commenced a scramble by many a family, trust and controlling group to determine if it was a BHC and, more often than not, how not to be a BHC.

---

35. As discussed in Chapter 3, *supra*, all national banks are members of the Federal Reserve by virtue of the charter. State banks may choose to be members. Section 23A is discussed as a part of prudential regulation in Chapter 6, *supra*.
36. S. Rpt. No. 91-1084, Aug. 10, 1970, p. 5521, U.S. CODE CONG. AND ADMN. NEWS, 91st CONG., 2nd sess.
37. *Id.* at 5521–5522.
38. Pub. Law 91-607, Dec. 31, 1970, 84 Stat. 1760.

Becoming a BHC

A company becomes a BHC by application to the Board on form FR Y-3 (or 3N, if the conditions for expedited approval are met). Upon approval, a BHC becomes subject to supervision and enforcement by the Board and becomes subject to the requirements and activities limitations of the BHCA and Regulation Y.

The role of a BHC is to own and control and manage the affairs of banks. It must serve as a "source of strength" for its subsidiary insured depository institutions.

Source of Strength

The Federal Reserve embraced a policy for many years referred to as the "source of strength doctrine" that obligated BHCs to act as a source of financial and managerial strength to depository institution subsidiaries and to commit resources to support such subsidiaries in circumstances where the BHC might not otherwise do so. The policy was made law as a result of Section 616(d) of Dodd-Frank[39] and goes all the way to the top company in a financial institution family. Dodd-Frank defines the term as "the ability of a company that directly or indirectly owns or controls an insured depository institution to provide financial assistance to such insured depository institution in the event of the financial distress of the insured depository institution."

Thus, under source of strength as embraced by Dodd-Frank, a parent company that is an insurance company or an investment bank or any other company has the legal obligation to provide capital to its bank/thrift subsidiaries as the highest priority, regardless of the needs of its other businesses.

BHC and Bank Acquisitions—Section 3 of the BHCA

Acquisitions of an in-state or out-of-state BHC or bank by a BHC must receive prior approval from the Federal Reserve under Section 3 of the BHCA.[40]

It is important to note that FHCs, discussed below, which are really just BHCs "on steroids," play by the same rules as BHCs under Section 3 of the BHCA. It is also noteworthy that the acquisition of a savings and loan association or an S&LHC by a BHC or FHC is considered a nonbank activity under Section 4 of the BHCA, discussed below.

---

39. Codified at Section 38A of the FDI Act (12 U.S.C. § 1831). *See also* 12 C.F.R. § 225.4(a) and 12 C.F.R. § 238.8, the Board's source of strength regulations for BHCs and S&LHCs, respectively.
40. 12 U.S.C. § 1842.

Obviously, there must be an application in order to vet would-be acquirors. It is on form FR Y-3 or 3N and must be filed with the Federal Reserve Bank with jurisdiction over the acquiring BHC. The Federal Reserve Bank, if acting under delegated authority, or the Board must consider the following factors in connection with consideration of such an application[41]:

- competitive factors[42];
- financial and managerial resources;
- convenience and needs of the community to be served (including performance under the Community Reinvestment Act); and
- effectiveness of anti–money laundering activities.

As with bank mergers, there must be notice published in a local newspaper of general circulation in the location of both parties, public comment is invited, protest may be filed, and hearings may be held.[43]

The Board is authorized to approve the acquisition by a bank holding company of a BHC or bank in another state (the target bank) without regard to whether the acquisition is prohibited by the laws of any state, provided states may impose concentration limits and age requirements on such interstate acquisitions.

Concentration Limits. An acquisition by a BHC of a bank in another state may not be approved by the Board if:

- The BHC and its affiliated depository institutions either before the acquisition would control, or after the acquisition would control, more than 10% of the total amount of deposits of insured depository institutions in the United States; or
- The transaction falls within both of the following parameters:
    - Other than its first-time entry into the state, immediately before the acquisition, the BHC, including any of its affiliated depository institutions, controlled any depository institution or any branch in the home state of the target bank or in any other state in which in the target bank maintained a branch; and
    - Upon completion of the acquisition, the applicant and its depository institution affiliates would control 30% or more of the deposits of insured depositories in the host state of the

41. 12 U.S.C. § 1842(c) and 12 C.F.R. § 225.13.
42. Antitrust review for BHCs is handled the same way it is for bank mergers, as discussed in Chapter 9, *supra*.
43. 12 C.F.R. § 225.16.

target bank; or in any other state in which the target bank maintained a branch.[44]

A state may set a limit by law or policy that is higher than the 30% limits set forth above and may impose that limit on interstate mergers or acquisitions so long as the law or policy that sets this standard does not discriminate against out-of-state banks, BHCs, or their subsidiaries.

Age Laws and Shell Banks. A state may adopt a law or policy requiring that a bank must have been in existence for up to five years before it may be acquired by an out-of-state BHC. As is the case with transactions by individual banks, a bank that is chartered solely for the purpose of acquiring another bank and does not open for business until it acquires all or substantially all of the assets of the other bank is deemed to have the age of the acquired bank for purposes of acquisitions by out-of-state BHCs.[45]

Powers' Limitations—Section 4 of the BHCA

A hallmark of the BHCA is not only the fact that every entity that controls a bank gains Federal Reserve jurisdiction, but the fact that Section 4(c)(8) as to BHCs and Section 4(k) as to FHCs limit activities of all members of the holding company families. The significant restrictions in these sections make it impossible for a diversified commercial entity to control a bank and make it extremely difficult for even diversified financial companies to do the same because of "nonfinancial" activities that may lie somewhere within hundreds, or even thousands, of affiliates.

Specific Authority and Less than 5% Investments. Section 4(c) of the BHCA contains specific authority for BHC activities and investments. For instance, BHCs may expressly own shares of companies that hold its properties, or conduct a safe deposit business, or furnish service to the bank family, or hold DPC property (foreclosed collateral for debts previously contracted). The most interesting, in light of the wall between banking and commerce, is Section 4(c)(6), which permits BHCs to invest in shares of any company that does not include more than 5% of the outstanding voting shares of the company. Think about a 5% share in Coca Cola (SunTrust had one) or Apple or Amazon. All legal—with no regulatory notice or approval.

Section 4(c)(8). Of course, BHCs can do more. The 1970 amendments to the BHCA retained the 1956 activities restrictions quoted above virtually unchanged and applied them to one-bank holding companies. These restrictions are now found at Section 4(c)(8) of the BHCA ("Section 4(c)(8)").[46] The activities tests (there are technically two: (i) *so closely related*

44. 12 U.S.C. § 1842(d)(1)(B).
45. *Id.* at (C).
46. 12 U.S.C. § 1843(c)(8).

to banking (ii) *as to be a proper incident thereto*), just like the "*business of banking*" test for national banking powers discussed in Chapter 9, spawned decades of rulemaking by the Board and its fair share of litigation as the Board step-by-step determined the activities that met the tests. As with banks, the wall between banking and commercial activities is retained.

The list of approved activities, supplemented by Board interpretations over the years, is found at 12 C.F.R. § 225.28. Activities that are permissible for BHCs under Section 4(c)(8) include consumer, mortgage, and commercial lending; limited insurance sales; securities brokerage and certain securities activities (including a limited amount of underwriting of corporate equity securities); credit card operations; and ownership of a savings association.[47] Insurance activities of BHCs are extremely limited, much more so than for banks.[48]

The Gramm-Leach-Bliley Act of 1999 ("Gramm-Leach-Bliley," or "GLBA")[49] froze the powers as of November 11, 1999, so that Section 4(c)(8) now reads that a BHC generally may control the shares of any company:

> [T]he activities of which had been determined by the Board by regulation or order under this paragraph as of the day before November 12, 1999, to be so closely related to banking as to be a proper incident thereto (subject to such terms and conditions contained in such regulation or order, unless modified by the Board); . . .

November 11, 1999, is the day before the signing of Gramm-Leach-Bliley, which authorized BHCs that elect to become financial holding companies ("FHCs") to engage in an expanded list of permissible financial activities.

Generally, a BHC must file an application on form FR Y-4 or 4N with the Federal Reserve Bank in its district to acquire a nonbanking entity. Although well-capitalized and well-managed BHCs may file a notice,[50] others must file an application.[51] When a BHC seeks to commence a new activity *de novo*, it is typically the subject of a notice.[52]

---

47. The application procedures for acquiring a savings association are set forth in 12 C.F.R. § 225.14.
48. *See,* 12 C.F.R. § 225.28(b)(11), which lists seven limited activities, including sales of insurance from places of a population of 5,000 or less and the sale and underwriting of credit insurance. See chapter 4 of Karol K. Sparks, INSURANCE ACTIVITIES OF BANKS (2nd Ed. Wolters Kluwer Law and Business 2012) for an in-depth discussion of BHC insurance powers.
49. Public Law 106-102, Nov. 12, 1999, 113 Stat. 1338.
50. 12 C.F.R. § 225.23.
51. 12 C.F.R. § 225.24.
52. 12 C.F.R. § 225.23.

Financial Holding Companies

When Citicorp and Travelers Insurance merged, a BHC and an insurance conglomerate, respectively, it was technically illegal from a powers' perspective. Together, they formed Citigroup, the prototype for a domestic diversified financial services company, the likes of which had not been permitted in the United States since the Great Depression. The merger was structured to create a new BHC so that the favorable divestiture period of Section 4(a)(2) was triggered.[53] As a result, Citigroup, the combined company, had as long as five years before it was required to divest impermissible insurance underwriting activities acquired as part of The Travelers Group. The parties needed Gramm-Leach-Bliley to supply permanent legality.

And it did. Section 103(a) of Gramm-Leach-Bliley added Sections 4(k)–(o) to the BHCA,[54] creating the FHC as a vehicle to meld banking with insurance, securities, and capital markets activities as well as other activities financial in nature, or incidental or complementary thereto. The hallmark of the FHC is not only greater powers, but the ability to engage in them and even acquire companies that engage in them with only an after-the-fact notice to the Board in most cases. In other respects, an FHC remains a BHC, and, for instance, the definitions in Section 2 of the BHCA and the rules for bank acquisitions in Section 3 apply to FHCs, just as they do to BHCs. The examination, supervision, and enforcement authority of the Board is also the same, as discussed in the final section of this chapter.

While the FHC structure is enticing, it is not necessary in many events. Further, it is so replete with compliance obligations that institutions considering use of this structure need to truly understand the long- and short-term ramifications. Nevertheless, as of April 2008, 647 BHCs had chosen to become FHCs,[55] including most of the largest domestic BHCs and twenty-four foreign companies. Interestingly, almost 75% of the original FHCs had less than $500 million in assets and selected FHC status for the purpose of selling insurance or for no particular purpose except flexibility. As of October 26, 2016, the number of FHCs had shrunk to approximately 530,[56] the attrition due to acquisition but also to FHCs failing to continue to meet the requirements for such status, as discussed below.

---

53. Section 4(a)(2) of the BHCA (codified at 12 U.S.C. § 1843(a)(2)) permits any new BHC, for a period of two years, to engage in impermissible activities. By regulation, the Board may grant requests for three additional one-year extensions. 12 C.F.R. § 225.22(f).
54. 12 U.S.C. § 1843(k)–(o).
55. This is according to the Board, as reported in the Financial Services Fact Book, http://www.fsround.org/fsr/publications_and_research/files/2012FinancialFactBook.pdf.
56. A list of FHCs is posted at http://www.federalreserve.gov/bankinforeg/fhc.htm.

Perhaps the most interesting twist is that, as a result of the financial crisis of 2008–2009, the nation's largest investment banks, which did not become part of FHCs through acquisition previously, opted to themselves become FHCs (with some governmental persuasion). In connection with such a sea change in regulation, Morgan Stanley converted its nonbank bank to a national bank and Goldman Sachs sought a New York charter for its bank, both becoming FHCs.

Expanded Powers under Section 4(k)

Gramm-Leach-Bliley expanded the powers of FHCs to include all activities "financial in nature," or "incidental" or "complementary" thereto. Section 4(k) of the BHCA ("Section 4(k)"), as set forth in Section 103(a) of the GLBA, identified certain activities that Congress determined were financial in nature and, as a consequence, were permitted to FHCs by virtue of the BHCA:

- underwriting, dealing, and making a market in securities;
- acting as an agent, broker, or principal in connection with insurance;
- merchant banking or venture capital;
- mutual fund activities (advisor, distributor, administrator, seller, sponsor);
- securities lending, safeguarding, exchanging;
- issuing or selling asset-backed securities;
- travel agency;
- pension fund administrator; and
- underwriting and dealing in foreign government debt.

Merchant Banking.[57] FHC affiliates, other than depository institutions or their subsidiaries, may acquire up to 100% of the shares in a company engaged in commercial or other activities that are not permissible for the FHC so long as the shares are held in connection with a "bona fide underwriting or merchant or investment banking activity, including investment activities engaged in for the purpose of appreciation and ultimate resale or disposition of the investment." The shares may be held for as long as required to enable the affiliate to sell or otherwise dispose of the company "on a reasonable basis." The holding company may not actively manage the company as though it were a normal affiliate, but can manage it to the extent necessary to obtain a reasonable return on its sale or other disposition.

Portfolio Investments by Insurance Affiliates. These are investments—in shares, assets, or ownership interests—made in the ordinary course of

57. The discussion of merchant banking and portfolio investments is based in part on *A Summary of Gramm-Leach-Bliley Act*, Kirkpatrick & Lockhart Nicholson Graham LLP, Nov. 1999.

business and in accordance with state law, by insurance companies that are predominantly engaged in underwriting life, accident, and health, or property and casualty insurance (other than credit-related insurance) or providing and issuing annuities. During the period such shares, assets, or ownership interests are held, the FHC may not routinely manage or operate such company except as may be necessary or required to obtain a reasonable return on investment.

Identifying New Powers

The authority to determine whether an activity is financial in nature or incidental to a financial activity is shared by the Board and the Treasury Department. The Board may not determine that an activity has either of these characteristics if the Treasury objects to the determination. The Treasury may also make recommendations to the Board, which also may decline to take further actions. In deciding whether a service is financial in nature, the Board must consider:

- The purposes of the BHCA and the GLBA;
- Changes or reasonably expected changes in the marketplace in which FHCs compete;
- Changes or reasonably expected changes in the technology for delivering financial services; and
- Whether such activity is necessary or appropriate to allow an FHC and its affiliates to:
    - compete effectively with other financial services companies in the United States;
    - efficiently use technology to deliver financial information and services that are financial; and
    - offer customers any available or emerging technological means for using financial services or for the document imaging of data.

Regulation Y[58] permits three ways for the industry to expand FHC activities under this regime. One may:

- Request an advisory opinion of the Board under 12 C.F.R. § 225.88(e) that proposed activities are within the confines of the law as contemplated by the express authority of the GLBA. This process has a forty-five-day response window. It has been used successfully to add insurance risk management and claims adjusting to the powers' cadre.

58. 12 C.F.R. § 225.88-89.

- Request a determination that the activities are financial in nature or incidental to an express power. Under 12 C.F.R. § 225.88(a)-(d), this process requires consultation with Treasury, and the regulation says the Board will endeavor to make a decision within sixty days after Treasury chimes in. On December 7, 2000, the agencies entered into a memorandum of understanding to govern the way in which they would consider proposals for new powers.[59] The memorandum establishes additional time frames and clarifies that each agency may veto the other's proposal at any time during the process, but only in writing with an attached explanation of its reasoning. In the first rulemaking under this provision, the Board approved a rule defining "finder" activities as financial in nature. The rule allows FHCs to bring together buyers and sellers of products and services, leaving them to negotiate their own deals.[60] The Federal Reserve consulted with Treasury, as required, and Treasury made no objection.
- Request a determination that the activities are complementary under 12 C.F.R. § 225.89. This requires sixty days' prior notice and is deemed approved on the sixtieth day under 12 U.S.C. § 1843(j), unless the Board extends the period. The disadvantage to this alternative is that the factors are more demanding—the proposed activities may not pose a substantial risk to depository institutions or the financial system generally and the proposal must be expected to produce benefits to the public that outweigh possible adverse effects. The Board has approved health and disease management and mail-order pharmacy activities as complementary to permissible insurance activities under this authority.[61]

Notwithstanding the construct of Regulation Y in this regard, suffice it to say that the appetite of the Board to expand powers in the wake of the Global Financial Crisis has been exceedingly lacking.

---

59. Richard Cowden, *Treasury and Fed Agree by Memorandum on System for Approving Proposed Activities*, 76 BNA Banking Reports 6 (Jan. 8, 2001).
60. Codified at 12 C.F.R. § 225.86(d)(1); *see*, Adam Wasch, *Fed Adopts Final Regulation Allowing 'Finder' Role for Financial Holding Companies*, 75 BNA Banking Reports 783 (Dec. 18, 2000).
61. WellPoint Order Determining that Certain Activities Are Complementary to the Financial Activity of Underwriting and Selling Health Insurance (Sept. 7, 2007), https://www.federalreserve.gov/newsevents/press/other/other20070907a1.pdf.

Becoming an FHC

Before engaging in financial activities under Section 4(k), a BHC must qualify as an FHC under Section 4(1) of the BHCA.[62] To that end, it must ensure that:

- All banks and thrifts controlled or to be controlled by it are well-capitalized and well-managed. Section 606(a) of the Dodd-Frank Wall Street Reform and Consumer Protection Act of 2010 ("Dodd-Frank")[63] changed this rule such that as of July 21, 2011, a BHC itself is also required to be well-capitalized and well-managed before it may elect to become an FHC, and will be required to maintain that status in order to remain a FHC.
    - For purposes of the well-capitalized test, each depository organization (and the BHC under Dodd-Frank) must meet the requirements of Section 38 of the Federal Deposit Insurance Act as of the close of the previous quarter.[64]
    - For purposes of the well-managed test, each depository organization (and the BHC under Dodd-Frank) must have a composite CAMELS rating[65] of 1 or 2 and at least a 2 on the management component of that rating as of the date of filing the election.
- All of the banks and thrifts controlled or to be controlled by it have at least a "satisfactory" Community Reinvestment Act ("CRA") rating. In this regard, the BHCA directs the Federal Reserve to prohibit any FHC from establishing or acquiring a financial company if any bank or thrifts controlled by the FHC have received a less than satisfactory CRA rating in their most recent CRA exam. It also renders ineffective any FHC declaration made when the CRA test is not met.[66]

A BHC becomes an FHC through a simple certification process. Before engaging in both banking and financial activities under Section 4(k), a BHC must satisfy the conditions delineated above and qualify as an FHC under new Section 4(1) of the BHCA.[67] It must:

---

62. 12 U.S.C. § 1843(1); *see also,* 12 C.F.R. §§ 225.81 *et seq.*
63. Pub. L. No. 111-203 (2010), amending Section (l)(1) of the BHCA (codified at 12 U.S.C. § 18443(l)(1)).
64. Capital requirements and the concept of "well-capitalized" are discussed in Chapter 4, *supra.*
65. CAMELS and the concept of "well-managed" are discussed in Chapter 11, *infra.*
66. Section 103(b) of the Gramm-Leach-Bliley amends Section 804 of the Community Reinvestment Act of 1997 to this end (codified at 12 U.S.C. § 2903).
67. 12 U.S.C. § 1843(1).

- File an election with the Federal Reserve, stating its intention to operate as an FHC;
- File a certification with the Federal Reserve, in which it affirms that it and all of its subsidiary banks and thrifts are well-capitalized and well-managed; and
- Assure that all of its subsidiary banks and thrifts have received a satisfactory examination result on their most recent CRA exam.[68]

The election is effective generally on the 31st day after it is filed, unless the BHC fails to meet any of the qualifications, in which event the Federal Reserve will notify the company that the election is ineffective.[69]

An FHC may lose its status as an FHC if it or one or more of its depository institutions becomes less than "well-capitalized" or if it is rated as less than "well-managed." If the FHC does not correct these deficiencies within 180 days after notice from the Federal Reserve, or a longer period as prescribed by the agency, the FHC must either divest its depository institutions or stop engaging in activities other than the Section 4(c)(8) activities that are permissible for a BHC. This cessation requirement does not apply to activities conducted by the institutions themselves or by their subsidiaries, including financial subsidiaries.

FHC Nonbank Acquisitions

Obviously, the quest for FHC status typically means the BHC has its sights set on one more of the GLBA suite of special powers. In that regard, Gramm-Leach-Bliley presented FHCs with a reward of unprecedented value—no prior approval required to exercise most Section 4(k) powers. (There went our involvement in the preparation of messy applications—the app and publication of the deal came off the acquisition checklist.) However, the acquisition of banks and thrifts reverts to the same rules as discussed for BHCs.

After-the-fact Notice. An FHC may establish or acquire an entity without any prior notice to the Federal Reserve. It must merely give notice within thirty days *after* it commences or acquires a company engaged in a permissible activity.[70] The notice is made on Form FRY-10 and must describe, as relevant:

- The activity that was commenced and the identity of each subsidiary engaged in the activity; or
- The identity of the company acquired and the activities conducted by the company.

68. 12 C.F.R. § 225.82.
69. 12 C.F.R. § 225.82(a) and (b).
70. 12 C.F.R. § 225.87.

However, Dodd-Frank impacts this entitlement in connection with large acquisitions by systemically important FHCs and nonbanks under its supervision. Under Section 163(b)(1) of Dodd-Frank.[71] FHCs must provide notice to the Federal Reserve *before* acquiring a company engaged in financial activities if the target company has $10 billion or more of consolidated assets. Also, effective on the same date, under Section 163(b)(4), the Federal Reserve must consider the impact of acquisitions on U.S. financial stability in approving or disapproving proposed bank and nonbank acquisitions by such FHCs and nonbanks.

No Notice Required. It is noteworthy that there are two circumstances in which no notice to the Federal Reserve is required in order to engage in an activity:[72]

- First, no notice to the Board is required when an FHC acquires shares of a company *without acquiring control* of the company. This would always be the case when an FHC will acquire less than 5% of the voting securities of a company. Unlike prior law, no notice or clearance is required.
- The second exemption applies to an FHC that is engaged in securities activities, that makes merchant banking investments, or that makes insurance company investments and has provided the Federal Reserve with the appropriate notice regarding the relevant activity. Under those circumstances, the company need only submit a notice in connection with the acquisition of more than 5% of the shares of any company as part of the securities, merchant banking, or insurance investment activity if the cost of the acquisition exceeds the lesser of 5% of the FHC's Tier 1 capital or $200 million.

In cases where a financial holding company already has approval under Section 4(c)(8) to engage in an activity now available in an expanded scope under Section 4(k), the company must provide the Federal Reserve with a post-commencement notice as described above informing the Federal Reserve that the company has expanded the scope of the activity in accordance with Section 4(k). For instance, if a BHC has authority to sell insurance from a place of 5,000 under Section 4(c)(8) and sought to expand that activity, it would provide post-commencement notice once it is certified as an FHC.

Antitrust Review. Historically, all acquisitions that required approval under the Bank Merger Act, Section 3 of the BHCA, or Section 10 of the Home Owners Loan Act were exempt from the Hart-Scott-Rodino

71. Amends Section 4(k)(6)(B) of the BHCA to add (ii) (codified at 12 U.S.C. § 1843(k)(6)(b)(ii)).
72. 12 C.F.R. § 225.87(b).

("HSR") Act[73] pre-merger notification filing requirements because a federal regulator and the Department of Justice were reviewing the competitive effects. HSR also exempted from filing those transactions that required approval under Section 4 of the BHCA if copies of all materials filed with the federal banking agency were contemporaneously filed with the Federal Trade Commission ("FTC") and the Department of Justice at least thirty days prior to consummation of a transaction. As a consequence, banking organization acquisitions of nonbank entities did not generally require notices under HSR.

But, all of a sudden, there were no applications for FHCs to acquire a whole host of companies, including larger companies like investment banks and insurance companies—thus, no antitrust review of significant transactions. Section 133 of Gramm-Leach-Bliley addressed this issue and amended HSR to provide the FTC with jurisdiction over nonbank acquisitions by FHCs.

Hart-Scott-Rodino Filings. As amended by Gramm-Leach-Bliley, HSR requires pre-merger notification filings for transactions under Section 4(k) of the BHCA that do not otherwise require approval under Section 3 or 4 of the BHCA. While the acquisition of a nonbanking company by a BHC that is not an FHC continued to be exempt from the pre-merger notification filing requirement if copies of the application are filed under applicable law, the acquisition of such nonbank company by an FHC (assuming the transaction meets the HSR threshold tests) is subject to the pre-merger notification filing requirement.[74]

HSR filings in this regard are triggered based on the size of the parties and the size of the transaction. The FTC adjusts the threshold tests annually. The most significant threshold in determining reportability is the minimum size of transaction threshold. This is often referred to as the "$50 million (as adjusted)" threshold because it started at $50 million and is now adjusted annually. As of February 27, 2020, that threshold was $94 million *at the time of closing.*[75] For example, a deal valued at $92 million which closed on or after February 27, 2020, was not reportable because it was below the minimum size of transaction threshold, even though it would have been reportable a day earlier.

Furthermore, the FTC is subjecting the acquisition of a nonbank company through a bank merger or a bank acquisition to the same

73. 7a(c) of the Clayton Act (15 U.S.C. §18a(c)).

74. For large nonbank acquisitions of $10 billion and greater by systemically important FHCs and nonbanks, Dodd-Frank Section 163 (b)(5) eliminated the statutory exemption from the HSR filing requirement that is available in transactions for which prior Federal Reserve approval is required.

75. *See*, ftc.gov, HSR Threshold Adjustments and Reportability for 2020 (Jan. 31, 2020).

notification requirements.[76] As a result, if a target bank owns a nonbank subsidiary, the acquiring bank or BHC or FHC must review the acquisition under the size of transaction test and file notice with the FTC if the test is exceeded.

Reg Y "Gotcha's"

Oh, that Regulation Y can be tricky. It is best to assume that whatever course your client seeks to take, they best not go forth until you check the fine print in Regulation Y. Most of this is legacy, and there have been promised fixes for more than a decade, but here we are in the Reg Y land of lore and gotcha's.

1. Did you know that state banks may not acquire less than 100% of any subsidiary without applying to the Board under Section 4 and abridging the power to that of a BHC under Section 4(c)(8)?
2. Did you know that a merger of BHCs when the subsidiary banks are merging (so it will be a one-bank holding company owning one bank) requires not only a Bank Merger Act application to the primary federal regulator but also an application or waiver from the Board?
3. Did you know that a reverse merger is treated as the acquisition of a new bank under Section 3? A reverse merger is a favorite structure for tax reasons, where the BHCs merge and, at the bank level, the target bank is the continuing charter.
4. Did you know a BHC needs prior approval for a stock redemption?
5. Did you know a BHC needs merger approval to dissolve a subsidiary?

Savings and Loan Holding Companies

Legislation involving S&L holding companies evolved on a separate track from the BHCA. The first federal banking law relating to S&LHCs, the "Spence Act,"[77] which was enacted in 1959, imposed a two-year moratorium on the acquisition of additional savings associations by S&LHCs that already controlled one association. The Federal Home Loan Bank Board ("FHLBB") was directed to conduct a survey of the implications of holding company control of stock savings associations and submit a report to the

76. *See* FTC Formal Interpretation 17 (2000); *see also* R. Christian Bruce, *FTC Division Says It Has Broad Jurisdiction to Review Nonbank Deals by Banks, Thrifts*, 74 BNA Banking Report 15 at 645 (Apr. 10, 2000).
77. Publ. L. 86-374, Sept. 23, 1959, 73 Stat. 691.

House and Senate Banking Committees along with any draft legislation it deemed advisable.

Congressional concerns with S&LHCs were similar to those it had with BHCs in 1956, but the Senate report on the Spence Act acknowledged that the situation with S&LHCs was different from those involving other holding companies, both "[B]ecause of the nature of the [S&L] industry and because of differences in stage of development which savings and loan holding companies have reached, as compared with public utility holding companies or bank holding companies."[78] While the Senate report alluded to possible anticompetitive effects of increasing holding company ownership of savings associations, there was less emphasis on the harmful effects of combining banking and commerce (savings associations could not make commercial loans at that time, for example). There was concern, however, about: absentee ownership in an industry that is closely tied to the local community, "financial manipulation and intercorporate dealings," and entanglement of associations in schemes designed to promote interests unrelated to homeownership.[79]

THC Regulation

These concerns culminated in Congress enacting the Savings and Loan Holding Company Amendments of 1967,[80] which imposed limits on nonbanking activities of multiple S&LHCs but not on otherwise lawful activities of S&LHCs that controlled one savings association (so-called "Unitary THCs"). This ability to conduct unrestricted activities continued until the enactment of the Competitive Equality Banking Act of 1987 ("CEBA").[81] CEBA provided that Unitary THCs could no longer engage in unrestricted activities unless their savings association subsidiaries became and remained "qualified thrift lenders" ("QTLs").[82] Multiple S&LHCS, which were otherwise restricted to engaging in a limited set of activities, were free of activities restrictions after CEBA if all, or all but one, of their savings association subsidiaries had been acquired in supervisory acquisitions and all of the subsidiaries met the QTL test.

Source of strength applies to S&LHCs just like BHCs.[83] Moreover, even if the Federal Reserve requires an intermediate holding company to act as

78. S. Rpt. No. 810, Aug. 25, 1959, p. 2888, U.U. Code Cong. and Admn. News, 86th Cong., 1st sess.
79. *Id.* at 2887.
80. Publ. L. 90-255, Feb. 14, 1967, 82 Stat. 5.
81. Publ. L. 100-86, Aug. 10, 1987, 101 Stat. 552.
82. 12 U.S.C. § 1467a(c)(3).
83. 12 C.F.R. § 238.8.

the S&LHC, a unitary parent company must serve as a source of strength to the intermediate holding company.[84]

Qualified Thrift Lender ("QTL")

The QTL test was a response to Congressional concerns that savings associations were becoming more "bank-like" as a result of legislation in the early 1980s that had expanded their investment powers beyond mortgage lending to include, among other things, limited authority to make commercial and consumer loans. Congress devised the test to keep associations focused on housing finance and to make this focus the "price" for their unlimited unitary holding company powers. A QTL (as the test was amended)[85] is a savings association that qualifies as a domestic building and loan association under Section 7701(a)(19) of the Internal Revenue Code or that has at least 65% of its portfolio assets in "qualified thrift investments." Investments that are considered "qualified thrift investments" include, among other things, loans and investments relating to domestic residential real estate or manufactured housing and mortgage-backed securities relating to the same, home equity loans, small business loans, educational loans, loans made through credit cards or credit card accounts, and shares of stock issued by any Federal Home Loan Bank, without limitation; and shares of stock issued by the Federal Home Loan Mortgage Corporation or the Federal National Mortgage Association, and 50% of the dollar amount of residential mortgage loans originated by the association and sold within ninety days, the aggregate of which is subject to a 20% of portfolio assets limitation.

Unitary THCs after Gramm-Leach-Bliley

Section 401 of Gramm-Leach-Bliley[86] ended unrestricted activities of Unitary THCs that were organized after May 4, 1999 (not so coincidently, a date picked to assure that Wal-Mart would not be able to own an S&L) and that did not have on or before that date, an application pending at the OTS to organize a unitary holding company. Unitary THCs and QTL-qualified multiple S&LHCs that were in existence on May 4, 1999 (or established thereafter pursuant to an application pending before OTS at that date) may continue to engage in activities in which they were engaged on that date and in any activities in which *they could have engaged* under the S&LHCA on that date so long as: they control at least one association that they controlled on that date (or that they acquired pursuant to an application filed on or

84. Section 626 of Dodd-Frank. Codified at Section 10A of HOLA (12 U.S.C. § 1467b).
85. 12 U.S.C. § 1467a(m)(4)(c); 12 U.S.C. § 1464(c)(1).
86. Amending Section 10(c) of HOLA.

before that date); and the association or associations under their control are qualified thrift lenders.

Unitary THCs that were organized after May 4, 1999, and those that were organized before that date that lost their grandfathered status, were limited to engaging in the "post-Gramm-Leach-Bliley" activities listed below. Grandfathered Unitary THCs lose that status if they are acquired by a company or other entity that is engaged in activities other than "post-Gramm-Leach-Bliley" activities. These post-Gramm-Leach-Bliley activities are:

- Section 4(k) activities permissible for FHCs;
- Section 4(c)(8) activities permissible for BHCs; and
- The permissible activities for multiple S&LHCs, i.e.:
    - furnishing or performing management services for a savings association subsidiary of such company;
    - conducting an insurance agency or escrow business;
    - holding, managing, or liquidating assets owned or acquired from a savings association subsidiary of such company;
    - holding or managing properties used or occupied by a savings association subsidiary of such company;
    - acting as trustee under deed of trust; and
    - activities permissible for multiples by regulation on March 5, 1987.[87]

"Nonbank" Holding Companies

There are specialized banks, such as credit card banks and industrial loan companies ("ILCs"), which are excluded from the definition of "bank" for purposes of the BHCA. Companies that control these banks are therefore not BHCs and are not subject to the Section 4(c)(8) activity restrictions of the BHCA, or to the Section 4(k) restrictions for FHCs. They are also not subject to Federal Reserve regulation and supervision. Yes, that creates an uneven playing field that has the potential to increase risk in the banking sector.

87. These activities, at 12 C.F.R. § 238.53(b), include acquisition of unimproved real estate for development, data processing, storage, and other services for affiliates and development and administration of employee benefit plans.

History of "Nonbank Banks"

Prior to 1987, Section 2(c) of the BHCA[88] defined a "bank" as an institution that:

- offered demand deposits *or*
- made commercial loans.

The loophole was apparent on the face of the statue—one could avoid coverage under the BHCA by declaring that the bank would offer either commercial loans or demand deposits, but not both. Essentially, any commercial entity could enter banking through any charter and conform activities to either not make commercial loans or not take demand deposits.

Moreover, because the BHCA definition referred to "demand deposits," some of these nonbank holding companies were able to make commercial loans *and* offer their customers check-like instruments drawn on time deposits rather than demand deposits. These instruments were generally referred to as negotiable orders of withdrawal, or NOWs, and this "NOW account loophole" effectively erased any distinction between banks that conformed to the BHCA definition and those that did not.[89]

The acquisition of these "nonbank banks" thus breached the wall between banking and commerce that Congress had intended to build in 1970. Congress addressed this issue in CEBA, which redefined "bank" in the BHCA to close the loophole. The new definition included all banks that are FDIC-insured, or institutions that both made commercial loans and offered deposit accounts from which the customer could pay third parties by check "or similar means for payment to third parties."[90]

---

88. Codified at 12 U.S.C. § 1841(c).
89. Before the enactment of CEBA, the Supreme Court held that the reference to "demand deposits" in Section 2(c) of the BHCA means, literally, deposits withdrawable on demand, and does not include NOW accounts. In an attempt to stop nonbank banks from evading BHCA coverage by offering NOW accounts, the Federal Reserve had amended Regulation Y to change the definition of "demand deposit" to cover NOW accounts by defining these accounts to include deposits that are payable on demand "as a matter of practice." The court noted that NOW accounts, although functioning like traditional checking accounts, are (as time deposits) subject to "a seldom but nevertheless absolute right to require prior notice of withdrawal," are not, therefore, withdrawable "on demand," and therefore are not, under the plain language of the statute, demand deposits. Board of Governors, FRS v. Dimension Financial Corp., et al., 474 U.S. 361, 368 (1986).
90. Publ. L. 100-86, Aug. 10, 1987, 101 Stat. 552. Section 101 of CEBA adopted a new Section 2(c)(1) of the BHCA (codified at 12 U.S.C. § 1841(c)(1)).

CEBA also carved out several exceptions from the definition of "bank" in the BHCA, including thrifts and credit unions, certain trust companies, and two types of limited-purpose institutions: credit card banks and ILCs.[91]

Credit Card Banks

Credit card banks are institutions with a state or national bank charter that limit their activities exclusively to credit card operations. They were a popular option for retailers to offer their own credit cards. To qualify for the BHCA exclusion, these banks may accept collateral to secure consumer credit card loans, but may not:

- accept demand deposits or other deposits on which the customer may write checks or similar instruments;
- accept time or savings deposits of less than $100,000;
- have more than one branch where deposits are accepted; and
- issue commercial credit cards or otherwise make commercial loans.

Organizers of these banks generally secure a regular national or state bank charter and voluntarily limit its activities to conform to the BHCA exclusion. Delaware, however, offers a special charter for credit card institutions that conforms to the BHCA requirements.[92] As insured institutions, credit card banks are subject to virtually all of the rules and regulations of the FDIC and their chartering agency, including those pertaining to transactions with affiliates, tying arrangements.

Industrial Loan Companies

As noted in Chapter 3 in the context of the ILC as a charter, ILCs are state-chartered institutions that may be organized currently in five states: California, Hawaii, Minnesota, Nevada, and Utah. The vast majority have FDIC insurance. But, it is really mostly about Utah, which became a favorite "nonbank bank" charterer for commercial companies that were not eligible to become BHCs because of the powers' restrictions of the BHCA. Most of the modern law regarding ILCs derives from these commercial companies that sought to enter banking through the ILC loophole.

Impact of CEBA. Congress addressed this issue in 1987 in CEBA by changing the definition of "bank" in the BHCA to include all FDIC-insured depository institutions. But, the law created a narrow exclusion

91. Credit card banks and ILCs are excluded from the definition of "bank" in Sections 2(c)(2)(F) and (H), respectively, of the BHCA (codified at 12 U.S.C. § 1841(c)(2)(F) and (H)).
92. Del. Code, Title 5, Ch. 15.

for ILCs.[93] In connection therewith, CEBA limited the availability of the exclusion to those that had been chartered in a state that had a law in effect or under consideration on March 5, 1987, that required, or would require, ILCs to obtain federal deposit insurance. ILCs chartered in these states are then excluded from coverage under the BHCA if they meet any one of the following conditions:

- the assets of the ILC must be less than $100 million;
- the ILC does not accept demand deposits that the depositor may withdraw by check or similar means for payment to third parties; or[94]
- control of the ILC has not been acquired by any company after August 10, 1987.

CEBA also provided that uninsured ILCs, like other nonbank banks, would be grandfathered as long as they refrained from engaging directly or through an affiliate in any activity in which they were not lawfully engaged on March 7, 1987. The exclusion of any grandfathered ILC will be defeated if the institution permits any overdraft on its account at a Federal Reserve Bank including intraday overdrafts, on behalf of an affiliate. There are several exceptions to this restriction, however, including overdrafts caused by inadvertent errors, overdrafts in connection with primary government securities dealers, and overdrafts in connection with activities permissible for financial holding companies.

Popularity of the Charter after CEBA. The industry experienced significant asset growth in the wake of CEBA. With uncertainty erased, between 1987 and 2006, according to the FDIC,[95] total assets held by ILCs grew from $4.2 billion to $213 billion. There were fifty-eight ILCs as of the end of 2006. Companies as diverse as BMW, Target, Pitney Bowes, and Harley-Davidson were able to enter banking by acquiring or chartering an ILC.

The joyride ended, and ILCs declined in number and size since 2006—from fifty-eight to thirty-four, with the assets of such institutions dropping

93. Codified at 12 U.S.C. § 1841(c)(2)(H)).

94. Section 2(c)(2)(H) of the BHCA (codified at 12 U.S.C. § 1841(c)(2)(H)). The General Accountability Office ("GAO") points out that this language permits ILCs that wish to do so to offer NOW accounts to their customers. ("Industrial Loan Companies—Recent Asset Growth and Commercial Interest Highlight Differences in Regulatory Authority" GAO-05-621, Sept., 2005, p. 6). *See also,* summary of *Dimension* case in note 56.

95. *See,* Parent Companies of Industrial Loan Banks, FDIC, Notice of Proposed Rulemaking, 85 Fed. Reg. 17,771, 17,773 (Mar. 31, 2020).

from $212.7 billion to $102.4 billion.[96] By the end of 2019, there were only twenty-three with $141 billion in total assets.[97] Part of this was because in 2008, in the midst of economic meltdown, parents of a number of ILCs converted into bank holding companies through expedited conversions permitted by the Federal Reserve due to prevailing emergency conditions in the financial markets. ILC parent companies that undertook expedited conversions to BHCs were Morgan Stanley, Morgan Stanley Capital Management LLC, and Morgan Stanley Domestic Holdings, Inc.; Goldman Sachs Group, Inc.; American Express Travel Related Services Company, Inc.; CIT Group Inc.; and GMAC LLC. Also, in 2008, Merrill Lynch, the parent company of an ILC, was sold to Bank of America.[98]

Moratoria. These entities, when owned by *commercial companies*, are controversial, and the charter has left in its wake a history of vigorous opposition from the banking industry. But the ire was particularly awakened in 2005, when Wal-Mart's application for FDIC insurance for an ILC generated overwhelmingly negative comments to the FDIC (13,800 comment letters to be exact) and equally negative testimony in public hearings. Home Depot then filed an application on June 28, 2006, to acquire an existing industrial loan company, EnerBank,[99] once again spawning hundreds of negative comments. Both applications were later withdrawn, but the FDIC self-imposed a six-month moratorium on applications for deposit insurance for new ILCs and applications to acquire existing industrial loan companies beginning on July 28, 2006, and ending on January 31, 2007. After much interest by Congress, the FDIC extended the moratorium on ILC applications for an additional year, but only with respect to applications filed by companies engaged in nonfinancial (commercial) activities.[100]

Enter Congress again, which imposed a moratorium on FDIC insurance of ILCs (and credit card banks and trust companies) and on changes in control of them in Section 603 of Dodd-Frank.[101] The moratorium ended

96. Government Accountability Office, *Report on the Regulatory Implications of Limited-Purpose Bank Charters* (Jan. 2012), discussed at http://www.gibsondunn.com/publications/pages/Limited-Purpose-Bank-Charters-for-Commercial-Firms-End-of-Dodd-Frank-Moratorium.aspx.

97. *Supra* note 91.

98. Statement of Martin J. Gruenberg, Chairman, Federal Deposit Insurance Corporation on *De Novo* Banks and Industrial Loan Companies before the Committee on Oversight and Government Reform; U.S. House of Representatives; 2157 Rayburn House Office Building (July 13, 2016), https://www.fdic.gov/news/news/speeches/spjul1316.html.

99. *Id.* at 3.

100. For an excellent discussion of the ILC backstory, see, Industrial Loan Companies after the Moratorium, https://www.cov.com/-/media/files/corporate/publications/2008/02/industrial-loan-companies-after-the-moratorium.pdf. *See also*, the FDIC's 2020 Notice of Proposed Rulemaking, *infra* note 27,17,774-17,775.

101. Title VI, Publ. L. No. 111-203 (2010),

on July 21, 2013, and thereafter it became technically legally permissible for any type of company—retailer, manufacturer, or any type of nonfinancial firm—to seek to acquire or establish such an FDIC-insured bank.

During the FDIC moratorium, one ILC was approved, but not for a commercial company, and that was the key. The FDIC approved an ILC for deposit insurance in 2007 for ARCUS Financial Bank, a proposed new Utah state-chartered industrial bank, to be owned by ARCUS Financial Holding Corp., which in-turn was a direct subsidiary of WellPoint Inc., Indianapolis, Indiana, a publicly traded health benefits company,[102] following the Federal Reserve's determination that the activities of ARCUS were complimentary to permissible activities for an FHC.[103] ARCUS was not a particularly controversial application in light of the powers determination by the Board because WellPoint was not a commercial firm trying to evade the BHCA.

2020 and Beyond Rules. The last moratorium expired in 2013, and the FDIC has announced on several occasions that it "is open for business" for ILC applications. On March 17, 2020, the FDIC released a Notice of Proposed Rulemaking[104] that laid out a construct of required conditions and commitments for deposit insurance applications, nonobjection to change in control notices, and merger application approvals that would result in an ILC becoming a subsidiary of a commercial company.

The rules, codified at 12 C.F.R 354, require "covered companies" (commercial companies) to enter into one or more agreements in which they agree to (in pertinent part)[105] submit to examination by the FDIC; provide annual reporting to the FDIC of financial condition, internal controls and risk management, affiliate transactions, and compliance; cause an independent audit of each ILC to be performed annually; limit board representation; maintain capital and liquidity; execute a tax allocation agreement; and maintain a disaster recovery plan. There are also restrictions on material changes, adding or replacing directors and senior officers, and entering into a service contract with the ILC.[106] In other words, submitting the ILC and its parent to the panoply of bank regulation and supervision addressed in this book by agreement.

Application Approvals. Although mixing commerce and banking remains controversial, the FDIC was as good as its word in the proposed

102. In Re: ARCUS Financial Bank (Proposed) Salt Lake City, Salt Lake County, Utah Application for Federal Deposit Insurance (Deposit Insurance Fund) Statement and Order (Sept. 11, 2007), https://www.fdic.gov/regulations/laws/bankdecisions/depins/arcus.pdf.

103. The citation to the Board order is, *supra*, note 61.

104. Parent Companies of Industrial Banks and Industrial Loan Companies, 85 Fed. Reg. 17,771 (Mar. 31, 2020).

105. *Id.* at 17,785 (to be codified at 12 C.F.R. § 354.3-354.4).

106. *Id.* (to be codified at 12 C.F.R. § 354.5).

rulemaking, approving two applications for ILC deposit insurance one day after the release (but before publication in the *Federal Register* and after their respective "marathon quests" for the charter): first to the fintech Square and then to student loan servicer Nelnet.[107] Square Financial Services, a Utah-chartered ILC, intends to make commercial loans to their payment customers.[108] Nelnet Bank, also a Utah-chartered ILC, will originate student and consumer loans.[109] The conditions of these approvals are comprehensive and read exactly as promised in the proposed rulemaking, but with more on lending practices.

Rakuten, the Japanese online shopping platform, with emphasis on rebates, refiled its FDIC application for ILC deposit insurance for Rakuten Bank America, Midvale, Texas, on May 29, 2020, and then withdrew it, proving again the controversy surrounding the charter.

Mutual Holding Companies

Mutual holdings companies ("MHCs") are unique entities, permitted to own savings associations. The MHC structure, another innovation enacted as a part of CEBA,[110] is designed to permit a mutual savings association to enjoy the advantages of being in a holding company structure, including issuance of stock and other access to capital markets, while preserving the advantages of mutual ownership, including insulation from hostile takeovers and proxy fights.[111]

Mutual S&L Holding Companies

To reorganize into a MHC, a mutual savings association must organize a mutual savings and loan holding company, which is an entity now chartered and supervised by the Board under Regulation MM. The savings association would then convert to a stock charter and transfers 100% of

107. Brendan Petersan, *ILC Freeze Breaks with Federal Approvals for Square, Nelnet*, Am. Banker, May 18, 2020.
108. Press Release, *FDIC Approves the Deposit Insurance Application for Square Financial Services, Inc.*, Salt Lake City, Utah, Mar. 18, 2020; FDIC Order Square Financial Services, Inc. (In organization) Salt Lake City, Salt Lake County, Utah Application for Federal Deposit Insurance, https://www.fdic.gov/news/news/press/2020/pr20033a.pdf.
109. Press Release, *FDIC Approves the Deposit Insurance Application for Nelnet Bank*, Salt Lake City, Utah, Mar. 18, 2020; FDIC Order Nelnet Bank (In organization) Salt Lake City, Salt Lake County, Utah Application for Federal Deposit Insurance, https://www.fdic.gov/news/news/press/2020/pr20034a.pdf.
110. Section 107(a), adding a subsection to the National Housing Act, which became Section 10(o) of the S&LHCA (codified at 12 U.S.C. § 1467a(o)).
111. Board MHC regulations are at 12 C.F.R. Part 239 (Regulation MM).

its voting stock to the MHC. The MHC, which would be controlled by the depositors of the subsidiary association, retains control of a majority of the voting stock, but may raise capital by issuing up to 49.9% of that stock, and any nonvoting stock the association may have issued, to the public.

MHCs may engage in activities permissible for the following:

- FHCs;
- multiple savings and loan holding companies;
- service corporations and operating subsidiaries of federal savings associations, which are discussed in Chapter 3; and
- service corporations of state-chartered associations in a state where the MHC has its home office.

In 1998, OTS issued regulations[112] to permit MHCs to create an "intermediate" stock holding company, commonly called a "mid-tier" stock holding company ("SHC"). In this structure, 100% of the stock of the savings association is held by the SHC, which can issue up to 49.9% of its own stock to the public. The parent mutual holding company must own at least 50.1% of the stock of the SHC.

Mutual Bank Holding Companies

CEBA also authorized mutual savings banks and cooperative banks to reorganize to form a mutual bank holding company, which is to be regulated on the same terms and subject to the same limitations "as any other bank holding company."[113] Bank MHCs, unlike savings associations MHCs, are organized under state law.[114]

Supervision, Examination, and Enforcement of Holding Companies in the Wake of Dodd-Frank

While the Board is the primary federal regulator of all holding companies, the holding company's depository institution subsidiaries continue to be regulated by their primary federal regulator. Since 1999, activities of regulated nonbank subsidiaries of BHCs were supervised by the "functional regulators," with oversight authority vested in the Board.

This "functional regulation" concept was a key component of Gramm-Leach-Bliley. The result was that a holding company family would have conceptual "buckets" of regulation: the banking agencies each had their

112. OTS, Mutual Holding Companies, Final rule, 63 Fed. Reg. 11,361 (Mar. 9, 1998).
113. Section 107(b) of CEBA, adding subsection (g) to Section 3 of the BHCA (codified at 12 U.S.C. § 1842(g)).
114. *See, e.g.*, Mutual Holding Companies, ch. 167H, title XXII, Part I., Mass. Gen. Laws.

buckets: OCC for national banks, and the Federal Reserve or FDIC for state banks; there might be a Securities and Exchange Commission bucket for investment advisers and a Financial Industry Regulatory Authority and SEC bucket for broker-dealers; and there might be a state insurance bucket for an insurance company or agency. While there were oversight features built into the law, they were relatively weak.

Much has been said about the failure of functional regulation and its contribution to the 2008–2009 financial crisis. It has been characterized, in fact, as a "co-conspirator" in the crisis. As a consequence, the buckets were ditched in favor of systemic, comprehensive regulation—essentially enterprise-wide oversight, ignoring corporate entities and looking horizontally and vertically through the entire organization. Title I of Dodd-Frank created the Financial Stability Oversight Council ("FSOC") to facilitate coordination of financial regulatory policy and tapped the Federal Reserve for this daunting duty with respect to systemically important financial entities. As a result, there will still be BHCs and FHCs, and the bank family will look a lot the same; however, the Federal Reserve will be watching over the entire enterprise.

As indicated, the Federal Reserve continues to be the regulator of BHCs and FHCs under Dodd-Frank and is also the regulator of S&LHCs. And more so. Taken together, Titles I and VI of Dodd-Frank significantly enhance the supervisory role of the Federal Reserve, especially over systemically important financial services providers, but, in turn, they subject the agency to a new level of transparency.

Role of the Federal Reserve

The Federal Reserve picked up unprecedented examination authority over the entire depository institution family top to bottom and side to side. The punch for much of this authority is found in Title VI of Dodd-Frank, carrying the moniker "The Bank and Savings Association Holding Company and Depository Institution Regulatory Improvements Act of 2010." Specifically:

- Section 604(b)[115] and (h),[116] respectively, of Dodd-Frank gave the Federal Reserve authority to examine BHCs and S&LHCs and each subsidiary in order to (i) inform the Board of the nature of the operations, financial condition, risks, and stability of the parent company and subsidiary; and (ii) monitor compliance with federal law by functionally regulated subsidiaries and insured depository institutions with respect to those federal laws that the Federal Reserve has specific jurisdiction to enforce, and other than in the

115. Amends Section 5(c)(2) of the BHCA (codified at 12 U.S.C. § 1844(c)(2)).
116. Amends Section 2 of HOLA (codified at 12 U.S.C. § 1462).

case of an insured depository institution or functionally regulated subsidiary, any provision of federal law. The Federal Reserve's examination authority over compliance is made subject to the authority of the Bureau of Consumer Financial Protection's in respect of federal consumer financial law.

- Section 604(c)(2)[117] eliminated the perceived culprit in keeping the Federal Reserve removed from effective enterprise risk oversight of the BHC family under the auspices of functional regulation by deleting Section 10A of the BHCA. Section 10A only permitted the Federal Reserve to take action against a functionally regulated affiliate if its actions posed a threat to the depository institution. No longer.
- The hedge in the expanded authority is that Section 604[118] required the Board to rely to the fullest extent possible on reports and other information available from sources other than the subsidiary, such as other federal regulators and publicly available information. The Federal Reserve is required to provide notice to and consult with the appropriate federal banking agency, the SEC, the Commodities Futures Trading Commission, or state regulatory agency, as appropriate, before commencing an examination with respect to a functionally regulated subsidiary or a depository institution subsidiary.
- To assure consistent oversight of activities of holding company subsidiaries, Section 605[119] of Dodd-Frank required the Federal Reserve to examine the bank permissible activities of each nondepository institution subsidiary that is not a functionally regulated subsidiary or a subsidiary of a depository institution in the same manner, subject to the same standards, and with the same frequency as would be required if such activities were conducted in the lead insured depository institution. The Federal Reserve's examination authority is made subject to the Bureau's authority in respect of Federal consumer financial law.

In connection with the special examination powers it ceded to the Board, Dodd-Frank requires coordination with state supervisors, and permits the Federal Reserve to conduct examinations in a joint or alternating manner with a state regulator, if the Federal Reserve determines that an examination of a nondepository institution subsidiary conducted by a state carries out the purpose of Section 605. The appropriate federal banking agency for the holding company's largest depository institution subsidiary

117. Strikes Section 10A of the BHCA (12 U.S.C. § 1848a).
118. Amends Section 5(c)(1) of the BHCA (codified at 12 U.S.C. § 1844(c)(1)).
119. Adds a new Section 26 to the FDIA.

may exercise back-up authority to examine the activities of the nondepository institution subsidiary if the Federal Reserve does not conduct the required examinations. The examination must consider whether the activities pose a material threat to the safety and soundness of any insured depository institution, are conducted in accordance with applicable state law, and are subject to appropriate monitoring and control. The appropriate federal banking agency may recommend that the Federal Reserve take enforcement action against the nondepository institution subsidiary. If the Federal Reserve does not take action within 60 days, then the federal banking agency may take the recommended enforcement action.

Enhanced Prudential Standards and Tailoring

Another feature of Dodd-Frank aimed at preventing or mitigating risks to the financial stability of the United States, is Section 165(i),[120] which required the Board to establish "enhanced prudential standards" for institutions with total consolidated assets of $50 billion or more as well as nonbank financial companies designated for supervision by the Board. Standards required by Congress included risk-based capital and leverage limits, liquidity requirements, overall risk management requirements, resolution plans, and concentration limit credit exposure report requirements. For the most part, these requirements are addressed in the appropriate chapters of this book. The Economic Growth, Regulatory Relief and Consumer Protection Act of 2018 ("Regulatory Relief Act")[121] rightsized the threshold for this regime to $250 billion in assets. However, tailoring is required for those of $100 billion and above.

To this end, on October 10, 2019, the Federal Reserve and the FDIC each released final rules to tailor the application of the enhanced prudential standards to large banking organizations to more closely match their risk profiles. The Federal Reserve, on its own, issued rules that finalize the application of the enhanced prudential standards, which include capital planning and stress testing, liquidity risk management and stress testing, single counterparty credit limits, and enterprise risk management to U.S. bank holding companies, certain savings and loan holding companies, and foreign banking organizations.[122] The FDIC, jointly with the Federal Reserve

---

120. Codified in 12 C.F.R. § 252 (Regulation YY).
121. Publ. L. 115–174, S. 2155.
122. *Prudential Standards for Large Bank Holding Companies, Savings and Loan Holding Companies, and Foreign Banking Organizations* (Oct. 10, 2019), https://www.federalreserve.gov/aboutthefed/boardmeetings/files/tailoring-rule-fr-notice-20191010a2.pdf.

and the OCC, released a separate final rule that tailors the application of capital and liquidity rules to those same banking organizations.[123]

The rules establish a framework that sorts large banking organizations into four different categories based on several factors, including asset size, cross-jurisdictional activity, reliance on short-term wholesale funding, nonbank assets, and off-balance sheet exposure. The rules are intended to build on the Federal Reserve's existing rules and policies aimed at tailoring its requirements and are consistent with changes made by the Regulatory Relief Act.

In materials published along with the final rules, the Federal Reserve produced a chart detailing the requirements and standards for each of the four categories of banking organizations.[124]

The four categories of U.S. banking organizations are as follows:

Category I: U.S. Global Systemically Important Banks as determined by the Financial Stability Board;

Category II: Total assets greater than or equal to $700 billion or greater than or equal to $75 billion in cross-jurisdictional activity;

Category III: Total assets greater than or equal to $250 billion or greater than or equal to $75 billion in nonbank assets, weighted short-term wholesale funding, or off-balance sheet exposure;

Category IV: Other firms with total assets of $100 billion to $250 billion.

The Federal Reserve estimated the changes set forth in the final rules would, in the aggregate, result in a 0.6% decrease in required capital and a reduction of approximately 2% of required liquid assets for banking organizations with assets of $100 billion or more. At the same time, the Federal Reserve clarified that the rules do not reduce capital or liquidity requirements for firms in the highest risk categories, which include U.S. global systemically important banks.

---

123. *Changes to applicability thresholds for regulatory capital and liquidity requirements* (Oct. 10, 2019), https://www.federalreserve.gov/aboutthefed/boardmeetings/files/tailoring-rule-fr-notice-20191010a1.pdf.

124. https://www.federalreserve.gov/aboutthefed/boardmeetings/files/tailoring-rule-visual-20191010.pdf. The chart indicates that firms in the lowest risk category will have reduced compliance requirements, owing to their smaller risk profile. As the risk of a firm increases and it moves into a new risk category, its requirements will increase.

11

Bank Examination and Enforcement

John M. Geiringer and Stanley F. Orszula,
Barack Ferrazzano Financial Institutions Group

How to Police Compliance and Safety and Soundness?

Who can forget the "flinty-eyed" examiner—Mr. Carter—who almost cost Jimmy Stewart his building and loan association in *It's A Wonderful Life*? (If you don't understand that reference, watch the movie at your earliest convenience—it's required watching for every bank regulatory lawyer!)

We all recognize that the federal subsidies do not come without a price. That is the essential theme of this book—protect the bank and the system. Critical components of that protection are the supervisory and enforcement roles of the bank regulators, who send in troops of examiners to evaluate compliance with law and safety and soundness, armed with an array of examination manuals and checklists. On that note, examination manuals are one of the best sources of informal guidance on every banking subject imagined by the regulators. They are housed on the various regulatory websites listed at the end of Chapter 2, and many are on the Federal Financial Institutions Examination Council ("FFIEC") website.[1]

1. The FFIEC is an interagency body composed of the bank regulatory agencies and empowered to prescribe uniform principles, standards, and reporting forms for the federal supervision and examination of financial institutions. *See,* http://www.ffiec.gov.

Examination Types

To help ensure the public confidence in, and the overall stability of, the American banking system, Congress, state legislatures, and federal and state bank regulatory agencies have created a thorough and often complex statutory and regulatory framework of requirements and limitations relating to bank holding companies ("BHCs") and their subsidiary banks' operations. Evaluating a bank's adherence to these requirements is best accomplished through periodic onsite examinations, which allow examiners to obtain information not contained in the bank's financial statements or other means of self-reporting. Indeed, the largest BHCs and banks have resident examiners permanently stationed on-site. The primary BHC inspections (as those examinations are known) are to determine the overall enterprise's financial condition and whether the entity is complying with its applicable laws and regulations, while bank-level examinations are generally comprised of safety and soundness, compliance, and other specialty examinations.

Bank Holding Company and Saving and Loan Holding Company Inspections

The Board of Governors of the Federal Reserve System (thc "Federal Reserve"), through its constituent Federal Reserve Banks, conducts inspections of BHCs and saving and loan holding companies, now under similar processes.[2] Holding company inspections is unique insofar as that they require the Federal Reserve to cooperate with the other banking regulators.[3] The Federal Reserve is also charged with examining nonbanking subsidiaries of the BHCs.[4] Additionally, as a result of the Dodd-Frank Act, the Federal Reserve must determine whether a holding company poses risks to the U.S. financial system.[5] The Federal Reserve's assessment factors include:

- The holding company's financial condition to serve as a source of strength;
- Whether the holding company is complying with its own internal governance, federal banking laws and regulations, as well as Federal Reserve policy statements;
- The consolidated financial condition of the enterprise;

2. 12 U.S.C. § 1844(c)(2); Federal Reserve, SR 14-9, *Incorporation of Federal Reserve Policies into the Savings and Loan Holding Company Supervision Program*, (Nov. 7, 2014) available at https://www.federalreserve.gov/supervisionreg/srletters/sr1409.htm.
3. 12 C.F.R. § 225.5(c).
4. 12 U.S.C. § 5361(b).
5. 12 U.S.C. § 5365(a).

- The financial condition of the subsidiary bank (utilizing the examination conducted by the bank's primary regulator);
- The effectiveness of the holding company's and bank's (again utilizing the examination conducted by the bank's primary regulator) management and board of directors;
- Compliance with any existing supervisory actions; and
- The holding company's ability to meet financial obligations and whether it would have a negative impact on the subsidiary bank.[6]

The Federal Reserve uses two rating systems to examine holding companies, based on size and other characteristics. A large financial institution rating system ("LFI") is used for BHCs, noninsurance savings and loan holding companies with greater than $100 billion in total consolidated assets, and U.S. intermediate holding companies of foreign banking organizations established under Regulation YY with $50 billion in total consolidated assets. For smaller holding companies, the Federal Reserve uses a rating system known as "RFI/C(D)" to examine holding companies.[7]

The LFI rating system has the following three components:

Capital Planning and Positions. This component measures "(i) the effectiveness of a firm's governance and planning processes used to determine the amount of capital necessary to cover risks and exposures, and to support activities through a range of conditions and events; and (ii) the sufficiency of a firm's capital positions to comply with applicable regulatory requirements and to support the firm's ability to continue to serve as a financial intermediary through a range of conditions."[8]

Liquidity Risk Management and Positions. This component evaluates "(i) the effectiveness of a firm's governance and risk management processes used to determine the amount of liquidity necessary to cover risks and exposures, and to support activities through a range of conditions; and (ii) the sufficiency of a firm's liquidity positions to comply with applicable regulatory requirements and to support the firm's ongoing obligations through a range of conditions."[9]

Governance and Controls. This final metric "assesses a firm's effectiveness in aligning strategic business objectives with the firm's risk appetite and risk management capabilities; maintaining effective and independent risk management and control functions, including internal

---

6. Federal Reserve Bank Holding Company Supervision Manual, Section 1000.
7. Federal Reserve, Supervisory Rating System for Holding Companies with Total Consolidated Assets Less Than $100 billion, SR 19-4.
8. Federal Reserve, Large Financial Institution (LFI) Rating System, SR 19-3 (Feb. 26, 2019), available at https://www.federalreserve.gov/supervisionreg/srletters/sr1903.htm.
9. *Id.*

audit; promoting compliance with laws and regulations, including those related to consumer protection; and otherwise planning for the ongoing resiliency of the firm." Additional focus is placed on the board of directors, management of business lines, independent risk management, and with respect to a limited number of U.S. holding companies subject to the Federal Reserve's Large Institution Supervision Coordinating Committee (LISCC) Framework, recovery planning.[10] Each of the foregoing factors is rated on the following descending scale: Broadly Meets Expectations, Conditionally Meets Expectations, Deficient-1, and Deficient-2.[11]

Non-LFIs are rated differently. RFI/C(D) stands for: **R**isk, **F**inancial condition, potential **I**mpact of the holding company, and other non-bank subsidiaries on the bank, **C**omposite rating, and **D**epository institution.[12] Each component of the RFI/C(D) rating is also based on the "1" to "5" scale, and some components may be given more weight than others depending on the bank's size, complexity of operations, and risk profile. A rating of "1" indicates superior condition and a rating of "5" shows grave concern by the Federal Reserve. Described below are the components of the RFI/C(D) rating system:

Risk: The holding company's ability to manage risk, including board and management oversight, policies and procedures, risk monitoring and internal controls.

Financial Condition: The overall financial condition of the holding company, which includes capital, earnings, liquidity and asset quality.

Impact: Whether the holding company could adversely affect the subsidiary bank.

Composite Rating: The holding company's overall condition and potential impact on the U.S. financial system.

Depository Institution: This rating is derived from the subsidiary bank's examination and is essentially the same as the bank's primary regulator's rating.[13]

Larger holding companies are generally examined once a year, while smaller ones are generally examined on a bi-annual basis, with thresholds based on asset size generally established at the $100 billion, $10 billion, and $3 billion levels.[14]

---

10. *Id.*
11. *Id.*
12. Federal Reserve, SR 13-21, *Inspection Frequency and Scope Requirements for Bank Holding Companies and Savings and Loan Holding Companies with Total Consolidated Assets of $10 Billion or Less,* (Dec. 17, 2013, rev'd Mar. 6, 2019), available at https://www.federalreserve.gov/supervisionreg/srletters/sr1321.htm.
13. *Id.*
14. *Id.*

Safety and Soundness Examinations

The purpose of safety and soundness examinations is to evaluate the overall financial condition of a bank or savings and loan association (referred to collectively as "banks" in this chapter). Examiners assign to banks examination ratings that are based on the Uniform Financial Institutions Rating System ("UFIRS"). Under UFIRS, a bank is assigned a composite rating between "1" and "5" based on an evaluation of six financial and operational components: **C**apital Adequacy, **A**sset Quality, **M**anagement, **E**arnings, **L**iquidity, and **S**ensitivity to Market Risk (collectively, "CAMELS").

Each component of the CAMELS rating is also based on the "1" to "5" scale, and some components may be given more weight than others depending on the bank's size, complexity of operations, and risk profile. A rating of "1" indicates superior condition and "5" shows a strong likelihood of failure. Described below are the components of the CAMELS rating:

Capital Adequacy: A bank's ability to maintain capital commensurate with its risks.

Asset Quality: The quantity of existing and potential credit risk associated with loan and investment portfolios, other real estate owned, other assets, and off-balance-sheet transactions.

Management: The capability of the board of directors and management to identify, measure, monitor, and control the risks of a bank's activities, and to ensure a bank's safe, sound, and efficient operation in compliance with applicable laws and regulations.

Earnings: The quantity, trend, and factors that may affect the sustainability or quality of earnings.

Liquidity: The adequacy of a bank's liquidity position, with consideration given to the current level and prospective sources of liquidity compared to funding needs, and the adequacy of funds management practices relative to the bank's size, complexity, and risk profile.

Sensitivity to Market Risk: The degree to which changes in interest rates, foreign-exchange rates, commodity prices, or equity prices can adversely affect a bank's earnings or economic capital.[15]

Under the UFIRS, as noted above, each bank is assigned a composite of "1" to "5" based on the evaluation and rating of the six CAMELS components. Following is a summary of these ratings:

Composite 1: A rating of "1" indicates that a bank is sound in every respect and generally has components rated "1" or "2." Any weaknesses are minor and can be handled in a routine manner by the board of directors

15. *See* http://www.kc.frb.org/banking/membership/statememberbanks/how-will-i-be-rated.cfm.

and management. These banks are the most capable of withstanding the vagaries of business conditions and are resistant to outside influences, such as economic instability in their trade area. These banks are in substantial compliance with laws and regulations. As a result, these banks exhibit the strongest performance and risk management practices relative to the bank's size, complexity, and risk profile, and give no cause for supervisory concern.

Composite 2: A bank with a composite rating of "2" is fundamentally sound. For a bank to receive this rating, generally no component rating should be more severe than "3." In addition, a bank with a "2" rating has only moderate weaknesses that are well within the board of directors' and management's capabilities and willingness to correct. Also, "2"-rated banks are stable and are capable of withstanding business fluctuations and are in substantial compliance with laws and regulations. Overall risk management practices are satisfactory relative to the bank's size, complexity, and risk profile. These banks have no material supervisory concerns and, as a result, the supervisory response is informal and limited.

Composite 3: Banks that are rated "3" exhibit some degree of supervisory concern in one or more of the component areas. These banks exhibit a combination of weaknesses that may range from moderate to severe; however, the magnitude of the deficiencies generally will not cause a component to be rated more severely than a "4." Management may lack the ability or willingness to effectively address weaknesses within appropriate timeframes. Banks in this group generally are less capable of withstanding business fluctuations than those banks rated a composite rating of "1" or "2." Additionally, these banks may be in significant noncompliance with laws and regulations, and risk-management practices may be less than satisfactory relative to their size, complexity, and risk profile. Failure appears unlikely, however, given the overall strength and financial capacity of these banks.

Composite 4: These banks generally exhibit unsafe and unsound practices or conditions. There are serious financial or managerial deficiencies that result in unsatisfactory performance. The problems range from severe to critically deficient. The weaknesses and problems are not being satisfactorily addressed or resolved by the board of directors and management. Banks in this group generally are not capable of withstanding business fluctuations and there may be significant noncompliance with laws and regulations. Risk management practices are generally unacceptable relative to the bank's size, complexity, and risk profile. Close supervisory attention is required, which means, in most cases, formal enforcement actions are necessary to address the problems. Banks in this group pose a risk to the Deposit Insurance Fund. Failure is a distinct possibility if problems and weaknesses are not satisfactorily addressed and resolved.

Composite 5: These banks exhibit extremely unsafe and unsound practices or conditions; exhibit a critically deficient performance; and often contain inadequate risk management practices relative to the bank's size, complexity, and risk profile. In addition, the volume and severity of problems are beyond management's ability or willingness to control or correct. Immediate outside financial or other assistance is needed in order for the bank to be viable. Ongoing supervisory attention is necessary. Banks in this group pose a significant risk to the Deposit Insurance Fund and failure is highly probable.[16]

Banks are generally required to undergo a full scope, onsite[17] safety and soundness examination every 12 months except for certain eligible institutions that are examined every 18 months.[18] The larger banks have resident examiners who are constantly engaged in the examination process. Examination findings are issued in a confidential Report of Examination ("ROE") to the bank. The bank's overall composite rating, and particularly its management component, also reflect its scores on compliance and specialty examinations.

Consumer Compliance Examinations

Banking agencies utilize compliance examinations as the primary means to determine whether a bank is meeting its responsibility to comply with the requirements of federal consumer protection laws and regulations. With the advent of the Consumer Financial Protection Bureau ("CFPB"), consumer compliance exams have increased in importance. The CFPB examines banks with over $10 billion in consolidated assets for consumer compliance; while the appropriate primary federal bank regulatory agencies examine smaller institutions.

Ratings for consumer compliance examinations are based on the Uniform Interagency Consumer Compliance Rating System. Under this system, a bank is assigned a consumer compliance rating predicated on an evaluation of the nature and extent of its present compliance with consumer protection and civil rights statutes and regulations, and the adequacy of its operating systems, which are designed to ensure compliance on a continuing basis. The rating system is based on a scale of "1" to "5" in increasing order of supervisory concern. Thus, "1" represents the highest rating and consequently the lowest level of supervisory concern, while "5" represents

---

16. *See, e.g.*, FDIC Risk Management Manual of Examination Policies, Federal Deposit Insurance Corporation, Basic Examination Concepts and Guidelines, Section 1.1-20.
17. In light of the COVID-19 pandemic, the bank regulatory agencies are now conducting "virtual" examinations in certain cases.
18. *See, e.g.*, 12 U.S.C. § 1820(d). *See, also,* Federal Reserve, SR 18-7: *Updates to the Expanded Examination Cycle for Certain State Member Banks and U.S. Branches and Agencies of Foreign Banking Organizations* (Jan. 23, 2019).

the lowest, most critically deficient level of performance, and therefore the highest degree of supervisory concern.[19]

Community Reinvestment Act Examinations

The Community Reinvestment Act ("CRA") encourages banks to help meet the credit needs of the communities in which they operate, including low- and moderate-income neighborhoods, consistent with safe and sound banking operations. Banking agencies are required to evaluate banks' compliance with the CRA periodically. This evaluation is publicly available and is referred to as a "public evaluation." The bank's rating, which may be "Outstanding," "Satisfactory," "Needs to Improve," or "Substantial Noncompliance," is included in the public evaluation. The public evaluation is taken into account in considering an institution's applications for branching and other expansionary activities.[20]

Consumer compliance and CRA examination cycles are based on a bank's number of years in operation, the bank's size, and the bank's previous consumer compliance rating.[21]

Specialty Examinations

The bank regulatory agencies also conduct a number of specialty examinations that focus on one area of law or one aspect of banking.

Bank Secrecy Act of 1970 and Anti-Money Laundering

The purpose of the Currency and Foreign Transactions Reporting Act of 1970 (commonly known as the "Bank Secrecy Act" or "BSA"), which was substantially amended and enhanced by the Uniting and Strengthening America by Providing Appropriate Tools Required to Intercept and Obstruct Terrorism Act of 2001 (commonly known as the "USA PATRIOT Act"), is to ensure that banks maintain appropriate records and file certain reports involving currency transactions and a bank's customer relationships, and that these records and reports are sufficient enough to reconstruct the transactions, if necessary. These records and reports have a high degree of usefulness in criminal, tax, money laundering, illegal drug and terrorist financing, and regulatory investigations or proceedings.

---

19. *See, e.g.*, FDIC, Compliance Examination Manual, Overview of Compliance Examinations, Section II-12; Supervision and Examination Manual, CFPB, Part I.
20. *See*, http://www.ffiec.gov/cra/default.htm.
21. FDIC, Compliance Examination Manual, Examination and Visitation Frequency, Section II-11.

Findings from BSA examinations are generally included within the safety and soundness examination; however, separate BSA examinations can be conducted.[22] Adverse BSA findings can affect both the safety and soundness management rating and the overall composite rating of the institution. They also must be factored into approvals on applications for mergers and acquisitions. These examinations have no fixed schedule.

Trust Examinations

A bank's trust department acts in a fiduciary capacity when the assets that it manages are not the bank's, but belong to and are for the benefit of others. This type of relationship necessitates a great deal of confidence on the part of customers, and demands a high degree of good faith and responsibility on the bank's part. The primary objective of a trust department examination is to determine whether its operations, or the administration of its accounts, give rise to possible or contingent liabilities, or direct liabilities (estimated losses), which could reduce the bank's capital accounts.[23]

Examinations of trust activities are conducted and scored on the basis of the Uniform Interagency Trust Rating System ("UITRS") adopted by the FFIEC in 1998.[24] The UITRS has five components: **M**anagement Ability; **O**perations, Internal Controls, and Auditing; **E**arnings; **C**ompliance; and **A**sset Management (collectively, "MOECA"). Each of these components and the composite rating are based on a scale of "1" to "5," with a "1" being the highest rating and indicating the strongest performance and risk management practices and the least degree of supervisory concern. Banking agencies generally conduct trust examinations on the same cycle as safety and soundness examinations.

Information Technology Examinations

Information technology ("IT") services apply to virtually all recordkeeping and operational areas in banks. These IT services may be managed internally on a bank's own in-house computer system, or outsourced, wholly or in part, to an independent data center that performs most IT functions. Although some or all IT services may be outsourced, management and the board retain oversight responsibilities. IT has become an ever-increasing area of critical concern for the banking agencies, given recent publicized data breaches, cyber-attacks on banks and related cybersecurity issues.

---

22. *See*, https://bsaaml.ffiec.gov/manual.
23. FDIC, RMS Manual of Examination Policies, Basic Examination Concepts and Guidelines, Section 1.1-15 to 1.1-16.
24. Federal Financial Institutions Examination Council, Uniform Interagency Trust Rating System, Notice, 63 Fed. Reg. 54,704 (Oct. 13, 1998).

The potential consequences of receiving faulty data, suffering an interruption of services or a cyber-attack are serious, and warrant comprehensive IT policies and procedures and thorough IT examinations. A primary objective of an IT examination is to determine the confidentiality, integrity, and availability of records produced by automated systems. Examination priorities include an evaluation of management's ability to identify risks and maintain appropriate compensating controls. IT operations are generally evaluated on the basis of the FFIEC Information Technology Examination Handbook. Recently, the FFIEC also introduced the Cybersecurity Assessment Tool ("CAT").[25] The CAT is meant to be used by banks to assess their cybersecurity preparedness, but as discussed below, the banking agencies are trending toward using the CAT as an examination tool.

IT operations are rated in accordance with the Uniform Rating System for Information Technology ("URSIT"), which is based on an evaluation of four critical components: audit; management; development and acquisition; and support and delivery. The composite IT rating is influenced by the performance of the four component functions and reflects the effectiveness of a bank's IT risk management and information security programs and practices. A scale of "1" through "5" is used, wherein "1" indicates strong performance and "5" denotes critically deficient operating performance.

Most IT examinations are embedded in risk management ROEs and only include an URSIT composite rating. Banking agencies may, however, direct examiners to conduct full-scope IT examinations that include composite and component ratings. Banking agencies generally conduct IT examinations on the same cycle as safety and soundness examinations. Nevertheless, the banking agencies are trending toward utilizing the CAT in IT examinations.[26]

Financial Technology ("Fintech") Examinations

Financial Technology ("fintech") is a new area for both banks and the bank regulatory agencies, and as such, is a new area for examinations.

As more banks utilize fintech as a solution, or offer banking-as-a-service ("BaaS") to fintechs, the federal bank regulatory agencies are conducting fintech-focused examinations. Although there are no uniform requirements

---

25. *See*, https://www.ffiec.gov/cyberassessmenttool.htm. Discussed in Chapter 8, *supra*, in connection with cybersecurity risk management.

26. OCC Bulletin 2015-31, *FFIEC Cybersecurity Assessment Tool* (Jun. 30, 2015), available at https://www.occ.gov/news-issuances/bulletins/2015/bulletin-2015-31.html; Federal Reserve, SR 15-9, *FFIEC Cybersecurity Assessment Tool for Chief Executive Officers and Board of Directors*, (Jul. 2, 2015), available at https://www.federalreserve.gov/supervisionreg/srletters/sr1509.htm.

for fintech examinations, guidance is drawn from various IT, third-party relationships, and vendor management guidance.[27] Fintech examinations are evolving, but nevertheless, the federal bank regulatory agencies in fintech examinations have focused on BSA/AML issues, compliance management system evaluations, board and senior management education and involvement, sufficiency of bank infrastructure, fintech-related policies and procedures, and third-party relationships.

Post-Examination Actions

In addition to a composite rating, an examination may result in the banking regulator directing the holding company or bank to address Matters Requiring Immediate Attention ("MRIA") or Matters Requiring Attention ("MRA").[28] MRIAs, are as the name suggests, matters that a bank must immediately address, while MRAs are less critical and more time is allowed to rectify the particular issue. Additionally, the FDIC has a similar concept styled Matters Requiring Board Attention ("MRBA").[29]

---

27. *See, e.g.*, OCC Bulletin 2013-29, *Third Party Relationships: Risk Management Guidance*, (Oct. 30, 2013), available at https://www.occ.gov/news-issuances/bulletins/2013/bulletin-2013-29.html; OCC Bulletin 2020-10, *Third-Party Relationships: Frequently Asked Questions to Supplement Office of the Comptroller of the Currency Bulletin 2013-29* (Mar. 5, 2020), available at https://www.occ.gov/news-issuances/bulletins/2013/bulletin-2013-29.html; Federal Reserve, SR 13-19, *Guidance on Managing Outsourcing Risk*, (Dec. 5, 2013), available at https://www.federalreserve.gov/supervisionreg/srletters/sr1319.htm; FDIC FIL-13-2014, *Technology Outsourcing: Informational Tools for Community Bankers*, (Apr. 7, 2014), available at https://www.fdic.gov/news/news/financial/2014/fil14013.html; Appendix E to the Retail Payment Systems booklet of the Federal Financial Institutions Examination Council Information Technology Handbook, Mobile Financial Services (Apr. 2016), available at https://ithandbook.ffiec.gov/it-booklets/retail-payment-systems/appendix-e-mobile-financial-services.aspx; FDIC FIL-50-2016, *Seeking Comment on Proposed Guidance for Third-Party Lending*, (Jul. 29, 2016) available at https://www.fdic.gov/news/news/financial/2016/fil16050.html; FDIC FIL-19-2019, *FDIC Technology Service Provider Contracts* (Apr. 2, 2019) available at https://www.fdic.gov/news/news/financial/2019/fil19019.html.
28. OCC Bulletin 2018-18, *Comptroller's Handbook Examination Process series: Updated Booklets and Rescissions*, (June 28, 2018), available at https://www.occ.treas.gov/news-issuances/bulletins/2018/bulletin-2018-18.html; Federal Reserve, SR 13-13, *Supervisory Considerations for the Communication of Supervisory Findings* (June 17, 2013), available at https://www.federalreserve.gov/supervisionreg/srletters/sr1313.htm.
29. FDIC, RMS Manual of Examination Policies, Section 16.1-1.

Confidentiality of Supervisory Ratings and Other Nonpublic Supervisory Information

ROEs are confidential and are the property of the agency issuing the report. Accordingly, the written approval of the issuing agency is generally required to disclose to third parties such reports or the information derived from them, as well as other information broadly deemed to be nonpublic supervisory information. There are exceptions related to disclosure to the bank's holding company, insiders, and certain advisors. The inappropriate disclosure or use of nonpublic supervisory information may subject individuals to certain criminal penalties.[30]

It may not appear to rank up there in severity or complexity with safety and soundness and prudential regulation at first blush, but the bank regulatory agencies take a fierce stance on confidentiality of ROEs, examination ratings and other nonpublic supervisory materials[31]—so serious in fact that the Federal Reserve Board on August 3, 2016, ordered Goldman Sachs Group to pay a $36.3 million civil money penalty for its unauthorized use and disclosure of confidential supervisory information, and to implement an enhanced program to ensure the proper use of confidential supervisory information.[32] As scary, the Federal Reserve Board announced that it was instituting enforcement proceedings against a former managing director at Goldman Sachs, seeking to impose a fine and permanently bar him from the banking industry stemming from his and his subordinates' unauthorized use and disclosure of confidential supervisory information.[33] States have the same sensitivity. Goldman had earlier (October 28, 2015) reached a settlement agreement with the New York State Department of Financial Services in connection with the unauthorized possession of its confidential supervisory information.[34]

Appeals of Material Supervisory Determinations

Section 309(a) of the Riegle Community Development and Regulatory Improvement Act of 1994 (the "Riegle Act") required each of the federal banking agencies to establish an independent intra-agency appellate process

30. 18 U.S.C. § 641.
31. *See, e.g.*, the Board's regulation on the confidentiality of these materials at 12 C.F.R. Part 261, Subpart C. All bank regulatory agencies, including the CFPB and the states, have similar rules.
32. *See,* In the Matter of the Goldman Sachs Group, Inc. New York, New York and Goldman, Sachs & Co, New York, New York 2016 WL 4432523 (Aug. 2, 2016); *see also,* http://www.federalreserve.gov/newsevents/press/enforcement/20160803a.htm.
33. *Id.*
34. *See,* http://www.dfs.ny.gov/about/press/pr1510281.htm.

to review material supervisory determinations made at the insured depository institutions that it supervises.[35] Material supervisory determinations include:

- CAMELS ratings;
- IT ratings;
- trust ratings;
- CRA ratings;
- consumer compliance ratings;
- registered transfer agent ratings;
- government securities dealer ratings;
- municipal securities dealer ratings;
- consumer compliance ratings;
- allowances for loan and lease losses ("ALLL") adequacy determinations;
- significant loan classifications;
- determinations relating to violations of a statute or regulation that may affect the capital, earnings, or operating flexibility of an institution, or otherwise affect the nature and level of supervisory oversight accorded an institution;
- Truth in Lending (Regulation Z) restitution;
- certain filings made pursuant to 12 C.F.R. § 303.11(f);
- decisions to initiate informal enforcement actions (such as memoranda of understanding);
- determinations regarding the institution's level of compliance with a formal enforcement action; however, if the FDIC determines that the lack of compliance with an existing formal enforcement action requires additional enforcement action, the proposed new enforcement action is not appealable;
- matters requiring board attention; and
- any other supervisory determination (unless otherwise not eligible for appeal) that may affect the capital, earnings, operating flexibility, or capital category for prompt corrective action purposes of an

35. 12 U.S.C. § 4806(a). This section of the Riegle Act also required each federal agency to appoint an ombudsman to act as a liaison between the agency and any affected person with respect to any problem that party may have in dealing with the agency resulting from the regulatory activities of the agency, and to assure that safeguards exist to encourage complainants to come forward and preserve confidentiality. 12 U.S.C. § 4806(d). *See also* FDIC FIL-42-2017, *Revised Guidelines for Appeals of Materially Supervised* Determinations, (Sept. 6, 2017), available at https://www.fdic.gov/news/news/financial/2017/fil17042.html.

institution, or otherwise affect the nature and level of supervisory oversight accorded an institution.[36]

Material supervisory determinations do *not* include:

- decisions to appoint a conservator or receiver for an insured depository institution;
- decisions to take prompt corrective action pursuant to Section 38 of the Federal Deposit Insurance ("FDI") Act;
- determinations for which other appeals procedures exist (such as determinations of deposit insurance assessment risk classifications and payment calculations);
- decisions to initiate informal enforcement actions, as discussed below; and
- formal enforcement actions and decisions, *including determinations and the underlying facts and circumstances that form the basis of a recommended or pending formal enforcement action*, and agency determinations regarding compliance with an existing formal enforcement action.[37]

A formal enforcement action or decision commences, and therefore becomes unappealable under Section 309(a) of the Riegle Act, when the applicable federal agency initiates a formal investigation or provides written notice to the institution indicating its intention to pursue a formal enforcement action.[38] Regulatory enforcement actions and the appeal mechanisms related thereto are described below.

Regulatory Enforcement Actions

When a bank regulatory agency determines—typically, but not necessarily, in connection with an examination—that an institution's overall financial condition has deteriorated, and/or that one or more of its CAMELS component ratings have decreased, such that a composite and/or component rating of "3" is warranted, the agency is likely to impose, or otherwise require the institution to enter into, an enforcement action.[39] This action will allow the agency to direct and monitor the activities to be taken or avoided by the institution to correct the identified issues. Enforcement actions may

36. 12 U.S.C. § 4806(f). *See also*, FDIC Guidelines for Appeal of Material Supervisory Decisions, available at: http://www.fdic.gov/regulations/laws/sarc/sarcguidelines.html.
37. *Id.* (emphasis added.)
38. *Id.*
39. *See* FDIC Formal and Information Enforcement Actions Manual; OCC Bulletin 2018-41, *Enforcement Action Policies and Procedures Manuals* (Nov. 13, 2018), available at https://www.occ.treas.gov/news-issuances/bulletins/2018/bulletin-2018-41.html.

also arise from practices or activities deemed to be unsafe and unsound, or that represent a breach of a fiduciary duty.

Regardless of the nature and terms of an enforcement action, it should be taken seriously by the institution's board of directors, management, and advisors, as it reflects an unsatisfactory condition or an unsafe and unsound practice that must be remedied or ceased before the applicable agency will be willing to terminate the enforcement action and its related requirements and restrictions, which can be quite onerous and resource-consuming. With knowledge of the legal foundations of, and regulatory practices related to, enforcement actions, a legal practitioner can, however, help to reduce the adverse impact of an enforcement action on an institution, and in some cases, reduce the severity of certain terms or the overall nature of the enforcement action.

Overview

Regulatory enforcement actions are considered to be either "informal" or "formal." Informal enforcement actions are normally associated with less serious regulatory issues and reflect a bank's willingness to self-correct those issues, rather than the largely involuntary and directive-based nature of formal enforcement actions. Accordingly, informal enforcement actions are generally corrective in nature, whereas formal enforcement actions may also be punitive in nature or include such elements.

Typically, the terms of informal enforcement actions that involve safety and soundness and/or compliance issues closely resemble the terms of formal enforcement actions. The primary difference between informal and formal enforcement actions is that informal enforcement actions are considered to be confidential supervisory information that is not, and generally may not, be publicly disclosed,[40] whereas a formal enforcement action is published by each applicable regulator on its website and otherwise. Moreover, formal enforcement actions have statutory roots, mechanisms, and implications, whereas informal enforcement actions generally do not. Accordingly, material noncompliance, even if involuntary, with the terms of an informal enforcement action will often result in the imposition of a formal enforcement action to provide for greater supervisory oversight.

As further described below, there is a federal statutory framework for formal enforcement actions, and each federal banking agency has policies and practices that supplement this framework and that address informal enforcement actions. Additionally, in most instances, there are state law equivalents (which are beyond the scope of this book) for each type of

40. In certain instances, however, federal securities laws may permit and/or require the disclosure of certain information pertaining to enforcement actions.

enforcement action; accordingly, enforcement actions are typically issued jointly, where applicable. For example, enforcement actions involving state nonmember banks will generally be imposed or entered into by the FDIC and the applicable state banking agency, whereas the applicable state banking agency and the Federal Reserve Bank will impose or enter into enforcement actions with respect to state member banks.

Because national banks and federal thrifts are not directly regulated by the states, the Office of the Comptroller of the Currency ("OCC") will typically be the sole regulatory agency involved in enforcement actions related to such institutions. Similarly, the applicable Federal Reserve Bank will generally be the sole regulator with respect to enforcement actions involving a BHC. Also, the applicable federal regulator will often be the sole agency involved with a consumer compliance enforcement action. Notwithstanding the typically joint nature of enforcement actions, sometimes a state bank's federal and state regulators do not always reach the same preliminary or final conclusion regarding the condition of a bank and the warranted enforcement action, if any.

Additionally, as a result of the global financial crisis, Congress created another layer of regulatory enforcement, specifically, the Special Inspector General for the Troubled Asset Relief Program ("SIGTARP").[41] The purpose of SIGTARP is to investigate banks and individuals and prosecute financial crimes related to illegal uses of Troubled Asset Relief Program ("TARP") funds under various federal financial institution laws.[42] SIGTARP prosecutions have yielded numerous criminal convictions and fines against both individuals and banks, and have included lengthy prison sentences.

Importantly, when a target bank is presented with a proposed informal enforcement action, or if the target is willing to stipulate or consent to the issuance of a formal enforcement action (as further described below), the applicable regulatory agencies are generally willing to engage in discussions and negotiations with the target and its legal advisors regarding the nature and terms of the enforcement action. It should be noted, however, that more discussion, negotiation, and resultant change is permitted in connection with proposed informal enforcement actions. The formal enforcement actions issued by each federal agency generally reflect the same form and content, although the agencies may be willing to consider changes to items, such as the time permitted for completion of, or compliance with, certain requirements, or the dollar threshold for loan review or workout plan requirements, for example.

Obviously, the more severe the issues relating to an enforcement action target, the less amenable to negotiation the agencies will be, notwithstanding

41. Emergency Economic Stabilization Act of 2008, 12 U.S.C. § 5201 *et seq.*
42. *See,* http://www.sigtarp.gov.

the target's contrition and/or cooperation. Accordingly, a bank regulatory lawyer must understand and be fully aware of the challenges and issues facing the target institution so that any discussions and negotiations with the applicable regulatory agencies can yield the most favorable result for the target institution.

As described below, there is a hierarchy of severity for both informal and formal enforcement actions.

Informal Enforcement Actions

Informal enforcement actions, in order of ascending severity, generally consist of corrective board resolutions or memoranda of understanding. They are nonpublic.

Corrective Board Resolutions

Corrective board resolutions are the least severe of all enforcement actions. They are often developed with the significant involvement, and adopted at the strong direction, of the institution's regulator(s). Notwithstanding this regulatory involvement, the primary advantage of corrective board resolutions over other forms of enforcement actions is that they have the external appearance of originating solely from the institution, rather than being imposed by the institution's regulator(s).

Memorandum of Understanding

A Memorandum of Understanding ("MOU") is the most severe form of informal enforcement action, and is likely to be imposed on any institution that has received a composite CAMELS rating of "3" and/or if the institution has deficiencies in other areas that warrant direction and close supervision by regulators. A MOU is essentially a contractual agreement between an institution and its regulator(s) that sets forth specific corrective actions to be taken or restrictions to be observed by the institution. Like contracts, MOUs are generally executed by representatives of the institution and each applicable regulatory agency.

Formal Enforcement Actions

As discussed above, formal enforcement actions constitute more severe, and public, remedial and restrictive actions against an institution or an institution-affiliated party ("IAP")[43] by banking regulators, and are generally

43. 12 U.S.C. § 1818(b)(7). The definition of an IAP is set forth in 12 U.S.C. § 1813(u) and includes attorneys.

imposed when the related deficiencies or violations are more serious, or have not been satisfactorily resolved under a previous informal enforcement action. Moreover, and also as noted above, formal enforcement actions are either: (i) corrective, and thus direct a bank to take, or refrain from, certain actions; or (ii) punitive, which impose monetary penalties and/or have a prohibitive impact with respect to individuals. The rules, mechanisms, and implications relating to formal enforcement actions are primarily prescribed in Section 8 of the FDIA.[44]

Types

Corrective formal enforcement actions include:

- written agreements;
- cease and desist orders;
- prompt corrective action directives; and
- temporary cease and desist orders.

Punitive formal enforcement actions include:

- suspension, removal, and prohibition orders; and
- civil money penalties.

Written Agreements

Written agreements are bilateral contractual agreements between a federal regulator and an institution or an IAP, the structure and terms of which are typically very similar to MOUs. In response to violations of, or substantial noncompliance with, written agreements, federal regulators may issue or impose more stringent enforcement actions, as described below. Written agreements are generally treated and enforceable as cease-and-desist orders under Section 8 of the FDIA. Moreover, during the last banking crisis, assuming a target's stipulation, the Federal Reserve's initial formal enforcement actions involving troubled state member banks and BHCs typically consisted of written agreements (again, enforceable under Section 8 of the FDIA[45]), rather than cease-and-desist orders.

Similarly, the OCC's initial formal enforcement actions imposed against, and upon the stipulation of, troubled national banks during the last crisis were typically in the form of written agreements referred to by the agency as "formal agreements." Despite their recent respective practices regarding written agreements, when warranted and appropriate, the Federal Reserve

44. 12 U.S.C. § 1818(a) *et seq.*
45. 12 U.S.C. § 1831aa.

and the OCC may also utilize cease-and-desist orders and other formal enforcement actions, as described below.

Cease and Desist/Consent Orders

Under federal law, the federal banking regulators may issue cease-and-desist orders (a "C&D") that prohibit, restrict, or require certain activities or functions of an institution or an IAP. In addition, through or in connection with a C&D, the federal banking regulators have broad authority to require the subject of a C&D to:

- make restitution or provide reimbursement, indemnification, or guarantee against loss if the institution or the subject was unjustly enriched in connection with the violation or practice at issue, or if the violation or practice involved a reckless disregard for the law or any applicable regulations or prior order;
- restrict the institution's growth (as applicable);
- dispose of any loan or asset involved;
- rescind agreements or contracts;
- employ qualified officers or employees (who may be subject to approval by the applicable federal regulator); and
- take such other action as the federal regulator determines to be appropriate.[46]

Notably, during the last banking crisis, if target state nonmember banks stipulated (*i.e.*, consented) to the issuance of a C&D, the FDIC began referring to, and labeling, such enforcement actions as "consent orders."[47] This nuanced change by the FDIC served to synchronize the apparent practice of each of the federal banking agencies to generally label a C&D as such only when a target does not stipulate to its issuance or if the basis for the order is particularly egregious.

Prompt Corrective Action Directives

If a financial institution's capital decreases to the point that it becomes "undercapitalized," "significantly undercapitalized," or "critically undercapitalized," pursuant to Section 38 of the FDIA and the prompt corrective action ("PCA") regulations of each federal banking agency, the applicable agency may issue a PCA directive that typically requires the institution to increase its capital to certain levels within a certain timeframe and to provide to the agency a written plan for achieving such

46. 12 U.S.C. § 1818(b)(6).
47. Consent orders are therefore, for all practical purposes, C&Ds, and enforced accordingly.

capital levels.[48] Generally, the federal regulator will provide the institution with notice of its intent to issue the PCA directive and an opportunity to respond to it.[49] If an institution against which a PCA directive has been issued fails to achieve compliance with it, the applicable federal banking agency may seek judicial enforcement, assess civil money penalties (as described below), or pursue any other judicial or administrative enforcement mechanism authorized by applicable law.[50]

Temporary Cease and Desist Orders

The federal banking regulators may also issue temporary C&Ds, which become immediately effective and remain until the federal regulator either rescinds the order or issues a standard C&D or other formal enforcement action to replace the temporary C&D.[51] The actions or omissions that warrant temporary C&Ds are those that are likely to:

- cause an institution's insolvency or a significant dissipation of an institution's assets or earnings;
- weaken the institution's condition; or
- prejudice the interests of an institution's depositors.[52]

A federal regulator also may issue a temporary C&D if it determines that an institution's books and records are so incomplete or inaccurate that the federal regulator cannot ascertain the current financial condition of the institution or the details or purpose of any transaction(s) that may have a material effect on the institution's financial condition.[53] Accordingly, temporary C&Ds are typically issued only in rare cases where an activity or inaction must be ceased immediately to prevent potentially irreparable harm to the institution and/or the rapid deterioration of depositors' interests (and thus also those of the FDIC's Deposit Insurance Fund).

The subject of a temporary C&D may seek review of it by the appropriate U.S. District Court, within 10 days of the imposition of such order.[54] Similarly, federal banking regulators may apply to the applicable U.S. District Court to enforce a temporary C&D.[55]

---

48. *See, e.g.*, 12 C.F.R. § 6.20 *et seq*. (OCC regulations applicable to national banks).
49. *See, e.g.*, 12 C.F.R. §§ 6.21, 6.22.
50. *See, e.g.*, 12 C.F.R. § 6.25.
51. 12 U.S.C. § 1818(c)(1).
52. *Id.*
53. 12 U.S.C. § 1818(c)(3).
54. 12 U.S.C. § 1818(c)(2).
55. 12 U.S.C. § 1818(d).

Removal, Suspension, and Prohibition Orders

The federal regulators are also authorized by law to issue removal, suspension, and prohibition orders against IAPs regarding their current or future bank-related responsibilities. The criteria for issuing a removal order consist of whether the subject institution-affiliated party has:

- violated any law, regulation, final C&D order, written regulatory application condition, or formal written agreement;
- engaged or participated in any unsafe or unsound practice; or
- committed or engaged in an activity or an omission that constitutes a breach of the IAP's fiduciary duty.[56]

The applicable federal regulator next must determine whether the activity or omission resulted in:

- actual or potential financial loss or damage;
- prejudice to the interests of the institution's depositors; or
- the IAP receiving financial gain or other benefit as a result of such activity or omission.[57]

Lastly, the federal regulator must demonstrate that the activity or omission at issue involved personal dishonesty or demonstrated a willful or continuing disregard for the safety and soundness of the institution.[58]

Although removal orders involve the process and determinations described above, suspension orders against IAPs are effective immediately, much like temporary C&Ds. A suspension order may be imposed when the applicable federal regulator determines that such action is necessary to protect the institution or the institution's depositors.[59] A suspension order is effective until it is overturned by a court, or until the applicable federal regulator dismisses the charges or issues a removal and/ or prohibition order.[60]

Federal banking regulators also have the authority to suspend or prohibit an IAP from further participation in any manner in the conduct of the affairs of any depository institution. A prohibition order may be issued if:

- the IAP is charged in any information, indictment, or complaint with the commission of or participation in: (a) a felony crime involving dishonesty or breach of trust or (b) a violation of 18 U.S.C. § 1956 (laundering of monetary instruments), 18 U.S.C. § 1957 (monetary transactions in property derived from specified unlawful activity), 18 U.S.C. § 1960 (illegal money transmitting

56. 12 U.S.C. § 1818(e)(1)(A).
57. 12 U.S.C. § 1818(e)(1)(B).
58. 12 U.S.C. § 1818(e)(1)(C).
59. 12 U.S.C. § 1818(e)(3)(A).
60. 12 U.S.C. § 1818(e)(3)(B).

businesses), 31 U.S.C. § 5322 (BSA violations) or 31 U.S.C. § 5324 (illegal structuring of transactions to avoid BSA reporting requirements); and
- the applicable federal regulator believes that continued service or participation by that person may threaten the interests of the institution's depositors or impair public confidence in the institution.[61]

A prohibition order remains effective until the disposal of information, indictment, or complaint involving the subject, or until the order is terminated by the federal regulator.[62] An acquittal of the subject defendant by an applicable court does not, however, prevent or preclude a federal regulator from suspending or removing an IAP from an institution, or from prohibiting further involvement with any financial institution.[63]

Civil Money Penalties

Depending on the nature and severity of committed violations, federal law authorizes the federal banking regulators to issue civil money penalties ("CMPs") against institutions and IAPs. CMPs are structured into three tiers, based on the severity of the violation(s).

First-tier CMPs of up to $5,000 per day may be issued against any institution or IAP for violations of any:

- law or regulation;
- final or temporary C&D or any suspension, removal, or prohibition order;
- written condition imposed by a regulator in connection with the approval of any application or other request by a bank; or
- written agreement between a bank and its regulator(s).[64]

Second-tier CMPs of up to $25,000 per day may be issued against any institution or IAP that commits any first-tier CMP violation described above, recklessly engages in an unsafe or unsound practice with respect to the institution's affairs, or breaches any fiduciary duty that:

- demonstrates a pattern of misconduct;
- causes or is likely to cause more than a minimal loss to the institution; or
- results in pecuniary gain or other benefit to such party.[65]

61. 12 U.S.C. § 1818(g)(1)(A).
62. 12 U.S.C. § 1818(g)(1)(B)(ii).
63. 12 U.S.C. § 1818(g)(1)(D)(ii).
64. 12 U.S.C. § 1818(i)(2)(A).
65. 12 U.S.C. § 1818(i)(2)(B).

Third-tier CMPs of up to the lesser of $1 million or 1% of the institution's total assets per day, subject to a limit of $1 million for individuals, may be issued against an institution or IAP that knowingly:

- commits any violation described above for first-tier CMPs;
- engages in any unsafe or unsound practice in conducting the affairs of the bank; or
- breaches any fiduciary duty, *and* knowingly or recklessly causes a substantial loss to the bank or a substantial pecuniary gain or other benefit to the IAP by reason of such violation, practice, or breach.[66]

Prior to imposing a CMP, the applicable federal regulator will provide the institution or IAP with what is commonly known as a "15-day letter," which gives the target an opportunity to submit relevant information to the agency prior to the ultimate CMP assessment decision. When determining whether to assess a CMP and the amount thereof, the federal regulators will consider:

- the size of financial resources and good faith of the insured depository institution or other person charged;
- the gravity of the violation;
- the history of previous violations; and
- such other matters as justice may require.[67]

These "other matters," which should be thoroughly addressed when responding to the potential assessment of a CMP, include the following:

1. Evidence that the violation or practice or breach of fiduciary duty was intentional or was committed with a disregard of the law or with a disregard of the consequences to the institution;
2. The duration and frequency of the violations, practices, or breaches of fiduciary duty;
3. The continuation of the violation, practice, or breach of fiduciary duty after the respondent was notified or, alternatively, its immediate cessation and correction;
4. The failure to cooperate with the agency in effecting early resolution of the problem;
5. Evidence of concealment of the violation, practice, or breach of fiduciary duty or, alternatively, voluntary disclosure of the violation, practice, or breach of fiduciary duty;

66. 12 U.S.C. § 1818(i)(2)(C).
67. 12 U.S.C. § 1818(i)(2)(G).

6. Any threat of loss, actual loss, or other harm to the institution, including harm to the public confidence in the institution, and the degree of such harm;
7. Evidence that a participant or his or her associates received financial gain or other benefit as a result of the violation, practice, or breach of fiduciary duty;
8. Evidence of any restitution paid by a participant of losses resulting from the violation, practice, or breach of fiduciary duty;
9. History of prior violation, practice, or breach of fiduciary duty, particularly where they are similar to the actions under consideration;
10. Previous criticism of the institution or individual for similar actions;
11. Presence or absence of a compliance program and its effectiveness;
12. Tendency to engage in violations of law, unsafe or unsound banking practices, or breaches of fiduciary duty; and
13. The existence of agreements, commitments, orders, or conditions imposed in writing intended to prevent the violation, practice, or breach of fiduciary duty.

The banking agencies utilize various matrices for assessing CMPs against financial institutions and IAPs.[68] Ultimately, the amount of a CMP should both serve a remedial purpose and provide a deterrent to future misconduct.

Procedural Matters Relating to Formal Enforcement Actions

Stipulation Agreement

A proposed formal enforcement action will typically be accompanied by a proposed stipulation agreement. A stipulation agreement allows the banking regulator to impose a formal enforcement action without the issuance of a notice of charges and the administrative law process described below. By stipulating (*i.e.*, consenting) to the issuance of the enforcement action, the target is not required to admit wrongdoing and avoids the public disclosure of the specific examination or other findings that the bank's regulator(s) deem severe enough to warrant the issuance of an enforcement action. In addition, stipulation will generally result in substantial cost and

68. Federal Financial Institutions Examination Council, Interagency Policy Regarding the Assessment of Civil Money Penalties by the Federal Financial Institutions Regulatory Agencies, 63 Fed. Reg. 30,227 (June 3, 1998); *see also,* OCC Bulletin 2018-41, *infra.*

time savings that would be incurred if the matter were to proceed to an administrative hearing.

If the target of a formal enforcement action agrees to execute a stipulation agreement, the target must agree to waive certain rights to which the target would otherwise be entitled, such as:

- the issuance of a formal notice of charges by the regulator;
- an administrative law hearing and the final agency decision on the matter;
- judicial review of the administrative law and agency decision;
- contesting the validity of the enforcement action;
- claims for fees, costs, or expenses against the regulator; and
- assertion of a "double jeopardy" claim in the event of a criminal prosecution.

As noted above, because stipulation prevents the facts, circumstances, and issues that are the basis for the proposed enforcement action from being made public, and reduces the expenditure of time and funds, the vast majority of formal enforcement actions are issued with the stipulation of the target. Moreover, and also as discussed above, a target's willingness to stipulate to a formal enforcement action will generally allow the target and its legal advisors to discuss and negotiate the provisions of the enforcement action with the issuing regulator(s).

Notice of Charges

Because of the serious nature and implications of formal enforcement actions, the target of any such action is statutorily provided the opportunity to request both administrative and judicial review of the issuance of the formal enforcement action. As part of this legal process, prior to the issuance of a nonstipulated formal enforcement action, the applicable federal banking regulator is required to provide the target of the action with a notice of charges.[69] The notice of charges will contain a recitation of the facts surrounding the alleged violations or practices, and must set forth a date and venue for an administrative hearing regarding the appropriateness of the issuance of the formal enforcement action.[70] The administrative hearing will generally be scheduled for 30 to 60 days from the service of the notice of charges, unless the parties agree otherwise.

Because issuing a notice of charges results in the public disclosure of the facts and circumstances relating to the alleged violations and/or unsafe and unsound practices, the vast majority of institutions and

69. 12 U.S.C. § 1818(b)(1), (e)(4).
70. *Id.*

institution-affiliated parties that are the targets of formal enforcement actions attempt to confidentially negotiate the terms of these actions and then stipulate or consent to the issuance of the action (and thus forego the notice of charges and administrative hearing), as described above. Accordingly, challenging a formal enforcement action through the statutorily provided administrative and judicial process should generally be reserved for instances in which the target has strong facts to demonstrate that the regulatory agency's findings and proposed enforcement action are arbitrary and capricious, an abuse of discretion, or unconstitutional, for example.[71]

Administrative Review

If a bank believes that the issuance of a formal enforcement action against it constitutes, *inter alia*, an arbitrary and capricious act by a banking regulator, and is willing and able to expend the time and funds, the bank may request an administrative hearing to contest the issuance of the formal enforcement action.

Each of the federal banking regulators has promulgated regulations that direct the administrative hearing process related to a contested formal enforcement action.[72] These regulations address issues such as informal settlement procedures, discovery, motions, and conflicts of interest. The Office of Financial Institution Adjudication ("OFIA") oversees the administration of enforcement hearings by the federal banking regulators. An administrative law judge from the OFIA conducts the administrative law hearings related to contested formal enforcement actions.

Judicial Review

Judicial review of the issuance of formal enforcement actions, which can occur only after the completion of the administrative law procedure described above, is extremely rare. Moreover, a banking lawyer and his or her client should recognize that federal courts give tremendous deference to administrative interpretation and decisions.[73]

If the result of an administrative hearing is that the appropriateness of a formal enforcement action is confirmed, upon issuance of the final enforcement action, it will generally remain effective and enforceable until it is "stayed, modified, terminated or set aside by action of the agency or a reviewing court."[74]

---

71. 5 U.S.C. § 706(2), discussed *infra*.
72. *See*, 12 C.F.R. Part 308 (FDIC); 12 C.F.R. Part 263 (Federal Reserve); 12 C.F.R. Part 19 (OCC); 12 C.F.R. Part 1081 (CFPB).
73. *See, e.g.*, Chevron USA, Inc. v. National Resources Defense Council, Inc., 476 U.S. 837 (1984), and its progeny.
74. 12 U.S.C. § 1818(b)(2).

The federal Administrative Procedures Act sets forth the criteria for reversing the final decision of federal banking regulators. These criteria, which represent a high and difficult threshold for the target of a formal enforcement action to overcome, allow the reviewing court to reverse the regulator's decision only if, after reviewing the entire record, the court determines that the agency's decision was:

- arbitrary, capricious, an abuse of discretion, or otherwise not in accordance with law;
- contrary to constitutional right, power, privilege, or immunity;
- in excess of statutory jurisdiction, authority, or limitations, or short of statutory right;
- without observance of legal procedure;
- unsupported by substantial evidence; or
- unwarranted by the facts to the extent that the facts are subject to trial *de novo* by the reviewing court.[75]

Publication

Once a federal banking regulator has finalized and issued a formal enforcement action, federal law requires the publication of the action.[76] The federal banking regulators may delay the publication of an action for a reasonable amount time if the publication of the action in accordance with the regulator's normal timing and procedures would present a serious threat to the target or related institution's safety and soundness.[77] Publications of certain actions may be avoided altogether if the publication would be contrary to the public interest.[78] Moreover, competitive disadvantage or the potential for an adverse liquidity event (*i.e.*, a run on the bank) will generally *not* constitute a sufficient reason for a federal banking regulator to delay or avoid the publication of a formal enforcement action.[79] Accordingly, to the extent possible and permitted, the practitioner should diligently attempt to negotiate the language in, and terms of, formal enforcement actions.

Indemnification

Federal law and regulations generally prohibit a financial institution from indemnifying an IAP for the liability or legal expense in connection with an enforcement action or civil action brought by a federal banking regulator

75. 5 U.S.C. § 706(2).
76. 12 U.S.C. § 1818(u)(1).
77. 12 U.S.C. § 1818(u)(4).
78. 12 U.S.C. § 1818(u)(1)(A).
79. In fact, we are not aware that a publication delay based on these factors has ever been granted.

that results in the issuance of a C&D, removal or prohibition order, or civil money penalty against the IAP.[80] A financial institution may, however, purchase an insurance policy or fidelity bond that will pay for the legal or professional expenses incurred by an IAP in connection with the defense of an enforcement action, or with respect to restitution of the financial institution, but this policy or bond may not provide reimbursement for any final judgment or civil money penalty.[81] Of note, there is no ban on an IAP purchasing his or her own insurance policy for a potential CMP or reimbursement for a final judgment.

In addition, a financial institution *may* indemnify an IAP for legal or professional expenses relating to violations for which the IAP was ultimately determined not to be responsible.[82] Notwithstanding the foregoing, an institution may also indemnify a target IAP for expenses (but not for the payment of a civil money penalty or restitution) related to a formal enforcement action prior to the "commencement" of such action, which is deemed to be the issuance of a notice of charges.[83]

Advising Troubled Banks

Although all bank regulators have criteria under which they may take possession and control over their supervised institutions (capital and liquidity impairment being the most common), it is generally a bank's chartering authority, namely the OCC or the applicable state banking agency, that ultimately makes that decision. Once that decision is made, the FDIC is appointed receiver or conservator and handles the disposition of the former institution's assets. Federal laws and regulations prescribe the roles and responsibilities of federal regulators as a bank approaches insolvency.

Troubled Condition Status

As the condition of a bank deteriorates, there reaches a point at which its federal regulator deems the bank to be in "troubled condition." This designation places certain restrictions on these institutions. Troubled condition status means that a bank:

---

80. *See, e.g.*, 12 C.F.R. §§ 359.1(l)(1), 359.3.
81. *See, e.g.*, 12 C.F.R. § 359.1(l)(2)(i).
82. *See, e.g.*, 12 C.F.R. § 359.1(l)(2)(ii), FDIC FIL-47-2013, *Director and Officer Liability Insurance Policies, Exclusions, and Indemnification for Civil Money Penalties* (Oct. 10, 2013), available at https://www.fdic.gov/news/news/financial/2013/fil13047.html.
83. Federal Deposit Insurance Corporation, Regulation of Golden Parachutes and Other Benefits Which May Be Subject to Misuse, 60 Fed. Reg. 16,069, 16,077 (Mar. 29, 1995), 61 Fed. Reg. 5,926, 5,930 (Feb. 15, 1996).

- has a composite rating, as determined in its most recent report of examination, of "4" or "5" under the UFIRS, or in the case of an insured state branch of a foreign bank, an equivalent rating;
- is subject to a proceeding initiated by the FDIC for termination or suspension of deposit insurance;
- is subject to a C&D or written agreement issued by its regulator(s) that requires action to improve the financial condition of the bank, or is subject to a proceeding initiated by its regulator(s) that contemplates the issuance of an order that requires action to improve the financial condition of the bank, unless otherwise informed in writing by its federal regulator; or
- is informed in writing by its federal regulator that it is in troubled condition on the basis of information available to its federal regulator.[84]

Banks that are in troubled condition, as well as their subsidiaries and holding companies, generally may not enter into contracts to pay and to make golden parachute and indemnification payments to IAPs except in accordance with 12 C.F.R. Part 359. In addition, an institution deemed to be in troubled condition must obtain prior regulatory approval before appointing any new director or senior executive officer or before materially changing the responsibilities of any senior executive officer.[85]

Prompt Corrective Action

As referenced above, each of the federal banking regulators has established prompt corrective action regulations for the institutions that they regulate.[86] Under these regulations, an institution's capital strength is segregated into the following categories:

- well-capitalized;
- adequately capitalized;
- undercapitalized;
- significantly undercapitalized; and
- critically undercapitalized.

Institutions that fall into the significantly and critically undercapitalized categories are subject to numerous and onerous restrictions because of the elevated risk of the institution's failure resulting from its diminished capital levels. Even institutions that are considered undercapitalized will be

84. *See, e.g.*, 12 C.F.R. § 303.101(c).
85. 12 U.S.C. § 1831i.
86. 12 C.F.R. § 6.20 *et seq.* (OCC), 12 C.F.R. § 208.40 *et seq.* (Federal Reserve), 12 C.F.R. § 325.101 *et seq.* (FDIC).

subject to substantive restrictions and safeguards imposed by the federal banking regulators.[87]

The determination of an institution's capital category under the PCA regulations is normally made upon the filing of each quarterly Report of Condition and Income (a/k/a "Call Report"), although it can also occur in connection with an examination or any other instance in which the applicable federal regulator is made aware of an institution's current capital levels. If an institution becomes undercapitalized (or a lesser PCA category), the applicable federal regulator will notify the institution of such PCA category in writing, which will also typically summarize the restrictions and requirements that will immediately apply to the institution.[88] For example, undercapitalized institutions are generally required to submit a capital plan to their federal banking regulator within 45 days following receipt of notice of their undercapitalized status. A capital plan required pursuant to the prompt corrective action regulations must include:

- the actions that the institution will take to restore itself to at least adequately capitalized status;
- target capital ratios and/or levels for each year in which the capital plan is in effect;
- how the institution will comply with the restrictions and requirements now applicable to it;
- the nature and extent of activities in which the institution intends to engage during the pendency of the capital plan; and
- any other information that the federal regulator requires.[89]

For a capital plan to be accepted by a federal regulator, it must be likely to succeed, be based on realistic assumptions, and cannot appreciably increase the risk to the institution.[90]

Prepayment of Salary or Legal Expenses in Contemplation of Insolvency

Banks and their holding companies may not prepay the salary, or any liability or legal expense, of any IAP if such payment is made:

- in contemplation of the insolvency of the bank or holding company or after the commission of an act of insolvency; and
- with a view to, or has the result of:

87. 12 U.S.C. § 1831o(e).
88. Such notice may be independent of a notice relating to the proposed issuance of a PCA directive, as discussed *supra*.
89. 12 U.S.C. § 1831o(e)(2).
90. *Id.*

- preventing the proper application of the assets of the institution to creditors; or
- preferring one creditor over another.[91]

The determination of when such payments are made in contemplation of insolvency is not always clear. One court held that a bank is in contemplation of insolvency "when the fact becomes reasonably apparent to its officers that the concern will presently be unable to meet its obligations, and will be obliged to suspend its ordinary operations."[92] In the absence of any statutory or regulatory guidance, and except for certain obvious situations such as when a bank is critically undercapitalized, this issue will remain highly fact-specific. Practitioners should note that the FDIC has indicated a willingness to bring suit against law firms seeking the recovery of funds paid to them by banks in alleged violation of this provision.[93]

Other Issues Affecting Attorneys

In addition to the banking regulators taking action against attorneys who received retainers pre-failure, other issues affect attorneys representing banks. For example, the former Office of Thrift Supervision (the "OTS") alleged that a law firm committed malpractice, among other things, representing the infamous Lincoln Savings and Loan Association ("Lincoln") pre-failure.[94] The OTS attempted to freeze the law firm's assets, which resulted in a quick settlement of $41 million and a prohibition against two of the law firm's partners from representing federally insured depository institutions. Some of the alleged conduct that made the law firm an IAP was that the law firm, among other things, positioned itself between the OTS and Lincoln pre-failure. The lesson from this case for attorneys is to be careful with respect to the boundaries between representing a bank and becoming an IAP.

In a more recent case involving in-house counsel, the OCC issued a consent order of prohibition and a $50,000 CMP against the former General Counsel of Rabobank, a California-based national bank. He was accused of participating in the continuous concealment of a third-party report assessing Rabobank's BSA program from the OCC, and making false statements to the OCC. The previous year, Rabobank pled guilty to conspiracy to obstruct

91. 12 U.S.C. § 1828(k)(3).
92. FDIC v. Goldberg, 906 F.2d 1087, 1091 (5th Cir. 1990), *citing* Kullman & Co. v. Woolley, 83 F.2d 129, 132 (5th Cir. 1936).
93. *See, e.g.*, FDIC as Receiver for George Washington Savings Bank v. The Coleman Law Firm, et al., (Case No. 11-CV-08823, N.D.Ill.) (FDIC aggressively sought recovery of $150,000 retainer paid pre-failure to attorney to defend directors and officers; attorney's estate agreed to a stipulated judgment against estate).
94. OTS v. Kaye, Scholer, Fierman; Hags & Handler; Misc. No. 92-101 (D.C. Cir. 1992).

an OCC examination and paid a forfeiture in the amount of $368,701,259, and a CMP to the OCC in the amount of $50 million.[95]

Another issue is whether the attorney-client privilege between a bank and its counsel is preserved when privileged material is sought by, or disclosed to the banking regulators.[96] The federal banking regulators assert that they can seek attorney-client privileged material in an examination and that such production does not destroy the attorney-client privilege.[97] Also, the CFPB is active in pursuing law firms for violations of consumer financial law, specifically in the consumer debt collection, mortgage foreclosure prosecution and mortgage foreclosure defense arenas.[98] Accordingly, as illustrated by these matters, attorneys are increasingly becoming the targets of the federal banking regulators.

Bank Records

In March 2012, after observing directors and officers of failing banks making and removing copies of bank and supervisory records in anticipation of personal litigation or enforcement actions, the FDIC issued *Guidelines Regarding the Copying and Removal of Confidential Financial Institution Information* (FIL-14-2012). While acknowledging that these individuals need access to bank records to carry out their official duties, the FDIC cautioned those individuals and legal counsel that such actions may violate their fiduciary duty to the institution and "may violate laws and regulations, constitute an unsafe or unsound banking practice, and violate the financial institution's information security program." This guidance leaves many unanswered questions and remains controversial.

---

95. OCC Issues Consent Order of Prohibition and $50,000 Civil Money Penalty Against Former General Counsel of Rabobank N.A. (July 23, 2019).
96. *See, e.g.*, 12 U.S.C. § 1828(x).
97. CFPB Final Rule, Confidential Treatment of Privileged Information (June 28, 2012) ("Final Rule") (effective Aug. 6, 2012), 77 FR 39617 (July 5, 2012).
98. For a list of CFPB enforcement actions, *see*, http://www.consumerfinance.gov/policy-compliance/enforcement/actions/.

12

Bank Resolution and Orderly Liquidation Authority

Sara A. Kelsey, former FDIC General Counsel

What Happens When a Bank Fails?

Introduction

A key safeguard of our financial system is the stability provided by the Federal Deposit Insurance Corporation's ("FDIC") deposit insurance and its resolution authority. Prior to the creation of the FDIC in 1933,[1] the Comptroller of the Currency ("OCC") supervised national bank liquidations and state regulators supervised the liquidations of state-chartered banks, usually under the legal provisions for general business insolvencies. Between 1865 and 1933, depositors were treated like other creditors, receiving their funds after the bank liquidation was completed. On average, for federal liquidations, this might take six years, although it took up to, in one instance, twenty-one years. Even when depositors were paid, the amount they received was considerably less than the money they had deposited in the bank. For the period of 1921 to 1930, during which more than 1,200 banks failed, depositors in state banks received an average of 62% of their deposits back and depositors in national banks received an average of 58%.

Depositors' knowledge of the delays and losses that occurred upon the failure of a bank led the depositors to withdraw all of their funds from a bank if there were any rumors that the bank might fail, leading to runs on bank deposits, which, in turn, could *cause* a bank to fail. With its creation

1. Chapter 5 includes an in-depth background on deposit insurance. The legislation that created the FDIC, the Banking Act of 1933, is commonly known as the Glass-Steagall Act, 48 Stat. §162 (1933). During the Great Depression, from 1929 to 1933, nearly 9,000 banks suspended operations or failed.

of the FDIC, Congress established an agency that insured deposits up to a pre-determined amount[2] and immediately paid off the insured depositors upon a bank failure. Since the inception of FDIC insurance, no depositor has lost any insured deposits as a result of a bank failure. Just as importantly, Congress also endowed the FDIC with sufficient authority to resolve failing banks as quickly and as smoothly as possible. Finally, Congress centralized the role of Receiver for the assets and liabilities of failed banks in the FDIC, to create an agency with specialized expertise and gave it "superpowers" to enable it to do this job efficiently and effectively.[3]

Following the bank and thrift crisis, from 1986 to 1994 ("Bank and Thrift Crisis"),[4] Congress passed the Federal Deposit Insurance Corporation Improvement Act ("FDICIA"),[5] which made substantial changes to how failing banks were resolved. In response to the Global Financial Crisis, from 2007 to 2011, Congress passed the Dodd-Frank Wall Street Reform and Consumer Protection Act of 2010 ("Dodd-Frank"),[6] which made further changes to this authority and added provisions to deal with the resolution of nonbank Systemically Important Financial Institutions ("SIFIs"). Each of these Congressional actions increased the tools available to the FDIC should the failure of banks and other important nonbank financial institutions pose a threat to the stability of the U.S. financial system.

Failure and Appointment of the Receiver

Bank failures are announced by the FDIC in a press release, usually issued after the close of business on a Friday afternoon.[7] But as a rule, it is the chartering authority that gave birth to a bank that signs the bank's death warrant. It is the chartering authority that makes the determination that

2. Originally set at $2,500, now $250,000 per depositor, per bank, per category of legal ownership.
3. Previously, a separate regulator resolved savings and loan institutions. Following the Bank and Thrift Crisis, Congress put the FDIC in charge of resolving all insured savings and loan, savings, and commercial bank institutions. For purposes of this chapter, the term "bank" includes all of these insured institutions.
4. During the Bank and Thrift Crisis, 1,617 banks and 2,295 savings and loan institutions failed or required financial assistance.
5. 105 Stat. 2236.
6. 124 Stat.1376-2223.
7. The press release includes information on the acquirer, how many bank failures have occurred year to date nationwide, and gives an estimate of the cost of the failure to the FDIC fund. Linked to the press release is information about the acquiring financial institution, including contact information, general information about FDIC deposit insurance coverage, the availability of banking services, instructions on how to file a claim and the priority of any such claims, the purchase and assumption agreement for the transaction, bid and balance sheet summaries, information concerning brokered deposits, and Q's & A's.

a Receiver should be appointed and then appoints the FDIC. In rare instances, the appropriate federal regulator of a state-chartered bank may appoint the FDIC as Receiver or the FDIC may exercise its back-up self-appointment authority with respect to any FDIC-insured bank.[8] In all cases, the bank loses its charter and a Receivership for the bank's assets and liabilities is created. Unlike in bankruptcy, where a corporation may survive throughout and following the bankruptcy proceeding, when a bank loses its charter, its corporate identity is dissolved.

Bank Failures in Brief—Summary 2001 to June 2020. Source: fdic.gov

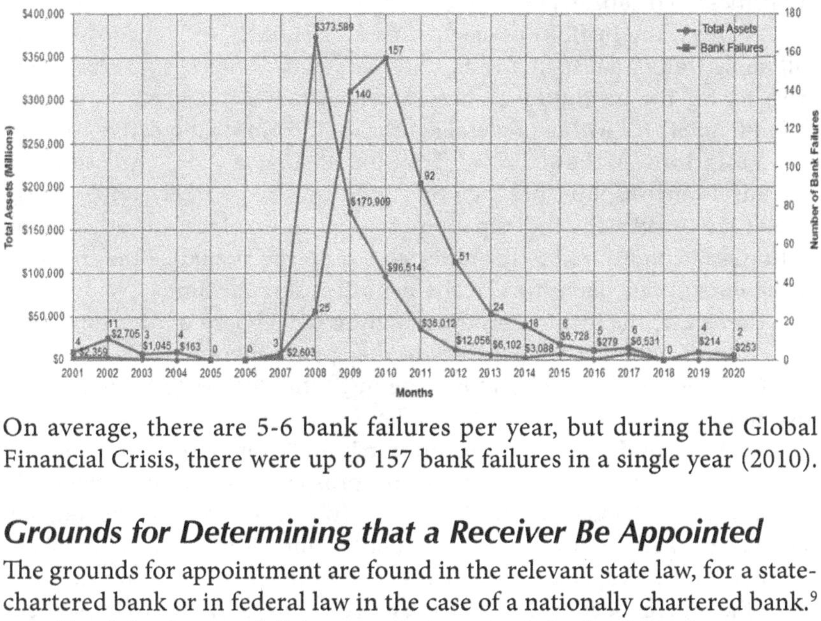

On average, there are 5-6 bank failures per year, but during the Global Financial Crisis, there were up to 157 bank failures in a single year (2010).

Grounds for Determining that a Receiver Be Appointed

The grounds for appointment are found in the relevant state law, for a state-chartered bank or in federal law in the case of a nationally chartered bank.[9]

The federal grounds[10] for appointment include the following:

Assets Insufficient to Meet Obligations. The institution's assets are less than the institution's obligations to its creditors and others. **(Insolvency)**

Substantial Dissipation. Substantial dissipation of assets or earnings due to: (i) any violation of statute or regulation; or (ii) any unsafe or unsound practice.

Unsafe or Unsound Condition. An unsafe or unsound condition to transact business.

---

8. 12 U.S.C. §1821(c)(10).
9. Federal law is also the source of the grounds in the instance of a determination made by the appropriate federal regulator or the FDIC for a state-chartered bank or thrift, 12 U.S.C. § 1821(c).
10. 12 U.S.C. §1821(c)(5).

Cease and Desist Orders. Any willful violation of a cease-and-desist order that has become final.

Concealment. Any concealment of the institution's books, papers, records, or assets, or any refusal to submit the institution's books, papers, records, or affairs for inspection to any examiner or to any lawful agent of the appropriate federal banking agency or state bank or savings association supervisor.

Inability to Meet Obligations. The institution is likely to be unable to pay its obligations or meet its depositors' demands in the normal course of business. **(Illiquidity)**

Losses. The institution has incurred or is likely to incur losses that will deplete all or substantially all of its capital, and there is no reasonable prospect for the institution to become adequately capitalized (as defined in Section 38(b))[11] without federal assistance. **(Prompt Corrective Action)**

Violations of Law. Any violation of any law or regulation, or any unsafe or unsound practice or condition that is likely to: (i) cause insolvency or substantial dissipation of assets or earnings; (ii) weaken the institution's condition; or (iii) otherwise seriously prejudice the interests of the institution's depositors or the deposit insurance fund.

Consent. The institution, by resolution of its board of directors or its shareholders or members, consents to the appointment.

Cessation of Insured Status. The institution ceases to be an insured institution.

Undercapitalization. The institution is undercapitalized (as defined in Section 38(b)), and: (i) has no reasonable prospect of becoming adequately capitalized (as defined in that Section); (ii) fails to become adequately capitalized when required to do so under Section 38(f)(2)(A); (iii) fails to submit a capital restoration plan acceptable to that agency within the time prescribed under Section 38(e)(2)(D); or (iv) materially fails to implement a capital restoration plan submitted and accepted under Section 38(e)(2).[12] **(Prompt Corrective Action)**

The Institution: (i) is critically undercapitalized, as defined in Section 38(b); or (ii) otherwise has substantially insufficient capital.[13] **(Prompt Corrective Action)**

Money Laundering Offense. The Attorney General notifies the appropriate federal banking agency or the FDIC in writing that the insured depository institution has been found guilty of a criminal offense under

11. 12 U.S.C. § 1831o.
12. *Id.*
13. *Id.*

Section 1956 or 1957 of title 18, United States Code, or Section 5322 or 5324 of title 31, United States Code.[14]

Prompt Corrective Action

Following the Bank and Thrift Crisis, Congress included so-called prompt corrective action (or "PCA") provisions in FDICIA. PCA requires the FDIC and federal regulators to close a bank when the bank's capital falls to certain levels. Congress was concerned that regulators might otherwise allow some banks to stay open even after the bank's capital had become so depleted that the resolution of the bank ultimately could prove costly to U.S. taxpayers. PCA provisions,[15] discussed in detail earlier in this text, **mandate** that the appropriate federal banking agencies and the FDIC appoint a Receiver not later than 90 days after an insured depository institution becomes critically undercapitalized. There can be up to two 90-day extensions. A critically undercapitalized institution **must** be closed not later than 270 days after notice. [16] The appropriate federal banking agency may take such other actions as the agency determines, with the concurrence of the FDIC, would better achieve the purpose of PCA provisions, after documenting why the action would better achieve that purpose. There must be periodic redeterminations and a Receiver **must** be appointed if the other action fails to restore capital.

The Dual Roles of the FDIC in a Bank Failure

The FDIC is responsible in its corporate capacity for administering the FDIC insurance fund[17] and in its capacity as Receiver for resolving failed banks and acting as Receiver for the Receivership.[18] When a bank fails, the FDIC quickly pays the insured depositors in its corporate capacity, and becomes subrogated to the claims of those paid-off depositors in the Receivership. But what happens to the bank, its shareholders and its non-FDIC-insured creditors?[19] To find out, we need to study how the FDIC acts in its capacity as a Receiver.

---

14. 18 U.S.C. §§ 1956 or 1957 or 31 U.S.C. §§ 5322 or 5324.
15. 12 U.S.C. § 1831o.
16. *Id.*
17. The FDIC insurance fund derives its funding from risk-based insurance premiums charged to insured banks by the FDIC, as discussed earlier in this text. Should the fund ever fail, it is backstopped by a line of credit from the U.S. Treasury.
18. In addition to these roles, the FDIC also serves as the primary (or "appropriate") federal regulator of state-chartered banks that are not members of the Federal Reserve System ("nonmember banks") and state-chartered savings banks.
19. The FDIC website contains in-depth information on the bank resolution process, including a Resolutions Handbook ("FDIC Resolutions Handbook"), with links to additional information. It can be located at: https://www.fdic.gov/bank/historical/reshandbook.

Resolution

Preparation for & Selection of the Winning Bid

When the FDIC becomes aware that a bank may need to be closed, it prepares for the potential resolution in great secrecy, so as not to adversely affect the bank, its depositors, the community and the financial system. This can make it challenging to obtain the best outcome.

During the period of time prior resolving a bank (ideally 90-105 days, but it can be much shorter) the FDIC seeks to understand and value a failing bank's assets and ascertain its liabilities. The more information the FDIC is able to learn about the bank's assets and liabilities and to communicate to potential bidders, the better price the FDIC will be able to achieve in the transaction. If there is little time to perform the due diligence for a transaction, as is the case if there is a liquidity run on a bank, it will be very difficult for the FDIC to do as complete a valuation as would be necessary to maximize value.

The FDIC traditionally limits those it invites to bid on a bank resolution transaction to potential acquirers who would qualify to own a bank. Usually, this means that the potential pool of bidders is limited to existing banking organizations. During the Global Financial Crisis, there were innovations aimed to increase the field of potential bidders, including the use of pre-approved "shelf charters" for banks, that could be activated for a successful nonbank bidder. In addition, small banks were acquired by prospective nonbank bidders and used as acquisition vehicles to acquire larger failed banks.

After gathering information, the FDIC distributes confidential bid packages. This and the subsequent exchange of information and performance of due diligence often takes place on the internet. Bids are submitted 1-2 weeks before the bank is scheduled to be closed. The FDIC quickly determines the winner among the competing bids. More than one potential resolution transaction structure may be offered by the FDIC to all prospective bidders, in an attempt to get more and better bids.

FDIC Resolution vs. Bankruptcy

You may have noticed that the steps outlined above are performed swiftly and unilaterally by the FDIC, without the prior knowledge or consent of the failing bank. *This is because the goal of resolution is to limit the impact of the failure on the financial system, while seeking to minimize loss to the FDIC fund.* This is quite different from the goals of bankruptcy, which are to try to maximize returns to creditors, while giving a debtor a fresh start. Bankruptcy takes place in a full and fair proceeding, with many opportunities to negotiate and appeal. In bankruptcy, a debtor may voluntarily choose to go into bankruptcy or creditors may force it into bankruptcy upon default. The FDIC resolves a bank after the bank has been involuntarily placed into Receivership. Although a bank may consent to resolution, it cannot initiate resolution and its directors, officers and shareholders do not have a role in the resolution. In bankruptcy, creditors, shareholders and management all have a role. The proceedings take place in a court, subject to judicial oversight and review, with notice and hearing. The FDIC proceeding is administrative, with extremely limited grounds for appeal. Shareholder rights and powers are eliminated, and creditors have no role. Resolution is swift and sure and the FDIC is in charge, although subject to the requirement that it deliver a result that is the "least cost" to the FDIC fund.

Least Cost Test and Other Limits on Resolution Transactions

The FDIC is required to adhere to the "least cost" test, which requires it to determine that a resolution is the least costly alternative to the deposit insurance fund of all possible methods of resolving the bank.[20] This test is calculated as of the date on which the FDIC makes the determination to provide such assistance to the bank. Valuation is calculated on a present value basis, using a realistic discount rate.[21] This test has in the past operated to require the FDIC to choose an insured-deposit-only bid over a rival all-deposits bid, if the all-deposits bidder was not willing to pay a premium for the uninsured deposits. This is because the test is applied to the cost of providing insurance coverage for the insured deposits, rather than to the cost of paying off all of the deposits in the bank. A winning bid for the assumption of uninsured as well as insured deposits can be a difficult result to achieve, especially in situations where the asset value does not cover all of the deposits. The least cost test was imposed in 1991 by Congress in FDICIA,[22] and differs from the pre-FDICIA, more general cost test, which allowed the FDIC to consider other factors, including the availability of banking services, so long as the bid was less costly than liquidation.[23]

20. 12 U.S.C. § 1823(c)(4).
21. The least cost test is based on a calculation of the total loss. This loss is based on the total gross assets, less the asset losses and receivership expenses, plus the bid (which will consist of the deposit premium and/or the asset discount), less the liabilities (claims) on the receivership. FDIC Resolutions Handbook.
22. 12 U.S.C. § 1823(c)(4).
23. FDIC Resolutions Handbook.

In addition, the FDIC is prohibited from benefitting uninsured depositors and creditors[24] and shareholders[25] of a particular institution.

Systemic Risk Exception to the Least Cost Test[26]

The Systemic Risk Exception to the least cost test, as well as to the prohibitions against benefitting creditors and shareholders (as applied to a particular institution), existed at the beginning of the Global Financial Crisis. The barriers to its use were high. To come within the exception the following hurdles had to be overcome:

- Supermajority (2/3) approval of both the FDIC Board and the Board of Governors of the Federal Reserve System;
- Approval of the Secretary of the Treasury, in consultation with the President; and
- A determination that the use of the exception would avoid or mitigate "serious adverse effects on economic conditions or financial stability."

Examples from the Global Financial Crisis where this exception was used for a single institution were the FDIC assistance for the acquisition of Wachovia by Citibank (which did not occur, due to a successful competing non-assisted bid by Wells Fargo); and the FDIC assistance for the ring-fenced troubled loans of Citibank and Bank of America (Bank of America later returned the assistance, plus a usage fee). Following the passage of Dodd-Frank, Congress eliminated the use of this exception by the FDIC for a particular institution.[27]

Types of Resolution Transactions

There are several types of resolution transactions commonly used by the FDIC. The FDIC usually is able to realize the most value from the assets

---

24. 12 U.S.C. § 1823(c)(4)(E).
25. 12 U.S.C. § 1823(a)(4)(B).
26. 12 U.S.C. § 1823(c)(4).
27. During the Global Financial Crisis, the FDIC also used Systemic Risk Determinations as authority for its Temporary Liquidity Guaranty Program, which guaranteed in full noninterest-bearing transaction deposits, and the Debt Guarantee Program, an FDIC guarantee of certain newly issued senior unsecured debt. The FDIC's authority to do so survives, but only for a widely available program, not for particular banks. The decision-making process for the widely available program is similar to that outlined above. Dodd-Frank § 1105. Although the Dodd-Frank also made it subject to Congressional review, this requirement was removed by the CARES Act, H.R. 748, Public Law 116-136, § 4408.

of a failed bank if they can be sold to a healthy bank. But the ability of the FDIC to realize this value depends upon how much information the FDIC is able to provide to prospective bidders, the structural choices it can provide for how the assets may be acquired and, sometimes, whether or not the FDIC is willing to share the risk the buyer is assuming with the assets through a loss-sharing arrangement.

Purchase and Assumption. This type of transaction involves the purchase of all, or insured only, deposits, as determined by the application of the "least cost" test. The FDIC may or may not provide loss sharing for the assets purchased. The institution may be broken up for multiple purchasers. Or a transaction may involve only the purchase of loans under a separate loan sale agreement.

- *"Clean" Purchase and Assumption Agreement.* Purchaser acquires insured-only or all deposits, but no assets. Typically used when there is a limited time to arrange a transaction or substantial risk of fraud.
- *Whole Bank Purchase and Assumption Agreement.* Purchaser acquires insured-only or all deposits and the same purchaser acquires all or substantially all of the loans and branches under one agreement.

Bridge Bank. The FDIC can organize a new "bridge" bank to facilitate resolution and transfer most assets and liabilities to the newly chartered institution. The FDIC has two years (with extensions, up to five years) to resolve the institution. This can be useful for an institution for which there is insufficient time to find an acquirer. A single bridge bank can handle multiple bank failures.

Deposit Payoff (Liquidation). Insured deposits only are paid out by mail to insured depositors.

Insured Deposit Transfer. Insured deposits are transferred to an agent institution in the community that pays off the insured depositors.

Deposit Insurance National Bank ("DINB"). As a stopgap measure, the FDIC may organize a bank solely for the purpose of paying out insured deposits in an orderly manner, where there is no other local organization that can do so.

Pass-through Receivership/Conservatorship. Rarely used. A failed institution is "passed through" a receivership to a newly chartered institution, which is placed into conservatorship. Shareholders' claims are not passed to the conservatorship and are fixed to a date certain. Operates similarly to a bridge bank but cannot contain multiple institutions. This method was used for thrift institutions before the law was changed to allow the use of a bridge bank for thrift institutions.

Previous Resolution Transactions No Longer Used by the FDIC

Open Bank Assistance. This option involved direct FDIC assistance provided to open (not failed) banks.[28] The least cost requirement and the prohibitions against protecting uninsured depositors and other creditors [29] or benefiting shareholders [30] have effectively eliminated the FDIC's ability to use open bank assistance except in the case of a Systemic Risk determination. During the Global Financial Crisis, this provision was used for both Citibank and Bank of America, following findings of Systemic Risk by the FDIC. Under Dodd-Frank, this option no longer is available with respect to a single bank.

Open Bank Conservatorship. FDIC becomes conservator without a receiver being appointed. This option puts the institution under FDIC's control without displacing shareholders. Unlikely to be used because of FDICIA prohibitions on benefiting shareholders.

Pass-Through Receivership/Conservatorship. This structure has not been used since mid-2008, when thrift institutions became eligible for the bridge bank structure.

Other resolution alternatives that have been used in the past include: income maintenance agreements; capital forbearance; merger assistance, including yield maintenance; capital loss coverage; negative net worth payments and indemnifications.[31]

Closing the Bank

Prior to closing the bank, the FDIC Board approves its closure as well as a number of related resolutions, generally delegating to FDIC staff the ability to determine the least costly method for resolution and delegating to the FDIC staff the authority to accept the appointment by the bank's chartering authority of the FDIC as Receiver for the bank. The winning bidder is notified (as are unsuccessful bidders and the chartering authority of the bank) and the winning bidder signs the legal documents to close the transaction.

Generally, bank closures occur on a Friday. The chartering authority closes the bank and appoints the FDIC as Receiver. The FDIC balances the accounts of the closed institution immediately after closing. The FDIC then transfers those assets and liabilities to the winning bidder, consistent with

28. 12 U.S.C. § 1823(c)(8).
29. 12 U.S.C. § 1823(c)(4)(E).
30. 12 U.S.C § 1823(a)(4)(B).
31. Resolutions Handbook, with links to additional information, https://www.fdic.gov/bank/historical/reshandbook.

the signed transaction and begins the process of settling various accounts between the winning bidder and the FDIC.

The winning bidder opens the bank usually on the next business day and, depending upon the transaction, the failed bank's customers become customers of the winning bidder, with immediate access to their insured deposits.

Determination of the Final Balance of the Failed Bank/Receivership

Upon the failure of an FDIC-insured bank, the FDIC must determine the amount of the assets and liabilities (including insured and uninsured deposits) on the final balance sheet of the failed bank, which will become the opening balance sheet of the receivership.

The FDIC has a specific responsibility to determine the total insured amount for each depositor.[32] In order to make this determination, the FDIC must ascertain the balances of all deposit accounts owned by the same depositor in the same ownership capacity at a failed institution as of the day of failure and then applies the standard maximum deposit insurance amount ("SMDIA") of $250,000.[33] This is necessary because the FDIC must make insurance payments to depositors as soon as possible up to the amount of their insured deposits.[34] For those bank depositors in an FDIC-insured bank who wish to keep track of the amount of deposit insurance to which they are entitled, the FDIC provides an interactive application on its website, the Electronic Deposit Insurance Estimator ("EDIE").[35]

The FDIC's practices for determining the value and the nature of the final account balances of deposits and other liabilities in the event of a failure of an insured bank generally have been consistent over the years, but have had to evolve to meet the challenge of larger, more complex banks with increasingly complicated deposit products. The FDIC has issued a regulation that details this determination method.[36] In the event of a bank failure, the FDIC will base its determination of deposit and other liability accounts upon the bank's end-of-day ledger balances for each account using, except as expressly provided otherwise, the bank's normal posting procedures.

32. 12 U.S.C. § 1821(f)(1).
33. 12 U.S.C. § 1821(a)(1)(C), 1821(a)(1)(E).
34. The FDIC becomes subrogated to the rights of the insured depositors up to the amount of the payout and joins the other depositors in the receivership for any *pro rata* amount of recovery that this class of liabilities receives in the receivership.
35. https://www.fdic.gov/EDIE.
36. Method for determining deposit and other liability account balances at a failed insured depository institution. 12 C.F.R. § 360.8.

In doing so, it will use the bank's own internal cutoff times for different accounts as would occur in the bank's normal processing routine. However, the FDIC also will establish an FDIC cutoff point that it will use to take all best efforts to stop the generation of any new liabilities or the extinguishing of existing liabilities for the bank. A simplistic way of thinking about this is that the FDIC will allow all transactions *internal to the bank* to take their natural course through the end of the bank's normal daily processing cycle, but will seek to stop all transactions that occur after the FDIC takes control of the bank (the FDIC cutoff point) that would involve liabilities being assumed or extinguished by the bank, that is, that would involve transactions *external to the bank.* In the FDIC's notice of its final rule on its determination method, the treatment of specific types of transactions and accounts are detailed.[37] Helpfully, the FDIC explains how it will deal with various types of sweep accounts,[38] including deposit-to-deposit sweeps within and outside of the bank; [39] Eurodollar and IBF sweep accounts;[40] repo sweep accounts;[41] money market mutual fund sweep accounts;[42] Fed Funds

37. 74 Fed. Reg. 5,797 (Mar. 4, 2009). An example of one such treatment is that all checks (whether collected or uncollected) that are deposited into and posted to the bank's end-of-day ledger will be considered as part of the end-of-day ledger for insurance purposes. *Id.* at 5,800.
38. A sweep account is defined by the FDIC as "an account held pursuant to a contract between an insured depository institution and its customer involving the pre-arranged, automated transfer of funds from a deposit account to either another account or investment vehicle located within the depository institution (*internal sweep account*), or an investment vehicle located outside the depository institution (*external sweep account*)." 12 C.F.R. § 360.8(a)(4).
39. Retail or "reserve sweeps" (between deposit and MMDA or between MMDA and NOW accounts) are not considered sweeps by the FDIC, as they involve only a single customer account, although the bank conducts a sweep between two subaccounts of the account that the bank creates for various regulatory reasons. 74 Fed Reg. 5,797 (Mar. 4, 2009) at 5,801.
40. Funds that have been swept will be considered as general creditor claims, since obligations at a foreign branch (unless payable in the United States) or IBF are not deposits for purposes of FDIC deposit insurance. *Id.* at 5,801.
41. If the repo transaction is properly secured, the customer will own a security or a perfected interest in a security, either of which will be recognized by the FDIC. If the bank has not properly executed the security interest for such deposits, the FDIC will treat the swept funds as if they had not left the deposit account from which they originated. Such improperly swept funds should be treated as deposit accounts in the bank's Call Report. *Id.* at 5,802. *See also,* FDIC FIL-39-2009: Frequently Asked Questions, discussing proper execution of a repo sweep arrangement, at pp. 4-5, https://www.fdic.gov/news/news/financial/2009/fil09039a.html.
42. Money market mutual fund sweeps may take various forms and may be internal or external, which will affect their treatment. *See, Id.* at 5,802 for examples.

sweep accounts;[43] holding company commercial paper sweep accounts;[44] and loan sweep accounts.[45]

The FDIC requires banks to prominently disclose in writing to sweep account customers whether their swept funds are deposits within the meaning of 12 U.S.C, § 1831(l) for all new sweep account contracts; in renewals of existing sweep accounts contracts, and at least annually. If the funds are not deposits, pursuant to the FDIC's rule, the bank must disclose the status such funds would have if the bank failed, for example, general creditor status or secured creditor status.[46]

The FDIC has published rules aimed at improving the recordkeeping of the largest banks so that it can better make this determination. Such rules include recordkeeping requirements for the FDIC's timely deposit insurance determination, which apply to insured banks that have two million or more deposit accounts.[47] Another recordkeeping rule assists the FDIC in identifying Qualified Financial Contracts ("QFC's") to which an insured bank is a party.[48]

FDIC as Receiver

Marshaling the Assets

The FDIC, as Receiver, then assumes charge of the Receivership, which involves collecting all of the assets retained by the Receiver, as well as gathering the additional funds as discussed below. This process is called "marshaling the assets."

FDIC Special Defenses Superpowers

The powers of the FDIC are similar to those of a Bankruptcy Trustee. Like a Trustee, the FDIC as Receiver steps into the shoes of the insolvent party. Congress has given the FDIC as Receiver some "superpowers" beyond those available to a Bankruptcy Trustee, in the interests of achieving a swift and sure resolution in order to maintain confidence in the banking system, while minimizing the costs to the FDIC fund. Some of these powers include:

---

43. The amount swept into Fed funds will be considered nondeposit liabilities. *Id.* at 5,803.
44. The status of the swept funds depends upon the ownership of the account into which they are swept, e.g., whether the account is held for the benefit of the sweep customers or in the name of the holding company. *Id.* at 5,803
45. This consists of an internal sweep of excess deposit balances to automatically pay down a loan or other credit account. Balances left in the deposit account after the sweep will be treated as deposits. *Id.* at 5,804.
46. 12 C.F.R. § 360.8(e).
47. 12 C.F.R. § 360.9, *See* 73 FR 41180 (July 17, 2008) and 12 C.F.R. § 370.
48. 12 C.F.R. Part 371.

Ipso Facto Clauses Unenforceable.[49] Clauses allowing acceleration upon appointment of a Receiver or Conservator are unenforceable against the FDIC as Receiver.

Cross Guaranty Liability.[50] The FDIC has up to two years to assess commonly controlled insured banks for a bank failure in an effort to recoup its losses. The assessment is generally equal to the estimated loss to the FDIC insurance fund for the resolution of the affiliated institutions. This may cause the affiliated bank to fail, making its assets available to the FDIC. The FDIC will assess cross guaranty liability only where such an assessment is determined to result in the lowest cost to the FDIC insurance fund. The FDIC's Board must approve the assessment of cross guaranty liability. This assessment is subject to judicial review. Cross guaranty liability has not been widely assessed. Instead a practice of waivers and settlement has developed.[51]

Director and Officer Liability.[52] The FDIC may hold directors and officers personally liable for gross negligence. But the FDIC can also take advantage of any state laws that may hold directors and officers to a higher standard. Before bringing a claim, the FDIC will consider the probability of the FDIC's success on the merits of the claim and the ability of the insider to pay. The insider payment may be from the insider's own assets or from insurance, such as a Directors and Officers ("D&O") liability policy or a bankers bond.

Side Agreements May Be Unenforceable.[53] Side agreements that would diminish the FDIC's interest in an asset are not valid unless in writing, executed contemporaneously by both parties, approved by the bank's board of directors, and have been continuously a bank record since the execution of the contract.[54]

Courts May Not Enjoin Receiver.[55] The Receiver is allowed to continue to carry out its resolution and liquidation work, even if there is a court challenge to an aspect of the FDIC's performance.

Capital Maintenance Claims. The FDIC has brought a number of capital maintenance claims using various authorities including its cease-and-desist authority.[56]

---

49. 12 U.S.C. § 1821(e)(13).
50. 12 U.S.C. § 1815(c).
51. The FDIC assessed cross guaranty liability against Advanta Corp.
52. 12 U.S.C. § 1821(k).
53. 12 U.S.C. § 1823(e).
54. D'Oench Duhme v. FDIC, 315 U.S. 447 (1943); FDIC Policy Statement on 12 U.S.C. § 1823(e).
55. 12 U.S.C. § 1821(j).
56. IndyMac Bancorp Inc.; Franklin Bank Corp.; Guaranty Financial Group; BankUnited Financial Corp.; Downey Financial Corp.; and UCBH Holdings Inc.

QFC Special Rules.[57] QFCs are securities and commodities contracts, forwards, swaps, and repurchase contracts. Similar but not identical rules apply to bankruptcy and FDIC Receivership for QFC's. Permits set off, termination, and close out for the counterparty, but only if the FDIC does not affirm or transfer the QFC by 5 pm on the business day after the failure. In Bankruptcy, such rights are immediately available to the counterparty. The Receiver may not cherry pick, but must affirm or transfer all or none of the QFC's with respect to a counterparty and its affiliates. FDIC rules require recordkeeping by insured banks to enable the FDIC to make this determination.

Satisfying Creditor Claims

In addition, the FDIC is responsible, to the extent possible, for satisfying creditor claims, in order of the priority set forth in the FDIC Act. In cases where the FDIC has agreed to share losses on assets that were transferred to the winning bidder, the FDIC manages the assistance payments throughout the period of the assistance agreement.

FDIC Claims Process Superpowers. The FDIC, as Receiver, has the administrative power to allow or disallow claims. A holder of a disallowed claim can litigate its claim in Federal District Court, but the FDIC can continue with its receivership without delay. In a Bankruptcy proceeding, a Bankruptcy Trustee can object to a claim, but the Bankruptcy Court decides whether or not to allow the claim in a judicial proceeding.

> *Contract Repudiation.* The FDIC as Receiver can repudiate any burdensome contract within a "reasonable time" of its appointment. A Bankruptcy Trustee can only repudiate executory contracts.[58]
>
> *Stay of Litigation.* The FDIC as Receiver can request a stay of legal proceedings of up to 90 days. The automatic stay in bankruptcy becomes effective immediately upon the filing of a bankruptcy petition.
>
> *Avoidance Powers.* The FDIC and a Bankruptcy Trustee can pursue fraudulent transfers. The FDIC's powers extend to transfers made five years before or after the date of the Receiver's appointment.[59]

---

57. 12 U.S.C. § 1821(e)(8).
58. 12 U.S.C. § 1821(e).
59. 12 U.S.C. § 18211821(d)(17) and (18).

Priorities of Claims. The very first items paid in a Receivership are the secured claims. As a result, any first priority secured lien on property of the bank will be satisfied, including claims of the Federal Reserve and any Federal Home Loan Bank to the extent of the failed institution's collateralized borrowings. At that point, the priority of claims in an FDIC Receivership is, first to last[60]:

- Administrative Expenses of the Receiver;
- Deposit Liabilities: Insured and uninsured. The FDIC is subrogated to all of the rights of any depositor to the extent that the FDIC has paid the insured amount of the deposit and its claims are equal to all other depositors. The FDIC is usually the largest creditor of a failed bank, because it has paid off the insured depositors. U.S. deposit claims are given priority over the claims of general creditors (known as the "national depositor preference"). Foreign deposit liabilities are treated as general creditors, unless the deposits are dually payable in the U.S. International Banking Facility ("IBF") deposits are not considered U.S. deposit liabilities and are treated as general creditors.
- General Creditors (including foreign deposits, unless dually payable in the U.S. and IBF deposits);
- Subordinated Debt of the Bank;
- Shareholders.

Claims Process. Claims must be filed within 90 days of notice and a determination by the Receiver is made within 180 days. Late-discovered claims are barred, but the Receiver may allow them. A disappointed claimant has sixty days to seek judicial review in Federal District Court.

SIFI Failures

Prior to and during the Global Financial Crisis, the FDIC only had authority to resolve a failing federally or state-chartered bank that was insured by the FDIC. But the FDIC did not have any authority to resolve the large holding companies that controlled the banks, or a subsidiary of the bank, or any of the holding company's subsidiaries other than the bank. And the FDIC had no authority to resolve other types of financial institutions, no matter how serious an effect on the financial system such a failure might have. All of these entities could only be resolved through a bankruptcy proceeding.

Yet many of the failing financial institutions that were at the core of the Global Financial Crisis were not FDIC-insured banks. These legal distinctions were lost in the alarming news headlines of "Bank Failure!"

60. 12 U.S.C. § 1821(d)(11)(A).

as these nonbanks failed. The failed entities were broker-dealers, such as Bear Stearns and Lehman, under the jurisdiction of the SEC. Or they were holding companies or their nonbank subsidiaries, such as AIG and its subsidiary, AIG Financial Products Corporation, which were regulated by the Office of Thrift Supervision or the Federal Reserve. None of these other regulators had resolution powers over these entities, nor did the FDIC. In addition, some of the worst of the Global Financial Crisis occurred, not in the banking system at all, but rather in the capital markets, or within what is sometimes known as "shadow banking."

Why Did This Gap Exist?

Our financial markets have evolved considerably over the years. In the beginning, prior to the creation of the FDIC in 1933, our financial system consisted primarily of depository institutions (banks), whose deposits were uninsured. When a bank failed, its chartering authority managed its failure, under the bankruptcy laws. As we discuss above, the FDIC became the insurer of deposits and resolver of banks to avoid the runs that occurred on banks and to stabilize our financial system.

It was not thought that a non-depository institution would require the swift and efficient resolution process needed for a depository institution and the law did not provide for it. After all, these other financial institutions did not play the "special" role of banks: they did not hold transactional accounts, including the deposits of large and small depositors; they did not play a role in the payments system; and they were not instruments for the execution of the monetary system. It was thought that the failure of such a nonbank financial institution should not require any protections beyond those provided to creditors under bankruptcy law. Yet in the financial Global Financial Crisis, the failures of these institutions threatened to bring down the entire financial system, including banks.

A lesson of the Global Financial Crisis was that we needed to rethink whether our existing system was sufficient to deal with future financial crises. Up until the Global Financial Crisis, the system appeared to be working: if a holding company or a broker-dealer were to have failed, the failure would have been dealt with in a Bankruptcy Court proceeding (and, in the case of a broker-dealer, some additional protections for investors were provided under SIPC).[61] Accordingly, if a holding company that controlled a bank went into bankruptcy, the FDIC sought to protect the bank from the failed holding company. But in many such instances, the bank was healthy and continued to operate. If a bank failed and was resolved by the FDIC, it was possible that its holding company remained solvent and continued

61. Securities Investor Protection Corporation.

to operate. Sometimes both the bank and the holding company failed, in which case the holding company failure was dealt with in Bankruptcy Court and the failed bank was swiftly resolved by the FDIC. There have been extended legal battles between the FDIC as Receiver and the creditors of a failed holding company and/or a Bankruptcy Trustee over whether assets that survive the failure(s) belong in the receivership of the bank or the holding company. But in the past, so long as the bank was resolved quickly, confidence in the banking system was maintained and the FDIC insurance fund remained strong.

What Happened in the Global Financial Crisis?

In the Global Financial Crisis, panic quickly spread from a few failed broker-dealers to the entire financial system, including banks. It became clear to both the financial market participants and regulators that the largest banks had become interconnected with and exposed to the risks posed by their holding companies and by less-regulated nonbank and shadow banking institutions that played a large role in the financial markets. It also became clear that there could be a "run" on one of these nonbank financial institutions that could potentially bring down the financial system.

Some examples of this were:

- As holding companies and broker-dealers all had become thought of as banks by the public, the failure of one of these entities could cause a loss of confidence in banks and the banking system.
- This was not just the result of fuzzy distinctions made by the public between these legal entities. It also reflected the fact that large and complex banking organizations were increasingly doing business holding-company-wide, across legal entities, with little separation between legal entities, including banks.
- The business of broker-dealers increasingly involved trading, investing, lending and large-scale underwriting and securitization of assets. These activities required a large amount of money. Broker-dealers engaged in transactions with affiliated and unaffiliated banks. Broker-dealers also maintained all of their deposit and clearing accounts at banks. In addition, broker-dealers funded themselves through the repo market. That is, they funded their balance sheet daily by selling securities in their possession (but not necessarily securities that they owned) and receiving funds in exchange. Each night, they purchased the securities back again. Many banks as well as other broker-dealers provided this financing. This daily transaction could only continue if there was confidence in the broker-dealer. The broker-dealers were highly

leveraged (that is, they had a large amount of debt compared to their capital). Consequently, they were very vulnerable to any adverse financial shocks.

- The banks also had become financially exposed through providing loans to a number of affiliated and non-affiliated nonbank mortgage companies, which were originating residential mortgages for securitization, using poor credit standards. Broker-dealer affiliates and non-affiliates of those banks were securitizing those mortgage loans.
- Banks had created special purpose, off-balance sheet entities that issued commercial paper to fund their corporate customers. This commercial paper was purchased by insurance companies and by mutual funds, which also were bank customers. The banks provided back-up lines of credit to the special purpose entities, to be used in the event there were any problems with the funding arrangements. When such problems developed, the banks were obligated to fund the special purpose vehicles, bringing the assets and liabilities of the vehicles out of the "shadows" and onto the banks' balance sheets.
- The banks were the largest participants in the trillion-dollar unregulated derivatives markets, with credit exposures to many counterparties, including other banks, broker-dealers, insurance companies, foreign banking organizations and large corporate derivatives users.

What do all of these examples have in common? They illustrate that large and complex banks had become inextricably interconnected not only with other banks, but, more significantly, with nonbank financial institutions, such as their holding companies, broker-dealers, insurance companies, and other financial companies. In other words, the banks were intertwined with other systemically important financial institutions, whose failure might trigger a financial crisis. Not until after the Global Financial Crisis was a formal legal mechanism for dealing with this put into place by Congress.

Regulatory Reaction and "Too Big to Fail"

Three federal agencies—The Federal Reserve System (including both the Federal Reserve Board and the Federal Reserve Bank of New York), the U.S. Treasury, and the FDIC—attempted to use their existing authorities on an *ad hoc* basis to try meet this challenge. Not having the swift and sure resolution authority and "superpowers" for nonbank resolution that were possessed by the FDIC for insured banks, the agencies tried to do the best they could to deal with the crisis without them. What some see as a catalyst for the crisis—the failure of Lehman—was an example of how bankruptcy law was insufficient to deal, in a manner that could quiet market panic, with resolving an entity that was important within the financial markets, that had been brought down by a "run." Other large financial participants were "bailed out" so as to avoid "runs" on them due to lack of confidence, or to avoid their failure, which it was thought could quickly spread to banks or to nonbank financial institutions. Following the Global Financial Crisis, Congress removed or sharply curtailed many of those authorities that were used by these agencies during the crisis.

The Dodd-Frank Act, passed in the wake of the Global Financial Crisis, includes several provisions to try to address the issues of what agency has the authority to resolve which institutions and pursuant to what process in a financial crisis. To this end, Congress:

- Created a process for identifying those financial entities that are not banks, but yet, were they to fail, could pose a threat to the financial system. The new multi-agency authority responsible for this is the Financial Stability Oversight Counsel ("FSOC"). It is charged with identifying and responding to systemic risks and promoting market discipline. Under the leadership of the U.S. Treasury, it is comprised of the heads of all the federal financial regulatory agencies.[62] The term created for these newly identified entities is "Systemically Important Financial Institutions," which also include bank holding companies with $50 billion or more in assets (collectively, "SIFIs").[63]
- Decided that it needed to provide for resolution-like authority to deal with SIFI failures. But Congress could not decide between bankruptcy and resolution as the preferable legal process for failing SIFIs, so it provided for both. Accordingly, the legal process for dealing with a failing SIFI would be bankruptcy law (the default option) unless a determination is a made that bankruptcy law would not be appropriate. There is a 24-hour window to appeal this determination. Congress created an Orderly Liquidation Authority ("OLA") process, which could be used as an alternative to bankruptcy law.[64]
- Opted to use the term "liquidation" rather than "resolution" in the new resolution-like authority it created, to make certain that an institution was not bailed out, but rather was liquidated at the end of the process.
- Prohibited taxpayer funding of bailouts.[65]

62. Title I, Subtitle A of Dodd-Frank.
63. Title I, Subtitles A and C of Dodd-Frank.
64. Title II, Dodd-Frank.
65. Title II, § 214, Dodd-Frank.

- Congress declined to create a pre-funded source of funds for Orderly Liquidations, not wanting to enable the bailout of a SIFI. Should such funding be required for a resolution, it must come in the form of a loan from the U.S. Treasury. The loan is to be repaid from the assets in the SIFI Receivership or, should this prove insufficient, through a risk-based assessment of the SIFIs remaining after the Orderly Resolution.[66]
- Congress assigned multiple agencies in charge of making the determination that a SIFI's failure would present systemic risk and must be resolved, depending upon the type of failing entity and its regulator.[67]
- Put the FDIC in charge of carrying out the process of OLA.
- Left in place the FDIC-administered resolution process for failing insured banks.

Orderly Liquidation and Resolution Planning under Title II of Dodd-Frank

In support of the two potential legal processes that Congress put in place for dealing with failing SIFIs, Congress has required two parallel types of preparation on the part of the Federal Reserve, the FDIC and SIFIs. First, Congress has established the Living Will process, whereby SIFIs must submit plans to the FDIC and the Federal Reserve demonstrating that the institution's failure could be handled under Bankruptcy Law.[68] Simultaneously, the FDIC was given the authority to prepare plans for how it would handle the resolution of a SIFI under OLA. The FDIC was authorized to obtain the necessary information for this from the institutions. Finally, the FDIC is working to establish plans for the resolution of banks with assets of $50 billion or more.

The FDIC has been diligently working on its OLA planning and has gathered advice on how it would administer OLA. The FDIC has decided upon a "single point of entry," whereby it would take control of a failed financial institution at the top of the structure of the consolidated organization, leaving the subsidiaries to continue in operation during the resolution. Over time, parts of the organization might be sold or put into bankruptcy. The FDIC has made this plan public and has sought comment on it.[69]

66. Title II, § 210(n), Dodd-Frank.
67. Title II, § 203, Dodd-Frank.
68. Title I, § 165(d), Dodd-Frank.
69. 78 *Fed. Reg.* 76,614.

Workings of Orderly Liquidation

In § 206 of Dodd-Frank, entitled "The Mandatory Terms and Conditions for All Orderly Liquidation Actions," Congress clearly stated that it wants to avoid future bailouts. The FDIC must "determine that such action is necessary for purposes of the financial stability of the United States, and not for the purpose of preserving the covered financial company" and ensure that management and the board of directors responsible for the failed condition of the covered financial company is removed.[70] The Systemic Risk Determination required to be made by the Secretary of the Treasury bears some similarity to the Systemic Risk Determination that the FDIC is empowered to make in connection with the resolution of FDIC-insured banks. But because the scope of the Treasury Secretary's action extends beyond FDIC-insured banks to companies that have not been operating with the prospect of being resolved by federal financial regulatory agencies, its list of findings is much longer and the process more involved. The recommendation for making a Systemic Risk Determination[71] for a SIFI is made upon the request of the Secretary of the Treasury or upon the initiative of the FDIC and the Federal Reserve, except for cases involving brokers or dealers (where the SEC takes the place of the FDIC) or insurance companies (where the Director of the Federal Insurance Office takes the place of the FDIC).[72] Upon receiving this written recommendation, the Secretary of the Treasury, in consultation with the President, determines that:

---

70. Title II, § 206, Dodd-Frank.
71. Title II, § 203, Dodd-Frank.
72. Each recommendation must be made upon a two-thirds vote of the agency. The written recommendation must contain:
    - An evaluation of whether the financial company is in default or in danger of default;
    - A description of the effect that the default of the financial company would have on the financial stability in the United States;
    - A description of the effect that the default of the financial company would have on economic conditions or financial stability for low income, minority, or underserved communities;
    - A recommendation regarding the nature and the extent of actions to be taken regarding the financial company;
    - An evaluation of the likelihood of a private sector alternative to prevent the default of the financial company;
    - An evaluation of why a case under the Bankruptcy Code is not appropriate for the financial company;
    - An evaluation of the effects on creditors, counterparties, and shareholder of the financial company and other market participants; and
    - An evaluation of whether the company satisfies the definition of a financial company.

- The financial company is in default or in danger of default;
- The failure of the financial company and its resolution under otherwise applicable Federal or State law would have serious adverse effects on financial stability in the U.S.;
- No viable private sector alternative is available to prevent the default of the financial company;
- Any effect on the claims or interests of creditors, counterparties, and shareholders of the financial company and other market participants as a result of actions to be taken under Title II of the Dodd-Frank is appropriate, given the impact that any action taken under Title II would have on financial stability in the U.S.;
- Any action under Section 204 of the Dodd-Frank would avoid or mitigate such adverse effects, taking into consideration the effectiveness of the action in mitigating potential adverse effects on the financial system, the cost to the general fund of the Treasury, and the potential to increase excessive risk taking on the part of creditors, counterparties, and shareholders in the financial company;
- A federal regulatory agency has ordered the financial company to convert all of its convertible debt instruments that are subject to the regulatory order; and
- The company satisfies the definition of a financial company under Section 21 of the Dodd-Frank.

This decision-making process must be fully documented and reported to Congress. The FDIC then assumes the responsibility of directing the OLA process, in consultation with any appropriate agencies, such as the regulators of the failed company. The detailed OLA authority largely is based upon the resolution authority that the FDIC follows for failed insured banks, although there are some provisions that are derived from Bankruptcy Law.[73] The FDIC may borrow from Treasury initially to fund the liquidation, but must repay the funds. First, funds must be reclaimed from the Receivership. Second, the FDIC must make risk-based assessments on the remaining SIFIs.

73. Notably, in an effort to bring creditors closer to the outcome that they might have received had the proceeding been under Bankruptcy Law, Title II of the Dodd-Frank provides that a creditor shall receive at least what they would have received in a liquidation proceeding under Title 7 of the Bankruptcy Code.

Prospects for Change

From time to time, there is mumbling that this process requires rethinking or at least amending, and thankfully, it has not yet been needed, but financial crises appear to be part of our makeup, and time will tell how OLA works out. In the meantime, momentum seems to be building for a new Subchapter V of the Bankruptcy Code, which would be "Chapter 14," to resolve large financial institutions and narrow the path to OLA. There are a number of issues of national importance that need to be in the rearview mirror before this happens, but it is worth watching.

Banking Law: Acronyms, Lingo, and Jargon (2020)

Banking TERM	REFERENCE	DEFINITION	Keys' Chapter[1]
§ 24 (Seventh)	12 U.S.C. § 24 (Seventh)	The general powers authority for national banks that requires their activities to be the "business of banking" or "incidental thereto." Many state banks have the same powers by virtue of state parity or wild card statutes.	3, 9
ACH	Automated Clearing House	A processing network whereby interbank transactions are cleared through batch electronic file entries. The ACH Network allows billions of direct deposit and direct payment transactions to be sent in account-to-account transfers.	8
Advanced Approaches		Refers to the large or "core" international banks (generally defined for U.S. purposes as having total assets of $250 billion or more, or consolidated foreign exposures of $10 billion or more) that are subject to Basel II and are required to hold additional capital buffers.	4
AIB	American Institute of Banking	Provides adult program education and training to bankers.	

1. The indication of a chapter(s) relates to the primary focus in *Keys* on the topic. It is not exclusive. The term may not appear in the Table of Contents for the referenced chapter.

Banking TERM	REFERENCE	DEFINITION	Keys' Chapter[1]
ALLL	Allowance for Loan and Lease Losses	The reserve financial institutions must maintain against loan and lease losses. It is a contra account on the asset side of the bank balance sheet to reduce gross loans to net loans and absorb loan and lease losses.	4
AML	Anti-Money Laundering	Usually referred to with the Bank Secrecy act as "AML-BSA," part of the regulatory regime aimed at money laundering, terrorist financing, tax evasion, and other criminal activities.	7
AOCI	Accumulated Other Comprehensive Income	A bank earnings entry that reflects unrealized gains and losses on bank available-for-sale securities. Under Basel III, AOCI flows through capital unless the bank opted out in the first quarter of 2015.	4
ATR	Ability to Repay	Required by sections 1411 and 1412 of Dodd-Frank and the CFPB's amendments to Reg Z, which generally compel creditors to make a reasonable, good faith determination of a consumer's ability to repay any consumer credit transaction secured by a dwelling (excluding an open-end credit plan, timeshare plan, reverse mortgage, or temporary loan) and establishes certain protections from liability under this requirement for "qualified mortgages." *See also* QM.	2
BaaS	Banking as a Service	A fintech term comprising relationships with banks where the fintech provides banking services to its customers.	8
Bank-eligible	12 U.S.C. § 24 (Seventh) 12 C.F.R. Part 1	Refers to the types of securities in which banks may invest under 12 C.F.R. Part 1–generally high-grade debt instruments.	9

Banking TERM	REFERENCE	DEFINITION	Keys' Chapter[1]
BASEL	The Basel Committee on Banking Supervision	Provides a forum for cooperation on banking supervisory matters. Its objective is to enhance understanding of key supervisory issues and improve the quality of banking supervision worldwide. It seeks to do so by exchanging information on national supervisory issues, approaches, and techniques, with a view to promoting common understanding. At times, the Committee uses this common understanding to develop guidelines and supervisory standards in areas where they are considered desirable. The Committee is best known for its international standards on capital adequacy, the Core Principles for Effective Banking Supervision, and the Concordat on cross-border banking supervision.	4
BASEL I	The original Basel Committee Framework for Capital Adequacy	The original risk-based capital guidelines, based on the 1988 capital accord adopted by the international Basel Committee on Banking Supervision. It imposed minimum capital standards on banks and thrifts, and for the first time, it required a risk-weighting of assets in connection with the calculation of required capital ratios. It also required off-balance sheet exposures to be weighted and brought back on the balance sheet.	4
BASEL II	The Basel II Framework for Capital Adequacy	In 2008, the U.S. banking agencies collaboratively began to phase-in capital standards based on a second capital accord, referred to as "Basel II," for Advanced Approaches institutions. Basel II emphasized internal assessment of credit, market, and operational risk, as well as supervisory assessment and market discipline in determining minimum capital requirements.	4
BASEL III	The Basel II Framework for Capital Adequacy	The capital reform implemented internationally in response to the Global Financial Crisis. The rules require banks and holding companies to hold more and better quality capital. The U.S. Basel III rules became effective on January 1, 2015. See Reg Q, 12 C.F.R. 217.	4

Banking TERM	REFERENCE	DEFINITION	Keys' Chapter[1]
BHC	Bank Holding Company	Any entity "controlling" a financial institution whose deposits are insured by the Federal Deposit Insurance Corporation. *See also* FHC.	3, 10
BHCA	Bank Holding Company Act of 1956 12 U.S.C § 1841 et seq.	Contains relevant definitions and governs the activities of companies that control banks, including Bank Holding Companies and Financial Holding Companies.	10
BHCA § 3	12 U.S.C. § 1842	The section of the BHCA that applies to companies becoming BHCs and acquiring banks.	10
BHCA § 4(c)(8)	12 U.S.C. §1843(c)(8)	The section of the BHCA that restricted BHCs to activities "closely related to banking or a proper incident thereto." The list of activities permitted under 4(c)(8) was frozen by Gramm-Leach-Bliley. It is in Reg Y at 12 C.F.R. 225.28.	10
BIF	Bank Insurance Fund	Created by FIRREA; the part of the FDIC insurance fund that insured the deposits of banks as opposed to thrifts. Now combined with SAIF as one DIF fund.	5
BIS	Bank for International Settlements	Owned by sixty central banks from around the world, who meet on a regular basis in Basel, Switzerland. Founded in 1930, the mission of BIS "is to serve central banks in their pursuit of monetary and financial stability, to foster international cooperation in those areas and to act as a bank for central banks." The Basel Committee on Bank Supervision is a part of BIS.	4
BMA	Bank Merger Act	A part of the FDIA and NBA that provides the rules for banks to merge and consolidate.	9
Board	Board of Governors of the Federal Reserve System	Overall governing board of the various Federal Reserve banks located around the country and responsible for U.S. monetary policy. Also the regulatory authority for BHCs and THCs and primary federal regulator of state banks that are members of the Federal Reserve System. *See also* Fed and FRS.	2, 3, 5, 10

Banking TERM	REFERENCE	DEFINITION	Keys' Chapter[1]
BOLI	Bank-Owned Life Insurance	Refers to limited types of life insurance that banks and thrifts may legally own. Such products may not be held for investment purposes but may be held to hedge liabilities, for instance, employee benefit obligations of a bank/thrift. The bank regulatory agencies have released interagency guidance on BOLI.	
BOPEC	**B**anks, **O**ther Subsidiaries, **P**arent, **E**arnings, **C**apital	The former examination rating system used by the Fed for bank holding companies.	11
BSA	Bank Secrecy Act of 1970	Requires financial institutions to keep records of cash purchases of negotiable instruments, to file reports of cash transactions exceeding $10,000 (daily aggregate amount), and to report suspicious activity that might signify money laundering, tax evasion, or other criminal activities.	7
Bureau	Bureau of Consumer Financial Protection	*See also* CFPB.	2
C&D	Cease and Desist Order	Issued by regulators to a bank, thrift, holding company or its Institution Affiliated Parties (Officers, Directors, etc.) to require affirmative action or stopping actions that violate law or are unsafe and unsound.	11
C&I	Commercial and Industrial	Bank commercial loans.	
Call Report	Periodic Reports of Condition	Quarterly financial report filed by financial institutions.	11
CAMELS	**C**apital Adequacy, **A**sset quality, **M**anagement, **E**arnings, **L**iquidity and Market **S**ensitivity	The examination rating system used by bank regulatory agencies with numerical ratings of 1 to 5. 1 is best, 5 is worst.	11

Banking TERM	REFERENCE	DEFINITION	Keys' Chapter[1]
CARD Act (or Credit CARD Act)	Credit Card Responsibility and Disclosure Act of 2009	Addresses abuses in credit card practices including imposing limits on changes in terms and raising rates; limits fees and expiration dates on gift cards.	
CARES Act	Coronavirus Aid, Relief, and Economic Security Act of 2020	The $2 trillion coronavirus economic stimulus bill, signed into law by President Trump on March 27, 2020. The Act included elements aimed at helping keep people engaged in the economy with direct cash for many, plus expanded unemployment benefits and loans to small and large businesses.	2, 5, 7
CBLR	Community Bank Leverage Ratio	Basel III "off-ramp" for institutions with total consolidated assets of less than $10 billion provided by Section 201 of the Regulatory Relief Act. The banking agencies set the CBLR at 9% of tangible equity to total assets for a qualifying bank to be well-capitalized. A community banking organization is eligible to elect the framework if it has less than $10 billion in total consolidated assets, limited amounts of certain assets and off-balance sheet exposures, and a CBLR greater than 9%. The electing institution would not be required to calculate the existing risk-based and leverage capital requirements of the Basel III Rule and would not need to risk-weight its assets for purposes of capital calculations.	4
CCAR	Comprehensive Capital Analysis and Review	A supervisory assessment by the Fed of the capital planning processes and capital adequacy of the larger, complex BHCs (over $250 billion). One component is testing against a severely adverse macroeconomic scenario specified by the Fed. It is intended to demonstrate that the banks have robust, forward-looking capital planning processes that account for their unique risks and sufficient capital to continue operations throughout times of economic and financial stress.	4
CCyB	Countercyclical Buffer	A capital buffer, intended to operate as an additional amount of the Capital Conservation Buffer for Advanced Approaches institutions.	4

Banking TERM	REFERENCE	DEFINITION	Keys' Chapter[1]
CDD	Customer Due Diligence	Required as a part of AML-BSA compliance, a bank's responsibility to verify the identity of a bank customer. It is the process where relevant information about the customer is collected and evaluated for any potential risk for the organization or money laundering/ terrorist financing activities.	7
CDFI	Community Development Financial Institutions	Program to use federal resources to invest in and build the capacity of CDFIs to serve low-income people and communities lacking adequate access to affordable financial products and services.	
CDO	Collateralized Debt Obligation	A type of derivative, used to repackage individual loans into a product that can be sold to investors on the secondary market.	
CDS	Credit Default Swaps	A swap agreement between two counterparties. "Covered CDS" are purchased by a buyer with an interest in the underlying reference obligation as a hedge against the buyer's risk of loss on such reference obligation. A buyer may purchase a CDS on a reference entity in which the buyer does not hold any interest, in order to speculate (rather than hedge against the risk of loss) on the future creditworthiness of the reference entity (e.g., buying a CDS on a security issued by an entity in financial distress).	
CEBA	Competitive Equality Banking Act of 1987	Established new standards for expedited funds availability; recapitalized the Federal Savings & Loan Insurance Company (FSLIC); expanded FDIC authority for open bank assistance transactions, including bridge banks.	2

Banking TERM	REFERENCE	DEFINITION	Keys' Chapter[1]
CECL	Current Expected Credit Loss	CECL is a controversial GAAP accounting standard adopted by FASB in the wake of the Global Financial Crisis that changes how depository financial institutions of any size account for expected credit losses. CECL requires financial institutions to record "life of loan" loss estimates at origination or purchase. This replaces the "incurred loss" accounting model and changes the way in which financial institutions manage the ALLL by requiring forecasting on loan performance. It also applies to credit losses on held-to-maturity securities. CECL took effect in Q1 2020 for large IDIs with holding companies that are registered with the SEC. Effectiveness was otherwise delayed for smaller reporting BHCs and banks and credit unions until 2023. The CRES Act included a further optional delay for two years.	4
CET 1	Common Equity Tier 1	Basel III not only increased most of the required minimum capital ratios, but it introduced the concept of "Common Equity Tier 1 Capital," which consists primarily of common stock, related surplus (net of Treasury stock), retained earnings, and Common Equity Tier 1 minority interests, subject to certain regulatory adjustments. As of January 1, 2015, the Basel III Rule requires CET 1 to risk-weighted assets of 4.5%.	4
CFPB	Bureau of Consumer Financial Protection	The Bureau that operates as an independent part of the Federal Reserve and regulates consumer financial products and certain providers of such products under Title X of Dodd-Frank. Its regulations are codified at 12 C.F.R. 1000 et seq.	2, 3

Banking TERM	REFERENCE	DEFINITION	Keys' Chapter[1]
C.F.R.	Code of Federal Regulations	Federal banking regulations are codified in 12 C.F.R. under the part assigned to the federal banking regulator promulgating the regulation. Certain interpretations of statutes are also included in 12 C.F.R.	2
Check 21	Check Clearing for the 21st Century Act 12 C.F.R. 229	A law that allows banks to handle paper checks electronically through check images and has given rise to remote and mobile deposit of checks and the use of substitute checks and image replacement documents in connection with check clearing and settlement.	5
CIP	Customer Identification Procedures	Know your customer requirements imposed by the USA Patriot Act. *See also* KYC.	7
CLA	Consumer Leasing Act	Provides for uniform disclosure of terms and costs of consumer leases; similar to Truth in Lending; requires lease agreements to include certain terms, including a statement of the number of lease payments and their dollar amounts, penalties for not paying on time and whether a lump sum payment is due at the end of the agreement.	
CLAR	Comprehensive Liquidity Analysis and Review	A supervisory assessment by the Federal Reserve of the liquidity planning processes of the larger, complex BHCs.	5
CMP	Civil Money Penalty	Fines imposed by regulators against financial institutions and IAPs under the FDIA.	11
Collins Amendment	DFA §171(b)	A provision of DFA that requires bank and thrift holding companies (except those with under $3 billion in assets) to hold capital on a consolidated basis as stringent as that required for insured depository institutions.	4

Banking TERM	REFERENCE	DEFINITION	Keys' Chapter[1]
Comptroller	Comptroller of the Currency	The Comptroller is the chairman of the Office of the Comptroller of the Currency, which charters and regulates all national banks and federal thrifts.	2, 3, 9
Correspondent Bank		Depository institutions hold deposits of each other and provide services to others and to their customers. These arrangements are generally contractual in nature and involve banks as "correspondents" of each other. Upstream correspondent banks provide services to smaller institutions, known as downstream correspondents.	
Council	Financial Stability Oversight Council	*See also* FSOC.	2
CP	Commercial Paper	Short-term corporate debt of less than nine months' duration.	
CRA	1. Community Reinvestment Act 2. Consumer Reporting Agency	1. Requires a financial institution to provide lending and banking services to the entire community it serves, in particular to low- and medium-income neighborhoods. It is the subject of a separate compliance exam by the applicable regulator with exam ratings: outstanding, satisfactory (high and low), needs to improve, and substantial noncompliance. Unlike other exam ratings, CRA ratings are published. The Act permits protests to be filed in connection with certain merger and acquisition applications. 2. Companies that collect information and provide reports on consumers that are used to decide whether to provide consumers credit, insurance, or employment, and for other purposes. Equifax, Experian, and TransUnion and the large national CRAs.	7, 9, 10

Banking TERM	REFERENCE	DEFINITION	Keys' Chapter[1]
Crapo	The Economic Growth, Regulatory Relief and Consumer Protection Act of 2018	Also known as the "Regulatory Relief Act," Crapo was enacted in May 2018 to modify or remove certain financial reform rules and regulations. The law roles back a number of Dodd-Frank provisions, especially dealing with community and regional banks: the SIFI test was increased to $250 billion (from $50 billion); less than $10 billion are generally exempt from Volcker Rule and risk committee requirement; between $50 billion and $100 billion are exempt from enhanced prudential standards (resolution planning, stress tests, single party credit limits) immediately and no longer subject to stress testing; less than $10 billion may adopt CBLR only (off-ramp for Basel III) of 9% (as set by agencies); small BHC rules apply to $3 billion and less; mortgage relief; reciprocal deposit relief from brokered deposit restrictions.	2, 4
CRE	Commercial Real Estate	Generally, refers to commercial lending secured by real property. The bank regulatory agencies have released guidelines for banks to develop risk management practices and levels of capital that are commensurate with the level and nature of their concentrations.	
CSBS	Conference of State Bank Supervisors	A clearinghouse for ideas to solve common problems of state bank regulators and to advocate for the continuation of the Dual Banking System.	3
CSI	Confidential Supervisory Material	The agencies view any information included in an examination report (including CAMELS ratings), and any information derived therefrom to be confidential. They also consider informal enforcement proceedings and information gathered from investigations as CSI. Sharing of this information without permission of the regulatory agency is a violation of Federal law.	11

Banking TERM	**REFERENCE**	**DEFINITION**	**Keys' Chapter**[1]
CTR	Currency Transaction Report	A report that U.S. financial institutions are required to file for each deposit, withdrawal, exchange of currency, or other payment or transfer, by, through, or to the financial institution which involves a transaction in currency of more than $10,000.	7
CUNA	Credit Union National Association	Nongovernmental, not-for-profit, trade group representing and lobbying for credit unions.	
CUSO	Credit Union Service Organization	Subsidiaries of credit unions that may engage in a broader range of activities than the credit union itself.	
DCC	Debt Cancellation Contracts	A type of credit insurance recognized as not being insurance by the banking agencies. DCCs are a contract between the financial institution and the debtor pursuant to which debt is paid off a death or disability, and sometimes on termination of employment. OCC regulations on the product are in 12 CR Part 37.	
DDA	Demand Deposit Account	A transaction deposit account, better known as a checking account. Banks must hold reserves on transaction accounts under Reg D.	5
de novo	Latin: new	Used as a reference to newly formed banks and newly formed branches.	9
DFA	The Dodd-Frank Wall Street Reform and Consumer Protection Act of 2010	*See also* Dodd-Frank.	2, 4, 5
DFAST	Dodd-Frank Annual Stress Testing	A test that banks with total consolidated assets of more than $100 billion must run annually against a severely adverse macroeconomic scenario to determine the ability of the financial institution to deal with an economic crisis. Required by Section 165(i)(2) Dodd-Frank.	4

Banking TERM	REFERENCE	DEFINITION	Keys' Chapter[1]
DIDMCA	Depository Institutions Deregulation and Monetary Control Act of 1980	Established "NOW Accounts." Began the phase-out of interest rate ceilings on deposits. Established the Depository Institutions Deregulation Committee. Granted new powers to thrift institutions. Raised the deposit insurance ceiling to $100,000.	2
DIF	Deposit Insurance Fund	The DIF is administered by the FDIC and provides deposit insurance for all insured banks and thrifts in the United States. Various categories of deposits are insured up to $250,000.	5
Discount Window		Credit facilities in which financial institutions go to borrow funds from the Federal Reserve. These loans, which are priced at the discount rate, are often structured as secured loans to alleviate pressure in reserve markets. It helps to reduce liquidity problems for banks and assists in assuring the basic stability of financial markets.	5
Dodd-Frank	The Dodd-Frank Wall Street Reform and Consumer Protection Act of 2010	The major financial reform package enacted in 2010, Dodd-Frank boasts 16 titles and creates 13 new Federal offices, with its principal mission to prevent systemic risk from threatening the financial system.	2, 4, 5
DPC	Debt Previously Contracted	Property banks are permitted to own for a limited number of years after they take it as collateral for a loan that defaults.	9, 10
DRP	Disaster Recovery Plan	IDIs and their vendors are required to maintain and test DRPs for business continuity.	8
DRR	Designated Reserve Ratio	The FDIC manages the DIF with a DRR goal as a percentage of insured deposits. The current goal is to obtain a DRR of 2%.	5

Banking TERM	REFERENCE	DEFINITION	Keys' Chapter[1]
Dual Banking System		A system of bank regulation unique to the United States whereby banks may be chartered either by each of the fifty states and territories or by the federal government and each of those jurisdictions has certain regulatory controls over the banks and charters. Also true of savings and loan associations and credit unions.	3
ECOA	Equal Credit Opportunity Act	Consumer protection statute with implementing regulations that prohibits discrimination in lending practices.	
EDD	Enhanced Due Diligence	As a part of AML-BSA compliance, bank due diligence policies, procedures, and processes should be enhanced for customers that pose higher money laundering or terrorist financing risks to present increased exposure to banks.	7
EDGE	Edge Act Corporation	Created by the Edge Act, § 25 of the Federal Reserve Act, it is a subsidiary of a bank, federally chartered by the Fed, which is established in the United States to offer services to only non-U.S. residents and institutions. The services offered include deposit and loan services. Implementing regulation is Reg K (12 C.F.R. Part 211) under the Federal Reserve Act. It is a subsidiary of a bank.	
EESA	Emergency Economic Stability Act of 2008	Created TARP and guarantee programs to stabilize the economy during the Global Financial Crisis.	2
EFTA	Electronic Fund Transfer Act Reg E (12 C.F.R. Part 1005)	Establishes the rights and liabilities of consumers as well as the responsibilities of all participants in EFT activities; provides for the establishment of minimum standards for the transmission of funds electronically, and provides for the establishment of regulations to deal with the manner and effect of such transfers.	2, 3

Banking TERM	REFERENCE	DEFINITION	Keys' Chapter[1]
EPS	Enhanced Prudential Standards	Section 165 of the Dodd-Frank Act required the Board to establish enhanced prudential standards for bank holding companies and foreign banking organizations with total consolidated assets of $50 billion (changed to some $100 billion and all $250 billion by Crapo) or more and nonbank financial companies that were designated by FSOC for supervision by the Board. The standards include enhanced risk-based and leverage capital, liquidity, risk management, and risk committee requirements; a requirement to submit a resolution plan; single-counterparty credit limits; stress test requirements; and others as the Board determines.	8, 10
***e*SLR**	Enhanced Supplementary Leverage Ratio	A rule to strengthen the leverage ratio standards for the largest, most interconnected U.S. banking organizations. It applies to U.S. top-tier bank holding companies with more than $700 billion in consolidated total assets or more than $10 trillion in assets under custody (covered BHCs) and their insured depository institution (IDI) subsidiaries (the eight large U.S. banking organizations meet the size thresholds and their IDI subsidiaries). Covered BHCs must maintain a leverage buffer greater than 2 percentage points above the minimum supplementary leverage ratio requirement of 3%, for a total of more than 5%, to avoid restrictions on capital distributions and discretionary bonus payments. IDI subsidiaries of covered BHCs must maintain at least a 6% supplementary leverage ratio to be considered "well capitalized" under the agencies' prompt corrective action framework.	4

Banking TERM	REFERENCE	DEFINITION	Keys' Chapter[1]
FACT Act	Fair and Accurate Credit Transactions Act of 2003	Extensive amendments to the then existing Fair Credit Reporting Act to improve the accuracy and transparency of the national credit reporting system and prevent identity theft and assist victims; restricts sharing of consumer information among affiliates without an opt-out; contains provisions enhancing consumer rights in situations involving alleged identity theft, credit scoring, and claims of inaccurate information; allows consumers to request and obtain a free credit report once every twelve months from each of the three nationwide consumer credit reporting companies (Equifax, Experian, and TransUnion).	7
FASB	Federal Accounting Standards Board	The organization primarily involved in developing Generally Accepted Accounting Principles.	4
FBO	Foreign Banking Office(s)	Refers to a foreign banking office of a domestic bank.	
FCRA	Fair Credit Reporting Act	Consumer protection statute and regulations relating to the reporting of credit history.	
FDCPA	Fair Debt Collection Practices Act	Provides rules for debt collection practices under regulations of the CFPB.	
FDIA	Federal Deposit Insurance Act of 1950	Revised and consolidated earlier FDIC legislation into one act. Embodies the basic authority for the current operation of the FDIC.	2, 5
FDIC	Federal Deposit Insurance Corporation	Provides federal insurance for deposits of virtually all commercial banks and thrifts, i.e., savings banks and savings and loans and serves as receiver in bank and thrift failures. The FDIC is also the principal federal regulator of state-chartered banks that are not members of the Federal Reserve System and state-chartered thrifts.	2, 3, 5

Banking TERM	REFERENCE	DEFINITION	Keys' Chapter[1]
FDICIA	Federal Deposit Insurance Corporation Improvement Act of 1991	Increased the powers and authority of the FDIC; recapitalized the Bank Insurance Fund; created new supervisory and regulatory examination standards; established new capital requirements for banks; ordered the creation of a risk-based deposit insurance assessment scheme; mandated a least-cost resolution method and prompt resolution approach to problem and failing banks; and created new Truth in Savings provisions. Also limited the authority of state banks and their subsidiaries to act as principal in activities prohibited to national banks without approval of the FDIC and prohibited insurance underwriting through state banks, except to the extent permitted to national banks.	2, 5
Fed or Federal Reserve	Federal Reserve System	Refers to the central bank of the United States composed of the Board and twelve Federal Reserve Banks. Also the regulatory authority for BHCs and THCs and the primary federal regulator of state banks that are members of the Federal Reserve System. *See also* FRS.	2, 3, 5, 10
Federal Funds Rate		A fluctuating interest rate per annum equal to the weighted average of the rates on overnight Federal Funds transactions with members of the Federal Reserve System which are arranged by Federal funds brokers, all as published for a particular day by the Federal Reserve Bank of New York.	
FEMA	Federal Emergency Management Agency	Oversees the National Flood Insurance Program, which requires participating communities to adopt and enforce ordinances that meet or exceed FEMA requirements to reduce the risk of flooding. *See also* NFIP.	

Banking TERM	REFERENCE	DEFINITION	Keys' Chapter[1]
FFIEC	Federal Financial Institutions Examination Council	Interagency body composed of the FED, FDIC, and OCC empowered to prescribe uniform principles, standards, and report forms for the federal examination of financial institutions regulated by each of them and to make recommendations to promote uniformity in the supervision of financial institutions; was given additional statutory responsibilities by section 340 of the Housing and Community Development Act of 1980 to facilitate public access to data that depository institutions must disclose under HMDA and the aggregation of annual HMDA data, by census tract, for each metropolitan statistical area.	8
FHC	Financial Holding Company	A bank holding company that has requested and qualified to become a financial holding company and has elected to engage in "financial activities" as defined in the Gramm-Leach-Bliley Act. In effect it is a holding company that may have subsidiaries engaged in commercial banking, investment banking, and insurance. It and its subsidiary banks/thrifts must be well-capitalized and well-managed and in compliance with CRA and must maintain compliance with those tests or be subject to loss of powers.	3, 10
FHFA	Federal Housing Finance Agency	The independent agency created in 2008 to regulate and supervise the GSEs. *See also* FHFB.	2
FHFB	Federal Housing Finance Board	Created by FIRREA. Is under HUD and supervises the twelve FHLBs.	2
FHLB	Federal Home Loan Banks	Twelve Regional Banks regulated by FHLBB until FIRREA. Now regulated by Federal Housing Finance Board. Primarily serve as source of residential mortgage credit.	2
FHLBB	Federal Home Loan Bank Board	Established in 1932 as the regulator of federal and state savings and loan association or "thrifts." FIRREA replaced it with the OTS.	2

Banking TERM	REFERENCE	DEFINITION	Keys' Chapter[1]
FHLMC	Federal Home Loan Mortgage Corporation	Commonly known as Freddie Mac, it is a federal government-sponsored enterprise (GSE) of the U.S. Government authorized to make loans and loan guarantees. Freddie Mac buys mortgages on the secondary market, pools them, and sells them as mortgage-backed securities to investors on the open market.	2
FICO	The Financing Corporation	A mixed-ownership governmental corporation chartered by the former Federal Home Loan Bank Board pursuant to the Competitive Equality Banking Act of 1987 to function as a financing vehicle for the recapitalization of the former FSLIC. FICO issued thirty-year noncallable bonds of approximately $8.1 billion that matured in September 2019. FICO's authority to issue bonds ended on December 12, 1991. Since 1996, federal legislation has required that all FDIC-insured depository institutions pay assessments to cover interest payments on FICO's outstanding obligations. The final payment was in March 2019.	5
FinCEN	Financial Crimes Enforcement Network	The U.S. Department of the Treasury established the Financial Crimes Enforcement Network in 1990 to provide a government-wide multisource financial intelligence and analysis network. The organization's operation was broadened in 1994 to include regulatory responsibilities for administering the Bank Secrecy Act.	7
FINRA	Financial Industry Regulatory Authority	The largest self-regulatory organization (SRO) for broker-dealers. It was created in July 2007 through the consolidation of the National Association of Securities Dealers (NASD) and the member regulation, enforcement, and arbitration functions of the New York Stock Exchange. Broker-dealers and their registered representatives and associated persons must hold licenses issued by FINRA, for instance, Series 7 and 24. FINRA produces and enforces the FINRA Rulebook.	

Banking TERM	REFERENCE	DEFINITION	Keys' Chapter[1]
Fin Sub	Financial Subsidiary	A type of subsidiary of a bank created by the Gramm-Leach-Bliley Act that has greater securities powers than the parent bank. The bank must be well capitalized and well managed to own a fin sub and must meet other prudential requirements.	3
FIO	Federal Insurance Office	Created by Dodd-Frank as a part of Treasury. Its mandate is not to be a regulator or supervisor—that role stays with the states—but to monitor all aspects of insurance, assist Treasury and coordinate efforts in certain respects, recommend insurers who may be nonbank companies subject to supervision by the Federal Reserve, make preemption determinations, and consult with state insurance regulators	2
FIRIRCA	Financial Institutions Regulatory and Interest Rate Control Act of 1978	Created the FFIEC. Established limits and reporting requirements for bank insider transactions. Created major statutory provisions regarding electronic fund transfers.	2
FIRREA	Financial Institutions Reform, Recovery, and Enforcement Act of 1989	Abolished FSLIC and gave FDIC the responsibility of insuring the deposits of thrift institutions in its place; created the Savings Association Insurance Fund (SAIF) as part of the FDIC insurance fund to cover thrifts, while the fund covering banks was called the Bank Insurance Fund (BIF) and was kept separately; abolished the FHLBB and created two new agencies, the Federal Housing Finance Board (FHFB) and the Office of Thrift Supervision (OTS), to replace it; created RTC as a temporary agency to manage the assets of failed thrifts.	2, 5, 11
FNMA	Federal National Mortgage Association	Commonly known as Fannie Mae, FNMA is a GSE that purchases qualifying residential home mortgages on the secondary market, pools them, and sells them as mortgage-backed securities to investors on the open market.	

Banking TERM	REFERENCE	DEFINITION	Keys' Chapter[1]
FOMC	Federal Open Market Committee	Part of the Federal Reserve Board that sets economic policy.	5
FRS	Federal Reserve System	The central banking system of the United States. It is a quasi-public (government entity with private components) banking system composed of (i) the presidentially appointed Board of Governors of the Federal Reserve System in Washington, DC; (ii) the Federal Open Market Committee; (iii) twelve regional Federal Reserve Banks located in major cities throughout the nation acting as fiscal agents for the U.S. Treasury; (iv) numerous private U.S. member banks, which subscribe to required amounts of nontransferable stock in their regional Federal Reserve Banks; and (v) various advisory councils.	2, 3, 5, 10
FSA	Federal Savings Association	A federal depository institution charter originally established to focus on consumer real estate lending under the Home Owners' Loan Act. Chartered by and regulated by the OTS before Dodd-Frank and the OCC after July 21, 2011. Also, an abbreviation that a federal saving association can use in its name.	2, 3
FSB	Federal Savings Bank	A federal depository institution charter originally established to focus on consumer real estate lending under the Home Owners' Loan Act. Chartered by and regulated by the OTS before Dodd-Frank and the OCC after July 21, 2011. Also, an abbreviation that a federal saving association can use in its name.	2, 3
FSLIC	Federal Savings & Loan Insurance Corporation	A subsidiary of the FHLBB that provided deposit insurance to S&Ls. Abolished by FIRREA, it was replaced by the FDIC, as insurer of all U.S. deposits.	2

Banking TERM	REFERENCE	DEFINITION	Keys' Chapter[1]
FSOC	Financial Stability Oversight Council	Council created by Title I of Dodd-Frank and chaired by the Secretary of the Treasury. It is composed of representatives from the principal federal financial regulatory agencies and a representative of the insurance industry, with its principal mission to prevent systemic risk from threatening the financial system. In so doing, the Council will fill gaps in supervision, monitor financial market developments, identify emerging risks in firms and market activities, and facilitate coordination of interagency policy and resolution of disputes.	2
GAAP	Generally Accepted Accounting Principles.	Accounting standards adopted by FASB.	4
Garn-St Germain	Garn-St Germain Act	Deregulated the limitations of S&Ls to take demand deposits and establish money market accounts; S&Ls were authorized to make commercial, corporate, business, or agricultural loans up to 10% of assets; expanded the powers of thrift institutions into a broader scope of activities and limited the insurance powers of bank holding companies; expanded FDIC powers to assist troubled banks.	2
Glass-Steagall	Glass-Steagall Act	Established the FDIC as a temporary agency. Separated commercial banking from investment banking, establishing them as separate lines of commerce. Gramm-Leach-Bliley revised and eliminated most of the Glass-Steagall act relating to affiliations between investment banking organizations and commercial banks. The provisions dealing with limitations on bank activities were not modified by GLBA.	2, 9

Banking TERM	REFERENCE	DEFINITION	Keys' Chapter[1]
GLBA	Gramm-Leach-Bliley Act of 1999	Repealed most of the Glass-Steagall Act of 1933. Allows national banks to underwrite municipal bonds. Allows FHCs to engage in underwriting and selling insurance and securities, conducting both commercial and merchant banking, investing in and developing real estate and other "complimentary activities." Preserves authority of states to regulate insurance, but prohibits state actions that have the effect of preventing bank-affiliated firms from selling insurance on an equal basis with other insurance agents. Makes significant changes in the operation of the Federal Home Loan Bank System, easing membership requirements and loosening restrictions on the use of FHLB funds. Restricts the disclosure of nonpublic customer information by financial institutions.	2, 9
GSE	Government-Sponsored Enterprise	Entities that are government related: Freddy Mac, Fanny Mae, and the Federal Home Loan Banks.	2
G-SIB	Global Systemically Important Bank	A financial institution whose distress or disorderly failure, because of its size, complexity, and systemic interconnectedness, would cause significant disruption to the wider financial system and economic activity. They must hold additional loss absorption capacity tailored to the impact of their default, to be met with common equity. The list is updated from time to time and includes JPMorgan Chase, Citigroup, and Bank of America.	2, 4, 10
Hedge		An investment strategy to reduce the risk of adverse price movements in an asset. A hedge consists of taking an offsetting position in a related security, such as a futures contract.	9

Banking TERM	REFERENCE	DEFINITION	Keys' Chapter[1]
Hedge Fund		An investment vehicle that pools capital from a number of investors and invests in securities and other instruments. They are administered by a professional management firm and often structured as a limited partnership, limited liability company, or similar vehicle. They are typically structured to avoid registration under the federal securities laws.	9
HMDA	Home Mortgage Disclosure Act of 1975	Establishes minimum and uniform disclosures of the terms and related charges for home mortgages.	
HOEPA	Home Ownership and Equity Protection Act of 1994	Amends TILA to require additional disclosures and additional protections for closed end not-purchase money mortgages on principal residences; targets high interest and high fee loans mainly in the home equity area. Assignees of such loans are also liable for penalties. Fed issues regulations defining rates which trigger the applicability and setting forth of required disclosure forms and information.	
HOLA	Home Owners Loan Act	Established the savings association charter and provides the rules for their supervision and regulation. The OCC now is the regulator with supervisory responsibility.	2
HQLA	High-Quality Liquid Assets	A liquidity objective arising from the Global Financial Crisis to provide an incentive for banks and holding companies to increase their holdings in unencumbered high-quality liquid assets like Treasury securities and other sovereign debt as a component of assets.	5
IAP	Institution Affiliated Party	Officers, Director, Principal Shareholders, Independent Contractors (which can include attorneys and accountants under some situations). The banking regulators may take enforcement actions against IAPs in certain circumstances, including imposing CMPs.	11

Banking TERM	REFERENCE	DEFINITION	Keys' Chapter[1]
IBF	International Banking Facility	A banking entity that any U.S. bank, or a U.S. branch/subsidiary of a foreign bank, or an Edge Act Corporation establishes in the United States to offer services to only non-U.S. residents and institutions. The services offered include deposit and loan services.	
IDI	Insured Depository Institution	Refers to banks and thrifts, any financial institution with FDIC-insured deposits. Frequently used in rulemaking by the banking agencies.	3
IHC	Intermediate Holding Company	As part of the Dodd-Frank Act's enhanced prudential standards, foreign banking organization with $50 billion or more in U.S. non-branch/agency assets were required to place virtually all U.S. subsidiaries underneath a top-tier U.S. intermediate holding company. IHCs are subject to U.S. Basel III, capital planning, Dodd-Frank stress testing, liquidity, risk management requirements, and other U.S. EPS on a consolidated basis.	
ILC	Industrial Loan Company	State-chartered institutions that originated in the early 1900s as finance companies for lower-income borrowers. ILCs were chartered in seven states as of mid-2004: California, Colorado, Hawaii, Indiana, Minnesota, Nevada, and Utah. These early ILCs offered relatively high-interest unsecured loans to factory workers who could not otherwise obtain credit. They were not originally FDIC insured and, for historical reasons, may be owned by commercial companies.	2, 10

Banking TERM	REFERENCE	DEFINITION	Keys' Chapter[1]
KYC	Know Your Customer	The due diligence that financial institutions and other regulated companies must perform to identify their clients and ascertain relevant information pertinent to doing financial business with them. In the United States, KYC is typically a policy implemented to conform to a customer identification program mandated under the Bank Secrecy Act and USA PATRIOT Act and to prevent identity theft fraud, money laundering, and terrorist financing. It is a process that banks must continually undertake from the start of a customer relationship to the end.	7
LCR	1. Liquidity Coverage Ratio	1. Liquidity is a measure of the ability and ease with which bank assets may be converted to cash. Liquid assets are those that can be converted to cash quickly if needed to meet financial obligations. The LCR is designed to ensure that the banking entity has an adequate stock of unencumbered high-quality liquid assets that can be converted easily and immediately in private markets into cash to meet liquidity needs for a thirty-calendar-day liquidity stress scenario. The U.S. bank regulatory agencies implemented the LCR in September 2014 for the large banking organizations.	5
	2. Least Cost Resolution	2. Refers to the requirement that the FDIC determine the least costly manner in which to resolve a failed IDI.	12
Leverage Ratio		A ratio of Tier 1 capital to book assets used to identify capital adequacy.	4

Banking TERM	REFERENCE	DEFINITION	Keys' Chapter[1]
LFI	Large Financial Institution	A rating system imposed by the Federal Reserve in 2019 that replaces RFI/C(D) for holding companies $100 billion in assets or over. The LFI rating system is designed to: (i) align with current supervisory programs and practices for LFIs; (ii) enhance the clarity and consistency of supervisory assessments and communications of supervisory findings and implications; and (iii) provide greater transparency to firms regarding the supervisory consequences of a given rating.	11
LH&A	Life, Health and Accident	Types of insurance some financial institutions and holding companies may sell (depending on the powers of the charter) that cover risks associated with death, accidents, and health. Certain kinds of life insurance with investment characteristics are considered to be NDIPs. Bank sales are subject to Consumer Protections in the Sale of Insurance, adopted by all the agencies. See 12 C.F.R. Part 14 for national banks and federal thrifts.	
Living Will		Required by Dodd-Frank for the largest institutions. All BHCs with over $250 billion in assets (and on a case-by-case basis, some over $100 billion) are required to submit and obtain approval of a plan to unwind the organization in the event of insolvency.	12
Line of Business		Refers to an activity of a company that is reasonably separable. The SEC requires that there be separate breakdowns of key economic data for each line of business of a registered company that accounts for more than 20% of the company's revenues.	
LMI	Low and moderate income	Bank lending and investing in LMI neighborhoods is the objective of CRA and fair lending laws.	7
Loans-to-One Borrower	12 USC § 84 for national banks.	The lending limit that a bank may extend credit to one borrower.	6

Banking TERM	REFERENCE	DEFINITION	Keys' Chapter[1]
LTOB	See Loans-to-One-Borrower		6
Member bank	Member of FRS	State banks that choose to become members of the FRS and have the Fed as their primary federal regulator. They purchase stock in the FRB in their area to become members.	3
MBS	Mortgage-Backed Security	An asset-backed security that is secured by a mortgage, or more commonly a collection of hundreds of mortgages. The mortgages are sold to a group that "securitizes," or packages, the loans together into a security that can be sold to investors. In the United States, they may be issued by government-sponsored enterprises like Fannie Mae or Freddie Mac, or they can be "private-label," issued by structures set up by investment banks.	
MMDA	Money Market Deposit Account	A type of savings account under Reg D. Certain transfers are limited to six per month.	5
MRB	Marijuana-Related Business	An acronym one would not have expected to find in banking, but, as states legalize marijuana, MRB's as bank customers becomes a bigger risk and AML-BSA issue.	7
MOU	Memorandum of Understanding	Agreement between regulator and institution regarding required change in practices and operations.	11
MRA	Matter Requiring Attention	An examiner instruction to management of an examined entity to correct a violation of law or other commission or omission.	11
MRIA	Matter Requiring Immediate Attention	An examiner instruction to management to correct a problem immediately.	11
MRC	Minimum Required Capital	Refers to the capital needed to be held by IDIs and holding companies to be adequately capitalized.	4

Banking TERM	REFERENCE	DEFINITION	Keys' Chapter[1]
MSB	Mutual Savings Bank	These institutions originated in the states and were organized on a philanthropic basis to provide wage earners with a safe place to deposit funds and earn interest. More than 95% of MSBs were concentrated in nine states—Connecticut, Maine, Massachusetts, New Hampshire, New Jersey, New York, Pennsylvania, Rhode Island, and Washington. Many have the power to issue and underwrite Savings Bank Life Insurance, a power not permitted generally to other IDIs.	2
N.A.	National Association	An abbreviation that a national bank can use in its name instead of national bank.	3
NACHA	National Automated Clearinghouse Association	The administrator of the ACH Network. It manages and enforces the ACH Operating Rules and is a payments industry trade association. The NACHA Rules provide the legal foundation for the ACH Network.	5
NAFCU	National Association of Federal Credit Unions	Trade Association of Federal Credit Unions	
NASCUS	National Association of State Credit Union Supervisors	A professional regulators association composed of State credit union regulators, which is the primary resource and lobbyist for the forty-seven state governmental agencies that charter, regulate, and examine the nation's state-chartered credit unions. (Delaware, South Dakota, and Wyoming have no laws permitting state-chartered credit unions.) Also acts as the liaison to federal agencies, including the NCUA.	
NASD	National Association of Securities Dealers	Formerly, the SRO for most broker-dealers. Now FINRA.	
NBA	National Bank Act of 1864	Established a national banking system and the chartering of national banks; established the Office of the Comptroller of the Currency (OCC) as the administrator of national banks.	2

Banking TERM	REFERENCE	DEFINITION	Keys' Chapter[1]
NCUA	National Credit Union Administration; National Credit Union Act	The primary supervisor of federal credit unions. It insures deposit of both state and federal credit unions and the administrator of the National Credit Union Share Insurance Fund (NCUSIF), the insurer of most state-chartered credit unions. The Act establishes and provides authority for NCUA and provides the legal framework for the charter of federal credit unions and the regulation of federal and state credit unions.	2
NCUSIF	National Credit Union Share Insurance Fund	Equivalent of FDIC deposit insurance for customers of credit unions.	2
NDIP	Nondeposit Investment Product	Includes securities, mutual funds, annuities, and life insurance with investment features. Typically referred to in the context of bank direct or indirect sale of the products to retail customers, which is the subject of the Interagency Statement on Retail Sales of Nondeposit Investment Products.	9
NFIP	National Flood Insurance Program	Provides a means for property owners to financially protect themselves against floods. The Federal Emergency Management Agency (FEMA) oversees the program, which requires participating communities to adopt and enforce ordinances that meet or exceed FEMA requirements to reduce the risk of flooding. Homeowners must secure the flood insurance policy before closing on a property and renew it every year to cover the principal balance on the loan. When financial institutions make mortgage loans on properties in flood zones, they have an obligation to place flood insurance and force-place such insurance if the mortgagor fails to do so.	

Banking TERM	REFERENCE	DEFINITION	Keys' Chapter[1]
Nonmember bank		State banks that do not choose to be members of the FRS and have the FDIC as their primary federal regulator.	3
NOW	Negotiable Order of Withdrawal	A type of transaction account like a checking account. Banks must hold reserves on transaction accounts under Reg D.	5
NPR	Notice of Proposed Rulemaking	Required by administrative law, it is a notice published in the *Federal Register* when one of the agencies of the U.S government, including the banking agencies, wishes to add, remove, or change a rule or regulation as part of the rulemaking process. NPRs give the public the opportunity to submit comments that must be considered in connection with final rulemaking.	2
NSF	Nonsufficient Funds (bad check charges)	Refers to a fee charged when there are insufficient funds to settle a check or card obligation.	
OCC	Office of the Comptroller of the Currency	A bureau of the Treasury that charters and supervises national banks and federal thrifts. It has rulemaking authority under the NBA and HOLA.	2, 3
ODP	Overdraft Protection	A service many banks offer so that depositors can overdraw their bank accounts and have the overdraft covered, subject to fees. If structured properly, the service has historically been exempt from federal law regarding consumer open-end credit, but overdrafts of ATM and debit card transactions are subject to an opt-in under Reg E, 12 C.F.R. 1005.	
OFAC	Office of Foreign Assets Control	An agency of the U.S. Department of the Treasury. OFAC administers and enforces economic and trade sanctions based on U.S. foreign policy and national security goals against targeted foreign states, organizations, and individuals.	7

Banking TERM	REFERENCE	DEFINITION	Keys' Chapter[1]
Op Sub	Operating Subsidiary	A subsidiary controlled by a bank or thrift that may only engage in the activities of the parent bank.	3
OREO	Other Real Estate Owned	Classification for assets of a financial institution acquired in foreclosure of collateral securing a loan.	9
OTS	Office of Thrift Supervision	A part of Treasury that regulated federal thrifts and thrift holding companies and was the federal regulator for state thrifts before the DFA transfer date, when it merged with the OCC.	2
Overdraft		When there are insufficient funds in an account and the bank makes the payment. Overdraft practices and charges are restricted by Reg E.	
Overline	Overline Loan	A loan that exceeds the bank's lending limit.	6
Oversight Council	Financial Stability Oversight Council	*See also* FSOC.	2
Part 1	12 C.F.R. Part 1	Generally refers to the regulations of the OCC at 12 C.F.R. Part 1 that restrict the investments national banks, federal thrifts, and state member banks may make. Many state nonmember banks are subject to the same rules if state law so provides.	9
P&C	Property and Casualty Insurance	Type of insurance some financial institutions and holding companies may sell that covers risks of destruction or loss of personal and commercial properties. Bank sales are subject to Consumer Protections in the Sale of Insurance, adopted by all the agencies. See 12 C.F.R. Part 14 for national banks and federal thrifts.	

Banking TERM	REFERENCE	DEFINITION	Keys' Chapter[1]
PCA	Prompt Corrective Action	Federal law provides the federal banking regulators with broad power to take prompt corrective action to resolve the problems of undercapitalized institutions. The extent of the regulators' powers depends on whether the institution in question is "adequately capitalized," "undercapitalized," "significantly undercapitalized," or "critically undercapitalized," in each case as defined by regulation. Depending upon the capital category to which an institution is assigned, the regulators' corrective powers include: (i) requiring the institution to submit a capital restoration plan; (ii) limiting the institution's asset growth and restricting its activities; (iii) requiring the institution to issue additional capital stock (including additional voting stock) or to sell itself; (iv) restricting transactions between the institution and its affiliates; (v) restricting the interest rate that the institution may pay on deposits; (vi) ordering a new election of directors of the institution; (vii) requiring that senior executive officers or directors be dismissed; (viii) prohibiting the institution from accepting deposits from correspondent banks; (ix) requiring the institution to divest certain subsidiaries; (x) prohibiting the payment of principal or interest on subordinated debt; and (xi) ultimately, appointing a receiver for the institution.	4
PPP	Paycheck Protection Act	A key stimulus program in response to the coronavirus pandemic, PPP was added by Section 1102 of the CARES Act to the Small Business Act. It was designed as an SBA loan to provide direct incentives for small businesses to keep their workers on the payroll. SBA will forgive loans if all employees were kept on the payroll for eight weeks and the money was used for payroll, rent, mortgage interest, or utilities. The Federal Reserve also created a facility to purchase the loans to allow banks to remove them from their balance sheets.	2, 5, 7

Banking TERM	REFERENCE	DEFINITION	Keys' Chapter[1]
QFC	Qualified Financial Contract	Refers to swaps, derivatives, and repurchase agreements that the FDIC must determine to affirm or unwind within one day of receivership of a failed IDI.	12
QM	Qualified Mortgage	The CFPB's QM requirement implements sections 1411 and 1412 of Dodd-Frank, which generally require creditors to make a reasonable, good faith determination of a consumer's ability to repay (ATR) any consumer credit transaction secured by a dwelling (excluding an open-end credit plan, timeshare plan, reverse mortgage, or temporary loan) and establishes certain protections from liability under this requirement for QMs.	2
QTL	Qualified Thrift Lender	A test that savings associations must meet to be regulated as thrifts instead of banks or BHCs. The test requires a majority of assets to be dedicated to mortgage and consumer lending. DFA imposes more severe sanctions on savings associations that do not meet the test, including prohibiting dividend payments to shareholders.	9
Reg or Reg.	Regulation	Abbreviation used to reference a particular regulation. Bank regulatory agencies promulgate regulations under most statutes for which they have rulemaking authority. Under the Administrative Procedures Act, such proposed regulations are subject to notice and comment. They are published in the *Federal Register*. Federal banking regulations are codified in 12 C.F.R. in the part dedicated to the regulator promulgating the regulation.	

Banking TERM	REFERENCE	DEFINITION	Keys' Chapter[1]
Reg B	Equal Credit 12 C.F.R. Part 1002	Former Fed regulation transferred to CFPB that implements the Equal Credit Opportunity Act. The purpose of Reg B is to promote the availability of credit to all creditworthy applicants without regard to race, color, religion, national origin, sex, marital status, or age (provided the applicant has the capacity to contract under state law). The regulation also prohibits the denial of credit merely because an applicant's income is derived from public assistance sources, such as Social Security disability payments. Reg B focuses on the fair treatment of customers in the granting of credit. At its heart, the regulation says the decision to grant credit is to be based on the borrower's ability to meet the lender's credit standards. Matters such as the race, age, or marital status of the borrower or the borrower's reliance on public assistance to repay the loan have no place in the decision to lend.	
Reg C	Home Loan Disclosure 12 C.F.R. Part 1003	Requires banks and thrifts to collect and report information as to loan applications received and mortgage loans made by or purchased by them. Information as to income level, race, gender, and other similar information is collected and compared to determine if discriminatory practices exist.	
Reg D	1. Fed regulation on deposit accounts 12 C.F.R. 204 2. Regulation promulgated by the SEC that constitutes a significant private offering exemption under the Securities Act of 1933	1. Under Fed Reg D, the various kinds of deposit accounts are defined and reserve requirements are established. Also, limitations apply to transaction in savings accounts. 2. Under SEC Reg D substantial amounts of capital may be raised by private sales of equity securities to accredited investors so long as offers to other persons are limited.	5

Banking TERM	REFERENCE	DEFINITION	Keys' Chapter[1]
Reg E	Electronic Funds Transfers 12 C.F.R. Part 1005	Former Fed regulation transferred to CFPB that implements the Electronic Funds Transfer Act. Provides for disclosures and limitations on activities in connection with devices that access accounts. Also implements the CARD Act on gift card limitations and overdraft requirements.	2
Reg K	International Banking 12 C.F.R. Part 211	Fed regulation that provides for the regulation of banking activities of U.S. Banks offshore; activities of foreign banks within the United States; and sets capital requirements for international structures.	
Reg O	Insider Transactions 12 U.S.C. § 375	Fed regulation implementing legal limitations on loans to officers, directors, and principal shareholder of banks and certain affiliates.	6
Reg P	Privacy 12 C.F.R. Part 1016	Implements the GLBA Title V privacy provisions by requiring all financial institutions to institute privacy policies with respect to consumer nonpublic personal information (NPPI) and disclose the same annually and upon account opening. Reg P is for bank holding companies and state member banks. The federal banking agencies have virtually identical regulations.	7
Reg Q	Federal Reserve capital rules under Basel III and DFA 12 C.F.R. 217	Provides for the capital regime for U.S. banks, thrifts, and their parent companies effective January 1, 2015. *See also* Basel III.	4

Banking TERM	REFERENCE	DEFINITION	Keys' Chapter[1]
Reg R	Joint Fed/SEC Regulation dealing with Securities Activities of Banks required by GLBA 12 C.F.R. 218 (Fed) 17 C.F.R. 247 (SEC)	Defines the scope of securities activities that banks, thrifts, and credit union may conduct without registering with the Securities Exchange Commission as a securities broker and implements the most important exceptions from the definition of the term broker for banks under section 3(a)(4) of the Securities Exchange Act of 1934. Specifically, the regulation implements the statutory exceptions that allow a bank, subject to certain conditions, to continue to conduct securities transactions for its customers as part of its trust and fiduciary, custodial, and deposit "sweep" functions and to refer customers to a securities broker-dealer pursuant to a networking arrangement with the broker.	9
Reg W	Affiliate Transactions (12 U.S.C. 371 c and c-1) 12 C.F.R. Part 223	Federal Reserve regulation that implements Sections 23A and 23B of Federal Reserve Act. These related laws restrict covered transactions between a bank and its affiliates and require many affiliate transactions to be on market terms.	6
Reg X	Implements RESPA 12 C.F.R. 1024	Regulation originally by HUD but with CFPB as successor, sets out requirements under RESPA, including disclosure requirements and anti-kickback provisions.	
Reg Y	Implements the BHCA 12 C.F.R. Part 225	Regulation by Fed that implements the Bank Holding Company Act, including application requirements and the list of activities permitted under section 4(c)(8).	3, 10

Banking TERM	REFERENCE	DEFINITION	Keys' Chapter[1]
Reg DD	Truth in Savings 12 C.F.R. Par 1030	Former Fed regulation transferred to CFPB that implements the Truth in Savings Act. Provides for uniform disclosures to depositors so they can easily compare rates and restrictions regarding savings accounts.	
Repo	Repurchase Agreement	A financial transaction in which one party "purchases" a government security form another party and then resells it the next day (overnight repo) or at a specified term (term repo) for the purchase price plus interest. Often an IDI is the repos seller to a customer and the repos is accomplished through a sweep of funds from the customer's DDA as a means to earn interest on the deposit or provide safety of the funds above the FDIC-insured amount. Repos must be secured on behalf of the purchaser with a priority lien on the government securities as if a secured financing.	5
Reserves	12 C.F.R. Part 204	Federal Reserve regulations require insured depository institutions to maintain reserves against their transaction accounts (primarily NOW and regular checking accounts). The reserve requirements are subject to annual adjustment by the Federal Reserve.	5
RESPA	Real Estate Settlement Procedures Act	Sets out required disclosures for mortgage loans and prohibits illegal steering of loans and kickbacks for home mortgage referrals.	
RFC	Resolution Funding Corporation	Created by FIRREA to provide funding for RTC operations during and after the thrift crisis when FSLIC, the insurer for savings and loan associations, ran out of funds.	2

Banking TERM	REFERENCE	DEFINITION	Keys' Chapter[1]
RFI/C(D)	Federal Reserve BHC Rating System for holding companies under $100 billion	The main components of the RFI rating system are risk management practices (R component) and financial condition (F component) of the consolidated organization, and an assessment of the potential impact (I component) of a holding company's nondepository entities on its subsidiary depository institution(s). A holding company under the RFI rating system is assigned a composite rating (C) based on an evaluation and rating of its managerial and financial condition and an assessment of future potential risk to its subsidiary depository institution(s). A holding company under the RFI rating system is also assigned a depository institution (D) component rating that generally mirrors the primary regulator's assessment of the subsidiary depository institution(s).	11
Riegle-Neal	Riegle-Neal Interstate Banking and Branching Efficiency Act of 1994	Eliminates state barriers to national expansion of banks and BHCs. Allows interstate mergers between banks, subject to concentration limits, state laws, and CRA evaluations.	2, 9
ROA	Return on Assets	A ratio of an institution's net earnings to total assets. Often used as a benchmark to indicate how well a bank is earning.	11
ROE	1. Return on Equity 2. Report of Exam	1. A ratio of a bank's net earnings to total equity. Often used as a benchmark to indicate how well a bank is earning. 2. The report examiners deliver to financial institutions following an examination. The report will include exam findings and the rating assigned to the institution. It must be signed by the directors and is considered the confidential property of the banking agency that examined the institution.	11

Banking TERM	REFERENCE	DEFINITION	Keys' Chapter[1]
RTC	Resolution Trust Corporation	Created by FIRREA; given the responsibility of managing and disposing of the assets of failed institutions. An Oversight Board was created to provide supervisory authority over the policies of the RTC.	2, 5
RWA	Risk-Weighted Assets	The denominator of the capital requirements, except for the leverage ratio. Assets are assigned risk-weighting amounts that are then applied to determine total assets. Off-balance sheet exposures are also brought on the balance sheet and risk weighted.	4
S&L	Savings and Loan Association or Savings Association	Refers to a state or federally charted savings and loan association. A depository institution that historically focused its business on mortgage lending and savings. Now it is regulated by the OCC if it is a federal association and the FDIC and the state if it is state chartered.	2, 3
S&LHC	Savings and Loan Holding Company	A company that owns one or more savings associations. SLHCs were regulated by the OTS until July 21, 2011, and are now regulated by the Federal Reserve.	2, 3

Banking TERM	REFERENCE	DEFINITION	Keys' Chapter[1]
Safety and Soundness or S & S		The catch-all prudential rules applicable to banks/thrifts to assure the health of our financial system. The federal banking agencies have adopted guidelines that establish operational and managerial standards to promote the safety and soundness of federally insured depository institutions. The guidelines set forth standards for internal controls, information systems, internal audit systems, loan documentation, credit underwriting, interest rate exposure, asset growth, compensation, fees and benefits, asset quality, and earnings. In general, the safety and soundness guidelines prescribe the goals to be achieved in each area, and each institution is responsible for establishing its own procedures to achieve those goals. If an institution fails to comply with any of the standards set forth in the guidelines, the institution's primary federal regulator may require the institution to submit a plan for achieving and maintaining compliance. If an institution fails to submit an acceptable compliance plan, or fails in any material respect to implement a compliance plan that has been accepted by its primary federal regulator, the regulator is required to issue an order directing the institution to cure the deficiency.	8, 11
SAIF	Savings Association Insurance Fund	Created by FIRREA; insured the deposits of thrifts but later consolidated with BIF into a single fund administered by the FDIC, the DIF.	2, 5
SAR	Suspicious Activity Report	Report required to be filed where deposits or other activities may, but not necessarily, indicate the violation of law or regulation.	7

Banking TERM	REFERENCE	DEFINITION	Keys' Chapter[1]
SCB	Stress Capital Buffer	In April 2018, the Federal Reserve proposed replacing the Capital Conservation Buffer for those firms that go through the CCAR stress test process with a new "stress capital buffer" consisting of: maximum projected decline (peak-to-trough) in a firm's CET1 ratio during the nine-quarter stress horizon under the "severely adverse" scenario, plus four quarters of the firm's planned common stock dividends.	4
SEC	Securities and Exchange Commission	The SEC is a federal agency created to protect investors and maintain the integrity of the securities markets (exchanges and over-the-counter markets). It has rulemaking authority and enforces the Securities Act of 1933 and the Securities Exchange Act of 1934, as well as the Investment Advisor Act of 1949, the Investment Company Act of 1940, and the Trust Indenture Act.	9
SFHA	Standard Flood Hazard Area	The areas for which flood insurance is available under the NFIP as determined by FEMA. Lenders must document the flood hazard determination as part of the mortgage lending process.	
SICC	Standard Industrial Classification Code	A numerical code developed by the Department of Commerce whereby virtually any business activity has a numerical indicator. This code can be found in financial reference manuals and is utilized by the SEC as part of the periodic filings it requires of registered companies. It is also used by a number of other governmental authorities including the Federal Trade Commission and the Antitrust Division of the Department of Justice.	
SIDD	Separately Identifiable Department or Division	Has relevance in connection with certain advisory activities under GLBA that banks may either conduct through a subsidiary or through a SIDD.	
SIFI	Systemically Important Financial Institution	FHC or nonbank supervised by the Federal Reserve as systemically important under Dodd-Frank.	2

Banking TERM	REFERENCE	DEFINITION	Keys' Chapter[1]
SLA	Shared Loss Agreement	Used by the FDIC in connection with the resolution of failed institutions to keep assets in the banking sector and minimize losses. Winning bidders for the deposits of failed institutions enter into SLAs with the FDIC.	12
SMDIA	Standard Maximum Deposit Insurance Amount	It is the amount of FDIC insurance on accounts at banks and thrifts. Single accounts (owned by one person with no beneficiaries): $250,000 per owner; Joint Accounts (two or more persons with no beneficiaries): $250,000 per co-owner; IRAs and other certain retirement accounts: $250,000 per owner; Revocable trust accounts: Each owner is insured up to $250,000 for each unique eligible beneficiary named or identified in the revocable trust, subject to specific limitations and requirements.	5
Spence Act	Savings and Loan Holding Company Act of 1959	Created a temporary moratorium on acquisition of additional thrifts by multi–thrift holding companies and limited S&L Holding Companies to a single thrift. Established the regulatory framework for holding companies that owned more than one thrift.	2
SRO	Self-regulatory Organization	A membership-based organization that creates and enforces rules for members based on the federal securities laws. SROs, which are overseen by the SEC, are the front line in regulating broker-dealers.	
Sweep		Refers to a number of financial transactions between a bank and its customers pursuant to which funds above a target balance are moved out of a customer account and then are returned the next morning or at the term. Sweeps allow DDA funds to earn interest and/or provide safety above the FDIC-insured amount. Sweeps can be into repos, money market funds, MMDA's, affiliate banks, etc.	5

Banking TERM	REFERENCE	DEFINITION	Keys' Chapter[1]
TAG	Transaction Account Guarantee	A guarantee of the FDIC that provided customers of participating institutions with full coverage on transaction accounts. It was one of the arsenal of programs put in place to avert the financial crisis, especially to prevent liquidity crises. Dodd-Frank continued TAG until December 31, 2012, and the CARES act permitted the FDIC to reinstate it until December 31, 2020.	5
Tailoring	12 C.F.R Part 252	Under Crapo, the process by which the Federal Reserve determines what holding companies are subject to what types of enhanced prudential regulation. For this purpose, the Federal Reserve identified categories I–IV for holding companies of $100 billion in assets and above, with GSIBs as Category I.	10
TARP	Troubled Asset Relief Program	Established under EESA and was intended to provide a mechanism for the purchase of troubled assets from financial institutions under either an auction option (if there is a market price) or a direct purchase option and, in the latter situation, may take a nonvoting equity interest in the selling institution. It turned into a mechanism to infuse capital into institutions through Treasury's purchases of preferred stock and warrants.	2
TBTF	Too Big to Fail	A widespread belief that certain very large financial institutions would cause widespread systemic problems if they were to fail. Title II of DFA is dedicated to mitigation of TBTF.	2
Texas Ratio		A leading indicator of financial institutions that may fail—adversely classified assets plus OREO divided by tangible equity capital plus reserves. A Texas ratio of 100% is the sign of a troubled bank.	11
THC	Thrift holding company	*See also* S&LHC.	3, 10

Banking TERM	REFERENCE	DEFINITION	Keys' Chapter[1]
Thrift		A term used generally to apply to S&Ls.	3
Tier 1	Tier 1 Capital Ratio	The core measure of a bank's financial strength from a regulator's point of view. It consists primarily of shareholders' equity but may also include preferred stock that is irredeemable and noncumulative and retained earnings.	4
Tier 2	Tier 2 Capital	Capital not included in Tier 1, typically subordinated debt, preferred stock that is not perpetual or accumulates skipped dividends, and part of the ALLL. It is used to calculate the Total Risk-based Capital Ratio.	4
TISA	Truth in Savings Act	Part of the larger Federal Deposit Insurance Corporation Improvement Act of 1991 that is implemented by Reg DD. It established uniformity in the disclosure of terms and conditions regarding interest and fees when giving out information on or opening a new savings account to allow the consumer to make informed decisions.	5
TILA	Truth in Lending Act	Initial and subsequent legislation establishing uniform nationwide consumer protection in lending and subsequently leasing of family homes and household items by requiring uniform disclosures of information as to the terms of the loans/leases. Subparts are: FCBA Fair Credit Billing Act, FCCCPA Fair Credit and Credit Card Protection Act, HELCPA Home Equity Lines of Credit Protection Act, HOPEA Home Ownership, and Equity Protection Act.	
TLAC	Total loss-absorbing capacity	For domestic GSIBs, DFA requires the Federal Reserve to set a minimum level of long-term debt that could be used to recapitalize these firms' critical operations upon failure. The TLAC requirement can be met with both regulatory capital and long-term debt. The debt would convert to equity upon failure so that shareholders, not taxpayers, would absorb the losses.	4

Banking TERM	REFERENCE	DEFINITION	Keys' Chapter[1]
Transfer Date		The date under Dodd-Frank on which many of the bank regulatory changes occurred—July 21, 2011.	2
Treasury	U.S. Department of the Treasury	Supervises the federal banking system.	2
TRID	**T**ruth-in-Lending **R**ESPA **I**ntegrated **D**isclosure	Includes integrated home mortgage disclosures required to be created by the CFPB under Dodd-Frank.	
TRuPs	Trust Preferred Securities	These instruments, which were issued by a special purpose entity ("SPE") created by a BHC, qualified under GAAP as minority interests in a consolidated subsidiary and therefore as regulatory capital. In 1996, the Federal Reserve expanded the definition of cumulative preferred stock to TRuPS, which could count as capital within a 25% Tier 1 sublimit. However, under both DFA and Basel III, TRuPS were excluded from capital, except securities that were issued prior to May 19, 2010, by bank holding companies with less than $15 billion of assets, as of December 31, 2009, may be retained as Tier I Capital subject to certain restrictions.	4
UFIRS	Uniform Financial Institution Rating System	Internal supervisory tool for evaluating the soundness of financial institutions on a uniform basis and for identifying those institutions requiring special attention or concern, adopted by the FFIEC on November 13, 1979.	11
UIGEA	Unlawful Internet Gambling Enforcement Act of 2006	The law prohibits "any person engaged in the business of betting or wagering from knowingly accepting payments in connection with the participation of another person in unlawful Internet gambling." The Federal Reserve has rulemaking authority.	5
Unitary S&LHC	Unitary Thrift/ Savings Association Holding Company	A holding company of only one federal or state savings association that was grandfathered under GLBA and may engage in any activity, including any commercial activity.	2, 3

Banking TERM	REFERENCE	DEFINITION	Keys' Chapter[1]
USA PATRIOT Act	Uniting and Strengthening America by Providing Appropriate Tools Required to Intercept and Obstruct Terrorism Act of 2001	Expands the authority of U.S. law enforcement agencies for the stated purpose of fighting terrorism in the United States and abroad. Among its provisions: increases the ability of law enforcement agencies to search telephone, email communications, medical, financial, and other records; eases restrictions on foreign intelligence gathering within the United States; expands the Secretary of the Treasury's authority to regulate financial transactions, particularly those involving foreign individuals and entities; and enhances the discretion of law enforcement and immigration authorities in detaining and deporting immigrants suspected of terrorism-related acts; also expands the definition of terrorism to include domestic terrorism, thus enlarging the number of activities to which the USA Patriot Act's expanded law enforcement powers can be applied. Title III of the Act is known formally as the International Money Laundering Abatement and Anti- Terrorist Financing Act of 2001 (IMLA Act). Expands the duties of banks in reporting high-risk activities; it also substantially raises the stakes for noncompliance with federal money laundering legislation and increases the scope of businesses now required to participate in anti–money laundering efforts.	7
USPAP	Uniform Standards of Professional Appraisal Practice	Quality control standards applicable for appraisal analysis and reports in the United States and its territories and Canada.	
VaR	Value-at-risk	Banks and BHCs whose trading activity equals 10% or more of its total assets or equals $1 billion or more are subject to holding capital for market risk. They must measure their market risk using a VaR measurement model and, subject to parameters in the market risk rule, hold sufficient levels of Tier 3 capital to cover the exposure.	4

Banking TERM	REFERENCE	DEFINITION	Keys' Chapter[1]
Volcker Rule	Section 619 of Dodd-Frank, known colloquially as the "Volcker Rule" because of its patronage by former Federal Reserve Board chairman Paul Volcker	An amendment to the BHC Act that restricts banks from making certain kinds of speculative investments that do not benefit their customers. Specifically, it prohibits insured depository institutions and their affiliates from: (i) engaging in "proprietary trading"; (ii) acquiring or retaining any equity, partnership, or other ownership interest in a hedge fund or private equity fund; and (iii) sponsoring a hedge fund or a private equity fund.	9
Well-capitalized		Banks/thrifts and their holding companies (except for BHCs with less than $3 billion in assets) must be well-capitalized for numerous regulatory purposes. BHCs and all bank/thrift subsidiaries must be well-capitalized to be FHCs. The measures under Basel I are: A leverage ratio of Tier 1 Capital to total assets of 5% or greater; a ratio of Tier 1 Capital to total risk-weighted assets of 6% or greater; and a ratio of Total Capital to total risk-weighted assets of 10% or greater. In order to be well-capitalized under Basel III, a bank/thrift and holding company must maintain a Common Equity Tier 1 Capital ratio of 6.5% or more (a new category); a Tier 1 Capital ratio of 8% or more; a Total Capital ratio of 10% or more; and a leverage ratio of 5% or more.	4, 5, 10, 11
Well-managed		Banks/thrifts and their holding companies must be well-managed for numerous regulatory purposes. BHCs and all bank/thrift subsidiaries must be well capitalized to be FHCs. It means that the Management rating in the CAMELS ratings was a 1 or 2.	10, 11
Wild card		A law that matches powers of one type of financial institution to another. Usually, a state law that permits a state bank to engage in the activities permissible to a national bank by interpretation of the OCC. However, it may work the other way as well.	9

Table of Cases

A

B

C

D

F

G

H

I

K

L

M

N

O

P

R

S

T

U

V

W

About the Author, Contributors, and Editors

Karol K. Sparks is a partner in the Financial Institutions Group of Barack Ferrazzano, LLP, Chicago, Illinois. Her practice concentrates on corporate activities and regulatory issues of financial institutions, about which she has counseled banks for over 40 years.

A past chair of the Banking Law Committee of the Business Law Section of the American Bar Association (1998–2002), she has been an active member of the committee since 1985. She was a member of the Council of the Business Law Section of the ABA, the governing body of that organization, for a term ending in August 2008. She chaired the Publications Board of the Business Law Section of the ABA for a term ended in August 2014.

In addition to KEYS TO BANKING LAW, Karol is the author of the legal treatise INSURANCE ACTIVITIES OF BANKS, published by Aspen Law & Business in 1998 and the second edition published in 2012, which is updated annually. She is a frequent lecturer on issues relating to the regulation of financial institutions and in 2008–2009 served as Distinguished Practitioner in Residence at Elon University School of Law, Greensboro, North Carolina. From 2009 until 2013, she was an Adjunct Professor at Wake Forest University School of Law, having previously taught at the University of Iowa College of Law as an Adjunct from 2001 to 2007. Starting in January 2014, she joined the Graduate Program in Banking and Financial Law of the Boston University School of Law as a Lecturer in Law in the LL.M program, from which she retired in 2017. She is a member of the founding faculty of Banking Law Basics, an ABA-CLE course offered in June and October of each year from 1998 to 2011, and its successor course, Banking Law Fundamentals, sponsored by the Boston University School of Law on the east coast and, until 2020, by the University of California at Berkeley Law School on the west coast.

Harding de C. Williams is the author of FEDERAL BANKING LAW AND REGULATION, published by the ABA Business Law Section in 2006, which is no longer updated, but, with his permission, served as the original base for this book. He is a graduate of Middlebury College and the University of Michigan Law School. He is the author of *Directors and Trustees Handbook*, written in 1990 and updated quarterly through January 2003, and editor of three editions of *Bank Director's Manual*, both for the former National Council of Savings Institutions and its successor, America's Community Bankers.

Harding was Counsel for the Association of Financial Services Holding Companies and General Counsel for the former National Savings and Loan League. Before joining the National League, he was Washington Representative, Industrial Relations for the National Association of Manufacturers and Manager of the Washington Office of the Del Monte Corporation. Harding has written extensively on corporate governance, banking, and accounting issues. He lives in San Antonio close to family.

Sara A. Kelsey is the author of Chapter 12 of *Keys*, Bank Resolution and Orderly Liquidation Authority. As a former FDIC General Counsel, she brought her expertise to this book.

Sara established her solo practice in 2012, specializing in domestic and international bank regulatory law. She advises on legislative and regulatory developments and restructuring, resolution, compliance, and enforcement matters affecting bank and nonbank financial firms. Previously, she was counsel in WilmerHale's Regulatory and Government Affairs Department and a member of the firm's Financial Institutions Group. In early 2007, she was appointed General Counsel of the Federal Deposit Insurance Corporation and served in that capacity until late 2008. Before that, Sara served as Deputy Superintendent and General Counsel of the New York State Banking Department (now part of the NYSDFS) from 1998 to 2007. Previously, she was counsel in the Financial Institutions Regulatory and Enforcement Group at Skadden, Arps, Meagher & Flom, and prior to that she was regulatory counsel with a predecessor bank (Chemical Bank) to JP MorganChase Bank. She began her career as an attorney in the Federal Reserve Board's Legal Division.

Sara has been an active member of the Banking Law Committee of the Business Law Section of the American Bar Association since the 1980s and has served in a number of leadership positions in the committee. Ms. Kelsey is now an adjunct professor at New York University Law School and New York Law School, and she is a member of the permanent faculty of Banking Law Basics and its successor course Banking Law Fundamentals.

John M. Geiringer is a co-author of parts of Chapters 7 and 11 of *Keys*. John is a partner in Barack Ferrazzano, Chicago, Illinois. As the Regulatory Section Leader of the Firm's Financial Institutions Group, John concentrates his practice on regulatory, governance, and investigative matters involving financial institutions.

He is a frequent speaker and author in the financial institutions area on issues surrounding banking regulations, examinations, and enforcement actions. He teaches banking law and regulation at Chicago-Kent College of Law's Graduate Program in Financial Services Law and serves on the board of advisors of its Institute for Compliance. He is the co-editor of the two-volume edition, *Advising Illinois Financial Institutions*, in which he wrote a chapter on bank enforcement issues. John is a vice-chair of the American Bar Association's Banking Law Committee and a past chairman of its Enforcement, Insider Liability and Troubled Banks Subcommittee and its Bank Secrecy Act/Anti–Money Laundering Subcommittee. He also is a former chairman of the Chicago Bar Association's Financial Institutions Committee.

John also devotes significant time to Bank Secrecy Act and anti–money laundering issues. He is on the advisory board of the Anti–Money Laundering Association and is the president of its Midwest chapter. He has frequently lectured on the subject, including at Georgetown University's Center for Security Studies, Boston University School of Law, and Chicago-Kent College of Law, where he serves as a co-director of its Center for National Security and Human Rights Law. He is the editor and author of a chapter in the upcoming book, *Countering the Financing of Terrorism: Law and Policy*, and is a Certified Anti–Money Laundering Specialist (CAMS).

Prior to joining the Firm in 1999, John was both a bank regulator and a compliance consultant. He served as legal counsel for the Illinois bank regulatory agency. John also obtained practical experience with respect to bank operations and compliance issues as a regulatory consultant with a regional accounting firm, performing compliance reviews and training for a variety of financial institutions.

Stanley F. Orszula updated and edited the Second and Third Editions of Chapter 11 of *Keys*, Examination and Enforcement. He is a partner in the Barack Ferrazzano Financial Institutions Group with extensive experience providing strategic counsel to banks on compliance and regulatory issues, fintech, banking-as-a-service (BaaS), general banking corporate matters, secured lending, government lending programs, distressed loans and assets, failed bank receiverships, and note sales. Stan's background includes experience serving as a Lieutenant in the United States Navy Judge Advocate Corps, counsel with the FDIC, sitting on the board of a financial institution, and representing banks in private practice for almost twenty years. Stan frequently speaks and writes about fintech and BaaS developments affecting banks.

J. Brent McCauley contributed to Chapter 10. He is a partner in the Barack Ferrazzano Financial Institutions Group. Brent has over twenty years of experience in the financial services industry. He began his career as an examiner with the Office of Thrift Supervision in 1989, where he also worked as a fraud investigator. After law school, Brent was senior regulatory counsel in the legal department of the Federal Reserve Bank of Chicago, handling complex regulatory and supervisory matters. He represents all types of financial institutions including securities broker-dealers, insurance companies, investment advisors, as well as banks, thrifts, and their holding companies in mergers and acquisitions/corporate regulatory matters.

Andrea Sill originally authored, and in the Second and Third Editions edited, the discussion of Regulation O in Chapter 6. Andrea is a partner in the Barack Ferrazzano Financial Institutions Group and concentrates her practice on bank regulatory, securities, and corporate matters. She has experience working on a variety of regulatory and securities matters, including mergers and acquisitions, equity and debt offerings, trust preferred securities transactions, regulatory applications, and enforcement matters. Prior to joining the firm, Andrea served as legal counsel to the Illinois Office of Banks and Real Estate.

K. Fritzi Getz authored the update on interest rate exportation in Chapter 3, Structure Choices in the Bank Family, and served as editor of that chapter. Fritzi is an associate in the Barack Ferrazzano Financial Institutions Group. She represents clients in the sale and acquisition of businesses, capital raising transactions, and in connection with the review and negotiation of business contracts. She also advises public companies on reporting obligations and has represented issuers in public and private offerings of equity and debt securities.